The Rise
of the
Medieval World
500–1300

The Rise
of the
Medieval World
500–1300

A Biographical Dictionary

Edited by
JANA K. SCHULMAN

The Great Cultural Eras of the Western World
Ronald H. Fritze, Series Adviser

GREENWOOD PRESS
Westport, Connecticut · London

Library of Congress Cataloging-in-Publication Data

The rise of the medieval world, 500–1300 : a biographical dictionary / edited by Jana K. Schulman.
    p. cm.—(The great cultural eras of the Western world, ISSN 1534–9527)
    Includes bibliographical references and index.
    ISBN 0–313–30817–9 (alk. paper)
    1. Biography—Middle Ages, 500–1500—Dictionaries. 2. Civilization,
Medieval—Dictionaries. 3. Europe—History—476–1492—Biography—Dictionaries. I.
Schulman, Jana K., 1959– II. Series.
    CT114.R57   2002
    940.1'092'2—dc21   2001037633

British Library Cataloguing in Publication Data is available.

Library of Congress Catalog Card Number: 2001037633
ISBN: 0–313–30817–9
ISSN: 1534–9527

First published in 2002

Greenwood Press, 88 Post Road West, Westport, CT 06881
An imprint of Greenwood Publishing Group, Inc.
www.greenwood.com

Printed in the United States of America

The paper used in this book complies with the
Permanent Paper Standard issued by the National
Information Standards Organization (Z39.48–1984).

10 9 8 7 6 5 4 3 2 1

Contents

Introduction

This volume, in Greenwood's series The Great Cultural Eras of the Western World, covers the period from A.D. 500 to 1300, the period of time generally referred to as the Middle Ages. While the scope of this volume is western Europe, it is impossible to discuss the Middle Ages without including the people from Byzantium, Baghdad, and the Arab world who contributed so much to the politics, religion, and culture of western Europe as these eight centuries passed.

Borders and peoples were never quiescent during these tumultuous times. By 500, the Germanic tribes had invaded and settled in the former Roman Empire, and the synthesis of three cultures—the classical, Christian, and Germanic—had begun. In the sixth century, *Theodoric the Ostrogoth ruled a relatively tolerant Ostrogothic-Arian kingdom in Italy; *Clovis had completed the Frankish conquest of Gaul; the Vandals controlled North Africa; the Visigoths, forced to retreat from southern Gaul by the Franks, continued to dominate Spain; and the Angles and Saxons had settled in Britain. (In this volume, an asterisk indicates a cross-reference to another entry.) At the same time, the emperors of the Eastern Empire, Constantinople, thrived. In fact, Emperor *Justinian tried to reconquer the West and unite the two halves of the empire; while he was somewhat successful, after his death, problems arose. Although Byzantium retained much of southern Italy, the Lombards took northern Italy in 568; the Visigoths retook what they had lost to Justinian in southern Spain; and in the 690s, the Muslims took Byzantine North Africa.

At the same time, the Roman papacy began to play an independent role in European society. Pope *Gregory the Great began to send out missionaries throughout Europe to convert the non-Christian tribes to Christianity. One of the first missions from Rome was to *Æthelbert of Kent; *Augustine of Canterbury arrived in Britain in 597 and slowly began the process of converting the people there. The spiritual life developed rapidly in Ireland and in Britain, and in later centuries, Irish and English missionaries went forth to Christianize the

Frisians and others. *Willibrod from Northumbria in the late 600s was one of the first. The second wave of missionaries included a Benedictine monk, Saint *Boniface, who, with the support of *Charles Martel and his sons, worked in Frisia, Thuringia, Hesse, and Bavaria from 716 until his death in 754. He served as a representative of the Anglo-Saxon Church, the Benedictine Rule, and the papacy. Moreover, he established the monastery of Fulda, a center of learning and evangelism.

The papacy and the various kings supported monasteries like Fulda because they served several important functions: The monks copied classical texts, transmitted classical learning, and taught; the monasteries themselves served as places of prayer, meditation, and learning and offered service to humanity and to God. The founder of Western monasticism was Saint *Benedict of Nursia, who established a monastic foundation at Monte Cassino and composed the Rule of St. Benedict, which became the guide for monasticism for centuries. The Benedictines' impact on the world was substantial. Not only did their schools produce literate people, but also the monks themselves served as scribes and advisers to princes. In fact, the leading scholars of the era were bishops: *Gregory of Tours (d. 594), Pope Gregory the Great (d. 604), and *Isidore of Seville (d. 636), among others.

While Christianity spread throughout Europe during the sixth and seventh centuries, in the Arabian city of Mecca, a man was born, c. 570, who would change the shape of the religious map. *Muhammad, the prophet of Islam, brought monotheism to his people; he taught the followers of Islam to submit to the will of the single, almighty God of the universe, Allah. Unlike Christianity, however, Islam had no priesthood, no Church apart from the state. Unlike Europe, then, no tension developed (or existed) between Church and state; the caliphs were defenders of the faith and guardians of the faithful.

Islam spread widely over the next century; Muslims conquered Syria, the Persian Empire, and Egypt between 632 and 655, North Africa around 661, and entered Spain in 711. From there, they moved into southern Gaul and threatened the Merovingian Franks. In 732, Charles Martel halted their advance. By the ninth century, Baghdad was a metropolis where intellectual life flourished. Islamic scholars studied and synthesized the traditions of Greece, Rome, Persia, and India while *Charlemagne struggled to educate his people.

When Charlemagne came to the throne, he had inherited from his father *Pepin III an expanded and unified kingdom. However, it took a while for the Carolingians, named after Charles Martel (Carolus), to become the rulers of the Franks. For many years, they had served as "mayor of the palace" to the reigning Merovingian kings, who, as time elapsed, became more and more their puppets. Gradually, they became masters of Austrasia, adding control of Neustria in 687. Charles' son Pepin III deposed the last Merovingian king, with papal support, and had himself elected king of the Franks in 751.

Pepin needed papal support to become king. However, the papacy benefited from this as well. For many years, the papacy had been trying to establish its own state in central Italy, the "Republic of St. Peter." However, the campaign had not been going well, and the papacy could no longer count on the Byzantine emperor who controlled Italy for his help. On the one hand, the Lombard attacks were too strong, keeping the emperor otherwise occupied; on the other hand, the emperor had embraced the idea of "iconoclasm" and decided to end the veneration of religious icons. The pope found this alarming and declared it heretical. Therefore, papal support of Pepin's cause garnered the papacy a champion to fight on its behalf and the so-called Donation of Pepin, a grant of land in central Italy to the papacy.

The pope crowned Pepin's son Charlemagne emperor of the Romans, an act that resulted in two major changes: It recreated the Holy Roman Empire in the West and firmly united the Frankish Empire and the papacy. However, this latter act infused the papacy with power; if it could make emperors, it could also depose them. The popes saw themselves as supreme and above the emperors. Charlemagne did not agree with this and, in fact, crowned his own son emperor, excluding the pope. This disagreement over supremacy and subordination marks the beginning of conflict between the papacy and empire as to their appropriate relationship that came to a head with the Investiture Controversy.

As emperor and master of the West, Charlemagne worked to improve the intellectual life of his people. He gathered scholars from all over Europe—his biographer *Einhard, *Paul the Deacon, *Theodulf of Orléans, and *Alcuin of York—and forced the cathedrals and monasteries to run schools. He himself established a school at Aachen, his capital, to preserve and transmit classical and Christian culture.

After Charlemagne's death, this intellectual revival, called the Carolingian Renaissance, continued. *Benedict of Aniane led a movement of monastic reform in Aquitaine; his piety influenced Charlemagne's surviving son, *Louis the Pious, who gave him free reign. Benedict's reform and Louis' religiosity mark a shift from a more superficial concern with religion to a deep commitment to a Christ-centered life. Churchmen like *Hrabanus Maurus prepared encyclopedic accounts of existing knowledge. Others, like *Hincmar of Rheims, were involved in the religious controversies of the day: He refuted the double predestination preached by *Gottschalk of Orbais and involved himself in a discussion of marriage and divorce—an important debate that focused on *Lothar and his concubine *Waldrada.

Charlemagne's hard-won empire disintegrated under Louis the Pious' sons; they rebelled against him, throwing the empire into civil war. Throughout Europe, unity began to break down, and invasions were rampant. The Vikings, from Scandinavia and those settled in England, began raiding the Continent. They attacked coastal cities at will, Antwerp in 837, Rouen in 841, Hamburg and Paris in 845, and Aachen in 881. The Danes invaded France and England; the Norwegians raided and settled in Scotland, Ireland, and the North Atlantic; and the Swedes went east to the Baltic Shores, Russia, and the Byzantine

Empire. This series of invasions began in England in 793 when the Danes attacked the monastery of Lindisfarne and continued, on and off, for centuries.

When the Danes first attacked England, they raided the monasteries because they possessed material goods. Eventually, though, a desire for land motivated their attacks, and by 870, they had conquered all of England with the exception of Wessex. *Alfred the Great, king of Wessex, fought against the Danes, eventually forcing their leader, *Guthrum, to convert to Christianity. After peace came to Wessex and England, Alfred turned to a revival of learning. However, as a result of the Viking depredations, literacy and Christianity were threatened. Very few people could read Latin, so even fewer heard or understood sermons. Alfred, like Charlemagne, a patron of learning, gathered scholars to teach Latin and to translate classical works into Anglo-Saxon. His program to translate Latin works into Anglo-Saxon resulted in translations of the Psalms, *Boethius' *Consolation of Philosophy*, Gregory the Great's *Pastoral Care*, and *Bede's *Ecclesiastical History*, among others.

Alfred died in 899, and by the mid-900s, his successors ruled all of England, which enjoyed a time of peace and prosperity from 955 to 980. From these invasions came the unification of the royal kingdom, which—no matter how many more invasions England saw—did not collapse. However, during the reign (978–1016) of one of Alfred's descendants, *Æthelred the Unready, the Danish invasions began again. By 1016, King *Cnut of Denmark sat on the English throne. Nonetheless, when his son died in 1042, *Edward the Confessor, a descendant of Wessex, took the throne. However, he was the last English king; the Norman *William, later William I the Conqueror, invaded in 1066.

France, like England, saw many invasions. Not only did the Vikings invade France, but, again in the ninth and tenth centuries, Muslims, settled in North Africa, Spain, and the Mediterranean, attacked merchant vessels, plundered cities, and set up bases on the southern coast of France from which to raid inland. However, the invasions there were responsible, in part, for a breakdown of political authority into regional and local units. As mentioned above, the Carolingian Empire started to dissolve under Louis the Pious' sons; in fact, the Carolingian kings became less and less powerful over time. The only one to negotiate successfully with the Norse invaders was *Charles III the Simple, the king of West Francia; in 911, he concluded a treaty with *Rollo, who then founded the duchy of Normandy. In 987, the crown passed to *Hugh Capet, founder of the Capetian dynasty. At first, their power was limited and their dynasty weak; while they were the kings of the French in theory, in reality, they had limited jurisdiction and were, essentially, one of many princelings. Fewer and fewer princes held more and more of the land. However, by conquest and intermarriage, the Capetian kings controlled much of France by the end of the thirteenth century.

Kingship in Germany, however, was a complicated system of election. In Germany, the Carolingian line ended with the death of King Louis the Child in 911. At that time, there were five duchies that dominated: Saxony, Swabia,

Bavaria, Franconia, and Lorraine (or Lotharingia). Louis was succeeded by the duke of Franconia; then, in 919, the duke of Saxony, Henry the Fowler, was elected king and took the throne (as *Henry I). His line ruled Germany until 1024. Like the English and French, Germany, too, faced invaders: Seminomadic Hungarians had begun raiding Germany, northern Italy, and France as early as the late 800s. They continued unchecked until they were defeated by *Otto I in 955. During his reign, Otto accomplished three important goals: He defended Germany against the Hungarians; he recovered royal lands within the remaining royal duchies; and he extended royal control over Italy. In 962, he was crowned as Holy Roman emperor, which marks the beginning of the medieval Holy Roman Empire. Otto also encouraged an intellectual revival that continued throughout the reigns of his son, *Otto II, and grandson, *Otto III. Otto I's court produced able administrators and scholars and he endowed abbeys and nunneries. For example, Gerbert of Aurillac, later Pope *Sylvester II, brought Arab thought into Western Christendom. *Hrotsvit of Gandersheim, a canoness at the abbey of Gandersheim that Otto's ancestors had established, wrote plays and legends extolling Christianity.

By the eleventh century, the Church had parishes in villages throughout Europe, and most Europeans would have understood themselves to be Christians. The Benedictines continued their work, and many of their monks played major roles in political life. However, not all within the Church hierarchy was rosy. Many lay lords appointed bishops and archbishops in their domains; as a result, many of these ecclesiastic men had interests more secular than spiritual. Abuses in the Church, at all levels, were rampant. However, many abbots preached reform of the Church; one abbey in the forefront of the reform movement was Cluny, which spread reform monasteries across Europe.

By the second half of the eleventh century, the reform movement had reached the papacy. There were two groups who sought reform: the moderates and the radicals. Those favoring moderate reform desired to reform the Church itself, but without challenging the traditional collaboration between kings and princes. Pope *Leo IX, appointed by Emperor *Henry III, was a moderate. In the interlude following the death of Henry III but during the minority of *Henry IV, the reformers created the College of Cardinals, a body independent of the emperor that elected the pope. While the popes who succeeded Pope Leo were also reformers, *Gregory VII was a radical reformer who wanted to see the papacy in control of all things ecclesiastical, including lay appointments. He saw a world where emperors, kings, and princes deferred to bishops who, in turn, received their orders from the pope. In fact, Gregory banned lay investiture, which infuriated Emperor Henry IV, who responded with a letter of defiance. The Investiture Controversy did not find a resolution until 1122, when Emperor *Henry V negotiated a compromise between empire and papacy, the Concordat of Worms.

As the power of the empire declined, the papacy became a major political force. Pope *Urban II rebuilt the papacy and united Christian Europe. In the eleventh century, the Seljuk Turks swept into Persia, became Muslims, and enslaved the ʿAbbāsid caliphs of Baghdad. In 1071, they defeated a Byzantine army at the battle of Manzikert and occupied Asia Minor. While the loss of Byzantine lands alarmed Byzantine Emperor *Alexius Comnenus, the stories of Turkish atrocities against Christian pilgrims eventually filtered west. When Alexius asked for help, Europe responded. Pope Urban II called the First Crusade in 1095, urging European Christians to take up the cross and reconquer the Holy Land, promising the glory of the kingdom of heaven as a reward.

While glad for the help, the arrival of some 25,000 Christians disturbed Alexius, who extracted a promise of homage for all the lands they might capture. Friction developed immediately between the crusaders—who wanted the conquest of the Holy Land—and the Byzantines, who wanted, merely, to retake what lands they had lost in Asia Minor. The two factions split, and the crusaders headed to Syria, defeated the Muslims, besieged and took Antioch, and in 1099, took Jerusalem. They divided the conquered lands into four Crusader states: the county of Edessa; the principality of Antioch; the county of Tripoli; and the kingdom of Jerusalem—all of which they ruled for some forty-five years. However, over the years, the Muslims began to recover their lands; Edessa fell to the Muslims in 1144. The loss of Edessa revived the crusading fervor in Europe.

However, the Second Crusade, inspired by *Bernard of Clairvaux, led by the kings of France and Germany in 1147–49, failed utterly. The 1170s and 1180s saw the rise of a new, unified Islamic state led by *Saladin and centered in Egypt. He negotiated a truce with the rulers of the Crusader States, but a Christian baron broke it in 1187. The battle of Ḥaṭṭīn, fought on 4 July 1187, ended with a decisive Muslim victory. Saladin destroyed the crusader army and seized large parts of the Crusader States. Three months later, he occupied Jerusalem.

Led by three European monarchs, Emperor *Frederick I Barbarossa, King *Philip II Augustus of France, and King *Richard the Lionheart of England, the Third Crusade, to retake Jerusalem, began in 1189 and lasted until 1192. Unfortunately, Frederick drowned on the way, and most of his army returned home. Philip quarreled with Richard and went home. Richard, although he won back much of the Holy Land, failed to take Jerusalem. As a result, Pope *Innocent III instigated the Fourth Crusade, which was led not by kings but by territorial princes like *Baldwin IX, count of Flanders.

This army, although it never reached the Holy Land, succeeded where no one had before: It captured Constantinople. Originally en route to the Holy Land, the crusaders landed in Venice. In debt to the doge, the leaders agreed to retake the Christian city of Zara for him. The pope, infuriated by the attack on a papal vassal, excommunicated the crusaders en masse. They, however, took Zara in 1202 and went on to Constantinople to help one of the two claimants to the Byzantine throne. After their candidate assumed the throne but was killed by his own anti-Latin countrymen, the crusaders decided to take Constantinople, doing so in 1204, and placed one of their own, Baldwin himself, on the throne. He and his successors ruled for over fifty years, until the Greek Empire in exile overthrew the Latin Empire and returned a Greek emperor to the throne in 1261.

The Crusades, however, did not end here. There were several others over the next eighty years, but none were successful. The Fifth Crusade, against Egypt, ended in disaster. The Seventh and Eighth Crusades, led by Saint *Louis, the former against Egypt in 1248 and the latter against Tunisia in 1270, both failed. In 1291, the fall of Acre finally brought an end to the Crusader States in the Holy Land.

The Christian piety that motivated the Crusades also gave rise to religious orders of Christian warriors, bound by monastic rules and dedicated to fighting the Muslims: the Knights Hospitaler, the Knights Templar, and the Teutonic Knights. In addition, lay piety became more and more intense; people, devoted to the Christian faith because it offered eternal salvation, an explanation for human suffering, and the promise of a better life in the present, became less tolerant of those who deviated from it. At the same time, as the papacy became more and more involved in secular matters, it became more difficult to view the papacy as a holy institution. The abuses of the upper echelons of Church hierarchy, unchecked, resulted in new forms of monasticism and heresy.

Heresy developed out of criticism of the Church itself. Many heresies began in the towns of southern Europe and spread; their members denounced ecclesiastical wealth and preached without approval, either episcopal or papal. In addition, many of the heretical sects disagreed with the Church about who could perform sacraments. Two heretical movements worth mentioning are the Waldensians (see Peter *Waldo) and the Cathars/Albigensians. The former group allowed untrained laypeople to preach and advocated a life of religious mendicancy. The latter protested against ecclesiastical wealth and also preached a dualist theology derived from Persia. They were quite popular and became enough of a threat that Pope Innocent III called a crusade against them, the first to be called against European Christians.

Ardent reformers founded new orders. *Bruno the Carthusian founded the Carthusian order, a particularly stark and austere one. Robert of Molesme founded the Cistercian order, which was less severe than that of the Carthusians but far more rigorous than the Cluniacs'. Bernard of Clairvaux, who called the Second Crusade, was a member of the Cistercians. In addition, orders devoted to poverty, teaching, and charitable deeds, the Dominicans and Franciscans, arose. Unlike the other orders mentioned above, these two did their religious works outside of the cloister and in the towns. Known as mendicant orders, they proved as alluring as the heretical movements, and their orthodox Christianity was compelling.

The Dominicans, also known as the Order of Friars Preachers, preached throughout Europe, among heretics and non-Christians. By the thirteenth century, they had sent their evangelical missions into the Holy Land, central Asia, Tibet, and China. They joined the universities and were the leading proponents of Aristotelian philosophy. Their order included such notables as *Albertus Magnus and Thomas *Aquinas. The Franciscans based their order on the imitation of Christ and, originally, practiced poverty and the simple life. For instance, Saint *Francis, unlike Saint *Dominic, viewed intellectual aspirations as irrelevant. As time passed, practicality forced a change: Poverty limited the Franciscans' movement. However, not all the Franciscans favored the move away from poverty, and some continued to imitate Francis. This group split off and later became known as the "Spiritual Franciscans." The former group, far larger, began to acquire goods with which to maintain their members. In addition, they embraced the idea of learning and scholarship.

While the earliest schools taught the trivium and quadrivium, a basic program in the seven liberal arts that included astronomy, geometry, arithmetic, music, grammar, rhetoric, and logic, the pursuit of higher learning saw the development of universities. By the twelfth century, the locus of learning had shifted from the monasteries to the cathedral schools, which led to the eventual development of the universities. During the twelfth century, *studia generalia* developed, at places like Paris, Bologna, Salerno, Oxford, and Cambridge, among others, where students could pursue the liberal arts plus advanced study in one or more of the higher disciplines: civil law, canon law, medicine, or theology. The age of European science dawned, and philosophers and theologians flourished.

The study of civil and canon law began at the University of Bologna. Emperor Justinian's *Corpus iuris civilis* formed the basis of Roman or civil law. After the promulgation of the *Corpus iuris civilis*, glossators wrote commentaries on it, produced textbooks, and reorganized the code into a coherent series of topics. Later still, glossators glossed the glosses. While collections of decretals had long existed, canon law became a serious discipline only in the eleventh century. The Investiture Controversy stimulated scholars to systematize, clarify, and reconcile their sources, the canons, or laws of the Church, the writings of the Church Fathers, and other documentary sources relevant to the Church. Canon lawyers needed to produce a single, coherent work. In 1140, *Gratian completed the definitive collection, called the *Decretum*, which was, in turn, supplemented by Pope *Gregory IX in 1234 and others after that. The *Decretum* and its supplements were given the title *Corpus iuris canonici*, the ecclesiastical equivalent of Justinian's *Corpus iuris civilis*.

The study of philosophy and theology, which had existed, albeit informally, for centuries, became standard. Philosophers and theologians explored the relationship between reason and faith. They built their arguments on the works and men who preceded them: the philosophical systems of Plato (rendered acceptable to Christian thought by Saint Augustine of Hippo) and Aristotle (whose works became available in translation in the thirteenth century); Greek scientific and philosophical works made available through translations from the Arabic that came into the West from the Islamic world; the works of the early Church Fathers; the works of early medieval scholars like Gregory the Great, Isidore of Seville, Bede, Alcuin, Hrabanus Maurus, *John Scottus Eriugena, and Gerbert of Aurillac; and the Bible. These "modern" theologians wondered about and investigated the nature of human beings, morality, the existence of God, and the relationship between man and God.

With Latin control of Constantinople came access to the intellectual legacy of Greek and Byzantine civilization. A conflict between the Christianized Plato and Aristotle developed in the thirteenth century when all of Aristotle's writings came into the West. Many Christians were suspicious of him and viewed his works as pagan and ominous. While the Franciscans favored Plato and Augustine, the Dominicans tended to espouse Aristotle. In fact, both Albertus Magnus and Thomas Aquinas worked toward reconciling Aristotle's philosophy with Christianity. The work of *Averroës, a Muslim who followed Aristotle, emerged as well; he, like Aristotle, produced followers and dissenters.

The High Middle Ages, from 1050 to 1300, the time of the rise of the universities and the philosophical debates and condemnations, saw parallel developments in other areas of culture. Mystery plays on religious themes spread. The mystic *Hildegard of Bingen produced Christian music and musical theater. Music itself saw the development of the first musical notation and, in the thirteenth century, the earliest polyphony (music for two voices). Literature, written in Latin and in vernaculars, was varied and changed to reflect differences. War-like epic poetry flourished, especially in France (*Song of Roland*) and England (*Beowulf*). As time passed, the lyric reappeared, and the romance emerged, paralleling a rise in emotionalism. The mid- and later twelfth century saw romantic lyric poetry from southern France, sung by troubadours, spread into northern France, England, and Germany. The troubadours focused on the love for one's lady, a theme also explored in the romances, which led to the idea of courtly love (see the entry for Andreas *Capellanus). Stories of King Arthur and his court abounded and did not recognize geographical boundaries; romances were written in French, English, and German. In fact, German poets, called Minnesingers, influenced by French lyric and romance, produced their own versions of the Arthurian stories (see the entries for *Wolfram von Eschenbach, *Gottfried von Strassburg). Architecture, too, reflected the emotional intensity of the times. The eleventh and early twelfth century saw the building of the massive Romanesque cathedrals. In the later twelfth century, the building of the delicate, seemingly freestanding, Gothic cathedrals commenced. Abbot *Suger designed St. Denis in around 1140; most consider this cathedral the first Gothic church. Others include Westminster Abbey, Chartres, and Notre Dame, just to name a few. These beautiful cathedrals brought separate arts into one place—architecture, sculpture, stained glass, liturgical music—where churchgoers could view and hear them when they went to Mass.

By the end of the early Middle Ages, the period between 500 and 1050, Europe was on the brink of change. The rise in population and food production led to the development of cities, to urbanization. By 1300, the cities had become crucial factors in the economy, culture, and social structure. They expanded their commercial districts and developed political and legal institutions. The earliest and largest commercial towns were in northern Italy, then Milan and Florence. Flanders specialized in the production of cloth; Scandinavia exported timber; Poland, salt; Burgundy, wine; and England exported beer and wool. The cities continued to venerate their saints and worked hand in glove with the religious centers. In fact, money and piety contributed greatly to the building of the cathedrals and the financing of the crusades.

Europe changed from a preliterate to a literate society. By 1300, even those who could not read depended on written records. This led to systematized record keeping with a subsequent need for skilled men. Skills like reading, writing, and mathematical calculation became vital to the function of secular and ecclesiastical governments and urban businesses. Schools sprang up everywhere, and they needed teachers. A new class developed, that of the professional intellectuals, the professors and scholars.

With these changes came a new sense and awareness of self. People began to collect and preserve their own letters. The first autobiographies since Saint Augustine's *Confessions* appeared: *Guibert of Nogent's *Memoirs* followed by Peter *Abelard's *History of My Misfortunes*. As one develops a sense of self, one also begins to see the world differently. It is Abelard who argued that the cosmos could be viewed rationally, that what God had created had an order and rules of its own, that it did not require frequent divine intervention.

These fundamental changes produced more opportunity and greater social mobility. The poor and the serfs went to the cities. Devout Christians joined monastic and religious orders. The social boundaries between the upper class, in particular the nobles and knights, became blurred. The idea of the knight grew in stature. The Church emphasized the idea of Christian knighthood, whereas the Crusades highlighted them as "the knights of Christ." Fictional knights like Roland and Lancelot became heroes of medieval literature, resulting in the so-called code of chivalry.

This volume covers 800 years, a time of incredible change in all areas of life. As a result, it is not exhaustive in its coverage. The people included are men and women who made contributions to European culture, some perhaps smaller or less significant than others but still worthy of inclusion for what they tell of their society. Others have been omitted, including popes, kings, and queens, if their cultural contributions were in only one arena. The biographies of the men and women in this volume will provide the reader with images of dynamic movement and countermovement, of a time and culture that, by its end, would prepare the way for the Renaissance.

The bibliography for this volume includes general titles in addition to a full list of specific titles. It is also worth noting that several entries refer to a specific title, the *Patrologia cursus completus. Series Latina* (abbreviated *PL* in text). This is a compilation of Latin writings from Late Antiquity through the Middle Ages that was compiled by J.-P. Migne, a French cleric, in the nineteenth century. It is a prime source for those writings that have not yet been the subject for modern critical editions.

Let me conclude by thanking all of the contributors, especially those who took on added entries late in the day as well as those who comforted and guided me. You know who you are.

Chronology

c. 496	Clovis converts to Catholic Christianity.
c. 500	Salic laws of the Franks are formulated.
c. 505	Anicius Manlius Severinus Boethius, a Roman philosopher, writes *The Fundamentals of Music*, a treatise summarizing classical theories about music.
507–510	Clovis unites all the Franks on the left bank of the Rhine under his rule and moves his capital to modern-day Paris.
511	Death of Clovis.
c. 521	Birth of Saint Columba, Irish abbot and missionary.
522	Boethius becomes chief minister to Theodoric the Great, the Ostrogothic king of Italy.
524	Boethius writes *On the Consolation of Philosophy*.
526	Priscian (c. 526) compiles a Latin and Greek grammar that becomes the standard text during the Middle Ages; death of Boethius; death of Theodoric.
527	Justinian becomes emperor of Byzantium and declares his wife Theodora, an actress, empress.
c. 529	Saint Benedict of Nursia establishes the first Benedictine monastery at Monte Cassino near Naples, Italy; promulgation of the first edition of the *Codex Iustinianus* by Justinian.
532	Emperor Justinian begins building the Church of Holy Wisdom, Hagia Sophia, in Constantinople.
533	Emperor Justinian issues the *Digesta*, extracts of Roman law, together with a guide to the *Codex*.
c. 538	Birth of Gregory of Tours, French bishop and author of the *History of the Franks*; Cassiodorus, a Roman statesman and historian, retires and founds a monastery at his estate in Calabria.
c. 540	Birth of Pope Gregory the Great; birth of Venantius Fortunatus.

542	Death of Caesarius of Arles.
c. 543	Birth of Saint Columbanus, Irish abbot, writer, and missionary.
c. 546	Saint Gildas writes *De excidio et conquestu Britanniae*, which criticizes the evils of contemporary British society.
547	The church of San Vitale in Ravenna is completed with mosaics depicting Justinian and Theodora; death of Saint Benedict of Nursia (c. 547).
c. 554	Jordanes, a Gothic historian, writes a history of the Goths, *Getica*.
c. 561	Before his death, Clothar I, king of the Franks, divides the Frankish kingdom into three parts: Austrasia (the Rhineland); Neustria (western France); and Burgundy.
563	Saint Columba establishes the monastery of Iona and sends missionaries to mainland Britain.
565	Death of Emperor Justinian.
c. 570	Death of Saint Gildas; birth of Muhummad, founder of Islam.
573	Germanic Lombards take Verona, Milan, and Florence and end the Eastern Roman rule of Italy.
575	Death of Saint Brendan; birth of Emperor Heraklios I.
c. 584	Death of Cassiodorus.
591	Pope Gregory the Great writes *Book of Pastoral Care*.
597	Saint Augustine's mission to England; death of Saint Columba.
600	Birth of ʿAlī ibn Abī Tālib.
604	Death of Pope Gregory the Great and his canonization.
c. 607	Birth of Ildefonsus of Toledo.
c. 609	Baudonivia writes a *Life* of Saint Radegunde.
613	Saint Columbanus founds the monastery of Bobbio in Lombardy.
c. 614	Birth of Saint Hild of Whitby.
615	Death of Saint Columbanus.
616	Death of King Æthelbert of Kent.
c. 622	Bishop Isidore of Seville compiles his *Etymologies*—though unreliable, its influence is significant throughout the Middle Ages.
632	Death of Muhammad.
639	Death of Dagobert I, the last "effective" Merovingian king.
642	Death of Oswald of Northumbria.
668	Theodore of Tarsus is appointed archbishop of Canterbury.
c. 673	Birth of Bede, Anglo-Saxon theologian, historian, and chronicler.
c. 675	Birth of Saint Boniface, English missionary and reformer.
687	Pepin II of Herstal, mayor of the palace, becomes the effective ruler of all the Frankish kingdom (except Aquitaine).

c. 690	Willibrod travels to Utrecht to convert the Frisians.
c. 700	King Ine of Wessex issues one of the earliest written Anglo-Saxon law codes.
c. 703	Bede compiles *On Times*, a treatise on chronology and the calculation of Easter.
704	Death of Adamnan of Iona.
711	The Arabs and their Moorish allies invade the Visigothic kingdom of Spain; all of Spain except for the Northwest comes under Muslim control by 713.
711–714	Arabs besiege the city of Constantinople.
714	Birth of Pepin III.
720	Foundation of the monastery of St. Gall.
721	Production of the Lindisfarne Gospels.
726	Byzantine Emperor Leo III issues an edict forbidding the veneration of religious images.
c. 730	Gradual alienation of the Greek Orthodox and Roman Catholic Churches begins; birth of Alcuin, Anglo-Latin poet, educator, and cleric.
731	Bede completes his *Ecclesiastical History of the English People*.
732	Charles Martel defeats the Arabs at the battle of Poitiers, halting the advance of the Arabs into Europe.
735	Death of Saint Bede.
742	Saint Boniface begins reforming the Church in France; birth of Charlemagne.
744	Foundation of abbey of Fulda.
751	Pepin III deposes the last Merovingian king and is crowned king of the Franks.
754	Martyrdom of Saint Boniface.
755	Pepin III invades Italy in response to Pope Stephen II's appeal for help against the Lombards.
757	Pepin defeats the Lombards again and gives the city of Ravenna to the pope, the so-called Donation of Pepin.
759	Pepin expels the Arab and Moorish invaders from southern France.
768	Death of Pepin III.
772	Charlemagne begins the campaign against the Saxons, destroying the sacred tree, the Irminsul.
773	Historian Paul the Deacon begins his *History of the Lombards*.
774	Charlemagne assumes the crown of Lombardy.
778	King Offa of Mercia introduces the English silver penny; the battle of Ronceveaux, and the slaughter of Charlemagne's rearguard, takes place—it is later immortalized in the *Song of Roland*.
785	King Offa of Mercia builds a massive dyke as a defense against invaders from Wales; birth of Paschasius Radbertus, whose *On the Body and Blood of the Lord* became the main Eucharistic interpretation.

786	Hārūn al-Rashīd succeeds as caliph, ruler of the Islamic world; a revival of the sciences begins under his reign.
787	Charlemagne initiates a school program encouraging the study of Latin literature and language; the palace school at Aachen becomes one of Europe's greatest centers of scholarship and learning.
793	Vikings sack the monastery at Lindisfarne.
800	Charlemagne arranges for the defense of the channel coast against the Vikings; he is crowned emperor of the Romans on Christmas Day; birth of Otfried of Weissenburg.
801	Hārūn al-Rashīd sends Charlemagne an elephant.
c. 803	Charlemagne reforms the law codes of the Ripuarian Franks, Saxons, Frisians, and Thuringians; Hrabanus Maurus becomes the head of the monastic school at Fulda.
804	Death of Alcuin of York.
809	Death of Hārūn al-Rashīd.
c. 810	Birth of John Scottus Eriugena, Irish theologian, translator, and commentator.
813	Charlemagne gives the imperial crown to his only surviving son, Louis; al-Ma'mūn, son of Hārūn al-Rashīd, reunites the ʿAbbāsid Arab caliphate by capturing the ʿAbbāsid capital, Baghdad.
814	Death of Charlemagne; all monasteries in the Frankish Empire are required to observe the Rule of St. Benedict; reforms administered by Benedict of Aniane.
816	Louis I crowned king of the Franks and emperor of the West.
822	The caliph al-Ma'mūn founds the House of Wisdom at Baghdad, a center for translation of philosophical and scientific works from Greek to Arabic.
c. 830	Einhard, one of Charlemagne's advisers, begins his *Life of Charlemagne*.
833	Louis I is deposed and imprisoned with his youngest son by his older sons: Lothar I, Louis the German, and Pepin; Death of al-Ma'mūn.
834	Vikings sack Dorestadt, near Utrecht, the Frankish Empire's richest and largest port; Hamburg becomes the seat of Archbishop Anskar and a base for Christian missionary activity in Scandinavia.
840	Vikings sack the city of Rouen; death of Louis I the Pious; succeeded by his son Lothar I, who finds himself involved in territorial disputes with his brothers over their share of the empire; death of Einhard; Norwegian Vikings found a permanent base at the mouth of the River Liffey in Ireland, which grows into the city of Dublin.
842	Oaths of Strasbourg.
843	Treaty of Verdun resolves the claims of Louis I's heirs.
847	Hrabanus Maurus completes *On the Nature of Things*.
849	Birth of Alfred the Great, king of Wessex; Gottschalk of Orbais is condemned as a heretic.

851	Danish Vikings sack London and Canterbury; John Scottus Eriugena writes *On Predestination* to refute Gottschalk of Orbais.
853	Vikings burn the city of Tours.
856	Death of Hrabanus Maurus.
858	Pope Nicholas I strengthens papal authority by declaring that bishops are not subject to secular authorities.
c. 860	Hincmar, archbishop of Rheims, writes *On Lothar's Divorce*, a defense of the Christian law of divorce; death of Paschasius Radbertus.
863	The mission of Saints Cyril and Methodius to convert Moravia; translation of the Bible and Liturgy into Slavonic; schism between the Roman Catholic and Greek Orthodox Churches deepens when the pope excommunicates the patriarch of Constantinople.
865	John Scottus Eriugena writes *On the Division of Nature*; death of Saint Anskar, patron saint of Scandinavia.
866	Danish army that had arrived in England in 865 takes York.
869	Death of Gottschalk of Orbais.
870	Settlement of Iceland; birth of al-Fārābī.
871	Danes occupy London; the West Saxons, under Kings Æthelred and Alfred, defeat the Danes at Ashdown; later in the year, Alfred becomes king of Wessex.
c. 877	Death of John Scottus Eriugena.
878	Alfred defeats the Danes; their leader, Guthrum, is baptized.
882	Death of Hincmar of Rheims.
c. 883	Notker Balbulus, a monk at the monastery of St. Gall, may have written the *Gesta Karoli Magni imperatoris*, a life of Charlemagne, at this time.
885–900	King Harald I Fairhair brings most of Norway under his direct control.
886	Alfred expels the Danes from London; in a treaty with Guthrum, the Danish king, defines the frontier of the "Danelaw," the area of eastern England to be ruled by the Danes.
890	The court of Alfred the Great becomes a center of learning and translation.
c. 894	Asser writes a *Life of King Alfred*.
899	Death of King Alfred the Great.
903	Vikings burn the city of Tours.
906	Regino of Prüm publishes *Two Books on Synodal Cases and Ecclesiastical Discipline*, a handbook for bishops.
908	The "tribal duchies" arise in Germany; Magyars from the Danube Basin defeat the Bavarians and raid Saxony and Thuringia.
909	Foundation of the abbey of Cluny.
911	Æthelflæd, Lady of the Mercians, succeeds her husband; Rollo agrees to defend the arena around the Seine from other Vikings and is baptized;

	Charles III the Simple of France grants him the county of Rouen in exchange; Rollo's lands become known as Normandy.
919	Henry the Fowler, duke of Saxony, is elected King Henry I of the Germans.
923	Vikings raid Aquitaine and areas in southern France.
927	Æthelstan, king of Wessex and Mercia, receives the submission of the Northumbrians, becoming the first king to rule over all of England; Saint Odo becomes abbot of Cluny and gains papal recognition of the abbey's independence.
930	The Althing (parliament) is established in Iceland.
936	Otto I succeeds his father, Henry I, as king of Germany.
937	Otto I of Germany founds the monastery of St. Maurice at Magdeburg.
c. 940	Saint Dunstan, appointed abbot of Glastonbury, begins the revival of English monasticism.
c. 945	Birth of Abbo of Fleury.
948	Otto I of Germany establishes bishoprics at Brandenburg and Havelberg in Germany, and then at Ribe in Aarhus and Schleswig in Germany.
c. 950	Birth of Notker Labeo.
951	The Magyars devastate the duchy of Aquitaine.
954	The Magyars raid through Bavaria, Lorraine, Burgundy, Flanders, and as far as Utrecht; Eiríkr Bloodaxe, the last Scandinavian king of York, is murdered.
955	Otto I defeats the Magyars at the battle of Lechfeld.
958	Chartres Cathedral, built in 743, is destroyed by fire; rebuilding is completed in 1022.
c. 960	Harald Bluetooth is baptized, and he establishes Christianity as the official religion of Denmark.
961	Otto I is acknowledged as king of Italy; the caliph of Cordova establishes a center for higher studies.
962	Otto I crowned Holy Roman Emperor, which marks the foundation of the Holy Roman Empire; c. 962, Hrotsvit of Gandersheim writes six comedies in imitation of Terence to provide moral guidance and entertainment for her fellow nuns.
c. 965	Liutprand of Cremona writes *Retribution*, a history of Europe from 886 to 958, and the *Book about King Otto*, in praise of Otto I; birth of Burchard of Worms.
968	Liutprand of Cremona's embassy to Byzantium fails; he writes *Account of the Embassy of Constantinople*; archbishopric of Magdeburg is created.
c. 970	Æthelwold, bishop of Winchester, writes *A Guide to Concord*, rules for English monastic life.
972	Otto I's son marries Theophano, a niece of the Byzantine emperor.
973	Otto II succeeds his father as king of Germany and Holy Roman Emperor; c. 973, Widukind of Corvey writes the *Deeds of the Saxons in Three Books*.

978	Æthelred the Unready becomes king of England.
980	Vikings renew their raids on England; Otto II of Germany begins to extend his authority in southern Italy; birth of Ibn Sīnā (Avicenna).
983	Sven I Forkbeard deposes his father, Harald Bluetooth, and becomes king of Denmark; Otto III of Germany succeeds his father; his mother Theophano is his regent.
984	Otto III elected king of Germany.
985	Basil II defeats a palace conspiracy and begins his personal reign as emperor of Byzantium.
987	Hugh Capet is elected as king of France and founds the Capetian dynasty.
991	Norwegian Viking leader Óláfr Tryggvason defeats and kills Byrhtnoth, alderman of East Anglia, in the battle of Maldon; Gerbert of Aurillac appointed archbishop of Rheims.
994	King Sven of Denmark and Óláfr Tryggvason besiege the city of London and leave upon receiving payment.
995	Óláfr Tryggvason becomes king of Norway; Olof Skötkonung becomes king of Sweden.
998	Stephen succeeds his father, Géza, as duke of Hungary.
999	Gerbert of Aurillac is elected as Pope Sylvester II.
1000	Iceland adopts Christianity; Otto III makes his permanent residence in Rome and creates the first archbishopric for Poland; King Sven of Denmark kills King Óláfr Tryggvason and conquers Norway; Duke Stephen of Hungary becomes king; French cathedral schools develop in Tours, Orléans, Utrecht, Rheims, Chartres, and Paris; birth of Pope Benedict IX.
1002	Henry of Bavaria is crowned as king of the Romans (king of Germany); King Æthelred the Unready of England massacres the Danes living in southern England.
1003	Brian Boru becomes high king of Ireland; King Sven of Denmark invades England to take revenge for the "St. Brice's Day Massacre"; Moorish forces devastate the kingdom of León; death of Pope Sylvester II.
1007	Foundation of Bamberg Cathedral.
1013	King Sven of Denmark, having been accepted as king in Northumbria and the Danelaw, conquers Wessex; King Æthelred flees to Normandy.
1014	Death of King Sven of Denmark; his sons succeed him—Harald in Denmark and Cnut in England; King Æthelred returns to England and forces Cnut to leave; King Henry II of Germany and Italy is crowned emperor; the Irish king Brian Boru defeats a Viking coalition at the battle of Clontarf but is killed; Wulfstan, archbishop of York, writes his *Sermon of the Wolf to the English*, which attacks the immorality of the English.
1016	On the death of Æthelred's son King Edmond Ironside, Cnut is accepted as sole king of England.
1019	Cnut succeeds his brother Harald and becomes king of Denmark.

1024	Duke Conrad II, the first of the Salian dynasty, is crowned king of the Germans.
c. 1028	Death of Fulbert of Chartres.
1030	King Óláfr II of Norway is killed in the battle of Stiklestad; King Cnut succeeds him as king of Norway.
1033	King Sancho III of Navarre creates the kingdom of Castile for his son, Ferdinand I.
1040	Birth of Rashi; birth of Alfonso VI of Castile.
1042	Edward the Confessor succeeds Harthacnut as king of England.
1046	Henry III of Germany officially crowned as emperor; the practice of simony is denounced at a council held in Pavia.
1047	Duke William I assumes personal rule of the duchy of Normandy; death of Magnús the Good, king of Denmark and Norway; Sven Estridsen succeeds him as king of Denmark; Harald Hardråde succeeds him as king of Norway.
1050	King Edward the Confessor orders the rebuilding of Westminster Abbey; Berengar of Tours is excommunicated for his controversial teaching on transubstantiation.
1054	Death of Hermann of Reichenau.
1057	Henry IV of Germany's regents are unable to interfere with the election of Pope Stephen IX, which begins the process of freeing the papacy from secular control; King Macbeth of Scotland is killed in battle.
1058	Birth of al-Ghazālī; birth of Bohemond I, prince of Antioch.
1059	Robert de Hauteville (Guiscard) becomes a papal vassal and duke of Apulia and Calabria and count of Sicily; the College of Cardinals is established to elect subsequent popes.
1061	Roger de Hauteville begins the Norman conquest of Sicily.
1066	1 January—King Henry IV takes personal control of the government in Germany; 5 January—King Edward the Confessor dies; 6 January—Harold Godwinson elected as king of England; 25 September—King Harold of England defeats Harald Hardråde of Norway at the battle of Stamford Bridge; 28 September—Duke William I of Normandy lands in Pevensey; 14 October—Duke William I kills King Harold of England at the battle of Hastings; 25 December—William I crowned king of England.
1070	Lanfranc of Bec becomes archbishop of Canterbury.
1071	The Turks defeat the Byzantines at the battle of Manzikert.
1072	Death of Peter Damian.
1073	Deacon Hildebrand, a radical Church reformer, is elected as Pope Gregory VII.
1075	King Henry IV of Germany defies Pope Gregory VII's ban against lay investiture, thereby initiating the dispute between the papacy and the empire known as the Investiture Controversy; birth of Orderic Vitalis.
c. 1076	Adam of Bremen writes his *History of the Archbishops of Hamburg*.

c. 1078   Byzantine philosopher and historian Michael Psellos writes the *Chronography*, a historical narrative of events in the Byzantine Empire from 976 on.

1079   The improved calendar computed by poet and astronomer ᶜUmar Khayyām is introduced in Persia; birth of Peter Abelard.

c. 1080   Birth of William of Conches.

1081   King Alfonso VI of Castile exiles Rodrigo Díaz, also known as the Cid; Robert Guiscard defeats the Byzantine emperor Alexius I Comnenus near Durazzo (in modern Albania); birth of Suger, abbot of St. Denis.

1084   Saint Bruno founds the Carthusian Order.

1085   William I the Conquerer orders a survey of England's resources subsequently recorded in the Domesday Book.

c. 1087   Death of Constantine the African.

c. 1090   The Bayeaux Tapestry, a pictorial record of the Norman Conquest of England, is embroidered; birth of Saint Bernard of Clairvaux.

c. 1092   Birth of Peter the Venerable.

1095   Pope Urban II considers Alexius I Comnenus' second request for help against the Turks, and later in the year, he proclaims the First Crusade; Bologna emerges as a center for legal studies.

1095–1099 The First Crusade.

1096   Robert d'Arbrissel founds the Fontevrault Order.

1098   Robert of Molesme founds the Cistercian Order; death of Adhémar of Le Puy.

1099   The crusaders take Jerusalem; pontificate of Pope Paschal II begins.

1100   William I's son, Henry, is crowned king of England; birth of Peter Lombard.

1103   Death of Frutolf of Michelsberg.

1105   Birth of Alfonso VII of Galicia, Castile, and León; death of Raymond IV of Toulouse.

c. 1108   William of Champeaux founds a theological school in the abbey of St. Victor.

1109   Death of Saint Anselm of Canterbury.

1111   Henry V officially crowned emperor; Guibert of Nogent writes his history of the First Crusade, *The Deeds of God through the Franks*.

c. 1113   Peter Abelard opens a school for the study of rhetoric, philosophy, and theology in Paris.

1114   Emperor Henry V marries Matilda, daughter of Henry I of England; birth of Gerard of Cremona.

1115   Guibert of Nogent writes his autobiography, *On His Life*; death of Saint Ivo of Chartres.

c. 1117   Death of Anselm of Laon.

c. 1118   Death of Alexius I Comnenus, Byzantine emperor.

1121   William of Champeaux becomes the first master of the cathredal school of

Paris; Peter Abelard is condemned at the council of Soissons; Saint Norbert of Xanten founds the Premonstratensian Order of Conventual Canons.

1122   The Concordat of Worms ends the Investiture Controversy; Peter Abelard writes *Yes and No.*

c. 1125   Ari Þorgilsson's chronicle *Íslendingabók* (Book of the Icelanders) is recorded.

1126   Adelard of Bath translates and adapts the *Astronomical Tables* of the ninth-century Muslim astronomer al-Khwārizmī; birth of Ibn Rushd (Averroës); Saint Bernard of Clairvaux writes the sermon "On the Love of God."

1127   Fulcher of Chartres completes the *Deeds of the Franks on Their Pilgrimage to Jerusalem*; The English barons confirm their allegiance to Henry I's daughter, Matilda, as his heir.

1131   Louis VII is crowned as king of France and rules jointly with his father; Saint Gilbert of Sempringham founds the Order of Sempringham.

1135   King Alfonso VII of Castile and León is acclaimed as emperor of Spain; Henry I of England's nephew, Stephen of Blois, is crowned king of England, thereby initiating civil war in England between his and Matilda's supporters.

1137   Louis VII marries Eleanor of Aquitaine; becomes sole king of France; c. 1137, Geoffrey of Monmouth completes his *History of the Kings of Britain.*

1139   Arnold of Brescia, an ardent Church reformer, is condemned at the Second Lateran Council.

1139–1141 Gratian compiles the *Concordia discordantium canonum*, known as the *Decretum*, the first systematic codification of canon law.

c. 1140   Peter Abelard writes his "Letters" to Héloïse as well as his autobiography.

1142   Adelard of Bath translates Euclid's *Elements* from Arabic; William of Malmesbury revises his *Deeds of the Kings of the English.*

1145   Suger, abbot of St. Denis, writes *On the Things Done in His Administration*; pontificate of Eugenius III.

1146   Otto of Freising writes his *Chronicle* or *History of Two Cities.*

1147   Hildegard, a Benedictine nun, founds a monastery near Bingen.

1147–1149 Second Crusade, called by Pope Eugenius III, supported by Bernard of Clairvaux, is forced to retreat.

1148   Anna Comnena completes *The Alexiad*; the theologian Gilbert of Poitiers is called to appear before the pope; birth of Béla III, king of Hungary.

1152   Frederick I Barbarossa is elected king of Germany; Louis VII of France and Eleanor of Aquitaine dissolve their marriage; Henry Plantagenet (later Henry II of England) marries Eleanor, thereby controlling more of France than Louis VII; John of Salisbury writes the *Historia Pontificalis.*

1153   Stephen of England recognizes Henry Plantagenet as his heir.

1154   Cardinal Nicholas Breakspear is elected as Pope Hadrian IV (the first and only English pope); Henry II Plantagenet crowned king of England; Thomas

Becket is appointed chancellor of England; al-Idrīsī, geographer to Roger II of Sicily, writes *The Book of Roger.*

1155   King Frederick I Barbarossa of Germany is crowned king of Italy; he captures and executes as a heretic Arnold of Brescia and is crowned as Holy Roman Emperor by Pope Hadrian IV; the Norman monk Wace completes the *Roman de Brut*; birth of Alfonso VIII of Castile.

1158   Holy Roman Emperor Frederick I grants his charter to the University of Bologna; Otto of Freising completes his *Deeds of Emperor Frederick I*; Peter Lombard writes *Four Books of Sentences*, which eventually becomes one of the most popular theological textbooks of the Middle Ages.

1159   A majority of cardinals elect Orlando Bandinelli as Pope Alexander III, while a group favoring the Holy Roman Emperor Frederick I elects Cardinal Octavian as Pope Victor IV; neither is able to control Rome; John of Salisbury writes the *Policraticus.*

1160   Pope Alexander III excommunicates the Holy Roman Emperor Frederick I; Averroës writes his great medical encyclopedia; death of Bernard Silvester; foundation of the University of Paris.

1163   Thomas Becket, now archbishop of Canterbury, supports the rights of the Church against the monarchy.

1164   Pope Alexander III confirms the Order of Knights of Calatrava to fight against the Muslims in Spain; King Henry II of England issues the Constitutions of Clarendon.

1165   Marie de France writes the *Lais*, verse narratives of Celtic and other legends.

c. 1166   Saint Ælred of Rievaulx writes the *Mirror of Charity.*

1168   Moses Maimonides, a Jewish philosopher, begins his commentary on the Mishna.

1170   Murder of Thomas Becket in Canterbury Cathedral; c. 1170, Chrétien de Troyes writes *Erec and Enide*; Heinrich von Veldeke writes "Servatius"; birth of Robert Grosseteste; birth of Saint Dominic; birth of Boncompagno of Signa.

1173   King Henry II of England's sons rebel against him with the help of Louis VII of France; Benjamin of Tudela, a Spanish Jew, writes the story of his travels to Constantinople and India; Peter Waldo initiates a Christian movement called the Waldensians.

1174–1186   Andreas Capellanus writes the *Art of Courtly Love.*

1175   Saladin is recognized as the sultan of Egypt and Syria by the caliph of Baghdad; Gerard of Cremona translates Ptolemy's astronomical work the *Almagest* from Arabic into Latin.

1176   Pope Alexander III is recognized as the legitimate pope by the Holy Roman Emperor Frederick I, thereby ending the schism between the papacy and empire; Chrétien de Troyes writes "Cliges."

1177   King Alfonso VIII of Castile takes the city of Cuenca from the Muslims; the king of Jerusalem, Baldwin IV, defends Jerusalem against an invasion by Saladin.

1179   Philip Augustus is crowned as Philip II and rules jointly with his father, Louis VII; Hildegard of Bingen writes *Physics*, an encyclopedia of natural history.

1180   Philip II becomes sole king of France; Walter of Châtillon writes the *Alexandreis*.

c. 1181   Birth of Saint Francis of Assisi.

1181–1183   King Henry II of England's sons rebel against him again, this time with the help of Philip II Augustus of France.

1183   William of Tyre writes a history of the Latin kings of Jerusalem.

1187   Saladin institutes the policy of doctors' neutrality; he destroys the army of the kingdom of Jerusalem at the battle of Ḥaṭṭīn and takes Jerusalem.

1188   The loss of the city of Jerusalem persuades King Henry II of England and Philip II of France to make peace and go on crusade; Holy Roman Emperor Frederick I also takes the Cross; Gerald of Wales begins his *Journey through Wales*.

1189   Richard I the Lionheart is crowned as king of England after his father dies, then leaves England to join the Third Crusade; c. 1189, Heinrich von Veldeke completes his High German poem *Eneit*, which is based on Virgil's *Aeneid*.

1189–1192   The Third Crusade.

1190   The Holy Roman Emperor Frederick I drowns on his way to Jerusalem to participate in the Third Crusade; Moses Maimonides completes *A Guide for the Perplexed*.

1191   Henry VI is crowned as Holy Roman Emperor upon the death of his father; King Richard I the Lionheart leads the crusaders to victory over Saladin at Arsuf, Palestine.

1192   King Richard I the Lionheart defeats Saladin outside Jaffa; they negotiate a three-year truce, thereby ending the Third Crusade.

1193   Death of Saladin.

c. 1195   Hartmann von Aue writes *Poor Henry*; death of Bernart de Ventadorn, a troubadour.

1196   King Philip II of France renews the war with Richard I the Lionheart of England by seizing lands in Normandy; the Holy Roman Emperor Henry VI's son Frederick II is elected king of Germany.

1198   Pontificate of Pope Innocent III begins; preparations begin for the Fourth Crusade.

1199   Death of Richard I; his brother, John, is crowned as king of England.

c. 1200   Birth of Albertus Magnus; Jean Bodel writes the *Play of St. Nicholas*; Wolfram von Eschenbach writes *Parzival* in Middle High German.

1201   Birth of Beatrijs of Nazareth.

1202   Death of Joachim of Fiore, an Italian theologian and mystic; King Philip II of France declares that John of England has forfeited his French lands by refusing to appear in his court to answer charges; John's vassals revolt against him; the crusaders agree to help the deposed Byzantine emperor regain the throne.

1202–1204 The Fourth Crusade.

1203 Death of Alan of Lille.

1204 The crusaders take Constantinople and Baldwin, count of Flanders, is crowned as Latin emperor of Constantinople; Philip II of France completes his conquest of Normandy.

c. 1207 Geoffrey of Villehardouin writes *The Conquest of Constantinople*, an account of the Fourth Crusade.

1208 Pope Innocent III declares a crusade against the heretics, the "Albigensian Crusade"; he places an interdict against England because King John refuses to accept the pope's choice, Stephen Langton, as archbishop of Canterbury; Saint Francis of Assisi is called to preach and live in complete poverty.

1208–1229 The Albigensian Crusade.

1209 A group of English academics leave Oxford after riots and move to Cambridge, where they establish a new university; Pope Innocent III excommunicates King John.

1210 Pope Innocent III excommunicates Holy Roman Emperor Otto IV, whose subjects then rebel against him; Pope Innocent III sanctions the Franciscan Order, the Friars Minor.

1211 The German princes offer the crown to Frederick II, duke of Hohenstaufen, king of Sicily.

1212 The Spanish kings win a decisive victory against the Muslims in Spain, and Muslim power there is permanently broken; Frederick II is crowned king of Germany; c. 1212, Gottfried von Strassburg writes *Tristan and Isolde* in Middle High German.

1213 King Philip II of France decides to conquer England with papal support; Pope Innocent III proclaims the Fifth Crusade; King John of England renders England a papal fief and agrees to accept Stephen Langton as archbishop of Canterbury; Simon of Montfort, the Elder, and the Albigensian crusaders defeat Raymond VI, count of Toulouse.

1214 King Philip II of France soundly defeats King John's allies at the battle of Bouvines; birth of Roger Bacon; birth of Sturla Þorðarson.

1215 English barons demand that King John restore their "liberties"; King John agrees to the Magna Carta; Pope Innocent III annuls the Magna Carta; at the Fourth Lateran Council, Pope Innocent III legislates for finances for the Fifth Crusade, for the suppression of heresy, and for the regulation of religious orders, among other things.

1216 Louis, Philip II of France's son, lands in England with the hope of being recognized as king of England; death of Pope Innocent III; Henry III, King John's son, is crowned king of England; the Magna Carta is reissued; Pope Honorius III recognizes the Dominican Order, the Order of Friars Preachers; c. 1216, Saxo Grammaticus writes the *History of the Danes*.

1217	Hákon IV Hákonarson becomes king of Norway; William Marshall, Henry III of England's guardian, defeats Louis' forces; Louis is paid to leave England; Queen Berenguela of Castile abdicates in favor of her son; Alexander Neckham, an English scholar, writes *De naturis rerum*, an encyclopedia; birth of Saint Bonaventure.
1217–1221	The Fifth Crusade.
1220	Frederick II of Germany is crowned as Holy Roman Emperor; Michael Scot translates Averroës' commentaries on Aristotle from Arabic into Latin; John of Garland writes the *Parisiana poetria*.
c. 1222	The Icelander Snorri Sturluson writes the *Prose Edda*, a manual on poetic meters; foundation of the University of Padua.
1223	Philip II's son, Louis VIII, is crowned king of France.
1224	Louis VIII of France declares war on Henry III of England.
1225	Saint Francis of Assisi writes the "Canticle of Brother Sun"; c. 1225, Eike von Repgow writes the *Sachsenspiegel*; Snorri Sturluson writes *Heimskringla*.
1226	On the death of his father, Louis IX becomes king of France; his mother, Blanche of Castile, serves as his regent during his minority.
1227	Pontificate of Gregory IX begins; he excommunicates Frederick II for his failure to fulfill his promise to go on crusade.
1229	The Holy Roman Emperor Frederick II negotiates the return of Jerusalem to Christian control; the Treaty of Paris brings an end to the Albigensian Crusade; foundation of the University of Angers in France.
1231	The Holy Roman Emperor Frederick II promulgates the *Liber Augustalis* for the kingdom of Sicily; King Henry III of England and Louis IX of France make a truce; Pope Gregory IX gives privileges to the University of Paris, exempting it from the local bishop's control and exempts the Friars Preacher and Friars Minor from episcopal jurisdiction.
c. 1232	Birth of Ramon Llull.
1233	Pope Gregory IX confirms the establishment of the University of Toulouse.
c. 1235	William of Auvergne, a scholastic philosopher, writes his *Teaching on God and Wisdom*; birth of Pope Boniface VIII.
c. 1237	Guillaume de Lorris writes the first 4,000 lines of the *Romance of the Rose*.
1240	The Englishman Bartholomaeus Anglicus composes an encyclopedia of natural philosophy, *On the Properties of Things*; death of Jacques de Vitry.
c. 1244	Appearance of the first edition of Vincent of Beauvais' *Great Mirror*.
1245	Pope Innocent IV holds a council in Lyons and legislates for reform, calls for a new crusade to liberate Jerusalem, and deposes the Holy Roman Emperor Frederick II; Pope Innocent IV sends John of Plano Carpini to the Mongol court, hoping to convert them; death of Alexander of Hales, an influential philosopher and theologian.
1247	King Louis IX of France initiates the *enquêteurs*; Pope Innocent IV confirms the new rule for the Carmelite Friars.

1248   King Louis IX sails from France on the Seventh Crusade; birth of Angela of Foligno.

1248–1254 The Seventh Crusade.

1249   Roger Bacon, an English scholar, argues that the curriculum of Oxford University should include scientific studies.

1250   Death of the Holy Roman Emperor Frederick II; Louis IX of France is captured while on crusade; the Dominicans establish the first school of Oriental studies at Toledo, Spain.

1253   William of Rubruck travels to the court of the Great Khan of the Mongols; Ottocar II becomes king of Bohemia; death of Saint Clare of Assisi, who founded the Poor Clares.

1254   King Louis IX of France issues ordinances to prevent corruption among his regional governors; King Alfonso X of Castile and León publishes the *Royal Law Code* and establishes a school of Latin and Arabic studies in Seville; Conrad IV, Holy Roman Emperor, dies and is succeeded by his son, Conrad V (Conradin); birth of Marco Polo.

c. 1255   Henry de Bracton writes *On the Laws and Customs of England*.

1256   Foundation of a theological college at the University of Paris, which will later bear the name of its founder, Robert of Sorbon.

1258   The Provisions of Oxford establish baronial control over King Henry III of England's government; Manfred of Sicily, the illegitimate son of Frederick II, takes the crown of Sicily.

1259   The Provisions of Westminster, a plan for legal reforms in England, are enacted by the baronial council; King Louis IX of France and King Henry III of England make peace in the Treaty of Paris; death of Matthew Paris; Saint Bonaventure writes his *Mind's Road to God*.

1263   Simon de Montfort, the Younger, returns to England to lead a new baronial movement against King Henry III; later in the year, he and his allies occupy London; death of King Hákon IV of Norway; his son Magnús Hákonarson succeeds him.

1264   King Louis IX of France, mediating between Henry III and the barons, decides in favor of Henry; Simon de Montfort and the barons go to war against Henry III, capturing him; he agrees to give control to Simon de Montfort's party; Thomas Aquinas writes the hymn "The Praise of Zion."

1265   King Henry III and his son Edward kill Simon de Montfort at Evesham; c. 1265, Jacobus de Voragine compiles the *Golden Legend*; birth of Dante Alighieri.

1266   Charles of Anjou kills Manfred, former king of Sicily, and is crowned king himself; King Magnús of Norway cedes his claims to the Hebrides and the Isle of Man; birth of John Duns Scotus.

c. 1267   Brunetto Latini writes the *Book of Treasure*.

1267–1270 Roger Bacon writes his *Greater Work*.

1268   Conradin invades Italy to recover the kingdom of Sicily; Charles of Anjou defeats him and has him executed.

1270   King Louis IX of France sails to Tunisia and dies there; his brother, Charles of Anjou, signs a peace treaty with the emir of Tunis, intending to head toward Constantinople, but the fleet is destroyed; birth of William Wallace.

1272   Edward Plantagenet, Henry III's son, returns to England from Jerusalem and is crowned as Edward I of England; Ramon Llull writes the *Book of Contemplation*, originally in Arabic and then translates it; John of Joinville begins the first section of the *Life of St. Louis*.

1274   Death of Saint Thomas Aquinas leaves his masterpiece *Summary of Theology* incomplete.

1275   King Edward I of England holds his first parliament; Pope Gregory X persuades Alfonso X of Castile and León to renounce the title of Holy Roman Emperor; death of Eudes Rigaud.

1276   King Magnús establishes a common law in Norway; Pope Gregory X approves Charles of Anjou's acquisition of the kingdom of Jerusalem; Ramon Llull founds a college of friars for the study of Arabic; death of King James I of Aragon.

1277   King Edward I of England begins the first of many Welsh campaigns; Roger Bacon is tried for heresy and imprisoned until 1292; Bishop Stephen Tempier condemns 219 radical Aristotelian propositions; Siger of Brabant is condemned for his Averroistic writings.

1278   Charles of Anjou is crowned king of Jerusalem; death of King Ottocar II of Bohemia; Jean de Meun finishes the second part of his continuation of Guillaume de Lorris' *Romance of the Rose*.

c. 1280   Mechthild of Magdeburg, a Cistercian nun, records her mystical visions in the *Flowing Light of the Godhead*; death of Saint Albertus Magnus.

1282   A Welsh revolt against King Edward I of England leads to war; Charles of Anjou is forced to relinquish the crown of Sicily to Aragon after the massacre of the "Sicilian Vespers."

c. 1283   Philippe de Beaumanoir writes the *Customs of Beauvaisis*.

1284   King Edward I of England's Statute of Rhuddlan provides English government for Wales; death of King Alfonso X of Castile.

1285   Giles of Rome writes *On the Rule of Princes*; birth of William of Ockham.

1286   Guillelmus Durandus (William Durand) compiles the *Rationale divionorum officiorum*, a guide to the Divine Offices; death of William of Moerbeke; death of Gregorius Bar Hebraeus.

1287   Salimbene of Parma writes his *Chronicle*.

1291   Fall of Acre and the end of the Crusader kingdoms in Palestine.

1292   King Edward I of England makes John of Balliol king of Scotland; Guillelmus Durandus writes the *Pontifical*; death of John Peckham, archbishop of Canterbury.

1297	William Wallace, a Scottish nationalist, leads a rebellion against King Edward I of England; Pope Boniface VIII canonizes Louis IX of France.
1298	King Edward I of England defeats William Wallace and the Scots but is unable to subdue the country.
1300	Pope Boniface VIII declares a "Jubilee Year."

The Rise
of the
Medieval World
500–1300

A

ABBO (ABBON) OF FLEURY, SAINT (C. 945–1004). Abbo was a French Benedictine monk renowned for his learning and considered one of the two "lights" of the tenth century (the other being Gerbert of Aurillac/Pope *Sylvester II). His diplomacy helped maintain monastic independence in the transitional years of the Capetian dynasty. This Abbo should not be confused with Abbo of St. Germain (d. c. 921), the monk who wrote *De bellis Parisiacae urbis* (The Siege/Battle of Paris).

Born in the vicinity of Orléans, Abbo entered the Abbey of Fleury school (famous for its intellectual activity—present-day St.-Benoît-sur-Loire) at a young age and excelled in the traditional curriculum. He left Fleury to continue his education, first in Rheims and then in Paris. Around 970 he returned to Fleury and spent the next twelve to fifteen years as a scholastic. His abbot, Oylbold, sent him to England as a teacher to help Oswald with the English Church's reform movement. Abbo taught at the Abbey of Ramsey from 985 to 987. The moribund Oylbold called him back to Fleury and appointed him abbot, an appointment challenged by a fellow monk with Capetian favor. In September 988, however, Abbo did receive the abbotship, which was his until his death.

As abbot, he served at several Church councils (St. Basle in 991, St. Denis in 993). His vehement defense of the rights and privileges of monasteries, especially their independence from both episcopal and secular powers, as well as his denunciation of simony and lay possession of Church properties earned him the animosity of Arnulf, bishop of Orléans, and brought him to the king's (*Hugh Capet) attention, to whom Abbo was summoned to defend himself. For this defense, Abbo wrote his *Apologia*, in which he gives a classification of ecclesiastic society. This work in turn led to his compiling a "canonical collection" (*Canones Abbonis*), wherein he expounds on the fifty-two canonical laws most needing clarification in his day. Abbo fell in favor with the royal household and in 997 was sent to Italy as the new king's (Robert II, the Pious) ambassador to the pope to plead for his divorce from Bertha. Abbo found Pope Gregory V in Umbria, banished there by the antipope, John XVI. Again, Abbo won a friend in the pope, who, although he denied Robert II's divorce, issued a bull that ensured the autonomy of monasteries from Episcopal and lay powers. Moreover, the Abbey of Fleury was recognized as the premier Abbey of the Gauls (housing as it did the remains of Saint *Benedict). Abbo spent much of the rest of his life reforming monasteries. On 13 November 1004, during his second sojourn to reform the monastery of La Réole (Gascony), Abbo was killed trying to settle a confrontation between the monks from Fleury and those from La Réole. He was later canonized.

Abbo was a precursor of later Church reformers (such as *Peter Damian), and his *Apologia* and *Canones* presaged such twelfth-century writers on jurisprudence as *Gratian and Peter *Abelard. Abbo was renowned for his knowledge, both in his own day and well through the fifteenth century. He wrote on several subjects—astronomy, logic, arithmetic, computation, grammar, saints' lives, popes' lives, law—and a number of his letters are still extant. Unfortunately, the majority of his works were lost over the years. Through the efforts of Van de Vyver, however, many of them have been identified. Perhaps chief among his identified writings are his *Quaestiones grammaticales* and his *Life* of the English king and martyr Saint Edmond. His own life was chronicled shortly after his death by his fellow monk Aimoin.

Bibliography: Abbo de Fleury, *Questions grammaticales*, 1982.

Paul B. Nelson

ABELARD, PETER (1079–1142).

Abelard, a French philosopher and theologian, was probably the most influential teacher of the Middle Ages, laying the foundation of what was to become the University of Paris. Much of his popular fame stems from his tragic love affair with and later marriage to his student *Héloïse.

Abelard recounts the events of his life to about age fifty-four in his autobiography *Historia calamitatum* (Story of My Misfortunes). He was born in Le Pallet, near Nantes, Brittany, to members of the minor nobility. His desire to become a scholar and a philosopher caused him to reject his inheritance and a military career. He focused his studies on logic and proved to be a brilliant but extremely difficult student. He was involved in bitter quarrels with two of his teachers, *Roscelin of Compiégne and *William of Champeaux. Roscelin was a Nominalist, believing that universals are merely words. In contrast, William followed a type of Platonic Realism and believed that universals existed. Apparently, Abelard pointed out weak areas in William's argument, forcing him to modify his ideas. This victory over one of the foremost philosophers of the time enhanced Abelard's reputation as a scholar and attracted many students to him, including some formerly taught by William. Abelard started his own school in Paris on Mont Ste. Geneviève, marking the beginning of what would eventually grow into the University of Paris. His rivalry with William continued, and William tried to keep Abelard from succeeding him as the head of the Cloister School. After a trip home to Brittany, Abelard returned to France to study theology, choosing to go to Laon in 1113 or 1114 to hear *Anselm of Laon, the most respected theology teacher of the time. However, Abelard was disappointed in Anselm's teaching and with the school at Laon in general and soon began to cause trouble. Two students convinced Anselm to ban Abelard from teaching at Laon. Abelard returned to Paris, taking several of Anselm's students with him. After Anselm's death, Abelard became the foremost authority on theology.

By his midthirties, Abelard had become one of the most popular and respected teachers in Paris, and he was hired by Canon Fulbert to teach his teenage niece Héloïse as a private student. Héloïse had a brilliant mind and was especially educated for a girl during that time. Abelard and Héloïse soon fell in love and began an intensely passionate affair. Although their love was well known in Paris, Fulbert was ignorant of it. They became even more daring until Fulbert caught them together. By that time, Héloïse was pregnant. Abelard took her away to Brittany, where their son Astralabe was born. Fulbert demanded that the pair marry. However, Abelard would only agree to a secret marriage, and Héloïse did not believe in marriage at all. Finally, they did marry in secret. Abelard moved her out of her uncle's house and into the convent of Argenteuil, where she had studied as a child. He continued to meet her at the convent. Strangely, he asked that she wear a nun's habit. Fulbert, probably thinking that Abelard meant to put Héloïse away for good, became violently angry with Abelard and ordered his servants to break into Abelard's room while he was asleep and castrate him.

Abelard's castration marks the beginning of the third period of his life. He entered the royal Abbey of St. Denis in 1119 and took holy orders. He forced Héloïse to remain at Argenteuil and become a nun. Although she had no vocation, she was very successful, eventually becoming abbess. Abelard repented of his relationship with Héloïse and claimed that his castration was fortuitous. In contrast, Héloïse never felt any shame about the affair and missed the physical part of their relationship. The couple did remain in contact, and their letters provide an insight into these brilliant, tragic lovers.

At St. Denis, Abelard continued his teaching and the study of theology. He once again proved himself to be difficult and constantly criticized the monks' way of life. However, despite his quarrels with the other monks, Abelard fit in well with the monastic lifestyle. His conversion appears to be sincere, and he was once again doing what he loved best—teaching. His life was far from serene, for his biblical research and reading of the Fathers of the Church led him to compile a collection of quotations representing inconsistencies in Church teachings. He organized the results of his study in *Sic et non* (Yes and no), which he intended to be used as a teaching manual in the study of disputation of difficult questions. In this work, he sets out 158 problems where authorities conflicted. He does not provide any solution, for he believed that young minds could be sharpened by working out the problems on their own. During this period in his life, he also wrote the first version of his *Theologia*, a work that was judged heretical and burned at the Council of Soissons in 1121 for what the council declared was its false analysis of the Trinity, presented by Abelard as divine attributes rather than as divine persons. Abelard was arrested and held briefly at the Abbey of St. Médard. Upon his release, he returned to St. Denis, where he continued to cause trouble, this time by applying his methods of disputation to the study of the community's patron saint. He concluded that Saint Denis of Paris, martyred apostle of Gaul, was not the same as Denis of Athens, who was converted by Saint Paul. This challenge to their traditional claims so provoked the monastic community that Abelard had to flee to avoid being brought to trial before the king of France.

Abelard found asylum with Count Theobald of Champagne. In Champagne, Abelard tried to lead a hermit's life, but he was convinced by students to resume his teaching. In 1125 he accepted the position of abbot of the monastery of Saint-Gildas-de-Rhuys, located in a remote part of Brittany. However, he was not successful there either. Attempts were made on his life, and he fled back to France. Back in Paris, he resumed his teaching, once again drawing large crowds and inciting the wrath of the clergy and other teachers. *William of St. Thierry, a former admirer of Abelard's who had turned against him, recruited the aid of Saint *Bernard of Clairvaux, the most influential religious figure of the time. In 1140, Abelard was condemned at a council held at Sens, and Pope Innocent II upheld the decision. Abelard retreated to the monastery of Cluny in Burgundy. There, through the mediation of *Peter the Venerable, Abelard made peace with Bernard of Clairvaux. Abelard retired from teaching and lived out the rest of his life as a Cluniac monk. Upon his death in 1142, Héloïse was granted permission to bury him in her convent at Paraclete, a community provided for her by Abelard. In the nineteenth century, the bodies of Abelard and Héloïse were buried side by side in the cemetery of Pére-Lachaise in Paris.

Abelard contributed greatly to the development of the University of Paris and to the medieval scholastic movement, although the extent of his contributions is subject to debate. His major theological writings include *Sic et non, Theologia, The Dialogue between a Philosopher, a Jew and a Christian*, and *Ethica* or *Know Thyself*. His major writings on logic are his *Dialectica* and commentaries on Aristotle's logic. However, Abelard is most popularly remembered for his tragic love affair with Héloïse, and translations of their letters remain his most widely read achievement.

Bibliography: É. Gilson, *Héloïse and Abelard*, 1953; L. Grane, *Peter Abelard*, 1970; D. E. Luscombe, *The School of Peter Abelard*, 1969.

Leah Larson

ADAM OF BREMEN (D. C. 1081). Historian and geographer, his *Gesta Hammaburgensis ecclesiae pontificum* is a detailed account of the see of Hamburg and the spread of Christianity in the North.

Adam was born in the mid-eleventh century. Details of his early life are obscure, many gathered from internal references in his writing and from the occasional appearance of his signature on documents. He is believed to have been raised in eastern Franconia. In the mid-1060s, he moved to Bremen at the invitation of Archbishop Adalbert of Bremen. On a document of 1069, he is noted as a canon of the cathedral and director of schools. Adam traveled to Denmark, where he obtained information about the northern regions: Russia, the Baltic, Scandinavia, and the northern isles. There is no evidence that he visited northern regions himself, although he gathered extensive information about them from contemporaries.

Between 1072 and 1076, he wrote his Latin history, *Gesta Hammaburgensis ecclesiae pontificum*, an account in four volumes of the see of Hamburg and its missionary role in the northern regions, the spread of Christianity northward, as well as the conversion of the Slavs and Scandinavians. Adam based his account on oral sources from firsthand visitors and knowledgeable sources including the Danish king *Sven Estridsen, whom he visited in the early 1070s, and Archbishop Adalbert of Bremen, whose life he details in Book III. Adam also made use of the written records of his church, official external ecclesiastical documents, contemporary chronicles, ancient Roman historians, and the Church Fathers.

The work is in four parts, three concentrating on history, one on the geography of the northern regions. In Book I, Adam relates the early history of the Saxons, their conversion to Christianity, and the progress of the sees of Bremen and Hamburg. Book II discusses the careers of the archbishops from Adaldag (937–988) to Alebrand (1035–1045) and offers a survey of contemporary Slavic nations and territories. Adam also discusses the power struggles between the Church and the Saxon aristocracy and German political affairs between 940 and 1045. A substantial portion of Book III delineates the character and accomplishments of Archbishop Adalbert (1043–1072), whom Adam portrays with psychological detail rare in his age. Book III also includes a substantial amount of information regarding Nordic history. Of interest to English historians is his account of Danish expansion under *Cnut, the battle of Stamford Bridge, and the Norman Conquest. Book IV describes Scandinavian geography and culture based in large part on recent explorations. Here Adam is openly skeptical of the mythical creatures described in the late antique Latin sources. He offers unprecedented information about the northern lands and islands, ending the book with an account of a Frisian expedition to the northern oceans. Adam offers his own interpretation of the northern gods.

Adam's *Gesta* provides valuable information and contemporary insight into what was known about the northern lands. He discusses a variety of topics including the establishment of Christianity, contemporary German politics, contemporary Church affairs, and the cultural practices of the Swedes. His is the earliest mention of "Winland," the land visited by Leif Eriksson. In his work, Adam adopts a critical approach to his sources, attempting to establish a credible chronology and noting discrepancies between sources. Although Adam's style is derivative and depends on Latin models, his history, informed by firsthand accounts of the cultural practices and geography of the northern lands, offers a valuable addition to northern sagas and earlier chronicles.

Bibliography: Adam of Bremen, *History of the Archbishops of Hamburg-Bremen*, trans. F. J. Tschan, 1959; C. F. Hallencreutz, *Adam Bremensis and Sueonia: A Fresh Look at* Gesta hammaburgensis ecclesiae pontificum, 1984.

Patricia Price

ADAMNAN (ADOMNÁN) OF IONA (623/624–704). Adamnan, the Abbot of Iona, is now best known for his *Life* of Iona's founder Saint *Columba and for the treatise *De locis sanctis*, a description of the Holy Land ostensibly based on the recollections of Frankish bishop Arculph but drawn almost exclusively upon Adamnan's own extensive reading.

Adamnan, despite the waning influence of Iona resulting from the growing power of Armagh in Ireland and the outcome of the Council of Whitby in England, was an influential figure throughout northern Britain and the whole of Ireland. He was author and moving force of the *Cáin Adomnáin* (or Canon of Adamnan), promulgated in 697–698, which legally enforced the protection of noncombatants. A member of the northern Ui Neill, Adamnan revived the traditional Iona connection with the Northumbrian monarchy during the reign of Aldfrith, the Iona-trained son of an Ui Neill mother. He presented the king with a copy of *De locis sanctis*, who made it available to *Bede. According to Bede, Adamnan, admonished by the Northumbrian clergy, attempted to introduce the Roman Easter and tonsure to Iona but was unable to bring his community to accept them. This has been disputed recently by a number of scholars who stress, however, Adamnan's ability to maintain good relations with those following the Roman Easter in southern Ireland and England. It has been argued that he was the editor/compiler of the so-called *Vergil Sylloge*, the remains of which still form an important body of Vergilian commentary, but the basis of this ascription is tenuous.

Bibliography: M. O. Anderson, *Adomnán's Life of Columba*, 1991; J.-M. Picard, "Adomnán, and the Writing of History," *Peritia* 3 (1984): 50–70.

Helen Conrad-O'Briain

ADELAIDE (ADELHEID) OF BURGUNDY (C. 930–999). Daughter of Rudolf II of Upper Burgundy, Adelaide married Lothar, king of Italy, and, after Lothar's death, *Otto I the Great of Germany. An active political leader throughout her career, she was regent for her grandson, *Otto III, from 991 to 994.

Adelaide's first marriage was part of Hugo of Provence's plan to unite Provence, Burgundy, and Italy. Otto I, who took Upper Burgundy under his protection, and Berengar of Ivrea, who also claimed the throne of Italy, opposed it. After the deaths of Hugo (947) and Lothar (950), leadership of the Provencal faction fell to Adelaide, and she managed to persuade Otto to intervene against

Berengar. After their marriage (951), Adelaide acted in partnership with Otto—decisions regarding Italy were made only with her consent, and she also exerted considerable influence on non-Italian affairs. Adelaide's role continued during the reign of her son *Otto II (972–983), although she had to accommodate the influence of her daughter-in-law *Theophano. When Theophano died in 991, Adelaide became regent for the eleven-year-old Otto III until he reached majority (at fifteen) in 994.

Adelaide's reputation as an effective leader has suffered from comparison to her daughter-in-law Theophano. Viewed on her own terms, her career demonstrates many of the possibilities open to aristocratic women and emphasizes the importance of cognatic, in addition to agnatic, relationships in early medieval noble families. Her marriage to Otto made the German kings heir to Burgundy and Provence (inherited by *Conrad II in 1029) as well as providing the basis for later claims to the so-called Matildine lands in Tuscany (those left by *Matilda of Tuscany).

Bibliography: T. Reuter, *Germany in the Early Middle Ages c. 800–1056*, 1991.

Edward J. Schoenfeld

ADELARD OF BATH (C. 1080–after 1142). A philosopher, translator, and educator of the twelfth century, Adelard acquired philosophical, mathematical, and astronomical knowledge from the Islamic world and transmitted it to the Latin West. His accomplishments in the area of natural philosophy have led him to be described as the first English scientist.

Adelard was probably born in the city of Bath, England, in the year 1080. After being educated at a monastery school in Bath, he attended the cathedral school in Tours, France. He then went on to study and teach at Laon, a well-known center of learning in northern France with close ties to England. Laon was an important locus of philosophical and theological studies, as well as a center of mathematical research. It was during his stay at Laon that Adelard wrote a treatise on the use of the abacus. Early in his career, he also wrote a treatise entitled *De eodem et diverso* (On the Same and Different), which addressed a number of issues in metaphysics and natural philosophy. From these two treatises, it is clear that he was deeply interested in the use of mathematics to understand the relationships of things in the universe.

Sometime before 1115, Adelard left Laon and spent seven years traveling. He made his way through southern Italy, Sicily, and Greece to Syria. During his travels, he conversed with Islamic scholars and acquired Arabic manuscripts. He may have also gathered material for the composition of the *Mappae clavicula*, a compendium of alchemical formulas and techniques sometimes attributed to him.

Upon his return to England, Adelard composed the *Quaestiones naturales* (Questions on Nature). In this work, he stressed the application of reason to the solution of scientific questions and justified the study of natural causes as a discipline distinct from theology. The topics of the book were derived from a list of popular contemporary questions such as the cause of motion, meteorological phenomena, human physiology, and sense perception. The *Questions on Nature* was very popular, widely read both in Latin and in a Hebrew translation. He also wrote a treatise on falconry, which provides a wealth of information about the taming, handling, and care of birds of prey. He translated the *Elements* of Euclid from an Arabic manuscript, the astronomical tables of al-Khwārizmī, and several Arabic works on astrology. Adelard's translation of al-Khwārizmī's astronomical tables is the only surviving version of this text, as the original has been lost.

He was attached to the court of *Henry I of England, possibly as an accountant or as an astrologer. Late in his career, Adelard composed *On the Use of the Astrolabe*, which explains not only the workings of the device but also the arrangement of the heavenly bodies and the orientation of the planets as understood at this time.

Adelard was a significant figure in the cultural interchange between scholars of the Latin West and the Islamic world. His travels in Greece and Asia Minor brought him into contact with a variety of contemporary thinkers, and he brought their knowledge and methods back to Europe. The European educational system of his time was considerably enriched by his incorporation of knowledge gained from contact with the Islamic world into the quadrivium. The translations he made from the Arabic included not only ancient Greek wisdom long lost to the West but the original contributions of the Islamic thinkers themselves.

His translation of Euclid greatly advanced the development of scientific thinking in Europe, as it informed its readers not only of specific mathematical facts but of the general method of proving mathematical theorems. His treatise *On the Same and Different* demonstrates a sophisticated epistemology, including an attempt to solve the problem of universals later known as the philosophy of "non-difference." It also provides a detailed and eclectic account of the seven liberal arts and their classical foundations. In the *Questions on Nature*, he often went beyond standard responses to a deeper investigation of topics such as accidental qualities, the problem of infinite movement, and the nature of the soul. Its emphasis on reason and its synthesis of Arabic, Neoplatonic, and Aristotelian sources were influential in the development of Scholastic philosophy. His account of hawking, *On the Care of Falcons*, is the first of its kind that can be attributed to a known author. It is especially valued by modern scholars for the way it illustrates the differences between Norman and Anglo-Saxon handling of hawks.

Bibliography: Adelard of Bath, *Conversations with His Nephew*, ed. and trans. C. Burnett, 1998; L. Cochrane, *Adelard of Bath: The First English Scientist*, 1994.

Anne Collins Smith and Owen M. Smith

ADHÉMAR OF LE PUY (D. 1098). The apostolic legate on the First Crusade, Adhémar of Monteil, bishop of Le Puy, was the first to take the vow at

Clermont on 27 November 1095 and was an instrumental figure in the formulation of the Crusade until his death at Antioch in 1098.

Adhémar's entry into the affairs of the First Crusade appears to have come when *Urban II stayed with him at Le Puy in August 1095, where the pope celebrated the Feast of the Assumption and issued letters of invitation to the Council of Clermont. This would seem to imply that Adhémar was already a trusted supporter of the reformist papacy. Adhémar, who may have been a member of the family of Valentinois, had replaced the simoniac bishop of Le Puy, Stephen of Polignac, in the early 1080s. Since at least 1087 he was closely associated with *Raymond IV of Toulouse, who was also to play a central role in the leadership of the Crusade. In 1087 he is reputed to have visited the Holy Land—though this is not mentioned in local chronicles. If so, such prior knowledge of the region may have promoted him to his central role in the planned expedition. On 28 November 1095, Urban II named Adhémar as his legate, with extensive powers, which he further outlined in his letter to the Flemings of December 1095. Adhémar departed for the east with Raymond in October 1096, passing through North Italy and down the eastern shore of the Adriatic, arriving in Thessaloniki in April 1097. He was robbed and assaulted en route by the Pechenegs, which is probably the cause for his delaying to rest in Thessaloniki before joining Raymond's forces at Nicaea on 16 May 1097.

As a religious leader, almost the archetypal "knight of Christ," who died on crusade, Adhémar's career lent itself to exaggeration and overstatement in later historiography. There seems no reason to doubt, however, that he was active in military planning, nor is there any serious reason to doubt that he led military forces, either of his own or of Raymond. Raymond of Aguilers claims that he played a crucial role in undermining a tower in the siege of Nicaea and, according to the *Gesta Francorum*, outflanked the troops of Kilij Arslan at Dorylaeum on 1 July 1096, by leading his men through a mountain pass.

Taken ill with typhoid in June 1098, Adhémar died at Antioch on 1 August 1098. It is probable that his death led to a rebalancing of leadership amongst the crusaders. Adhémar may have been temporarily replaced as the pope's vicar by Bishop William of Orange, but it is almost certain that his official replacement was Daimbert of Pisa in 1099—by which time the new kingdoms were established. Claims that Adhémar had been the overall leader of the Crusade, or that he might have brokered a rapprochement between the Eastern and Western churches, are unverifiable and probably overstate papal political ambitions for the expedition. Adhémar's role is, if anything, to be viewed as a moderating influence. His recorded skepticism at the finding of the Holy Lance at Antioch typifies the image of him as an urbane leader who sought to maintain the authority of ecclesiastical hierarchy over the religious vision of the Crusade. Urban's own words at Clermont suggest that the Church had no vision of states ruled by the legate—his was not the imperialist vision of *Gregory VII. On the contrary, he was concerned that churches under colonial rule observed the ideals of the reform movement. That they did not, in the final event, do so may or may not have been the consequence of the death of Adhémar.

Bibliography: J. A. Brundage, "Adhémar of Puy. The Bishop and His Critics," *Speculum* 34 (1959): 201–212; J. Richard, "La papauté et la direction de la première croisade," *Journal des Savants* (April–June 1960): 49–58.

Jonathan M. Wooding

ÆLFRIC OF EYNSHAM (MID-TENTH CENTURY–AFTER 1010).

Ælfric was the abbot of Eynsham and the greatest prose stylist of the Old English period whose literary concern was to instruct the laity—who knew no Latin—in the Christian faith.

Relatively little is known about the specific facts of Ælfric's life. He was born sometime around the middle of the tenth century, educated at Æthelwold's monastery in Winchester, and after serving for some time at Cernel in Dorset, became abbot of Eynsham around 1005. Ælfric lived at a time of renewed political and military unrest in Anglo-Saxon England, with the resumption of Viking attacks in the late tenth century, followed by the Danish conquest of 1013–1016. He saw as his mission as a writer the preservation and spread of learning among the English in the face of domestic moral and spiritual failings, coupled with the renewed threat of barbarian invasion; he was also a prominent figure in the Benedictine reform movement set into motion in the mid-ninth century by *Dunstan and furthered by Æthelwold. Perhaps because of his motivation as an educator and social critic, Ælfric wrote the majority of his works in Old English rather than Latin.

Ælfric's Old English prose is characterized by a great simplicity of diction and syntax, as compared, for example, to the Alfredian translations of the ninth century (see *Alfred the Great); at the same time, Ælfric does not hesitate to make extensive use of alliteration in his prose, so that it at times resembles Old English poetry in its sound. His major works include two series of *Catholic Homilies*, a collection of exegetical homilies arranged according to the religious calendar; the *Lives of Saints*, a collection of hagiographies so poetic in composition that some have argued they were indeed intended as poetry; the Old English *Heptateuch*, a translation and commentary on various books of the Bible; the *Grammar*, the first Latin grammar known to have been written in the vernacular; and the *Colloquy*, a set of dialogues on the occupations intended as exercises to teach Latin to Old English speakers and provided with an Old English gloss that has itself become a well-known tool for teaching Old English today.

Ælfric's writings are unmistakable, both for their calm, compassionate piety and their concern for the difficulties of the student laboring over a difficult subject. His works both provide a substantial portion of late Old English prose and add tremendously to its quality.

Bibliography: S. B. Greenfield and D. G. Calder, *A New Critical History of Old English Literature*, 1986.

David Day

ÆLRED OF RIEVAULX (AILRED, ÆTHELRED, ÆTHELRED, ETH-ELRED) (1109–1167). A mystic, historian, homilist, and spiritual adviser, Ælred was extremely influential in the development and spread of affective (emotive) piety in England.

He came from a clerical family (his father was a married priest) in Hexham, county Durham, and had some connection with northern nobility. As a youth he was in contact with the Scottish royal family, and at one time he was sent to live at the Scottish court. King David wanted to make Ælred a bishop and offered him the chance for his own see. But Ælred perceived political life, whether episcopal or secular, to be shallow and difficult, and instead he became a Cistercian monk. In 1134, he entered the monastery in Rievaulx (Yorkshire), which had only been in operation a few years at the time. He was soon in charge of the novices, a position for which he was remembered fondly for his patience and kindness. Despite a short absence from that house, he was elected abbot of Rievaulx in 1147, a move that also made him head of all Cistercian abbots in England. In about 1164 he went as a missionary to the northern parts of Galloway. Hagiographical legend has it that while there he so impressed a fierce Pictish chieftain with his piety and gentle demeanor that the chieftain converted instantly and became a Cistercian monk himself.

Ælred is best known for his prodigious writings, which included many sermons, letters, and ascetical treatises, histories, a biographical sketch of King David of Scotland, and a lengthy *Life* of Saint *Edward the Confessor, whose translation Ælred witnessed at Westminster Abbey. Probably best known and most often quoted are his chief works, *Speculum caritatis* (The Mirror of Charity) and *De spirituali amicitia* (Of Spiritual Friendships). In all of these writings, however, the aspect that is particularly Ælred's own is his gentle tone and his admonition for kindness and charity toward others. At a time when many medieval spiritual writers recommended an otherworldly detachment from earthly relationships and "special friendships" were discouraged for those in religious vocation—and indeed ideally for all Christians—Ælred wrote his treatise *Of Spiritual Friendships* in defense of fraternal love. Using Christ's own friendships with John, Mary Magdalene, Martha, and Lazarus as his exempla, he celebrated the goodness of camaraderie and human affection as being one more aspect of Christ's humanity to be emulated.

Ælred was also the author of "A Rule for Recluses," a long epistle to an anchoress, or spiritual hermit, living in voluntary contemplative exile and solitude. The recipient of his letter was most likely his biological as well as spiritual sister, and this work is probably the seminal document behind the Anchoritic movement in all of England during the High Middle Ages. Its influence is undeniable in the early-twelfth-century *Ancrene Wisse*.

Bibliography: B. P. McGuire, *Brother and Lover: Ælred of Rievaulx*, 1994.

Zina Petersen

ÆTHELBERT OF KENT (C. 560–616). The first king of Kent for whom we have any reliable knowledge, Æthelbert is noteworthy both as the first Anglo-

Saxon king to accept Christianity and as the first to promulgate a written law code.

It is unknown precisely when Æthelbert became king of Kent, although the date of his death in 616 is better attested. While still a pagan, he married Bertha, Christian daughter of the Merovingian Frankish king Charibert, but did not convert at that time. Instead, as *Bede memorably records in the *Ecclesiastical History*, he accepted the mission of *Augustine, sent by Pope *Gregory the Great in 597, perhaps seeking thereby to avoid a tacit admission of Frankish overlordship. After his conversion, he promulgated the first of the Anglo-Saxon codes, unusual among the law codes of the barbarian kingdoms for being written in the vernacular. Subsequent Anglo-Saxon law codes would build on Æthelbert's code and also follow its example of being written in Old English. According to Bede, Æthelbert was the preeminent king in southern England during the early seventh century, and he certainly established a Kentish political ascendancy over the East Saxon kingdom; he also seems to have attempted to convert the East Angles to Christianity. Æthelbert is really the first Anglo-Saxon king to emerge with any distinctness from the historical record, and his acceptance of Roman Christianity was of the highest importance for the future political and ecclesiastical history of England.

Bibliography: B. Yorke, *Kings and Kingdoms of Early Anglo-Saxon England*, 1990.

David Day

ÆTHELFLÆD OF MERCIA (C. 918). Lady of the Mercians, Æthelflæad was the daughter of King *Alfred the Great of England (d. 899) and was married to Æthelred, ealdorman of the Mercians, c. 884 as part of her father's political policy. Alfred was the only native English king to withstand the Viking onslaught, and as such he was able to rally Anglo-Saxons from outside his territory of Wessex; he was especially successful in Mercia. Æthelflæd's mother was Mercian, and like her mother, she served to tie the two English regions closer together. More important, as the lady of the Mercians, Æthelflæd helped her husband rule, and after his death in 911, she ruled the territory herself.

Æthelflæd cooperated with her brother King Edward the Elder (r. 899–924) in the reconquest of England from the Danes. Æthelflæd was instrumental in establishing alliances with neighbors, leading the Mercian forces in battle, and building at least ten fortresses in the newly conquered territories. The combination of the Mercians under Æthelflæd and the West Saxons under Edward was formidable enough to drive back the Danes and to prevent the Welsh from invading. Æthelflæd was so well respected in her own time that shortly before her death the Danes of York submitted to her. Her death ended this arrangement and also the near independence of Mercia because her only heir was a daughter who could not successfully fight Edward the Elder's consolidation of the two territories. In short, Æthelflæd helped her brother to unite all of England south of the Humber River and thereby develop the kingdom of England.

Bibliography: C. Fell, *Women in Anglo-Saxon England*, 1984; F. T. Wainwright, "Æthelflæd, Lady of the Mercians," in *Scandinavian England: Collected Papers*, ed. H.P.R. Finberg, 1975.

Janet Pope

ÆTHELRED THE UNREADY OF ENGLAND (ÆTHELRÆD "UNRÆD") (968–1016).

Æthelred was king of England from 978 until 1016 and oversaw a period marked by political and military disasters and localized cultural flourishing but that ended in Viking rule of England.

Still a young boy in 978, Æthelred acceded to the throne after the murder of his half brother Edward at a time of national crisis due to Scandinavian incursions. While a century earlier *Alfred the Great handled the Viking attacks decisively and successfully, Æthelred's ineffectual hesitancy and inability to handle the disloyalty of his noble retainers led to numerous disbursements of silver to the Vikings under leaders like *Sven I of Denmark. Both military solutions and attempts to pay off the invaders failed, or at best delayed their attacks, and in 1002, Æthelred, again fearing for his life, ordered all Danes killed. Although in many parts of England this order could not be carried out because the towns themselves were under Danish control, the slaughter incited a violent response. Attacks continued, and by 1013, Æthelred was driven into exile in Normandy. He returned to England but died in battle in London in 1016, and the Dane *Cnut (Sven's son) was crowned king of England. Æthelred's inept and treacherous leadership earned him the nickname Æthelred Unræd, Old English for "Noble-counsel Non-counsel (or bad counsel)."

Despite the instability and disastrous English losses under Æthelred, the Benedictine revival of the late tenth century reached its culmination in scholars and writers like Byrhtferth, *Ælfric of Eynsham, and *Wulfstan of York as well as in exceptional monastic book production, including most of the major extant Old English poetic manuscripts.

Bibliography: S. Keynes, *The Diplomas of King Æthelred "the Unready" 978–1016: A Study in Their Use as Evidence*, 1980.

Matthew Hussey

ÆTHELSTAN OF ENGLAND (C. 895–939; KING OF THE ANGLO-SAXONS 924/925–927, KING OF THE ENGLISH 927–939).

Æthelstan was one of four strong kings of Wessex in the first half of the tenth century who, with his father Edward the Elder (r. 899–924, eldest son of *Alfred the Great) and his brothers Edmund (r. 939–946), and Eadred (r. 946–955), was responsible for conquering Scandinavian England and laying the basis for the unified English state.

Æthelstan's reign is most notable for strengthening the unity of the various kingdoms and regions of England under a single West Saxon regime. It reinforced Wessex's relationship with Mercia, of which Æthelstan was independently crowned king and which showed no evident dissatisfaction with his rulership, despite the old rivalry of the two kingdoms. Æthelstan also established a tributary relationship with the various rulers of Wales and defeated the Britons of Cornwall. He invaded Northumbria in 927 and took York, beginning the West Saxon absorption of the Scandinavian north into greater England, which his brothers would complete. But his most important achievement in this regard was the great victory over the forces of Scandinavian Dublin, allied with Scotland and Strathclyde, at Brunanburh in 937, which left eventual West Saxon control over Scandinavian England a virtual certainty. This battle is poetically described by the author of the "Battle of Brunanburh," which remains one of the most famous examples of Old English battle poetry extant. The same battle may be described much later in *Egil's Saga*, in which Æthelstan figures prominently as *Egill Skallagrímsson's patron in England.

Not all of Æthelstan's achievements were military. He further unified his kingdom by convening regular assemblies consisting of the major thanes, nobles, and churchmen of both Wessex and the newly conquered regions. Diplomatically, he extended the influence of England much farther abroad, establishing marriage relationships with the Carolingian Franks and the new Ottonian dynasty in Germany, and according to Norse tradition, acting as foster father to Hákon, youngest son of *Harald I Fairhair of Norway. He also added considerably to the corpus of the Anglo-Saxon laws dealing with theft, and his reign saw the beginning of the religious reforms of the Anglo-Saxon Church that would culminate in the work of Saint *Dunstan later in the tenth century.

Æthelstan was recognized as an especially important and effective king within a few generations of his death by no less a person than *Ælfric of Eynsham, who saw him as a good example of an English king who protected his people and made them secure.

Bibliography: F. Stenton, *Anglo-Saxon England*, 3d ed., 1971.

David Day

ALAN OF LILLE (ALAIN DE LILLE, ALANUS DE INSULIS) (C. 1120–1203).

Known as *Doctor universalis*, Alan was widely influential in western Europe as a poet and as a theologian. Little evidence exists for Alan's early life. He probably was born in Lille, given his first education in the cathedral schools of the Loire valley, and placed under Parisian masters for his theological training. Alan himself is listed among the masters teaching at the University of Paris after 1150. He moved to the south of France, probably Montpellier, around 1170. At the end of his life, Alan became a Cistercian. He died at the motherhouse of his order, the Abbey of Cîteaux, and is considered blessed within the order. Alan's body was exhumed in 1960; from the skeletal remains, he was estimated to have been five feet tall and eighty-eight to ninety-two years of age at his death.

Alan's reputation as a major Latin poet may have overshadowed his theological writings in the later Middle Ages, much as his poetry now receives the most attention from readers. His two long poems *The Complaint of Nature* and *Anticlaudianus* survive in over 100 manuscripts apiece. *The Complaint* attracted a preface and a sequel written by later readers; *Anticlaudianus* received numerous commentaries, including a full and weighty response from Raoul of Longchamps. These poems echo through most of the great vernacular poems of the next two centuries in western Europe, and they are regularly cited as models by medieval treatises on rhetoric. Alan's influence as a theologian was also substantial during the later Middle Ages. He was a founder of systematic theology, the earliest extant voice attacking the Albigensian heresies sweeping southern France, and one of the first authors of manuals for priests on preaching and penitential instruction. Running through all his work is a profound concern for the relationship between the natural world and divine truth. Alan returns constantly to questions of how this relationship is constructed by the human mind and expressed by human language.

Alan's two poems cannot be firmly dated. *The Complaint of Nature* appears to be his first. Modeled on the *prosimetrum* form of the *Consolation of Philosophy*, *The Complaint* narrates a dream vision dialogue in alternating sections of verse and prose. The Dreamer opens the poem with a lament that the world has fallen into illicit desires; he then describes the arrival of Nature, adorned with the created world; the Dreamer falls into an ecstatic state, during which Nature complains in much greater detail that humankind has fallen away from sanctioned reproduction into vile sexual practices encouraged by a lawless Venus; Genius arrives, displays his ability to produce art on the right hand and on the left hand, and formally excommunicates all the sinners Nature has lamented; the Dreamer then wakes from his ecstasy. The creations of Nature and Genius illustrate an important twelfth-century argument that God and humankind can be linked through the mind's journey from perception to contemplation. Yet agents of both Nature and Genius can send the mind on a false, even sodomitical path. The Dreamer's vision fades with no ending to frame his experience or to resolve the problem of perverse paths of knowledge.

Alan's second poem, *Anticlaudianus* (c. 1179–1183?), uses the epic form to explore at length the mind's journey toward divine truth and redemption. As the poem opens, Nature once again laments the sinful state of humankind. She assigns Prudence the journey to Heaven, where God will give Nature the soul of the New Man to combat the world's moral demise; Prudence is carried heavenward in a chariot constructed by the seven liberal arts, drawn by the five senses, and driven by Reason; at Heaven's gate Prudence abandons the chariot to enter Heaven alone and falls into an ecstatic state; Faith conducts Prudence before God, where she is given the requested soul; upon her return Nature creates the New Man, who receives the gifts of the Virtues and the Liberal Arts along with a controlled selection from Fortune and her good daughter Nobility. Enticement marshals an army of vices against this new threat; the New Man, single-handedly, defeats this army; Love rules. Here Alan argues for a causal relationship between prudential thought, carried by proper academic training toward the divine, and humankind's defeat of evil in the world.

Alan's philosophical positions are everywhere apparent in his poetry, but his work as a theologian is even more versatile than his triumphs as a poet. This work falls roughly into three groups that may have come in a chronological sequence related to his poetry. The first group includes the summa *Quoniam homines* (c. 1155–1165) and the *Theologicae regulae*. In these writings Alan tries to establish logical rules for theology, including such mystical topics as the Trinity and angelology. He adapts the "negative" terminology of *Pseudo-Dionysius the Aeropagite and *John Scottus Eriugena, whose work contends with the unknowability of God, to explain epistemological problems such as the division between reason and sensory perception. These issues and terms also pervade the brief treatise *De virtutibus et vitiis et de doni spiritus sancti* and even a collection of maxims in verse known as the *Parabolae*.

More immediate and earthly concerns dominate Alan's second group of writings, apologia for the Church against contemporary heretics. These writings are compiled into one work titled *De fide Catholica contra haereticos* (c. 1172–1180). Alan devotes a separate book each to the errors of the Cathars, Waldensians, Jews, and Muslims. His discussion of the first two groups represents our earliest known source on this remarkably successful movement in southern France. The third group consists of reference works for priests. The *Distinctiones dictionum theologicarum* (c. 1179–1195) conveniently indexes useful scriptural topics and quotations by an alphabetical list of key words. Priests composing sermons could also turn to Alan's *Ars praedicandi*, the first known preaching manual. Alan supplies rhetorical methods and applies those methods to forty-eight sample sermons in a format, which spawned many imitators throughout the later Middle Ages. The *Liber poenitentialis* (c. 1183–1193), which guided priests in the methods of confession and penance, was also a first of its kind: positioned at the front of the Church's massive new interest in penitential instruction for the laity.

Alan's complex philosophical concerns echo through his poetry and his theology and may offer ways to chart his shifting interests over a long and distinguished career. His writings can stand alone effectively in a remarkable variety of disciplines, but their whole presents a much greater achievement in the kind of synthetic thinking that attracted so many scholars of his time.

Bibliography: Alan of Lille, *Anticlaudianus, or the Good and Perfect Man*, trans. J. J. Sheridan, 1973; Alan of Lille, *Plaint of Nature*, trans. J. J. Sheridan, 1980; G. R. Evans, *Alan of Lille: The Frontiers of Theology in the Later Twelfth Century*, 1983; W. Wetherbee, *Platonism and Poetry in the Twelfth Century: The Literary Influence of the School of Chartres*, 1972.

Joel Fredell

ALBERTUS MAGNUS (ALBERT THE GREAT), SAINT (C. 1200–1280).

Albert was a scholastic philosopher and theologian known as *Doctor universalis*.

Albert was born in Lauingen on the Danube near Ulm, the son of a noble German family. After his early education, Albert entered the nascent University of Padua while his father served Emperor *Frederick II. Despite opposition from his family, in 1223 Albert joined the recently formed Order of Friars Preachers (cf. *Dominic). He entered the novitiate, was sent to Germany to study theology, and taught successively at Hildesheim, Freiberg, Ratisbon, and Strassburg.

In 1241, Albert was sent to the University of Paris to complete his theological training. It was probably here where he first encountered the "new Aristotle," recently translated from the Greek and Arabic, and the works of the famous Muslim commentator of Aristotle, *Averroës. Albert incepted in theology in 1245 and taught at Paris for the next three years as a regent master. He also became the mentor of Thomas *Aquinas. In 1248, Albert was summoned to Cologne to found a studium for the Dominicans there; Thomas accompanied him. In 1252, he was elected provincial of the German Dominicans and held that post for three years. In 1256 he went to Rome to defend the mendicant orders against the attacks by the Parisian secular theologians, in particular by *William of St. Amour. He returned to teach at Cologne from 1257 to 1260, and at the Dominican General Chapter of 1259 he helped to organize a comprehensive plan of study for all the Order's members.

In 1260, he was reluctantly installed as bishop of Ratisbon but was allowed to resign the position two years later. Pope Urban IV ordered him to preach a crusade in Germany and Bohemia in 1263–1264, and Albert lived consecutively in Würzburg and Strassburg until he returned to Cologne in 1269. He attended the Council of Lyons in 1274 and returned to Paris in 1277 at the height of the Averroistic controversy to defend the teachings of his pupil Thomas. He died in Cologne three years later. He was beatified in 1622 and canonized in 1931.

Albert is perhaps best remembered today as the teacher of Thomas. However, Albert himself was a prolific writer who was recognized as Magnus even within his own lifetime. Convinced that the new scientific material translated from the Greek and Arabic would benefit Christian thought, Albert assumed the task of interpreting and explaining the "new Aristotle" to the Latins. In so doing, he commented extensively on almost the entire Aristotelian corpus, including many of the spurious works such as *De plantis*. Albert also encouraged scientific experimentation and wrote many original works on natural science. His work *De mineralibus* shows that he himself did personal research in chemistry. In large measure, Albert helped to introduce Aristotle's scientific treatises and scientific methods to the West.

Albert was also a trained theologian and wrote expositions on Scripture, sermons, and a commentary on *Peter Lombard's *Sentences* and lectured on the complete works of *Pseudo-Dionysius. Because of his reputation as a writer, throughout the centuries many spurious works have been ascribed to him. His written corpus is currently being edited and when finished will comprise forty volumes.

To a large extent, the success of Aristotle in the thirteenth century was due to Albert. He is today recognized as the patron saint of students of the natural sciences.

Bibliography: J. A. Weisheipl, "Albert the Great and Medieval Culture," *The Thomist* 44 (1980): 481–501; J. A. Weisheipl, ed., *Albertus Magnus and the Sciences. Commemorative Essays*, 1980.

Andrew G. Traver

ALCUIN OF YORK (C. 730–804). Eighth-century theologian, liturgist, poet, and educator, Alcuin was an important figure both in the history of pre-Conquest English letters and in the cultural flowering of the Carolingian Renaissance.

Details of his early life are vague: We do know that he was kin to *Willibrod and was born in Northumbria sometime around 730 (or at least in the second quarter of the eighth century). His early education was conducted at the cathedral school of York; Ecgberht and then Ælberht were his early mentors. Ælberht rose to bishop and later archbishop of York; Alcuin succeeded his mentor as master of the York school in 778. He would later provide a detailed portrait of York and its school, including the contents of its fine library, in his poem the *Versus de patribus regibus et sanctis Euboricensis ecclesiae* (Bishops, Kings, and Saints of York). Alcuin was a deacon (a position of greater prestige in the Middle Ages than today) but probably was never confirmed as a priest or monk.

Alcuin traveled to Rome and the Continent several times, making a number of important intellectual and ecclesiastical contacts. In 780 he went to Rome in order to bring back the pallium for Eanbald, Ælberht's successor at York; he also made *Charlemagne's acquaintance on one of these trips. But the turning point of Alcuin's life came during his second meeting with the emperor: On the way back from Rome in 781, he encountered Charlemagne at Parma. Apparently quite impressed with the English scholar, Charlemagne asked him to head his palace school at Aachen, and Alcuin accepted, spending the rest of his life in his service. He left England probably in 781 or 782 and devoted his considerable intellectual gifts to the community of scholars at Charlemagne's court, an array of international poets, theologians, and intellectuals: These included *Paul the Deacon, Peter of Pisa, Paulinus of Aquileia, Angilbert, *Theodulf of Orléans and *Einhard, the biographer of Charlemagne. Alcuin's circle gave each other classical or biblical "nicknames": Alcuin was known as "Flaccus" (and also "Albinus"). Alcuin's central role in the Carolingian Renaissance was an important eighth-century link between England and the Continent.

Alcuin was based in Aachen by 794, but he most likely traveled with the court throughout Charlemagne's kingdom, acting as the personal teacher for the royal family and promoting any number of ecclesiastical and educational programs. In Charlemagne's service, Alcuin produced a wide range of documents bearing upon an even wider range of political, ecclesiastical, theological, and administrative subjects. He undertook to reform and standardize the liturgy, the text of the Bible, even scribal practices and scripts. The exact extent of his role in the Carolingian ecclesiastical reform is still debated, but he was certainly an important force in the cultural renaissance under Charlemagne. Alcuin always maintained his ties with his native Northumbria, traveling to York at least twice during his life in Francia, in 786 and 790–793. For his efforts, Charlemagne rewarded him with the abbacy of St. Loup at Troyes, and he also became the abbot of Ferrières. In 796, near the end of his career, he was named the head of the Abbey of St. Martin's at Tours, where he retired until his death on 19 May 804.

Alcuin's extant corpus of Latin works is large, existing in many manuscripts. More than 300 letters survive, written from his influential position in Europe to his many contacts. These letters include his famous consolation to the English monks at Lindisfarne upon the destruction of their monastery by Viking raiders in 793. Alcuin also produced a poem on the subject, a part of his large surviving body of verse. He wrote a long narrative poem on the history of York (*Versus de patribus regibus et sanctis euboricensis ecclesiae*, 780–782), drawing mainly from *Bede and his own recollections. This text is an important source for the history of eighth-century Northumbria, York, and Alcuin's life. He also composed a number of shorter lyric poems. Alcuin was also a hagiographer: He composed *vitae* of Saint Vedastus, Saint Richarius, and Saint Martin of Tours and a life of Saint Willibrod, in both prose and verse (an *opus geminatum*). He wrote various theological treatises, including a tract on the virtues and vices (*De virtutibus et vitiis*) that was translated into Old English in the tenth century, as well as works on the trinity (*De trinitate*) and the soul (*De animae ratione*). Alcuin was also known for his exegetical commentaries including works on Genesis, Ecclesiastes, the Song of Songs, the Gospel of John, and various New Testament letters (Ephesians, Titus, Philemon, and Hebrews). Alcuin was also quite concerned with establishing an accurate text of the Latin Bible and worked diligently to improve the transmission of scripture. To this end he composed educational tracts, treatises on spelling, rhetoric, and grammar (*De orthographia, De rhetorica, Ars grammatica*), and an exploration of dialectic (*De dialectica*). An important figure in the history of letters and learning in the early Middle Ages, on both the Continent and in England, Alcuin deserves further study to properly assess his achievements.

Bibliography: Alcuin, *The Bishops, Kings, and Saints of York*, ed. P. Godman, 1982; L. Wallach, *Alcuin and Charlemagne: Studies in Carolingian History and Culture*, 1959.
Andrew Scheil

ALDHELM (BEFORE 640–709). Poet, abbot, and bishop, Aldhelm was praised by *Bede, his younger contemporary, as a man of great learning.

The biographical details of Aldhelm's life are few. He was born sometime before 640, but his place of birth is unknown. The circumstances of Aldhelm's early education are likewise a matter of conjecture; he perhaps studied under an Irish teacher at Malmesbury, perhaps with Archbishop Hadrian at Canterbury.

At any rate he did go on to study under Hadrian at Canterbury, from about 670 to 673. At the renowned Canterbury school, Aldhelm presumably polished and developed his already formidable education, perhaps learning Greek, although this is still a matter of some dispute.

Aldhelm probably attended the Council of Hertford in 672, and he apparently made at least one pilgrimage to Rome. By 673 we find him established as abbot of Malmesbury. He was abbot from about 673 to 705, then was appointed the bishop of Sherborne in 705 until his death in 709. We can assume that in these years he was consumed by ecclesiastical responsibilities, but he also found time to compose a large body of influential Latin texts.

His poetic corpus includes the *Carmina ecclesiastica*, the *Carmina rhythmica*, his *Enigmata* ("riddles" or "mysteries"), as well as the prose *Epistola ad Acircum* and other letters. He also wrote an *opus geminatum* (two works on the same subject, in prose and verse), entitled *De virginitate*. His complex Latin, in the so-called hermeneutic style, exerted a pervasive influence on eighth-century (and subsequent) Anglo-Latin letters.

Bibliography: A. Orchard, *The Poetic Art of Aldhelm*, 1994.

Andrew Scheil

ALEXANDER III, POPE (C. 1105–1181, PONTIFICATE 1159–1181).

Orlando Bandinelli assumed the name Alexander III upon his election on 20 September 1159. His election resulted in a schism lasting throughout much of his pontificate. Alexander, the first of a series of lawyer popes, constantly remained at odds with Holy Roman Emperor *Frederick I Barbarossa, supported Thomas *Becket against *Henry II of England, and presided over the Third Lateran Council (1179).

Alexander served as chancellor and papal legate under his predecessor *Hadrian IV and was a cardinal-priest at the time of his election. Hadrian had broken ties with the emperor, dividing the curia into two camps. Upon Hadrian's death, supporters of Alexander attempted to invest him with the papal mantle. The opposing candidate and imperial choice, Octavian, took the mantle from Alexander and proclaimed himself pope. Alexander fled to Ninfa and was consecrated, while Octavian was consecrated at Farfa, taking the name Victor IV.

Frederick I Barbarossa called a synod of German and Italian bishops at Pavia in 1160, which excommunicated Alexander and supported Victor. Alexander, having previously excommunicated Victor and condemned Barbarossa, met with Western leaders and received support from such leaders as Henry II and *Louis VII of France. Alexander resided in France from 1162 to 1165, during which time he presided over the Council of Tours (1163). The purpose of the council was to show continued support of Alexander in the face of mounting pressure from Barbarossa. The council was elaborate and well attended, and it produced canons against such offenses as pluralism, usury, granting of offices to laypersons, and heresy. The council also voided all decrees by the antipope Victor.

He died the following year, but the schism continued with the succession of antipopes Paschal III (1164–1168), Callixtus III (1168–1178), and Innocent III (1179–1180).

Thomas Becket's quarrel with Henry II placed Alexander in a difficult position. After the dispute over the Constitutions of Clarendon in 1164, Becket fled to France. Alexander supported Becket but did not want to alienate one of the more powerful rulers in Europe. Henry continually threatened to ally with Barbarossa, but a shaky peace was concluded that allowed Becket to return to England. Becket's murder in 1170 gave Alexander the opportunity to intervene more decisively. Henry did penance for his deed, and thus the pope reasserted his spiritual authority over England.

Alexander returned to Rome in 1165 for only a brief time. Barbarossa entered Italy the following year and accepted the submission of many Italian cities. The pope fled to Benevento in 1167, and Barbarossa returned to Germany. The northern Italian cities then joined to form the Lombard League to defend against Barbarossa and support Alexander. Barbarossa returned to fight the Lombard League at Legnano in May 1176, and the emperor suffered a crushing defeat. In the Peace of Venice of 1179, Barbarossa recognized Alexander as pope, and Alexander lifted the emperor's excommunication.

Now the undisputed ruler of the Church, Alexander called the Third Lateran Council, which was held in March 1179. The council attempted to resolve problems the schism created and eventually produced twenty-seven canons. The most important canons called for a two-thirds majority of voting cardinals for election, support of university and cathedral schools, cancellation of antipope orders, and punishment for heretics, such as the Albigensians and Waldensians. Alexander issued numerous decretal letters throughout his reign resulting in numerous additions to canon law.

Alexander left Rome in 1179 due to riots and traveled throughout the Papal States for the next two years. He died in Velletri on 30 August 1181, and his body was desecrated by a Roman mob on its way to burial in the Lateran Basilica.

Bibliography: P. G. Maxwell-Stuart, *Chronicle of the Popes*, 1997; R. P. McBrien, *Lives of the Popes*, 1997; R. Somerville, *Pope Alexander III and the Council of Tours*, 1977.

Paul Miller

ALEXANDER OF HALES (C. 1186–1245). Alexander was a Franciscan theologian and teacher known as *Doctor irrefragibilis* (irrefutable teacher).

He was born into a wealthy family of Halesowen, Shropshire, England. The details of his early life are unknown, but by 1210 he was teaching in the Faculty of Arts at the University of Paris. Sometime between 1210 and 1215, Alexander entered the Faculty of Theology as a student, and by 1222, he was a teaching master. His teaching was interrupted in 1229, when the university called a strike in protest over the civil authorities' treatment of a student. He traveled to Angers, along with a number of other university masters, then on to Rome, where he was part of a commission established to resolve the strike. He may have aided in the writing of the papal bull, *Parens scientiarum* (1231), which asserted the rights of the university and affirmed its autonomy from any secular power. After a short sojourn in England (1231–1232), Alexander returned to Paris. Around 1236, Alexander, for some unknown reason, entered the Franciscan Order. Since he was still part of the Faculty of Theology, his conversion provided for the Order an institutional link with the university and a place where they could send their members for a theological education. He was the teacher of a number of prominent Franciscan theologians, including John of La Rochelle, William de Melitona, and *Eudes Rigaud. Alexander continued to teach theology until 1245. He attended the Council of Lyons in that same year, where he served on the commission that recommended the canonization of Edmund of Canterbury. While traveling back to Paris, Alexander took ill and died.

Alexander was a prolific teacher, providing traditional lectures on the Bible, in particular the Gospels. His disputed questions, from the period before his entrance into the Franciscan Order, cover three large volumes in their modern edition, and they engage almost every topic of interest to scholastic theologians. They are partly the reason why he earned the title *Doctor irrefragibilis*. He also preached university sermons, some of which have survived. Roger *Bacon later described him as the person who introduced the *Sentences* of *Peter Lombard as a textbook for theology, although Alexander was clearly not the first person to lecture publicly on this text. As the Franciscan master of theology, he continued to participate in theological disputations, and these became the basis of his major project—a *summa theologiae*. Alexander envisioned this work as a comprehensive survey of theology for his students. Although it remained unfinished at his death and it was left to his leading students to complete it, this work is still known as the *Summa fratris Alexandri* (The Summa of Brother Alexander). Alexander's influence on the Franciscans was extensive: He contributed to the first commentary on the Rule of Saint *Francis (known as the *Commentary of the Four Masters*), and his theological outlook ensured that the Order remained committed to the theology and philosophy of Saint Augustine.

Bibliography: K. B. Osborne, "Alexander of Hales," in *A History of Franciscan Theology*, ed K. B Osborne, 1994; B. Smalley, "The Gospels in the Paris Schools in the Late Twelfth and Early Thirteenth Centuries: Peter the Chanter, Hugh of St-Cher, Alexander of Hales, John of la Rochelle," *Franciscan Studies* 39 (1979): 230–254; 40 (1980): 298–369.

James R. Ginther

ALEXIUS I COMNENUS (1057–C. 1118). Byzantine emperor of Constantinople (from c. 1081), Alexius I repelled Norman advances through alliances with Venice and Germany (1081–c. 1093) and ruled Constantinople during the meeting of Byzantium and the West during the First Crusade.

Alexius I served in the Byzantine military as a general under Michael VII (Doukas) and Nikephoros III Botaneiates. With his brother Isaac, and with the assistance of members of the military aristocracy, he revolted, took the throne, and was faced with numerous internal and external threats. Internally, he withstood the challenge and revolt of the bureaucratic and civil aristocracy and managed to centralize state administration based on the power of a few military families. He attempted to restructure the ruling class, debased the value of aristocratic honorifics and titles through their excessive use, successfully reformed the monetary situation, and challenged the Church's exemptions from fiscal taxation in order to strengthen the imperial treasury. These measures were essential to Alexius I's resistance to external threats. After the Byzantine loss to the Seljuks at Manzikert in 1071, the Seljuk Empire of Rum occupied most of Asia Minor, displacing the Anatolian magnates, alienating their estates, and thrusting a heavy blow to Byzantine defenses.

In the western regions, the Normans, under the leadership of *Robert Guiscard, had taken control of southern Italy and were moving east toward Constantinople. Norman activity in the Adriatic, including the taking of Dyrrachium, caused great concern for both Byzantium and Venice. Thus, a natural alliance with Venice helped the Byzantines repel Norman advances. Payment for this cooperation, however, was unrestricted trading privileges throughout the Byzantine Empire, thus setting the stage for Venetian maritime dominance and colonization in the Eastern Mediterranean. Henceforth, Venetian actions and policies assumed great importance for the fate of the Byzantine state.

Alexius I also faced a major struggle against the Pechenegs, nomadic Turkic-speaking peoples. While the Pechenegs threatened the Danubian provinces, Alexius I's calculated diplomatic decision to utilize another nomadic tribe, the Cumans, against the invaders resulted in the complete annihilation of the Pechenegs in c. 1091.

Although there has been some debate as to whether Alexius I requested aid from the West to recapture the Holy Lands, Alexius I desired and requested mercenary troops to help him fight the Pechenegs and Cumans, who, indeed, threatened the Empire. After requests for mercenary troops, and overtures toward religious union with Rome, the Western response, however, was the First Crusade called by Pope *Urban II at the Council of Clermont. The vast number of pilgrims who arrived first alarmed Alexius I, who adroitly dispensed with the riotous rabble accompanying *Peter the Hermit, by transporting them across the Bosphorus to be mowed down by the Turks of Asia Minor. Meanwhile, large contingents of west European knights including Godfrey of Boullion, the Duke of Lorraine, *Raymond IV of Toulouse, and the Norman prince *Bohemond I, the son of Robert Guiscard, had also arrived. Alexius also managed to force them to pledge an oath of allegiance to him and to promise to restore conquered towns to imperial Byzantine control. Thus, many of the cities of western Asia Minor, such as Nicaea, Smyra, Ephesus, Sardes, and a number of towns in Lydia, were restored to Byzantine imperial control.

Even with their pledge, however, he could not prevent their establishing independent Crusader kingdoms in Palestine, including the taking of Jerusalem (c. 1099) and the placement of Godfrey of Bouillon as Defender of the Holy Sepulcher. The capture of Antioch by the crusaders in c. 1098 led to an internal conflict out of which Bohemond, Guiscard's son, firmly established himself as independent ruler and renewed his father's plan of conquest. After securing his nephew Tancred in Antioch, Bohemond launched a major public relations campaign in western Europe against Alexius I, denouncing him as having betrayed the Crusade. Bohemond's military campaign led him again to Dyrrachium, in front of which he suffered complete defeat at the hands of strong Byzantine forces in c. 1108.

Although the prestige and authority of the emperor increased under Alexius I's rule, his reliance on the feudalization process to consolidate power eventually undermined the strength of the Byzantine state. Spurred by contacts with the Western crusaders, and vassal relationships, the feudal system became the mainstay of the late Byzantine state.

Alexius I Comnenus was memorialized in *Anna Comnena's famous work *The Alexiad*, a panegyric to her father, including detailed accounts of struggles with the Normans, and the crusaders as they established independent states in Palestine.

Bibliography: M. Angold, *The Byzantine Empire, 1025–1204*, 2d ed., 1997.

Tom Papademetriou

AL-FĀRĀBĪ. *See* FĀRĀBĪ, AL-.

ALFONSO VI OF CASTILE AND LÉON (C. 1040–1109).

The reign of King Alfonso VI (1065–1109) saw the rise of León and Castile as the most powerful kingdoms on the Iberian Peninsula. Alfonso was the son of King *Ferdinand I of Castile, whose realm extended across the northwestern part of the peninsula. Upon Ferdinand's death in 1065, his territories were divided among his three sons, with Alfonso inheriting León. A civil war ensued, and in 1072, his older brother, the Castilian King Sancho II, temporarily deposed Alfonso. Sancho was assassinated later that same year, an event in which Alfonso and his sister Urraca may have played a part. The murder of Sancho returned Alfonso to power in León in 1072 and entitled him to inherit the kingdom of Castile as well.

Once in power, Alfonso strove to fortify his authority and extend his domain. He married several times into the French nobility; he worked to strengthen religious ties with Rome; and he was the first ruler of León to mint a coinage. Alfonso's armies also conquered a number of Muslim-controlled territories. The most important conquest occurred in 1085, when Alfonso forced the capitulation of Toledo, a city of great strategic and cultural importance. Although Alfonso attempted to pacify the Muslims of Toledo by allowing them to retain their mosque, he eventually permitted it to be converted into a Christian cathedral, thus magnifying the significance of the taking of Toledo as a symbol of the progress of the Reconquest.

In 1086, a group of fundamentalist Muslims from Africa, the Almoravids, was summoned by the Islamic princes of Spain to halt the Christian advances. Later that same year Alfonso's armies were defeated at Zalaca, and by the mid-1090s the Almoravids had succeeded in fortifying their hold on the southern part of the peninsula. The arrival of the Almoravids was not as inauspicious for Alfonso's most renowned vassal, *Rodrigo Díaz de Vivar, also known as the Cid. The Cid, who had been loyal to Sancho II, entered into the service of Alfonso VI after Sancho's assassination. However, the king's possible complicity in the murder of his brother contributed to the development of a tenuous relationship with the Cid, who was exiled in 1081 and 1089. The Cid returned to royal favor in 1092 and, in 1094, defeated the Almoravids and captured the city of Valencia, over which he ruled in Alfonso's name until his death in 1099.

Alfonso's succession was not determined until the end of his lifetime. The death of his son Sancho in 1108 left his eldest daughter, Urraca, as heir to the throne. Alfonso died a year later, in 1109, leaving behind a Castilian-Leonese alliance that, in spite of the defeats suffered at the hands of the Almoravids, was at the forefront of the Reconquest. Moreover, Alfonso oversaw one of the greatest moments of that campaign, the capture of Toledo, the city that became the political and religious center of Christian Spain.

Bibliography: B. F. Reilly, *The Kingdom of León-Castilla under King Alfonso VI: 1065–1109*, 1988.

Gregory B. Kaplan

ALFONSO VII OF CASTILE AND LEÓN (EL EMPERADOR—"THE EMPEROR") (1105–1157).

The king who regained Castilian-Leonese hegemony through peaceful accords with the neighboring Christian kingdoms of Spain and through conquests of Muslim territories in the southern part of the peninsula, increasing Castilian-Leonese power to a degree previously not achieved, Alfonso VII reigned from 1126 to 1157.

Born in 1105 to Urraca and Prince Raymond of Burgundy, Alfonso VII was granted by his grandfather *Alfonso VI (d. 1109) the rule of Galicia jointly with his mother. Raymond died in 1107, and Urraca married the Aragonese king Alfonso I, el Batallador ("the Battler"), essentially submitting León and Castile to Aragonese rule. Their union, however, produced no heir. Alfonso was declared king of Galicia in 1111 and, upon his mother's death in 1126, king of León and Castile. As king, he first submitted the nobles to his authority. He next sought an accord with his stepfather, el Batallador, asserting Castilian-Leonese independence from Aragon and thus averting war. He then proceeded to check the Almoravid encroachment on Castilian territory. In 1133, Alfonso took up arms against Muslim Spain. When el Batallador died in 1134, Alfonso

VII occupied areas in both Navarre and Aragon and subjugated the counts of Barcelona. He had himself declared emperor in 1135, asserting Leonese supremacy over the other Spanish kingdoms. He spent the rest of his life fighting the Muslims of southern Spain. His greatest conquest was that of the Mediterranean port city of Almería in 1147. Ten years later, Alfonso successfully defended Almería against the invading Almohades from Morocco. On his return to León, he fell ill, dying in Fresnada in 1157.

Alfonso VII's reign experienced two low points: The first was Portugal's independence from Leonese authority in 1143. The second was his dividing his kingdom between his two sons, Sancho III (Castile) and Fernando II (León). The division contributed to the turmoil after Alfonso's death that undid a life's worth of political achievements.

Bibliography: B. F. Reilly, *The Kingdom of León-Castilla under King Alfonso VII, 1126–1157*, 1998.

Paul B. Nelson

ALFONSO VIII OF CASTILE (1155–1214). Spanish King Alfonso VIII turned the tide in favor of the Christians in the Christian-Muslim struggle for territory in the Iberian Peninsula.

Born in 1155 to Sancho III of Castile (d. 1158), Alfonso succeeded his father at the age of three, and a civil war over his guardianship ensued for the next eleven years. Both Muslim and Christian factions (kings of León and Navarre) took advantage of the turmoil to seize strongholds in Castile. At fourteen, Alfonso had himself proclaimed king, thus settling his kingdom's civil strife, and he wed Eleanor, daughter of *Henry II of England, receiving Gascony as dowry. Alfonso then formed an army and recaptured the Castilian strongholds the Christian kings had usurped. He next took up arms against the Muslims, spending the rest of his reign essentially in a state of war. The treaty he signed in 1179 with Aragon (Treaty of Cazorla) pertaining to the distribution of Muslim lands foreshadowed the two kingdoms that would emerge to dominate the peninsula from the thirteenth century on: Castile-León and Aragon-Catalonia. Due to Alfonso's overall success in his campaigns against the Muslims, the leader of the Almohad dynasty, Mahomed ben Yacub, rallied troops in 1195 and invaded the peninsula with a powerful army that completely devastated the Christian army. After this defeat, Alfonso's resolve to rid the peninsula of Muslims was stronger than ever. Peace was established among the Christian kingdoms of Spain in order to unite their efforts against the Muslims, who requested aid from Yacub. Yacub invaded Spain again with an enormous army. This time, however, the Muslim armies were completely destroyed by the Castilians with the aid of the kings of Aragon and Navarre. This decisive defeat occurred in Navas de Tolosa in 1212 and weakened the Muslim hold over the peninsula, giving the Christians the upper hand from then on. Alfonso died in 1214 while preparing for a new assault against the Muslims.

Although he dedicated much of his life to war, Alfonso showed foresight and did not ignore his kingdom. He supported education and founded a university in Valencia. He also began the *Fuero Real*, a body of laws completed by his successors. Furthermore, both to promote peace and to unite the two kingdoms of Castile and León as they had previously been, he wed his daughter *Berenguela to Alfonso IX of León.

Bibliography: J.-M. Jover Zamora and M. A. Ladero Quesada, *Historia de España Menéndez Pidal: Tomo IX. La Reconquista y el proceso de diferenciación política (1035–1217)*, 1998.

Paul B. Nelson

ALFONSO X OF CASTILE (1221–1284). King of Castile, Alfonso X earned the title "el Sabio," meaning "the Wise" or "the Learned," not for the astuteness with which he ruled the central Iberian kingdom of Castile but rather for the multiplicity of cultural works, many written in vernacular Castilian, produced during his reign.

Alfonso X was born in Toledo in 1221, the son of King Fernando III of Castile and Beatriz of Swabia, granddaughter of the Holy Roman Emperor, *Frederick I Babarossa. His father was later canonized as "San Fernando," less for his piety than for his great success as a crusader in reconquering much of Andulusia and Murcia from Muslim rule. In 1244, Alfonso married Violante, daughter of King *James I of neighboring Aragon. This union produced six sons and four daughters.

Alfonso added no new territory to the kingdom he inherited from his father in 1252. His reign was taken up instead with the difficult task of bringing unity and order to newly conquered territories in which Christian and Jewish settlers intermingled with a large Mudejar population. To this end, he reorganized the royal chancellery and treasury, imposed new taxes, and promulgated a new royal law code, the *Especulo*. He also met more regularly with the Cortes, the Spanish Parliament. His new initiatives did not prove popular with the nobility, however—nor did his efforts to claim the crown of Holy Roman Emperor based on his mother's Hohenstaufen lineage. A faction of the Imperial Electors elected Alfonso emperor in 1257. However, despite a large expenditure of time and money, Alfonso was never able to secure papal confirmation of his election, and the imperial crown eluded him. The latter part of his reign saw other disappointments as well: a Mudejar revolt, a Moroccan invasion, and the death of his eldest son and heir, Fernando de la Cerda, in 1275. The last precipitated an extended succession crisis as Alfonso vacillated between favoring his second son Sancho and his de la Cerda grandsons. By 1282, with the support of disgruntled Castilian nobles, Sancho captured the reins of government from his father. However, he declined the title of king until after Alfonso's death in 1284.

What Alfonso lacked as a statesman, he made up for as a poet and a scholar. Bringing together a host of collaborators—translators, poets, jurists, musicians, painters, philosophers, scientists, and historians—he oversaw the creation of a vast array of literary, legal, and historical works unparalleled in thirteenth-century Europe. Even more striking was his choice to employ vernacular in place of Latin as the language of his chancellery and library, making him the "father" of Castilian. His interests were eclectic; he oversaw the translation of both Arabic scientific texts and game manuals including the book *Chess, Dice, and Backgammon*. His compilation of astronomical observations, the *Alfonsine Tables*, would be consulted by astronomers and sailors well into the modern era. He produced two major historical works, the *General Chronicle*, a history of the world from antiquity through the time of Jesus, and the *General Chronicle of Spain*, a history of Spain through the reign of his father. Both works were innovative for their use of multiple sources and their concern for social and cultural as well as political history.

Alfonso was also a great champion of Roman law and sought to reintroduce it in his kingdom. His greatest legal achievement was the *Siete Partidas*, a monumental encyclopedia of law that included hundreds of didactic essays on such diverse topics as religious practice, the conduct of kings and knights, warfare and castle building, regulations for Jews and Muslims, and how to run a university. This work became the foundation of legal practice in Spain and the Americas and is still in use today. Alfonso's most unique and creative accomplishment was the *Canticles of Holy Mary*. In this work written in Galician, Alfonso became a troubadour, singing the praises of the Virgin Mary. Included are over 400 lyric and narrative poems, the latter relating tales of Marian miracles. Many of the poems are set to music, and the entire text is lavishly illustrated. The almost 1,300 illustrations are often gathered into groupings for a particular poem, narrating the action in a comic-book-style with detailed depictions of daily life in Alfonso's court. Thus, in a time and place more noted for conquerors, this wise king left his people a rich cultural heritage.

Bibliography: R. I. Burns, *Emperor of Culture: Alfonso X the Learned of Castile and His Thirteenth-Century Renaissance*, 1990; J. Keller, *Alfonso X el Sabio*, 1967.

Linda A. McMillin

ALFRED THE GREAT (849–899, R. 871–899). Anglo-Saxon king Alfred the Great repelled the attempt by Danish Vikings to conquer Wessex, laid the foundation for the unification of England under his son Edward the Elder and grandson *Æthelstan, and presided over a circle of scholars who made his royal household one of the most learned in ninth-century Europe.

Born on the royal estate of Wantage (Berkshire), Alfred (or Ælfræd) came into the world with little apparent chance of occupying the throne of Wessex. He was the youngest son of Æthelwulf (839–858) and his first wife Osburh, and he had four older brothers. Æthelstan (the eldest) died before his father, but Æthelbald (858–860), Æthelberht (860–865), and Æthelred I (865–871) preceded Alfred as king, and the last left two minor sons, Æthelwold and Æthelhelm. Further complicating the succession was the practice, dating to the reign of Alfred's grandfather Egbert, of dividing responsibility for eastern and western Wessex between the king and a son or brother.

Alfred spent much of his youth traveling about the kingdom with his father, who also sent him to Rome in 853 and took him along in 855–856 when visiting Rome and the court of *Charles II the Bald of France. Although Alfred's biographer *Asser claimed that he had little education as a boy, he did have tutors and was literate in English by the age of twelve. He also received military training. Relatively little is known about Alfred during the reigns of Æthelbald and Æthelberht, though under the latter the remaining brothers reached an agreement whereby Alfred was to inherit the entire kingdom of Wessex if he outlived the others.

Æthelred's reign coincided with an important new phase in the Viking threat. Viking raiders had plagued the British Isles since the late eighth century; however, about 865 the Danes shifted to a strategy of actual conquest, and over the next five years they conquered East Anglia and Northumbria and forced Mercia to accept peace. King Burgred of Mercia, who was married to Alfred's older sister Æthelswith, sought an alliance with the West Saxons. One result was that in 868 Alfred married Ealhswith, whose mother was a member of the Mercian royal family. In late 870, the Danes attacked Wessex. Early in 871, Æthelred and Alfred fought a series of battles against them but were unsuccessful except for a victory at Ashdown. Soon after Æthelred's death in April 871, the new king found it necessary to make peace, probably by paying the Danes to go away. However, the Danes invaded Wessex again in 875, and Alfred made peace once more in 877. A third invasion in 878 forced Alfred to flee to Athelney in the Somerset marshes. From there he organized the counterattack that led to his victory at Edington, the baptism of the Danes' leader *Guthrum, and the Danes' withdrawal into East Anglia. That area, together with Northumbria and eastern Mercia, subsequently became known as the Danelaw.

From 878 to 892 Wessex was mostly at peace, and Alfred was able to devote himself to strengthening the kingdom in various ways. He built the extensive network of burhs (fortresses) later detailed in the Burghal Hidage, reorganized the fyrd from an occasional levy into a standing army in which half the force were always on duty, and built longships capable of countering Viking attacks from the sea. He also took steps to revitalize religion, education, and justice. During the same period he became overlord of western Mercia, and following the Viking capture of London in 886, he obtained recognition as king of all Anglo-Saxons outside the Danelaw. This peaceful interlude came to an end in 892, when a Viking force that had been active on the Continent invaded England. However, thanks to Alfred's reforms and the military leadership he and his son Edward now provided, the Anglo-Saxons were much more effective on land and sea. The Vikings were unable to maintain dependable bases for their raids or to penetrate his network of fortifications, and they eventually gave up and went away in 896. Though the sources say little about them, Alfred apparently spent his final three years in peace, dying on 26 October 899. He is buried at Winchester.

Alfred's contribution to Western culture is multifaceted. While the learned circle he assembled at his court was not the equal of that which *Charlemagne had summoned to Aachen a century earlier during the Carolingian Renaissance, it was impressive nonetheless. It included several Mercian priests: Plegmund, whom Alfred appointed archbishop of Canterbury in 890; Werferth, bishop of Worcester; Æthelstan; and Werwulf. Asser, who became Alfred's biographer and the bishop of Sherborne, came to his court in 885 from Wales, where he may already have held the see of St. David's. Alfred also called upon continental scholars, among them Grimbald the Frank and John the Old Saxon. By assembling this group, Alfred apparently sought to restore religion and learning in England to the greatness he believed they had enjoyed in the seventh century. The king himself learned to read Latin and was personally involved in the translation into Old English of the first fifty Psalms, Saint Augustine's *Soliloquies*, *Boethius' *Consolation of Philosophy*, and Pope *Gregory the Great's *Pastoral Care*, whereas others at court translated Gregory's *Dialogues*, Paulus Orosius's *Histories against the Pagans*, and *Bede's *Ecclesiastical History*. Alfred also instigated the compilation of the *Anglo-Saxon Chronicle*. Alfred's law code is of considerable significance in early medieval legal history. It drew upon Mosaic and Church law, Frankish law codes, and the dooms of *Ine of Wessex, *Offa of Mercia, and *Æthelbert of Kent, and of course it continued to influence the subsequent development of English law.

Not unlike George Washington, Alfred (in some ways the "father of his country") is the subject of numerous myths. One of the most famous is the story that while he was in Athelney in 878, he sought refuge in the hut of a swineherd whose wife left him in charge of some cakes that she was baking, then scolded him for allowing them to burn. Another concerns his receiving a visit (in the flesh), a vision, and miraculous assistance against the Danes from Saint Cuthbert of Lindisfarne. There is also a tale about him conducting reconnaissance in a Danish camp disguised as a minstrel. He is often portrayed as the founder of the English navy, though he was not the first Anglo-Saxon king to build ships for war. In the nineteenth century he became the subject of a different sort of mythology when various patriotic historians depicted him as an early proponent of English nationalism.

More recently, he has been the subject of historiographical debate stemming from challenges to the authenticity of Asser's biography. In 1964, V. H. Galbraith advanced the argument that Leofric, bishop of Devon and Cornwall (1046–1072) was the real author, though Dorothy Whitelock effectively refuted that argument. Then in 1995, Alfred P. Smyth published a massive and highly controversial biography contending that the real author of "Pseudo-Asser" was the Benedictine monk Byrhtferth of Ramsey. Smyth questions all information about Alfred for which Asser is the exclusive source and is particularly hostile to the notions that Alfred was troubled by ill health and that he was poorly educated before meeting

Asser, arguing instead that he received a very thorough education as a child. By and large other, however, other historians have rejected Smyth's account.

Bibliography: R. Abels, *Alfred the Great: War, Kingship and Culture in Anglo-Saxon England*, 1998; S. Keynes and M. Lapidge, trans., *Alfred the Great: Asser's* Life of King Alfred *and Other Contemporary Sources*, 1983; A. P. Smyth, *King Alfred the Great*, 1995.

William B. Robison

ALGAZEL. *See* GHAZĀLĪ, AL-.

AL-IDRĪSĪ. *See* IDRĪSĪ, AL-.

'ALĪ IBN ABĪ TĀLIB (600–661). 'Alī is the son-in-law and paternal first cousin of the prophet *Muhammad as well as the father of Muhammad's grandchildren, Hasan and Husayn. Questions about 'Alī's position in the early history of Islamic rule led to the division of the Muslim community into Sunni and Shiite factions. Whereas Shiite Muslims recognize 'Alī as the first imam (the legitimate religious and political leader of the Muslim community), Sunni Muslims consider 'Alī the fourth and last of the so-called rightly guided caliphs.

'Alī ibn Abī Tālib, born around the year 600, competes with Abū Bakr al-Siddiq, the first rightly guided caliph of Sunni Islam, over the claim to be the first male convert to Islam after Muhammad. 'Alī's father, Abū Tālib, had taken care of Muhammad after the latter lost his parents and his grandfather. Although Muhammad is about thirty years older than 'Alī, early sources describe the relationship between the two as being very close.

Muslim sources depict 'Alī as a brave Muslim and valiant warrior. During the night when Muhammad set out on his emigration to Medina in order to escape persecution and death threats, 'Alī, reportedly ready to die for the Prophet Muhammad, slept in Muhammad's bed to hide the fact that Muhammad was escaping from his Meccan enemies. In different accounts of the various battles in which he participated, 'Alī always is portrayed as fighting bravely and fiercely. Shiite traditions report that 'Alī was designated to be the successor of Muhammad by the latter in 632; however, 'Alī's claim to leadership was, according to Shiite tradition, usurped by three other caliphs before 'Alī finally became caliph in 656. Almost immediately after his accession, his claim to authority was being questioned. In 656, 'Alī had to move into battle against an army of challengers to his authority, led by the Prophet Muhammad's favorite wife, 'Ā'isha bint Abī Bakr, daughter of the first caliph. 'Alī emerged victorious from this battle, only to be challenged in the following year by Mu'āwiya ibn Abī Sufyān, founder of the Umayyad dynasty, who alleged that 'Alī had not adequately dealt with the assassins of his predecessor, 'Uthmān ibno 'Affān, a relative of Mu'āwiya. Although the ensuing battle between 'Alī and Mu'āwiya ended in a stalemate, the latter won the upper hand in subsequent arbitration; he succeeded 'Alī to the caliphate after ʿAlī was assassinated by disenchanted elements formerly associated with his own camp, in 661. The dispute between the families of ʿAlī and Muʿāwiya reached its peak in 680, when ʿAlī's second son Husayn, grandson of the Prophet Muhammad, was killed by an army led by Yazid, the son of Muʿāwiya, near the city of Karbalāʾ. This event, in which the grandson of the Prophet Muhammad was killed by the grandson of a former archenemy of Muhammad and Islam, constitutes a pivotal event in the memory of Shiite Islam and is reenacted in the Shiite Muslim world in words and symbolic action annually on the anniversary, the tenth day of the month Muharram.

ʿAlī's significance lies not so much in the political arena but in the religious sphere; for both Sunni and Shiite Muslims ʿAlī became a role model of valor, dedication, and sincerity. Shiites additionally regard ʿAlī as the first of a line of infallible imams who have inherited the "Light of Muhammad," an esoteric knowledge of the hidden meanings of the Qur'an.

Bibliography: E. L. Petersen, *ʿAlī and Muʿāwiya in Early Arabic Tradition*, 1964.

Alfons Teipen

AL-MA'MŪN. *See* MA'MŪN, AL-.

AL-RASHĪD. *See* HĀRŪN AL-RASHĪD.

AMALSWINTHA (AMALASUNTHA) (born after 495–535). *Theodoric's daughter by *Clovis's sister Auflade, she encouraged greater integration of Goths and Romans.

In 515 Amalswintha married Eutharic (d. 523), an Amal kinsman. They had two children, Athalric, king of the Ostrogoths (526–534), and Matasuentha, married first to Witigis, king of the Ostrogoths (536–540), and then to Germanus, nephew of Emperor *Justinian. When Athalric succeeded his grandfather, the widowed Amalswintha acted as regent. Amalswintha had been given a careful Roman literary education, apparently usual among her generation of Amal ladies. Even allowing for Cassiodorian (see *Cassiodorus) flattery in the *Variae*, she was apparently fluent in Latin and Greek as well as Gothic and more than competent in public affairs. She attempted to give her son the same training. However, Ostrogothic nobles, who believed Roman education would make him unfit to rule, removed him from her control and gave him a warrior's upbringing. Resenting this interference, she banished and then procured the secret murder of the three leading members of the Ostrogothic opposition.

Athalric, torn between two traditions, died 2 October 534, probably of drink. Amalswintha, who had foreseen the death of her son, had been in negotiation with Justinian for the surrender of the Italian kingdom in return for his support. In the end, she associated her cousin, Theodahad, a hyper-Romanized Ostrogoth, whose land grabbing she had censured and thwarted, with her on the throne. Despite his oaths, Theodahad quickly moved against his cousin, eliminated her supporters, imprisoned her, and then organized her murder.

Bibliography: T. Burns, *A History of the Ostrogoths*, 1991; Cassiodorus, *Variae*, trans. S.J.B. Barnish, 1992.

Helen Conrad-O'Briain

ANDREAS CAPELLANUS. *See* CAPELLANUS, ANDREAS.

ANGELA OF FOLIGNO (C. 1248–1309). Angela was one of the most influential female mystics of her day; she described her relationship with Christ as an ascent to mystical union.

Angela was a well-to-do woman, from an affluent family, who experienced her conversion in her midthirties. The conversion began with her fear of hell; she had been leading a superficial, pleasure-seeking life and, according to her own confession, had committed some kind of mortal sin, which she feared would require absolution from a bishop. We do not know what this sin might have been, but whatever it was did not in fact require episcopal absolution. Nonetheless, this fear of hell gradually transformed into anxiety about Christ's love. After the deaths of her mother, husband, and sons, whom she perceived as obstacles to her spiritual growth, she began to give away all her possessions, in order to become truly poor. So strict were her sufferings that others feared demonic possession. But Angela was experiencing visions of God's love, had pledged chastity to her new lover Christ, and was trying to move as far away from her old life as she could. She was eventually allowed to take the habit and make her profession in the third order of Saint. *Francis.

Her visionary experiences were becoming increasingly public, most notably the one she had in the Basilica of St. Francis at Assisi: she cried out in words that became ever less intelligible and writhed on the floor. Her confessor again suspected demonic possession and pressed her to tell him what was going on. Her answer surprised him; Angela had been undergoing nineteen of an eventual thirty steps towards mystical union with Christ and described so much torment and joy that he doubted her and convinced her to doubt herself. Nevertheless, she kept dictating, and he kept copying her *Memorial* and eventually became convinced that she was, as she said, God's Dear One. Angela died on 4 January 1309, which became her feast day. Her grave became a cult site, and she was given the title of "Blessed" by popular acclaim, but this was not formalized until 11 July 1701. She was never canonized.

Angela played a considerable role as a spiritual mother. A small community gathered around her, the most famous member of which was Ubertino of Casale, who credits her with his conversion. But Angela is best seen in the context of the many female mystics who defined their relationship with God in personal, almost erotic terms and who changed the spiritual options open to women.

Bibliography: Angela of Foligno, *The Complete Works*, trans. P. Lachance, 1993.

Andrea Schutz

ANNA COMNENA (1083–1153). The eldest daughter of Byzantine Emperor *Alexius I Comnenus and Irene Ducas, Anna was a scholar and historian who wrote *The Alexiad*, a political history of the reign of her father.

Born in 1083, Anna was the heir apparent to the Byzantine Empire until 1092, when her five-year-old brother John was proclaimed *basileus*. She had three sisters: Maria, Eudocia, and Theodora. Her mother came from an important noble family, the Ducas, and for a while Anna was betrothed to a Ducas cousin. She married Nicephorus Bryennios in 1097 at the age of fourteen; he was two years her elder. They had four children, Alexius, John, Irene Ducas, and another daughter whose name is not recorded. Nicephorus Bryennios was smart and ambitious, and Anna became involved in a conspiracy to have him take the Byzantine throne in 1118, upon the death of her father Alexius. Bryennios himself was responsible for composing the *Historical Materials*, an accounting of Byzantine political history from 1069 to 1079. For a long time, historians believed Anna's history, which extended from 1069 to 1118, to be overly dependent on the work of her husband. In the nineteenth century, however, historians began to accept that Anna's work was her own and credit her with a valuable historical work.

The failure of the plot to overthrow her brother John resulted in Anna's withdrawal to a convent with her mother in 1118. There she completed *The Alexiad*, a fifteen-book chronicle of the reign of her father using Homer's *Iliad* as a model and a great number of important primary sources. Her history considers not only firsthand knowledge of court life and imperial affairs from her position as a Byzantine princess but also letters, government correspondence, military records, and diplomatic summaries as well as materials from the imperial archives. She also considers several Latin sources so must have been able to read Latin as well as Greek. Anna's scholarship, her mastery of Greek philosophy, mythology, and literature as well as medicine, was not unusual for a Byzantine princess.

In writing *The Alexiad* Anna claimed she wanted to document her father's achievements so that they would not be lost or underestimated. She also wanted later historians to distinguish her father from the previous generation of emperors, who she termed inefficient militarily, so he would not be blamed for their mistakes. Her work is unapologetically pro-Byzantine and pro-Greek. Events, such as the Crusades, are recounted with a distrustful bias against the achievements of what she calls "Latins," the western Europeans who traveled to the Middle East to recapture the Holy Land from the Muslims. Her work extols her father's accomplishments without much criticism for his faults, personal or political. Yet it is a valuable study of life at court, particularly the role of Anna Dalassena, her paternal grandmother, the "Mother of the Komemnoi," and the real power behind the throne until 1100.

Bibliography: R. Dalven, *Anna Comnena*, 1972.

Alana Cain Scott

ANSELM OF CANTERBURY (1033–1109). Theologian, saint, and Doctor of the Church, he was the first major scholastic philosopher. He set forth in his *Proslogion* an ontological argument for the existence and nature of God that was based on reason alone. His conviction that reason and faith were compatible made him an important pioneer in the development of high medieval rationalism. As he put it, "I believe so that I may know" (*crudo ut intelligam*).

Born to a noble family at Aosta on the Burgundy-Savoy border, Anselm, having quarreled with his Lombard father, left home and traveled first to his mother's family in Burgundy and then to Normandy, where he became a pupil of *Lanfranc at the monastery of Bec sometime before 1059. He became a monk in 1060, and when Lanfranc moved to Caen in 1062, Anselm succeeded him as prior and schoolmaster the following year. In 1077–1078, he wrote the *Monologion* and *Proslogion*, which revealed his originality and prepared the way for his later theological works. When Bec's founder and abbot Herluin died in 1078, Anselm was elected abbot in his place.

During his tenure at Bec, Anselm combined efficient administration with ideals of universal friendship and love. Bec became the wealthiest and most respected monastery in Normandy; its monks became abbots and bishops throughout Normandy and England, spreading Anselm's growing reputation. Shortly after he became abbot, Anselm journeyed to England, where his monastery had several possessions. There he visited his old teacher Lanfranc, who had become archbishop of Canterbury in 1070. He was also brought into contact with English ecclesiastical affairs. On Lanfranc's death in 1089 the English clergy wanted Anselm to be his successor, but the English king, William II Rufus (d. 1100), kept the see open for four years, seizing Church revenues and granting Church lands to his followers. Only when William seemed mortally ill did he agree to Anselm's appointment.

As archbishop, Anselm was embroiled in a series of disputes with William and his successor, *Henry I of England, about papal jurisdiction, investiture, and the primacy of the spiritual world over the temporal. Anselm refused to consent to William's exploitation of the Church, nor would he endorse the antipope Wibert at William's request when, as abbot of Bec, he had already recognized *Urban II as pope. He was totally committed to what he saw as the cause of God and the Church, to which he owed and gave absolute obedience. Relations between king and archbishop continued to be strained, and in 1097 William brought a false charge of disloyalty to the crown against Anselm. Rather than travel to court to meet this charge, Anselm requested permission to travel to Rome—a self-imposed exile that the king eventually granted.

It was in Rome that Anselm wrote his important theological treatise *Cur Deus homo* (Why God Became Man), in which he subjected the doctrines of the incarnation and atonement to rigorous logical analysis. He attended the council at Bari, where, at the pope's request, he successfully defended the doctrine of the Double Procession of the Holy Spirit against the Greeks. Anselm was also introduced to the controversial arguments against investiture during his stay in

Rome, where new canons were passed against this practice and excommunication decreed the punishment for offenders.

Following William Rufus' accidental death in 1100, his successor Henry I recalled Anselm to Canterbury. However, Anselm adopted the papal position on investiture and refused to countenance the ceremony of royal investiture of prelates. Henry declined to abandon this long-accepted royal prerogative of investing abbots and bishops, and Anselm was once again forced into exile (1103–1107). The English investiture controversy pitted king, archbishop, and pope in a three-way struggle. It did not end until 1107, when Anselm was finally able to negotiate compromises among all parties. In a council at London, Henry I agreed to relinquish his right of investiture of abbots and bishops in their offices, while the Church allowed those prelates to do homage to the king for the temporal possessions they received from him. The abdication of this symbol of real power by the English king prepared the way for the later solution of the same controversy in Germany at the Concordat of Worms (1122). Anselm achieved primacy for the archbishopric of Canterbury in all Church matters in England, as well as Wales, Ireland, and the Orkney Islands. He also established a new episcopal see at Ely. He died on 21 April 1109 and was buried at Canterbury next to Lanfranc.

Anselm was fortunate in his biographer, Eadmer, a monk of Canterbury, who wrote an intimate, personal life that took the literary genre of biography in a new direction. Thomas *Becket, Anselm's later successor, promoted his canonization at Tours in 1163, but Pope *Alexander III referred it to a provincial council, and no formal record survives. However, a Canterbury calendar dated c. 1165 listed both St. Anselm's feast day of 21 April and his translation of 7 April.

A dedicated Augustinian, Anselm applied reason to faith based on the Platonic tradition transmuted and transmitted by Augustine of Hippo (d. 430) to the medieval world. He took Augustine's realist position on the question of universals and the superiority of meditation to observation. Anselm taught that faith must guide reason but that reason could help to illuminate faith. His lasting monuments are treatises on logic and a series of theological works in which a powerful logic dominated. His ontological argument is an a priori one, based not on sense experience but on a definition of God from which it follows that God exists. It is deceptively simple and, as such, was largely ignored from the late medieval period. It was rejected by Thomas *Aquinas and his followers, although supported by *John Duns Scotus. It was revived in another form by Descartes and later defended by Hegel. Anselm was made a Doctor of the Church in 1734 as the most important writer between Augustine and Thomas Aquinas.

Bibliography: Eadmer, *The Life of St. Anselm of Canterbury*, ed. and trans. R. W. Southern, 1962; S. N. Vaughn, *Anselm of Bec and Robert of Meulan: The Innocence of the Dove and the Wisdom of the Serpent*, 1987.

Marguerite Ragnow

ANSELM OF LAON (D. C. 1117). Anselm was an erudite biblical scholar and teacher. Little is known about this teacher and theologian, and it may be more accurate to speak of the "school of Anselm." His actual name is recorded as "Ansellus," but later generations referred to him as "Master Anselm." Sometime between 1106 and 1109 he became dean of Laon cathedral, where he may have been teaching since 1080. In 1115, cathedral documents describe him as archdeacon of Laon as well. Anselm remained in Laon for another two years until his death.

Anselm's fame and reputation were based on his teaching in the cathedral school, and he attracted a large number of students. Contemporary accounts report that he was an excellent teacher and well versed in theology. Even Peter *Abelard, who considered Anselm to be a second-rate theologian, conceded that he was an excellent communicator. While there is no complete record of his teaching, the scattered collections of his *Sententiae* (recorded theological opinions) reveal a robust and engaging school of theology at Laon. The disputed question was central to Anselm's pedagogy, though it had not yet reached the rarified form it would take on in later centuries. Nonetheless, Anselm appears to have been concerned with presenting rational arguments for doctrinal points, which were founded upon biblical citations and the concordance of disparate patristic opinions. The issues and concepts he debated ranged from ideas about human nature and the Incarnation to the juridical issues in Church practice, including practical items concerning correct ethical behavior.

Many of these questions emerged from reflection upon Scripture, as biblical exegesis was at the center of theological education. Perhaps the greatest contribution made by Anselm and his school to medieval theology was the creation of the glossed Bible. Anselm's careful readings of patristic sources were deployed as exegetical markers in the biblical text; soon manuscripts of the Bible surrounded the biblical text with extracts from the Fathers, which were to act as the definitive interpretation. It would seem that Anselm was responsible for compiling the glosses for the Psalter and the Pauline Epistles and possibly for the Gospel of John. Near the end of his life, he permitted one of his students, *Gilbert of Poitiers, to revise the gloss for the Psalter—but under his supervision. Eventually, Anselm's work became known as the *parva glossatura* (the small gloss), to distinguish it from the work of Gilbert (whose own commentaries were known as the *media glossatura*—the middle gloss) and the later *magna glossatura* (the great gloss) of *Peter Lombard.

In addition to the *Sententiae* and the glossed Bible, Anselm may have also written a separate commentary on the Psalms. However, his authorship remains disputed in the modern scholarship. Regardless of what be counted among his written works, later theologians held Anselm in high regard as an example of erudition and biblical scholarship.

Bibliography: A. Landgraf, *Introduction à l'histoire de la littérature théologique de la scolastique naissante*, ed. L. Geiger and trans. A. Landry, 1973; O. Lottin, *Psychologie et morale aux XIIe et XIIIe siècles, tome V: Problèmes d'histoire littéraire. L'école* *d'Anselme de Laon et de Guillaume de Champeaux*, 1957; R. W. Southern, *Scholastic Humanism and the Unification of Europe, Volume 1: Foundation*, 1995.

James R. Ginther

ANSKAR (ANSGAR), SAINT (801–865). The patron saint of Denmark, Germany, and Iceland, he was responsible for Christianizing the people of northern Europe and working to eliminate the Viking slave trade.

Born into a noble family in Picardy, Anskar was sent to the nearby Benedictine monastery of Corbie, where he received his formal education under Paschasius *Radbertus. He became a monk and moved to New Corbie (Corvey) in Westphalia, where he taught and first performed pastoral work. When Harald, king of Denmark, sought refuge with *Louis the Pious during a dispute over the right of succession, Harald and his entourage were baptized in 826. Upon his return to Denmark, Harald took Anskar and another monk, Autbert, to convert the Danes.

After leaving Denmark, Anskar went to Sweden at the invitation of King Björn to preach there. In 831 King Louis established a bishopric in Hamburg and named Anskar to head the see. Three years later Pope Gregory IV raised the see to the rank of an archbishopric that was to include Germany, Greenland, Iceland, and Scandinavia. Anskar remained there as archbishop until 845 when an invasion of Vikings destroyed Hamburg. Anskar traveled over Germany for several years tending his churches until *Louis the German appointed him to the see of Bremen and Pope *Nicholas I confirmed him as archbishop of Hamburg and bishop of Bremen. He spent the remainder of his life preaching in Denmark and Sweden, trying to reverse the damage done to the Church by the Vikings.

Bibliography: C. H. Robinson, *Anskar: The Apostle of the North*, 1921.

Clinton Atchley

AQUINAS, THOMAS, SAINT (C. 1224/1225–1274). Thomas Aquinas was a Dominican scholastic theologian known as the Angelic Doctor and the most prominent intellectual figure of the later Middle Ages.

Thomas was born in Roccasecca, Italy, into a minor noble family in the service of Emperor *Frederick II. In 1230, his family offered him as an oblate to the ancient Benedictine monastery of Monte Cassino founded by Saint *Benedict in the sixth century. His family hoped that Thomas would one day become abbot of this prestigious house. From 1230 to 1239, Thomas began his studies at Monte Cassino; in 1239, he was sent, along with other oblates, to the newly founded imperial University of Naples to complete his studies. At Naples, Thomas first came into contact with the "new" Aristotle—those works that had recently been translated from the Greek and Arabic—along with those of the famous Aristotelian commentator *Averroës. Thomas also came into contact with the Order of Friars Preachers (cf. *Dominic). By spring 1244, Thomas had decided to enter the Dominican Order. Thomas' family, however, was distressed by his plans; his brother abducted young Thomas and brought him back to the family estate at Roccasecca while he was en route to Bologna. Unable to change his decision, in 1245, his family allowed him to rejoin his friars.

Thomas proceeded to Paris and studied under the tutelage of Albert the Great (*Albertus Magnus). In 1248, when Albert was asked to direct a new house of studies at Cologne, Thomas accompanied him there. From 1248 to 1252 Thomas studied at Cologne. Here he composed his first works, two short treatises on logic. He also reported on Albert's lectures on Aristotle's *Ethics* and *Pseudo-Dionysius' *On the Divine Names* and may have begun lecturing on Scripture. While at Cologne, he was ordained a priest.

In 1252, Albert recommended that he return to Paris and finish his theological training. Thomas then resumed his studies at Paris and lectured on *Peter Lombard's *Sentences*. He completed the requirements for the theological degree by 1256 but, like *Bonaventure, was not recognized as a regent master until the following year due to the opposition of *William of St. Amour and other secular theologians. In response to William, Thomas wrote his first polemical work *Contra impugnantes Dei cultum et religionem* (Against Those Who Attack the Religious Profession) in 1256. While at Paris, Thomas also completed his first metaphysical text, *De ente et essentia* (On Being and Essence), and completed an explanatory handbook of Aristotelian terms, *De principiis naturae* (On the Principles of Nature). Thomas also wrote expositions on Isaiah and Matthew and determined quodlibetal questions and his disputed questions *De veritate* (On Truth). At Paris, he also began his monumental *Summa contra Gentiles*, a work to be used by Spanish missionaries to help convert Jews and Muslims to Christianity. Thomas lectured at Paris until 1259, when he was sent to teach in the Roman province of the Dominicans. For the next nine years, he taught at Anagni, Orvieto, Rome, and Viterbo and was frequently attached to the papal curia.

During this Italian period, Thomas finished his *Summa contra Gentiles*. He also wrote the *Catena aurea* (Golden Chain), a running commentary on all four Gospels, and lectured on Scripture. While in Italy, Thomas produced his *Contra errores Graecorum* (Against the Errors of the Greeks), which demonstrated that there was a theological harmony between the Greek Church Fathers and the Latin Church. This work also proves that while Thomas was in Italy, he had access to new translations of Greek Patristic authors. In Italy Thomas also began his *Summa theologiae*. He intended this work to be used for students of theology within the Dominican schools. Thomas probably began most of his Aristotelian commentaries in Italy but may have finished some of them in Paris. He also composed a liturgical work, the *Office of the Feast of Corpus Christi*.

In 1269 Thomas was sent to Paris again, and here he had to face two serious threats to his Order: the attacks of the Parisian theologians led by Gerald of Abbeville and Nicholas of Lisieux on the mendicant life and the radical Aristotelian or "Averroistic" movement led by *Siger of Brabant and *Boethius of Dacia. Against Gerald and Nicholas, Thomas wrote two polemical works, *De* *perfectione vitae spiritualis* (On the Perfection of the Spiritual Life) and *Contra doctrinam retrahentium a religione* (Against the Teaching of Those Drawing People away from Religion); against Siger, Thomas wrote *De unitate intellectus* (On the Unity of the Intellect). Some manuscripts of this latter work contain the phrase *contra Sigerum* (against Siger). Thomas also wrote *De aeternitate mundi* (On the Eternity of the World) against the more conservative theologians who objected to the use of Aristotle in theology. Not all of Thomas' works from his second Parisian regency were polemical, and he also wrote expositions on Job and John. By the end of his second period at Paris, Thomas had commented on most of the major works of Aristotle including *Physics, Ethics, Metaphysics, Politics, De anima*, and *De interpretatione*.

Thomas was asked to help found a new Dominican studium in Naples and in 1272 left for that city. He remained there for two years. Here he lectured on Psalms and the Pauline epistles and wrote commentaries on Aristotle's *On Generation and Corruption, On the Heavens and Earth*, and quite possibly *Meteorology*. He also preached a Lenten cycle of sermons and wrote expositions on the prayers Hail Mary and Our Father. He was summoned to help organize a Church council to reunite the Greek and Latin Churches (Second Council of Lyons), but he fell sick and died along the way in March 1274. A few months before he died, Thomas allegedly explained that all he had written was "straw." He was canonized in 1323 and recognized as a Doctor of the Church in 1567. He was made the patron of Catholic schools in 1880.

As an intellectual figure, Thomas is the most prominent philosopher and theologian of the Middle Ages. Thomas wrote so much throughout his lifetime that during the late medieval period and even to the present day his works have had a broad impact on Western society. His *Summa contra Gentiles* and unfinished *Summa theologiae* form classic systemizations of Catholic theology. These two works, which were so influential as medieval manuals of the faith, still provide important explanations on basic points of Christian doctrine.

Like Albert, Thomas was convinced that Aristotle could be used in the service of the faith, and his Aristotelian commentaries showed that the Greek philosopher could be interpreted in a way palatable to Christians. While Thomas argued that philosophy was important, he always viewed it as a servant of theology, for the former relies on human reason, whereas the latter requires faith and revelation. Although Thomas believed in the compatibility of faith and reason, he argued that due to sin some theological truths, such as the Trinity, cannot be grasped by the human mind and require supernatural aid for understanding. Thus while faith and reason work in tandem, the latter is subservient to the former, especially in regard to theological truths. As an example of Thomas' penchant for using philosophy in the service of theology, in the *Summa theologiae* he advances five proofs for the existence of God. Proof four, based on motion, derives from Aristotle.

Thomas had little sympathy for the Latin "Averroists" and sought to repudiate them on their own terms by clarifying Aristotle, noting in *De aeternitate mundi* that even Aristotle thought the issue of the world's eternity was debatable. He likewise opposed the critics of the friars and proved himself not only as an able polemicist but also as an expert defender of his Order. Thomas' greatest contribution to medieval thought was his theological synthesis of reason and faith.

Bibliography: J.-P. Torrell, *Saint Thomas Aquinas: The Person and His Work*, vol. 1, trans. R. Royal, 1996; J. A. Weisheipl, *Friar Thomas d'Aquino: His Life, Thought, and Work*, rev. ed., 1983.

Andrew G. Traver

ARI ÞORGILSSON (ARI THE WISE, ARI THE LEARNED) (1068–1148).

The author of the *Íslendingabók*, the first work in Icelandic and the first history of Iceland, the priest Ari Þorgilsson not only preserved much of Iceland's earliest history, including the establishment in 930 of the Althing, the Icelandic parliament, but also established the rich tradition of historical literature in Iceland.

In 1068, Ari the Wise was born into a noble family, whose genealogy he treats as an appendix to his book. This genealogy contains many important figures in Iceland's early government, which may have influenced Ari's interest in history. When Ari's father, Þorgils, drowned when Ari was still young, he went first to live with his grandfather Gellir and then the man who later sources call his foster father, Hallr Þórarinsson. However, Ari called another man, Teitr Ísleifsson, his foster father, and it is Teitr who was a profound influence on Ari's life and learning. Teitr was a priest and ran a renowned school at Haukadalr; Ari lived there with his tutor and schoolmaster Teitr for fourteen years and received a clerical education. In Haukadalr, Ari also became close to a leading aristocratic family in Iceland, the Mosfellingar, who worked to further education and Christianity through the national Icelandic Church. In school, under Teitr's tutelage, Ari was known for being extremely intelligent and having an exceptionally good memory. Ari left school in 1089, and though little is known about his later life, he probably settled near his ancestral home in Snaefellsnes, married, and had at least one son, Þorgils, a priest. Besides the date of his death on 9 November 1148, it is only known that he wrote the *Íslendingabók*.

The *Íslendingabók* was written in two versions between 1122 and 1132 at the request of two bishops, Þorlákr Rúnólfsson and Ketill Þorsteinsson, perhaps to instruct and preserve Iceland's early history and strengthen Christianity and its laws. Only Ari's second recension of the history is extant in two much later manuscripts. Ari cites many sources for the materials in the history and seems to have begun gathering information for the book when he was still in school with Teitr, whom he often quotes. In the *Íslendingabók*, Ari records the migration from Scandinavia, the settlement of Iceland, and the establishment of the Althing in 930, the first parliament of its kind in Europe. He discusses the establishment of the calendar, the division of the island, the colonization of

Greenland (c. 985), and the coming of Christianity to Iceland (c. 1000). Taking care to trace the secular and religious leadership in Iceland, the *Íslendingabók* culminates with the great Bishop Gizurr Ísleifsson, whose popularity and wisdom helped establish a number of laws. The history concludes with three genealogies: one of kings, one of bishops, and Ari's own. In so doing, Ari traced the beginnings of his nation up to his present moment and thus laid the foundations for Icelandic historical literature.

Bibliography: Ari Þorgilsson, *The Book of the Icelanders*, ed. and trans. H. Hermannsson, 1930; K. Hastrup, *Culture and History in Medieval Iceland*, 1985.

Matthew Hussey

ARNOLD OF BRESCIA (C. 1094–1155).

Italian churchman and reformer, he was part of the reform movement that swept through the Catholic world in the early twelfth century. His preaching and activism against the worldliness of the Church, particularly at the papal level, led to his exile, excommunication, and finally death by hanging.

Arnold was a tireless critic of abuses in the Church, especially its possession of worldly goods and its exercise of temporal power. Educated in France, Arnold returned to Brescia in northern Italy and became a canon regular, a secular clergyman living under a modified form of monasticism. He took a leading role in a conflict between local politicians and Manfred, bishop of Brescia, concerning the bishop's involvement in city affairs, which in 1138 led to an insurrection against the bishop. For this activity, Pope Innocent II at the Second Lateran Council condemned Arnold in 1139. Ordered to leave Brescia, Arnold took refuge in France, where, according to *John of Salisbury (Historia pontificalis), he allied himself with Peter *Abelard and the Italian Hyacinth Boboni (the future Pope Celestine III) against *Bernard of Clairvaux, who secured his condemnation, along with that of Abelard, at the Council of Sens in 1140. Arnold, supposedly confined to Mont Sainte-Genevieve in Paris, held public discourses on moral theology, declaring that wealth and temporal power infected the Church like a virus. Once again he was challenged by Bernard of Clairvaux, who convinced King *Louis VII to banish Arnold from France. After a brief exile in Zurich, Arnold returned to Rome in 1143 upon the death of Innocent II, reconciling with the Church.

However, a conflict between the Roman Senate and the papacy had led to an insurrection whose leaders wanted to drive out the pope and reestablish the ancient Roman Republic. This revolt soon fell under Arnold's leadership. Although he was excommunicated on 15 July 1148 by Pope *Eugenius III, a former pupil of Bernard of Clairvaux, Arnold and his supporters continued their struggle against papal authority in secular affairs. In 1152, however, with the support of Holy Roman Emperor *Frederick I Barbarossa, Eugenius once again gained control. Although Arnold's revolution briefly reasserted itself in 1154, when Pope *Hadrian IV put the entire city of Rome under interdict, ordering the suspension of church services throughout the city, Arnold's revolution collapsed, and driven from the city, he retired to Campania. Hadrian joined forces with Frederick Barbarossa to hunt Arnold down. He was arrested and, in 1155, condemned to death and turned over to the prefect of Rome, who hanged him, burned his body, and threw his ashes in the Tiber River.

Like other reformers of his time, Arnold's goal was the revival of the ideal of apostolic poverty. He believed that wealth and temporal authority corrupted the Church. His reforming zeal led him to become a political activist, characterized by *Otto of Freising, among others, as an "enemy of the Catholic Faith."

Bibliography: G. W. Greenaway, *Arnold of Brescia*, 1931.

Marguerite Ragnow

ASSER (D. C. 909). Asser was a Welsh monk and priest who became the servant of *Alfred the Great, was bishop of the Anglo-Saxon diocese of Sherborne, and is best known as the author of the *Life of King Alfred*, one of the principal sources for ninth-century England.

Though his birthdate is unknown, Asser apparently was a native of St. David's in the Welsh kingdom of Dyfed. His name is Hebrew, derived from Jacob's eighth son Asher in the Old Testament. He may have served as bishop of St. David's after the death of his kinsman Nobis vacated the see in 873 or 874. It is also possible that he was suffragan in Sherborne before succeeding Wulfsige in the episcopal dignity there sometime between 892 and 900. If he was bishop of St. David's, that would explain why he initially insisted on spending part of each year there after he entered Alfred's service.

Asser first met the West Saxon king in 885 on his estate at Dean in Sussex; at the time he may have been involved in talks that led several Welsh kings to submit to Alfred as their overlord. In any case, he agreed to enter Alfred's household, where the king was assembling a learned circle, including Plegmund of Mercia (whom Alfred made archbishop of Canterbury) and numerous scholars from the Continent, among them Grimbald the Frank. Asser read to Alfred, perhaps taught him to read Latin, assisted him in translating *Boethius' *Consolation of Philosophy* and Pope *Gregory the Great's *Pastoral Care*, helped him promote education, and may have been directly involved in government and diplomacy during the king's struggle against the Danes. Eventually he settled permanently in Wessex, though he traveled extensively, often with the king.

Alfred rewarded him well for his services. Among other things, the king gave him control in 886 of the monasteries of Banwell and Congresbury in Somerset and later of the powerful house in Exeter. Though the exact year that Asser became bishop of Sherborne is unknown, it is almost certain that Alfred appointed him sometime before his own death. The diocese was the largest in Wessex, including the shires of Cornwall, Devon, Dorset, and Somerset; therefore, Asser's acquisition of the see indicates that the king put great trust in him. He remained in the post until his death during the reign of Alfred's son and heir Edward the Elder.

Asser began his education at St. David's but no doubt was influenced by continental scholars at Alfred's court. His writing reveals some knowledge of the Church Fathers, earlier Anglo-Saxon historians (probably including *Bede), Frankish chroniclers, and *Einhard's *Life of Charlemagne*, which may have been the model for his own *Life of King Alfred*, though he was more familiar with the Old Latin Bible than Jerome's Vulgate. Asser's biography drew heavily upon the *Anglo-Saxon Chronicle* for events up to 887 and then more on his own knowledge, though he also questioned Alfred and others of his household about various aspects of his reign. Like Einhard, Asser finds no fault with his monarch and patron, consistently presenting him as the exemplary king. For some reason, Asser stopped his account at the year 893; thus, he omits Alfred's later victories over the Danes and his death.

What survives is apparently a draft, and it is possible that a more complete version once existed; however, there is very little hard evidence for this. Keynes and Lapidge suggest that Asser wrote the life for a Welsh audience, though its only known circulation in the Anglo-Saxon period was in England. Regrettably, the original manuscript is not extant, and the only known medieval copy (from about 1000) was part of the Cotton Manuscripts destroyed by fire in 1731. The present-day version is a reconstruction based on modern editions.

There have been two major challenges to the authenticity of Asser's life of Alfred. V. H. Galbraith argued in 1964 that Leofric, bishop of Devon and Cornwall (1046–1072), is the real author. Alfred P. Smyth insisted in 1995 that the Benedictine monk Byrhtferth of Ramsey forged it in the late tenth or early eleventh century to provide support for the reforms championed by his order and that everything except the passages drawn from the *Anglo-Saxon Chronicle* is pure fabrication (Byrhtferth in fact did excerpt it for his *Historical Miscellany*). However, other scholars have pointed out serious flaws in Galbraith's and Smyth's arguments, and most regard Asser's *Life of King Alfred* as genuine. It thus remains an essential source for that king's reign.

Bibliography: R. Abels, *Alfred the Great: War, Kingship and Culture in Anglo-Saxon England*, 1998; S. Keynes and M. Lapidge, trans., *Alfred the Great: Asser's* Life of King Alfred *and Other Contemporary Sources*, 1983; A. P. Smyth, *King Alfred the Great*, 1995.

William B. Robison

AUGUSTINE OF CANTERBURY, SAINT (D. C. 604).

Sent by Pope *Gregory I as a missionary to the Anglo-Saxons in 597, Augustine became the first archbishop of Canterbury and later a saint. Although little is known of his family and upbringing, Augustine (sometimes called the Lesser, to distinguish him from Augustine of Hippo) entered the famous monastery of St. Andrew, established by Pope Gregory at his ancestral home on Caelian Hill, and eventually became its prior. In 596, Gregory the Great chose Augustine to head the mission to England.

After a yearlong journey from Rome through Gaul, Augustine and about forty priests landed at Ebbsfleet, Kent, in 597 and were greeted cautiously by the Kentish King *Æthelbert, who ruled the tribes south of the Humber. As reported by *Bede, although Æthelbert did not accept the Christian faith immediately, he was impressed both by the distinguished procession of Augustine's group to the meeting place and by the great distance they traveled for the mission. As a result, Æthelbert granted Augustine a house and provisions in Canterbury and allowed the group to preach freely among his subjects. In Canterbury, Augustine organized the monks under a modified version of the Benedictine Rule and probably worshipped at the site of the present day Church of St. Martin, whose Roman and Anglo-Saxon brickwork is still visible.

The evidence is unclear as to whether or not Bertha, Æthelbert's queen and a Frankish Christian, and her chaplain Liudhard, aided in proselytizing Æthelbert; however, within a year Æthelbert was baptized, probably at St. Martin's Church, according to tradition on 2 June 597, Whitsunday. On the following Christmas, many of the English were also baptized. After the baptism of the king, according to Bede, Augustine traveled to Arles and was consecrated archbishop of the English by Etherius, although this could be an error in that Etherius was bishop of Lyon and Virgilius was bishop of Arles.

Once instituted as archbishop, Augustine set about a number of pastoral works: He built the first cathedral at Canterbury, established the monastery of SS. Peter and Paul (later called St. Augustine's), founded a school that produced manuscripts, and failed ultimately to reach an agreement with the Celtic Church concerning matters of discipline and practice, including the reckoning of Easter on the Roman calendar and the evangelization of the other peoples of England. Augustine died on 26 May 604. A number of miracles were attested to Augustine so that by the Council of Clovesho in 747 the day of his death was decreed to be a feast day. Pope Innocent VI in 1356 made it a double observance, and in 1882, Saint Augustine's feast day was to be celebrated by the whole Church.

A storied figure not only in the history of the English Church, Augustine is also noteworthy for his missiology, derived from Pope Gregory I's instructions (detailed in their well-known correspondence). Primary among these was Gregory's famous admonition that pagan idols, but not pagan temples, should be destroyed, and Christian rites and feasts should gradually replace the native forms of religious practice. Thus, at the same time Æthelbert did not compel the immediate conversion of his subjects, so too Augustine instituted the measured substitution of Christian practice rather than the forced assimilation of Christianity upon the indigenous peoples.

Bibliography: N. Brooks, *The Early History of the Church of Canterbury: Christ Church from 597 to 1066*, 1984; P. Hunter Blair, *The World of Bede*, 1970; H. Mayr-Harting, *The Coming of Christianity to Anglo-Saxon England*, 1972.

Daniel Kline

AVERROËS. *See* RUSHD, IBN.

AVICENBRON. *See* SOLOMON BEN JUDAH IBN GABIROL.

AVICENNA. *See* SĪNĀ, IBN.

B

BACON, ROGER (C. 1214–C. 1293). Bacon was an English master of arts in Paris, a philosopher and experimental scientist, and a Franciscan friar. He proposed a general reorganization, based on Aristotelian philosophy and secular subjects, of all the sciences and religious teaching of his time, with emphasis on experimental procedures and research. In his plan, the foundation of theology must come from the knowledge of nature and physical properties, as well as from Scripture. A polemical and energetic personality, he gave up a traditional university career in order to pursue his scientific interests, which makes his life highly unique among thirteenth-century scholastics.

Independent information on Bacon's life is rather scarce, and most facts must be deduced from his own writings. He was born c. 1214 at Ilchester, Somerset, into a family of small nobility with royalist tendencies. From an early age, he mastered classical authors such as Cicero and Seneca and showed a propensity for the science of the quadrivium (geometry, mathematics, music, and astronomy), which were part of the medieval secondary education. He enrolled at the Arts Faculty of the University of Oxford around 1228 and acquired an interest for sciences, especially the medieval optical science of *Perspectiva*, which was taught from translations of Arabic treatises. In Oxford he was greatly influenced by Robert *Grosseteste.

After receiving his M.A. either in Oxford or in Paris around 1237, he taught in Paris as a master of arts between 1237 and 1247 on grammar, logic, natural philosophy, and metaphysics. He lectured extensively on the books of Aristotle, which had been just made available for teaching after their earlier prohibition. In later works, he complained about the gap between the Arts and Theology Faculties regarding their different reception of the new Aristotelian writings. In 1247 he resigned from his university position and devoted himself to a life of study and research, at his own expense. Perhaps influenced by the French poet Richard Fournival, who owned a large collection of books on science and magic, he turned to experimental science and astronomy and also examined astrological treatises and "secret" books on magic. In 1256 he joined the Franciscan Order and taught arts at the Franciscan Studium in Paris.

This activity did not leave Bacon the time to continue his own research on sciences and language, nor did the Order promote intellectual freedom for its members, for fear of spreading heresies among its members, particularly that of *Joachim of Fiore. Thus, around 1263, Bacon contacted Cardinal Guy le Gros de Foulques, papal legate to England, to promote his own reform project of higher education based on a scientific and philosophical curriculum. In 1265 the cardinal became Pope Clement IV, and Bacon received a request to submit "quickly and secretly" the material of his project. Between 1267 and 1270 Bacon produced an impressive literary output: the major works *Opus maius* (Greater Work), *Opus minus* (Minor Work), and *Opus tertium* and other treatises on perception, optics, alchemy, and natural philosophy.

Following Pope Clement IV's death in 1268, Bacon found himself under scrutiny by his Order, and suspicions about his secretive activity led to a formal condemnation of his doctrines by a Franciscan chapter meeting presided over by the Minister General James of Ascoli between 1277 and 1279. The main issue in Bacon's condemnation seems to have been an astrological theory on the birth of Christ similar to that of the Arabic astrologer Albumasar, although his general views on astrology and alchemy, his interest for the Joachimite heresy, and his scathing criticism of contemporary theologians may have well played a role. Perhaps his condemnation was connected in some way with the 1277 censure of Radical Aristotelianism in Paris, which had also targeted black magic practices. Bacon was also imprisoned, or at least put into house confinement, at a certain stage of his career. In his last work, the *Compendium studii theologiae*, composed in 1292 shortly before his death, he again expressed contempt for the sterility and narrowmindedness of theological studies after Robert Grosseteste, attacking in particular Richard Rufus of Cornwall, who had been an influential Franciscan thinker and theologian, particularly important for *Bonaventure's teachings.

In Bacon's early works, which reflected his teaching at the Arts Faculty, the interpretation of Aristotle's philosophy was influenced by the Neoplatonic doctrines expounded in the *Liber de causis*, which in Bacon's time was thought to be genuinely Aristotelian, and the *Fons vitae* by the Jewish philosopher *Avicenbron. Bacon supported a doctrine of universal hylomorphism, eclectic in its sources, which stated that all creatures, even the "separated substances" or angels, are essentially a composite of matter and form, while God is essentially simple. For Bacon, the distinction between the essence and existence of any given reality is merely logical and not a real one. Thomas *Aquinas had opposite views on both issues. Bacon's notion of prime matter is that it is a reality that is to some degree actual and predetermined, not a mere potential one. In man, the rational soul is created, while the vegetative and sensitive souls derive from the potency of matter through the natural process of generation. These souls form a composite and not simple, substantial form. Bacon's psychology appears to be within the tradition of the English Franciscan teaching of the plurality of substantial forms in any given substance.

While teaching in Paris, Bacon also developed an interest in philology and languages. He reported a small incident that occurred at one of his lectures, when he had taken a word—*benenum*, henbane—of a Pseudo-Aristotelian treatise to be Arabic instead of Hispanic, prompting the derision of some students of Hispanic origin. To Bacon's eyes, this episode was a definitive proof of the necessity of going back to the original languages of revelation, science and philosophy, Greek and Hebrew, and of the inadequacy of translations. He himself wrote a grammar of the two languages.

In the works composed after 1267, Bacon's main preoccupation is to outline a grand reform of education and society. Philosophy, which for him is largely identified with Aristotle, *Avicenna, and the scientific knowledge available with the translations from the Arabic, must be the "servant" of theology, but at the same time it provides the only useful way by which man can come to know God and creation. Theologians who are oblivious of Aristotle, or actively condemn his scientific works, are in fact destroying the very basis of Christian education. On the other hand, Bacon also attacked Latin Averroism, although not directly *Averroës. His interest in logic and languages provides the ground for his theory of signs and the signification of language. For Bacon, words are signs that can be divided into naturally and artificially signifying; the names of a physical thing signify primarily only the thing itself and only secondarily its mental concept; the result of the latter use of words is equivocation. Bacon's semantic doctrines paved the way for the successive elaboration of William of Ockham and Thomas Hobbes.

Bacon's rationalistic mentality led him to emphasize the role of mathematics in human knowledge. True mathematical sciences, like geometry and astronomy, must not be confused with magic or superstition; however, the movement of the heavenly bodies do affect, as natural causes, human actions. Mathematics does provide a key to the knowledge of nature in the sense that its object, the category of quantity, accounts for the other categories. Mathematics only warrants certainty of judgment, whereas all the other sciences, like physics, or even theology, do not provide clear and distinct knowledge. To mathematics and geometry is connected also Bacon's treatment of the theory of vision, or *Perspectiva*. After the introduction to the West of the work of the Arabic scientist Ibn al-Haytham (Alhazen), this science had been studied extensively in Oxford, especially by Robert Grosseteste in connection with his metaphysics of light. Bacon devoted many studies and experimental observations to the nature of light, refraction, and reflection and put his studies in the wider context of the theory of knowledge and philosophy in general. For him, the *Perspectiva* was the most important physical science, providing evidence of the regularity of the laws of nature, which only experience could grasp. Bacon also wrote tracts on medicine, using

Arabic sources, and on moral and social philosophy, where he showed influences from Avicenna and classical authors, such as Cicero and Seneca.

Bibliography: S. C. Easton, *Roger Bacon and His Search for a Universal Science. A Reconsideration of the Life and Work of Roger Bacon in the Light of His Own Stated Purposes*, 1952; J. Hackett, ed., *Roger Bacon and the Sciences: Commemorative Essays*, 1997.

Roberto Plevano

BALDWIN IX OF FLANDERS (1172–1205). Count of Flanders, Hainaut, and Namur, Baldwin took part in engineering the overthrow of Greek administration after the infamous Fourth Crusade in 1204. He was elected emperor of Constantinople but was slain the following year.

Son of Baldwin V, count of Hainaut, and Margaret of Flanders, young Baldwin inherited both counties by 1195, after the death of his parents. However, because the counts of Flanders had ceded large portions of Flanders to the king of France, *Philip II Augustus, Baldwin's early career was witness to delicate maneuvering between his oath of fealty to his king and his deflection of Philip's encroachments into his territory.

Baldwin sought outside support by allying himself with *Richard the Lionheart and *John of England in their wars against France. He met with success in 1200 when, after repeated routs of Philip's forces, the French king agreed to the Treaty of Péronne, returning to Baldwin large portions of Artois.

To make Hainaut more easily governable, Baldwin also issued two charters that were the county's first effort at codifying its ancient laws and traditions. One (the feudal code) he intended to prevent the outbreak of private war; the other (the criminal code) imposed penalties for murder and mutilation, acts in which his more powerful subjects were often involved.

His reputation for compassion and piety coexisted with his well-known political savvy; both Baldwin and his wife took the cross for the Fourth Crusade in 1200. Baldwin's marriage to Marie, daughter of the count of Champagne, was an unusually happy one; though she was compelled to stay in Flanders with the birth of their second daughter, Baldwin's devotion to Marie while crusading was well known. Marie later left both children, Jeanne and Margaret, in the hands of Baldwin's younger brother to join Baldwin on crusade. Neither Baldwin nor Marie would ever return.

Baldwin and the rest of the crusaders, forced to wait in Venice for transport, were embroiled in Italian politics and eventually attacked the Christian city of Zara to pay off their Venetian hosts in a notorious lapse of judgment. Afterward, Baldwin was a leading voice in favor of restoring young Alexius IV, the rightful heir to the imperial throne of Constantinople, dispossessed at the hands of his treacherous uncle, as part of the Crusade's mission prior to reaching the Holy Land.

However, the mission was transformed again by the murder of young Alexius at the hands of his subject, Mourtzouphlus, who became Alexius V. The new design of the Crusade featured the installation of a Latin emperor and the appointment of a Latin patriarch. The bloody conquest of Constantinople in 1204 left a power vacuum that the European forces were quick to fill. Baldwin of Flanders, considered honest and free of Byzantine connections, was chosen. Baldwin was crowned with great ceremony in the rich halls of the Great Palace in May. Sadly, the envoys sent to escort Marie to Constantinople as empress arrived with only her corpse; she had succumbed to plague while awaiting Baldwin at Acre.

Baldwin reigned as emperor only until 1205; Ioannitsa, king of the Bulgarians, captured him near Adrianople. His cause of death is unknown, but he did not survive captivity, leaving the newly latinized throne of Constantinople to his brother Henry.

Bibliography: D. E. Queller and T. F. Madden, *The Fourth Crusade: The Conquest of Constantinople*, 2d ed., 1997.

Laura L. Gathagan

BAR HEBRAEUS, GREGORIUS (1226–1286). A powerful Christian figure in the Middle East, Bar Hebraeus was a prolific writer in many disciplines.

He was born at Meletine in Asia Minor, the son of a Jewish physician who had converted to the Monophysite Jacobite faith (hence his surname, which means "Son of the Hebrew"). In 1246, he became a bishop in the Jacobite church, and in 1264 he was elevated to the post of Primate of the East. He was instrumental in keeping Syrian Christians on good terms with other Christian groups, including the Nestorians and Armenians, as well as the Syrian Muslim community and powerful neighbors such as the Mongols and Persians.

Bar Hebraeus also wrote a number of well-received scholarly works. In the *Granary of Mysteries*, a biblical commentary, he attempted to establish a sound text by using many different manuscripts before proceeding to doctrinal analysis. The *Cream of Science* is an encyclopedic work encompassing almost every branch of human knowledge. Another major work, the *Chronicon*, is a history of the world from its creation to his own day. In addition, he composed numerous other works on theology, grammar, mathematics, astronomy, cosmography, and medicine.

Bar Hebraeus was a unifying force in the Syrian Christian community of his day and a capable administrator who skillfully maneuvered among the complex political factions of the thirteenth-century Middle East. His written works are especially valued today for his synthesis of the works of his predecessors; he is an important source for many texts that survive only in his reproductions or condensations. His *Chronicon* provides scholars with reliable information about the medieval history of the Middle East.

Bibliography: T. Nöldeke, *Sketches from Eastern History*, trans. J. S. Black, 1892.

Anne Collins Smith and Owen M. Smith

BARTHOLOMAEUS ANGLICUS (FL. THIRTEENTH CENTURY). Friar, teacher, and encyclopedist, he is known primarily for compiling the important medieval encyclopedia *De proprietatibus rerum* (On the Properties of Things).

Bartholomaeus Anglicus (Bartholomew the Englishman) was a friar, probably born in England. He studied at Oxford and later became a professor at the University of Paris in the mid-thirteenth century. *De proprietatibus rerum* was likely compiled during residence in Saxony where he had been sent in 1231 to organize the Franciscans there. This nineteen-book encyclopedia, which draws on the earlier work of *Isidore of Seville and Robert *Grosseteste, systematically recounts the divine and human universe, beginning with the Trinity in book one and proceeding through the angels, the senses, the human body, its components and infirmities, before detailing the constellations, the monthly and Christian calendar as well as the characteristics of the elements, air and water, and the entities engendered there. The encyclopedia then specifies sacred and secular geography, gems and metals, plants and animals, the attributes of color, heat, liquid, and other physical properties.

As such, it is a veritable compendium of medieval learning and lore, theology and polity, science and myth. It is no wonder that John of Trevisa translated *De proprietatibus rerum* into Middle English in 1389; this work also was translated into French, Dutch, and Spanish.

Bibliography: M. C. Seymour, *Bartholomaeus Anglicus and His Encyclopaedia*, 1992.

Daniel Kline

BASIL II (958–1025). Emperor of Constantinople (crowned as a minor in 960 and ruled independently from 985), he was known also as the Bulgar-Slayer (Bulgaroktonos). He oversaw expansion of the Byzantine Empire from Armenia to the Adriatic, and from the Euphrates to the Danube. He was responsible for annexing the Bulgarian kingdom, consolidating the Balkans, and bringing the state of Kiev under Prince Vladimir I into the spiritual and cultural orbit of Constantinople. Finally, he sought to consolidate Italian possessions and increase Byzantine influence in western Europe.

Basil II was the son of Romanos II Lekapenos and the grandson of Constantine VII Porphyrogenitos. He and his brother Constantine VIII were rightful heirs to the throne. While they were crowned emperors as children, they were overshadowed first by the regency of their mother, Theophano, then by the military co-emperors Nicephoros Phokas, and John I Tzimiskes, and throughout by their powerful uncle, the eunuch Basil Lekapenos, until the latter's exile in 985. When Basil II reached his maturity, he had to confront the rise of the powerful Bulgarian Empire ruled by Samuel, the youngest of four sons of a provincial governor of Macedonia who revolted against Byzantine rule. Taking over large territory between the Danube and Balkan Mountains, Thessaly, Epirus, and Albania, Samuel repelled Basil II's counteroffensive at Trajan's Gate and ruled over territory extending from the Black Sea to the Adriatic.

At this time, Basil II was also faced with the rebellions of Bardas Skleros and Bardas Phokas, which he overcame with the help of Vladimir I of Kiev. He rewarded Vladimir I with marriage to his sister Anna, an unprecedented action as she was the first Byzantine princess born in the purple to be married to a foreigner. Additionally, the condition placed on the marriage was that Vladimir I and his people would convert to Christianity, accept baptism, and come under the spiritual jurisdiction of Constantinople. Thereafter, Byzantine culture was to heavily influence Russia's cultural development.

As a result of the bitter civil struggles that challenged his rule for thirteen years, Basil II turned inward, became suspicious and withdrawn, rejected advice of the court, shunned court ceremonial, art, and learning, and ruled as a complete autocrat. He turned his attention to undermining aristocratic and dynastic landholdings as part of his agrarian and fiscal policies by going so far as to require landlords to pay the taxes of their insolvent peasant neighbors. While this ensured the peasantry would remain in one place, it also weakened the hand of the landed aristocracy and prevented further rebellion.

After overcoming the internal challenges to his throne, he again focused externally but this time faced the unsavory prospects of threats from two fronts. With Antioch and Aleppo under siege by the Fatimids in 995, Basil II went in person and eventually was able to create a peace with the Fatimids that reestablished the previous, though unsatisfactory, status quo.

Samuel, the Bulgarian king, seized the opportunity to move south as far as the Peloponnese and to annex the state of Kiev and make Vladimir I into his vassal. Upon his return from the East in 1001, Basil II opened a counteroffensive that cut off the lifeline to Samuel's power base on the Danube and proceeded to reduce drastically the size of Samuel's holdings. The final blow to Samuel's Bulgarian Empire came in 1014 at Kleidion (near the river Struma), where Basil captured over 14,000 Bulgarian troops; he allegedly blinded them, allowing only one man in a hundred to keep an eye so as to be able to guide the others home to Samuel in Prilep. Shocked by the sight of his troops, Samuel died two days later.

Basil II's rule over the former Bulgarian territory was relatively moderate, making it into an administrative province, or *theme*, governed by a military official. He relieved his subjects from the heavy burden of paying taxes in gold by accepting payments in kind. In addition, although he reduced the Bulgarian Patriarchate to the status of an archbishopric, he allowed it to remain autocephalous and not become subordinate to the Patriarchate of Constantinople.

Towards the end of his career, Basil II was able to capitalize on disorder in the Caucasus region and annex part of Georgia and the Armenian kingdom. In the West, he found opportunity in the person of *Otto III, the son of the Byzantine princess *Theophano, to gain ground in Italy by consolidating their holdings and planning for an invasion against Arab-held Sicily. He died in 1025, unmarried and without an heir.

Bibliography: G. Ostrogorsky, *History of the Byzantine State*, rev. ed., trans. J. Hussey, 1969.

Tom Papademetriou

BAUDONIVIA (FL. SEVENTH CENTURY). A seventh-century nun at the convent of the Holy Cross at Poitiers, Baudonivia composed a life of Saint *Radegunde (d. 587), founder of that convent. The life, known as *Vita II*, was written 609–614 and is the earliest known saint's life written by a woman. It was a conscious supplement to *Vita I* by the Italian poet and bishop of Poitiers, Venantius *Fortunatus, to which it is often negatively compared. While Fortunatus wrote to elevate the former queen to saint and martyr, Baudonivia wrote of Radegunde as the holy woman and spiritual mother who the nuns saw daily.

Nothing is known of Baudonivia's parentage or life in the convent. All we know about her is derived from internal references within her work. She knew Radegunde and had lived within her convent for many years. She may have been an oblate, "nourished familiarly from the cradle as her [Radegunde's] own child at her feet" (McNamara et al., 86).

Baudonivia was well read in hagiographical literature. Within *Vita II* are numerous quotations from or references to the lives of Saints Martin of Tours and *Caesarius of Arles, and other works such as the *Inventio S. Crucis.* She often reworked events from such sources to show Radegunde acting in a manner similar to Martin, Caesarius, and the Empress Helena.

Vita II is dedicated to the abbess and the nuns of the convent and quickly spread to nuns in other Frankish houses. Baudonivia's work was among the most widely read in Francia—at least nine manuscripts survive from the early Middle Ages, testifying to its popularity.

Bibliography: J. Kitchen, *Saints' Lives and the Rhetoric of Gender: Male and Female in Merovingian Hagiography*, 1998; J. A. McNamara, J. E. Halborg, and E. G. Whately, "Radegund, Queen of the Franks and Abbess of Poitiers," in *Sainted Women of the Dark Ages*, ed. and trans. J. A. McNamara, J. E. Halborg, and E. G. Whately, 1992.

Janice R. Norris

BEATRIJS OF NAZARETH (C. 1201–1268). A mystic, she was abbess of the convent of Our Lady of Nazareth near Antwerp and author of several works, of which one survives, *The Seven Manners of Minne.*

She was born in Tienen, Belgium, youngest of three daughters of a merchant, Barthelmy de Vleeschouwer, and his wife, who died when Beatrijs was seven. Her education began early; by the age of five she had knowledge of Latin. She continued her studies, first at the convent of Beguines at Zoutleeuw, then at the Cistercian convent at LaRamee, where she was instructed in calligraphy in order to produce liturgical choir books. After becoming a Cistercian novice in 1215, she studied further at Florival. Finally, in 1236, along with her sisters, she went to Our Lady of Nazareth near Antwerp where she was to spend the remainder of her life, part of it as the convent's abbess. An anonymous scribe produced her biography from a diary in Flemish kept by Beatrijs but no longer in existence, making it impossible to know what may have been deleted as "heresy" or otherwise unsuitable.

Although she is credited with several works, only one, *The Seven Manners of Minne* (The Seven Degrees of Love), remains. It is an example of a genre practiced by other women mystics of the period, often women associated with the Beguines. *Minne* describes a kind of German courtly love convention in which a prostrate lover pleads with Lady Minne to pity him. As employed by the thirteenth-century mystics, the form becomes a cross between exegetical commentaries on the voluptuous imagery of the *Song of Songs* and the often erotic poetry of the *Minnesang*. As the latter frequently uses the language of religion—the lover as martyr, the beloved as angel—so the writings of *minnemystik* are couched in the diction of courtly love poetry as the soul pleads for union with God. In her work Beatrijs defines the stages by which the soul makes that ascent. Beginning with the soul's first yearning, it proceeds through suffering and rapture to serene joy and is finally immersed in love on reaching the mystic's goal of union with God.

Bibliography: R. Bradley, "Beatrice of Nazareth (c. 1200–1268): A Search for Her True Spirituality," in *Vox Mystica: Essays on Medieval Mysticism in Honor of Professor Valerie M. Lagorio*, ed. A. C. Bartlett, 1995.

Patricia Silber

BEAUMANOIR, PHILIPPE DE (C. 1250–1296) A *bailli* and seneschal, he was the author of the legal treatise *Coutumes de Beauvaisis*.

Philippe de Beaumanoir should be distinguished from his father, Philippe de Remy. Each was a lawyer and *bailli* (administrator and judge of a county, employed by the king or a high-ranking nobleman for terms of about three years), and a considerable body of works has been attributed to them. Most modern scholars agree, however, that it was the father who authored the poetical works (including the two romances *Jehan et Blonde* and *La Manekine*), while it was the son who wrote the legal treatise *Coutumes de Beauvaisis*. This entry deals only with the son, who was a *bailli* in the service of Robert, count of Clermont (and son of *Louis IX), then subsequently a royal seneschal or *bailli* in the districts of Poitou, Saintonge, Vermandois, Touraine, and finally Senlis, where he died.

Philippe was a very minor nobleman whose education and early career remain obscure, although the object of speculation. Did he study law at the university, perhaps in Orléans? Did he practice law, perhaps in the ecclesiastical courts? Did he travel? Almost the first we hear of him is that in 1279 he is appointed as *bailli* to the county of Clermont, under its count. Beauvais itself, in the same county, was administered by its bishop. In Clermont, Beaumanoir acted not only as the local administrator but as a judge in the county court, using local noblemen as a kind of jury or panel of judges to decide cases, whether brought in his court or appealed from lower courts. He may have had very great autonomy, since the count had been incapacitated by a blow to the head he had received in a tournament. While in this post, Philippe wrote his great book on the customs of his county, which he signed and dated in 1283 as he left the county at the end of his term to take up a post elsewhere.

All customary compilations from the thirteenth century have unique characteristics, and none is simply a list of the laws remembered as being in force at the date of the compilation. Beaumanoir himself says in his preface that his book is intended for litigants (perhaps especially defendants) in local courts. He not only tells these readers what the law is in their district but also gives many practical hints for the proper ways of doing things and for avoiding costly procedural mistakes. For example, a challenge to a jury verdict given at the wrong moment might result in the challenger's having to fight several opponents at once in a judicial duel; but Beaumanoir pinpoints the exact moment when this danger is avoided and urges his reader to choose this moment to object (§§1752–1755). These pieces of practical advice suggest that Beaumanoir had long frequented the courts, either as an advocate or as a judge. Nor is Beaumanoir afraid of theoretical issues. On several occasions he gives his opinion on serfdom, the king's obligations to his subjects, and the relation between the lay and ecclesiastical jurisdictions in his county.

Although there are many indications in the *Coutumes* that Beaumanoir knew some Roman law, he never invokes its authority and never acknowledges borrowings from it. This places him in marked contrast with several other customary writers of his time, who freely translate and approve portions of the *Corpus iuris civilis*. For Beaumanoir, who may be among the last French jurists to hold this view, a custom will always prevail as law over a contrary view in Roman law, and a custom is established either by many instances of application without challenge or by a judicial decision in an actual case where the custom is challenged. Custom, therefore, is judge-made law. In support of his exposition of the customs of his district, Beaumanoir cites a hundred different cases, some decided in his own court, many or most by a jury. In a typical "case" he cites the issue involved, then recites some facts, the differing outcomes requested by plaintiff and defendant based on their claim of what the custom is, and then a verdict. In many of the hundred cases, Beaumanoir then adds a commentary provided by the jury or himself and even some hypotheticals based on a slight change in the facts. The status of these cases as records of actual cases is somewhat undermined by the use of generic names Pierre and Jehan for the opposing parties; but some cases name names and places and even involve well-known figures such as the king.

Bibliography: P. de Beaumanoir, *The* Coutumes de Beauvaisis *of Philippe de Beaumanoir*, trans. F.R.P. Akehurst, 1992; A. Salmon, ed., *Philippe de Beaumanoir*: Coutumes de Beauvaisis, 2 vols., 1974.

F.R.P. Akehurst

BECKET, THOMAS, SAINT (1118–1170). Becket is best known as the archbishop of Canterbury who was murdered by knights in the service of his former companion, King *Henry II, and who later inspired Chaucer's *General Prologue to the Canterbury Tales* and T. S. Eliot's *Murder in the Cathedral.*

Born in England of Norman parents, Becket studied at Merton Abbey and later at the University of Paris. He entered the service of Theobald, archbishop of Canterbury, in 1141 and later studied civil and canon law at Bologna and Auxerre. Theobald ordained Becket a deacon in 1154; the same year, Henry II named him chancellor of England, the highest political appointment in the land.

Although more than a decade older than the new young ruler, Becket and Henry II were close personal companions and political allies. Known for his quick mind, confident judgment, and administrative efficiency, Becket faithfully served Henry II in domestic matters and foreign warfare. When Theobald died in 1161, Henry appointed his compatriot to the archbishopric of Canterbury, the highest ecclesiastical position in England. Soon thereafter, to the king's displeasure, Becket surrendered the chancellorship, marking the first step in an escalating series of famous controversies that led to Becket's murder and eventual sainthood. Upon taking the see of Canterbury, Becket adopted a life of personal austerity, which, though not absent earlier in his life, now came clearly to the fore, and he pursued the interests of the Church with the same vigor and clarity of purpose with which he had previously served Henry.

This conflict between the archbishop and the king, the Church and the state, came to a culmination in Becket's opposition to the Constitutions of Clarendon in 1164. Appealing to the customs of his grandfather and namesake *Henry I as a political pretext, Henry II attempted to consolidate power over the realm in the Constitution's sixteen provisions. In a brief but pointed list, Henry called for disputes between secular and clerical parties to be settled in the king's court rather than by ecclesiastical justice; required that churches and ecclesiastical offices be given at the favor and consent of the king; obliged clerics already punished in the Church court to come under obligation of secular justice, apart from further protection of Church; commanded all ecclesiasts to seek the king's permission to leave the realm and required them to pledge that they would not act contrary to the king's wishes at any point during their trip; disallowed excommunication for any secular official without the king's consent; put the court of the archbishop under the king's court; declared that the Church hierarchy, like the barony, held their possessions at the pleasure of the king and required their attendance at court; determined that vacant benefices revert to the king and be filled by an election of the clergy held at the king's pleasure and in his court; and mandated that new archbishops, bishops, abbots, and priors pay homage and swear lifelong fealty to the king prior to being consecrated.

After privately assenting initially to the terms to reach a compromise with the king, Becket, seeing the implications of the Constitutions, later publicly withdrew his support from the agreement and doggedly fought their institution. Recriminations followed in which the king required Becket to surrender the ecclesiastical benefices he earlier held and account for monies spent during his chancellorship, while Becket sought to recapture holdings traditionally within the purview of the archbishopric. At a council in Northampton in the fall of 1164, Becket refused to accept the king's demands. Henry insisted that the council pass judgment on Becket, but in the ensuing discord, Becket escaped and went into exile in France, where he was welcomed by *Louis VII and appealed to Pope *Alexander III. Becket's exile first at Pontigny and later at Sens lasted six years, during which the king persecuted Becket's supporters and family in England while the archbishop used ecclesiastical censures against the king's faction. Finally, Alexander fashioned a fragile truce, and Becket returned to England late in 1170.

The peace, however, was short-lived. The king had his son crowned at York, defying the primacy of Canterbury, and Becket responded by excommunicating the bishops involved. It is unclear exactly what the king's intentions were when he uttered the seemingly offhand remark to the effect, "Who will rid me of this troublesome priest?" on 20 December 1170, but it is clear that four of the king's knights took this potentially rhetorical statement literally and murdered Thomas Becket in Canterbury Cathedral, a deed graphically recounted in the accounts of Edward Grim, William of Newburgh, Roger of Hovenden, Gervase of Canterbury, and Benedict of Peterborough. Public reaction to the popular priest's murder was extreme, and miracles were attributed to the martyr almost immediately. Devotion to Becket spread quickly throughout Europe, and in February 1173, he was canonized. In an extraordinary display of public penance, Henry II made pilgrimage to Becket's shrine and was scourged in July 1174. Henry II died in 1189, having kept much of his power, and Becket's bones were probably scattered in 1538.

Bibliography: F. Barlow, *Thomas Becket*, 1986; J. Butler, *The Quest for Becket's Bones: The Mystery of the Relics of St. Thomas Becket of Canterbury*, 1995; D. C. Douglas and G. W. Greenaway, eds., *English Historical Documents, Volume II: 1042–1189*, 1981; C. Duggan, *Canon Law in Medieval England: The Becket Dispute and Decretal Collections*, 1982.

Daniel Kline

BEDE (672/673–735). Frequently referred to as the Venerable Bede, he was a monk at the monastery of Wearmouth-Jarrow in Northumbria responsible for writing an enormous range of works covering Latin grammar, cosmology, metrics, computus, biblical exegesis, hagiography, and especially history. Bede is probably the best-known example of the flowering of Christian Latin scholarship in Northumbria during the seventh and eighth centuries and is today the single best known Anglo-Latin writer of Anglo-Saxon England. This is primarily due to his *Historia ecclesiastica gentis Anglorum* (Ecclesiastical History of the English People), chronicling the conversion of the Anglo-Saxons late in the sixth century and the spread of Christianity in England up to Bede's own day.

Very little is known of Bede's life beyond what he tells us of himself in the *Ecclesiastical History*. He became an oblate at Wearmouth-Jarrow at the age of seven, studied there under Abbots Benedict Biscop and Ceolfrith, was ordained deacon and then priest, and beyond this spent the bulk of his life at the monastery writing and teaching. It is probably because of Bede's concern with teaching that his works are almost invariably clear and straightforward in their exposition of their individual subjects.

These works cover virtually all of the standard subjects of Anglo-Latin literature. His concern with Latin instruction is brought out in *De orthographia*, a treatise on correct Latin spelling, and *De arte metrica*, on Latin versification. He also wrote *De natura rerum*, a work on basic cosmology. The latter two works were extremely influential, becoming standard medieval textbooks for the teaching of their respective topics. Bede was also one of the best writers on the subject of computus, the mathematical procedures for calculating the moveable feasts of the Christian year, first in *De temporibus* and later in *De temporum ratione*, which became a standard work on the subject. Bede also wrote a large number of individual works of biblical exegesis, commenting on various books of the Bible. In the Old Testament, these include Genesis, Exodus, Samuel, Kings, Chronicles, Ezra, Nehemiah, Tobit, Proverbs, Song of Songs, and Habbakuk. In the New Testament, he wrote commentaries on Mark, Luke, Acts, the Pauline and Catholic Epistles, and Revelation. All of Bede's exegetical writings were obviously valued for their characteristic clarity and conservative approach, as they survive in numerous manuscripts. He also wrote a number of saints' lives, the best known of which is his *Vita S. Cuthberti*, a life of the seventh-century English ascetic. Finally, Bede was a better-than-average writer of Latin verse, most of them hymns, a very few of which have survived preserved in other texts, such as the *Ecclesiastical History*.

But it is as an historian that he is best known today, due almost solely to his *Ecclesiastical History*. This is one of his last works and is modeled partly on *Gregory of Tours' *Historia Francorum* in its emphasis on a single geographic area and people. Bede divides it into five books: the background to the sixth-century Augustinian mission to the Anglo-Saxons; the conversion of *Æthelbert of Kent and his kingdom; the growth of the Northumbrian church and its contacts with Irish Christianity; the histories of Archbishop *Theodore of Canterbury and of Saint Cuthbert; and an account of the state of the English Church in Bede's own day. The work was enormously popular in the Middle Ages and was translated into Old English as part of *Alfred's late-ninth-century program to revive learning in England. It also has proven invaluable in our own day, as without it much of the history of the English people, both lay and ecclesiastical, for the first century or so following the conversion would simply be lost to us. Bede includes in his text a wide variety of papal and political correspondence, acta, anecdotes, and verse quotations, much of which is not otherwise preserved. Many of these, such as his account of Pope *Gregory the Great's chance meeting with the English slave boys, his simile of man's life as that of a sparrow passing through a hall on a cold night, or the miraculous poetic awakening of *Cædmon, have achieved virtually independent existence as part of the Anglo-Latin and Old English literary corpus. It is difficult to imagine what the study of Anglo-Saxon England might have been like without the writings of Bede.

Bibliography: S. B. Greenfield and D. G. Calder, *A New Critical History of Old English Literature*, 1986; P. Hunter Blair, *The World of Bede*, 1970.

David Day

BÉLA III OF HUNGARY (1148–1196). Béla was king of Hungary from 1172 and, under the name Alexius, briefly heir apparent to the Byzantine emperor Manuel I Comnenus during the 1160s. Béla maintained strong connections with Byzantium, asserted royal power at home, and secured Hungary's frontiers in the West while expanding into the Balkans.

The son of Géza II and Euphrosyne of Kiev, Béla was exiled in Constantinople from 1165 to 1172. He still nominally controlled his *ducate* (Croatia, Dalmatia, and the region around Belgrad), which the Byzantines also claimed, and was briefly betrothed to Maria, the heiress of Manuel I. Modern speculation that Manuel intended the prospective marriage to unify Hungary and Byzantium cannot be proven.

In 1172 Béla took the Hungarian throne with Byzantine help but soon overcame internal opposition by following an independent policy. His support of Pope Alexander II and Sobêslav of Bohemia against *Frederick I Barbarossa turned these former enemies into allies. Béla's effective diplomacy also led to peace with Frederick and security along the western frontiers after 1175, despite significant disputes caused by German expansion into southern Italy and Sicily. After Manuel's death in 1180, Béla reasserted Hungary's claim to his former *ducate* and eventually expanded his influence as far south as Nis, sometimes in opposition to and sometimes in alliance with Serbian Prince Stephen Nemanja. Despite this, relations with Byzantium continued to be cordial—his daughter Margaret married Emperor Isaac II Angelus, and Béla successfully mediated disputes between the Byzantines and the leaders of the Third Crusade. Beginning in 1187, he resisted Venetian efforts to take the Dalmatian town of Zara, making it part of the *ducate* of his heir, Emeric (Imré). An attempt (1187–1193) to gain the Russian principality of Galicia (Halich) for his younger son Andrew (András) failed. Domestically, Béla asserted the political authority of the monarch over the nobility and the Church but was unable to introduce the cult of an orthodox saint due to ecclesiatical opposition.

Modern efforts to characterize Béla as an agent of the Byzantines or lackey of the pope do not conform to the evidence. Béla III was a wide-ranging diplomat and skillful administrator, fully the equal of contemporaries such as *Henry II of England, Frederick Barbarossa, or *Philip II Augustus. His policies were independent and always promoted the interests of the Hungarian monarchy, which (for Béla) superseded any friendship or alliance. He was, arguably, medieval Hungary's greatest king.

Bibliography: F. Makk, *The Árpáds and the Comneni: Political Relations between Hungary and Byzantium in the 12th Century*, trans. G. Nóvak, 1989.

Edward J. Schoenfeld

BENEDICT IX, POPE (C. 1000–C. 1055, PONTIFICATE 1032–1044, 1045, 1047–1048).

As the third consecutive layman pope, Benedict IX concerned himself with family matters before spiritual duties, and his reign marked the end of a corrupt period of family-dominated papal politics.

In one of the more confusing and scandalous periods of papal history, the influential Tusculan family placed the eighteen-year-old Theophylact, nephew of Popes John XIX and Benedict VIII, on the papal seat, where he took the name Benedict IX. Benedict attained his exalted position at an early age and soon achieved a reputation for being cruel and immoral. Holy Roman Emperor *Conrad II concentrated on German affairs, and therefore allowed the papacy to fall into disrepute. By 1044, the Roman populace had grown tired of Benedict's immorality and revolted in September. Benedict fled the city, and the Romans elected John, bishop of Sabina, as Sylvester III. Benedict excommunicated Sylvester and returned to Rome in March 1045, reclaiming the papacy. His triumphant return lasted two months, however, because he accepted a bribe of 1,000 pounds of silver to abdicate in favor of his godfather, John Gratian. The new pope, taking the name Gregory VI, attracted the attention of the emperor because of the manner in which he took office.

Conrad II had died in 1039 to be succeeded by *Henry III of Germany. Henry wanted to be crowned by the pope and also address the recent papal corruption, and he finally came to Italy in 1046. He held a synod at Sutri in December that deposed Sylvester, Gregory, and Benedict. Henry then appointed Suidger, bishop of Bamberg, to the papal throne; he served as Clement II until his death eight months later. Reformers, most notably Cluniacs, were pleased with Henry's involvement and interruption of the string of bad popes. Benedict was not through, however, and gained control of Rome and the papacy by November 1047. Henry removed Benedict in July 1048 and appointed Poppo of Brixen, who became Damasus II. His reign lasted only twenty-three days. The subsequent synod of Worms chose Bruno, bishop of Toul, and he took the name *Leo IX. Leo was a reformer and created the idea of crusading with his attack on the Normans in Sicily.

Benedict continued to claim that he was pope but was later excommunicated for failing to answer a charge of simony. He never returned to the papacy and eventually died in 1055. Benedict's reign marked the end of a period of papal corruption dominated by the powerful Roman families Crescentii and Tusculani and began a period of papal reform. Europe was coming out of the dark ages and experienced an increase in scholarly activity, which positively affected the papacy.

Bibliography: R. P. McBrien, *Lives of the Popes*, 1997; W. Ullmann, *A Short History of the Papacy in the Middle Ages*, 1972.

Paul Miller

BENEDICT OF ANIANE (C. 750–821). A Frankish abbot and monastic reformer, he is best known for the reforms he instituted under *Charlemagne and for the monasteries he founded. Although very few of his writings survive, they appear to have influenced contemporary and later writers.

Benedict (prebaptismal name Witizia) was born, of noble parents, in Languedoc. His father, Aigulf, unnamed in the *Vita* composed after Benedict's death, was duke of Maguelone and a military leader who, among other successes, crushed marauding Basques in the region. Benedict was brought up at the court of King *Pepin III, educated there under the tutelage of Pepin's queen Bertrada, and entered military service. In his early twenties, he underwent a religious experience, as a result of watching his brother drown in a fast-flowing river. The *Vita* suggests that he himself nearly drowned as well, and this probably led to his decision to become a monk. He made his monastic profession in the abbey of St.-Seine near Dijon in 773 and served there as cellarer for several years. He quickly developed a reputation for austerity, believing that the Rule of St. *Benedict was for weaklings and preferring to follow the harsher rule of Saint Basil instead. As cellarer, he was generous with those who sought help legitimately, but not with those who tried to take advantage of him, and as a result he become quite unpopular with some of the monks.

However, when the abbot of St.-Seine died in 779, the community asked him to take over the position, but Benedict refused. Instead, he returned to his father's estate at Aniane in Languedoc and founded a small monastery. At first, this community followed a strict ascetic rule, but from about 782, Benedict seems to have undergone a conversion, and he began to follow the less rigorous Rule of Saint Benedict. His monastery became the motherhouse of a number of other foundations that followed Benedict's example. From this period also dates a major building program at Aniane; during the next three decades, Aniane became the center of monastic reform in the Frankish kingdom, a reform that was supported by Charlemagne's successor, *Louis the Pious.

In 816–818, Benedict presided over a series of Church councils at Aachen, which officially approved his version of the Benedictine Rule. One of his most important writings is a collection of early monastic rules, known collectively as the *Codex Regularum monasticarum et canonicorum* (Book of Monastic and Canonical Regulations), which he compiled in preparation for his own revision of the Benedictine Rule; this is a work that remains our primary source of knowledge for these important texts. He himself remained profoundly ascetic in his own life, to the point where people often spoke of his filthy clothing and lack of personal hygiene. A life of Benedict was written by one of his fellow monks and followers, Ardo of Aniane.

Bibliography: A. Cabaniss, trans., *The Emperor's Monk: A Contemporary Life of Benedict of Aniane*, 1979.

William Schipper

BENEDICT OF NURSIA, SAINT (C. 480–C. 547). Benedict of Nursia, a saint, was the founder of western European monasticism.

The earliest source for the life of Benedict is Pope *Gregory the Great's *Dialogues*. Although Gregory's primary purpose was hagiographical, the details of Benedict's life as he presents them are not generally disputed. Benedict was born, probably about 480 in Nursia, near Spoleto (northeast of Rome) and educated in Rome. In his late teens or early twenties, and unhappy with the sinful life of Rome, he became a hermit in a cave near Subiaco, about forty-seven miles east of Rome. As the number of his followers grew, he organized them into twelve small groups. After a number of years, as a result of local rivalries, he moved with some of his monks to Monte Cassino, a hill above Cassino, between Rome and Naples. Here he founded a monastery that became the model for monasticism in the West and developed a reputation for holiness and wisdom. He also founded a monastery for his sister Scholastica at Plombariola, near Monte Cassino. Benedict did not himself ever contemplate founding a monastic order (the "Benedictines" were known simply as "Black Monks" during the Middle Ages), but the set of regulations he composed, known as the *Regula Sancti Benedicti* (Rule of Saint Benedict), became the guide for monasticism in Europe for many centuries.

The author of the Rule of Saint Benedict, disputed in the 1930s, has now been generally accepted as Benedict, although the manuscript tradition does not go back to before the eighth century, and the Rule is only cited once before then, albeit anonymously, by Gregory the Great in his Commentary on 1 Kings. Benedict drew on earlier monastic rules, such as the Rule of Saint Basil (as transmitted by Rufinus) and of John Cassian (d. 435), as well as writings of Saint Augustine. The earlier part (Cap. 1–7) of the Rule is based largely on the earlier anonymous *Regula magistri* (Rule of the Master), which is widely accepted as by Benedict himself. The sections the two have in common embody Benedict's central ideas on how a monastery should be run. It is here that he assigns a central place to the abbot and develops the central monastic notions of obedience, silence, and humility. The rest of Benedict's Rule provides regulations for all aspects of a monk's life, from the work outside of the monastery to the need for study, when to sleep, when to pray, and how to relate to the world outside the monastery through charitable works. Moreover, the emphasis on education and reading indirectly ensured that the monasteries that followed the Rule would become the repositories of learning and centers of education in the West.

Although Benedict is universally regarded as the "founder" of western European monasticism, his influence was not immediately apparent. It is not certain that his Rule saw immediate widespread use: The earliest use recorded for Rome is only from the tenth century, for example. It was promoted by *Benedict of Aniane in the eighth century, with the support of a set of decrees issued from Aachen in 816–817, but again there is no direct evidence that this had any immediate lasting effect. Nor is there any direct evidence that the Rule was brought to England by *Augustine of Canterbury; instead, it may have been introduced to England by Wilfrid of Ripon. Oxford, Bodleian Library, MS Hatton 48, a copy made in Worcester about 750, is the earliest extant copy of the rule, but the text preserved in this manuscript represents a mixed version probably originating in Italy. Benedict's Rule remained the foundation of reforms subsequent to the Carolingian period, in England (tenth century) through the *Regularis concordiae*, and the reforms begun with the foundation of Cluny (from 910). The Rule also inspired new orders, such as the Cistercians (begun under the influence of *Bernard of Clairvaux at Cîteaux). Most new monastic orders formed during the Middle Ages adopted the Rule of Saint Benedict for their own use.

Saint Benedict's legacy lives on in a number of ways, aside from the influence his Rule had on European monasticism. Wynfrith (Saint *Boniface) brought Benedictine monasticism to the Franks in the eighth century. Throughout Europe, during the early Middle Ages, monks following the Rule of Saint Benedict were instrumental in preserving classical and patristic learning through their libraries, and they and their successors were continually involved in education throughout medieval Europe. From the last half of the seventeenth century, moreover, Benedictine monks and scholars, and especially those in the Congregation of St. Maur, devoted themselves to the historical and literary scholarship of the Christian Church, and their editions of the writings of the Church Fathers have sometimes still not been superseded. One of them, moreover, Jean Mabillon (1632–1707), placed the study of palaeography and diplomatic on a firm scientific footing.

The Reformation put an end to Benedictine monasticism in northern Europe and England; the French Revolution greatly diminished its influence in France, and the loss of territories west of the Rhine caused rulers in Bavaria and other German states to close many monasteries in order to compensate their aristocracies for the loss of those territories to the French. But Benedictine monasticism saw a revival in the late nineteenth and early twentieth centuries, and the Black Monks have continued to play a significant if more muted role in education and spiritual life. The influence of Benedict cannot easily be underestimated; it was given symbolic recognition by the Vatican when he was declared "Patron Saint of Europe" in 1964.

Bibliography: P. Batselier, ed. *Saint Benedict, Father of Western Civilization*, 1981; E. R. Elder, ed., *Benedictus: Studies in Honor of St. Benedict of Nursia*, 1981; T. Lindsay, *Saint Benedict, His Life and Work, 1950*.

William Schipper

BENJAMIN OF TUDELA (FL. TWELFTH CENTURY).

The most famous Jewish traveler and travel writer of the Middle Ages, he was a native of Tudela in Spain and a rabbi.

Little is known about Benjamin of Tudela other than his account of his travels that took place from 1160 to 1173. He set out from Saragossa in Spain in 1160 on a long journey that antedated the travels of Marco *Polo, *John of Plano

Carpini, and *William of Rubruck by many years. Why Rabbi Benjamin went on his travels is never stated, but he does relate that he kept a record of what he observed and also interviewed many reliable persons along the way to gain further information. After leaving Spain, he traveled through southern France and into Italy where he visited Rome. From there he proceeded eastward to Constantinople, Antioch, Damascus, Jerusalem, Baghdad, and on to Samarkand. Turning south into India he went all the way to Ceylon and then journeyed westward to Ethiopia and up the Nile River to Egypt. Before returning home, he visited Sicily and Germany. All along the way he lists and describes the various Jewish communities he encountered along with trade, industry, and curious phenomena. Descriptions of the Assassins and sandstorms are provided along with a mention of China. His book was first translated into Latin in 1543 and has been further translated into many other languages. It provides an invaluable description of Christendom and the lands of Islam during the twelfth century that agrees very well with the writings of Arabic geographers of that era. While the accuracy of Rabbi Benjamin has been borne out when it can be checked, he was no practitioner of analytical geography as were some contemporary Arab scholars.

Bibliography: M. N. Adler, *The Itinerary of Benjamin of Tudela*, 1907, reprint 1964.

Ronald H. Fritze

BERENGAR OF TOURS (C. 1000–1088).

Rector of the cathedral school of St. Martin of Tours, he was condemned as a heretic for his teachings on the Eucharist, but his method of argument had some influence on the development of later medieval philosophy and theology.

Berengar was born in Tours, but in his youth he went to study under the famous *Fulbert who was rector at the cathedral school of Chartres. There he studied and excelled in, among other things, Latin poetry and dialectical logic. Sometime in the 1030s, he returned to his native city and became the rector of the cathedral school of St. Martin of Tours. Some of his students who went on to enjoy great careers in the Church were Eusebius Bruno, bishop of Angers; Hildebert, archbishop of Tours; and *Bruno, the founder of the Carthusian order of monks and a teacher of the future Pope *Urban II. Around 1039, Berengar also became archdeacon of Angers, and he enjoyed the favor and protection of Geoffrey Martel, the count of Anjou, in the early years of the persecution for his teachings on the Eucharist.

Around 1047, Berengar became involved in a debate over the nature of the Holy Eucharist. In a letter to *Lanfranc, abbot of Bec, who was a colleague and friend of his, Berengar defended the teachings of the monk Ratramnus and *John Scottus Eriugena on the Eucharist. These men had taught that the real body and blood of Christ were not present in the bread and wine of the sacrament of Holy Communion. They believed that Christ was only present in a spiritual sense. Berengar's doctrine was examined at several councils of bishops, and Berengar was found to be in error, and consequently he was branded a heretic. Berengar spent the rest of his life alternating between acceptance and rejection of the Church's doctrine of the real presence, which would later come to be known as transubstantiation. In later years, Lanfranc of Bec led the fight against Berengar's ideas, writing the *De corpore et sanguine Domini* (Book on the Body and Blood of the Lord), which was widely read. Berengar responded with his own treatise, the *De sacra coena adversus Lanfrancem* (On the Holy Meal against Lanfranc), where he responded line by line to Lanfranc's earlier treatise. In 1080 Berengar made his final rejection of his own teachings on the subject, and he died in communion with the Church on the island of St. Cosme, near Tours, in 1088.

At the time, Berengar's ideas and writings had a profound influence on theologians who both defended and contested his position. His ideas and his refusal to give them up altogether helped bring about the Church's more specific doctrine of transubstantiation. His teachings on the Eucharist were not his only heretical ideas, however. He also taught that baptism and marriage were unimportant ceremonies. Perhaps even more than these false teachings themselves, what really inflamed Berengar's detractors was his spreading of them throughout France.

Bibliography: A. J. MacDonald, *Berengar and the Reform of Sacramental Doctrine*, 1930.

Ryan P. Crisp

BERENGUELA OF CASTILE (C. 1180–1246). Although she was afforded the opportunity of becoming queen of Castile herself, Berenguela is perhaps best remembered for unselfishly abdicating the throne in favor of her son Ferdinand, an act that led to the permanent political unification of Castile and León.

Berenguela was one of four children born to King *Alfonso VIII of Castile and Eleanor Plantagenet of England. In 1197, Berenguela's marriage was arranged to King Alfonso IX of León in order to secure a peace between that region and Castile. However, due to the fact that Berenguela and Alfonso were second cousins, Pope *Innocent III annulled the marriage in 1198. The couple had four children whose legitimacy was recognized by the pope in spite of his disapproval of the marriage. In 1204, the couple conceded to papal pressure by separating, and Berenguela returned to Castile. After the death of Alfonso VIII ten years later, Berenguela's younger brother Enrique, who was only eleven years old at the time, became king of Castile. Berenguela served as guardian to her younger brother until his untimely death in 1217. Enrique's death left Berenguela as heir to the Castilian throne. Although she could have rightfully claimed the throne, Berenguela elected to pass the crown to her son, who became King Ferdinand III of Castile. By renouncing power, Berenguela set the stage for the reunification of Castile and León under one ruler, an event that occurred when Ferdinand inherited the Leonese throne in 1230. Berenguela served as an adviser to Ferdinand until her death in 1246.

Bibliography: J. C. Parsons and B. Wheeler, eds., *Medieval Mothering*, 1996.

Gregory B. Kaplan

BERNARD OF CLAIRVAUX, SAINT (1090–1153).

Bernard was a Cistercian monk and an abbot of Clairvaux and was named, in 1830, a Doctor of the Church.

Bernard was born to a noble family in Fontaines-lès-Dijon in Burgundy, France. After completing his schooling at the chapter school of Notre Dame de Châtillon, he decided on a monastic vocation; he persuaded a brother and several of his companions to join him, and in 1112, they entered the austere new community of Cîteaux near Dijon. After a year's novitiate and two years of the monastic profession, Stephen *Harding, the abbot of Cîteaux, persuaded Bernard to make a new monastic foundation at Clairvaux in Champagne. As abbot of Clairvaux, Bernard oversaw a period of rapid expansion within the Cistercian Order; during his tenure, Clairvaux established sixty-eight daughter houses.

It was also at Clairvaux that Bernard began his career as a writer, composing his *De gradibus humilitatis et superbiae* (The Degrees of Humilty and Pride) c. 1121 and his *Homilies in Praise of the Virgin Mary* shortly thereafter. Around 1124 Bernard wrote an *Apologia* that criticized the Cistercians for their criticism of the Benedictine religious at Cluny but nevertheless reproached the latter for their laxity. Bernard attended the Council of Troyes in 1128, which approved a monastic rule for the Knights Templar, and for this new order he wrote *In Praise of the New Knighthood*.

In 1130, Bernard became involved in the contested papal election between Anacletus II and Innocent II. Bernard defended Innocent so successfully at the Council of Étampes in this year that he won over the support of the king of France, *Louis VI. The grateful pope then made Bernard a counsellor, and Bernard spent much of the 1130s traveling either with him or on his behalf throughout France, the German lands, and northern Italy. Wherever Bernard ventured to support the beleaguered pope, he formed new Cistercian daughter houses. Bernard left for Italy in 1137 and was instrumental in ending the papal schism, in Innocent's favor, in 1138.

After the papal election had been settled, *William of St. Thierry warned Bernard of the dangers of the teachings of Peter *Abelard. Bernard vigorously defended traditional theology, writing letters to prelates denouncing Abelard's teachings as a threat to the faith. Bernard then secured his condemnation at the Council of Sens in 1140. Bernard once again assumed the role of defender of academic orthodoxy in 1148 at the Council of Rheims. Although this council did not condemn the philosopher *Gilbert of Poitiers, it nevertheless averted him from the potential dangers of his teachings.

In the years 1144–1145, Bernard began a preaching tour directed against the success of two popular anticlerical preachers, Peter of Bruys and *Arnold of Brescia. The election of *Eugenius III, a former disciple of Bernard, to the pontificate in 1145 brought Bernard to the forefront of papal politics. Pope Eugenius charged Bernard with the preaching of a new crusade, and in 1146 and 1147, Bernard traveled throughout France and the German lands making preparations for the Second Crusade. Bernard met personally with King *Louis VII about this matter, encouraging him to take the cross. The failure of the Second Crusade was one of Bernard's greatest disappointments. He died at Clairvaux on 20 August 1153 and was canonized by Pope *Alexander III in 1174.

Bernard's influence and personality loom large over the entire twelfth century. He kept correspondence with popes, kings, abbots, and bishops and composed over 500 letters. He actively sought Church orthodoxy and unity by opposing dissident belief (Peter of Bruys, Arnold of Brescia) and dissident thought (Abelard and Gilbert of Poitiers) and by stressing the role that the pope played as the spiritual leader of Christendom. He wrote and dedicated his *On Consideration* to Eugenius III, outlining in it the duties of a pope. Bernard preached over 332 sermons, the most famous of which are his eighty-six *Sermons on the Song of Songs*.

Bibliography: A. Bredero, *Bernard of Clairvaux: Between Cult and History*, 1996; J. Leclercq, *The Love of Learning and the Desire for God*, 1962.

Andrew G. Traver

BERNARD SILVESTER (D. C. 1160). Although little is known of his life, Bernard was a poet and commentator whose philosophical mythmaking had a substantial influence in western Europe during the later Middle Ages. According to Matthew of Vendôme, Bernard was his teacher of poetry and letter-writing (an important branch of medieval rhetoric known as the *ars dictaminis*) in St. Martin at Tours around 1130 to 1140. Bernard's other institutional connection seems to be with Chartres. His greatest work, the *Cosmographia*, is dedicated to Thierry of Chartres, who became chancellor of Chartres in 1141; this dedication led some earlier scholars to confuse Bernard Silvester with Bernard of Chartres, a teacher and writer from an earlier generation. Bernard Silvester either lived or maintained property in Tours to the end of his life, according to records that show a nephew selling a house in Tours willed to him by Bernard. The absence of other records suggests that Bernard lived a quiet life as an academic at St. Martin until his death.

Two important texts, the *Cosmographia* and the *Mathematicus*, are certainly Bernard's work; commentaries on the first six books of Virgil's *Aeneid* and on Martianus Capella's *De Nuptiis* are very probably his; a number of shorter works (the *Experimentarius, De gemellis,* and *De paupero ingrato*) have been less convincingly attributed (in part or whole) to him. Bernard also refers, in his commentary on Martianus, to another commentary of his on Plato's *Timaeus*;

no such commentary has yet been found. However, the influence of the *Timaeus* on Bernard's writing is pervasive and profound. Bernard is fascinated by the problem of knowing the universe in its forms and its processes of creation. He both explains and adapts pagan classical stories to produce hybrid literary texts. His *Cosmographia* alternates sections of Latin poetry and prose in the *prosimetrum* format (a genre familiar from the *Consolation of Philososphy* by *Boethius). Bernard's commentaries similarly combine classical poetic texts with his prose interjections. In both cases, Bernard combines mythic narrative with philosophizing, scientific inquiry, encyclopedialike discussions of arcane details, panegyric, and other features. His approach to all these elements depends heavily on Platonic ideas of form and knowledge from the *Timaeus*, as these ideas were shaped by medieval Neoplatonic writers before him (notably Boethius and *John Scottus Eriugena).

Bernard's *Mathematicus*, an elegiac poem, is notable for its attempt to discuss the philosophical questions of necessity and destiny in mathematical terms. The *Cosmographia* is even more ambitious and, judging by its wide circulation (more than fifty medieval copies survive today), much more influential. This poem is divided into two sections. In the first section, *Megacosmos*, Nature journeys to Nous, a personification of the mind of God, to request that Nous transform the universe. Nous obliges by defining the four elements, shaping matter into forms that correspond to divine ideas, and creating the world soul. *Microcosmos*, the second section, follows this process of divine creation to humanity. Nature meets Genius; together they set out to find Urania and Physis, who help Nature and Genius locate the soul of humankind in the heavens and deliver it to humankind on earth. Taken together these allegories argue that creation follows the same divine order in the microcosm of human experience that shapes the primeval matter of the cosmos itself. Human knowledge of that order, according to Bernard's commentaries on Virgil and Martianus, is driven by a desire to attain divine knowledge. The promise and the problems of attaining a higher state of knowledge, personified by Bernard in the mythic figure of Vulcan, parallel those between earthly and heavenly love. Despite the optimistic allegory of creation in the *Cosmographia*, Bernard's commentaries argue that heaven and earth are not so easily joined in mortal experience.

Bernard's greatest influence may be through another Latin poet and philosopher writing later in the twelfth century: *Alan of Lille. Alan's two major poems, *The Complaint of Nature* (*De planctu naturae*) and *Anticlaudianus*, were read and imitated by many, positioning Bernard as an indirect but still important figure in the vernacular dream visions of the later Middle Ages. Alan revamps Bernard's allegories; nonetheless, Alan's personifications once again include Nature, Genius, and a figure receiving the soul of the New Man from the divine presence. Also, Alan's poetry is broadly indebted to Bernard's Platonism and his concern with creation and knowledge. Bernard's student, Matthew of Vendôme, frequently praises Bernard's poetic excellence as a matter of rhetorical style; however, Bernard's use of myth, philosophy, and commentary in a complex poetic narrative may be his most important contribution to later poets.

Bibliography: *The Cosmographia of Bernardus Silvestris*, trans. W. Wetherbee, 1972; B. Stock, *Myth and Science in the Twelfth Century: A Study of Bernard Silvester*, 1972.
Joel Fredell

BERNART DE VENTADORN (FL. MID-TWELFTH CENTURY). Bernart
was a troubadour, poet, and musician whose work has been translated into German, French, and English.

As with most troubadours not of noble birth, relatively little is known of this poet–musician except what we can learn from the *vida* (life) written by his (unreliable) thirteenth-century biographer, from a stanza of Peire d'Alvernha, and from his own poetry. The first states in part that Bernart was of poor birth, a son of servants in the castle of Ventadorn; he fell in love with the wife of the lord of the castle, and she with him; for a long time he was a successful courtier and singer, but the lady's husband eventually found them out and forced him to leave; he went to the court of the duchess of Normandy (*Eleanor of Aquitaine), and she received him well, and he fell in love with her and she with him; then she married King *Henry II of England and became queen; and Bernart served the count of Toulouse and later entered the order of Dalon, where he died. In a poem composed of stanzas each discussing a troubadour of his day, Peire d'Alvernha estimates that Bernart is only slightly inferior to Guiraut de Bornelh.

More important than the historical Bernart, however, is the body of verse he left to posterity, consisting of over forty songs. The music for eighteen of these songs has also been preserved. The texts are written in the style later called "trobar leu" or "easy style." This contrasts with the more complicated style of "trobar clus," with its interweaving rhyme schemes, rare rhymes, and obscure, even hermetic expression. Bernart's poetry deals almost exclusively with love and with the poetry that celebrates it. Written from the male lover's point of view, the poetry tells of the successes and failures, the hopes and despair, of the lover, generally in the first person. Whether the feelings expressed in the poems are an accurate reflection of the real feelings of the historical Bernart may be doubted; but they have a ring of sincerity, which is not the least of their charms.

Belonging to the third generation of troubadours, namely, those who flourished from about 1150 until the Albigensian Crusade, Bernart is the consummate poet–musician. Almost all his preserved poems are *cansos*, lyrical expressions of feeling probably meant for performance by a single singer. His rhyme schemes are simple, and he favors the style known as *coblas unissonans* in which not only the rhyme scheme but the very sounds at the rhymes are repeated from stanza to stanza. His poems mostly include six or seven stanzas. He avoids very short lines but mixes freely lines of different lengths. Bernart sings of all the different stages a courtly love affair can go through, from first sight through acquaintance and shared love, even to parting. His tone is often elegiac, regretting his lack of progress or success with his lady but remembering also the joy of love and hoping for better things in the future.

Bernart has been edited (with translations) in German and in French and has also been translated into English. Many of his poems appear in modern anthologies, and his "Lark" poem, many times recorded by different artists, is among the best known of all troubadour poems.

Bibliography: C. Appel, *Bernart von Ventadorn, Seine Lieder mit Einleitung und Glossar*, 1915; M. Lazar, ed., *Bernard de Ventadour, Troubadour du XIIe siècle, Chansons d'amour*, 1966; S. G. Nichols et al., eds., *The Songs of Bernart de Ventadorn*, 1962.

F.R.P. Akehurst

BERNO OF REICHENAU (D. 1048). Berno of Reichenau, abbot of Reichenau from 1008 to 1048, a music scholar, composer, and poet, was an important figure in monastic reform at Reichenau. He is also responsible for the rebuilding of the cathedral, which had been damaged by fire, and for the construction of the West transept of the cathedral, which remains today.

Berno, educated at Fleury-sur-Loire and Prüm, was appointed as abbot by Emperor Henry II in 1008. Berno's efforts to restore monastic life to its more disciplined ways centered on making clerical tasks once again the center of monastic life. In 1014, when he was in Rome for Henry II's coronation, he gathered materials for *De quibus dam rebus ad missae officium pertinentibus*, a monograph on the Mass. He was particularly concerned with scholarship at the abbey and was the teacher of *Hermann of Reichenau.

Berno's major musical work, done between 1021 and 1036, is a compilation of a tonary, a musical guide to regulate liturgical chant and describe the system in which chant was sung. The work, which includes a lengthy prologue, appears to have been widely distributed in the surrounding area during the eleventh and twelfth centuries.

Bibliography: H. Oesch, *Berno und Hermann von Reichenau als Musiktheoretiker*, 1961.

Elaine Cullen

BLANCHE OF CASTILE (BLANCA DE CASTILLA) (1188–1252). Regent of France, she governed the nation on two occasions: during the minority of her son *Louis IX and from 1248, when he joined the Seventh Crusade, until her death in 1252. Blanche proved to be a dynamic, competent monarch, dealing successfully with both internal and external threats to her realm.

Blanche was born in the Spanish kingdom of Castile to King *Alfonso VII and Eleanor, daughter of the English King *Henry II. Well educated, reputedly beautiful and well mannered, and devout, she was chosen by her grandmother *Eleanor of Aquitaine to wed French heir apparent Louis in 1200 at the age of eleven. The marriage had been arranged by her uncle, King *John of England, in an attempt to settle a territorial dispute between England and France. The dispute continued, however, reaching a climax at the battle of Bouvines in 1214, in which the French defeated the combined armies of England and the Holy Roman Empire, enabling Blanche's father-in-law *Philip II Augustus to annex Normandy and Anjou.

That same year, Blanche gave birth to a son who was to become Louis IX and eventually be canonized Saint Louis. Her husband, the future Louis VIII, was plotting to seize the throne of England. He put his plans into motion, but his invasion was ultimately turned back by the English forces in a battle at Lincoln, and he returned to France in 1217. Here, he immediately joined the devout Blanche in her zealous suppression of the heretical Albigensian or Cathar sect, which had spread throughout southern France, especially in Provence and Languedoc. Pope *Innocent III approved a policy of using the crusade—previously reserved solely for use against Muslims—as a tool of religious purification. Louis undertook a series of military expeditions in the south, continuing the crusade after he succeeded his father in 1223, and was crowned Louis VIII. He extended his sovereignty all the way to the Mediterranean. However, he paid the ultimate price for this expansion in 1226, dying of dysentery upon returning home from the crusade.

Louis VIII's will specified that Blanche rule as regent until his son, crowned Louis IX at the age of twelve, reached adulthood. Assuming the foreign-born regent and child king to be weak, a group of barons joined a rebellion under the leadership of Philip Hurepel. They were supported by England's *Henry III, who was eager to reclaim lands his father had lost to France. While Blanche proved to be a shrewd negotiator, she was quite capable of using force, riding into battle at the head of her troops in an attack on the castle of Peter Mauclerc in January 1229. Her efforts ultimately resulted in a triumph over the rebellion, and a series of treaties secured northern territories and established a peace with England that lasted until 1240. Blanche also concluded the Albigensian Crusade in 1229 and signed the Treaty of Paris with Raymond VII of Toulouse, solidifying the throne's claim over the south.

Although Blanche stepped down as regent when Louis IX came of age and assumed the throne in 1236, she remained a powerful influence, guiding and supporting her son the rest of her life. She selected his wife, Margaret of Provence, but was not a very supportive mother-in-law. In 1244, Louis and Margaret vowed to undertake a crusade against the Muslims, a move that displeased Blanche. When the couple departed in 1248, Blanche once again assumed the regency. The crusade was unsuccessful, however, and Louis was captured and imprisoned after losing a battle at Al-Mansurā, Egypt, in 1250. Two years later, in 1252, Blanche died in Paris and was buried in Maubuisson Abbey.

Blanche of Castile, like her grandmother, Eleanor of Aquitaine, was a powerful woman who affected history through both her public and private efforts. She not only maintained the kingdom with which she was entrusted, but she extended and strengthened it. She ushered in a period of peace and prosperity during which many of France's great cathedrals were built. Even when she was not officially in power, she was an important influence in her son's decisions; the successes of the beloved Louis IX's reign are attributed largely to her. Educated and creative, she wrote songs that have survived to this day. Carrying on the devout faith in which Blanche raised them, Louis IX and his sister Isabel both led lives that led to their canonization.

Bibliography: R. Pernoud, *Blanche of Castile*, trans. H. Noel, 1975.

Leah Larson

BODEL, JEAN (JEHAN) (C. 1176–1210). Jean Bodel was a French poet, jongleur, author of fabliaux, and playwright whose drama *Le Jeu de saint Nicolas* (Play of St. Nicholas, c. 1200) is thought to be the first French miracle play.

Bodel was born in Arras, Artois (France), and may have held public office there. He belonged to one of the literary confraternities there. His plans to take part in the Fourth Crusade were curtailed when he contracted leprosy. He was admitted to a lazar house where he lived for the rest of his life. In addition to *Le Jeu de saint Nicolas*, Bodel's literary works include nine fabliaux (1190–1197), "La Chanson des Saisnes" (The Song of the Saxons, written sometime before 1200), and five pastourelles (four in 1190–1194 and one in 1199). His final work is *Les Conges* (Leave-Takings, 1202), a forty-two-stanza lyrical poem sadly bidding farewell to his friends probably at the time of his entrance into the lazar house.

Bodel's *Le Jeu de saint Nicolas* is the oldest extant French miracle play (a real or fictitious portrayal of the life, miracles, and martyrdom of a saint). In this play, Bodel treats a theme already presented in Latin by Hilarius (fl. 1125), among others; however, Bodel updates and expands this theme by connecting it to the Crusades. In this play, the only survivor of a defeated Christian army battling with the Saracens is found praying to an image of Saint Nicholas. The image later becomes the agent of a miracle. The Saracens find the image and place it on top of the king's treasure. However, the statue does not prevent the treasure from being carried off by thieves. The thieves are shown drinking, gambling, and fighting in several tavern scenes. These scenes represent what may be the first time that comic scenes based on contemporary life appear in religious drama. The comic characters and probably the tavern itself represent the people and manners of Arras. In the end, Saint Nicholas himself appears and convinces the thieves to return the treasure. This miracle causes the Saracen king and all his people to convert to Christianity. *Le Jeu de saint Nicolas* is remarkable for its religious devotion, its zealous support of the Crusades, its satirical humor, and its depiction of local color. In addition, it may be the first of the Latin college plays to be translated into the vernacular.

Among his other important works, *La Chanson des Saisnes*, an epic, provides additional chapters to the historical account of *Charlemagne's Saxon wars. In addition, one of Jean Bodel's fabliaux, *De Gombert et les ii clers*, is a close analogue to Chaucer's *Reeve's Tale*. However, it has not been established whether Bodel's fabliau influenced Chaucer or if the resemblance is coincidental.

Bibliography: O. Mandel, trans., *Five Comedies of Medieval France*, 1982; H. S. Robertson, "Structure and Comedy in *Le Jeu de Saint Nicolas*," *Studies in Philology* 64 (1967): 551–563.

Leah Larson

BOETHIUS, ANICIUS MANLIUS SEVERINUS (C. 480–526). A Roman statesman and scholar, Boethius became an important figure for medieval poets, philosophers, and teachers through his writings. Boethius was born into a consular family, orphaned, and then adopted by Symmachus, another Roman aristocrat. Boethius married the daughter of this patron, Rusticana, and took up the life of public service expected from men in the senatorial class. He served with distinction under *Theodoric (493–526), the Ostrogothic king of Italy. Boethius was made consul in 510 and the head of government and court services in 522; he also participated in the ceremony that named his two sons consul in 522. However, not long thereafter he was accused of treason against Theodoric, possibly based on his own stated intention to preserve Roman liberties under Ostrogothic rule and sacrilege based on his alleged practice of astrology. Theodoric himself was in conflict with Emperor Justin (519–527) in Constantinople during this period. The reasons for this conflict and their relationship (if any) to the imprisonment of Boethius remain in dispute among modern scholars, but in medieval Europe the widely accepted explanation was that Boethius suffered a Christian martyrdom due to his adherence to the Catholic faith supported by Justin and Symmachus (who was executed shortly after Boethius) and resisted by the Arian Theodoric. Boethius was clubbed to death, at the order of Theodoric, in Pavia in August 526.

   Although Boethius does not receive much notice from his near contemporaries, in the ninth century a remarkable circulation of Boethian manuscripts and ideas began. The most famous work of Boethius, the *Consolation of Philosophy*, is traditionally dated from the period its author spent in jail awaiting execution, and numerous biographical details in the work support that dating. A man of high standing, clearly identified with Boethius, is in prison awaiting his fate when Lady Philosophy appears to him. Philosophy claims the role of physician to the man's despairing mind. They discuss a sweeping range of issues surrounding the problem of evil in a world created and controlled by divine good— true and false goods, the movement from concrete to abstract thought, the differences between instinct and reason, the relationship of language to truth, the possibility of free will in a predestined universe, the nature of godhead. The *Consolation* concludes with a powerful speech by Philosophy summing up her argument that all events of worldly fortune are for the good; neither the voice of the imprisoned man nor any indication of his ultimate fate interferes with this closing.

Virtually everything about the *Consolation* was to have an impact on medieval writers. Individual passages, such as the description of Lady Fortune and her wheel, took on their own life as literary conventions from the scholastic writers of the twelfth century to the great vernacular poets of the late Middle Ages. The *Consolation*'s strategy of setting up a dialogue between a human struggling for meaning and a personification of divine wisdom on earth also made its way into countless later adaptations. Its combination of poetry and prose, called *pro-simetrum*, found imitators in *Bernard Silvester, *Alan of Lille, and other writers. The work as a whole continued its influence in several languages besides its original Latin: The *Consolation* was translated into Anglo-Saxon by *Alfred the Great, into Old French by *Jean de Meun, into Old High German by *Notker Labeo (Teutonicus), and into Middle English by Geoffrey Chaucer.

Other writings by Boethius helped shape medieval thought and education. His theological work *De trinitate* (along with several other tracts medieval readers ascribed to him) was an important source for Neoplatonic ideas among poets as well as philosophers. Among scholastic philosophers the reputation of Boethius was based not only on treatises but also on translations and commentaries. His treatises, such as *De categoricis syllogismis*, were crucial to the development of medieval logic and philosophical terminology generally. Boethius translated from the Greek Aristotle's logical treatises and Porphyry's *Isagoge* and supplied his own commentaries. All these works played an important part in medieval schools, since lessons were often based on definitions established by Boethius. Several additional works by Boethius served as bulwarks for the medieval liberal arts curriculum. His widely used texts on mathematics include the *De institutione arithmetica* and the *Geometria Euclidis*. The *De institutione musica* established Boethius as one of the few medieval authorities on music theory and composition.

The reputation of Boethius continued to prosper after the Middle Ages. An edition of what was believed to be his complete works was first published in Venice in 1497. Queen Elizabeth I of England herself translated the *Consolation*. The tradition of his martyrdom, kept alive in a cult of worship at Pavia, was sanctioned by the Catholic Church in 1883 with his canonization as Saint Severinus Boethius. His life and writings, particularly the *Consolation*, remain topics of lively interest to this day.

Bibliography: A.M.S. Boethius, *The Consolation of Philosophy*, trans. P. G. Walsh, 1999; H. Chadwick, *Boethius: The Consolations of Music, Logic, Theology, and Philosophy*, 1981; M. T. Gibson, ed., *Boethius: His Life, Thought and Influence*, 1981; N. H. Kaylor, *The Medieval Consolation of Philosophy*, 1992.

Joel Fredell

BOETHIUS OF DACIA (FL. 1270s).

Boethius was a thirteenth-century Aristotelian philosopher and a follower of *Averroës.

He was born in the first half of the thirteenth century, but little else is known about the life and early career of Boethius. Although often referred to as Boethius of Sweden, he probably in fact hailed from Denmark. By 1270 he had become a master of arts at the University of Paris and proceeded to teach philosophy within the Faculty of Arts there. He soon became associated with his colleague *Siger of Brabant and the "Averroistic" or radical Aristotelian movement. While Boethius' teaching career may have ended as early as 1272–1273, many medieval manuscripts list him as an advocate of several of the 219 philosophical propositions condemned by Bishop Stephen *Tempier of Paris in 1277. After 1277, Boethius fled Paris and appealed to the papacy. After detention at the papal curia at Orvieto, Boethius joined the Dominican Order.

Boethius himself strongly defended the philosopher's right to discuss any topic under reason even if it seemingly contradicted the Christian faith. He thus separated philosophy from theology by discussing the tenets of the faith, such as *creation ex nihilo*, and the Resurrection as a philosopher (by reason) and not a theologian (by recourse to supernatural revelation and miracles). Although accused of teaching the "double truth"—that is, that philosophy may prove false what the Christian religion teaches as true—Boethius himself remained Christian and avoided calling true a philosophical conclusion contrary to the faith. He thus taught that while faith teaches the truth, human reason sometimes cannot demonstrate it and may instead seem to indicate the contrary.

Boethius wrote commentaries on Aristotle and the works *De summo bono* (On the Supreme Good), *De aeternitate mundi* (On the Eternity of the World), and *De sompniis* (On Dreams). His career bears witness to the difficulties that thirteenth-century intellectuals had in incorporating the new Aristotle into a Christian milieu.

Bibliography: Boethius of Dacia, *On the Supreme Good, On the Eternity of the World, On Dreams*, trans. J. Wippel, 1987; S. Jensen, "On the National Origin of Boethius of Dacia," *Classica et Mediaevalia* 24 (1963): 232–241.

Andrew G. Traver

BOHEMOND I OF ANTIOCH (C. 1058–1111). The eldest son of the Norman adventurer *Robert Guiscard, he was one of the leaders of the First Crusade.

According to a description by Byzantine princess *Anna Comnena, Bohemond had gray eyes, light brown hair cut short, was very tall, well built, and of a light complexion (compared with the Greeks at least). The anonymous author of the *Gesta Francorum*, a popular, contemporary account of the Crusade, idealized him. Bohemond inherited Robert Guiscard's lands on the eastern shore of the Adriatic, while his younger brother, Roger, received Apulia. He lost much of his inheritance in his war with the Byzantine Empire over these lands in 1085. Among his possible motives for participating in the First Crusade was the desire to replace this lost inheritance, especially at the expense of the Byzantines.

During the First Crusade, Bohemond proved himself a more than able commander, especially at the battle of Dorylaeum and the siege of Antioch. He led
a rather small contingent of Normans to the east, accompanied by his nephew
Tancred, who served loyally as his second in command. When he arrived in
Constantinople, he was treated with some suspicion by the Byzantine emperor
*Alexius I due to their earlier conflicts, but Bohemond was willing enough to
take an oath of loyalty to the emperor; it is thought that he hoped to be named
as the commander in chief of the Greek forces that were to accompany the
crusaders, although this never came to pass. However, when the crusaders finally
took the city of Antioch from the Muslims in 1098, it was due to an arrangement
Bohemond had made with a traitor on the inside. He then claimed Antioch for
himself, promising only to yield it to the emperor if he should come in person
to claim it. Bohemond did not complete his pilgrimage to Jerusalem until December 1099 where he cooperated with the papal legate Daimbert, the archbishop of Pisa, and participated in installing Daimbert later as the patriarch of
Jerusalem. Daimbert suggested Bohemond as a possible successor to the king
of Jerusalem in 1100, but before any action could be taken in this direction,
Bohemond was captured by the Danishmends. He was not released until 1103,
and Tancred served as the regent of Antioch in Bohemond's absence. In 1106,
Bohemond traveled back to Europe, seeking western aid against both the Muslims and the Byzantines. He visited France, and while he was there he not only
organized a new crusade but married Constance, the daughter of King Philip I.
This new crusade only got as far as Albania, where Bohemond tried to take
Durazzo from the Byzantines, but he was forced to surrender. By signing the
treaty of Devol, he acknowledged the Byzantine emperor as his feudal overlord
for Antioch. Bohemond did not return to Antioch, however, and he died on his
estates in southern Italy in 1111. He was succeeded in Antioch by his infant
son Bohemond II, although Tancred continued to serve as regent until his own
death in 1112.

Bibliography: R. B. Yewdale, *Bohemond I, Prince of Antioch*, 1924.

Ryan P. Crisp

BONAVENTURE (GIOVANNI DI FIDANZA), SAINT (C. 1217–1274).

Bonaventure was a Franciscan theologian, the "second founder" of the Franciscan Order, and was known both as the Devout Doctor and as the Seraphic
Doctor.

Born at Bagnoregio in Italy, Bonaventure was the son of a physician. He fell
seriously ill at the age of ten and was cured through the intervention of Saint
*Francis. He received his early schooling at the Franciscan friary in Bagnoregio
and in 1234–1235 entered the Faculty of Arts at Paris. He became a master of
arts in 1243 and joined the Franciscan Order in the following year. He studied
theology at Paris under the Franciscan masters *Alexander of Hales and John
of La Rochelle and lectured on Scripture in the late 1240s and on *Peter Lom-

bard's *Sentences* in the early 1250s. By spring 1254, he had completed the requirements for the theological degree at Paris but, like Thomas *Aquinas, was not recognized as a university master due to the opposition of *William of St. Amour and other secular masters of theology.

From 1254 to 1257 Bonaventure taught and preached at the Franciscan house at Paris (in 1256 the university officially recognized him as master). Here he defended disputed questions on Christ, the Trinity, and evangelical perfection. In February 1257, he was elected Minister General of the Franciscans. In this capacity, he played a pivotal role in quelling the internal divisions within the Order and helped to repair the damage done by his brethren who championed a radical interpretation of *Joachim of Fiore.

In his first years of office, Bonaventure visited the provinces of his Order. In 1259 he made a pilgrimage to La Verna where Francis had received the stigmata. Here he wrote his *Itinerarium mentis in Deum* (The Mind's Road to God), a mystical return to God. In 1260, at the General Chapter at Narbonne, Bonaventure reorganized and codified the constitutions of his Order. Here he was commissioned to write a new biography of Francis, and he subsequently traveled to Italy to visit the places of Francis' life and interview the early friars. In 1262–1263 he wrote two new lives of Francis, *Legenda maior* and *Legenda minor*, both of which were approved by the Order in 1263. In 1266, the Franciscan General Chapter ordered that all other legends about Francis be destroyed.

In 1267, Bonaventure returned to Paris and delivered his Conferences on the Ten Commandments against *Siger of Brabant and the "Averroists" (cf. *Averroës) within the Faculty of Arts. Bonaventure continued his attack in the following year in his Conferences on the seven gifts of the Holy Spirit. In 1269, the Parisian secular theologians once again challenged the validity of the mendicant form of religious life; Bonaventure responded with his *Apologia pauperum*, his classic defense of voluntary poverty.

In 1272, Bonaventure assisted Pope Gregory X in the calling of a Church council to reunite the Greek and Roman churches but returned to Paris in the following year to deal yet again with the Averroistic challenge within the Arts Faculty. Here Bonaventure delivered his Sermons on the six days of Creation, chastising those who preferred the wisdom of the world to the true wisdom of Christ. In this same year, he was nominated a cardinal bishop of Albano and was consecrated by Pope Gregory in Lyons. Hereafter, Bonaventure helped prepare for the Council of Lyons in 1274 and resigned his position as Minister General. Bonaventure preached sermons at this Council and probably presided over several of its sessions. He fell ill in Lyons and died on 15 July while the Council was still in session. He was canonized in 1482 and made a Doctor of the Church in 1587.

As a writer, Bonaventure was prodigious. Although he had received a thorough training in the philosophical literature recently translated from the Greek and Arabic, Bonaventure remained faithful to the theological tradition of Augustine and eschewed the "new" Aristotle. During the "Averroistic" crises within the Arts Faculty at Paris, Bonaventure in fact became a strident opponent of Aristotle and Averroës. In his *Reduction of the Arts to Theology* (1256), Bonaventure explains how knowledge is not an end in itself but rather strengthens faith and leads to experimental knowledge of God through love. In his *Breviloquium* (1256–1257), he proposed a detailed program of scriptural study. Through his mystical theology, Bonaventure's legacy can be seen across northern Europe in the Devotio Moderna and the Brethren of the Common Life.

As an administrator, Bonaventure helped to provide the Franciscan Order with a firm institutional basis. As a polemicist, Bonaventure not only wrote vigorously against those who cast doubt upon Francis' conception of the religious life but also admonished those who sought to exalt reason over faith. Throughout his career, he preached over eighty sermons on scriptural themes: some to university audiences, some to the court of King *Louis IX, and some to ecclesiastical prelates. As an able administrator and a brilliant theologian, Bonaventure helped to shape the Franciscan tradition in the Middle Ages.

Bibliography: J. G. Bougerol, *Introduction to the Works of Bonaventure*, trans. J. de Vinck, 1963; J. F. Quinn, *The Historical Constitution of Saint Bonaventure's Philosophy*, 1973.

Andrew G. Traver

BONCOMPAGNO OF SIGNA (C. 1170–C. 1250).

A master of rhetoric at the University of Bologna in the early thirteenth century, he was a practioner of the *ars dictaminis*.

Born round 1170 at Signa (near Florence), he studied the liberal arts in Florence and Bologna, where he may also have learned law. He was notary to an Italian bishop for a time before deciding, around 1193–1194, to become a teacher of rhetoric. As he was only twenty-three or twenty-four when he began his first post in Bologna, his youth surprised his fellow masters. He taught there from 1194 to 1204, when he moved to Rome for two years. From 1206 to 1235, he held a succession of teaching positions in rhetoric at Vicenza, Bologna again, Venice, Padua, and outside Italy. He was legate to the papal curia between 1229 and 1234 but in 1240 had an appointment for a position there rejected. He died in poverty sometime after 1240 at the Hospital of S. Giovanni Evangelista in Florence.

Boncompagno's branch of rhetoric was the *ars dictaminis*, the art of composing letters and other prose documents. It first took in public correspondence, then personal letters, and finally oratory by the thirteenth century. Launched by the works of Alberic of Monte Cassino in the late eleventh century, *dictamen* was a response to the increasing need of Italian powers to communicate through public letters. The *ars dictaminis* was imported into France by the last decades of the twelfth century and became the preserve of grammar masters in places like Tours, Orléans, and Blois, where classical studies had long flourished. By the time that Boncompagno started teaching at Bologna in the early thirteenth century, the French approach had become the dominant one in Italy.

Boncompagno aroused hostility among the masters at Bologna by declaring war on the French school. He found its style to be too grammatical, too full of classical quotations and unusual vocabulary to be of much use outside of the study. Instead he advocated a simpler and clearer prose style that could be incorporated into public documents and civic oratory. He proclaimed his new approach rather belligerently in a series of rhetorical works over the course of his long career: the *Rhetorica antiqua sive Boncompagnus*, a collection of 1,000 model letters; the *V Tabulae Salutationum*, a model collection of salutations for letters (1194/1195); the *Palma* (1198), a textbook on the *ars dictaminis*; and the *Rhetorica novissima* (1235), on judicial oratory. His posturing so infuriated his enemies in Bologna that they smoked a copy of his *V Tabulae* in order to make the manuscript appear aged, implying that he had merely copied the whole thing from an ancient author. Although his reputation may always have been greatest in his own mind, his demand for a clearer, more oratorical style of rhetoric did eventually prevail in thirteenth-century Italy.

Bibliography: R. G. Witt, "Boncompagno and the Defense of Rhetoric," *Journal of Medieval and Renaissance Studies* 16.1 (1986): 1–31.

Kimberly Rivers

BONIFACE, SAINT (C. 675–754). Born Wynfrith, the greatest of the Anglo-Saxon missionaries on the Continent, he laid the foundation of the great Carolingian reforms.

According to a fourteenth-century tradition, he was born at Crediton near Exeter. His family furnished a number of important workers to the German mission, including the Abbess *Leoba and the brothers, Willibald and Wynnebald. He was educated at Minster, Thanet, and at Wimbourne in Dorset. He served as master of the school at Nursling, where he wrote his grammar and his poetry and was elected abbot there, against his will, in 717. The influence of *Aldhelm is obvious in his early works, although his later letters are in a sober prose style more reminiscent of *Bede. His literary career is characteristic of Southumbrian culture of the late seventh century.

He was already recognized as a man of ability, acting as an envoy of *Ine of Wessex at Canterbury. In 716 he sailed from London to Frisia. Unfortunately for his plans, Frisia was in revolt against Frankish lordship, and missionary activity was almost impossible. He joined *Willibrod, who retired to Echternach, and then he returned to Nursling. In 718 he followed Willibrod's precedent and went to Rome for permission to preach. He never returned to England. Gregory II changed his name to Boniface, and his letter of authority (15 May 719) charged him to preach to unbelieving gentiles.

From 719 to 722 he worked in Frisia with Willibrod under the protection of *Charles Martel and the local ruler Aldgisl. He began work in Thuringia, moving into Hesse, where he founded monasteries and destroyed the Oak of Donar (Thor) at Geismar in Hesse. Gregory invited him again to Rome and consecrated him bishop on 30 November 722. Boniface based his profession on the formula for bishops of the Metropolitan district of Rome, after consecration; although the obligations to the emperor were dropped, he swore obedience and fidelity to Peter, the pope, and his successors, to have no communion with bishops living in opposition to the fathers, and to oppose those who did with all his power. His oath was particularly significant because it brought the sphere of the new bishop into closer connection with Rome than any other Frankish dioceses. The close Roman connections of the English Church with its passionate emphasis on ecclesiastical unity would be an important influence in the developing institutions of the Carolingian Empire and its successors.

In 733 Gregory III sent him a pallium, although he would not have a proper see until he was made archbishop of Mainz in 747. In 738, Charles Martel defeated the Saxons of Westphalia, and with a new field opening to him, Boniface wrote home for prayers for their conversion since as they said of themselves and the English, "We are of one blood and one bone with you." In 739, Odilo of Bavaria invited Boniface to reform and reorganize the Bavarian church, where he had preached as early as 735. In 741, Charles Martel died. His sons Carloman (who later renounced the throne for the religious life) and *Pepin III both supported reform in their own halves of the Frankish kingdom. Carloman called a synod in Austrasia on 21 April 742. Earlier decrees became canon law by decision of the attending bishops; with these synods, decrees became proposals submitted to the secular ruler, who then published them under his own name, giving them the character of law. In 744, Pepin held a similar synod in Neustria. The 747 synod issued a formal declaration of adherence to Rome, and even opponents of Boniface now appealed to Rome. In 751, Chilperic, the last of the Merovingians, was deposed, and Boniface crowned Pepin with papal encouragement. In 753, Boniface retired and went to spend his last active years in the mission field. On 5 June 754, pagan Frisians martyred Boniface with his companions.

Important as his apostolic work was, his organizing and reforming activity was even more so. He was not a man of original thought, but he was one of enterprise, action, and integrity ready to denounce abuses whether among his own people or at Rome. Although he never returned to England, he kept in close contact with both the individuals and the Church there.

Bibliography: W. Levison, *England and the Continent in the Eighth Century*, 1946, reprint 1998; C. H. Talbot, *The Anglo-Saxon Missionaries in Germany*, 1954.

Helen Conrad-O'Briain

BONIFACE VIII, POPE (1235–1303, PONTIFICATE 1294–1303). Boniface was a pope whose creation of the doctrine of the supremacy of papal power led to a confrontation with Philip IV of France that resulted in the Babylonian Captivity of the papacy in 1309.

Benedict Gaetani (Boniface), a native of Italy, studied law and began his public career as secretary to the papal legate to France in the 1260s, who became pope as Martin IV in 1281. Benedict became a cardinal under Martin, and in 1290, Benedict became the legate to France and met for the one and only time his future nemesis Philip IV.

In 1291, Martin's successor, Nicholas, died, and the College of Cardinals deadlocked on the choice of his successor, settling finally in 1294 on a pious hermit who took the title Celestine V. His lack of political acuity made him a liability to the papacy, and he was forced to resign. Benedict, who probably had a hand in Celestine's resignation, was named as his successor on 24 December 1294 and became Boniface VIII.

England and France were shortly to embark upon the Hundred Years War and, to prepare for the coming hostilities, began to exact taxes from their clergy, an act Boniface saw as a deliberate transgression. He responded with the issuance of *Clericis Laicos* in February 1296, which forbade the taxing of clergy by secular rulers without the approval of the pope. Philip IV decided to forbid any monies to be sent to Rome, and knowing this would severely deplete his coffers, Boniface conceded that the French king could tax his clergy under emergency circumstances.

In 1300, Boniface declared a "Jubilee Year," and its popularity inspired him to once again meddle in secular affairs. When Philip IV convicted one of his bishops on charges of heresy and treason, Boniface demanded the reversal of the conviction and issued a bull stripping Philip of all privileges, subsequently indicting him for his misuse of power.

Philip responded by calling the pope a heretic and a fool and, over the next months, waged a war of words with the pope. On 18 November 1302, the pope issued the bull *Unam Sanctum*, which was a statement of papal supremacy, based on divine origin, on all matters spiritual and temporal. The French indicted the pope, and Philip sent his chief adviser, Nogaret, to arrest the pope in September 1303; though the pope was physically assaulted, the townspeople rose to his support and rescued him from Nogaret.

Several days later, the pope returned to Rome but was still in shock over the violent attack; a fever led to his sudden death in October 1303. It was clear that Philip had won the battle for supremacy. Boniface thus came to represent the deposition of the papacy and ecclesiastical power from world dominance; never again would the secular powers be challenged for it.

Bibliography: T.S.R. Boase, *Boniface VIII*, 1933.

Connie Evans

BRACTON, HENRY DE (D. 1268). A cleric and royal judge during the reign of *Henry III of England, he is traditionally identified as the author of the legal treatise *De legibus et consuetudinibus Angliae* (On the Laws and Customs of England), though that attribution is now controversial.

Henry de Bracton probably came from one of two Devonshire villages, Bratton Clovelly or Bratton Fleming, and thus the correct spelling of his surname is likely "Bratton." Though some scholars have speculated that he received a doctorate in civil and canon law at Oxford, there is no hard evidence that he ever attended the university. Bracton was an ecclesiastic, and by 1245 he had a dispensation allowing him to hold three benefices simultaneously. He served as a clerk to the royal justice William Raleigh, who was also bishop of Norwich and then Winchester and who probably helped him to enter royal service by introducing him to Henry III's brother Richard, earl of Cornwall. Bracton was a clerk of the court of King's Bench by 1240, a justice in Eyre by 1244, and a justice in King's Bench from 1247 to 1251 and again from 1253 to 1257. Why he left the bench is uncertain, though it may have been related to the political disturbances that led to the baronial revolt led by Simon de *Montfort, the Younger in 1258. In any case, he continued to enjoy ecclesiastical preferment, obtaining a series of benefices between 1259 and 1264 that culminated with him becoming chancellor of Exeter Cathedral, where he is buried.

The great constitutional and legal historian F. W. Maitland described the treatise long credited to Bracton as "the crown and flower of English medieval jurisprudence." It is the first work to comprehensively describe the common law as it stood following the many innovations introduced by *Henry II of England, and no one would attempt so full a treatment of the subject again until William Blackstone in the eighteenth century. Though the treatise shows some influence of civil law in its systematic approach, it is much more "English" than "Roman," making extensive use of cases recorded on the court rolls since the late twelfth century to explain the principles and operation of the common law in every area to which it applied. Though there were various texts in the later Middle Ages (including the fourteenth-century summary known as *Fleta*), it was not published until 1569 (by Richard Tottel). Sir Travers Twiss' edition and translation in the Rolls Series (1878–1883) is flawed; the authoritative Latin text is the twentieth-century edition by George E. Woodbine, upon which the definitive English translation by S. E. Thorne is based.

Recent scholarship has raised questions about the treatise and Bracton. Maitland believed that Bracton wrote the entire treatise between 1250 and 1256. However, Thorne claims that a clerk associated with the justice Martin of Pateshull (who retired in 1229) wrote parts of the treatise in the late 1220s or early 1230s and that Bracton merely added to it. He provides evidence that points to William Raleigh, who was one of Pateshull's clerks and whom Bracton, in turn, served as a clerk. J. L. Barton defends Maitland's views about Bracton's authorship and the dates of the treatise's production, but—unlike Thorne—he challenges Maitland's notion that the treatise accurately describes practice in Henry III's courts. Paul Brand largely agrees with Thorne about the authorship and dating of the treatise, though he argues more strongly that Raleigh wrote major portions of it. However, he supports Barton with regard to the treatise's accuracy, arguing that it is useful for the 1220s and 1230s if checked against the plea rolls but is unreliable thereafter. Brand also contends that Maitland exaggerated Bracton's importance as a justice, seeing him instead as a minor figure. All of this notwithstanding, the treatise itself remains historically significant.

Bibliography: J. L. Barton, "The Mystery of Bracton," *Journal of Legal History* 14 (1993): 1–142; H. de Bracton, *De legibus et consuetudinibus Angliae*, ed. G. E. Woodbine and trans. S. E. Thorne, 1915–1942; P. Brand, "The Age of Bracton," in *The History of English Law: Centenary Essays on "Pollock and Maitland,"* ed. J. Hudson, 1996; F. Pollock and F. W. Maitland, *History of English Law before the Time of Edward I*, vol. 1, 2nd ed., 1968.

William B. Robison

BRENDAN, SAINT (C. 486–575). Saint Brendan (Brénainn) is one of a number of sixth-century monastic founders of Munster origin who founded major churches in the midlands of Ireland. As the archetypal Irish voyaging saint, or *peregrinus*, Brendan's medieval and modern fame is sustained principally, however, by the internationally popular Latin prose tale *Nauigatio sancti Brendani abbatis* (The Voyage of St. Brendan the Abbot), a remarkable and original monastic romance that survives in over 125 medieval copies. The *Nauigatio* later gave rise to a popular belief that Brendan voyaged to the New World, for which he is still most commonly remembered.

The verifiable details of Brendan's life are few. He was certainly of the Alltraige, a sept based around Tralee, county Kerry. Later genealogies describe him variously as belonging to the Ciarraige and to the Corca Dhuibhne, but as the Ciarraige Luachra absorbed the Alltraige after the eighth century, then spread west into Corco Dhuibhne (the western part of the Dingle Peninsula, where Brandon Mountain represents the pilgrimage focus of his cult), we may regard these later attributions as reflecting the spread of the saint's cult after his death. He died in 575.

Saint Brendan's principal monastery was at Clonfert (county Galway), founded in 558. His cult links him also to monasteries Annaghdown (county Galway), Inishadroum (county Clare), Ardfert (county Kerry), as well as various other foundations in Ireland, Scotland, Wales, and Brittany, which are probably attributable to the later spread of his cult. Whether or not Brendan made a famous ocean voyage remains unclear. *Adamnan (d. 704) describes him as voyaging to Scotland, as does the *Life of St Malo* (c. 878). The *Nauigatio Brendani* (c. 780) describes a voyage to an ocean Promised Land near Ireland; it is a mixture of biblical eschatology combined with geographical details of Irish voyages to the Faroes and Iceland from later than Brendan's time.

Bibliography: J. M. Wooding, ed., *The Otherworld Voyage in Irish Literature and History*, rev. ed., 2000.

Jonathan M. Wooding

BRIAN BORU (C. 926–1014). The first high king of Ireland, Brian Boru was born Brian mac Cennétig, into the royal family of Munster. In 975, Imar, king of Limerick, killed Brian's brother, King Mahon. Brian pursued and slew Imar and his family, gaining both Munster, by right, and Limerick, by conquest, as his own kingdom. In the following years, Brian proceeded to grab both Connacht and Leinster, and finally, in 1002, he demanded that Mael Sechnaill, the last descendant in the 600-year dynastic rule of the O'Neills over Tara, recognize him as high king of all Ireland. The title Boru ("of the Tributes") he earned by exacting payments from former petty kings, using the money to rebuild Viking-sacked monasteries and libraries.

Though a hero to many for having unified Ireland and resisted the Vikings, Brian ruled by force and was not universally popular. His possession of Leinster, in particular, had angered many of its citizens. In 1014, some men of Leinster coordinated with the Vikings now settled in Dublin to overthrow what they perceived as Brian's tyranny. The two armies met on 23 April 1014 at Clontarf (incidentally where Mael had seceded half of his possessions to Brian in 997, five years before giving up the rest of his rule to the new high king). By the time of the battle of Clontarf, Brian was a fairly old man, and he could not fight as fiercely as he had before; his army beat the Leinster-Viking challengers in the battle, but Brian was killed in his tent that day.

Bibliography: R. C. Newman, *Brian Boru, King of Ireland*, 1983.

Zina Petersen

BRUNHILDE (545–613). Wife of Sigebert I, mother of and regent for Childebert II, she reappears in the legend of the Nibelung.

Brunhilde, the daughter of the Spanish Visigoth king Athanagild, became the wife of Sigebert I, king of the Frankish realm of Austrasia, while her sister Galswinthe became one of the wives of Sigebert's half brother Chilperic I of the Frankish realm of Neustria (566). Chilperic favored another wife, the freed slave *Fredegund, with the result that Galswinthe was found strangled in her bed, whether by Chilperic himself or by his servants is uncertain, in 567. Brunhilde urged Sigebert to seek compensation for the death of his sister-in-law; he was offered Galswinthe's dowry in recompense. Fredegund, displeased with this, launched numerous assassination attempts against her Austrasian in-laws (before and after her husband Chilperic's death by assassination in 584): against Sigebert (in 575: successful); against Brunhilde (in 584: unsuccessful); and against Childebert II, the son of Sigebert and Brunhilde, who succeeded Sigebert as king of Austrasia (in 585: unsuccessful; in 595: successful).

Following Sigebert's death in 575, Brunhilde became regent of Austrasia, serving as guardian to her son Childebert II and later to Childebert's two sons Theudebert II and Theuderic II. Part of this time she spent imprisoned and exiled by Fredegund in Paris and Rouen, where she met and married (her nephew) Merovech, son of Chilperic I of Neustria (but *not* of Fredegund) and half brother of Chlothar II; the couple later separated. Following a regency under his mother Fredegund, Chlothar II became king of Neustria at the age of thirteen upon her death in 597 and later ordered (his aunt and former sister-in-law) Brunhilde's torture and death in 613, as well as the death of her great-grandson Sigebert II (son of Theuderic II), who was Brunhilde's current choice for king of Austrasia. This brought all the Frankish realms temporarily together under Chlotar II.

The figures of Brunhilde and Sigebert are of particular interest to literary scholars and folklorists because of their reappearance in the legendary Nibelungen narrative in its German and Old Norse versions, as Brünhild/Brynhild and Siegfried/Sigurd. Chronicle and legend overlap in the following elements: S., the lover of B., is slain in treacherous fashion by his in-laws. The Nibelungen legend-complex has also attracted at least two other historical figures, who similarly appear out of context and chronology: Attila the Hun and Ermanaric the Goth.

Bibliography: *France before Charlemagne: A Translation from the Grandes Chroniques*, trans. R. Levine, 1990; Gregory of Tours, *The History of the Franks*, 1974.

Sandra Ballif Straubhaar

BRUNO THE CARTHUSIAN, SAINT (C. 1033–1101). Born in Cologne to a noble family, Bruno distinguished himself at the cathedral school at Rheims and was ordained as a priest before beginning to teach theology there. He became master of the schools in 1056 and chancellor of the archdiocese in c. 1075. In 1076 he and the archbishop had a major disagreement over the latter's appointment to his post. After calling the archbishop a simonist, Bruno lost his teaching post.

In 1084 Bruno and six friends built a religious center at Grande Chartreuse, a quiet wilderness area in the mountains near Grenoble, France. There the seven men lived quietly in the quasi-communal lifestyle combining prayer, labor, and repentance that characterize medieval and modern Carthusians. The name comes from the French word for "charterhouse," used by the English to describe these monasteries. In 1090 Bruno's former student Pope *Urban II called him to Rome but was convinced to allow Bruno to found another religious center with like standards at La Torre in Calabria. He was in the process of establishing another monastery at San Stefano-in-Bosco when he died. Eventually, Carthusian monasteries sprang up all over Europe, though they were generally more prevalent in France and Italy.

Many believed the Carthusian monks followed the strictest religious rule, though the order nevertheless attracted many followers. The Carthusians had separate individual living quarters and only convened as a group for nightly offices, mass, and dinner on special feast days. Each member prepared his own meals from food grown in his own garden and followed the daily offices, though some communal agricultural plots existed. In addition, the Carthusians were expected to take a vow of silence, and the Carthusian life was generally a lonely, quiet one with the motto "O beatitudo solitudo: O sola beatitudo." Frequently, Carthusians excelled as scholars, such as Ludolphus of Saxony, whose *Life of*

Christ was widely read in the fourteenth century. Saint Bruno himself is re-membered through the publication of two letters, one to his brethren at Grande Chartreuse and another to a friend. In these letters, Bruno praises the life of solitary contemplation, encourages others to remain steadfast in the Lord, and extols the joys of nature.

Bibliography: H. G. Koenigsberger, *Medieval Europe, 400–1500*, 1987.

Alana Cain Scott

BURCHARD OF WORMS (C. 965–1025). Bishop of Worms and canonist, he was the author of two legal collections, the *Decretum Burchardi* and the *Lex familiae Wormatiensis ecclesiae.*

He was born into an aristocratic family in Hesse and educated in Koblenz. After his initial education, he traveled from center to center to study, although none of these places has been identified with certainty. In 993, Archbishop Willigis invited him to Mainz to join his household, and he was made provost of St. Viktor in Mainz. In 995, he became a member of the royal court chapel until he was raised to the see of Worms by Emperor *Otto III in 1000, where he remained until his death in 1025.

Burchard appears to have been one of the most influential bishops of his time. He took part in Emperor Henry II's second invasion of Italy in 1013–1014 and was present at several significant councils, including the Council of Frankfurt in 1007 at which the bishopric of Bamberg was founded. His most important work, however, was concentrated on the city of Worms and its church. He rebuilt the Cathedral church of St. Peter, added several new churches and a monastery for women (and appointed his sister as abbess), multiplied the church's income, and divided the city itself into four parishes, which still form the basis of city government. His most important work, however, consists of two legal collections, the *Decretum Burchardi* and the *Lex familiae Wormatien-sis ecclesiae.*

Burchard's second work, the *Lex familiae Wormatiensis ecclesiae*, deals with a variety of legal issues that had arisen in the bishopric of Worms during his primature. The document includes a description of the variety of social groups dependent on the bishop, but although it sheds light on the organization of the bishopric, it is of more local significance than his *Decretum.*

The *Decretum Burchardi*, consisting of twenty books of questions on the sacraments and on penance, was completed before 1023. The systematic organ-ization of the *Decretum* would have made it relatively simple to find relevant information on specific topics, and the scope of the material he included (1,786 separate chapters), drawn from such diverse sources as early collections of church council decrees, penitential handbooks, and theological writings, ensured that other collections were superseded. In fact, Burchard's *Decretum* remained influential for several centuries after it was compiled. Nearly eighty manuscripts have survived from Germany, France, and Italy, and it continued to be copied until the thirteenth century, after which its influence seems to have waned, since no further manuscripts were produced. This decline was no doubt largely the result of the existence of *Gratian's *Decretals*.

Nonetheless, Burchard's *Decretum* exercised a lasting influence on medieval canon law. It is cited with authority in the *acta* of several church councils (e.g., Seligenstadt 1023). More important, it was used by a number of twelfth-century canon law specialists such as *Peter Damian, Humber of Silva Candida, and *Ivo of Chartres. The work of Ivo in turn deeply influenced Gratian (in his *Concordia discordantium canonum*, or *Decretals*).

Bibliography: H. Hoffmann and R. Pokorny, *Das Dekret des Bischofs Burchard von Worms: Textstufen, Frühe Verbreitung, Vorlagen*, 1991.

William Schipper

C

CÆDMON (FL. C. 675). Cædmon was a farm laborer at the monastery of Whitby during *Hild's tenure as abbess in the seventh century. He is said to have written poetic paraphrases of Bible stories from both Testaments. Other than this his dates are unknown, as is any evidence of his poetry apart from the example found in *Bede in conjunction with the following story.

Each time the harp was passed about after a feast and songs called for from each of the workers of the monastery, Cædmon was embarrassed at his inability to compose and slipped silently out of the room when his turn came. One night, having been assigned care of the cattle, he went to sleep in the barn. While sleeping he heard a voice call, "Cædmon! Sing me something." When Cædmon protested that he could not sing, the visitor repeated the command, insisting that he sing about the beginning of created things. Upon this, according to Bede, Cædmon sang the following:

Now we must praise the Maker of the heavenly kingdom, the power of the Creator and his counsel, the deeds of the Father of glory and how He, since he is the eternal God, was the Author of all marvels and first created the heavens as a roof for the children of men and then, the almighty Guardian of the human race, created the earth.

The following day, when Cædmon was brought to the abbess Hild with his story, she had him speak with scholars of the monastery, who decided that his gift was from the grace of God. He was given a scriptural passage from which to make a song and produced a fine poem. At Hild's urging, he entered the monastery and devoted his life to production of sacred poetry.

He died a holy death after producing many poems drawn from Scripture, none of which survive. The above example, known as "Cædmon's Hymn," exemplifies Old English metrics: alliterating half lines marked by formulaic diction and variation of conventional epithets, in this case for God.

Bibliography: S. B. Greenfield and D. G. Calder, *A New Critical History of Old English Literature*, 1986.

Patricia Silber

CAESARIUS OF ARLES (CAESARIUS ARELATENSIS), SAINT (C. 469–542).

Bishop of Arles from 502 until 537, he played a significant role in establishing Arles as a major ecclesiastical center during the early sixth century, while his many extant homilies are a primary source for the social history of the period.

Caesarius was born about 469 or 470 to a Gallic-Roman aristocratic family in the territory of Châlon, in Burgundy, where he also received his initial education. At about seventeen, he entered the local clergy (his *vita* suggests it was done secretly). Two years later, he entered the monastery of Lérins, a monastery with close connections to Arles in southern Gaul. A few years after his arrival, he was appointed cellarer and thereby made responsible for distributing food and wine to the monks. After only a short while, though, he was removed from the post, accused of being too niggardly by his fellow monks. For the remainder of his time at Lérins, Caesarius followed an increasingly excessive ascetic life, until the abbot ordered him to move to Arles to recover his health.

The bishop of Arles at the time of his arrival was Aeonius, a relative of Caesarius from Châlon. The latter's ambition, education, and his connection with Lérins convinced Aeonius to appoint Caesarius his successor. In 498, Caesarius was appointed abbot of the men's monastery in Arles, and upon Aeonius's death in 502, he was elected bishop, although opposition among the clergy delayed the election for more than a year. Because of his origins in Burgundy, he was considered somewhat suspect by the Visigothic rulers who controlled Arles, and he was arrested and charged with treason on several occasions. In 505, Alaric exiled Caesarius to Bordeaux, but he was allowed to return in 506. In 508, he undertook the building of a monastery for women in Arles, particularly at the urging of his sister Caesaria. Its completion was delayed by the outbreak of war between the Visigoths and an alliance of Franks and Burgundians. The Franks defeated the Visigoths, and besieged Arles, but were unable to capture the city, and the siege was lifted by an Ostrogothic force under *Theodoric.

Caesarius pawned or sold most of the silver and gold dishes that belonged to the bishop's palace and used the proceeds to ransom the many hostages the Franks had taken, an act that endeared him to the people of the city and helped him to reestablish his authority as bishop. Over the next two decades, he was able to found several monasteries in or near Arles, preside over several councils, and extend his episcopal influence over the Burgundian territories that had traditionally fallen under the control of Arles but since the wars with the Burgundians had been lost to that control. During these decades, Caesarius set in motion a concerted effort to depaganize the countryside around Arles and to convert the local population that had continued to follow their traditional worship of Roman and local deities to Christianity.

Between 526 and 535, a struggle took place between the Roman emperor ruling from Ravenna and the bishops of Rome over who should be pope. Although Caesarius had managed to consolidate his control over his own diocese, bishops of other cities frequently opposed him. In 533, Caesarius called a council of bishops at Marseilles to deal with charges of sexual misconduct and selling church property without authority against Contumelius, bishop of Riez. Although the council found Contumelius guilty, it could not agree on a suitable penalty. Caesarius appealed for a ruling to Pope John, but he died shortly after making a ruling, and his successors nullified the decision and ruled against Caesarius and for Contumelius. In succeeding years, this and similar lack of support from Rome helped undermine Caesarius' authority within his own diocese. His position was not helped by the new war that broke out in 535.

By 537, Arles was no longer under the direct control of the emperor at Ravenna but instead now formed part of the Frankish kingdom, with the result for Caesarius that he could no longer depend on support either from Rome or from Ravenna. He saw his status reduced to a subordinate one in the Frankish ecclesiastical province. He had always considered himself to be the papal legate to Provence, although political realities had never allowed him to exercise that power outside Provence, but that position changed dramatically once Provence, and Arles, came under the control of the Franks. Caesarius never participated fully in any of the Merovingian church councils held during the last years of his life, though Arles was represented at them. He died on 27 August 542, at age seventy-two.

Although Caesarius was not as successful in his episcopal control as he might have wished, and frequently battled both ecclesiastical and secular opponents, he remains one of the most important figures of his age. He succeeded in establishing Arles as the most important episcopal see in Provence and founded a number of churches and monasteries in the region, some of which continued throughout the Middle Ages. He was also mostly successful in regularizing such matters as ownership by priests of property, church discipline, and ordination. He appears to have been a dynamic preacher, and collections of his homilies circulated from an early time. These homilies today form a significant body of our knowledge about social and religious conditions among ordinary people in the late fifth and early sixth centuries.

Bibliography: W. E. Klingshirn, *Caesarius of Arles: Life, Testament, Letters*, 1994; W. E. Klingshirn, *Caesarius of Arles: The Making of a Christian Community in Late Antique Gaul*, 1994.

William Schipper

CALIXTUS II (CALLISTUS), POPE (C. 1050–1124, PONTIFICATE 1119–1124).
Guido, archbishop of Vienne, was confirmed as pope on 1 March 1119 and continued his struggle to end the lay Investiture Controversy with the Holy Roman Emperor. As Calixtus II, he eventually settled the investiture prob-

lem through the Concordat of Worms (1122), which allowed the papacy to retain spiritual authority and confine imperial authority to primarily secular German matters. The Investiture Controversy ended temporarily with the ratification of the Concordat at the First Lateran Council (1123).

Calixtus, who was related to many European sovereigns, began his attack on investiture by calling a council at Rheims in October 1119. He took a firm stance against Holy Roman Emperor *Henry V, reissuing his excommunication and banning lay investiture. Each side remained suspicious of the other even though an attempt at an agreement was made. Following the success at Rheims, Calixtus triumphantly marched into Rome in 1120. The antipope, Gregory VIII, fled but was captured and kept in a monastery. Calixtus was now secure in Rome and continued to receive support from his European relations.

Henry gradually became more conciliatory, and he and Calixtus made concessions to each other at Worms in 1122. Henry agreed to give up investiture and allow free elections and consecration of bishops. Ecclesiastical offices, symbolized by the ring and staff, were for clerics only. Calixtus allowed Henry to be present at elections, and the emperor could settle disputed elections. The benefice, with the sceptre as a symbol, was now separated from the ecclesiastical office. Henry recognized Calixtus, and a period of peace ensued for thirty years, allowing breathing room in the imperial-papal struggles.

The First Lateran Council, held in March 1123, ratified the Concordat of Worms, which secured papal supremacy in spiritual matters. This first council of the Church of the West reaffirmed reforming principles, and papal stature began to rise. Although Calixtus died on 13 December 1124, he helped strengthen the papacy's spiritual position against encroachments by the Holy Roman Emperor.

Bibliography: R. P. McBrien, *Lives of the Popes*, 1997; W. Ullmann, *A Short History of the Papacy in the Middle Ages*, 1972.

Paul Miller

CANUTE. *See* CNUT I.

CAPELLANUS, ANDREAS (FL. 1174–1186). Chaplain to *Marie de Champagne, daughter of *Eleanor of Aquitaine, Andreas Capellanus undertook to write a treatise on "the art of love" at the urging of his patroness. Little else is known of "Andreas the Chaplain" except that he signed several charters before 1186 and called himself "chaplain of the royal court."

In his late-twelfth-century treatise *The Art of Courtly Love* (*De arte honeste amandi*), Andreas drew upon a tradition as old as Ovid and sparked a critical controversy that extends into the present day, for it codified the rules of "courtly love." Distilled to its barest outline, "courtly love" delineates a medieval code of conduct concerning the attitudes and practices of love thought suitable especially for the members of the nobility. Its generic attributes in medieval romance call for a valiant knight or gallant courtier to seek the favor of a beautiful noblewoman, whom he adores from afar and for whom he overcomes numerous obstacles to prove his devotion. The lady, however, remains unattainable. Whether she is indifferent to the knight, is already married, or if unmarried, is kept aloof by her father, the knight suffers in his love for her while his respect for her purity prevents the consummation of the affair. The pangs of secret love ennoble the knight and drive him toward greater exploits, and although he may never gain the beloved, their relationship is often symbolized through a love token and memorialized in poetry or song. Thus, the perfect lover is ever in a state of unfulfilled desire. In C. S. Lewis's memorable summary, courtly love consists in "Humility, Courtesy, Adultery, and the Religion of Love."

Drawing for inspiration upon Ovid's *The Art of Love* (*Ars amatoria*) and *The Cure of Love* (*Remedia amoris*), Arab mystical philosophy brought back from the crusades, and popular devotion to the Virgin Mary, "amour courtois" seems to have flourished first among the troubadour poets of southern France, who found a willing patron in Eleanor of Aquitaine, the wife first of *Louis VII of France and then *Henry II of England. Through her influence, the ideas of courtly love spread into northern France and England. The *Lais* of *Marie de France ring the changes on all types of romance among nobles, ranging from puerile, illicit, or sterile love to mutual, mature, and idealized relationships, while the *Roman de la Rose*, one of the most influential literary texts of the medieval period, is an allegory of courtly love. Ideas of courtly love influenced the German "minnesinger" lyrics and epics such as *Gottfried von Strassburg's *Tristan und Isolde* (c. 1210), while the late thirteenth century found the "Stil-novisti" or "sweet new style" spread into Italy and influencing Dante and Petrarch, each of whom elevated their beloved (Beatrice and Laura) beyond the realm of physical into a symbol for divine love. This tradition fusing courtly values, social decorum, and moral ideals culminated in Castiglione's handbook of noble behavior, *The Courtier*, translated into English by Thomas Hoby in 1561, and can be seen in works by Spenser, Sidney, and Shakespeare.

The Art of Courtly Love itself is divided into three books: Book I, Introduction to the Treatise on Love; Book II, How Love May Be Retained; and Book III, The Rejection of Love. In Book I, Andreas is keen to begin by asserting that love is purely heterosexual, between persons of the opposite sex, for "Whatever nature forbids, love is ashamed to accept," and the chapter goes on to detail both the physical and psychological effects of love and the means by which women of different classes and social stations (from noblewomen to prostitutes) might be induced to love. Interspersing didactic material and letters with imagined dialogues between men and women, Book I is the longest section of *The Art of Courtly Love* and contains a secular dudecalogue of love:

1. Thou shalt avoid avarice like the deadly pestilence and shalt embrace its opposite.
2. Thou shalt keep thyself chaste for the sake of her whom thou lovest.

3. Thou shalt not knowingly strive to break up a correct love affair that someone else is engaged in.

4. Thou shalt not choose for thy love anyone whom a natural sense of shame forbids thee to marry.

5. Be mindful completely to avoid falsehood.

6. Thou shalt not have many who know of thy love affair.

7. Being obedient in all things to the commands of ladies, thou shalt ever strive to ally thyself to the service of Love.

8. In giving and receiving love's solaces let modesty be ever present.

9. Thou shalt speak no evil.

10. Thou shalt not be a revealer of love affairs.

11. Thou shalt be in all things polite and courteous.

12. In practising the solaces of love thou shalt not exceed the desires of thy lover.

Ever mindful of social and class distinctions, Book II continues with advice about how love, once consummated, may be maintained or even increased. Andreas' advice is that reticence, on the one hand, breeds desire, whereas charm, on the other, increases yearning. He completes Book II with thirty-one rules of love, of which the first six follow:

1. Marriage is no real excuse for not loving.

2. He who is jealous cannot love.

3. No one can be bound by a double love.

4. It is well known that love is always increasing or decreasing.

5. That which a lover takes against the will of his beloved has no relish.

6. Boys do not love until they reach the age of maturity.

The Art of Courtly Love concludes with Book III—The Rejection of Love— where Andreas seems to ironically undercut the previous discussion with a rather conventional and misogynistic rationale: "Read this little book, then, not as one seeking to take up the life of a lover, but that, invigorated by the theory and trained to excite the minds of women to love, you may, by refraining from so doing, win an eternal recompense and thereby deserve a greater reward from God." Depending upon the degree of veracity they posit for Book III, scholars continue to debate the degree to which the canons of courtly love constitute a medieval reality at one extreme or perhaps an elaborate and ironic joke. For feminist scholars, the canons of courtly love are no joke, but when compared to extraliterary texts like court proceedings and legal accounts, they appear to rationalize the powerlessness of women and to justify sexual exploitation.

Throughout the later Middle Ages the idea of courtly love is refracted through a wide variety of literary and historical texts, and it is possible to trace the devolution of this courtly ideal. In addition, many of the great romance cycles of the later Middle Ages, those of Arthur and the Round Table, Tristan and

Isolde, Troilus and Criseyde, have at their center the problem of love in its many forms, and they idealize, investigate, allegorize, spiritualize, criticize, and even subvert the notions of "amour courtois." One need only to compare Thomas Malory's fifteenth-century version of the Lancelot story, "The Knight of the Cart," with *Chrétien's twelfth-century "Lancelot, ou le chevalier de la charrette" to measure both the change in the social conditions of knighthood and the denigration of the ideal of courtly love. On one hand, in Chrétien's tale, Lancelot, after losing his horse in battle, hesitates for a moment before boarding a cart, representative of lower-class scandal, to find Guenevere. Guenevere later upbraids him for the moment's hesitation. For Chrétien, Lancelot's self-abnegation and public humiliation in mounting a cart piloted by a dwarf constitute a test of love different from, but no less challenging than, deeds of heroism. On the other, Malory's version of the story, 300 years later, finds a very different Lancelot. Having been unhorsed in battle, Lancelot demands that the cart take him to his destination. When the first carter delays, Lancelot strikes him dead and the other carter quickly accedes to the knight's command so that he and the queen can consummate their passion. In Chrétien, Lancelot is a hero in service to his lady; in Malory, he's a bully on his way to a tryst.

Bibliography: A. Capellanus, *The Art of Courtly Love*, trans. J. J. Parry, 1960; K. Gravdal, *Ravishing Maidens: Writing Rape in Medieval French Literature and Law*, 1991; C. S. Lewis, *The Allegory of Love: A Study in Medieval Tradition*, 1936; B. O'Donoghue, *The Courtly Love Tradition*, 1982.

Daniel Kline

CASSIODORUS, FLAVIUS MAGNUS AURELIUS (C. 490–C. 584).

Politician, scholar, and teacher, Flavius Magnus Aurelius Cassiodorus Senator was also the author of religious, historical, political, and pedagogical texts.

He was born into a noble, well-connected Italian family sometime between 484 and 490. His family lands were in Scyllacium (modern Calabria); it was there that he would eventually found the monastic community Vivarium upon his retirement. His initial calling, however, was secular: Cassiodorus' father rose to the position of praetorian prefect, and his talented young son served as his father's aide. In turn the young Cassiodorus moved quickly through the political ranks under *Theodoric the Ostrogoth, holding the offices of quaestor, consul, and magister officiorum, succeeding *Boethius to this final position upon the philosopher's imprisonment and execution. Cassiodorus was something of a political prodigy in his early career and was a confidant and adviser to Theodoric.

The circumstances of Cassiodorus' early education are unclear; he was perhaps taught by Dionysius Exiguus. In any case, he soon became indispensable at Theodoric's court for his epistolary skill; Cassiodorus' rhetorical style is ornate and rather baroque. Upon his retirement from public office c. 537–538, he collected his various official letters into a work of twelve books entitled the *Variae*. This miscellany is an important source for sixth-century Italian history and also exerted a certain influence in the later Middle Ages in terms of the conventions and models of official political discourse and correspondence. Near the end of his secular career he also wrote a treatise on the soul, the *De anima*, a work that shows his early interest in theological matters. Surviving works from this period also include the *Chronica* (an account of the rulers of Italy), the *Laudes* (fragments of panegyric poems), and a history of the Goths in twelve books, which for the most part has not survived—all that remains are extracts used by *Jordanes in his *Getica*.

After the collapse of Gothic rule in Italy, and the publication of the *Variae*, Cassiodorus retired from his political career and apparently felt an insistent call to the more deeply religious life. For reasons that remain unclear, he traveled to Constantinople and resided there for some portion of the years between 540 and 550. In Constantinople, he deepened his knowledge of letters, both sacred and secular, and composed a commentary on the Psalms, the *Expositio Psalmorum*. Cassiodorus' work was modeled on Augustine's *Enarrationes in Psalmos* but with a more clearly pedagogical purpose in mind. The *Expositio* was perhaps written with an eye to the next great endeavor of Cassiodorus' final years: his return to his ancestral home in Italy and the foundation there of the monastery Vivarium.

The exact date and circumstances of the monastery's foundation, as well as Cassiodorus' exact role in its creation, are matters of some dispute. It was founded, by Cassiodorus himself or with the help of others, at some time in the 540s or early 550s; at any rate, Cassiodorus retired to the monastery in 554. The monastery consisted of a social community organized, apparently, by a rule devised by Cassiodorus himself and an attached "outpost" for those embracing the strict isolation of the cenobitic path. Vivarium was a center for book production, collection, and translation of important Greek texts into Latin, including the work of John Chrysostom and the historian Josephus. Cassiodorus wished to merge the tradition of classical rhetoric and secular letters with theological discourse. To this end he produced his *Institutes* (c. 562), an introduction to divine and secular learning for educational use in the monastery, a guide to responsible education. The first book of the *Institutes* ("The Divine Letters") provides a guide to reading and interpreting the Scriptures, patristic authors, and sundry other basic matters of monastic life. The second book ("The Secular Letters") is a compact treatise on the seven liberal arts: grammar, rhetoric, dialectic, arithmetic, music, geometry, and astronomy.

Cassiodorus' monastery did not last past the seventh century, but his works were known and respected throughout the Middle Ages, some to a greater degree than others. The second book of the *Institutes* provided a popular compact introduction to the liberal arts; the *De orthographia* (a work on spelling and the scribe's art) found similar popularity in monasteries across Europe; the *Expositio Psalmorum* had a wide circulation; and the *Variae* was an important text in political philosophy of the later Middle Ages.

Bibliography: Cassiodorus, *An Introduction to Divine and Human Readings*, trans. L. W. Jones, 1966; J. J. O'Donnell, *Cassiodorus*, 1979.

Andrew Scheil

CHARLEMAGNE (742–814). Charlemagne, a Frankish ruler who established the first European empire of the Middle Ages, patronized the revival of ancient learning known as the Carolingian Renaissance and laid the foundation for medieval Latin Christendom, which fused classical influences, Christianity, and Germanic culture into a distinctively Western civilization. His name was Charles; only in later centuries was he known as Charlemagne ("Charles the Great").

For several generations Charlemagne's ancestors had served the increasingly feeble Merovingian kings of the Franks as mayors of the palace, governing the kingdom in their name. Pepin II (of Herstal) made the Carolingians the most powerful family in the kingdom during his ascendancy from 687 to 714, and his son *Charles Martel ruled from 714 to 741 with almost complete disregard for the Merovingians. Martel's sons, *Pepin III (the Short) and Carloman, shared the office of mayor until 747, when the latter became a monk. By this time, the family had earned papal goodwill by helping Anglo-Saxon missionaries, notably Saint *Boniface of Wessex, to replace residual Frankish paganism with Christianity. Thus, in 751 Pope Zacharias supported Pepin III when he seized the throne from Childeric III, and in 754 Pope *Stephen II crowned the new king at St. Denis. Pepin reciprocated by attacking the Lombards in Italy in 755 and 756, eliminating their threat to Rome, and handing over to the papacy the land subsequently known as the Republic of St. Peter, or Papal States—the Donation of Pepin. His eldest son Charlemagne accompanied him on this campaign.

Charlemagne was born to Pepin and his consort Bertrada before they were canonically married, which raised questions about his legitimacy. His younger, clearly legitimate brother Carloman was born in 751. Pope Stephen recognized both brothers as Pepin's heirs in 754 and referred to them as "kings" when calling upon Pepin for assistance in 756. Nevertheless, at his death in 768, Pepin bequeathed the main portion of his kingdom to Carloman, leaving Charlemagne a long strip of land along its western and northern borders, adjacent to the Atlantic and north of the Rhine. However, when Carloman died in 771, Charlemagne received the homage of his vassals and reunified the kingdom.

From this point, Charlemagne launched one of the most remarkable careers of conquest in history. He conducted around sixty campaigns, leading about half himself. In 770, at his mother's urging, he ended his first marriage to the Frankish woman Himiltrude and married Desiderata, daughter of the Lombard king Desiderius. However, a year later, he repudiated her as well and in 773, he invaded Lombardy, where his former father-in-law was harboring Carloman's heirs. In 774, he captured the Lombard crown, visited Pope Hadrian I in Rome, and confirmed the Donation of Pepin. Between 772 and 804, Charlemagne fought a long series of wars against the pagan Saxons in northern Germany, who bitterly resisted his rule and his attempt to convert them to Christianity. He defeated their chieftain Widukind in 779, put down a revolt in 782 with the massacre of over 4,500 rebels, and thereafter deported vast numbers of Saxons and repopulated the area with Franks. In 788, he subdued Duke Tassilo III of Bavaria, and from there he moved on to conquer the Avars (or "Huns") in Austria and Hungary, north of the Byzantine Empire. In 791, he drove them into the Danube valley, and in 795 his son Pepin expelled them from Carinthia and captured the vast Avar treasure. Charlemagne's only significant failure in this period came in his war against the Christian Basques south of the Pyrenees in 778. He also conducted campaigns against the Slavs in the northeast, and in 810, he was en route to war with the Danish Godofrid when the latter was assassinated.

By 800, Charlemagne ruled all of western and central Europe except for the British Isles (held by Anglo-Saxons and Celts), Scandinavia (occupied by Danish, Norwegian, and Swedish Vikings), southern Italy (still part of the Byzantine Empire), and the Iberian peninsula (largely in Muslim hands). He further extended his influence through diplomatic relations with a series of Byzantine rulers; the Anglo-Saxon *Offa of Mercia; *Hārūn al-Rashīd, the caliph of Baghdad; and others. In 800, he made his final visit to Rome (having done so earlier in 774, 781, and 787) to put down an antipapal rebellion that had erupted in 799. On Christmas Day, Pope *Leo III placed the imperial crown on his head as he knelt in prayer. While this might seem appropriate for the man who had created the Carolingian Empire, it has proven controversial. According to the *Annales regni Francorum*, it was the Franks who suggested the coronation, while Charlemagne's contemporary biographer *Einhard claims that his king was surprised and angry about it.

Whatever the case, it allowed Charlemagne and his Frankish heirs to claim the mantle of the ancient Roman emperors, and after the Saxon *Otto the Great acquired the crown in the tenth century, his descendants (somewhat inaccurately) described their German realm as the Holy Roman Empire. Charlemagne was also able to boast of equal status with the Byzantine emperors, and though the latter hardly welcomed this, by 813 he forced Michael I to recognize his title as emperor in the West. The coronation also became part of the long-running medieval debate about the relationship between imperial and papal authority.

The Carolingian Empire survived less than half a century after its creator's death, but Charlemagne's influence on the development of Western culture was more long lasting. Lacking the professional army and bureaucracy of the Roman Empire, he relied for military service and local administration upon a system of unpaid counts, margraves, and dukes, supervised through annual visitation by officials known as *missi dominici*. Desiring that these officials and the clergy be well educated, Charlemagne ordered the creation of schools in every bishopric and monastery within his realms. Using the Avar treasure (brought west in fifteen wagons, according to Einhard) and other wealth, he constructed a grand capital and palace at Aix-la-Chapelle (Aachen), built cathedrals and monasteries, and assembled an impressive group of scholars at his royal court. Eventually presided over by *Alcuin of York, this learned circle at various times included such early medieval luminaries as Einhard, *Paul the Deacon, Paulinus of Aquileia, Peter of Pisa, and *Theodulf of Orléans.

Charlemagne struggled to acquire as much learning as his demanding schedule would allow, eventually learning the rudiments of reading and writing. He patronized artists, Latin and vernacular literature, and music, and he amassed a considerable art collection and library. His stable of scholars preserved much of classical and patristic literature that survives today (often the earliest extant copy dates from the eighth or ninth century), and it was during his reign that scribes developed Carolingian miniscule, which became the standard script of the Middle Ages. Charlemagne's life is recounted in a variety of contemporary (or nearly so) biographies and chronicles, ranging from Einhard's useful (if overly flattering) *Vita Caroli magni* to the frequently dubious work of *Notker Balbulus. As the subject of medieval romantic literature, only the mythical Arthur rivals Charlemagne, whose exploits inspired many chansons de geste during the High Middle Ages (ironically, the most famous is the *Chanson de Roland*, which recounts the defeat of the Frankish king's rearguard at Roncevaux during his retreat from Spain in 778).

By his wife Himiltrude, Charlemagne produced a son named Pepin the Hunchback, who revolted after being barred from the succession and was forced into a monastery. His third wife Hildegarde was the mother of four sons, including Charles, another Pepin, Lothar, and *Louis the Pious, Charlemagne's eventual heir, as well as three daughters, including Rotrude, Bertha, and Gisela. His fourth wife gave him two more daughters, Theoderada and Himiltrude. Often a study in contrasts (e.g., his piety did not interfere with a good deal of carnal pleasure), this rough giant of a warrior (six feet four inches) was so fond of his daughters that he could hardly bear to be parted from them.

Bibliography: R. McKitterick, *The Frankish Kingdoms under the Carolingians, 751–987*, 1983; R. McKitterick, ed., *Carolingian Culture: Emulation and Innovation*, 1994; P. Riché, *The Carolingians: A Family Who Forged Europe*, trans. M. I. Allen, 1993.

William B. Robison

CHARLES II (THE BALD) (823–877).

One of the three sons of *Louis the Pious and his second wife Judith, Charles became king of the West Franks in 843 and emperor in 875 until his death in 877.

Charles was born without rights to the empire that his three older half brothers were to share. He was well educated and gained political experience early in his life when his father gave him lands in central Francia in 838. After Louis the Pious' death in 840, Charles allied himself with his half brother *Louis the German and in 841 defeated their brother *Lothar, who had claimed the throne. Charles' kingship was firmly established with the acquisition of many lands when he came to terms with Lothar and signed the Treaty of Verdun in 843.

This marked the end of civil war with his brothers, or at least a firm truce, and Charles could turn his attention to attempts to promote a revival of the Carolingian Renaissance.

However, the years from 845 were troubled by Lothar's continued attempts to overturn Verdun, as well as significant increase in Norman attacks in the west from 851. Charles faced a major crisis in his reign in 858 when Louis the German invaded his realm; his military failure was partly due to his own illness, and when he withdrew, he hoped to negotiate. Charles recovered much in the next campaigning season, and in the following decade, his skills as a military, political, and diplomatic leader served him well enough to hold on to most of his realm. After successfully containing his rebellious son and outlasting his brothers and their sons, Charles the Bald was able to triumphantly progress to Rome and be crowned emperor by Pope John VIII on Christmas Day 875. However, his years as emperor continued to be a struggle to maintain power, and he died after coming from Italy to Francia on 6 October 877.

Bibliography: J. Nelson, *Charles the Bald*, 1992.

Matthew Hussey

CHARLES III (THE SIMPLE) (879–929). The posthumous son of Louis II the "Stammerer," he was king of the West Franks from 898 to 923. The epithet "the Simple" means honest or straightforward.

Charles was passed over for the kingship in 884 and again in 888 because of his youth and the current Viking threat. In 893, Charles attempted to replace King Odo, but he lacked support among the Frankish nobles and had to wait for Odo's death (in 898) before he finally became king.

Charles' most lasting contribution to medieval history was his granting of the land around Rouen to the Viking chieftain *Rollo in 911. With this grant, Charles hoped to combat both the frequent Breton incursions in the northwest and other Viking raiders. Charles also became king of Lotharingia in 911 and chose a Lotharingian noble, Hagano, as his chief adviser. The West Frankish magnates resented Charles' preference for his Lotharingian kingdom and Hagano's influence upon the king, and in 920, they revolted, led by Robert of Neustria (Odo's brother). When Charles and they reconciled, the reconciliation was short-lived. In 922, Robert of Neustria was crowned king of the West Franks, and Charles fled to Lotharingia. He returned and killed Robert at the battle of Soissons in 923, but Charles lost the battle. Robert's son-in-law, Ralph of Burgundy, was elected king, and shortly thereafter, Herbert II of Vermandois captured Charles and imprisoned him for the remainder of his life. Charles' reign marked the beginning of the end of the Carolingian dynasty in the West Frankish kingdom.

Bibliography: P. Riché, *The Carolingians: A Family Who Forged Europe*, trans. M. I. Allen, 1993.

Ryan P. Crisp

CHARLES I OF ANJOU (1226–1285). Youngest brother of *Louis IX, king of France, he became king of Naples and Sicily and attempted to restore Latin domination over the Byzantine territory by recapturing Constantinople.

Charles received the appanage of Anjou and Maine in 1246, during a period when local barons were opposing Louis IX's rule and when *Henry III of England was pressing to regain the former English possessions. He also obtained Provence through a strategic marriage, with Beatrice, the daughter of the count of Provence-Farcalquier, thwarting the designs of the powerful Raymond of Toulouse, who wished to marry her, and emerging as ruler of a large and powerful principality. Charles supported Louis and joined him on crusade in 1248. Returning after the crusader's defeat in Egypt in 1250, he helped rule the kingdom in his brother's absence. His attitude toward his brother is unclear, although he has been described as not being particularly fond of him.

In 1263, Charles became a senator of Rome and soon realized the opportunity available to him by focusing on the Hohenstaufen holdings in southern Italy and Sicily. Soon after Manfred, the illegitimate son of *Frederick II, was crowned at Palermo in 1258, Pope Urban IV invested Charles of Anjou as Charles I, king of Naples and Sicily. He had the blessings of Louis IX and the support of Pope Clement IV when he defeated Manfred at Benevento in 1266, gaining the kingdom of Naples and Sicily in truth. However, he only secured the kingdom after defeating *Conradin in 1268, whereupon he executed him, to the dismay of the Ghibellines.

He became leader of the papal faction, the Guelphs, and gained control over large areas including cities in Tuscany, Piedmont, and Lombardy. His increase in power, however, led him to consider expanding his domains by establishing an actual empire. He allied with the former Latin emperor of Constantinople, Baldwin II, in an effort to remove Michael VIII Paleologos from the Byzantine throne. To shore up his support, he married his daughter to the son and titular heir to the Latin throne at Constantinople, Philip of Courtenay. In 1273, he sought to launch a crusade against Constantinople but was prevented by the union of the churches that took place at the Council of Lyons. He continued fighting for years in the Balkans and used the opportunity of the accession of the Angevin Pope Martin IV to prepare another expedition against Constantinople. In 1281, at Orvieto, he concluded an alliance that included Venice and Philip of Courtenay to assist him. However, due to the carefully crafted response of Michael VIII Paleologos, their plans were thwarted by a rebellion of Charles' subjects in Sicily, called the Sicilian Vespers, in 1282. Charles I was driven out of Sicily by Peter III of Aragon, Manfred's son-in-law, who had been chosen as king of Sicily by the rebels and who was an ally of Michael VIII. During the final three years of his life, Charles I attempted to regain his kingdom but finally had to renounce his designs to conquer Constantinople.

Even though Charles' dream of taking Constantinople did not materialize, poets and chroniclers viewed him as the model crusader of his generation. *Salimbene, in his *Chronicle*, depicts Charles as the perfect knight. While educated in Paris, he supported the University of Naples, which had been established by Frederick II. He wrote at least two love songs and was a patron to poets, including *Jean de Meun, the continuator of the *Romance of the Rose*.

Bibliography: J. Dunbabin, *Charles I of Anjou: Power, Kingship, and State-Making in Thirteenth-Century Europe*, 1998.

Tom Papademetriou

CHARLES MARTEL (C. 688–741, R. 714–741). The grandfather of *Charlemagne, he earned his nickname Martel (from the Latin *martellus*, meaning "hammer") through his defeat of Muslims at Moussais, near Poitiers, on 25 October 732. As the mayor of the palace, Charles Martel brought about the end of Merovingian rule; founded the Carolingian dynasty; restored Frankish unity and extended Frankish authority over surrounding regions; set the foundations for Frankish feudalism; checked Muslim expansion into Europe; and supported the missionary work of Saint *Boniface in Thuringia and Hesse, *Willibrod in Frisia, and Pirmin in Alemannia.

Charles Martel was born a bastard son to Pepin II of Herstal and his concubine Alpais (or Chalpaida). As mayor of the palace, Pepin was, in effect, the ruler of the Frankish kingdom despite the fact that a Merovingian king remained upon the throne. Pepin's death in 714 led to a power struggle within the kingdom, which led to invasions by the Frisians and the Aquitanians, and Pepin's wife Plectrude claiming the regency for her grandson, Theudobald. Fearing Charles might displace her grandchildren, Plectrude had Charles imprisoned. With the help of his supporters, however, Charles escaped and raised an army to battle the invading forces. Eventually defeating them, he then turned his attention to Plectrude and Pepin's royal treasury. In 718, he declared himself the Austrasian mayor of the palace and proclaimed the son of Theuderic III king, renaming him Chlothar IV. In order to secure his position as mayor of the palace, Charles appointed relatives and supporters to positions of power and seized control of ecclesiastical lands, filling abbeys and bishoprics with friends.

After having secured his position, Charles directed his efforts toward his borders and defeated the Frisians, Saxons, Alemanni, Bavarians, and Aquitanians. Realizing that christianizing the lands of Thuringia and Hesse would help to solidify his rule over them, Charles supported Boniface's missionary work there. As the policy was a success, Charles also supported Pirmin's missionary work in Alemannia, which helped solidify Charles' control over the eastern provinces.

In 732, Duke Odo of Aquitaine, once a supporter of Charles' enemies, now found himself in need of Charles' support against Spanish Muslims invading Aquitaine. This led to the famous battle of Poitiers on 25 October 732 where Charles checked Muslim expansion into western Europe. While the battle was not the crushing blow that "saved" Europe from Islam that it was once thought to be, it did halt Muslim advancement. The invasion, though repelled, sufficiently weakened Aquitaine to an extent that Charles was able to bring Provence under his control.

When the last of the Merovingian kings, Theuderic IV, died in 737, Charles did not appoint another king; neither did he take the throne himself. By not appointing a new king, Charles became, as Pope Gregory III called him in a letter written in 739, *vice regulus*—a substitute king. In that letter, Pope Gregory requested Charles' help against the Lombard King Liutprand. Though Charles had had warm relations with both Pope Gregory II and Gregory III because of his support of missionaries, Liutprand was a close ally of his, so Charles refused to aid the pope.

In preparation for his death, Charles divided most of his kingdom between his two sons, Carloman and *Pepin, his sons by his first wife. Carloman, the elder of the two, was made mayor of Austrasia, Alemannia, and Thuringia. Pepin (later Pepin III) was made mayor of Neustria, Burgundy, and Provence. To Grifo, a son by his second wife, Charles gave various lands scattered throughout the kingdom. On 22 October 741, Charles died at his palace in Quierzy. His remains were taken to St. Denis, where he was buried among the Merovingian kings.

Bibliography: P. Riché, *The Carolingians: A Family Who Forged Europe*, trans. M. I. Allen, 1993.

John Paul Walter

CHRÉTIEN DE TROYES (C. 1135–1180). Author of five Arthurian romances, he was responsible for shaping various Arthurian legends into the form most familiar to us today. Among his innovations are the introduction of Guinevere's affair with Lancelot, the first mention of the Holy Grail, and the first reference to Camelot.

Practically nothing is known of his life. It is almost certain that he wrote for the court of *Marie de Champagne, and for that of Philip of Alsace, count of Flanders. His familiarity with English folklore and topography points to a possible sojourn in England at some point in his career. Although there is little biographical material, readers can gain an insight into his personality through his writing. He reveals himself to be a man of wit and charm, one well versed in the intricacies of court life and knowledgeable of both Celtic folklore and existing Arthurian material, whose writing style is polished and sophisticated. His allusions and the dialectical structure of his love monologues indicate that he received clerical training at a church school and probably entered into the minor orders.

Although he wrote other works, including translations into French of the *Art of Love* and Ovid's *Commandments* as well as what is considered the first French version of the Tristan and Isolde story, he is best known for his five Arthurian romances: *Erec and Enide, Cligés, Yvain ou le Chevalier au lion* (The Knight with the Lion), *Lancelot ou le Chevalier à la charrette* (The Knight of the Cart), and *Perceval ou le Conte du Graal* (The Story of the Grail). Although these romances have Arthurian subject matter, their setting and focus are the courtly milieu of his day. His knights are twelfth-century knights. Thus, he begins a long tradition of authors whose Arthurian stories say more about the morals and concerns of their own time than they do about the period in which the events supposedly occurred. However, Chrétien had certainly read those Arthurian works available to him, and much of the basic story derives from *Wace's *Roman de Brut*. A translation of *Geoffrey of Monmouth's *Historia regum Britanniae*, Wace's work had made its first French appearance in 1155 and introduced the Arthurian legend to continental Europeans before Chrétien composed his first Arthurian romance.

Each of Chrétien's romances can be read as a separate adventure; however, because of their recurring characters, the stories also fit together into an interconnected whole. In *Erec and Enide* (c. 1170), the eponymous lovers become so involved in marital bliss that Erec no longer performs those duties necessary to fulfill his position as a knight; Enide convinces him that he must not shirk his duty, and the two embark on a series of adventures in which they are tested but are ultimately victorious. *Cligés* (c. 1176) concerns the adulterous but pure love of the lady Fenice for Cligés. This story provides a contrast to the adulterous but impure love of Tristan and Isolde. Its scene of the lady feigning death so she can start life over with her lover is a precursor to a similar incident in many later works, including *Romeo and Juliet*. Chrétien's next two romances, *Yvain* and *Lancelot*, are more interconnected than the others, with incidents in each romance only comprehensible if one has read the other work. However, other incidents seem to contradict each other. These connections and discrepancies have led many scholars to believe that the two works were composed simultaneously with Chrétien starting on *Yvain* and then switching to *Lancelot* and then coming back to *Yvain*. *Yvain* returns to the issue Chrétien first explored in *Erec and Enide*—the conflict between love and glory. In this romance, Yvain takes the opposite position from Erec and ignores his wife, concentrating instead on his pursuit of glory. Like Erec, Yvain must set out on a series of adventures accompanied by his wife. Through many tests, Yvain realizes that he is wrong to neglect his wife and turns over a new leaf. *Lancelot* introduces the adulterous relationship between Lancelot and Guinevere. Possibly Marie de Champagne suggested this plot to Chrétien. His final romance is the unfinished *Story of the Grail*, probably begun sometime in 1180, possibly at the request of Philip of Alsace, count of Flanders, to whom the work is dedicated. With its religious theme, this work marks a radical departure from the others, which concern secular love. In addition, this work is notable for its introduction of the Grail into the Arthurian tradition.

Judging from the number of extant manuscripts and fragments of manuscripts, Chrétien's works were enormously popular. Although his works later faded in popularity until their rediscovery in the nineteenth century, his many innovations have become the standards of the Arthurian legend as we know it today.

Bibliography: J. Frappier, *Chrétien de Troyes: The Man and His Work*, trans. R. Cormier, 1957, reprint 1982; L. Topsfield, *Chrétien de Troyes: A Study of the Arthurian Romances*, 1981.

Leah Larson

CHRISTINA OF MARKYATE (C. 1096–C. 1155/1166). A recluse, she later headed a Benedictine community at St. Albans. Our knowledge of her is derived largely from an anonymous manuscript of her life to 1142.

She was born on the feast of Saint Leonard (6 November) to a family of Anglo-Saxon nobles prominent in Huntingdonshire. She was originally called Theodora and probably became Christina at the time she entered religious life about 1131.

At the age of five or six Christina took a vow of virginity at the monastery of St. Albans. When she was about sixteen, a friend of the family attempted to seduce her. Failing, he retaliated with machinations that led to her unwilling betrothal to one Burhred. She fled to take refuge with a hermit, Alfwen, and later with another, Roger, in his hermitage at Markyate, where she remained for four years in spite of efforts to find her and proceed with the marriage. Because her father, Autti, was both wealthy and distinguished in public affairs, she had great difficulty in evading her pursuers to maintain her vow of chastity, but ultimately she was permitted to enter religious life formally and to head a religious community at Markyate. Her reputation for holiness led prelates from distant parts of England and abroad to visit her, requesting, unsuccessfully, that she become abbess of monastic establishments in which they had an interest. She had a special friendship with Abbott Geoffrey of St. Albans, the monastery at which she made her religious vows; her influence may have accounted for changes in his character from overdue concern for the material to compassion for the poor and humble. Christina died sometime between 1155 and 1166.

Her story until 1142 is told in an anonymous twelfth-century Latin manuscript that may be the work of Abbott Geoffrey. It is distinguished by a wealth of biographical detail that indicates the author was familiar with Christina and with her family. Unlike conventional hagiography, the life is not marked by miracles or heroic feats of spirituality but rather by an intimate, almost conversational tone as it recounts her adventures.

Bibliography: C. H. Talbot, ed. and trans., *The Life of Christina of Markyate: A Twelfth Century Recluse*, 1997.

Patricia Silber

CLARE OF ASSISI, SAINT (C. 1194–1253). First of the Poor Clares, a Franciscan order of nuns, this "most faithful follower" of Saint *Francis spent nearly all of her religious life at the convent of San Damiano near Assisi.

Chiara (Clare), eldest daughter of the wealthy nobleman Favarone di Offreduccio of Assisi and his devout wife Ortolana, disappointed her family's expectations for her to marry a rich lord after having an encounter with the "Poverello." It is not known when or how Clare became acquainted with Francis of Assisi since they were separated by age and class differences, but she arranged a private meeting with him in 1211. Then on the evening of 18–19 March 1212 (Palm Sunday), Clare abandoned the security of her family to become his follower at the place known as the Portiuncula (cradle of the Franciscan order). She vowed to live a life of chastity and poverty, and Francis himself cut off her hair and provided her with a tunic of sackcloth. Afterward Clare was taken to a Benedictine monastery for temporary residence. Her family attempted to bring her home by force, but their efforts failed as they would again when Clare's younger sister Catherine (Saint Agnes of Assisi) soon joined her. Years later, another sister Beatrice and their widowed mother became members of the order.

It was not Clare's wish to live a cloistered life in a rich abbey. Clare wanted to live the way Francis and his followers did, to enjoy what she called the "privilege of poverty." She believed that women in religious orders could support themselves by their labors and by begging alms. In 1215, Francis presented Clare with a short Rule, and she reluctantly agreed to head a small community of her followers at San Damiano near Assisi. There the women lived in austere poverty.

From 1224 until her death, Clare was frequently ill and confined to bed. Yet her *Vita* indicates that it was her devotion to the Holy Eucharist that freed her convent and the entire city of Assisi from the Saracens in 1240 and 1241. She also continued to seek papal approval of a more elaborate Rule for the order that she had composed. Final approval came on 10 August 1253, the day before she died at San Damiano. She was canonized on 15 August 1255.

Some of Saint Clare's writings have survived, but only five have been authenticated—her Rule and four letters to Saint Agnes of Prague. These reveal her vision of a new kind of religious community. The Rule, which Clare preferred to call a *forma vitae* (way of life), was the first Rule to be written by a woman for a female religious community. Because she disliked the hierarchical structure of Benedictine communities, Clare rejected the title of abbess and contended that the sister in charge should not be empowered to make unilateral decisions but should seek advice from a council of "discreets." She does not use the word *enclosure*; her rule explicitly includes "the privilege of poverty."

Bibliography: R. J. Armstrong and I. C. Brady, trans. and eds., *Francis and Clare: The Complete Works*, 1982; E. A. Petroff, *Body and Soul: Essays on Medieval Women and Mysticism*, 1994.

Deanna Evans

CLOTILDA (CHROTILDA, CHRODECHILD, CHLOTHILD) (D. 544).

Burgundian princess, she was the youngest daughter of prince Chilperic and his

Gallo-Roman wife. Although most Germanic peoples were pagan or followers of Arian Christianity, Clotilda was a Catholic Christian.

The Salian Frankish chief Childeric had opened diplomacy with the court of Clotilda's uncle King Gundobad, and in 493, Childeric's heir, *Clovis, founder of the Merovingian dynasty and probably a pagan, married Clotilda. From the beginning of their marriage, she worked to convert Clovis to Catholic Christianity and at the birth of each of their sons contrived to have them baptized Catholic. Their first son died shortly after baptism, but at the birth of a second son, Chlodomer, Clotilda again requested the rite. According to *Gregory of Tours, after Clovis' victory against the Alamanni under protection of Clotilda's god (in 496), Bishop Remigius of Rheims publicly baptized Clovis, his sisters, and warriors. The religion of a king was of military and tribal importance, not just personal choice.

Clotilda helped convert Clovis to Catholic Christianity, giving Merovingian Franks common cause with a literate, Gallo-Roman aristocracy both within and outside of Francia. For early medieval Christians, she became the paradigm for Catholic "missionary-queen," converting a husband or son. Clotilda's thirty-three years of widowhood were spent mostly at Tours. She was active in dynastic politics and founded several religious houses. She died on 3 June 544 at Tours.

Bibliography: J. A. McNamara, J. E. Halborg, and E. G. Whately, "Clothild," in *Sainted Women of the Dark Ages*, ed. and trans. J. A. McNamara, J. E. Halborg, and E. G. Whately, 1992.

Janice R. Norris

CLOVIS (C. 466–511). Defeating both Goths and Gallo-Romans, Clovis united much of what is now France under his rule. After converting to Catholic Christianity in 496, he became the most important Catholic ruler in western Europe and leader of the opposition to Arianism.

Much of what is known about Clovis comes from *Gregory of Tours' *History of the Franks*, written more than fifty years after Clovis' death. Gregory reports that Clovis was the son of Childeric I, that he became king of the Salian Franks while still a youth, and that he embarked upon a campaign of military expansion. After defeating the Roman general Syagrius at Soissons in 486, Clovis proceeded to conquer much of Roman Gaul as well as the Riparian Franks and the Thuringians. According to legend, Clovis converted to Christianity in 493 as a result of a battlefield experience at Tolbiac where pleas to his Frankish gods did nothing, but a last-minute plea to Jesus Christ led to success. However, the influence of his Catholic wife, *Clotilda, and the growing reputation of miracles attributed to Saint Martin of Tours probably predisposed Clovis to conversion. In 496, Clovis and several thousand of his men went to Rheims to be baptized by Archbishop Remigius (Rémy). There, once again according to legend, after Clovis' baptism, a dove brought down from heaven a vial of holy oil with which

Remigius anointed Clovis as king of the Franks and conferred upon him the divine gift of thaumaturgic healing. These two elements, the consecration with holy oil at Rheims and the consequent "king's touch" by which sufferers could be healed of scrofula, became two earmarks of legitimacy for French royalty until the eighteenth century.

After his baptism and consecration, Clovis became a stout defender of Catholic orthodoxy against the Arian heresy held by Christian Visigoths. In turn, Catholic clergy in Clovis' newly conquered territories helped to secure the allegiance of their Gallo-Roman parishioners. In 507 at Vouillé, Clovis defeated the Visigothic leader Alaric II, adding the region (and treasury) of Toulouse to his domain. Afterward Clovis received the honorary, but nonetheless impressive, title of consul from Anastasius, the emperor of the Eastern Empire.

In his later years, Clovis turned to consolidating the lands he had conquered. From his headquarters in Paris, he authorized the compilation of the laws of the Salian Franks in a compendium known as *Lex Salica* (Salic Law). Shortly before his death in 511, Clovis met with Catholic bishops in Orléans to confirm the alliance of political and religious powers.

Clovis was "king of the Franks," not king of France, but he established the foundation on which the French kings would build. The "Salic Law" and a close political alliance with the Catholic Church would remain mainstays of French royal policy for over a thousand years.

Bibliography: J. Verseuil, *Clovis ou la naissance des rois*, 1992; J. M. Wallace-Hadrill, *The Long-Haired Kings*, 1962.

Olivia H. McIntyre

CNUT I (CANUTE) (C. 995–1035). At the peak of his power Cnut ruled a North Sea empire that included Anglo-Saxon England, Denmark, Norway, and perhaps parts of Sweden, Ireland, Scotland, and Wales.

Cnut was the son of *Sven I (Forkbeard), who seized the throne of Denmark from his father *Harald I Bluetooth in 988; his mother was probably the sister of King Boleslav of Poland and the widow of King Eric of Sweden. Between 991 and 1012, Sven conducted a series of raids against England, extorting the tribute known as Danegeld from *Æthelred the Unready, and in 1013 he conquered the kingdom, accompanied by Cnut. After Sven died in early 1014 and Æthelred returned from exile in Normandy, Cnut went back to Denmark. However, in 1015, he resumed the war. Æthelred died on 23 April 1016, and Cnut defeated his son Edmund Ironside at Assandun (either Ashdon or Ashingdon in Essex) on 18 October. The two agreed that Edmund should retain Wessex, but his death on 30 November made Cnut king of all England. Æthelred had left three other sons: Eadwig by his first wife, whom Cnut had killed, Alfred and Edward by his second wife *Emma, sister of Richard II, duke of Normandy. He put aside his own first wife Ælfgifu, daughter of ealdorman Ælfhelm of Northampton, and married Emma, whose sons were safe in Normandy (Alfred died while visiting England in 1036; *Edward the Confessor was king from 1042 to 1066). Edmund Ironside's two small sons found refuge in Hungary.

Cnut returned to Scandinavia on four occasions: in 1019, to secure the Danish throne after his older brother Harald's death; in 1023, to put down a rebellion by Thorkell the Tall; in 1026, to resist a threat from *Oláfr Haraldsson of Norway (Saint Oláfr) and Anund Jacob of Sweden; and in 1028, when he put Oláfr to flight and took Norway. In 1027, Cnut went on a pilgrimage to Rome, where he witnessed the coronation of Holy Roman Emperor *Conrad II by Pope John XIX. Cnut experienced considerable difficulty from the Scottish Malcolm II but eventually entered Scotland and forced his submission, possibly in 1031. Otherwise he remained in England, where he was generally well regarded, partly due to the large Scandinavian population already there but also because he was an effective king.

On the other hand, it is clear that he sometimes used brutal methods to enforce his rule, and his reliance upon paid soldiers may indicate that he faced more resistance in England than is recorded. It appears that he turned over less land in England to his Danish followers than *William I (William the Conqueror) did with his French supporters after 1066. He made considerable use of the existing Anglo-Saxon machinery of government, including the system for collecting the Danegeld. In 1017, he divided the kingdom into four parts. He kept Wessex himself, and tradition has it that he created earldoms in East Anglia, Mercia, and Northumbria, though that is uncertain. However, he did entrust considerable power to earls, both Danish and English; the most powerful of the latter was Godwin of Wessex.

Cnut's impact on Western culture is difficult to assess. His empire barely outlived him. He intended for Hardacnut, his son by Emma, to succeed him in all his dominions, but the threat to Denmark from Norway prevented him from coming to England to claim the throne. Thus Harold Harefoot, his son by Ælfgifu, ruled England from 1035 to 1040, followed at his death by Hardacnut, who ruled until his own demise in 1042 brought the return of Edward the Confessor. Otherwise, Cnut certainly promulgated laws, written for him by *Wulfstan, archbishop of York, though it is unclear to what extent these were original. Though the conversion of Scandinavia to Christianity was quite recent, Church chronicles suggest that Cnut was a generous patron, for example, supporting the monastery at Bury St. Edmunds and the cult of Edward the Martyr (king of England 975–978).

Cnut is the subject of an unusual legend wherein he failed to command the ocean waves, demonstrating the inefficacy of human rulers compared to God. He left letters of 1019–1020 and 1027, probably written for him by Wulfstan. He is remembered in skaldic poems like those of Ottar the Black and Sighvat (both titled "Knútsdrápa") and Thorarin Praise-Tongue ("Tøgdrápa," for which Cnut paid him fifty marks), Icelandic prose sagas, the *Encomium Emmae reginae* (composed for his wife), the *Anglo-Saxon Chronicle*, and various charters and writs. The epic *Beowulf* has been claimed for many eras, and at least one scholar has attributed it to Cnut's reign, but most experts reject this. In the long run, the impact of Cnut's conquest was much less than that of William I half a century later; however, had he lived longer or had more worthy heirs, the outcome might have been different.

Bibliography: M. K. Lawson, *Cnut: The Danes in England in the Early Eleventh Century*, 1993.

William B. Robison

COLUMBA, SAINT (520/521–597). Columba was a significant figure in the establishment of the early Irish colonies in Scotland and, via his cult, in the extension of Irish influence into the churches of Northumbria as well as the Pictish kingdom. His later life is documented in detail in the *Vita Columbae* of *Adamnan, and his monastic foundation on the Inner Hebridean island of Iona has left extensive remains. He is recorded as the founder of a number of monasteries in Ireland and the Hebrides.

Columba was born near Derry in 520 or 521. Gartan, county Donegal, is now claimed as his birthplace, but this is on the strength of a Middle Irish homily and cannot be verified. His father was named Fedelmid mac Ferguso, his mother Eithne, and he was a member of the immensely powerful Northern Uí Néill family—the most influential dynasty in Ireland at that time. He was the great-grandson of Conall Gulban, founder of the Cenél Conaill sept, whose territory is still commemorated in the name Tyrconnell. Whether he was born into a Christian or pagan family has been a matter for speculation. Later biographies record that his Irish birth name was Crimthann ("fox"). The Latin name Columba ("dove") was probably adopted on his ordination and is often now used in the Irish form Colum Cille ("dove of the church") to distinguish him from his younger contemporary and namesake *Columbanus. Typically for a nobleman of his era, he was fostered, in this case by a priest named Cruithnechán, before entering the tutelage of a churchman named Gemmán, in Leinster. Columba's early career is difficult to reconstruct, as Adamnan's *Vita Columbae* is principally concerned with his prophecies, miracles, and visions subsequent to his becoming a "pilgrim for Christ" in 563. Adamnan records that as a deacon Columba studied scripture with Finnian (Uinniau), a shadowy figure at the beginning of early Irish monasticism who was probably a British immigrant and who wrote a penitential as well as a fragment of a letter to *Gildas. Adamnan refers to Columba's excommunication for "trivial offences" at a synod around 560, almost certainly at Tailtiu (Teltown in county Meath). Later tradition has it that Columba's exile to Scotland was the result of his involvement in the events of the battle of Cúl Drebene (562), but while Adamnan closely associates the two events, a causal link cannot safely be inferred.

Whatever his status at the time of his exile, as a senior member of a powerful northern dynasty, his subsequent years saw him engaged in much diplomacy, the circumstances of which may be only partially disentangled. He was at the

Convention of Druim Cett in county Derry (traditionally dated to 575 but probably later) where he is alleged to have supported the king of Scottish Dalriada (in which his monastery of Iona was situated) against Uí Néill hegemony. He also made missions to the Pictish king Brude mac Maelchon at Inverness, though there is no definite evidence that these were primarily religious in focus or had any immediate effect upon the christianization of Pictland. His relations with the kings of Dalriada remain especially tantalizing, notably the question as to who granted him the territory of Iona, as well as his anointing of the king of Dalriada in 576—an event unprecedented in Christian coronation ritual in Europe. Though widely reputed as an author, Columba has left no works that can be securely attributed to his authorship. Traditions that he is the author of the hymn "Altus Prosator" and the scribe of the gospel text named the "Cathach of St. Columba" (Royal Irish Academy MS 12 R 33) remain possible if controversial. Early cult literature from the saint's *familia* is especially rich, comprising a substantial body of early poems and the biography of the saint by his kinsman Adamnan. His successors founded the houses at Lindisfarne, in Northumbria, and Kells, in county Meath, both famous for their illuminated gospel books.

Bibliography: Adamnan of Iona, *Life of St. Columba*, ed. R. Sharpe, 1995.

Jonathan M. Wooding

COLUMBANUS, SAINT (C. 543–615). An Irish monk, teacher, and founder of monasteries on the continent, his works contribute to our understanding of early Irish literary culture.

Columbanus was the first documented Irish *peregrini* on the Continent. From the Irish province of Leinster, he was educated in his parents' home. Entering monastic life, he went first to Abbot Sinell and then to Comgall's newly founded Bangor on Belfast Lough, where he eventually served as master of the school. From Bangor he left for France c. 591 with twelve companions. Supported by Childebert of Austrasia, his first foundation was Annegray in the Vosges Mountains, followed almost immediately by Luxeuil, which revitalized Frankish monasticism. The Rule used at these monasteries was adopted even by earlier foundations during the seventh century and eventually observed by fifty-three religious houses.

Columbanus was in almost constant conflict with the bishops of the Gallic province. He castigated their simony and laxity; they accused him of schism and heresy over his use of different tables for calculating the date of Easter, for interfering with episcopal rights over monasteries, and for introducing Irish penitential practices including auricular confession and private penance. Preparations were under way for a public accusation of heresy over his use of the Insular eighty-four-year Easter tables when in 600 Columbanus appealed to *Gregory the Great (Epistle 1). This placed his enemies in an awkward position; the French Church itself used tables that were different from Rome's, and Gregory was unlikely to support bishops whom he had repeatedly condemned for simony.

Gregory responded by commending Columbanus to the protection of Conon, abbot of Lérins.

The bishops continued their machinations against him and may have maneuvered Columbanus into the situation where his refusal to bless Theuderic's illegitimate sons, and concomitant outspoken condemnation of the king's lifestyle, lost him royal favor. He and his surviving Irish followers were finally exiled from France in 610. They worked along the shores of Lake Constance until expelled after the defeat of their patron Theudebert. One companion, Gall, however, stayed on, despite Columbanus' orders, to found the major monastic center of St. Gall.

Columbanus went to Italy in late autumn of 612 and was welcomed at the court of Agilulf, where he became involved in a Christological controversy. He was naturally suspicious of doctrinal innovation and complained to Boniface IV that Catholic dissension over the Justinian condemnation of certain theological works (the "Three Chapters") was hampering the conversion of the Arian Langobards to orthodoxy, warning the pope against supporting a Christological heresy (Epistle 5). Given land in the Apennines by Agilulf, Columbanus spent his last year at the newly founded Bobbio, refusing an invitation from Chlothar to return to France.

His works, vitally important for our understanding of early Irish literary culture, include five letters, a *Penitential*, a *Regula monachorum*, and a *Regula coenobialis*. The attribution to him of thirteen sermons has recently been shown to have a better basis than sometimes thought. The poems once used to adduce a school of classical studies in Bangor are now believed to have been written by Columbanus, abbot of St. Trond (fl. c. 780–c. 815).

Bibliography: M. Lapidge, ed., *Columbanus: Studies on the Latin Writings*, 1997; *Sancti Columbani Opera*, ed. and trans. G.S.M. Walker, 1957.

Helen Conrad-O'Briain

COMTESSA DE DIA, LA (BORN C. 1140). La Comtessa [Beatritz] de Dia (Die, northeast of Montélimar in southern France) was the most famous of a small group of *trobairitz* or female troubadours who wrote courtly songs of love during the twelfth and thirteenth centuries. The word *trobairitz* comes from two roots meaning "to compose" and "female"—hence, "a woman who composes."

The Countess and others appear to have been active from approximately 1170 to about 1260, during a time when women enjoyed a brief interlude of relative independence. As a group, female troubadours were virtually unknown, and certainly unappreciated, prior to the last century. Considered anomalies by earlier French scholars, these women have been brought into critical prominence since the publication of Meg Bogin's *The Women Troubadours* in 1976.

In the Countess' four surviving songs it is clear that she shared both the concepts and the vocabulary of her masculine counterparts. One song longs for a lost extramarital love ("I long to hold you instead of my husband"); two describe the joys of loving a knight of prowess and worth, despite the threat of slanderers and spoilsports; and one laments having been betrayed by a former and unfaithful friend. Although her poetic persona is modeled on that of the masculine courtier, she presents herself also as the troubadour *domna* or lady, employing feudal imagery to describe her feelings for a lover. All of her songs express an expectation of reciprocity and mutuality in a relationship as well as fidelity and appreciation of her worth as a countess and an intelligent woman.

Bibliography: M. T. Bruckner, "Fictions of the Female Voice: The Women Trouba- dours," *Speculum* 67 (October 1992): 865–891; W. D. Paden, ed., *The Voice of the Tro- bairitz: Perspectives on the Women Troubadours*, 1989.

Judith Davis

CONRAD II OF GERMANY (C. 990–1039). The first Salian emperor, a Frank rather than a Saxon, Conrad was elected German king in 1024, after the death of Henry II, the last Saxon king. He was made king of Italy in 1026, emperor in 1027, and king of Burgundy in 1033. His dealings with the Church precipitated many of the conflicts his descendants later faced.

Conrad owed his rights to the throne to his maternal lineage: He was a de- scendant of a daughter of *Otto the Great. He was well connected to the major houses of Europe through marriage: He married Gisela, daughter of the duke of Swabia (she died 1043), and his son married a daughter of *Cnut, king of England and Denmark. His wife's lineage provided a rather tenuous claim to the throne of Burgundy, which he exercised when the throne fell vacant in 1033. But he did not rely only on family connections for the expansion of royal power; for example, he won significant military victories over the Poles and became their overlord. He believed that Italy and Rome should be integral parts of the empire, even though the Italian nobles, the Church, and commercial centers resented German lordship. He spent the end of his reign subduing rebellions in northern Italy, supporting the lesser nobility against the magnates and prelates. By the time he died, Italy and Germany were relatively peaceful, the imperial treasury was wealthier than before, and the emperor was a force of great power. But his treatment of prelates and magnates sowed the seeds for many of the conflicts future emperors had to face.

In some respects a prime example of Christian kingship, Conrad was an able ruler well able to uphold royal authority. But his reign was also characterized by greed, corruption, and shortsightedness in his dealings with the Church, the magnates, and his lesser subjects. After the Italian campaign, he deposed a number of powerful Italian bishops, restricted the power of the nobles, and improved the position of the lesser nobility by making their fiefdoms hereditary. This policy was not long followed by his descendants, as it left the great mag- nates free to make alliances with other lords. Conrad considered the pope no more than his subject, and Pope John XIX was in fact Conrad's tool. Conrad made disastrous choices in his appointments of bishops in Italy and Germany;

they were frequently either illiterate or actually bought their sees. He occasionally forced monasteries to grant lands as fiefs to his friends, sometimes even granting royal abbeys as fiefs. This policy gravely offended the Church even though a number of these lands had once been part of the royal demesne. Gisela was also too interested in using Church property for personal gain, but she at least favored some of the reforms made necessary by her husband's style of dealing with the Church.

Shrewd enough to realize that neither his disaffected nobles nor coerced churchmen provided a sufficient power base, Conrad encouraged the formation of a class of lay servants, called *ministeriales*; these were peasants, usually serfs from the royal holdings, trained to be either warriors or administrators. *Ministeriales*, having no ties either to other nobles or to the Church, could be called upon as a corps of civil servants or an army, owing direct allegiance to the king. This strengthened the imperial position in many ways and, in contrast to his exaltation of lesser Italian nobles, was a policy continued by future emperors. But on the whole, Conrad may be seen as precipitating the conflicts between Church and state, and between emperor and nobles, which plagued the Holy Roman Empire for centuries to come.

Bibliography: F. R. Erkens, *Konrad II (um 990–1039): Herrschaft und Reich des ersten Salierkaisers*, 1998; K. Hampe, *Germany under the Salian and Hohenstaufen Emperors*, trans. R. Bennett, 1973.

Andrea Schutz

CONRADIN OF SWABIA (1252–1268). Also known as Conrad V and last of the Hohenstaufen dynasty, he was duke of Swabia and in name only king of Germany and Sicily (r. 1254–1268). His grandfather was the controversial Emperor *Frederick II, and his father was Conrad IV (1228–1254), the king of Germany and Sicily from whom he inherited their quarrel with the papacy. Conrad IV's premature death allowed Conradin's uncle Manfred, an illegitimate child of Frederick II, to take Sicily for himself while acting as a regent for his nephew. In Germany, powerful opposition prevented Conradin's recognition as king. As a result, Conradin spent his childhood obscurely in Swabia under the protection of relatives.

In 1266, *Charles of Anjou, with the support of Pope Clement IV, defeated and killed Manfred at the battle of Benevento. This event opened an opportunity for the young Conradin to regain Sicily from the uncertain control of Charles of Anjou. Old Hohenstaufen adherents helped him to raise an army in Germany, while the Ghibellines of Italy enthusiastically rallied to his cause. On 24 July 1268 he entered Rome. The rival armies of Conradin and Charles met at the battle of Tagliacozza on 23 August. Although Conradin's troops were winning during most of the battle, Charles prudently kept a body of cavalry in reserve and won the final victory. Charles considered the captive Conradin too dangerous to live and tried him on trumped-up charges of treason. The sixteen-year-old Conradin was executed at Naples on 29 October 1268, ending forever the Hohenstaufen threat. The ruthless act shocked thirteenth-century Europe, particularly the Germans, for centuries afterward. Dante condemned Charles' action and called Conradin a victim (*The Divine Comedy: Purgatory*, Canto XX, 67–68).

Bibliography: S. Runciman, *The Sicilian Vespers: A History of the Mediterranean World in the Later Thirteenth Century*, 1958.

Ronald H. Fritze

CONSTANTINE THE AFRICAN (C. 1010–C. 1087). Translator of medical texts, he was a major figure in eleventh-century medical writing whose influence on medical thought persisted for several centuries.

Born in North Africa around 1010, he spent over thirty years as a merchant and medical man traveling in the Middle East, Africa, and India. The last two decades of his life, he spent as a Benedictine monk at Monte Cassino, where he translated, adapted, and wrote over thirty treatises on medicine, covering topics as diverse as surgery, women's health, the eye, and lovesickness. Peter the Deacon of Monte Cassino, who devoted several sections of his work to Constantine's career, records what we know of Constantine's life. According to Peter, Constantine studied both the liberal arts and medicine in Egypt and traveled widely in India and Ethiopia. In Salerno, he was sponsored by Duke *Robert Guiscard and Archbishop Alphanus of Salerno, who recommended him to his friend, Abbot Desiderius (later Pope Victor III) of Monte Cassino. Desiderius received him as a Benedictine monk and sponsored his project, translating a large body of medical literature from Arabic into Latin. Constantine's work provides strong evidence of the active interest in medical matters sponsored at Monte Cassino in the late eleventh and early twelfth centuries. Constantine died in Monte Cassino around 1087.

Constantine made paraphrase translations and adaptations of medical works by Greek, Arab, and Jewish authors available to practitioners of medicine in the Latin West. These works were enormously popular, and more than twenty-five treatises are now known in many manuscripts. Constantine's main work, the *Pantegni*, is a ten-book free translation of the *Kitāb al-malikī* by ʿAlī ibn al-ʿAbbās al-Magūsī and is dedicated to Desiderius.

Bibliography: H. Bloch, *Monte Cassino in the Middle Ages*, vol. I, 1986; C. Burnett and D. Jacquart, eds., *Constantine the African and ʿAli ibn al-ʿAbbas al-Magusi: The* Pantegni *and Related Texts*, 1994.

Patricia Price

COURSON, ROBERT OF. *See* ROBERT OF COURSON.

CYNEWULF (FL. EARLY NINTH–LATE TENTH CENTURY). Cynewulf, an Anglo-Saxon author, used Anglo-Saxon poetic conventions of martial heroism in four poems about Christ, the Apostles, and saints Helen (Elene) and Juliana.

Cynewulf lived and wrote some time between the late eighth and middle tenth centuries; he may have been a monk. We can say with certainty of Cynewulf only that he wrote four poems, signed with runic letters embedded in the conclusions of those poems: *Fates of the Apostles, Juliana, Elene*, and *Christ II*. The runes are ancient letters used in England before the adoption of Roman script, each of which represents both a word and a sound, so that Cynewulf was able to weave the runes into the poems by having them represent simultaneously the concepts of their names as nouns within the text of the poem and an anagrammatic signature. Attempts to identify him with people of the same name who are known to have lived at various times and places in Anglo-Saxon England have faltered with the recognition that several dozen Cynewulfs lived during the period when the poems were written. We can observe that Cynewulf wrote in Anglian, though we cannot be sure if he wrote in Northumbria or in Mercia. He was literate and fairly well read, using a variety of Latin sources for each of his poems, but not extremely well educated, as evidenced by his misdating of various historical events.

While several other poems have been attributed to Cynewulf in the past, it is now generally accepted that the four mentioned above are his only surviving works. Each is an adaptation of Latin materials that combines Christian apostolic and hagiographical material with conventions drawn from Anglo-Saxon heroic poetry of the treatment of travel, battle, and the character of the fighter. *Christ II* treats Christ's harrowing of hell and ascension to heaven. *Juliana*, found, like *Christ II*, in the poetic compilation known as the Exeter Book, concerns the beautiful saint's refusal to marry a non-Christian and her subsequent verbal battle with the devil. Though burned at the stake, she suffers no harm and is finally killed with a sword stroke. Like *Juliana*, Cynewulf's *Elene* (which appears in the Vercelli manuscript) records the life of a female saint. In this poem, Helen journeys to Jerusalem on the request of her just-converted son Constantine to seek the cross on which Jesus is said to have been crucified. Once there, she calls an assembly of the Jews and demands the information of them. One, Judas, is thrown in a desert pit without food or water for a week until he consents to give her the information she wants (and is baptized as Cyriacus). Also in the Vercelli book is *Fates of the Apostles*, a brief description of the deaths of each of the Apostles.

Bibliography: E. R. Anderson, *Cynewulf: Structure, Style, and Theme in His Poetry*, 1983; R. E. Bjork, ed., *Cynewulf: Basic Readings*, 1996.

Heide Estes

CYRIL AND METHODIUS, SAINTS (827–869 AND 826–885). Called the "Apostles to the Southern Slavs," the brothers Cyril and Methodius were instrumental in the conversion of many eastern Europeans, particularly the Moravians, to Christianity. Originally named Constantine, the former was given the honorary name of Cyril before his death by Pope Hadrian II. He contributed to the linguistic evolution of the region through the development of a written Slavonic language.

Constantine and Methodius were born in Thessaloniki. Their father, Leo, was a military officer and well known at the Byzantine court. After the death of his father, Constantine traveled to Constantinople to be tutored by Theoctistus, the chancellor of the Byzantine empress Theodora. His impressive academic abilities won him a place in the imperial academy, where he was tutored by Photius, an important Byzantine theologian who later became the patriarch of Constantinople. Theoctistus had ambitious plans for Constantine, planning to have him marry his daughter and accept an office at court. Instead, Constantine chose a spiritual life yet tentatively accepted a position as librarian to the patriarch Ignatius; however, he rejected the position and disappeared after clashing with Ignatius over the latter's iconoclastic policies. By 850, at the age of twenty-three, he had reappeared. Records show that Constantine had been appointed a professor of philosophy at the imperial court. In 855, he left the post to join his brother in a monastery on Mount Olympus near the Bosphorus Straits.

The story of Methodius up to this point is a little mysterious. Not as intellectually gifted as his brother, Methodius had not been given the opportunity to study in Constantinople, though he was active politically and even served as a provincial governor before withdrawing to the monastery. Many historians state that although he did not have the same scholarly abilities as his brother, he nevertheless possessed the organizational leadership qualities necessary for his work in Moravia.

In 860, the Khazars asked the patriarch of Constantinople to send them Christian missionaries, and he chose the brothers. After learning the Khazar language, Constantine and Methodius attempted to convert the Khazars to Christianity, with mixed results. They must have met with a certain measure of success because the Moravians, in 863, asked them to come preach and conduct service in the Slavonic language. In fact, Rostislav, king of Great Moravia, specifically requested Constantine and Methodius because their reputation as preachers and scholars had reached him. Because they were already acquainted with the language, they traveled to Moravia after Constantine invented a new alphabet to use in translating the Bible and other devotional works into the Slavonic language. The Moravians had no written language, using the spoken Slavonic language. Constantine used the letters of the Greek alphabet to represent the same sounds the Greeks had and created new letters to represent the inflections and diphthongs of the spoken Slavonic language. The new alphabet, called the Glagolithic alphabet, eventually evolved into the Cyrillic alphabet.

In Moravia, Constantine and Methodius achieved much, and it is for their work there that they are best remembered. They not only preached but also trained new converts in the hopes that they could develop a new ecclesiastical hierarchy for the region. Their success concerned many traditional churchmen who believed Latin to be the only authoritative ecclesiastical language, so their use of the Slavonic language compelled Pope *Nicholas I to call them to Rome for a hearing. By the time they reached Rome, however, Nicholas had died, and the new pope, Hadrian II, had a different view of their evangelical activities. He sanctioned the Slavonic Liturgy they had developed and also had them consecrated as bishops, blessing their return to Moravia.

In addition, Hadrian II created a new archdiocese, the archdiocese of Moravia, by combining the territories of two Moravian princes, Rostislav and Svatopluk, and the Slavic prince Kocel of Pannonia and granting them independence from the German Church. Unfortunately, Constantine died soon after, and Methodius went on alone, newly appointed as archbishop of Moravia. In some ways, Constantine and Methodius had become political pawns of Rostislav and the Byzantine church. In addition to religious concerns, they had political motives for requesting the help of Christian missionaries. In the mid-ninth century, Rome and Constantinople vied for ecclesiastical control of Moravia, and up until this point the Franks, whose ecclesiastical loyalty belonged to Rome, had provided religious leadership in the region. The creation of the archdiocese of Moravia satisfied Rostislav, because it provided for independence from the Franks, yet disappointed the Byzantine emperor and patriarch because the new archdiocese was clearly under the authority of Rome.

Furthermore, the creation of the new archdiocese alienated the Holy Roman Emperor, *Louis the German. He reacted by attempting to discredit Methodius and, thus, his Moravian mission. In 870, he called Methodius to a synod in Ratisbon, thereafter deposing the archbishop and having him cast into prison. He spent three years in prison before being freed by Pope John VIII, who also reconfirmed him as archbishop of Moravia.

Once back in Moravia, Methodius endeavored to spread the Christian message to Bohemians and Poles but was summoned again to Rome on charges of heresy propagated by the ambitious German priest Wiching. This time John VIII affirmed papal sanction of the Slavonic Liturgy while mandating that the service should first be read in Latin and then in Slavonic. Wiching became one of Methodius' bishops and continued to harass him, though John VIII continually supported and praised the archbishop's efforts. On a visit to Constantinople, Methodius finished translating the Bible into Slavonic with the help of several scholarly priests and also translated works of Greek church law. He died in 885. Later popes would not be so willing to accept the Slavonic language and required the service to be read in Latin. However, the Slavonic language was used on several evangelical missions into eastern Europe, so thus was used to help convert many eastern Europeans to Christianity.

Bibliography: F. Dvornik, *Byzantine Missions among the Slavs: SS. Constantine-Cyril and Methodius*, 1970.

Alana Cain Scott

D

DAGOBERT I (C. 604–639). Merovingian king of Austrasia and later all of Francia, Dagobert was the son of Bertrude and Chlothar II. He nearly died of an intestinal infection at age nine but survived to rule Austrasia (in central Gaul) as a vassal of his father, Clothar II, from 623 to 629. At his father's death in 629, the entire Frankish kingdom was divided between Dagobert and his simpleminded half brother Charibert, king of Aquitaine, while Dagobert established his two-year-old son Sigibert III as the ruler of Austrasia. Shortly after his father's death, Dagobert dissolved his childless first marriage, made at his father's command to his stepmother's sister Gomatrude, to marry Nantechild, who would become the mother of Clovis II, the future king of Neustria. Dagobert later took several mistresses, including Ragnetrude, the mother of Sigebert III.

Dagobert's reign of Francia was characterized, like that of his father, by both internecine conflict and challenges along its borders. However, he found time to dispense justice and may have been responsible for the composition of the *Lex Ripuaria*. In addition, Dagobert strengthened relations with the Church in pursuit of both religious and secular stability, giving with particular generosity to the monastery of St. Denis, where he was eventually to be buried, beginning a tradition of royal burials there that would last into the eighteenth century. Dagobert's close ties with the Church led him to patronize the arts and learning in a century known as the most impoverished in these areas in all of Frankish history. In fact, Dagobert himself was probably the most effective of the Frankish kings in the seventh century.

Bibliography: M. Bouvier-Ajam, *Dagobert*, 1980; I. Wood, *The Merovingian Kingdoms 450–751*, 1994.

Heide Estes

DAMIAN, PETER. *See* PETER DAMIAN, SAINT.

DHUODA (FL. NINTH CENTURY). Dhuoda was born to Carolingian nobility early in the ninth century; she produced a handbook of conduct for her son that sheds a good deal of light on the society of her time and especially on the life of a woman of the aristocracy.

She was married to Bernard, son of William of Gellone, on 30 June 824, in Aachen. As a result of Bernard's involvement in the wars of succession waged by *Charlemagne's sons, he sent their son, William, who was about fourteen years old, as a hostage to *Charles the Bald. A second son was born to Dhuoda in 841 but was taken from her even before his baptism by Bishop Elefantus of Uzes to be brought to his father. Both Bernard and his elder son were killed in battle, William in 850 while trying to regain hereditary territories in Catalonia. We do not know the fate of the younger son.

Dhuoda began the *Liber manualis* as a letter to her son William to instruct him in moral virtue more than in courtly behavior. It was begun shortly after the birth of her second son and shows her to be both literate and capable of business affairs. The Latin in which it is written reveals significant learning, especially on theological topics. It is representative of the lay education supported by Charlemagne. In addition to familiarity with Scripture, Dhuoda's book demonstrates a knowledge of *Alcuin, *Isidore of Seville, *Gregory of Tours, and Augustine, among a number of others.

Dhuoda undertook in her book to provide moral and spiritual guidance to her son as a person of substance in the secular world; of the eleven books (or seventy-three chapters) in her book, the longest deal with "Social Order and Secular Success" and "Moral Life." The underlying premise of the work is religious obligation expressed here in terms of maintaining right order through duty to one's father, whose role is analogous to that of God. Although she employs the humility topos of unworthiness and limited ability, she is clearly capable.

Bibliography: M. A. Mayeski, *Dhuoda: Ninth Century Mother and Theologian*, 1995.

Patricia Silber

DIONYSIUS THE PSEUDO-AREOPAGITE. *See* PSEUDO-DIONYSIUS THE AREOPAGITE.

DOMINIC (DOMINGO DE GUZMÁN), SAINT (C. 1170–1221). Dominic was the founder of the Order of Friars Preachers, more commonly known as the Dominicans.

Dominic was born the son of Domingo de Guzmán and Juana of Aza. His father was a knight, reputedly of Visigothic origin, while his mother was of Castilian nobility. At Juana's insistence, Domingo allowed Dominic to join his two elder brothers in studying for the priesthood rather than following his father's military career. At about the age of seven, Dominic began his training under his uncle, an archpriest of Gumiel d'Izan. He entered higher studies at the cathedral school at Palencia at about the age of fourteen.

After ten years of study in the liberal arts and theology at Palencia, Dominic became ordained and subsequently appointed a canon, then prior, in the cathedral chapter at Osma. In 1203, Dominic accompanied his bishop on a diplomatic mission for King Alfonso IX of Castile. Alfonso had entrusted the bishop to secure a marriage alliance between his son Ferdinand and the daughter of the Lord of the Marches (presumably a Danish princess). While Dominic and Bishop Diego traveled through Languedoc, they came into contact with Albigensians (Cathars), dualist heretics whose teachings and ascetic lifestyle had placed the Catholic Church on the defensive in southern France. It was here that Dominic conceived of a religious order devoted to preaching and the refutation of heresy.

After the completion of their first mission, Diego and Dominic were dispatched on a second one, to bring the betrothed princess to Castile. As the princess either died or entered a convent, Diego and Dominic went instead to Rome, where they met Pope *Innocent III. Here, Diego requested permission to resign his bishopric so he and Dominic could devote themselves to the conversion of unbelievers in distant lands. Innocent, however, sent them back to Languedoc and asked them to help the Cistercian monks there entrusted with the conversion of the Albigensians. Dominic and Diego returned to southern France and quickly realized the shortcomings in the Cistercians' mission—their pomp, retinue, and worldly demeanor alienated them from the local Languedocians. Dominic indicated that they were proceeding poorly and suggested that they try to outdo the heretics in poverty and preaching. Along with the Cistercians, Dominic and Diego devised a new method of evangelical preaching in imitation of the apostles. Bishop Diego died in 1207, but Dominic remained in Languedoc, preaching and debating with the heretics. Dominic stayed in Languedoc after the assassination of the legate Peter of Castelnau (1208) and throughout the subsequent crusade against the Albigensians.

By 1215, Dominic established a religious community devoted to propagating true doctrine and extirpating heresy. Dominic traveled to Rome for confirmation of his order and was present at the Fourth Lateran Council. Although Pope Innocent III was sympathetic to Dominic's request, he could not confirm his new order as the canons of the Fourth Lateran Council had specifically prohibited the establishment of new religious orders. By December 1215, Dominic had taken the flexible Rule of Saint Augustine and had modified it slightly to address the needs of his brethren, adding his own constitutions. Pope *Honorius III confirmed this rule in the following year. Like the recently established order of Saint *Francis, Dominic's order was for mendicants. Unlike Francis' order, however, Dominic's consisted of priests who were trained in theology. Recognizing the need of a good theological education, Dominic began to disperse his brothers to the university towns of Paris and Bologna, later sending them to Spain, the Rhineland, England, eastern Europe, and Palestine. Pope Honorius facilitated

Dominic's plans by sending numerous letters of recommendation to the prelates of Europe.

Dominic continued to preach throughout Lombardy and traveled to the new congregations established at Paris and Bologna. Dominic's order began to grow rapidly as more and more young men at these university towns entered the order. In 1220, Dominic's order took a more cohesive appearance, and in that year, Dominic himself presided over the first Chapter General or general assembly of the order, which issued legislation governing the order. In the following year at the Chapter General in Rome, the order was divided into provinces, and a second order of Dominican nuns was created. Dominic died shortly thereafter in Bologna on 6 August 1221. By the time of his death, Dominic had established four monasteries, about twenty priories, and had divided his order into eight provinces. Pope *Gregory IX canonized him in 1234.

What Dominic established was something quite new—a mendicant order dedicated to preaching and teaching created specifically for an urban milieu. This order would play a large role in combating heresy over the next centuries by concentrating on reestablishing orthodoxy in the new, often turbulent, urban centers. The Dominican system of provincial and general chapters has been seen as democratic in spirit and allowed the order much flexibility while simultaneously preserving a centralized system of government. The influence of the Dominicans on the intellectual life of medieval Europe is incalculable. The Dominicans themselves, and especially at their Parisian convent of St.-Jacques, helped to create *pastoralia* or preaching manuals and aids, educational tools (e.g., biblical concordances), and scholarly exercises (e.g., quodlibetal questions). The Dominicans also took a leading role in helping to synthesize and explain the newly translated works of Aristotle to a Christian audience. The scholarly careers and activities of such early Dominicans as *Hugh of St. Cher, *Albertus Magnus, and Thomas *Aquinas only serve to emphasize that the followers of Saint Dominic very rapidly became the leading theologians of the thirteenth century.

Bibliography: W. A. Hinnebusch, *The History of the Dominican Order*, 2 vols., 1966; M.-H. Vicaire, *Saint Dominic and His Times*, trans. K. Pond, 1964.

Andrew G. Traver

DUNS SCOTUS, JOHN. *See* JOHN DUNS SCOTUS.

DUNSTAN, SAINT (C. 909–988). Archbishop of Canterbury, he was instrumental in the monastic reform movement both as abbot of Glastonbury and as archbishop.

Dunstan and his fellow reformers, Saints Oswald and Æthelwold, worked with the royal and aristocratic families to reestablish the Benedictine Rule as the guide to monastic life in Britain. Dunstan was almost certainly the motivating force behind the Council of Winchester (c. 973) where King *Edgar, Dunstan, and the major churchmen and -women of the day discussed the proper form of Benedictine monasticism that was to be followed in Britain; their conclusions were drawn up in the *Regularis Concordia*, which mandated the uniform observance of the Rule.

Dunstan was born c. 909 to a well-placed family; he was educated at Glastonbury and became the abbot there c. 940. As a prominent churchman, he often acted as an adviser to the king and on two occasions was banished: The first time he was forgiven before he actually left the kingdom; the second time, he went to Ghent in Flanders. His stormy career calmed when Edgar came to the throne and made Dunstan first bishop of Worcester, then bishop of London, and finally archbishop of Canterbury (959). Edgar valued the archbishop's opinion, and it seems likely that Dunstan influenced the king's support of the monastic reform. Dunstan's role as an adviser to the king extended beyond Edgar's death; the archbishop was involved in the succession dispute between Edgar's sons and played an important role in choosing Edward the Martyr (r. 975–978) over *Æthelred the Unready. Despite this partisanship, he served both Edward and then Æthelred until his death.

Bibliography: N. Ramsay, M. Sparks, and T. Tatton-Brown, *St. Dunstan: His Life, Times and Cult*, 1992.

Janet Pope

DURAND, GUILLAUME. *See* GUILLELMUS DURANDUS.

E

EADBURG (FL. EIGHTH CENTURY). Eadburg was an eighth-century abbess of the Minster in Thanet. Much of what we know of Eadburg is revealed in the letters she received from Saint *Boniface, bishop and later archbishop at Mainz. Boniface's letters, like those of his correspondents, reveal the interest the Anglo-Saxons took in his project—the conversion of the continental Saxons—in part via the textiles, clothing, and texts he frequently requested be sent abroad. Women played a significant part in Anglo-Saxon book production and, as a partial consequence, in education, as Boniface's many letters requesting manuscripts from abbey scriptoria demonstrate. In fact, among the manuscripts Boniface requests from England, he asks for the most elaborate—a text of the Epistles of Peter, written in gold, which he promises to supply—from Eadburg's scriptorium. Like other Anglo-Saxon nuns, Eadburg was highly educated (the standard for women's education drops in the later Middle Ages); not only did her correspondence with Boniface take place in Latin, but we also learn from one surviving letter written by *Leoba, one of Eadburg's students in the abbey, that she taught Latin using *Aldhelm of Malmesbury's difficult treatise on the writing of Latin verse, the text from which male clerics were also taught.

Bibliography: C. Fell, *Women in Anglo-Saxon England*, 1984.

Heide Estes

EADBURH (EADBURG) (FL. EIGHTH CENTURY). Eadburh was the daughter of *Offa, the powerful Anglo-Saxon king of Mercia who maintained frequent communication with *Charlemagne and received the first papal envoy to England in 200 years.

Most of what we know of Eadburh is recorded by *Asser in his biography of King *Alfred the Great; she is mentioned in the *Anglo-Saxon Chronicle* only as the daughter of Offa and wife of Beorhtric. According to Asser, West Saxons refused (albeit wrongly, Asser writes) to be ruled by any king who placed his wife on the throne beside him and refused to call any king's wife "queen," on account of the behavior of Eadburh. Eadburh was given in marriage to Beorhtric, king of Wessex, in 789, apparently to seal a treaty involving joint efforts to defeat the Kentish kings Ealhmund and Egbert, over whom Offa claimed supremacy. Asser records that Eadburh won Beorhtric's trust but then began to behave tyrannically, persuading Beorhtric to do away with nobles whom she disliked. Unable to persuade him to kill one of his favorites, she prepared poison for him, but Beorhtric also consumed some of the poison, and both were killed. Fleeing into exile, she brought immense treasure to the court of Charlemagne, from whom she sought protection. Asked to choose between Charlemagne himself and his son, she chose the son, whereupon Charlemagne instead made her the abbess of a large convent. According to Asser, however, she was caught in violation of her vows of chastity and kicked out of the nunnery, whereupon she lived out her days in poverty, dying many years later at Pavia.

Bibliography: S. Keynes and M. Lapidge, trans., *Alfred the Great: Asser's* Life of King Alfred *and Other Contemporary Sources*, 1983.

Heide Estes

EDGAR OF ENGLAND (943–975). King of the Mercians (r. 957–959) and king of the English (r. 959–975), often known as "the Peaceable," Edgar established a strong and relatively centralized government through his legal, political, economic, and ecclesiastical policies. Edgar's reign was marked by peace both within and without England, a fact that becomes remarkable when contrasted with the civil unrest that both preceded and succeeded his reign and with the resumption of the Viking incursions under his son *Æthelred the Unready. To what degree Edgar himself was responsible for the peace of his reign is unclear, but he certainly deserves a good deal of the credit.

Edgar was born in 943 to King Edmund and followed his older brother, Eadwig, to the throne. Eadwig's reign was marked by dissension, and in fact, the people of Mercia decided in 957 to replace him with his brother Edgar. Edgar succeeded Eadwig throughout the entire kingdom in 959 when the older brother died. As king of the English, Edgar became famous for revising the laws and for promulgating four law codes as well as for reissuing the coinage on a regular basis, which ensured the quality of the coins and allowed the government to make a profit in the process. Edgar also supported the monastic revival by placing Saints *Dunstan, Oswald, and Æthelwold in prominent ecclesiastical offices and by patronizing their reformed monasteries. Politically, Edgar worked to establish good relations with his nobility and with foreign rulers, such as his kinsman Emperor *Otto I. It has been argued that Edgar practiced serial monogamy in an attempt to strengthen the monarchy's political ties throughout England; if this is so, then the scheme ultimately failed after his death. Edgar was survived by two sons—Edward the Martyr (r. 975–978) by his first wife and Æthelred the Unready by his third wife. The succession dispute led to large-scale civil unrest and the eventual murder of Edward. This upheaval may well account for the renewal of Viking attacks under Æthelred.

Bibliography: P. Stafford, *Unification and Conquest: A Political and Social History of England in the Tenth and Eleventh Centuries*, 1989.

Janet Pope

EDWARD I OF ENGLAND (1239–1307, R. 1272–1307). One of medieval England's most powerful kings, Edward I conquered Wales, conducted wars against France and Scotland, expanded the role of Parliament, and is called the "English Justinian" because of his impact on the common law.

Edward was the son of *Henry III and Eleanor of Provence. Though a dissolute youth, he supported his father against Simon de *Montfort the Younger in the Barons' Wars and defeated the barons at Evesham in 1265. Edward helped restore royal authority before setting off in 1270 on an unsuccessful crusade that initially involved *Louis IX of France. Though Henry died in November 1272, Edward did not return to England until August 1274. Once there, he strove to preserve and extend his authority beyond English borders.

Because Llywelyn ap Gruffydd refused him homage, Edward invaded Wales in 1277. The Welsh Wars led to the deaths of Llywelyn in 1282 and his brother Dayfdd in 1283, and Edward annexed Wales and introduced English administrative and legal practices by the Statute of Wales in 1284, built a string of castles there, and in 1301 bestowed the title prince of Wales on his son, the future Edward II. Though lord of Ireland, Edward I paid little attention to that land and never went there. More important was that as duke of Aquitaine, he held Gascony as a fief from the French king. He was there in 1254–1255, 1260–1261 (twice), 1262 (probably), 1273 (returning from the crusade), and 1286–1289. Disputes between the French and Gascons in 1293 led Philip IV to summon Edward, whose refusal led to a perfunctory war. Pope *Boniface VIII intervened to end the hostilities in 1298. The formal peace concluded in 1303 led to the ill-fated marriage between the prince of Wales and Philip's daughter Isabella, whose son Edward III's claim to the French throne was one cause of the Hundred Years War.

Edward I's most bitter and unsuccessful war was with Scotland. The deaths of Alexander III in 1286 and his only heir Margaret, maid of Norway, in 1290 led to a disputed succession that the Scots called upon Edward as feudal overlord of Scotland to settle. In 1292 Edward awarded the Scottish throne to John of Balliol, who was initially so obedient to his English overlord that the Scots derisively nicknamed him "Toom Tabard" (empty coat). Later he proved recalcitrant, and in 1295–1296 the Scots began aiding France. Edward invaded Scotland in 1296, captured Balliol, and seized the Stone of Destiny upon which the Scots traditionally crowned their kings. However, William Wallace emerged to wreak havoc upon the English. Edward invaded again in 1300, 1301, and

1303, made peace in 1304 with most of the nobility, and captured and executed Wallace in 1305. But in 1306, Robert the Bruce, grandson of one of Balliol's rivals, assumed leadership of the Scots. Edward died on 7 July 1307 while en route to another invasion, and Bruce defeated Edward II at Bannockburn in 1314 and ruled an independent Scotland as Robert I. The depiction of Edward I ("Longshanks") in *Braveheart*, the Academy Award–winning movie about Wallace, is effective as drama but historically inaccurate.

Parliament first emerged under Henry III, but Edward I used it more extensively. As yet, there were no separate houses of lords and commons, and most of Edward's parliaments included only councilors, nobles, and prelates, making them difficult to distinguish from meetings of the great council. However, at times he did summon knights of the shire and burgesses, though the "Model Parliament" of 1295 is misnamed, for it also included the lesser clergy, who did not become a permanent part of the institution. Edward needed parliamentary taxation to finance his wars, but it also served as a court, provided him with the opportunity to seek advice and accept petitions, and produced legislation that made him the greatest innovator in the common law between *Henry II and the end of the Middle Ages.

The Statutes of Westminster I (1275) and II (1285) and Winchester (1285) dealt with a wide range of issues concerning law and order, legal procedure, property rights, and so on; the Statutes of Gloucester (1278) and *Quo Warranto* (1290) restricted nonroyal exercise of various liberties and franchises; the Statutes of Acton Burnell (1283) and of Merchants (1285) regulated trade; the Statute of Mortmain (1279) limited grants of land to the Church, while the Statutes of *Circumspecte Agatis* (1285) and Carlisle (1307) further circumscribed ecclesiastical power; and the Statute of *Quia Emptores* ended subinfeudation and strengthened the king's hand against the great nobles. However, the lawlessness of Edward's own officials frequently caused complaint, and his excessive demand for taxation provoked a revolt that forced him to issue the Confirmation of Charters in 1297, acknowledging that new taxes required the consent of the realm, and the subsequent Articles upon the Charters in 1300. Nevertheless, Edward produced a more coherent legal system and ended the haphazard process of judge-made law that characterized his father's reign.

Bibliography: M. Prestwich, *Edward I*, new ed., 1997.

William B. Robison

EDWARD THE CONFESSOR, SAINT (C. 1005–1066).

Edward was the last king of England to be a direct descendant of *Alfred the Great. As king, Edward suffered from the policies established by his predecessors and from the effects of his twenty-eight years of exile in Normandy. His failure to produce an heir opened the door for a succession dispute that resulted ultimately in the Norman Conquest. Nevertheless, after his death he was revered and canonized in 1161.

Edward was the son of King *Æthelred the Unready of England and his second wife *Emma, the daughter of Duke Richard I of Normandy. After Æthelred's death in 1016, the Dane *Cnut was crowned king of England, and Æthelred II's orphans, Edward, Alfred, and Godgifu, were exiled to Normandy. The new king married Emma, who returned to England, but her children by Æthelred remained in Normandy. Emma and Cnut produced a son, Harthacnut, and thus created a new heir to the English throne. In fact, Edward did not become king until 1042, after Cnut's sons were dead. These facts are extremely important for understanding Edward and his reign because his years of exile made him more Norman than English; and therefore, when he did become king, Edward brought several Frenchmen to England with him as political advisers and Church officials. The native English aristocracy resented these foreigners and extended their rancor to the king himself.

Edward's problems with the English nobles were exacerbated by the legacy of Cnut's administrative policies. Cnut had distributed large tracts of land to a handful of followers, including Earl Godwin, who along with his peers became major landowners with great political authority. For Edward, this meant that his nobles were almost as wealthy and powerful as he, which is a dangerous position for any king to be in. Godwin was a special threat because he was able to place his children in prominent positions. In particular, his two eldest sons, Sven and *Harold Godwinson, controlled large earldoms, and his daughter Edith was married to Edward in 1045. That Godwin and his family were a force to be reckoned with became clear in 1051–1052 when they rebelled against Edward and his foreign friends and relatives; Godwin succeeded in forcing Edward to accept his terms, and Anglo-Saxons replaced some powerful Frenchmen at court.

Godwin and his eldest son were both dead by early 1053, thus leaving Harold as the second-most-powerful man in England. By this time it was obvious that Edward and Edith would not produce an heir to the throne. This situation was especially disturbing because there were very few living male descendants of the royal line. From this point onward, the only male relative who was alive and old enough to rule was Edward's distant cousin through Emma, Duke *William of Normandy. When Edward died on 5 January 1066, William fully expected to succeed to the English throne and even claimed that Edward had designated him as his heir in 1051. William also said that Harold Godwinson had taken an oath in 1064 to respect William's claim.

Nevertheless, Godwinson and *Harald Hardråde, the king of Norway, had designs on the throne. Hardråde's claim was based on a treaty that his predecessor had signed with Harthacnut. Godwinson's right was founded on his being Edward's brother-in-law as well as the richest and most powerful man in England. Godwinson also said that, on his deathbed, Edward had chosen him as his heir. The English council of nobles selected Godwinson as the new king, and he was crowned by the archbishop of Canterbury on 6 January 1066. Neither William nor Hardråde accepted this decision, and both invaded in the fall of that year. King Harold was thus forced to fight two invading armies within three weeks' time, and although he defeated Hardråde at Stamford Bridge in September, he was killed at the battle of Hastings in October. In essence, Edward's greatest legacy is the Norman Conquest.

Despite the problems of his youth and his reign, Edward gained a reputation as a good king and saint. He became an ideal king because William and his heirs wanted to link themselves to a great figure and to revile Harold as a usurper. Edward was a generous patron of the Church, he oversaw the building of Westminster Abbey, and after his death, the legend began that he was childless because his great piety made him celibate. These factors combined to form his reputation for sanctity, which led to his canonization in 1161.

Bibliography: F. Barlow, *Edward the Confessor*, new ed., 1997.

Janet Pope

EGIDIUS COLONNA. *See* GILES OF ROME.

EGILL SKALLAGRÍMSSON (910–990). Egill was an Icelandic adventurer and skald, the eponymous hero of *Egils saga Skallagrímssonar*, which in turn was possibly authored by *Snorri Sturluson.

As is the case with other central personages found in the semihistorical Icelandic family sagas, Egill's actual life and works (in the form of poetry) are difficult to separate from the not entirely historical narratives and poems that have accrued to him. Some of the highlights of Egill's life as recounted in *Egils saga* include: his loss of temper at a ball game at the age of seven, resulting in several deaths; his first poem, composed on that occasion, declaring his intent to "fare with vikings"; first trips abroad, where he meets the Norwegian nobleman Arinbjörn and strikes up a friendship; his inimical encounters with King Eiríkr Blood-Axe in Norway and York and his forced composition of the poem "Head-Ransom" (*Höfuðlausn*) in Eiríkr's honor; his Rabelaisian adventures (e.g., throwing up in his host's beard) in Sweden; the loss of his sons and the poem he composed (*Sonatorrek*) to expiate that grief; his unwarlike death of old age; and the unnatural heaviness of his bones, as found by his successors. Egill was born in Borg and buried in Mosfell, both in western Iceland.

Höfuðlausn is unusual in that it is composed in a metrical form that contains not only the usual alliteration, but also end-rhyme. There is also a rhetorical strangeness about it: The deeds for which the king is praised are generically but not specifically described. This is perhaps not surprising, since it is supposed to have been composed under duress by a poet with no love for the king it honors. *Sonatorrek*, as might be expected, has an entirely different tone and is considered one of the finest elegies in Icelandic. Egill's loose stanzas (*lausavísur*) seem to be of varying authenticity and quality.

The figure of Egill as presented in his saga is perhaps the least stereotypically heroic of all such saga portraits. The saga does not present a grand, fair-haired warrior but rather a moody, charismatic poet, hardly good-looking, of strong attachments and capricious manners. It is perhaps because of the uniqueness of this characterization, as well as the excellence of the poetry, that *Egils saga* has remained one of the most widely read sagas down the centuries. How much the historical Egill resembled his saga portrait is, of course, impossible to know.

Bibliography: *Egils saga*, trans. E. R. Eddison, 1930.

Sandra Ballif Straubhaar

EIKE VON REPGOW (VON REPPICHOWE, HEICO VON REPE-CHOWE) (1180/1190–after 1235). Eike von Repgow was author of the *Sachsenspiegel* (The Saxon Mirror), the first medieval German vernacular legal text and the most important for all of late medieval central Europe.

Eike was born into a family of lesser nobility in the area of Repgow (present-day Reppichau). A layman, he studied the seven liberal arts, learned Latin, and may have studied in Magdeburg. It is clear from the *Sachsenspiegel* that he knew the Bible and canon law very thoroughly. While little is known about him, except from his work, his name appears in several charters from 1209 to 1233. He was connected with several important men in the area; one of these, Count Hoyer of Falkenstein, asked Eike to write a customal shortly after 1220.

In the rhyming preface to the *Sachsenspiegel*, Eike explains why he undertook this project: "to collect and preserve the inherited legal rules as a reference text for everyone." He and Count Hoyer believed that everyone—judge or someone bringing a case—needed a reference work and that reliance on oral repository of legal customs was no longer adequate. Eike did not receive formal training in jurisprudence according to the practice of the Italian law schools; he was not a legal scholar. He may have served as a *Schöffe*, a lay judge or juror. Regardless of his training, however, he knew the law. The text reveals his reflection upon legal custom, his knowledge of the Bible, canon law, and German literature, his incorporation of papal decretals and *Gratian's commentary, as well as his expertise in legal procedure. The narrative is shaped by his personal perspective.

The *Sachsenspiegel* does not present specific cases. Instead, Eike structured the text to present a framework that defines legal custom; then he explained legal procedures and outlined the conditions so that the reader would know how or when to apply this knowledge to specific cases. For Eike, legal custom existed in three dimensions: literal, moral, and metaphysical. At the literal level, customary law focuses on regulating events and providing solutions. At the moral level, law encompasses both rights and duties. By fulfilling their legal duties and learning proper conduct, people improve themselves. Customary law, education, and proper conduct are interdependent. At the metaphysical level, the source of law is God: "God is Law itself, therefore, justice is dear to him."

Although Eike's original text does not exist, it is clear that he revised the text himself. The revised one is similar to the first: five sequential books framed by two prologues and an epilogue. The late thirteenth-century version has a different format—two distinct parts, the first on general territorial law and the second on feudal law—which was followed in all subsequent redactions. By the end of the Middle Ages, some 450 complete or partial manuscripts of the *Sachsenspiegel* existed. The text had been translated into several dialects and languages and influenced legal systems in Prussia, Silesia, Poland, Bohemia, the Ukraine, and Hungary.

Bibliography: *The Saxon Mirror. A* Sachsenspiegel *of the Fourteenth Century*, trans. M. Dobozy, 1999.

Jana K. Schulman

EINARR SKÚLASON (FL. TWELFTH CENTURY). An Icelandic skald, he composed poems in praise of Norwegian kings. Like his celebrated predecessor and kinsman *Egill Skallagrímsson, he was said to be from Borgarfjord in the west of Iceland.

Only fragmentary information is available about Einarr's life. Starting in approximately 1114, he was intermittently in the retinue of various kings of Norway, including Sigurðr Jórsalafari ("Jerusalem-farer"), Haraldr gilli, Eysteinn Haraldsson, and Hákon herðibreiðr ("Broadshouldered"). A roster of Icelandic priests from 1143 includes Einarr, which seems to indicate that he was home at least that year. It is unknown whether Einarr received his priestly training in Iceland or in Europe.

Einarr's longest poem was *Óláfsdrápa*, also called *Geisli* (Ray of Light), in honor of *Óláfr Haraldsson, Norway's eleventh-century king and patron saint. Among the other poems of Einarr we retain are stanzas from two *Sigurðardrápa* poems, praising Sigurðr Jórsalafari and his pilgrimages to Compostela and Jerusalem; stanzas from two poems praising Haraldr gilli; stanzas on Haraldr's sons; part of a poem in end-rhymed meter; stanzas on King Eysteinn Haraldsson's quelling of peasant insurrections; stanzas on Eysteinn's killer, Símun skálpr; four stanzas on King Ingi; two stanzas of the battles of Hákon the Broadshouldered with King Ingi; and numerous fragmentary stanzas. Einarr is the single skald most often quoted by *Snorri Sturluson in *Heimskringla* and *Snorra Edda*; as might be expected from this fact, his poetry is consistently of fine quality.

Bibliography: P. Hallberg, *Old Icelandic Poetry: Eddic Lay and Skaldic Verse*, trans. P. Schach, 1975; F. Jónsson, ed., *Den norsk-islandske skjaldedigtning*, 1912–1915.

Sandra Ballif Straubhaar

EINHARD (EINHARD THE FRANK, EINHARTUS, AINHARDUS, HEINHARDUS; AND AFTER THE TENTH CENTURY, AGENHARDUS, EGINHARDUS, EGINHARTUS) (C. 770–840). After notable service at the court of *Charlemagne and his son, Einhard wrote a number of Latin works including one of the most important documents of the Carolingian age, the *Vita Karoli Magni* (The Life of Charlemagne the Great).

In around 770, Einhard was born into a relatively noble family of East Franconia in the Main River region and was educated in one of the famed cultural centers of northern Europe, the monastery at Fulda. He excelled there and was recommended by his abbot Baugulf to the court of Charlemagne and its palace school in 791 or 792. At the time, the Anglo-Saxon scholar and adviser to Charlemagne, *Alcuin of York was directing the school. Einhard's versatility and learning impressed Alcuin, and he eventually appointed Einhard to teach Charlemagne literature and mathematics. His erudition was matched by skill in architecture and handicrafts, as he oversaw the building at Aachen; indeed, Alcuin gave him yet another nickname (among many, most of which referred to his diminutive size), calling him "Bezaleel" in a letter to Charlemagne, after the workman in the biblical book Exodus. Einhard succeeded Alcuin directing the palace school upon the latter's retirement to Tours, and it is then that Einhard became close to Charlemagne and his family.

For Charlemagne, Einhard undertook a number of diplomatic missions to Rome: In 806 he secured approval from Pope *Leo III for Charlemagne to partition the empire, and in 813 he helped Charlemagne's son *Louis the Pious become recognized as regent. After Charlemagne's death in 814, he became secretary to Louis the Pious, who bestowed control of a number of abbeys on Einhard, including Seligenstadt, where he had a church built for the dubiously obtained bones of Saint Peter and Saint Marcellinus. Einhard, although he had the favor of Louis, grew to disrespect him, and when he became the tutor to Lothar, Louis' son, who he preferred over Louis, his position at court became difficult. Upon Lothar's open threats to his father's rule, Einhard had to retire to Seligenstadt with his wife Imma in 830. His married status did not prevent him from being abbot, and his wife abbess, of Seligenstadt, where he lived until his death in 840. He remained distant but still politically active up to near the end, effecting just before his death a reconciliation between Louis and Lothar.

It is in Seligenstadt between 830 and 836 that Einhard wrote his greatest work, the *Vita Karoli Magni*. The portrait of Charlemagne is often called the first and best secular biography in the Middle Ages. Not only does the work provide intimate and thoughtful details of Charlemagne's life and rule—after all, Einhard had been very close to the man and his family—but the biography reveals much about Frankish history, politics, language, and culture. Einhard drew heavily on the style and form of the Roman Silver Age biographer Suetonius, whose portraits of the Caesars in his *Lives* (especially those of Caesar Augustus and Titus) influenced Einhard's style and structure. Other influences include Cicero, Caesar, Ovid, and Tacitus, which attest to the renaissance of classical learning that Einhard helped foster under Charlemagne.

Indeed, the *Vita* looks back fondly at Charlemagne's rule and Charlemagne himself; he is characterized as a humble and devout man, moderate and pious, a Christian statesman and courageous soldier. This may have as much to do with Einhard's devotion and love of his king as with his dissatisfaction with the reign of Louis the Pious. He portrays Charlemagne's political successes, soldiery, and educational programs as they stem from the king's own character; it is a vivid and honorific picture of one of the Middle Age's greatest leaders. While there are some factual errors and Einhard did not witness Charlemagne's military campaigns, it remains a brilliant and personal profile, which reveals the great learning and intellect of its author.

Einhard produced a number of other works in Latin in addition to the *Vita*; he wrote the devotional work *Libellus de adoranda cruce* (Book on the Adoration of the Cross) and the *Translatio et miracula sanctorum suorum Marcellini et Petri* (The Translation and Miracles of Our Saints Mark and Peter). There also are a number of letters dating from 823 to 836 that reveal much about the politics of Louis' reign. The body of work Einhard left is crucial to our understanding of Carolingian history and culture.

Bibliography: Einhard, *Vita Karoli Magni/The Life of Charlemagne*, ed. and trans. E. S. Firchow and E. H. Zeydel, 1985.

Matthew Hussey

EKKEHARD I OF ST. GALL (C. 910–973). Ekkehard I was a liturgical poet and major monastic figure at the abbey of St. Gall in the Ottonian period.

Ekkehard I had long been considered the author of the *Vita Waltharii manufortis* (the *Waltharius*, or Walter of Aquitaine epic), leading to a "Waltharius problem" that produced a copious scholarly literature; however, scholars now reject Ekkehard's authorship of the epic poem. The continuation of Ratpert's chronicle of the abbey of St. Gall, the *Casus sancti Galli*, by Ekkehard IV (980/990–1056) that makes this attribution is nonetheless our main biographical source for the life of Ekkehard I.

Chapter 80 of Ekkehard IV's *Casus* attests to Ekkehard I's mild nature and poetic skill and his restoration to good health during a stay in Rome when the pope brought a relic of Saint John the Baptist to him. The relic is said (by Conrad of Fabaria in his *continuatio* ch. 5) to have come back with Ekkehard to St. Gall. Coming from a family in the area of Thurgau (a present-day canton of eastern Switzerland along Lake Constance), he entered the nearby monastery at St. Gall at a young age and spent most of the rest of his life there. Two of his nephews bore his name and were also connected with St. Gall: Ekkehard II "Palatinus" ("the courtier," as he was at the court of *Otto I) and his cousin Ekkehard III "Minor," a monk and later dean of St. Gall abbey.

Five of Ekkehard's hymns were included in the sequence of *Notker Balbulus (Notker the Stammerer): on Saint *Benedict (11 July), on the decollation of John the Baptist (29 August), on Saint *Columbanus (23 November), on the Trinity (*De sancta Trinitate*), and on Saint Paul (30 June); he also authored the hymn *O martyr aeterni patris*. He possibly also authored antiphons on Saints Andrew and Afra collected in the antiphonary of Hartker of St. Gall (d. 1011). Ekkehard IV quotes one hexameter from Ekkehard's hymn on the recluse Rachilda and mentions also a life of the recluse Wiborada.

Though he is not now connected with the genesis of the *Waltharius* epic,

Ekkehard I is nonetheless vital to the early medieval monastic, intellectual, and liturgical development of the great abbey at St. Gall.

Bibliography: H. Helbling, ed., *Ekkehard IV. Die Geschichten des Klosters St. Gallen*, 1958; W. von den Steinen, *Notker der Dichter und seine Geistige Welt*, 2 vols., 1948, 2d ed. 1978.

Joseph McGowan

ELEANOR OF AQUITAINE (C. 1122–1204). Political mastermind, patron of the arts, duchess and queen, consort and counselor of kings, Eleanor of Aquitaine was the most powerful woman of her time. As the daughter of William X, duke of Aquitaine and count of Poitiers, Eleanor was heir to domains larger than those of the French king. In 1137 she became queen of France through her marriage to *Louis VII; she remained married to the man she described as "a monk" for fifteen difficult years.

In 1147, Eleanor accompanied Louis on the Second Crusade, an adventure that introduced her to her uncle, Raymond of Antioch. Her obvious sympathy for a relative and a way of life antithetical to her ascetic husband's led to a growing estrangement that eventually led to an annulment in March 1152. Eleanor was then entitled to repossess Aquitaine; in June she married Henry Plantagenet, count of Anjou and duke of Normandy, who became *Henry II of England two years later. By Louis she had two daughters, Alix and Marie; by Henry, three daughters and five sons. Her daughter Mathilde married Henry of Saxony; Eleanor married *Alfonso VII of Castile; and Joan married first William II of Sicily and Raymond VI, count of Toulouse. Her son William died at the age of three, but Henry, *Richard I the Lionheart, Geoffrey, duke of Brittany, and *John survived. Eventually John inherited the throne of England after the death of his brothers.

Eleanor did not hesitate to participate in the administration of either realm in addition to managing her own domains. From the charters she signed under her own seal, notably to offer donations to religious establishments, it is clear that she disposed of her own properties and goods with the assistance of her own staff. After being sent by Henry to Aquitaine in 1169 to rein in the ambitions of her barons there, by the following year she had established a court at Poitiers, where she installed her son Richard as count and duke. *Marie de Champagne, her daughter, joined her there, and the two of them made her court the center of a rich and varied cultural life. Eleanor patronized troubadours, notably *Bernart de Ventadorn, and other writers including Thomas of Britain, the author of the romance of Tristan and Isolde. She influenced the epic *Girart de Roussillon*, and *Wace dedicated to her the *Roman de Brut*, a retelling of legends attributing the settlement of Britain to Aeneas's great-grandson Brutus. Benoît de Sainte-Maure probably referred to her when he spoke of a queen of beauty and generosity, the noble lady of a noble king, in his *Roman de Troie*.

After her sons (perhaps at her instigation) revolted against Henry II in 1173, her cultural activities ended; she was imprisoned in England from 1174 until Henry's death in 1189. She then resumed a lively political life, arranging for Richard's coronation as king and serving as administrator of the realm during his absence on crusade. When Richard was captured and held for ransom by the duke of Austria on his way back from the crusade, Eleanor raised an enormous ransom and delivered it herself, accompanying her son back to England.

In 1199 Richard died intestate, and John, known as Lackland, assumed the throne. The following year Eleanor, about eighty years old, crossed the Pyrenees to bring back her granddaughter *Blanche for marriage with the son of the French king. It was her hope that she could thus ensure peace between the two countries. In 1200 she also helped defend Anjou and Aquitaine against a threat from her grandson Arthur of Brittany, securing John's holdings in France. She continued to support John against Arthur until 1202, when John captured him at the castle of Mirebeau and ended the threat.

After Mirebeau, Eleanor retired to the abbey of Fontevrault. Like her forebears, she had long supported the abbey through donations; on the occasion of her son Richard's installation as duke of Aquitaine and count of Poitou, she had made a substantial contribution to Fontevrault, continuing to subsidize the establishment for the remainder of her life. She died at the abbey in 1204.

Never the favorite of clerical writers such as *William of Malmesbury and *Gerald of Wales who criticized her without mercy, she was given a regal tribute by the nuns of Fontevrault who said in eulogy: "She enhanced the grandeur of her birth by the honesty of her life, the purity of her morals, the flower of her virtues; and in the conduct of her blameless life, she surpassed almost all the queens of the world" (Kelly, 387).

Bibliography: A. Kelly, *Eleanor of Aquitaine and the Four Kings*, 1950; W. W. Kibler, ed., *Eleanor of Aquitaine: Patron and Politician*, 1976; R. Pernoud, *Aliénor d'Aquitaine*, 1965, R. Pernoud, *La Femme au temps des cathédrales*, 1980.

Judith Davis

ELISABETH OF SCHÖNAU (C. 1129–C.1164).

Benedictine nun and mystic, she had visions and wrote letters to bishops, abbesses, and abbots, as well as the popular *Revelations of the Sacred Band of Virgins of Cologne*, which tells the story of Saint Ursula and the 11,000 Virgins, among others.

Born in 1129 into a noble family from the Middle Rhine region, Elisabeth entered the convent attached to the Benedictine monastery of Schönau in Nassau, located southwest of Bonn. When she was twenty-three years old, in 1152, her first recorded visions began. She dictated her visions to her brother Ekbert, a priest in Cologne who later became abbot of the monastery at Schönau. Eventually, Elisabeth's works became quite well known and were widely distributed; there are at least 150 Latin manuscripts that contain Elisabeth's visions, though not all are complete.

Images of sickness characterize her visions, in the form of extreme pain as well as a sense of strangulation or suffocation. Elisabeth viewed the combination of illness and visionary experience as martyrdom that needed no priestly mediation; it is the visionary martyrdom that gives Elisabeth a "priestly" authority of her own. Elisabeth's visions are intricately connected with the seasons of the liturgical year. In addition to her visions, which are an account of her visions of Christ, Mary, and the saints and the *Revelations*, she also wrote the *Visiones de resurrectione Beatae Mariae Virginis*, on the Assumption of the Virgin, and the *Liber viarum Dei* (Book of the Ways of God), which is patterned on *Hildegard of Bingen's *Scivias*.

Elisabeth was born a generation after Hildegard of Bingen, with whom she is often compared. However, Elisabeth, while sharing ideas with Hildegard, has more in common with her twelfth-century contemporaries. Her visions contribute greatly to an understanding of this transitional period; they are important windows into the specifically Benedictine aspects of religious life during this time, as well as into the beginning of German women's mysticism.

Bibliography: M. Thiébaux, "Handmaid of God. Elisabeth of Schönau," in *The Writings of Medieval Women: An Anthology*, trans. M. Thiébaux, 2d ed., 1994.

Alexandra Sterling-Hellenbrand

ELIZABETH OF HUNGARY, SAINT (1207–1231).
Elizabeth was known for her many charitable works. After the death of her husband, under the influence of Conrad of Marburg, her spiritual director, she gave up her children, submitted to the mortification of the flesh, and lived austerely until her death.

Born the daughter of Andrew II, king of Hungary, Elizabeth, from an early age, displayed the piety and compassion that were to distinguish her later life. Around the age of four, Elizabeth was taken to the Thuringian court to be raised with her future husband, Louis, son of the Landgrave Herman of Thuringia. In 1221 at the age of fourteen, she married Louis, who was then twenty-one and had succeeded his father as landgrave, and they had three children. While married, Elizabeth performed many charitable acts. During a famine in 1225, she fed the poor by utilizing her own resources. She built hospitals and provided for children and orphans. When Emperor *Frederick II was organizing another crusade to the Holy Land in 1227, Louis went to join him but never saw combat. After contracting the plague, he died in Otranto. Early in 1228, Elizabeth became a tertiary of Saint *Francis at Eisenach, where she came under the authority of Conrad of Marburg, a domineering inquisitor of heretics, who attempted to break Elizabeth's will. Under these severe conditions, Elizabeth established the Fransiscan hospital at Marburg and drove herself relentlessly in her efforts to aid the poor, the sick, and the elderly. All of this took its toll on her health. She died on 17 November 1231 at the age of twenty-three.

Bibliography: E. R. Obbard, *Poverty, My Riches: A Study of St. Elizabeth of Hungary, 1207–1231*, 1997.

Clinton Atchley

EMMA OF ENGLAND (C. 985–1052). Queen of England, she was the daughter of Duke Richard I of Normandy. She married King *Æthelred the Unready of England in 1002 as part of Æthelred's attempt to gain the Normans' aid against Viking invaders. Emma and Æthelred had three children, *Edward (later called the Confessor), Alfred, and Godgifu. The marriage did not end England's Viking problems, however. After Æthelred died in 1016, the Dane *Cnut became king of England and married Emma in 1017. As Cnut's wife, Emma had two children, Hardacnut and Gunnhild. Perhaps the most significant contribution that Emma made was the family tie between the Norman dukes and the English kings; *William I the Conqueror's claim to the English throne was based on his kinship to Emma.

As queen, Emma gained a reputation for generosity to the Church as well as a reputation for political machinations that involved supporting one son's claim to the throne against another's. Emma, especially while she was Cnut's queen consort, gave lavish gifts to several monasteries, including altar pieces of gold, silver, and gems, various relics, and illuminated manuscripts. The implication seems clear; both Emma and Cnut, as foreigners ruling the realm, wanted to gain the support of the Church through the practice of gift-giving. As for her political endeavors, Emma tried to secure the English throne for Hardacnut, but when Cnut died in 1035, Harold I, his son by another woman, succeeded him. Harold's short reign saw Emma in exile, but she returned to England when Hardacnut ascended the throne in 1040. Hardacnut's death in 1042 resulted in Edward the Confessor's gaining the crown and in Emma losing her land. Exactly why Edward deprived his mother of her estates is not entirely clear, although she did not originally support his claim to the throne, and she was implicated as an accessory to his brother Alfred's murder. Despite this, he did allow her to live out her life in relative ease in Winchester.

Bibliography: P. Stafford, *Queen Emma and Queen Edith: Queenship and Women's Power in Eleventh-Century England,* 1997.

Janet Pope

ERIGENA. *See* JOHN SCOTTUS ERIUGENA.

ETHELBERT OF KENT. *See* ÆTHELBERT OF KENT.

ETHELFLED. *See* ÆTHELFLÆD OF MERCIA.

ETHELRED OF RIEVAULX. *See* ÆLRED OF RIEVAULX.

ETHELRED THE UNREADY. *See* ÆTHELRED THE UNREADY OF ENGLAND.

ETHELSTAN OF ENGLAND. *See* ÆTHELSTAN OF ENGLAND.

EUDES RIGAUD (ODO RIGALDUS) (C. 1200/1212–1275). Archbishop of Rouen, he was born at Courquetaines between 1200 and 1212. Eudes was appointed archbishop in 1248 and held that position until his death on 2 July 1275. His *Register of Visitations*, a day-by-day chronicle of the archbishop's interactions with his see from 1248 to 1269, is a rare and valuable source of insight into the ecclesiastical relations of his time.

Eudes' natal village of Courquetaines has been variously located in Lyons, Picardy, and the Île-de-France in the diocese of Meaux. Though his parentage is uncertain, it is generally believed that Eudes was born to a family of knightly status. Eudes had three sisters and two brothers: A sister Marie became abbess of *Héloïse's Paraclete, and a brother Adam became, like Eudes, a Franciscan. Eudes joined the Franciscan Order by 1236 and studied under *Alexander of Hales.

He then studied theology at the University of Paris and was regent of the Franciscan school in Paris from 1245 to 1247. Eudes was consecrated archbishop of Rouen at Lyons by Pope *Innocent IV in March 1248. The circumstances surrounding Eudes' election as archbishop are filled with speculation and debate. It is curious that a Franciscan was elected to such a high position when his Order was still at odds over the issue of whether or not the Rule allowed room for such a worldly role.

Eudes commented on the *Sentences* of *Peter Lombard in 1245. Along with Alexander of Hales, John de la Rochelle, and Robert de la Bassée, Eudes co-authored the *Exposition of the Four Masters*, which explores the meaning of the word "poverty" as used in the Franciscan Rule. But Eudes' greatest gift to posterity is his *Register of Visitations*, which shows the archbishop as a conscientious administrator of his see who sought to enforce canon law. His *Register* records over twenty-one years of inquiries into the workings of his see and provides insight into the social, political, and economic forces Eudes confronted on a day-to-day basis. It also contains commentary on *Louis IX's preparation for his crusade.

His talent for mediation and close relationship with Louis IX led Eudes to be appointed to a royal commission to help settle disputes between university factions. Eudes also served at least nineteen times in the Parliament of Paris, was a member of the Norman Exchequer, and performed such celebrated marriages as that of Philip, Louis' son, to Princess Isabella of Aragon. He also had a hand in the negotiations between Louis and *Henry III of England that resulted in the Treaty of Paris (1259). Near the end of his career, Eudes was ordered by Pope Gregory X to preside over the Second Ecumenical Council of Lyons, a task of great honor.

Eudes embarked on the Eighth Crusade with Louis IX and his army on 1 March 1270. After the army's defeat and Louis' death and internment in Tunis,

Eudes returned to Rome, where he died on 2 July 1275. He was buried in Rouen. His tomb was smashed in 1562, and his bones were scattered during the French Revolution.

Bibliography: S. Brown and J. O'Sullivan, eds., *The Register of Eudes of Rouen*, 1964.

Karolyn Kinane

EUGENIUS III (EUGENE), POPE (D. 1153, PONTIFICATE 1145–1153).

Bernardo Pignatelli, a Cistercian abbot from Pisa, was elected pope on 15 February 1145, the same day his predecessor Lucius II died. He was a pupil of *Bernard of Clairvaux and vigorously pursued papal reform. He also initiated the Second Crusade, which ultimately proved to be a failure.

Eugenius, son of the lord of Montemagno, eventually became vicar general of the bishop of Pisa and served as a monk at Clairvaux under Saint Bernard. He later came to Rome at the request of Innocent II to become the abbot of the monastery at St. Anastatius. The people of Rome were in revolt against the papacy at the time of his election in 1145, and thus Eugenius was consecrated at Farfa. He spent much of his pontificate outside of Rome due to continual revolts. *Arnold of Brescia led the most serious revolt in 1148, and he preached against the extravagance of the clergy and the temporal powers of the pope to such an extent that he angered Bernard and was excommunicated by Eugenius.

Problems also emerged elsewhere in the Christian world. Edessa fell to the Turks in 1144, and Eugenius called upon the French king, *Louis VII, to go on crusade. Bernard aided the pope in convincing Louis, but he also succeeded in convincing the Holy Roman Emperor, Conrad III, to join Louis. Eugenius expected Conrad to help subdue the rebellious Romans and the Normans in Sicily but was forced to flee to France because he could not fight the Romans alone. Louis and Conrad were on crusade in 1147 and 1148, but the crusade ended in failure due to problems between the rulers.

Conrad promised to come to Rome in 1151 to receive the crown and help Eugenius against the Romans, but the emperor died in February 1152. *Frederick I Barbarossa was elected, and problems between the empire and papacy began over his attempts to restore imperial rights. At a disputed ecclesiastical election at Magdeburg in 1152 Frederick appointed his own candidate, Winchmann, and the other candidate, Gerard, appealed to Rome. Papal legates were sent to Germany in 1153, and they deposed three bishops and began proceedings against Winchmann when Frederick ordered them to leave. Peace was temporarily achieved between the papacy and the emperor, and Frederick promised to come to Rome in 1154 and help Eugenius against the Roman populace in exchange for the crown. This meeting never took place, however, as Eugenius died of a violent fever at Tivoli on 8 July 1153.

Throughout his pontificate, Eugenius promoted reform as evidenced by synods at Paris (1147), Trier (1147–1148), and Rheims (1148), and he claimed temporal and spiritual authority through his crusading efforts and interference in the ecclesiastical affairs of most European nations. Conflicts with successive Holy Roman Emperors, however, impeded much of Eugenius' secular and ecclesiastical efforts. He was buried next to Gregory III in St. Peter's and beatified in 1872.

Bibliography: R. P. McBrien, *Lives of the Popes*, 1997. W. Ullmann, *A Short History of the Papacy in the Middle Ages*, 1972.

Paul Miller

EYVINDR FINNSSON SKÁLDASPILLIR (FL. TENTH CENTURY). A nobleman and skald from Hálogaland in northern Norway, he was descended on the maternal side from King *Harald I Fairhair. Eyvindr's best-known poem *Háleygjatal* (Enumeration of the Hálogalanders) is an enumeration of the great deeds of the ancestors of Jarl Hákon Sigurðarson of Hlaðir, one of the noble patrons at whose court Eyvindr served. Eyvindr's by-name, "Skáldaspillir" (Poet-Spoiler), often interpreted to mean "plagiarist," could just as easily mean that he shamed the competition because he was so good.

As is the case with many court skalds, much of what is known of Eyvindr's life concerns his patrons. They were all rulers of Norway: Eyvindr's kinsman Hákon inn góði, whose battles against the sons of his brother Eiríkr blóðøx ("Blood-Axe") Eyvindr memorialized; Haraldr gráfeldr ("Grey-Cloak"), who succeeded Hákon; and Jarl Hákon Sigurðarson, whose successful defeat of the Jómsvíkings (985) was the occasion of *Háleygjatal*.

Eyvindr composed *Háleygjatal* after the model of *Ynglingatal* (Enumeration of the Yngling Clan), composed by þjóðólfr hvinr for King Harald I. Both recount the deeds of the legendary (and divine) ancestors of prominent noblemen, and stanzas from both were used copiously by the Icelandic historian *Snorri Sturluson as sources throughout his compilation of kings' sagas called *Heimskringla* (The Circle of the World, after its first line). Eyvindr's other lengthy poem that has survived is *Hákonarmál*, in memory of King Hákon inn góði of Norway who fought Eiríkr's sons. Fourteen of Eyvindr's loose stanzas (*lausavísur*) recounting contemporary events have been preserved. Snorri Sturluson mentions in *Heimskringla* an additional poem by Eyvindr, *Íslendingadrápa* (Ode to the Icelanders), but it has been lost.

Bibliography: Snorri Sturluson, *Heimskringla: History of the Kings of Norway*, trans. L. M. Hollander, 1964.

Sandra Ballif Straubhaar

F

FĀRĀBĪ, ABŪ NASIR MUHAMMAD, AL- (C. 870–C. 950). This renowned Muslim philosopher was known among his coreligionists as "the second
teacher" (after Aristotle) and as Alfarabius or Abunaser among Latin scholastics.
Perhaps one of the most original of the medieval Islamic philosophers, his commentaries on Aristotle exerted a marked influence on the development of European thought.

Very little is known about al-Fārābī's life, save that he was of Turkish ex-
traction and spent the greater part of his philosophic career at the court of the
Shiite Hamdanid prince Sayf al-Dawla (d. 944) in Aleppo. He was born in the
village of Wasij in the district of the city of Farab in Transoxiana and eventually
settled in Baghdad. Here he studied logic and philosophy under two leading
Nestorian Christian Aristotelians, Yūhannā ibn Haylān (d. c. 932) and Abū Bishr
Mattā ibn Yūnus (d. 940). In 942, he took up residence at the court of the prince
Sayf al-Dawla, where he remained until moving to Damascus shortly before his
death in 950.

Al-Fārābī's literary output was vast, and his biographers list between seventy
and one hundred works to his credit. However, few are extant, and many have
proven to be spurious. Al-Fārābī's existing corpus can be divided into two
parts, the first concerning Aristotle and the study of logic and the second,
ancillary philosophic studies. Belonging to the first category are al-Fārābī's
commentaries and paraphrases of Aristotle's logical corpus, the *Organon*, which
in its Arabic recension included Aristotle's *Rhetoric* and *Poetics*. He also wrote
commentaries on some of Aristotle's other works including his *Nicomachean
Ethics, Physics*, and *Metaphysics* as well as Plato's *Laws* and Porphyry's
Isagoge. The second category includes works on metaphysics, ethics, mathematics, music, and politics. He also penned a number of important original
tracts; the most important are the *Reconciliation of Plato and Aristotle*, the
Great Book of Music, the *Virtuous City*, and the *Survey of the Sciences*. The

latter is the first attempt by a Muslim philosopher to classify the various branches of knowledge.

Al-Fārābī's philosophical thinking can be placed squarely within the Arabic Aristotelian teachings of tenth-century Baghdad. As the "second teacher," he continued the reconciliation of Greek philosophic thought and Islamic revelation begun by the first Muslim philosopher, al-Kindī (d. 873). He posits that his work aims to explain the principle of syllogism of Aristotle in terms familiar to the Arabs. Indeed, it is Aristotelian logic that forms the core of al-Fārābī's philosophic system. He firmly held that correctly applied logical methods could direct man away from error toward truth and that only through the judicious application of logic could one be completely sure that any given proposition, idea, doctrine, or theory was correct.

Al-Fārābī has rightly been characterized as the father of Islamic Neoplatonism. He developed a highly complex metaphysical system that centers on the so-called Theory of the Ten Intelligences. This theory hypothesizes a Supreme Being who created the world by way of contemplating Himself through an exercise of rational intelligence. The Supreme Being, identified as God, is held to be a necessary existent requiring no other for existence or subsistence. From this Supreme Being emanates a second hypostasis called the First Intellect, which, like God, is immaterial substance. This Second Being contemplates, through the exercise of rational intelligence, the Supreme Being in addition to its own essence, and it is this contemplation that allows for the emanation of the Second Intellect. This chain of emanation likewise continues down to the Tenth Intellect, which constitutes the bridge between the heavenly and terrestrial worlds. Each Intellect has an individual celestial sphere, and like the Greek Neoplatonists, al-Fārābī identifies each of the spheres with a celestial body.

Al-Fārābī gave considerable attention to political theory, adapting the Platonic system to the Muslim political situation in his work the *Virtuous City*. While not a complete reiteration of Plato's *Republic*, this work lays down the various qualities that constitute the ideal state. In the *Virtuous City*, al-Fārābī tackles the subject of what an ideal state would ultimately look like. He begins with the Aristotelian idea that mankind is by nature political. He goes on to posit that the ideal human society is one in which all members cooperate in a political collective to achieve the goal of the "highest happiness." Thus, by extension the ideal virtuous world can only be achieved when all its constituents, here the sundry virtuous cities, collaborate in the pursuit of the highest happiness. Al-Fārābī asserts that such a life can be attained only under the aegis of a good and virtuous ruler who embodies a number of qualities such as sound body, intelligence, eloquence, resolution, learning, and most important, a thorough understanding of philosophy and logic. Just as God rules the universe, so should the philosopher, as the most perfect kind of man, rule the state.

Al-Fārābī's work quickly gained popularity in the Muslim world, and by the eleventh century, its study was obligatory for all aspiring philosophers. His impact on those who followed him, most notably the celebrated *Avicenna, was considerable. He also exerted an influence on medieval Jewish philosophers; the great Jewish philosopher *Maimonides held him in high esteem. In the Christian West, al-Fārābī's works on logic, metaphysics, and psychology were translated into Latin and exerted a wide-ranging influence on Christian Scholastics. Gundissalinus, the spiritual leader at Segovia, translated many of his works and in addition produced his own *Classification of the Sciences* (*De divisione philosophiae*) modeled on al-Fārābī's system. This classification was subsequently followed in the then recently established Western universities. Through the translations of Gundissalinus and others, al-Fārābī came to influence Scholastics such as Thomas *Aquinas and *Albertus Magnus. Thomas Aquinas takes up al-Fārābī's arguments for the existence of God in his *Summa Theologiae*, and the so-called cosmological argument popularized by Aquinas is prefigured in al-Fārābī's discussion of the subject.

Bibliography: M. G. Galston, *Politics and Excellence: The Political Philosophy of Alfarabi*, 1990; I. R. Netton, *Al-Fārābī and His School*, 1992.

Erik S. Ohlander

FERDINAND I OF CASTILE AND LEÓN (C. 1018–1065). As the self-proclaimed first king of Castile (r. 1035–1065), Ferdinand I worked to expand his realm and establish the preeminence of Castile-León among the Christian kingdoms vying for superiority during the early centuries of the reconquest of Islamic Spain.

At his death in 1035, Ferdinand's father, Sancho "el Mayor" of Navarre, divided his lands among his sons, with Ferdinand inheriting Castile. Ferdinand soon set about restoring the territorial unity of his father's domain and increasing the size of his own. In 1037, Ferdinand defeated his brother-in-law Vermudo III and acquired León. After taking León, he officially named himself king of Castile, thus becoming the first person to possess that title. In 1054, Ferdinand vanquished his older brother García, who had inherited Navarre, and acquired lands in the northeastern part of the peninsula. Other conquests were made in Galicia in the years that followed. In 1063, Ferdinand's forces overcame those of one of his younger brothers, Ramiro, and captured the strategically important city of Zaragoza, whose Islamic ruler was made to pay tribute to Castile.

In the war against the Muslims, Ferdinand also oversaw the rise of Castile-León as the most powerful kingdom of the Christian Reconquest. On his western frontier, he made a number of conquests during the 1050s and 1060s, a campaign that culminated in the taking of Coimbra in 1064. He also captured territories on his southern frontier and set the stage for the taking of Toledo, which would occur in 1085 during the reign of his son *Alfonso VI. Moreover, Ferdinand forced the Muslim rulers of cities such as Badajoz and Seville to pay tribute to him in exchange for protection, thus impeding further advances of Navarre and Aragón, two neighboring Christian kingdoms.

Within his own kingdom, Ferdinand worked to achieve an ecclesiastical reform through policies designed to improve the quality of religious officiation and strengthen the authority over those dioceses and monasteries that were under the auspices of the monarchy. New bishops were appointed in order to ensure their loyalty to the king, and new canons concerning the qualifications of those in the clergy and the nature of religious education were enacted at episcopal councils. The most important of these took place in Coyanza, in 1055, a council over which Ferdinand himself presided.

Ferdinand will be remembered for founding the Castilian monarchy and for situating Castile-León at the forefront of the Christian Reconquest. Although he had successfully reunited much of his father's domain, before his death Ferdinand imitated his father by dividing his kingdom among his children: His eldest son Sancho became the new king of Castile, his second son Alfonso inherited León, his youngest son García received Galicia, and his two daughters, Urraca and Elvira, acquired monasteries over which they presided.

Bibliography: C. J. Bishko, *Studies in Medieval Spanish Frontier History*, 1980.

Gregory B. Kaplan

FORTUNATUS, VENANTIUS (C. 540–C. 601). Born in Venetia in northern Italy and educated at Milan and Ravenna, Venantius Honoratus Clementianus Fortunatus was the most prolific and "classical" poet of his time.

Although he wrote a life of Saint Martin and other works in prose, it is his "occasional" poems for which he is best known. Entitled *Miscellanea*, the eleven books of his poetry include two of the best-known hymns in the Christian Church, "Pange, lingua, gloriosi" (Sing, My Tongue, the Savior's Glory) and "Vexilla regis prodeunt" (The Banner of the King Goes Forth).

After leaving Italy in about 565, Fortunatus spent some time traveling through France. At Poitiers, he was ordained a priest and became chaplain of the convent of *Radegunde, a Thuringian princess who had fled her marriage to King Clothar. She became his patron and encouraged him to stay in Poitiers, where he became bishop in 599. After Radegunde's and Agnes' deaths, he began traveling again and stayed for some time at the court of Sigibert, king of the Franks.

In the long tradition of Latin elegaic writing, he addressed many works to male friends in ardent language; images of light and radiance pervade his poems to both men and women, and an important element in his verses is a sense of humor directed equally at himself and at others. The close friendship enjoyed by Fortunatus with Radegunde and her sister Agnes was the occasion of some of his most courtly and delicate poetry; in these lyrics the poet appears as an ardent and ineffably courteous admirer, pampered friend of the family, fond relative, and spiritual counselor perennially on call.

Bibliography: P. Dronke, *Medieval Latin and the Rise of European Love Lyric*, 2d ed., 2 vols., 1968; J. George, trans., *Venantius Fortunatus: Personal and Political Poems*, 1995.

Judith Davis

FRANCIS OF ASSISI, SAINT (C. 1181–1226). The "Poverello," the "Seraphic saint," founder of the Order of Friars Minor, the Poor Clares, and the Third Order, Francis embraced a life of poverty in imitation of the poor Christ. In September 1224 he claimed to have received the stigmata (the wounds of the crucified Christ) at Mount Alvernia.

Born in the Umbrian town of Assisi to the wealthy textile merchant Pietro di Bernardone and his wife Pica, daughter of a distinguished French family, he was baptized Giovanni (John), but afterward his father, a frequent traveler to France, chose to call him Francesco (Francis), then a rare name. He was provided with a basic education and had some knowledge of Latin and French. Talented in music, he enjoyed singing and composing songs throughout his life.

Before his conversion, Francis enjoyed the carefree lifestyle afforded to favored sons of the wealthy. His ambition was to become a knight. His first encounter with military service was to enlist in the troops of Assisi when it was attacked by the city of Perugia. He was taken prisoner and spent a year in prison (1202–1203), where he became ill. Francis turned to prayer and meditation while recovering. However, still aspiring to become a knight, he planned to engage in a campaign against Apulia at Spoleto but became ill on the journey and returned home.

After Spoleto, Francis grew increasingly devout and adopted an ascetic lifestyle. His medieval biographers relate several transforming experiences from this period of his life including an encounter with a leper. Francis, overcome by compassion, is said to have given the leper all his money and then kissed him. Another such experience is said to have taken place at the church of San Damiano, then in need of physical repair. Francis, standing before the altar in prayer, is said to have heard a voice from the crucifix bidding him to rebuild "my" church; Francis then performed manual labor to rebuild its crumbling walls. Whatever the authenticity of such accounts, lepers were of special concern to Francis throughout his ministry, and the church of San Damiano was restored enough to become part of the first convent for the Poor Clares. Moreover, it can be argued that in a metaphoric sense the saint's entire ministry was devoted to the task of restoring God's church. The culminating event of Francis' conversion is said to have occurred on 24 February 1208 at the little church of Santa Maria degli Angeli (called the Portiuncula) near Assisi. While hearing Mass, Francis was struck by the words of the Gospel reading, the account of Jesus commissioning the twelve disciples (Mt. 10:5–14), and believed it to be his personal call to discipleship. Thus the Portiuncula has become known as the birthplace of the Franciscan order.

Although derided by some, Francis was soon joined by followers. He composed a simple Rule now lost but believed to have been essentially a statement of strong commitment to the apostolic life delineated in the Gospel of Matthew. Francis and his small band of followers went to Rome, where their rule received the oral approval of Pope *Innocent III (1210), and thus the Franciscan order was born. Rigorously following the way of discipleship contained in the Gospel, they set out as poor, itinerant preachers, having renounced the ownership of property, and believed themselves led by the Holy Spirit. The optimism and simplicity of Francis' preaching touched the hearts of many. He stressed the need for penance and brought a message of peace; he taught his followers not to resist ill treatment. One person especially moved by Francis' preaching during the early period of his ministry was young *Clare, daughter of the powerful Favarone di Offreduccio. In 1212, she left the wealth and security of her family home to follow Francis in a life of poverty. He listened to her vows at the Portiuncula and provided her with a simple Rule, thereby establishing the Second Order, the Poor Clares.

Saint Francis sent his followers into the world on missionary journeys and ventured forth himself, sometimes encountering difficulties. In 1212 he was shipwrecked at Dalmatia en route to Syria. In 1213–1214 he set out for Morocco but became ill in Spain. During the Fifth Crusade, he journeyed to the Holy Land (1219–1220) but stopped first at Damietta in an unsuccessful attempt to convert the sultan of Egypt, Malikal-Kamil. Then his trip to Jerusalem was cut short by growing problems within the order at home.

After he returned to Italy in 1221, a great meeting was held in Assisi with about 3,000 friars in attendance. Francis chose to step down from his position of leadership, asking the pope to name as protector Cardinal Hugolino (who later became Pope *Gregory IX). During the next two years the Rule was revised, and a definitive Rule (*Regula bullata*) was approved by Pope *Honorius III on 29 November 1223.

Francis continued preaching and lent support to the emerging Tertiaries (the Third Order) intended for laypeople who promised to keep the principles of Francis' apostolic Rule. He contributed to the spiritual growth of his order by composing circular letters and writing the Admonitions (directives). During this period Francis was ordained a deacon and made his first public appearance as such on 25 December 1223 at Greccio, the occasion of his joyful "crib" celebration of Christ's Nativity, the beginning of a popular tradition.

What sets Francis apart is the stigmata. His is the first documented case and the only one celebrated with a special feast day in the Roman Catholic Church. It is said to have occurred on 14 September 1224 on Mt. Alvernia while the saint was in intense prayer. The marks were said to have remained visible on his body throughout the remainder of his life and were witnessed after his death by Saint Clare and others. Francis lived for about two more years at the Portiuncula. Although sick, blind, and in great pain, he awaited death with joy— singing and requesting songs. During his last days he presumably completed the mystical *Cantico del sole* (Canticle of Brother Sun), considered the first literary poem in Italian. Highly regarded, the Canticle conveys the saint's belief that all of creation is unified because God's love permeates all aspects of nature. On 3 October 1226 Francis embraced "Brother Death." Pope Gregory IX canonized him on 16 July 1228. The next day the cornerstone was laid for the Basilica being built to house his remains. His feast day is 4 October.

Establishing an accurate biography of Saint Francis has been of critical concern since the late nineteenth century. Thomas de Celano (c. 1190–1260), who joined Francis as a follower c. 1214, was commissioned to write the first *Life*, completing his task no later than January 1229, and Saint *Bonaventure finished his *legendae* in 1263. There are other medieval lives, one being the famous *Legend of the Three Friends* (1246), preserved only in fragments. Some twenty-eight writings by Saint Francis have been authenticated, and during the last half of the twentieth century, scholars turned to these for greater insight to the man. Saint Francis remains one of the best-loved saints in the world. Admired for his love of nature and his gospel of peace, he is held in high esteem by believers, nonbelievers, and followers of non-Christian religions.

Bibliography: R. J. Armstrong and I. C. Brady, trans. and eds., *Francis and Clare: The Complete Works*, 1982; A. Fortini, *Francis of Assisi*, 1981.

Deanna Evans

FREDEGUND (D. 597). Fredegund was the third wife of the Merovingian king Chilperic I (d. 584) and the mother of Chlothar II (d. 629) and a daughter, Rigunth. Fredegund seems to have been the servant of Chilperic's first wife and to have served Chilperic as a concubine before becoming his wife. Our chief source for the period, *Gregory of Tours, recounts various sordid tales about Fredegund and blames her for the murders of King Sigebert (Chilperic's half brother), Galswinthe (Chilperic's second wife), Galswinthe's sons, Chilperic himself, and various other members of the royal family as well as clergymen and aristocrats. She is also accused of trying to strangle her own daughter.

Despite this portrayal of Fredegund as an evil queen, even Gregory has to admit that she worked hard to secure her son's succession to the throne. When her elder sons died, Fredegund burned the tax records because she seems to have believed that collecting royal taxes angered God and that the death of her sons was a sign and a punishment. She then convinced Chilperic not to assess future taxes so that the royal couple would be blessed with a new son, which they were when Chlothar II was born. In a similar vein, Fredegund's ruthless treatment of Galswinthe and her sons cleared the stage of all rival claimants to the crown so that Chlothar could rule unimpeded. When Chilperic died, Fredegund became regent for her infant son, and one could argue that she trained Chlothar well; by her elimination of his cousins, he became the first Merovingian king to rule all of the Frankish territories in half a century. In sum, despite her humble beginnings and being a woman, Fredegund participated actively in the political arena and ensured her son's succession to the kingdom of the Franks.

Bibliography: S. F. Wemple, *Women in Frankish Society: Marriage and the Cloister, 500 to 900*, 1981.

Janet Pope

FREDERICK I BARBAROSSA (C. 1125–1190). Frederick I established the Hohenstaufen dynasty in Germany, revived the Holy Roman Empire, and brought it into conflict with the papacy.

Born a Staufen prince, Frederick favored his mother's family, the Welfs, who had challenged Frederick's uncle, Conrad III, for the German throne. Conrad made Frederick his heir to appease both families; Frederick was subsequently elected king of Germany in March 1152. The unanimity of his election allowed Frederick to begin his reign as a traditional king, following the policies laid down by Conrad; his main goals were to dispense justice, maintain law and order, and keep the peace. He made overtures to Pope *Eugenius III and worked on settling disputes between the German princes.

Frederick wanted the imperial crown and, to that end, signed a mutual assistance treaty in 1153 with the pope, who had earlier given Frederick permission to annul his first marriage due to his wife's infidelity. In 1154, the new pope, *Hadrian IV, found himself exiled from Rome, and Frederick traveled there to restore him to his throne. Having accomplished this task, Frederick was crowned Holy Roman Emperor in June 1155.

In 1156, Frederick settled on the idea of creating a geographic power base that would provide him with financial and military support, a plan called the Grand Design, which encompassed much of northern Italy. To concentrate on the Grand Design, Frederick allowed the development of new imperial princes in Germany who had sovereign powers within their territories, thus sacrificing the centralization of Germany. In addition, his attempt to achieve the Grand Design ultimately brought him into conflict not only with the German princes but with France and the papacy as well.

The pope resented Frederick's Grand Design, and Frederick in turn publicly rejected the pope's contention that the emperor was a vassal of the pope. In mid-1158, Frederick traveled to Lombardy to announce the Grand Design and to gain its acceptance. He reckoned without the communalization of the northern Italian towns and cities, which had become very independent; in addition, social mobility within the urban areas meant that Frederick could not play off the nobles against the commoners. Milan, which agreed after some hostilities to become an imperial city, resented Frederick's administrators, and war broke out again in 1160. When Milan surrendered in 1162, Frederick had the city destroyed.

After Pope Hadrian's death in 1159, the chaos in Lombardy led to a double papal election. The Sicilian candidate, *Alexander III, was the selection of the College of Cardinals, while Frederick supported the popularly elected pope, Victor IV. Alexander excommunicated Frederick and began a propaganda campaign to stir up the Lombards against Frederick. The German princes resented the problems with the papacy and put pressure on Frederick to come to terms with Alexander, and the schism clearly put the Grand Design in danger in Lombardy.

By 1166, Alexander was installed in Rome, and Frederick tried to capture him in 1167 but failed. The Lombards, meanwhile, formed a defensive coalition called the Lombard League, and Frederick retreated to Germany in 1167. The death of Rainald (his chancellor, adviser, and father-in-law) that year further exacerbated Frederick's indecision on what course to take, and problems in Germany with *Henry the Lion, duke of Saxony, added to his burden. Alexander threw his support behind the Lombard League, and Frederick made his first overtures to Alexander in 1169. However, it would take another campaign against Lombardy in 1174, which ended in an indecisive battle in 1176 at Legnano, to convince Frederick that his plan for a central European kingdom (the Grand Design) had failed and that he had to reach an accommodation with Alexander.

The Peace of Anagni was Frederick's official recognition of Alexander as pope, and Frederick began to concentrate on a new plan that centered on Germany. The emperor began to co-opt an incipient feudalism that had been growing in Germany for some years and eventually made it into a constitutional principle in which the new imperial princes became tenants-in-chief to the emperor. By 1180, Frederick was able to subdue his greatest rival, the duke of Saxony, and sentenced him to exile in Normandy in 1181. As a result of the trial, feudal law became the foundation of the German constitution, replacing tribal law. Feudalism eventually resulted in the creation of new territorial units that would preclude any hope of creating a centralized German state.

Having dealt with Germany, Frederick cemented a cordial relationship with the pope and Sicily in the Peace of Venice (1177) and arranged a marriage between the Sicilian heir, Constance, and his heir, *Henry (VI). Frederick then turned to what he had long considered as his main goal as a Christian ruler, the defense of the Church and the rescue of Palestine from the infidels. He took the cross at Pentecost in 1188 and departed for the Holy Land in May 1189, roughly at the same time that both *Philip II Augustus of France and *Richard I Lionheart of England did so.

Traveling overland, Frederick made it into Armenia by early June 1190; riding ahead of his forces, he stopped at a river to refresh himself and, inexplicably, drowned. His men buried him at the cathedral at Antioch, and most of his crusading force subsequently broke up. His heir, Henry, was unable to complete his father's plan, and over the next century, the German kings lost most of their powers to the imperial princes and became largely ceremonial figures. Thus, Frederick's ultimate legacy was the dismantling of the German empire and the end of any hope of centralization for many centuries to come.

Bibliography: P. Munz, *Frederick Barbarossa, a Study in Medieval Politics*, 1969.

Connie Evans

FREDERICK II (1194–1250). Holy Roman Emperor Frederick II's authoritarian rule of his lands and quarrels with the Catholic popes laid the foundations of instability and disunification in Germany and Italy that would last into the nineteenth century.

The grandson of *Frederick I Barbarossa, the young Frederick's inheritance of Germany and Sicily was threatened by his parents' early deaths. He became a ward of the pope, *Innocent III, and secured his claim to the Sicilian throne, though he had to battle *Otto IV to regain the German crown. Innocent concluded an alliance with *Philip II Augustus of France that allowed Frederick to be elected to the German throne in 1211.

Though still a young man, Frederick was already married and the father of a son, whom he named king of Sicily when he traveled to Germany to be crowned king in 1212. It took another three years to retrieve the entire German territory from the hands of Otto and his English supporters, but in 1215, Frederick was crowned again. In gratitude, Frederick took a crusading oath; however, his failure to fulfill this oath led to a division with the pope.

As the ruler of Germany, Frederick was to prove disastrous, and out of his thirty-eight years as emperor, he only spent nine years in Germany, most in the early years of his reign. He devolved his authority in Germany to the imperial cities, the German princes, and his bishops, a practice that decentralized the German territories. He spent most of his time building a northern Italian power base and focusing on his imperial ambitions, which included mounting a crusade and being crowned by the pope in Rome.

Frederick had plans to join the two crowns of Sicily and Germany, a plan that the pope, now *Honorius III, greatly opposed. In 1220, Frederick marched to Rome to be crowned Holy Roman Emperor in November and reaffirmed his crusading vow; he also freed the ecclesiastics in his territories from taxation and submission to secular courts. Even as he focused on his imperial ambitions, he still found time to patronize art and law schools. His court was a center of culture; he himself wrote a book on hunting and poetry. He supported translations from Greek and Arabic and engaged the poet *Walther von der Vogelweide to promote his political causes.

His first wife having died, Frederick negotiated to marry the daughter of the Latin king of Jerusalem; he would thus become heir to that throne on his father-in-law's death. Frederick planned to combine the marriage ceremony with the start of a crusade, but when Frederick finally went east in 1228, it was only to consummate the marriage and be crowned. By 1227, the new pope, *Gregory IX, who was less trusting of Frederick's motives, was growing weary of the emperor's promises, and when the crusade did not materialize by late 1228, he excommunicated Frederick.

Frederick crowned himself king of Jerusalem in early 1229, making it clear that the Holy Roman Emperor was superior to the pope. But the Latins rebelled against him, and after making a treaty with the Muslims, Frederick returned to Italy, where Gregory had been inducing insurrection against him. He was able to negotiate with the Sicilians in 1230 and granted them a centralized law code that implied that the ultimate power in the country rested in the monarch and not in the pope.

Frederick maintained a regent in Germany, and the German princes generally supported him, especially since he had granted them jurisdiction over their territories in 1232. They provided an army that Frederick used against the rebellious Lombards in 1235, an act that the pope saw as a threat to his power in Italy. The pope supported the Lombards against Frederick, whom he eventually came to view as the Antichrist. Frederick's refusal to withdraw from Lombardy led the pope to excommunicate him again in 1238, and the war became a crusade against the emperor, reaching a virtual stalemate by 1239.

Frederick made plans to subdue Rome and the pope and encircled the city by 1240. When Gregory summoned his cardinals to a meeting to address the situation in 1241, Frederick captured some of them and held them as hostages. Frederick had full run of Italy from north to south except for Rome, and though Gregory died in August, his eventual successor *Innocent IV remained committed to the cause and began a propaganda campaign against Frederick.

Frederick wanted peace by 1244, but Innocent avoided meeting with the emperor. The pope called a general council of the Church for June 1245, and Frederick was called before it; his attempt to present his case was rebuffed, and he was condemned by the council in July and stripped of his thrones, titles, and the allegiance of his people.

Negotiation attempts continued through 1250, though Innocent continued to stir up resistance to the emperor in both Sicily and Germany. The pope wanted a new crusade with Frederick as the first target, a plan that *Louis IX of France could not agree to, as it set a precedent that made secular power secondary to that of the pope's. The attempt of the pope to use a crusade to interject himself into the world of secular politics eerily foreshadowed the struggle between popes and kings in the fourteenth century that resulted in the Babylonian Captivity of the papacy by the kings of France.

Though Innocent was unable to get the German princes to overthrow Frederick, he was able to induce enough instability to keep Frederick off balance. All of Frederick's attempts to reach a peace settlement with the pope were rejected, though he was able to retain much of his control of Italy through 1250. By early 1250, Frederick was back in Sicily, and though he managed to assert his control there, he fell violently ill in December. He made a will that named his eldest son Conrad heir to Germany, Italy and Sicily, while his youngest son Henry was given the throne of Jerusalem; Frederick subsequently died on 13 December 1250.

Frederick had not achieved the peace he had dreamed of, but neither had he been defeated in his aims. Innocent died four years later, and his successors continued their efforts against the Hohenstaufen dynasty. Eventually, the Holy Roman Empire was to pass out of existence as a real entity, and the German king became a figurehead, factors that created disunity and instability in both Germany and Italy for centuries to come.

Bibliography: D. Abulafia, *Frederick II: A Medieval Emperor*, 1988; G. Masson, *Frederick II of Hohenstaufen, a Life*, 1957.

Connie Evans

FRUTOLF OF MICHELSBERG (D. 1103). Monk of Michelsberg, the first chronicler of the Middle Ages, he wrote a history of the world from the creation to his own time, two important treatises on music theory, and a book on the Divine Office.

Frutolf was a monk, and he may have been prior of Michelsberg at Bamberg. He might have taught the quadrivium at the monastery and was definitely well versed in music, astronomy, and mathematics. From the range of his works, he appears to have been interested in compiling information and making it available in a collected form to others. He also bequeathed books to his monastery, some on chant and others on musical theory.

His most well-known work is his history of the world from the creation to 1099. When he compiled this book, there had been no comprehensive world history written for two centuries; he is therefore considered the first chronicler of the Middle Ages. Frutolf worked to establish accurate chronologies and to find the truth when his sources disagreed; in these cases, he stated his view but also included others so the reader could judge. He followed in the traditional style of annals, presenting events year by year, but he did vary his style, providing elaborate and complete accounts of important people like Alexander the Great and *Charlemagne, among others.

The history reveals the breadth and depth of Frutolf's knowledge. Extensive coverage of the material from the beginning through the ninth century existed. His sources include Saint Jerome's translation of Eusebius' chronicle—which Saint Jerome continued up to his own time (378), *Isidore of Seville, *Bede, *Sigebert of Gembloux, *Jordanes, *Paul the Deacon, Frechulf of Lisieux, and *Widukind of Corvey. For the tenth and early eleventh centuries, he relied on a local chronicle from Würzberg, and the coverage is a bit thin. Starting with the middle of the eleventh century, though, Frutolf presents original information, which is a major, independent source for the years 1071 to 1098. The material that spans his own time indicates that he was more interested in political than ecclesiastical history. He treats the Investiture Controversy as more of a political event than a religious one, and he avoids taking sides.

His other works, also compilations, include the *Breviarium de musica* (a compendium of musical science), the *Tonarius* (a tonary), and the *Liber de divinis officiis* (Book of the Divine Office). His musical treatises owe much to *Boethius and *Berno of Reichenau. In fact, Berno's tonary served as a model for the *Breviarium* and the *Tonarius*. In the *Breviarium*, he discusses the origins and names of the pitches (following Boethius), the monochord, the proportions that govern consonances, tetrachords, modes, intervals, and names of notes; he also borrows from and includes various verse texts. The *Tonarius* actually exists in two versions, an abridged one and a much fuller one. The latter lists each tone, which is preceded by theoretical remarks from the *Breviarium*, and then Frutolf provides a list of pieces from the chant repository, including sequences from the Mass. His last known work, the *Liber de divinis officiis*, a list of responses for the Divine Office, consists of passages taken from the works of Amalar, *Hrabanus Maurus, and *Alcuin's *De divinis officiis.*

Frutolf's success as a compiler stands out; his history of the world serves as a reference work and influenced many chroniclers. His abridged *Tonarius* was transcribed into twelve German manuscripts. Historians and musicians owe him a debt of gratitude.

Bibliography: F.-J. Schmale and I. Schmale-Ott, *Frutolfs und Ekkehards Chroniken und die Anonyme Kaiserchronik,* 1972; C. Vivell, *Frutolfi Breviarium de musica et tonarius,* 1919.

Jana K. Schulman

FULBERT OF CHARTRES (C. 952/962–C. 1028). Fulbert was an eleventh-century bishop and theologian who led the theological school of Chartres to prominence.

Fulbert was born of poor parents around 960, probably in northern France or Rome. Like many poor but gifted intellectuals of his time, he found the church schools an avenue to success. He studied under Master *Gerbert of Aurillac at the school of Rheims, where his classmates included Prince Robert of France (later King Robert II). Fulbert moved to Chartres around 990, where he became an assistant in the cathedral school and held minor church offices. He became increasingly popular and well known as a theologian and administrator. By 1004, he had been made a deacon, and he was named chancellor between 1003 and 1006. In 1006 he became bishop of Chartres, while continuing to teach at the school.

Training at the school of Chartres focused on orthodox theology, moral training, and spiritual formation for young clergymen. Fulbert attracted and inspired many students. Under his guidance, Chartres was a stronghold of Platonic conservatism, untouched by the controversies that later arose from the introduction of Aristotelian ideas. Indeed, Fulbert lived in a halcyon period between two major collisions between faith and reason: after the great debates over the nature of the Eucharist and before the full flowering of the conflict between nominalism and realism. Fulbert's theological writings include exegetical sermons, polemics against the Jews, and exhortations to orthodoxy and reverence, especially reverence of the Blessed Virgin. He also wrote poetry, including humorous mnemonic jingles and a lovely ode "To the Nightingale."

Many insights into Fulbert's career as a bishop may be gleaned from his episcopal correspondence, from which 140 letters have survived. These letters demonstrate the range of problems presented to him by his diocese, which range from contentious clerical rivalries to the minutiae of sacramental procedure. They also display Fulbert's erudition; in the resolution of these matters, he brought to bear relevant material from the Church Fathers, canon law, and other scholarly sources. Moreover, Fulbert's personality is revealed in the letters as well; he responded compassionately to the wayward penitent but frankly condemned the corrupt and ambitious. He addressed high-ranking churchmen and secular politicians alike in a bold and forthright manner; his correspondence with dukes, nobles, and the king is highly revealing of the relationship between Church and state in eleventh-century France. He was a valued adviser to King Robert II, who granted Fulbert many favors; in return, Fulbert supported Robert in conflicts with the French nobility. In 1020, a disastrous fire destroyed much of Chartres, including the cathedral; its reconstruction was Fulbert's chief occupation for the remainder of his life.

Renowned for leading a saintly life, Fulbert inspired warm personal devotion among his students and colleagues. Although he was never formally beatified or canonized, he is sometimes known as "Saint Fulbert." Fulbert's erudition, compassion, and forthrightness made him both an effective administrator and a popular teacher; the school of Chartres flourished under his capable leadership. His writings are especially valued for the insights they provide into the relation between the Church and feudal society; they also furnish a wealth of information about liturgical practices and conflict resolution within the Church of Fulbert's time.

Bibliography: F. Behrends, ed., *The Letters and Poems of Fulbert of Chartres*, 1976; L. C. MacKinney, *Bishop Fulbert and Education at the School of Chartres*, 1957.

                                            Anne Collins Smith and Owen M. Smith

FULCHER OF CHARTRES (C. 1059–1127). Fulcher was chronicler of the First Crusade and chaplain to Baldwin of Bouillon, lord of Edessa, and king of the Latin kingdom of Jerusalem.

Fulcher was born around 1059 and was probably educated for the priesthood. He seems to have had the interest in classical literature associated with the school of Chartres. In 1095 he attended the Council of Clermont, which inaugurated the First Crusade. He then joined the Crusade himself, accompanying the army headed by Robert of Normandy and Stephen of Blois as far as Edessa, where he became Baldwin of Bouillon's chaplain. After the crusaders captured Jerusalem in 1099, Fulcher visited the Holy City and then returned to Edessa, where he stayed until Baldwin became king of Jerusalem in 1100. He remained Baldwin's chaplain until the king's death in 1118, when he may have become prior of the Mount of Olives. He probably died in 1127.

Fulcher's greatest contribution to scholarship is his *Gesta francorum Iherusalem peregrinantium* (Deeds of the Franks on Their Pilgrimage to Jerusalem, also known as the *Historia Hierosolymita* [*History of the Expedition to Jerusalem*] after the second redaction was made). It is one of three eyewitness Latin accounts of the First Crusade, along with the anonymous *Deeds of the Franks and of the Other Pilgrims to Jerusalem* and a history by Raymond of Aguilers. Fulcher's chronicle is particularly important because his is the only work that covers the early period of the crusaders in the East after the First Crusade.

Written in three books, it was probably started in 1101 and completed about 1127. Most historians consider it the most reliable account of the First Crusade.

Bibliography: E. Peters, *The First Crusade: The Chronicle of Fulcher of Chartres and Other Source Materials*, 2d ed., 1998.

Kimberly Rivers

G

GABIROL, IBN. *See* SOLOMON BEN JUDAH IBN GABIROL.

GEOFFREY OF MONMOUTH (C. 1100–1155). Geoffrey is best known for his *Historia regum Britanniae* (History of the Kings of Britain), completed between 1136 and 1138. He also composed a long verse "Life of Merlin" in about 1152. In addition to writing his *Historia* and his *Vita Merlini*, Geoffrey served as the archdeacon of Llandsaff, anointed in 1140. In 1152 he was consecrated bishop of St. Asaph, a place it is doubtful he ever saw or visited.

His *Historia* enjoyed a vast readership for hundreds of years, despite its dubious reliability as history. Its fame is primarily due to its emphasis on and glorification of King Arthur, to whom a majority of its pages are devoted. Since Arthur is a figure whose historical authenticity is still unverified, it is likely that as much fiction went into Geoffrey's work as fact. Thus, though the issue is still debated, many scholars credit Geoffrey of Monmouth with having actually invented the King Arthur of popular perception, by combining details from existing "local hero" stories into his tale of one great hero. Geoffrey also includes and gives importance to the character of Merlin, whom he probably borrowed both from Nennius' *Ambrosius* and from a body of poetry about a Welsh prophet named Merddyn.

It is clear from his own commentary that Geoffrey perceived the literary status of the Celts to be low compared to various continental peoples. He set about rectifying this by presenting purely British heroes in the first comprehensive, descriptive history of Britain from the Celtic point of view. In the *Historia*, Geoffrey establishes for Britain an equal literary importance with Greece and Rome by inserting the foundation of Britain into the tradition of the classical sources, claiming the founder of Britain to be Brutus, the great-grandson of Aeneas. This detail contributed to many vernacular verse "histories" of Britain, including *Wace's *Roman de Brut* and Layamon's *Brut*. The term "Brut" was adopted as a generic term for any heroic history of Britain.

Geoffrey's work begins with the arrival of Brut in 1100 B.C. and traces the legendary kings of Britain to the middle of the seventh century, a conveniently sparsely documented time span. The sources for Geoffrey's work are a mixed lot: Most scholars agree that he relied more on oral traditions than on written records. Some shared details in the *Historia*, however, show that he based his work partly on earlier works by *Gildas and Nennius (about whom little is known) and also on the *Annales Cambriae* and *Bede's *Ecclesiastical History of the English People*. Geoffrey himself writes that his history is a translation of "[a] very ancient book, written in the British language." Though there are a few speculative possibilities, no one has yet discovered such a book.

The *Historia* includes some of the best-known plots and characters in litera-ture and story—Leir (Shakespeare's Lear) and his daughters; Julius Caesar's attempt to gain Britain; and Coel (Mother Goose's Old King Cole) among them. But the histories of these kings are obviously preamble and stage-setting for the greatness of Arthur. Geoffrey's early chapters lead up to the infamously bad decisions of King Vortigern to oust Aurelius and Uther and to invite Saxon warriors to the island to help him fight invading Picts and Scots. In return for the assistance from Hengist and Horsa, the Germanic leaders, Vortigern offers them British land. The ensuing wars with these continentals bring the *Historia* to the tale of the return of Uther Pendragon from exile; his infatuation with Gorlois' beautiful wife Ygrain (Ygerna); and Uther's Merlin-assisted trickery, which leads to the conception of Arthur.

The Arthur of Geoffrey's version is the consummate warrior-chief, traveling to the Continent to battle with emperors and kings and conquering most of Europe, including Ireland, Iceland, and Scandinavia, before he is through. Geof-frey's hero is not a love rival with Lancelot (who is a much later French addition to the Arthur traditions); however, Guenivere's treachery in adultery is still central to Arthur's defeat, as she and Mordred conspire against him while he is on a continental campaign. Upon Arthur's return, Mordred is killed in battle still attempting to usurp Arthur's throne; Guenivere is not punished but enters a nunnery; and Arthur is borne to Avalon to tend his battle wounds.

It might be said that in presenting the world with King Arthur, Geoffrey laid the foundation for all of British nationalism and gave a name to the ultimate hero king.

Bibliography: M. J. Curley, *Geoffrey of Monmouth*, 1994.

Zina Petersen

GEOFFREY OF VILLEHARDOUIN. *See* VILLEHARDOUIN, GEOFFREY OF.

GERALD OF WALES (GIRALDUS CAMBRENSIS, GIRALDUS DE BARRI, GERALD DE BARRY, GERALD THE WELSHMAN) (1145/1146–1223).

Gerald of Wales was a prominent cleric and writer best known for his works on the history of Ireland and Wales in the twelfth century.

Gerald was the son of William de Barry, a Norman knight, and Angharad, the daughter of another Norman knight, Gerald of Windsor. Angharad's mother was Princess Nest, a daughter of the southern Welsh prince Rhys ap Towdwr and an influential mistress of *Henry I of England. The children of Gerald of Windsor and Nest participated in the conquest of Ireland and founded the powerful Fitzgerald interest there. Thus was Gerald of Wales well connected by birth into the power elites of both the Normans and the Welsh. Although largely of Norman blood, he seems to have identified more with his Welsh heritage. After spending his childhood in Pembrokeshire, Gerald received an excellent education in Latin grammar and literature under Master Haimo at the Abbey of St. Peter, Gloucester. From 1165 to 1174 he studied the trivium at Paris. After returning to Wales, he gained the office of archdeacon of Brecon in 1175 and from the start showed a strong interest in Church reform. When he failed to gain the bishopric of St. David's in 1175, he returned to Paris to study canon law from 1176 to 1179. When he returned to Wales, he resumed his clerical duties. *Henry II of England made him court chaplain in 1184, and in 1185–1186, he accompanied Prince *John (of England) on his invasion of Ireland. This experience inspired him to write his *Topographia Hibernica* (The History and Topography of Ireland) and his *Expugnatio Hibernica* (Conquest of Ireland). Both works presented an unfavorable view of the Irish. During the spring of 1188 he accompanied Archbishop Baldwin of Canterbury on a trip through Wales in which they preached the Third Crusade. Gerald described that journey and the Welsh with affection in his *Itinerarium Kambriae* (Journey through Wales) and soon added the *Descriptio Kambriae* (Description of Wales).

Gerald's great dream was to be the archbishop, not simply the bishop, of St. David's and thus restore Welsh ecclesiastical independence from England. From 1198 to 1203, he engaged in a bitter struggle to become bishop but ultimately was defeated. He spent the remaining twenty years of his life writing in relative obscurity.

During his long life, Gerald wrote seventeen books, all in Latin, and either started or contemplated many others. Most of these writings dealt with ecclesiastical concerns or the lives of various saints and bishops. He also wrote an autobiography entitled *De rebus a se gestis* (Events of His Own Life). Although he considered them to be his minor works, Gerald is best known for his books on Ireland and Wales. Those works were written in a lively, personal style and contain much information that would otherwise be lost. They were also attempts (although flawed) at objective ethnographic and topographic description and analysis that mark an original departure from previous practices. The sixteenth-century antiquarians David Powell and William Camden recognized the importance of Gerald's works and edited them for printed editions. Scholarly interest has remained strong ever since.

Bibliography: R. Bartlett, *Gerald of Wales, 1146–1223*, 1982.

Ronald H. Fritze

GERARD OF CREMONA (GHERARDUS CREMONENSIS, GHERARDUS TOLETANUS) (C. 1114–1187).

The most important twelfth-century translator of Arabic scientific and philosophical texts, Gerard of Cremona was born in the northern Italian city of Cremona in 1114.

According to the testimony of his friends, he came to Toledo around 1144, attracted by the possibility of studying Ptolemy's *Almagest*, the important Hellenistic work on astrology and astronomy not available in the Latin West but known to exist. Toledo in the twelfth century was a center of learning, which illustrated well the cultural exchanges of the "land of the three religions." Jewish, Muslim, and Christian scholars and theologians mutually read and translated writings of their traditions, sometimes in partnership. Wealthy patrons, such as the city's Archbishop Raymond, supported their studies, and the city possessed many libraries and manuscript repositories. Aware of the abundance of works of Greek science and philosophy in Arabic translation, and contemporary Arabic commentaries, Gerard learned Arabic with the help of Jewish and Mozarab associates and translators. He remained in Toledo for forty-three years, until his death in 1187.

Gerard is referred to in some documents with the title of "teacher" (*magister*), but this did not refer to his work as a translator. In Toledo there was no organized center for translations, only several scholars working on disparate projects—John of Seville's and Dominicus Gundissalinus' collaboration on the *De anima* of *Avicenna is a case in point—and Gerard did not establish his own school of translation. His extensive activity stemmed primarily from his interest, as a scientist and scholar, in scientific Arabic texts. He worked mainly alone when translating (he acknowledges the help of a collaborator only for his version of the *Almagest*) and probably used his translations in his own lectures on arts and sciences. However, he may have assembled a small group of assistants for jobs collateral to the translations, such as collecting Arabic manuscripts, and the delicate but tedious task of editing and copying his translations. In fact, a group of Gerard's friends (*socii*) left a eulogy after his death.

Like other translators of his time, Gerard's method of translating was literal, sometimes word for word. In trying to accommodate the Arabic language and expressions in Latin syntax, which tends to conciseness, medieval translations are often difficult to read and quite distant from the felicitous style of classical Latin. Gerard's translations retained the construction of the Arabic sentences; each Latin word carefully corresponds to an Arabic term. However, they possess an acceptable literary form and were readily welcomed to the West. More than seventy-one translations are attributed to him, covering mainly subjects and authors of natural science. Among the works of logic he translated are the version of an anonymous Arabic translation of Aristotle's *Posterior Analytics*, Themistius' commentary on that work, and al-*Fārābī's *De syllogismo*. Mathematics and geometry are represented by the translation of Euclid's *Elements*, together with some Arab commentaries: Archimedes' *De mensura circuli*, Theodosius' *Spherica*, and Banū Mūsā's *Geometria*. Astronomy and astrology are covered by Ptolemy's *Almagest*, which he translated with "the help of the Mozarab Galippus ('Galib')" (in a manuscript the year 1175 is given as date of completion of the work, but it should have been one of Gerard's early translations, or else Gerard revised his translation some time after); al-Farghānī's (Alfraganus) treatise on stars, which he achieved by editing and correcting an earlier Latin translation by John of Seville; Jābir ibn Aflah's *De astronomia*; Māshā' allāh's *De elementis et orbibus celestibus*, used later by *Albertus Magnus; Theodosius' *De locis habitationibus*; and Thābit ibn Qurra's *De expositione nominum Almagesti* and *De motu accessionis et recessionis*.

Gerard translated many works of optics such as Tideus' *De speculo*; al-Haytham's *De speculis comburentibus*; and al-Kindī's *De aspectibus*. Philosophy is represented by the translation of the pseudo-Aristotle's *Liber de causis*, which became very popular in the thirteenth century; Aristotle's *Physics* (which in the *corpus Aristotelicum* of the thirteenth century, or *Corpus vetustius*, was scarcely used and was replaced with the translation from the Greek by James of Venice); the *Commentary on the Physics of Aristotle* by al-Fārābī; Aristotle's *On Generation and Corruption, On the Heavens*, and *Meteorology* (the last two became a standard acquisition of the *Corpus vetustius*); several treatises by Alexander of Aphrodisias; al-Kindī's *De quinque essentiis*; and al-Fārābī's *De scientiis*, translated also earlier by Gundissalinus, who was less faithful to the original than Gerard.

Gerard's activity in the field of medicine was very important for the establishment of the canon of medical texts and curriculum in the West. He translated the whole corpus of Galen; Hippocrates' aphorisms; and fundamental treatises of Islamic medicine such as al-Rāzī's *Liber Almansorius and Liber divisionum*, Avicenna's *Canon*, Yahyā ibn-Sarāfyūn's (Filius Serapionis) *Breviarius*, al-Kindī's *De gradibus* on pharmacology, and Abu'l-Qāsim al-Zahrāwī's (Abulcasis) *De chirurgia*. The availability of the Arabic medical encyclopedias to the Latin West, and the progress they showed over Galen's corpus, was a powerful incentive for the diffusion of medical studies in the twelfth and thirteenth centuries. Islamic knowledge promoted the belief that medicine was a discipline with a close connection to philosophy and open to rational and methodological investigations. More generally, Gerard's corpus of translations paved the way and shaped the great movement of acquisition of classical and Arabic civilization by the medieval Latin world in the thirteenth century.

Bibliography: B. Boncompagni, *Della vita e delle opere di Gherardo Cremonese*, 1851; C. H. Haskins, *Studies in the History of Medieval Science*, 2d ed., 1927; M. McVaugh,

"A List of Translations from Arabic into Latin in the Twelfth Century. Gerald of Cremona," in *A Source Book in Medieval Science*, ed. E. Grant, 1976.

Roberto Plevano

GERBERT OF AURILLAC. *See* SYLVESTER II, POPE.

GERTRUDE THE GREAT (1256–1301/1302). Benedictine nun, mystic, and author, Gertrude the Great is also known as Gertrude of Helfta.

Gertrude is one of the Helfta mystics; the other two are Gertrude's older contemporaries *Mechthild of Hackeborn and *Mechthild of Magdeburg. Helfta was a Benedictine convent that became famous under the direction of Abbess Gertrude of Hackeborn as a center of mysticism and culture in thirteenth-century Germany. Gertrude the Great is still sometimes confused with her abbess, Gertrude of Hackeborn, who also happened to be the sister of Mechthild of Hackeborn (also at the same monastery in Helfta). Pope Benedict XIV, in his 1738 treatise *De servorum Dei beatificatione et beatorum canonizatione*, distinguished Gertrude from her contemporaries with the title "the Great" because of her mysticism and her major work, the *Legatus divinae pietatis* (Herald of Divine Love).

Renowned for her love of study and scholarship, Gertrude wrote two major works. The first is the *Legatus divinae pietatis*. The *Legatus* is an extensive work in five parts, of which only Book II is a spiritual autobiography written by Gertrude herself. The first book is Gertrude's vita, written as a memorial by one of Gertrude's friends following Gertrude's death. Books III through V contain Gertrude's teachings as recorded by Gertrude's sisters. These books deal with the soul's relationship to God, with the feasts of the Church, and with the community at Helfta, respectively.

Gertrude's second major work is the *Exercitia spiritualia* or *Spiritual Exercises*. In the seven exercises, Gertrude continues in her role as educator, offering a short volume of meditations and instructions for a Christian life of prayer. Gertrude was also the major compiler of Mechthild of Hackeborn's *Liber speciales gratiae* (Book of Special Grace). The fact that Gertrude dictated much of her work to members of her community ensured that her teachings were disseminated locally, though Gertrude's writings did not gain wider renown until the mid-sixteenth century.

Gertrude and the nuns at Helfta were instrumental in perpetuating the cult of the Sacred Heart. Gertrude invokes the Sacred Heart at the beginning of the seventh exercise in the *Exercitia*, believing the Sacred Heart to offer the source of everything she needed. In their visions and writings, the nuns at Helfta did not challenge the power of the clergy; on the contrary, their personal relations with Christ reinforced the Church's teachings. Gertrude's *Legatus* is a key document in the devotional literature of the Sacred Heart.

The arrival of Mechthild of Magdeburg at Helfta in 1270 seems to have acted as a catalyst for the writing talents of the nuns at Helfta. Certainly, Gertrude's work ensured Helfta's importance in the history of thirteenth-century German mysticism.

Bibliography: M. J. Finnegan, *The Women of Helfta: Scholars and Mystics*, 1991; Gertrude the Great, *Spiritual Exercises*, trans. G. J. Lewis and J. Lewis, 1989; R. Voaden, "All Girls Together: Community, Gender and Vision at Helfta," in *Medieval Women in Their Communities*, ed. D. Watt, 1997.

Alexandra Sterling-Hellenbrand

GHAZĀLĪ, ABŪ HĀMID MUHAMMAD, AL- (ALGAZEL) (1058–1111).

Al-Ghazālī was a celebrated Muslim theologian, philosopher, mystic, jurist, polemicist, religious reformer, and original thinker. An essential figure in the development of medieval Islamic thought, al-Ghazālī reconciled Islamic mysticism with speculative theology. Al-Ghazālī's greatest contribution to Western civilization lies in the influence of his philosophic and theological works on Christian scholastics, most notably Raymond Martin (d. 1285) and Thomas *Aquinas.

Al-Ghazālī was born in Tūs in Khurāsān, a district in northeastern Iran, in the year 1058. He was orphaned at a young age, and his care was relinquished to a family friend who saw to his early education. In 1077–1078, al-Ghazālī journeyed to the regional center of Nīshāpūr and became a pupil of the famous Ash'arite theologian al-Juwaynī (d. 1085). Here he studied natural science, theology, philosophy, and logic. From his boyhood, he tells us, he had been pushed by the desire to know the truth of things for himself and refused to rely on the words of authorities without first testing their arguments for himself. Accordingly, he applied himself vigorously to the pursuit of knowledge. It was here in Nīshāpūr where al-Ghazālī made a name for himself as a reputable scholar and thinker; in fact, it is related that upon showing al-Juwaynī his first book, the Shaykh remarked: "Do you want to bury me while still alive?"

Upon the death of al-Juwaynī, al-Ghazālī left to join the circle of Nizām al-Mulk (d. 1092), the vizier of the great Seljuq sultans. Nizām al-Mulk was a patron of scholars, thinkers, and mystics and had gathered around himself a collection of the most learned men in the empire. Al-Ghazālī's reputation followed him to the office of Nizām al-Mulk, and he was received with much enthusiasm and favor by the vizier. To recognize his greatness and talent, Nizām al-Mulk appointed him to the "Chair of Law" at the famous Nizāmiyya academy in Baghdad (c. 1091). As his fame grew, so did the size of his classes. He became the undisputed master of the circles of scholars that surrounded him, and many prominent figures sought his council and advice on everything from religious matters to political decisions.

It was during this time that al-Ghazālī wrote his famous critique of rationalistic philosophy, the *Incoherence of the Philosophers*, as well as his exposition of the main issues in Islamic philosophy, the *Aims of the Philosophers*. Destined to become a classic both in the Islamic world and the Christian West, the *Incoherence of the Philosophers* argued that rational philosophy cannot form a basis for interpreting religion. In defense of this assertion, al-Ghazālī worked out twenty points on which the philosophers' doctrines were either internally inconstant or against natural reason.

After lecturing for four years in Baghdad, al-Ghazālī experienced a profound spiritual and intellectual crisis. As he relates in his autobiography, his crisis of faith manifested in a devastating pathology: He found himself unable to speak and thus was forced to give up his lectures. After a period of brief recovery, he resigned from his prestigious post at the Nizāmiyya, gave away all he owned, and left Baghdad on the pretext of performing the pilgrimage to Mecca. He left the city in November 1095 and journeyed westward, spending time in Damascus, Jerusalem, Mecca, and Medina. During this time, he lived as a poor mendicant and spent most of his time in solitude, engaging in meditative and religious exercises. It was during this period of withdrawal that he wrote his magnum opus, the *Revival of the Religious Sciences*, a complete guide to the proper observance, theory, meaning, and practice of every single aspect of Islamic religious and spiritual life. In 1105–1106, he returned to formal lecturing and taught at Nīshāpūr for at least three years before retiring to his native Tūs in 1109. He spent his remaining years in Tūs among his disciples, where he died in the year 1111 at the age of fifty-three.

Al-Ghazālī was a prolific writer, authoring a multitude of scholarly works. He worked within many disciplines, including the spheres of jurisprudence, philosophy, logic, ethics, theology, religious orthopraxy, and Islamic mysticism. In the Islamic world, al-Ghazālī's works profoundly influenced the course of theological thinking, and his judicious and systematic treatment of philosophic and mystical doctrines helped to make them palatable to orthodox theologians. In the Christian West, however, it was mainly his philosophical and theological works that came to have any substantial impact. The first Latin translations of al-Ghazālī's works appeared in the middle of the twelfth century under his Latinized name Algazel. Both the aforementioned *Incoherence of the Philosophers* and *Aims of the Philosophers* were read widely by Christian scholastics, the latter being of particular importance in that it provided an authoritative summary of the philosophies of al-*Fārābī and *Avicenna.

Of special mention is al-Ghazālī's influence on the thought of Raymond Martin and Thomas Aquinas. Raymond Martin, a Catalan Dominican monk, quotes both al-Ghazālī's *Aims of the Philosophers* and his *Revival of the Religious Sciences* and reiterates al-Ghazālī's theses on the Beatific Vision and the spiritual character of the Hereafter. Aquinas studied Algazel while a student at the University of Naples, and many of his works, including the *Summa Theologiae*, resonate with ideas and arguments drawn from al-Ghazālī's works. Both al-Ghazālī and Aquinas, for instance, agree that the highest goal of man is the contemplation of God and that eternal bliss is commensurate with the intensity of one's love and knowledge of God. In addition, Aquinas adopted al-Ghazālī's arguments for *creatio ex nihilo*, the proof that God's knowledge comprises particulars, and the justification for the resurrection of the dead. He was also deeply influenced by al-Ghazālī's arguments against Aristotelianism, and his discussion on reason and revelation in the *Summa Theologiae* utilizes many of the same arguments proposed by al-Ghazālī.

Raymond Martin and Thomas Aquinas were not the only Christian Scholastics influenced by al-Ghazālī. In a number of his minor prose works, the poet Dante (d. 1321) also quotes him, and a number of views expressed in his *Divine Comedy*, such as the Beatific Vision, the inner light, and the seven Heavens are anticipated in al-Ghazālī's work. Toward the latter Middle Ages, three important skeptic philosophers, Peter of Ailly (d. 1420), Nicholas of Autrecourt (d. 1350), and William of Ockham (d. 1349), were influenced by al-Ghazālī's treatment of the issue of causality.

Bibliography: R. Frank, *Al-Ghazālī and the Ash'arite School*, 1994; W. M. Watt, *Muslim Intellectual: A Study of al-Ghazali*, 1963.

Erik S. Ohlander

GILBERT OF POITIERS (C. 1080–1154). Bishop, philosopher, teacher, and commentator on the Bible, Gilbert was born in Poitiers, where he studied the liberal arts. He studied philosophy at Chartres and then theology at Laon. It is unclear whether Gilbert remained in Laon after 1117 or returned to Poitiers. However, by 1124, one of his former masters, Bernard of Chartres, had arranged a teaching position for him at the cathedral church, where Gilbert remained until 1137. Gilbert then taught theology at Paris. He was elected bishop of Poitiers in 1141, a post he would hold until his death.

Gilbert's teaching was carefully examined by Pope *Eugenius III. A casual remark by Gilbert on the nature of the Trinity (apparently making a strong distinction between divine nature and person) eventually resulted in a full-scale investigation. In 1147, Eugenius III summoned Gilbert to a trial in Paris, but it was adjourned and reconvened at the Council of Rheims the following year. *Bernard of Clairvaux and his supporters pursued the case against Gilbert, focusing especially on his commentary on *Boethius' works. However, Gilbert's immense knowledge of patristic sources made the prosecutors look foolish and ill-prepared. With the trial going in Gilbert's favor, Bernard convinced Eugenius to introduce a creed as a test of Gilbert's orthodoxy and thereby limit the power of the trial judges. In the end, a compromise was reached so that Gilbert's reputation remained intact, but he was instructed to reedit his Boethian commentary in order to purge it of any possible heresy.

Although it is Gilbert's philosophy that has caught modern scholars' attention, he also made significant contributions to biblical exegesis, producing commentaries on the Psalms and the Pauline Epistles. One of his most famous students was *John of Salisbury, who would later include details of Gilbert's life in his *Historia pontificalis*.

Bibliography: T. Gross-Diaz, *The Psalms Commentary of Gilbert of Poitiers: From Lectio divina to the Lecture Room*, 1996; L. O. Nielsen, *Theology and Philosophy in the*

Twelfth Century: A Study of Gilbert Porreta's Thinking and the Theological Expositions of the Doctrine of the Incarnation during the Period, 1130–1180, 1982.

James R. Ginther

GILBERT OF SEMPRINGHAM, SAINT (C. 1085–1189). Saint and centenarian, Gilbert of Sempringham founded an English religious order, the Gilbertines, unusual in incorporating both men and women.

Born into a prosperous knightly family in Lincolnshire, Gilbert attended schools in both England and France, then entered the service of the bishop of Lincoln before 1123. Gilbert rose in the episcopal household but eventually left to embrace a life of poverty. In 1131, he used his wealth to found a small religious community of women in Sempringham. They lived a strictly cloistered life; Gilbert himself ministered to their spiritual needs, while to provide for their material welfare he attracted lay sisters and brothers. A second house was founded nearby in 1139.

In 1147, the aging Gilbert attempted to relinquish control of his houses to the Cistercians. They refused, but Gilbert received papal endorsement for his leadership. The next decade brought growth to Gilbert's nascent order, with the foundation of at least eight new houses, mainly in Lincolnshire and Yorkshire. Simultaneously, Gilbert added regular canons to his communities, who served as chaplains for the women and supervised the lay brothers. Gilbertine houses thus took their characteristic form as double monasteries, with both male and female religious.

The 1160s, in contrast, proved a time of trial. A nun at the house of Watton became involved in a scandalous affair. Around 1165, some Gilbertine lay brothers rose in revolt, rejecting Gilbert's authority and bringing charges of maltreatment to the papal court. The root problem was the lay brothers' new subordination to the canons. The English Church hierarchy and King *Henry II himself rallied around Gilbert, and his leadership was vindicated in 1169. Failing health convinced Gilbert to step down c. 1177, though he lived on until 4 February 1189. He was declared a saint in 1202.

Bibliography: B. Golding, *Gilbert of Sempringham and the Gilbertine Order, c. 1130–c. 1300,* 1995.

Donald Fleming

GILDAS, SAINT (C. 500–C. 570). The monk and historian Gildas Badonicus was born near Clyde but received his education in Wales. After many years there, he retired at a monastery, later called St. Gildas de Rhuys, in southern Brittany. Though he traveled to Ireland and Northumbria in his later years, he died and was probably buried at Rhuys.

Gildas was most famous for writing *De excidio et conquestu Britanniae,* a history of fifth-century Britain. In 410, Roman troops were withdrawn and the Roman emperor instructed the British to provide for their own defense and administration. In the 420s, a local leader named Vortigern came to power, but Gildas portrays him as an arrogant despot who provoked rebellion twenty years later through his dependence on German (Saxon) soldiers and government officials. Many of the British who survived fled to Europe. Ultimately, however, they routed the Germans, traditionally under the leadership of Arthur at the battle of Badon Hill, c. 497. In Gildas' view, victory came too late to maintain peace and security because the war destroyed Roman civilization and caused the triumph of corrupt Germanic elements in Britain.

Though maligned by some fellow medieval historians because of his reliance on oral history, Gildas acted as the voice of his contemporaries, speaking aloud what many people felt. He encouraged the contemplative life for those seeking to escape from the evils of his world, and some scholars credit him with the increased popularity of monasticism in South Wales, Ireland, and Northern Gaul.

Bibliography: L. Alcock, *Arthur's Britain*, 1971; A. Butler, *The Lives of the Fathers, Martyrs, and Other Principal Saints*, 6 vols., 1846.

Alana Cain Scott

GILES OF ROME (EGIDIUS, AEGIDIUS COLONNA) (C. 1243/1247–1316).

Giles was a scholastic philosopher and a political theorist later known as *Doctor fundatissimus*.

Giles was born at Rome and was descended from the noble Colonna family. He joined the Hermits of St. Augustine after 1260 and was sent to study at the Order's house in Paris. He completed the arts program in Paris and began studying theology there c. 1266. From 1269 to 1271, he probably attended the lectures of Thomas *Aquinas. He commented on *Peter Lombard's *Sentences* c. 1276. In 1277–1278, he wrote a treatise, *Liber contra gradus et pluralitatem formarum*, defending Aquinas' doctrine of a unicity of substantial form in material creatures. This teaching was one of the 219 philosophical propositions condemned by Bishop Stephen *Tempier in 1277. Refusing to retract, Giles was forced to leave Paris and retired to Bayeux (1278–1280) and then Italy (1281–1285). At the request of Pope Honorius IV, Giles was reinstated at the University of Paris in 1285 and completed his theological degree. He became the first Augustinian master of theology at Paris and taught there from 1285 to 1291. In 1287, the General Chapter of the Augustinians imposed Giles' teachings upon the teachers of the Augustinian Order. In 1291 he relinquished his teaching position and became the general of the Augustinian Order. In 1294, Pope *Boniface VIII made him archbishop of Bourges, and although he spent much of his time at the papal curia, he retained this position until his death at Avignon in 1316.

Giles was a very productive writer, composing commentaries on Aristotle's *Physics, Metaphysics, De anima*, and *Posterior Analytics*. He also commented upon the *Liber de causis* and wrote treatises against the Averroists, on angels, and Original Sin. His exegetical works include commentaries on John and the

Pauline Epistles. His disputations reflect the theological concerns of his day, often in opposition to his contemporaries *Henry of Ghent and *Godfrey of Fontaines.

King Philip III of France (1270–1285) appointed Giles as tutor to the future Philip IV, and he wrote the manual of princely advice, *De regimine principum* (On the Rule of Princes), c. 1286 for the dauphin. In it, Giles emphasized the Aristotelian conception of a ruler and relied heavily upon the *Politics* and *Ethics*. It was an immediate success and was translated into many vernacular languages. However, in the quarrel between Boniface VIII and Philip IV, Giles sided with the former and wrote the treatise *De renuntiatione papae* to defend the validity of Pope Celestine V's abdication. In 1301–1302 he wrote *De ecclesiastica potestate* in support of Boniface, defending in this work the supremacy of the spiritual power over the temporal. This work helped inspire Boniface's famous bull *Unam sanctam* of 1302.

Although an important theologian and a follower of Aquinas on many philosophical issues, Giles' most enduring legacy can be seen in the realm of political philosophy.

Bibliography: É. Gilson, *History of Christian Philosophy in the Middle Ages*, 1955.

Andrew G. Traver

GLABER, RADULPHUS (C. 980–C. 1046).

Glaber was a Cluniac monk who wrote a history of his times, intending it to be a universal history of events surrounding the Millennium.

Although Glaber's origins are obscure, his life can be pieced together from autobiographical passages in his works. It is possible that he was of noble birth; his concern with high birth and his denigration of the *rustici* indicate that he was or would like to be perceived as from the lower aristocracy. Shortly after 1000, Glaber was at the abbey of St. Germain of Auxerre, where it is likely he was educated. Expelled from St. Germain, Glaber took residence at St. Bénigne, where he became a protégé of its abbot, William. William was an international figure, intent on transmitting the Cluniac reforms to Italy, Western Germany, and Normandy. At William's urging, Glaber began his *Five Books of the Histories* (*Historiarum libri quinque*). By 1030, however, Glaber and William quarreled. Glaber left St. Bénigne for the abbey of Cluny, where shortly after William's death in 1031 Glaber reports that he received a vision of the saint that inspired him to write his *Life of St. William* (*Vita domini Willelmi abbatis*). After writing the *Life*, Glaber continued writing the *Histories*, which were finished shortly before his death in 1046.

Glaber uses as his principal sources what he himself saw and what he received by "certain report," and his text consequently seems burdened by a wealth of curious digressions. The chronology is variable, using general dates and dates of realms rather than a universal calendar; Glaber is also attached to allegory as a historical method. Sometimes inexact with its facts and geography, Glaber's

Histories nevertheless reflects a contemporary revival of learning, especially among the Cluniac houses, and it conveys as well a sense of anxiety that the world was changing rapidly as feudal principalities emerged and the Cluniac reforms were transmitted. For Glaber, the personal relationships among the principals of those reforms—Saints Mayol, *Odilo, and William—were more important than their actual accomplishments. These abbots are presented as friends and collaborators, working in concert for reform. Although the *Histories* is primarily concerned with Cluniac thinking, Glaber also describes contemporary political events. He focuses primarily on the West Frankish kings, particularly the Capetian dynasty and their vassals in Normandy and Burgundy, but he describes the activities of the German emperors as well.

Glaber was concerned not just with the powerful and famous; the *Histories* also provides a unique glimpse of the commonplace and local world of Burgundy. Glaber communicates how mass religious enthusiasm was beginning to create a new force in millennial society, and he is convinced that the heresies he describes are particularly odious because they stir up popular discontent. Glaber was a better biographer than historian, in part because history was a less familiar genre. Still, Glaber's *Histories* provides a contemporary voice that describes the inspiration, dissemination, and impact of the Cluniac reforms.

Bibliography: R. Glaber, *Five Books of the Histories*, ed. and trans. J. France, 1989.

James Countryman

GLANVILLE, RANULF DE (C. 1125–1190). A preeminent official of *Henry II of England, Ranulf de Glanville rose through royal service to the post of justiciar (in effect, viceroy) of England. Though he was active in all facets of government, he is best remembered for his role in administering justice during a formative period of English legal history; the earliest treatise on common law has long borne his name.

Glanville came from a substantial family of East Anglian landholders, not the high aristocracy. His father Hervey played a prominent part in local Suffolk courts and shared command of the Anglo-Norman contingent of crusaders involved in the capture of Lisbon from the Muslims in 1147. Ranulf's early years are obscure, but by 1162–1163 he was prominent enough that Richard de Anesty sought his support in a well-known lawsuit. Glanville first entered royal service in 1163, when he became sheriff of Yorkshire. He was, or soon became, linked to the shire through his marriage to Bertha de Valognes, whose family held lands there as well as in Suffolk. He remained sheriff until 1170, when an inquiry into malfeasance led to the dismissal of many officials; slightly later evidence suggests that he was engaged in considerable peculation. Despite losing his position, Glanville retained Henry II's confidence. When rebellion broke out in 1173 and a Scottish invasion threatened, Glanville received the strategic post of sheriff of Lancashire. He did not disappoint his master. Glanville was a key leader of the force that defeated and captured the Scots king, William the Lion, at Alnwick on 13 July 1174; William surrendered to him personally.

After this success, Glanville's rise was rapid. Henry II soon reappointed him sheriff of Yorkshire, which he remained until the reign's end. He was briefly (1177–1180) sheriff of Westmorland also. More significantly, after 1174 Glanville moved from local offices to those of national importance, acting in 1177 as one of Henry's envoys to Count Philip of Flanders. Most notably, Glanville became increasingly prominent in judicial affairs. He frequently served as an itinerant justice from 1175 and in the Eyre of 1179 was head of one of the four circuits. He also heard cases in the central court alongside such men as the justiciar Richard de Lucy. When Richard retired in 1179, Glanville likely succeeded immediately to his duties, though he did not officially become justiciar until the king left England in 1180.

As justiciar, Glanville's job was to execute royal policy, not to make it. Yet because the king was present in England for only one-third of Glanville's justiciarship, his viceregal responsibilities were large. He acted for the king in every kind of business, such as commanding an army against a Welsh rising in 1182, presiding over a meeting of English bishops with papal envoys in 1184, and negotiating with the French king, *Philip II Augustus in 1186. He oversaw the routine of English government, presiding at the Exchequer, and issuing grants to royal dependents. He headed the judiciary and, unlike his predecessor, served frequently as an itinerant justice. Though most of Henry II's legal innovations appeared before Glanville became justiciar, much work in implementing the reforms doubtless remained. Contemporary writers record the pride that Glanville took in the efficient workings of English justice. The king relied on Glanville as he did on few others, naming him as an executor of his will in 1182 and entrusting him for a time with the education of Prince *John of England. When Richard succeeded his father in 1189, Glanville's close association with Henry cost him the justiciarship; one chronicler states he resigned on his own, another that he was dismissed and fined a heavy sum. Perhaps under pressure from Richard, Glanville set out on the Third Crusade, fulfilling a vow made several years before. A member of the advance party, he died at the siege of Acre in October 1190.

In his origins among the lesser nobility, unwavering loyalty to his king, and effectiveness in bureaucratic, judicial, political, and military affairs, Glanville was an outstanding example of an Angevin civil servant. Typical too were his willingness to enrich himself through royal service, his advertisement of success by endowing churches (he founded religious houses at Butley and Leiston in Suffolk), and his patronage of relatives and neighbors. During his justiciarship, many of Glanville's connections received shrievalties or other offices; the future archbishop and justiciar Hubert Walter was Glanville's nephew and a member of his household. Competent and powerful Glanville surely was, but the balance of current historical opinion holds that he did not write the legal treatise that has been associated with him from the thirteenth century onward. Yet it was compiled during his justiciarship, perhaps under his direction, and remains a fitting monument to his achievement.

Bibliography: J. S. Falls, "Ranulf de Glanville's Formative Years, c. 1120–1179: The Family Background and His Ascent to the Justiciarship," *Mediaeval Studies* 40 (1978): 312–327; R. Mortimer, "The Family of Rannulf de Glanville," *Bulletin of the Institute of Historical Research* 54 (1981): 1–16.

Donald Fleming

GODFREY OF FONTAINES (FL. LATE THIRTEENTH CENTURY).
Godfrey was a philosopher and theologian at the University of Paris who flourished during the period between Thomas *Aquinas and *John Duns Scotus.

Godfrey was born into a noble family sometime before 1250 at the family estate of Fontaines-les-Hozemont in Liège, Belgium. He studied philosophy at the University of Paris in the early 1270s, moving on to theology by 1274. He served as a regent master in theology from 1285 to 1289, then again beginning in 1303. His philosophy and theology are characterized by a distinctive concept of act and potency that informs his views on issues from the nature of creation to the metaphysics of substance.

He opposed the special privileges accorded to members of the mendicant orders and thus did not enjoy the support accorded to scholars associated with those orders. Nevertheless, he was well regarded, holding several ecclesiastical offices (canon of Liège, canon of Tournai, provost of St. Severan in Cologne) and serving on a special commission charged with settling a dispute within the university.

His writings include fifteen *Quodlibets* (or formal exercises) and a set of *Ordinary Disputed Questions*. He also collected a large personal library, which he bequeathed to the Sorbonne at his death in either 1306 or 1309.

Godfrey of Fontaines stands out from his neo-Augustinian contemporaries like *Henry of Ghent and James of Viterbo as a boldly Aristotelian thinker who developed a thorough and internally consistent metaphysical-theological system. His impact on later philosophers and theologians has yet to be fully assessed by contemporary scholars.

Bibliography: J. F. Wippel, *The Metaphysical Thought of Godfrey of Fontaines: A Study in Late Thirteenth-Century Philosophy*, 1981.

Anne Collins Smith and Owen M. Smith

GOTTFRIED VON STRASSBURG (C. 1170–1220?).
The most renowned poet of the German Middle Ages, he composed *Tristan*, the region's greatest vernacular work of the era. Recent discoveries confirm that the romance, possibly begun about 1200, could not have been finished before 1212 but probably not later than 1220.

Nothing certain is known about Gottfried. Later literary sources mention his name, otherwise unwitnessed in any historical document of the age. Later poets called him "meister" (master), probably related to his education or to his profession. Rudolf von Ems and Konrad von Würzburg claim him as their teacher. The influence of the classics and also of French literature exhibited throughout his work reflect that he was highly educated as a "clericus" and "literatus" in the Latin tradition. His patron is obscure, though an unidentified Dieterich, possibly the benefactor, is spelled out in *Tristan*'s acrostic. The *Tristan* romance of Thomas of Britain served as his immediate model. The German text seems to have originated in the Strassburg area since the majority of surviving manuscripts come from Alsace.

The body of critical literature pertaining to Gottfried is large, frought with unsolved problems and disagreements. One of the knottiest difficulties is the significance of the acrostic. It proceeds through the text, spelling out the names of Tristan and Isolde in alternating fashion, but is cut short by the fragmentary nature of the poem's ending. This too is an important source of disagreement; is the text truly fragmentary or did Gottfried intentionally leave it open-ended? It stands uncontinued in only one manuscript; in other manuscripts it is completed by Ulrich of Türheim, Heinrich of Freiburg, and the conclusion of Eilhart von Oberg's rendition of the *Tristan* material.

Other popular topics of research include the various "excursus" that appear in the text, asides where Gottfried departs from his story line to comment on various themes. In one of these, the poet catalogs a number of his literary near-contemporaries, whose accomplishments he judges. In another he considers love and honor in the context of a woman's surveillance by her husband. Critics have disagreed as to the relationship of these excursus to the text. However, recent findings show an unequivocal structure, one shared by all the excursus and by the events of the narrative.

Critics have been unable to reach a consensus as to *Tristan*'s interpretation. Some scholars find the text secular, and some believe it to be religious in nature. The one point of agreement is that knightly accomplishments take a second place to artistic and intellectual talents. Adding to the frustration is the allegorical nature of the work, which Gottfried composed in accordance with the form of scriptural exegesis and allegoresis common in the Middle Ages, "typology."

New research affirms both a secular and a religious dimension, identifying Tristan with the Holy Roman Emperor *Frederick II, with Christ, and with Moses. Famous for its obscurity and beauty, the allegorical love grotto has until recently defied scholarly efforts. Friedrich Ranke and Julius Schwietering espoused the position that the grotto is related to the church building and to the mysticism of Saint *Bernard of Clairvaux. New scholarship dramatically confirms this, revealing in the grotto not only a cave but physical genitalia, the house of courtly love, the cloister of the heart, the literary work of art, the seat of the intellectual conception analogous to the conception of God's Word in Mary's womb, and the birthplace of God in the soul. At its supreme allegorical instance, Gottfried evokes the Christian interpretation of the Song of Songs and, though he precedes Dante, in Danteesque fashion, modulates and then transforms the love of Tristan and Isolde for each other into the union of the soul (Isolde) with God. Gottfried ultimately equates light, love, and honor with salvation and with God. Most significantly, Gottfried incorporates many aspects of human existence into the grotto excursus so that God and all things become "one thing without difference."

Research now stands at the threshold for a new understanding of *Tristan*. It is possible that no other poet of the Middle Ages employed the rules of Latin rhetoric so rigorously and successfully, that no other reached such a high intellectual plane. While Gottfried's work was imitated, it lost popularity in the fifteenth century. Nineteenth-century critics were slow to revive the poem, but Richard Wagner valued it as the foundation for his opera *Tristan und Isolde*. Frescoes in the castle Neuschwannstein commemorate the work, and a number of modern novels have employed the Tristan thematic.

Bibliography: M. Chinca, *Gottfried von Strassburg: Tristan*, 1997; R. Schnell, *Suche nach Wahrheit: Gottfrieds "Tristan und Isold" als erkenntniskritischer Roman*, 1992.

Kristine K. Sneeringer

GOTTSCHALK OF ORBAIS (C. 804–869). Gottschalk was a poet, lyricist, and theologian condemned of heresy for preaching an extreme form of predestination based on the ideas of Augustine, igniting a significant debate among the leading thinkers of his day.

Gottschalk, the son of a count of Saxony, was given to the monastery at Fulda as a boy, where he became friends with Walahfrid *Strabo. His studies there were thorough, and while he was still in his teens, he was sent to Reichenau to complete his education under highly qualified teachers. Gottschalk returned to Fulda around 827. In 829, Gottschalk wrote to the council in Mainz to request that he be released from his vows, arguing, among other things, that his father (a free man) was not entitled to commit his son to a life of servitude. The council agreed to release him, but his abbot, *Hrabanus Maurus, objected. The direct result of this is not known, but Gottschalk next appears in the records in the monastery at Orbais.

At some point between 835 and 845 Gottschalk was ordained as a priest. He then went off on a pilgrimage, apparently not authorized, to Italy, where he stayed for some time, studying the works of Augustine. Augustine mentions predestination, the doctrine that at Creation the fate of each individual had been determined. Some few elect individuals were predestined to salvation through the gift of God's grace, but the remainder were predestined, because of Adam's original sin, to eternity in hell. Though this did not, according to Augustine, deny the freedom to choose between good and evil, the idea of predestination was uncomfortable for western European Christians, who wanted to make room for the capacity of individuals to influence their eternal fate through actions (including good deeds as well as participation in Catholic sacraments). Gottschalk, however, preached an extreme version of predestination, that is, of double or dual predestination, much to the consternation of Hrabanus, who worried that if the recently converted Franks and Saxons were led to believe in predestination, they might neglect the Catholic sacraments and feel less compelled to act morally.

Out of practical as well as theological concerns, therefore, Hrabanus accused Gottschalk of heresy, with the result that in 848 Gottschalk was declared a heretic and given over to the responsibility of Archbishop *Hincmar of Rheims. The following year he was brought before a synod at Quiercy where he was deposed from the priesthood, placed next to a hot fire, and beaten until he agreed to burn a pile of books he had collected to support his ideas on predestination. He was then committed to prison in the monastery of Hautvilliers, where he was to remain until his death some twenty years later. Early in his imprisonment he was treated well, allowed to read and write and receive letters, and take communion. However, conditions were gradually tightened.

Gottschalk's interest in Augustine's ideas ignited a debate on predestination that involved many of the leading theologians of his time, with many of them coming down on his side; in 866 he wrote a letter to Pope *Nicholas I, with the result that Nicholas summoned Hincmar to bring Gottschalk before his deputies to defend his treatment of Gottschalk. Hincmar refused to appear but offered to send Gottschalk himself to the pope. Nicholas died before further action could occur, and Gottschalk remained in prison until his death, when he was denied the sacrament for a last time.

Bibliography: E. S. Duckett, *Carolingian Portraits: A Study in the Ninth Century*, 1962; D. E. Nineham, "Gottschalk of Orbais: Reactionary or Precursor of the Reformation?" *Journal of Ecclesiastical History* 40 (1989): 1–18.

Heide Estes

GRATIAN (GRATIANUS, JOHANNES) (D. C. 1179). Little is known concerning the life of the ecclesiastical lawyer who compiled a collection of Church laws, *Concordia discordantium canonum* (Concord of Discordant Canons) that came to be called the "Decretum [Gratiani]" or [Gratian's] *Decretals*.

He is presumed to have been born at Chiusi, Tuscany, perhaps becoming a Benedictine monk and teaching canon law (c. 1130–1140) at the noted legal center of Bologna where he was associated with the monastery of Saints Felice and Nabor. His work and that of his continuators exists in several hundred manuscripts dating from the twelfth century and constituting the first comprehensive collection of Church law in history. With additions and revisions through the centuries, it remained the primary compendium of canon law until the codification of 1918; however, despite its acknowledged importance and influence, it was not recognized as an official collection by the Church until Pope Gregory XIII finally recognized it in 1582, authorizing the printing of the first official edition of the *Corpus iuris canonici* or *Body of Canon Law*.

Before the time of Gratian, Church or canon law had been subsumed under theology, applying theological principles to specific cases. The increasing prominence and influence of Scholastic theology and a revival of interest in Roman law contributed to the climate of opinion in which Gratian worked to create his synthesis as practicing legal scholars began to distinguish between canon law and civil law. Just as civil law regulated the actions of secular rulers and their subjects, canon law was seen to pertain to the pope, bishops, and the faithful. By analogy with civil law, canon law—in Gratian's compilation—prescribed norms for the organization and governance of the hierarchy as well as the direction of the laity. (Under Roman civil law, the term *decretum* referred to a judgment of the emperor; in canon law, the word came to signify a papal pronouncement.)

It seems likely that Gratian worked on the *Decretum* between 1139 and 1149; it contains decrees of the Second Lateran Council held that year, and *Peter Lombard mentioned the work in his *Sentences* issued in 1150. The work contains nearly 4,000 *capitula* or chapters, assembled from materials dating from the period following the Edict of Milan in 313 and spanning nearly nine centuries: the writings of the Church Fathers; papal decretals or letters; the decrees of Church councils; earlier collections of canon law, notably those of Anselm of Lucca (c. 1036–1086), *Burchard of Worms, and *Ivo of Chartres; and fragments of Roman and civil law. Prior to the twelfth century, collections of legal and theological principles had been organized by subject, without substantial regard for resolving difficulties caused by differing opinions expressed at different times by opposing churchmen. Gratian organized and unified these disparate elements through commentaries that summarized the subject and cited pertinent authorities; when authorities differed on a question, he attempted to reconcile their positions, after which he drew conclusions about the subject.

Gratian's opus is divided into two parts. The first part comprises 101 *distinctiones*; the first twenty explain the origins, types, and definitions of law as well as Church laws regarding governance and discipline of prelates. The remaining 81 distinctions cover clerical morals, ecclesiastical elections, the ordination of bishops, and secular and ecclesiastical authority. The second part contains paradigmatic *causae* (cases) and *quaestiones* regarding problems in penal law and procedure with respect to property, members of the clergy, and matrimony. Some scholars question the authorship and origins of the treatments of penance (added to canon 33), the consecration of churches, and the sacraments (added as a third part, *De consacratione*), which differ from the rest of Gratian's work. If indeed these segments represent later additions by other canonists, they must have been added soon after the conclusion of his work, for the first commentators cite them.

The influence of the *Decretum* was permanent and widespread, the occasion of numerous amplifications and commentaries. By 1170 it was substantially complete, forming the first segment of the *Corpus iuris canonici*, the comprehensive text of Roman Catholic Church law. Gratian himself died perhaps as early as 1160 (one canonist refers to him as "he of renowned memory") but certainly before the Third Lateran Council in 1179. His disciples, known as "decretists," continued to study, comment upon, and spread his work, which served as a teaching tool as well as a legal code for centuries to follow. Dante included Gratian in his *Paradiso*, perhaps to offset the influence of later canonists who supported the concept of temporal power accruing to the papacy.

Bibliography: S. Chodorow, *Christian Political Theory and Church Policy of the Mid-Twelfth Century: The Ecclesiology of Gratian's* Decretum, 1972; E. Friedberg and A. Richter, contributors, *Corpus iuris canonici*, 2nd ed., 2 vols., 1879, reprint, 1959; S. Kuttner, *Gratian and the Schools of Law, 1140–1234*, 1943, reprint, 1983.

Judith Davis

GREGORY I (THE GREAT), POPE (C. 540–604, PONTIFICATE 590–604).

Saint and the first monk to be elected pope, his term as pope is often seen as the beginning of the medieval papacy. He worked feverishly to save the Romans from the depredations of the Lombards, reform the Church's administration, and spread the influence of the papacy throughout the West.

Around the year 540, Gregory was born into a wealthy and pious patrician family of Rome that included other saints (his mother Silvia, and two aunts, Tarsilla and Aemilians) and popes (his great-great-grandfather Felix III and a kinsman, Agapitus). Like most men of his rank, Gregory looked destined for a career in public service from early on. By 573, he had distinguished himself enough to be named as prefect of Rome. Shortly thereafter, in about 574, Gregory decided to become a monk. He founded several monasteries in Sicily, as well as converting his own home on the Caelian Hill in Rome into a monastery dedicated to Saint Andrew. There he lived as a monk until the pope (probably Pelagius II) ordained him as a deacon of Rome. In 579, he was sent to Constantinople as the ambassador (*apocrisarios*) of the pope at the Byzantine imperial court. He took with him to Constantinople several of his fellow monks of St. Andrew, and he lived like a monk as much as possible while there. His principal mission in the East was to induce the emperor to come to Italy's aid against the Lombard invaders. Gregory was relatively unsuccessful in this mission, but there were other positive results of his residence in Constantinople. It was at this time, at the request of Leander of Seville, who was also visiting the imperial city, that Gregory began writing his exposition on the Book of Job.

After close to six years in the imperial capital, Gregory returned to Rome and was elected abbot of his monastery. He completed and published his lectures on the Book of Job at this time. In 589, flooding and famine ravaged Rome, and as a result, Pope Pelagius II died in early 590. Gregory was unanimously elected as his successor, even though Gregory himself was hesitant to accept such a great responsibility and leave his monastery. The emperor confirmed his election, however, and Gregory was consecrated as bishop of Rome on 3 September 590. As pope, he worked tirelessly to comfort and feed the victims of the Lombard attacks, to deal with the Lombard threat, in the absence of any real activity by the emperor or his representatives, and to protect and extend the interests and influence of the papacy throughout the West.

Much of Gregory's papacy was spent in negotiating with the Byzantine emperor, with his exarch at Ravenna, and the Lombard king and his dukes of Spoleto and Benevento. Gregory continually sought to bring peace to Rome and Italy and even went so far as to negotiate a separate peace with the Lombards in order to end the deprivations of, and threat upon, Rome and the surrounding Italian countryside. Jeffrey Richards has argued that Gregory's worldview was greatly shaped by his loyalty to Rome and the empire, which was surpassed only by his devotion to God and the Church. Despite this loyalty, Gregory was often at odds with the emperor over the Lombard problem. Carole Straw has suggested that Gregory's disagreements with the emperor over this and other issues led Gregory to pay more attention to the Germanic kings of the West.

An important theme of Gregory's pontificate was reform and order. He employed monks and clerics in his administration, at the expense of the local clergy, in an effort to combat various abuses. His reforms and subsequent smooth-running administration of the papal estates and resources allowed him to perform many of the duties and services required of him during these turbulent times. He also made some minor reforms of the liturgy, including the Eucharistic prayer. Ultimately, Gregory was only moderately successful in implementing his policies. He died on 12 March 604.

Gregory had an influence on the papacy and the Christian Church, which was felt for many years after his death. He was a prolific letter writer, and the letters from all fourteen years of his pontificate were compiled and kept in Rome. Many of these letters are now lost or destroyed, but the 854 that remain are the main source for reconstructing the history of Gregory's pontificate. Other important writings of Gregory include the *Morals on the Book of Job, Pastoral Care, Homilies on the Prophet Ezekial, Forty Gospel Homilies*, and the *Dialogues*. It was for these many works that Gregory was chiefly remembered in the Middle Ages.

The *Dialogues* and *Pastoral Care* (*Regula pastoralis*) were perhaps his most popular works. *Pastoral Care* was Gregory's guide to becoming an ideal bishop, and it was very influential and widespread throughout the Middle Ages. Among his advice to bishops was to consider their audience when they preached. He advocated a simple and straightforward approach, which is evident in his own sermons and writings. For example, the *Dialogues* are conversations between Gregory and his loyal deacon, Peter, which relate various stories of miracles, visions, and prophecies. These stories were meant to teach and convert by example. Gregory was concerned with teaching morals, and calling people to repentance; this is most evident in the *Morals on the Book of Job* and his homilies on the Gospels. His writings, which reaffirmed and clarified the theology and doctrine of the earlier Fathers of the Church, especially Saint Augustine, led later writers to rank him as the fourth and last Latin Father, placing him in the company of Tertullian, Ambrose, and Augustine.

Arguably, Gregory's greatest accomplishment during his pontificate was the mission, in 596, to Anglo-Saxon England, headed by *Augustine, a monk from Gregory's own monastery. The mission was ultimately successful in converting the king of Kent, *Æthelbert, to Christianity, and later the English came to regard Gregory as their own apostle. The real significance of this mission was the example it set for the later missionaries who set out to convert the pagans living in Flanders and Germany. They tried to model their efforts after Augustine's mission and always looked to Rome for guidance and authority. Gregory's influence upon the early English Church, and the English Church's devotion and reverence for Gregory's memory, helps to explain, at least in part, England's early and fairly constant loyalty to the Roman Church and the pope throughout the Middle Ages.

However, Gregory's efforts at asserting papal authority extended beyond his efforts in England. One prevailing theme of Gregory's papacy was his claim and assertion of Rome's primacy as the highest authority of the Christian Church. He continually reasserted this belief in many of his letters. He helped enhance his own claim to supreme authority by taking up many secular concerns, in the absence of imperial control, including organizing the military defense of Rome against the Lombards, although he did not generally support ecclesiastical involvement in secular affairs. He accepted and supported the emperor as the head of the empire and all its secular affairs, but he was careful not to support serious encroachments of spiritual authority by the emperor.

Bibliography: F. H. Dudden, *Gregory the Great: His Place in History and Thought*, 1905; J. Richards, *Consul of God: The Life and Times of Gregory the Great*, 1980; C. Straw, *Gregory the Great*, in *Authors of the Middle Ages*, ed. P. J. Geary, vol. IV, no. 12, 1996.

Ryan P. Crisp

GREGORY VII, POPE (C. 1020s–1085, PONTIFICATE 1073–1085).

Gregory VII (Hildebrand) is the pope most closely identified with the changes to the Church in the eleventh century, which are known as the Papal, or "Gregorian," Reform. These changes, which resulted in a more imperial vision of papal leadership, in part emerged as a response to growing concerns over the perceived menace of simony (purchase of church office) but were also fueled by debate as to whether there should be a more apostolic character to papal leadership.

As an official at the Lateran Palace for three decades prior to his election as pope in 1073, the contribution of Hildebrand as sub- and archdeacon, and later chancellor of the apostolic see, was central in setting the terms of the reform process under the reformist papacies of *Leo IX (1049–1054), *Nicholas II (1059–1061), and Alexander II (1061–1073). His own accession to the papacy heralded a period of political brinkmanship that, though mostly unsuccessful in the short term, in the long term saw Gregory VII's actions pave the way for a new role for the papacy in European affairs.

Early details of Hildebrand's life are uncertain. He may have been of Tuscan or of Roman family. He was educated in Rome, first at the Lateran Palace and then at St. Mary Aventine. It was here that he probably professed as a monk; the suggestion, by Bonizo of Sutri, that Cluny was the site of his profession probably only reflects a rival claim for the source of his reformist vision. He first came to notice in the controversial reign of Gregory VI (1045–1046). When the latter was sent into exile in 1046, Hildebrand went with him to Germany, only returning to Rome on Gregory VI's death in 1047. Hildebrand was to become one of the key reformers in the curia of Leo IX, whose reign saw the commencement of many of the reforms that have often come to be, perhaps anachronistically, termed "Gregorian."

Hildebrand appears as something of an *eminence grise* in the reform process of Leo IX; his separate contribution is not easily distinguished from that of his contemporaries Humbert, *Peter Damian, Desiderius, and others. The emphasis of the reforming decree of 1059 on papal election and opposition to lay investiture, in reflecting concerns that would also be central to the early years of Gregory VII's pontificate, would seem to demonstrate his likely input; other initiatives of the papacy in Nicholas II's reign, such as renewed claims over the Eastern Church, the establishment of feudal relations with the Norman counts of Apulia and Calabria, as well as the establishment of a bureaucracy for international administration—with an increase of legates and correspondence issuing directly from the Holy See—are similarly paralleled in Gregory VII's pontificate.

Whether Hildebrand ever had a singular influence on policy will remain debated. His influence as a negotiator and diplomat is undoubted. Hildebrand's negotiations with the Empress Agnes were critical to brokering the election of Nicholas II in 1059. The death of Humbert in 1061 and Peter Damian's retreat into eremitic life saw Gregory's guidance become central to the determining of papal policy. He was made archdeacon of the Roman Church and, under Alexander II, chancellor of the Apostolic See. On the death of Alexander in 1073, he was elected pope. If the reforming decree of 1059 is correctly regarded as his work, it is notable that his election was directly in contravention of that decree in making no consultation with either Cardinal Bishops or the emperor. The latter, *Henry IV, who had attained his majority in 1066, was slow to react to this defiance of his authority, only coming into direct conflict with Gregory in 1075 over appointment to the strategically important see of Milan.

An assembly of the German court, including bishops, deposed Gregory in January 1076. At the Lenten Synod of the same year, Gregory, in turn, deposed Henry and excommunicated him, absolving Henry's subjects from oaths. Henry, avoiding attempts by dissident nobles to capture him, managed to come to Canossa in winter 1076–1077 and, in one of the more dramatic scenes in European history, confronted Gregory barefoot as a penitent on 25 January. Gregory absolved him, as he was bound to do, after three days. Events in Germany were to overtake both of them, as the German court elected Rudolf of Swabia as king in March 1077. After three years, Gregory acknowledged Rudolf, but Rudolf's death in the same year swung Henry back into a position of power. After appointing the archbishop of Ravenna as an antipope (Clement III), he besieged Rome, from where Gregory VII was rescued by his Norman allies, to die in exile in Salerno on 25 May 1085. On his death, Gregory VII is said to have stated: "I have loved righteousness and for this reason die in exile."

Gregory was a man of deeds whose desire for temporal leadership inspired distrust among other reformers. Peter Damian dramatically described Gregory as "Holy Satan"; Wido of Ferrara called him "false monk." His desire for a *passagium* against the east continued the martial vision of Leo IX and anticipated the Crusade of 1095. The document of twenty-seven articles known (from one of its rubrics) as the *"Dictatus papae,"* found among his letters, though not published in his lifetime, presents a clear image of Gregory as a pope of near imperial vision. His turbulent and frustrated reign marked a turning point in the history of the papacy.

Bibliography: E. Emerton, *The Correspondence of Pope Gregory VII*, 1932; A. J. Mac-Donald, *Hildebrand, a Life of Gregory VII*, 1932; C. Morris, *The Papal Monarchy*, 1989.
Jonathan M. Wooding

GREGORY IX, POPE (B. C. 1145, PONTIFICATE 1227–1241). A relative of Pope *Innocent III, Ugolino dei Conti, cardinal bishop of Ostia, was elected to succeed *Honorius III in 1227 and took the name of Gregory IX. He was extremely active in the compilation of canon law, encouraged the crusade against the Moors in Spain, and continued the struggle he shared with his predecessor and successors against Emperor *Frederick II of the Holy Roman Empire. Two kings with whom he was in contact during his reign as pope were later made saints: Ferdinand III of Castille and *Louis IX of France. *Dominic was made a saint during his papacy, and even his own confessor, chaplain, and penitentiary *Ramon Peñafort was later sanctified.

Gregory's stormy relationship with Frederick (he excommunicated him) included many attempts to get the emperor to set out as promised on a crusade. When Frederick eventually did reach the Holy Land, he recovered Jerusalem, but by treaty rather than by force of arms. The excommunication was lifted, but the conflict between the two men did not end there, and Frederick had been blockading the sea approaches to Rome when Gregory died. The latter also encouraged Ferdinand III to crusade against the Moors, driving them out of Cordova, Seville, and Cádiz. He also inspired Louis IX of France but was generally unsuccessful in gaining his help against Frederick. In 1240 Gregory raised the alarm concerning the approach of the Mongols. The pope also contributed to the elaboration of the rules for the Franciscans (by holding that they did not have to obey *Francis' injunctions concerning strict poverty as elaborated in his spiritual testament) and the Dominicans, for whom he helped lay down the rules for the rooting out of heresy, thus paving the way for the Inquisition.

In the famous bull *Parens scientiarum*, Gregory provided rules for the University of Paris, which were subsequently adopted by other universities. He caused to be revised some suspect and banned books of Aristotle and subsequently made the teaching of Aristotle so much a part of the university curriculum that the Philosopher, as he was called, dominated for the rest of the century and beyond.

In canon law, Gregory employed the Dominican Ramon of Peñafort in codifying the Church's legislation since the time of *Gratian. The various canons had been collected into five compilations, and Ramon culled out the repetitions and reconciled what was contradictory. The resulting *Decretales* were published in 1234, when copies were sent to the universities of Paris and Bologna. The text was declared to be official and was to be taught in the schools and applied as law. It forms the second part of the *Corpus iuris canonici* with the title of *Decretales Gregorii IX*. His successors were Celestine IV, who died only sixteen days after his election, and *Innocent IV.

Bibliography: E. Brem, *Papst Gregor IX bis zum Beginnen seines Pontifikats*, 1911; C. Morris, *The Papal Monarchy: The Western Church from 1050 to 1250*, 1989; F. Mourret, *Histoire genérale de l'église*, vol. 4, *La chrétienté*, 1928.

F.R.P. Akehurst

GREGORY OF TOURS (538/539–593/594). Gregory was the bishop of Tours and the author of *The History of the Franks*, a monumental work that incorporates both a defense of Christianity beginning with the Creation and a detailed and historically valuable account of contemporary events.

Gregory, named at birth Georgius Florentius, was born in 538 or 539, possibly in Clermont, the capital of Auvergne in central Gaul. On both sides of his family he was descended from Roman senatorial families long associated with service to the Church. His father was the Senator Florentius and his mother was Armentaria, who was in turn the descendant of two bishops of Langres who were also saints, among numerous members of Gregory's family (on both sides). Whether Gregory made the choice to join the clergy or was pledged by his parents is uncertain, but he seems to have done so early in life, taking the name Gregory at that point. Gregory's father apparently died when he was a child; at about age eight he was sent to his uncle Gallus, bishop of Clermont-Ferrand (another of the family's numerous saints). When, a few years later, Gallus died, Gregory went to the home of the archdeacon Avitus, who also later became bishop of Clermont.

He was educated thoroughly in Christian doctrine with some reading in pre-Christian Roman authors, of whom he makes particular reference only to Virgil. At age twenty-five, he was ordained a deacon. He became bishop of Tours in 572 or 573, a popular appointment, though he was, at about thirty-four, quite young for the honor, and held the position until his death some twenty years later in 593 or 594. Early in his bishopric, Gregory weathered political storms, beginning with the assassination of King Sigibert in 575. Sigibert's throne was taken by his brother Chilperic, who may also have been his killer and whose attempts to collect taxes from the townspeople of Tours Gregory fought. When Chilperic was in turn assassinated in 584, the surviving brother of the three, Guntram, reinstated as king Sigibert's son Childebert II (whom he considered his own adopted son, his own sons all having died). Gregory had been on good terms with Guntram, serving him as ambassador on more than one occasion, and at this point Gregory seems to have gained greater freedom and power in the administration of the affairs of Tours.

Gregory's best known work, *The History of the Franks*, is a polemic for the truth of Christianity and the justice of Church actions but also a compilation of historical documents drawing on both written sources (including the Bible, Jerome's Latin translation of Eusebius' Greek *Chronicles*, and Orosius' *Seven Books of History against the Pagans*) and oral histories. As the main contemporary source of documentation for sixth-century Gaul, Gregory's *History* is an invaluable (but by no means infallible) historical source. He began the work shortly after his ordination as bishop and continued work until his death, describing the reigns and challenges to the early Merovingian kings. While the earlier portions of the *History* are written from the perspective of a historian examining the past, at some point, perhaps with the death of Sigibert, Gregory begins in chroniclers' fashion to recount events, both secular and religious, as they occur. (His work is thus more comprehensive than *Bede's *Ecclesiastical History of the English People*, which, though comparable in its method of beginning far in the past with the birth of Christ and then collecting oral and written accounts of events closer to his own time, limits itself primarily to the history of Christianity in Britain.) Gregory concludes the *History* with a series of descriptions of the bishops of Tours and concludes with the plea, "Do not, I beg you, do violence to my Books. . . . Keep them intact." Gregory's other works include several works on miracles of saints; one on *The Lives of the Fathers*, a series of biographies of churchmen of Gaul; a commentary on the Psalms; and an astronomical treatise dealing with determining dates of festivals.

Bibliography: Gregory of Tours, *The History of the Franks*, trans. L. Thorpe, 1974; Gregory of Tours, *Lives of the Fathers*, ed. and trans. E. James, 1985.

Heide Estes

GROSSETESTE, ROBERT (C. 1170–1253).

Grosseteste was an English theologian, philosopher, and translator whose works were popular throughout the Middle Ages and after.

Born into a humble family from Stowe, Suffolk, this English theologian and philosopher went on to become a major leader in the English Church of the thirteenth century. The early years of Grosseteste's life are obscure, but it would appear that he completed the first stages of his education at a cathedral school in England, perhaps Hereford. In 1192, *Gerald of Wales recommended Grosseteste to the bishop of Hereford, noting that he excelled in the liberal arts, canon law, and even medicine. This seems to have guaranteed Grosseteste's first ecclesiastical appointment, as he remained part of the household of Bishop William de Vere until his death in 1198. At this point Grosseteste almost disappears entirely from the historical record, although there is evidence that he acted as judge-delegate in Hereford sometime between 1213 and 1216. There is also an early-thirteenth-century charter from Paris that names a Robert Grosseteste residing at a house in Paris; however, since this charter concerns the property claims of his children, some historians have suggested that this may be another Robert Grosseteste.

The next mention of Grosseteste is in the episcopal register of Hugh of Lincoln, when in 1225 Grosseteste was given a benefice with pastoral responsibilities in the diocese of Lincoln. In 1229, he was appointed archdeacon of Leicester and became a canon in the cathedral church of Lincoln. Three years later, Grosseteste was seriously ill. Taking this as divine warning against holding more than one benefice, he resigned all save his position of canon. During this period, Grosseteste also lectured in theology at Oxford. There has been some controversy as to when he became a master of theology, but the first documented evidence we have is his appointment to run the Franciscan school at Oxford in 1229–1230. The Franciscan chronicler Thomas of Eccleston wrote that Grosseteste's teaching was of considerable benefit to the convent, and it explains his influence on Franciscan theology for the century. When Hugh of Lincoln died in 1235, the cathedral chapter elected Grosseteste as the next bishop. He was consecrated in March of that year and remained bishop of the largest diocese in England for the next eighteen years. In October 1253, Grosseteste died at the ripe old age of eighty-three.

During his lifetime, Grosseteste was an avid participant in European intellectual life. His early education had given him a taste for natural philosophy. He began producing texts on the liberal arts and mainly on astronomy and cosmology. His most famous scientific text, *De luce* (Concerning Light), argued that light was the basis of all matter, and his account of Creation devotes a great deal of space to the biblical text of God's command, "Let there be light." Light also played a significant role in his epistemology, as he followed the teachings of Saint Augustine that the human intellect comes to know truth through illumination by divine light. Grosseteste's interest in the natural world was further developed by his study of geometry, and he is one of the first Western thinkers to argue that natural phenomena can be described mathematically. He also played a pivotal role in the introduction of Aristotle to scholastic thought, producing commentaries on a number of Aristotle's logical and scientific works. Later as bishop, Grosseteste translated the *Nicomachean Ethics*, making this important work available to the West in its entirety for the first time.

As important as science was to Grosseteste, his ultimate intellectual fascination was with theology. Before he became a professional theologian, Grosseteste produced treatises in pastoral theology. He was primarily interested in providing texts to educate the clergy in the sacrament of Confession. His most famous work from this period, the *Templum Dei* (Temple of God), survives in over ninety manuscripts from the thirteenth to the fifteenth centuries, a testament to its enduring popularity. The work contains the standard theology of confession but is also adorned with useful tables and diagrams that summarize some of the more complex theological discussions on penance. In total, Grosseteste wrote five major works on pastoral care throughout his long life. All reflect the most recent theological discussions but are mediated with a desire to make these ideas useful and applicable for parish priests.

At Oxford, Grosseteste lectured on Scripture, disputed theological questions, and preached university sermons—the three main duties of a scholastic theologian. Even after he became bishop of Lincoln, he retained links with theological discourse. He kept a watchful eye over the University of Oxford, as it was within his diocese, and ensured that the theology faculty was following in the footsteps of the faculty of theology at Paris. Around 1239–1241, he began to employ his knowledge of Greek (which he had acquired during his tenure at Oxford) to render a new translation of the works of the Byzantine theologian John Damascene. This was soon followed by a sophisticated translation of the entire corpus of *Pseudo-Dionysius the Areopagite, a set of writings that would have tremendous influence on mystical thought in the later Middle Ages. He also translated from the Greek the *Testament of the Twelve Patriarchs*, a text that Grosseteste considered to be further proof that Jesus was the promised Messiah.

During his eighteen years as bishop, Grosseteste became known as a brilliant but highly demanding Church leader. He insisted that all his clergy be literate and receive some training in theology. His high standards for Christian practice and ministry landed him in a number of disputes with various parts of his dioceses, especially monasteries and most notably his own cathedral chapter. When the cathedral chapter refused to allow an episcopal inspection in 1239, a long court case began that was eventually resolved in Grosseteste's favor in 1245. During this dispute, Grosseteste produced a treatise on his conception of Church leadership, now part of his letter collection, and this is one of the most comprehensive discussions of ministry and authority in the medieval Church. Further disputes over the activities of the archbishop of Canterbury in the 1240s led to Grosseteste's appearance at the papal court in 1250, residing at the time in Lyons. He lectured the pope on the major problems of the contemporary Church, indicting the papacy as a principal cause for the current malaise. While Grosseteste's practical demands were eventually met, in 1253 he once again clashed with the papal court over the appointment of a non-English-speaking cleric in the Lincoln diocese. Grosseteste's last letter is to the papal notary, outlining the theological and canonical reasons why he must resist this appointment. This letter is one of the main reasons why some sixteenth-century thinkers considered Grosseteste a hero for the antipapists.

In more recent years, scholars have rejected the image of Grosseteste as a proto-Protestant and have attempted to place him within the intellectual and institutional context of the thirteenth century. His thought had a significant impact on Oxford theology, and his influence can be visibly seen in the writings of John Wyclif. Of the 120 works he penned, a great number still survive only in manuscript form, but most of his major philosophical and theological works have been recently published in modern critical editions. His life and thought provide an important insight into the intellectual development of scholasticism and medieval science, as well as the theoretical and practical aspects of Church ministry.

Bibliography: J. McEvoy, *The Philosophy of Robert Grosseteste*, 1982; R. W. Southern, *Robert Grosseteste: The Growth of an English Mind in Medieval Europe*, 1986; F. Stevenson, *Robert Grosseteste: Bishop of Lincoln*, 1899.

James R. Ginther

GUIBERT OF NOGENT (C. 1053–C. 1124). The prolific writer Guibert of Nogent was a Benedictine commentator, theologian, and historian.

Guibert was born to a noble family in Clermont-en-Beauvais perhaps around 1053, according to his biographer and fellow monk of Nogent, Dom Jean Mabillon. Much of what we know of Guibert's life is related in his own works, particularly *De vita sua*, a first-person account of his early life. Guibert was promised to the Church as an infant. His early life was spent with his widowed mother whose attitudes regarding the body molded his character. He was educated at home by a tutor until around the age of twelve and had little contact with either siblings or contemporaries. Although connected by blood to aristocratic families, he was isolated as a child, under the primary influence of his mother and tutor. As a young adolescent, he entered the monastery of St.-Germer-de-Fly where he began to prepare for life as a monk. He dedicated himself to study and writing and was encouraged by Saint *Anselm of Bec (later of Canterbury), a frequent visitor to St.-Germer. Guibert began to consider the role of the mind and contemplation in theology. His commentary on Genesis reflects the influence of this concern.

For the next twenty years, he remained a monk at St.-Germer, writing numerous commentaries, histories, prayers, and other works. In 1104, he was offered the abbacy of the small Benedictine house of Nogent-sous-Coucy, where he wrote his most famous works: *Gesta Dei per Francos*, a history of the First Crusade; *De vita sua*, biblical commentaries, a tract in praise of the Virgin and her miracles; and *De pignoribus*, a treatise challenging the legitimacy of relics. He also engaged in technical debates against both Jewish and Christian opponents regarding articles of the faith. He involved himself in ecclesiastical affairs and had contact with the bishop of Laon and the pope. His stance was frequently adversarial to ecclesiastical authorities. At one point, he even withdrew from Nogent for a time. In contrast with the accounts of his early life, Guibert is reticent about his time at Nogent. After his return to Nogent, he continued to write prolifically, producing commentaries on the Old Testament prophets. He died in 1124 at Nogent, where he is buried.

Guibert read widely and as a young man admired the classical Latin poets, especially Virgil and Ovid, who influenced his literary style. He developed an interest in theology and wrote prolifically on issues of liturgical practice and Christian faith. He was a conservative commentator in the tradition of Pope *Gregory the Great. His work shows a fascination with sins of the flesh, sexual purity and bodily cleanliness, and visionary experiences. His *Gesta Dei per Francos* reflects a nascent national pride. Guibert's histories represent an intensely moral perspective and incorporate numerous literary and moral embellishments in support of his theological standards. His works reflect the complex and challenging political, social, and theological environment of the twelfth century.

Bibliography: J. F. Benton, trans., *Self and Society in Medieval France: The Memoirs of Abbot Guibert of Nogent*, 1970; R. Levine, *The Deeds of God through the Franks: A Translation of Guibert de Nogent's* Gesta Dei per Francos, 1997.

Patricia Price

GUILLAUME DE LORRIS (FL. C. 1230). Thirteenth-century French author of the first 4,058 lines of the *Roman de la Rose*, one of the most popular and important medieval allegorical poems.

Except that his name derives from a village near Orléans, nothing is known about Guillaume de Lorris outside of his authorship of the *Roman de la Rose*; this fact is known only because *Jean de Meun mentions it forty to fifty years later in his continuation of the poem. Guillaume de Lorris' section of the poem, often called the most poetic part, is an allegorical description of the course of a love affair. The poem's first-person narration, its May setting, its subjectivity, and its use of religious imagery to describe a secular love affair link it to the courtly love lyric tradition, a tradition that was waning in popularity in the thirteenth century. The connection to this tradition has caused some critics to propose that Guillaume left his poem in a finished state, since the ending of his section, with the Lover persevering in his love for the lady from afar, coincides with the traditional endings of several types of early courtly lyric.

Guillaume stresses that his poem is meant to be interpreted didactically. He places his poem alongside other treatises of love, such as *De arte honeste amandi* (The Art of Courtly Love) by Andreas *Capellanus, and in fact, the poem may be read as an illustration of the rules and theories proposed in that text. Told in the form of a dream vision, the poem is directly related to other didactic dream visions in classical and medieval literature; however, the *Roman de la Rose* is the first instance of such a form being used to express secular love.

Guillaume seems to seek validation for his work by using this form and by connecting his work to that of Macrobius, a fourth-century author who wrote a commentary on Cicero's *Dream of Scipio*, a work that was very popular and highly respected during the Middle Ages. The first-person narrator of the *Roman de la Rose* claims that his dream was prophetic and that everything actually happened as predicted. Although Guillaume's portion of the work may be read as a pleasant romance, there is evidence of a more complex meaning. All is not perfect in this world. Even the Garden of Pleasure has a dark aspect, and the God of Love at times seems sinister, setting traps for the Lover. Some critics suggest that Guillaume intended for his work to be read ironically and that instead of illustrating and supporting the ideal of courtly love, the poem is actually critical of it. Guillaume himself frequently implies such an ironic reading. Despite this possibility of the poem as an ironic criticism of courtly love, however, Guillaume's section is certainly gentler in tone than the section written by Jean de Meun. Although Love itself may be deceitful, the Lover is characterized as an innocent child. Guillaume also lacks the blatant antifeminism present in Jean de Meun's continuation.

Bibliography: H. M. Arden, *The Romance of the Rose*, 1987.

Leah Larson

GUILLELMUS DURANDUS (GUILLAUME DURAND, WILLIAM DURAND) (C. 1230–1296).

Bishop, lawyer, judge, and author, Durandus' works, especially the *Speculum iudiciale* and revised *Pontifical*, remained useful and popular for centuries.

Born in southern France in about 1230, Durandus became a canon regular of Maguelonne before going to study law in Bologna. He subsequently taught law there and at Modena. In the mid-1260s under Pope Clement IV he was appointed an appeals judge in Rome and held thereafter a number of high-ranking posts, of which the most arduous was that of papal governor of Bologna and the Romagna, always more or less in revolt against the civil authority of the pope. At this time he was also the absentee holder of benefices in France, including that of dean of Chartres. In 1285 the cathedral chapter of Mende in southern France, not far from his birthplace, elected him bishop, although he did not arrive there until 1291. He remained only a few years in Mende before being recalled in 1295 to the Romagna. For a time, he was both spiritual and temporal rector of that province, and also of the March of Ancona, but he did not succeed in putting an end to the troubles of the region before he died in Rome the following year. His tomb may still be seen in the church of the Minerva. His successor at Mende was his own nephew of the same name, Guillelmus Durandus the Younger.

Durandus' earliest work, reflecting his service as a lawyer, was the *Speculum iudiciale*, written in 1271–1276 and revised in 1289–1291. It gained for its author the nickname of "The Speculator." It is a manual of procedural law, including criminal procedure, in ecclesiastical courts. The procedural law of the newly rediscovered Roman law had been taught, but it had been combined with local procedure in different ways in different places. Durandus has the distinction of having produced a unified code, although a great deal of it is simply copied and borrowed from other authors. In spite of the reworking of the *Speculum*, it is still rather repetitious and even contains contradictions. However, this manual remained very popular for centuries and was printed about fifty times before 1678.

The Speculator's other works, mostly written toward the end of his life, include a digest of canon law, the *Repertorium aureum iuris canonici*, of uncertain date. He also produced, probably in the 1280s, a *Rationale divinorum officiorum*, which discusses all aspects of church worship and services, explaining the liturgy and the words and objects used in it from many points of view. This encyclopedic work collects and codifies a vast amount of medieval lore and became the uncontested authority on liturgy. It is estimated that more than 300 manuscripts of the *Rationale* may still exist. He prepared for the priests in his diocese a set of instructions and statutes, the *Constitutiones synodales*, probably completed soon after he arrived in his see in 1291 and clearly linked to his own diocese. This work was thought lost for centuries until a manuscript (annotated in Durandus' own hand) and even a printed edition were discovered in the late nineteenth century.

He further produced a revision of the *Roman Pontifical*, which served as a model for the authoritative 1485 edition of this set of instructions for the church services performed by a bishop. It was modeled on the *Pontificale romanae curiae*, but it omitted most of the sections that applied only to rituals conducted by the pope himself and included the whole range of church services and rituals that were performed by a bishop. It is an invaluable tool for understanding the Church at a time when it was still triumphant and its unanimity not yet seriously challenged. It is noteworthy that in his *Pontifical* Durandus makes reference to his *Constitutiones synodales*, showing that on his election to the see of Mende he first took care of the needs of his local clergy, then turned his attention to those of the bishop and of all Christian bishops.

Bibliography: Guillaume Durand, *Pontificale*, in *Le Pontifical roman au moyen-âge*, vol. 3, *Le pontifical de Guillaume Durand*, ed. M. Andrieu, 1940; Guillaume Durand, *Rationale divinorum officiorum*, ed. V. d'Avino, 1859; Guillaume Durand, *Speculum iudiciale*, 1574, reprint, 1975; P.-M. Gy, ed., *Guillaume Durand, évêque de Mende (v. 1230–1296)*, 1992; J. Neale, trans., *The Symbolism of Churches and Church Ornaments*, 1893.

F.R.P. Akehurst

GUTHRUM (D. 890). Viking leader of one of several armies that harried England, he carried out nearly annual raids during the summer followed by retreat during the winter, throughout much of the ninth century.

A large Viking army attacked England in 865, entering York in 866, then moving back and forth between York and Anglia over the course of the next few years. The Vikings further attacked Wessex in 870, London in 871, and Trent in 872–873. In 874, however, some of the Vikings, tired of nine years of continuous fighting and nomadic life, began to establish settlements in Northumbria. The remaining army continued their raids on Wessex in 875–876 and 877 but were defeated by *Alfred the Great and finally routed in 878. At this point Alfred and Guthrum negotiated a treaty establishing the boundaries of a permanent Viking settlement in England, which became known as the Danelaw. The treaty allows for trade between the Danelaw and the English but stipulates that Danes and English are not permitted to settle in each other's areas. Guthrum was also persuaded by Alfred to convert to Christianity and be baptized, which he did along with thirty of his men; Alfred showered him with gifts and made him his godson at this point, and Guthrum took the Anglo-Saxon name Æthelstan. Guthrum apparently took this conversion seriously, ruling in East Anglia until his death.

Bibliography: P. Hunter Blair, *An Introduction to Anglo-Saxon England*, 1966.

Heide Estes

GUÐMUNDR ARASON (1161–1237). Bishop of the northern see of Hólar from 1203 to 1237, he attempted to reform the Icelandic Church but met with little or no success.

Guðmundr, born in the north of Iceland, was the illegitimate grandson of a chieftain in Eyjafjord. His uncle, a priest, raised and instructed Guðmundr for the priesthood. In 1185, he was ordained and began working as a district priest almost immediately thereafter. Moreover, he taught clerics; as his fame and popularity increased, he traveled during the summer, often at the invitation of the rich and powerful.

By 1201, when the northern chieftains insisted that the candidate for the see of Hólar should be a northerner, Guðmundr had attracted quite a following as a miracle worker, and the chieftains named him to the see. Although he refused the appointment at first, he accepted it soon thereafter, which resulted in confrontation. Traditionally, the more powerful Icelandic chieftain in each region controlled the monies of the diocese; however, Guðmundr, while nominated as an easily controlled puppet, proved to be the opposite. He insisted on the liberties of the Church and charity for all, often depleting the revenues of Hólar. His defense of the Church's jurisdiction over its clerics led him to excommunicate the very chieftain who had nominated him three times; this led to Guðmundr's capture. Later released, his ability to control the finances of his diocese decreased, and he was often barred from his cathedral.

Prestssaga Guðmundar Arasonar and the saga of Bishop Guðmundr describe a man famous for his religious fervor and asceticism, a man who did not care that the chieftains regarded him with disdain and disfavor. Unlike other priests in Iceland, Guðmundr identified himself with the Church. His attempts at reform failed because other priests refused to throw off the trappings of the secular world. Moreover, the reformers found Guðmundr's behavior and actions objectionable because he generated confrontation and opposition both to himself and the ideals he represented.

A man loved by the common people, Guðmundr Arason found himself persecuted by the chieftains and members of the Church. He died in 1237 without having accomplished the reforms he had hoped to make.

Bibliography: O. Vésteinsson, *The Christianization of Iceland: Priests, Power, and Social Change 1000–1300*, 2000.

Jana K. Schulman

H

HADEWIJCH OF BRABANT (EARLY THIRTEENTH CENTURY). A Flemish Beguine and teacher, many of her letters, poetry, and recorded visions survive.

Little is known about Hadewijch, particularly since her writings include few autobiographical comments. She must have lived in the thirteenth century and must have composed her works before 1245 when the Muslims conquered Jerusalem; she calls Jerusalem the holiest of Christian cities and celebrates its leadership in one of her works. Her work shows an awareness of chivalric customs and court life and reveals a familiarity with language, rhetoric, numerology and astronomy, music theory, and theology. Thus, she must have come from an aristocratic family and must have obtained a broad education.

Hadewijch wrote in three genres. Her letters, of which thirty-one are extant, reveal her affection for the women of her Beguine community. She believed Christ had authorized her to lead and instruct younger women, so many of her letters are addressed to "Young Beguines" and encouraged the girls to live pious lives and submit to God's will. She commands them to make love the greatest force in their lives. Encouraging the development of self-awareness, she nevertheless reminds her readers that God's might is greater than any human power. Only through experiencing God can one truly know God; thus, Hadewijch stresses experiential knowledge of God over intellectual knowledge of him. Such ideas place her in the category of other mystics such as *Bernard of Clairvaux, and the letters to the young Beguines are perhaps the most well known of her works.

Many of Hadewijch's letters are serious and sorrowful. Accused of teaching quietism, condemning human effort in salvation, she probably faced exile. This would explain why she had to send letters to the young girls and why her letters are full of comments about her "travels" and "wanderings." Beguines faced some opposition in the thirteenth century because they resisted ecclesiastical control, and Hadewijch might have sought asylum from the Church authorities. Some scholars believe that her own Beguine community rejected her.

Hadewijch produced two kinds of poetry, forty-five in stanzas and sixteen in couplets. Her stanza poetry incorporates the symbolism of courtly love, and some scholars credit her with creating the "mystical love lyric." Like her letters, these poems were intended for the instruction and leadership of Beguines within her community. In addition, she published poems in rhyming couplets for public consumption. As letters, and treatises, these poems often provide a glimpse of Hadewijch's theology.

Lastly, she recorded fourteen visions in prose form. These visions yield the most information about Hadewijch's mystical experiences. All of the visions follow a general pattern. She is first seized by a desire to be with God, a desire so strong that she cannot interact with people. To communicate with God she partakes of the Eucharist, the consumption of which transports her to a different plane. In the new world, her senses are heightened, and she gains knowledge about God and his will. From a study of Hadewijch's visions, one can see that she both experienced the divine and believed herself to be called to share her experiences with others.

Bibliography: S. Madigan, ed., *Mystics, Visionaries, and Prophets: An Historical Anthology of Women's Spiritual Writings*, 1998.

Alana Cain Scott

HADRIAN IV, POPE (ADRIAN) (C. 1100–1159, PONTIFICATE 1154–1159).

Hadrian IV is unique in that he is the only Englishman ever to rise to the papacy, and during his brief tenure, he found himself in the midst of a political struggle that had abiding consequences for the rest of Europe.

Born Nicholas Breakspear near St. Albans, he entered the monastery of St. Rufus, Avignon, and took the habit of an Augustinian canon. Breakspear climbed the ecclesiastical ranks, becoming abbot of St. Rufus in 1137, cardinal bishop of Albano (c. 1150), and papal legate to Scandinavia (1152–1154), where he established an independent archepiscopal see for Norway and initiated reforms among local clergy. Soon after his successful return to Rome as Apostle of the North, Anastasius IV died; Breakspear was elected to the Holy See as Hadrian IV.

Immediately, Hadrian IV found himself under threat from the forces of *Frederick I Barbarossa to the north and William of Sicily to the south. Hadrian IV also faced the theological and popular opposition of *Arnold of Brescia, who opposed the temporal power of the papacy, within Rome itself. Employing the tools at his command, Hadrian IV took the extraordinary step of putting Rome under an interdict to quell Arnold of Brescia's followers; he later excommunicated William of Sicily. At the pope's behest, Barbarossa captured Arnold and delivered him to Rome, where he was executed in 1155; in return, Hadrian IV crowned Barbarossa Holy Roman Emperor after Barbarossa paid proper homage. After Barbarossa's withdrawal from Rome, Hadrian was left to fight William of Sicily, who captured Beneventum in 1156, made peace with the pope, and became his vassal—much to Barbarossa's consternation. *John of Salisbury claimed that during this time Hadrian made "the donation of Ireland" to *Henry II of England, who ruled the island as a papal fief, though the authenticity of *Laudabiliter*, the bull giving Henry II rights to Ireland, is doubted by many. Hadrian died in 1159, and his successor *Alexander III eventually excommunicated Frederick Barbarossa.

Bibliography: S. Malone, *Pope Adrian IV and Ireland*, 1899; A. Tarleton, *Nicholas Breakspear (Adrian IV), Englishman and Pope*, 1896; O. J. Thatcher, *Studies Concerning Adrian IV*, 1903.

Daniel Kline

HÁKON IV HÁKONARSON OF NORWAY (1204–1263). First king of Norway to rule without the threat of civil war, he revised the legal codes of Norway, had French Romances translated into Old Norse, and pursued international politics and friendships throughout the medieval world.

Hákon was born in 1204, the illegitimate and posthumous son of Hákon Sverrarson. He grew up at the court of King Ingi II Baardson and took the throne after Ingi's death in 1217. However, because of his illegitimacy, some factions supported Ingi's half brother, Skuli Baardson, as rightful king. In 1223, Skuli and his supporters received a crushing blow to their expectations; secular and religious leaders met in Bergen and acclaimed Hákon the rightful king of Norway. Hákon married Skuli's daughter in 1225 in an attempt to defuse the situation between himself and Skuli, a reconciliation that lasted, on and off, for some fourteen years. In 1239, Skuli had himself proclaimed king. In 1240, Hákon killed Skuli; with Skuli's death, the civil wars over the succession to the Norwegian throne ended.

When the civil wars ended, King Hákon involved himself more with legislative matters than he had done before. Historian Knut Gjerset believed that Hákon wished "to revise the old laws both in Church and state so as to bring them into harmony with the more enlightened concept of justice." Historians who followed Gjerset rejected his view of the king's motivation, but nowadays the consensus has shifted back to Gjerset's view. Another reason for Hákon to revise the laws was that the king's position did not match the "suggested" position or dignity of a king as put forth in those European laws following Roman law. According to Germanic law, the king, though he enjoyed certain privileges, was still a citizen. If he committed a crime, he had to pay compensation. By revising the laws in accordance with European laws, Hákon could have more power. Given these factors, King Hákon began to revise the legal texts, setting the stage for his son, *Magnús Hákonarson, to continue his undertaking. King Hákon left his son a changed office. The king was now the *vicarius dei*, the Lord's annointed, and held his office by the grace of God (according to Augustine) and had the right to legislate as he wished (according to *Justinian's *Digesta*).

In addition to legal revision and consolidation, King Hákon also brought chivalric literature to Norway. Hákon wanted the Norwegian court to be on a par with the rest of Europe, and he patronized the translation of foreign courtly literature to create a rich literary prose in his national language. The oldest translation is *Tristams saga* from 1226, a translation of the story of Tristan and Isolde. Hákon had his translators emphasize the court and the power of the king at the expense of the Romance elements, in some forty translations. King Hákon intended the Norse translations to glorify the position of the king and "inspire fear and respect in his subjects." In addition, Hákon had a book called the *King's Mirror* written. This book, organized as a dialogue between father and son, covers three major topics: loyalty to the king, a king's divine right to rule, and the proper demeanor or behavior at court.

Finally, Hákon engaged in international politics. After 1240, he expanded and solidified control over Norway's tributary colonies in the British Isles (the Isle of Man and the Hebrides) and the North Atlantic (Greenland and Iceland). Greenland accepted Norwegian rule in 1261 and Iceland quickly followed (1262–1264). In 1250, Hákon signed a trade agreement with the city of Lübeck. He exchanged letters and gifts with Holy Roman Emperor *Frederick II. *Louis IX of France sent *Matthew Paris to Hákon to invite him to join them on crusade. He was a friend of King *Henry III of England. He married off his children for political and dynastic connections. His son Hákon married the daughter of Earl Birger of Sweden; his son Magnús married the daughter of King Erik of Denmark; and his daughter Christina married the Infante Don Felipe, the brother of King *Alfonso X of Castile. King Hákon died in 1263 after leading a failed attack on Scotland to secure Norwegian control over the Isle of Man and the Hebrides.

Bibliography: S. Bagge, *From Gang Leader to the Lord's Anointed: Kingship in* Sverris saga *and* Hákonar saga Hákonarsonar, 1996; K. Gjerset, *History of the Norwegian People*, 1915; D. Sunnen, "Life and Letters at the Court of Hákon IV Hákonarson," *Medieval Perspectives* 8 (1993): 87–103.

Jana K. Schulman

HARALD BLUETOOTH GORMSSON OF DENMARK (R. C. 958–C. 988).

He was the second king of Denmark in the same dynastic line that continues unbroken today. His memorial stone at Jelling in Jutland claims the following: "Harald the king had this monument made in the memory of Gorm his father and Thyri his mother—that Harald who won all Denmark for himself, and made Christians of the Danes." This complements the text on the earlier stone found at the same spot: "Gorm the king made this monument in memory of Thyri his wife, Denmark's adornment."

The three portions of what became medieval Denmark—Scania (Skåne; now part of southern Sweden), Jutland (Jylland), and the islands in between—had in fact been united before at various times, for instance, under Godfred more than a hundred years before Harald, and possibly under Harald's own father Gorm the Old, though not permanently. It is even possible that the parts of Denmark that Harald "won" were simply parts of Jutland that had been temporarily taken by *Otto II of Germany.

The possibly legendary details of Harald's conversion to Christianity are recounted in sources written in subsequent centuries, including *Snorri Sturluson's *Heimskringla*. Harald is said to have converted (possibly in the 960s) after seeing Poppo, a Christian bishop, carry glowing iron in his hand and not be burned by it.

Harald's reign ended following an insurrection by his son *Sven I Forkbeard. He died of his wounds, probably in what is now northern Poland.

Bibliography: E. Roesdahl, *Viking Age Denmark*, trans. S. Margeson and K. Williams, 1982.

Sandra Ballif Straubhaar

HARALD I FAIRHAIR HÁLFDANARSON OF NORWAY (C. 854–C. 930).

Also known as Harald Finehair, he is given the credit of unifying Norway under his kingship. His consolidation of power is thought to have been the impetus behind the settling of Shetland, Orkney, the Hebrides, and Iceland by displaced chieftains. Though no doubt a historical figure, the details of his ascension to power and reign and consequently his legacy are blurred by legend and oral tradition.

*Snorri Sturluson's account of Harald in his thirteenth-century *Haralds saga*, though unreliable as history, is colorful and intriguing and may provide a few clues into this larger-than-life king. According to that tradition, Harald was descended from the Yngling dynasty, an even more legendary family with ties to Sweden and to the Norse gods, particularly Ing. At the age of ten, Harald is purported to have ascended to the throne of his father in the kingdom of Vestfold. Within a few years, he began successfully to make bold aggressive moves against his neighboring districts in order to increase his power. According to Snorri, after Harald's initial success, he sought as his bride the haughty and beautiful princess Gyða of Hordaland. She rejected his offer, stating that she would not give up her maidenhood to a petty king, but only to a king of a unified Norway. Rather than being incensed by her reply, Harald became more determined to increase his power and vowed that he would not cut or comb his hair until all of Norway was under his rule. After ten years and numerous battles, particularly against northern and southwestern territories, he fought and won against a coalition of kings and earls at the naval battle of Hafrsfjorðr (c. 885–890) and claimed total kingship, though territories particularly to the north continued to oppose him. He also claimed the hand of Gyða who finally assented and joined what seems to have been a long list of Harald's wives and concubines. Shortly thereafter he had his hair clipped and his sobriquet changed from Haraldr lúfa (mop hair) to háfagri (finehair).

During his reign, it is thought that Harald increased his economic and political power by confiscating private lands, thereby encouraging emigration to the Hebrides, Orkneys, Shetland, and Iceland. No doubt, he laid the foundations for provincial administration, and though a pagan, he encouraged ties between Norway and England by having his son Hákon (later Hákon the Good) fostered by King *Æthelstan of England. Only the idea of a unified Norway survived Harald's kingship. Upon his death, his many sons by his various wives divided his realm up; his son, the brutal Eiríkr Bloodaxe, was to be the so-called high king. In short, he left Norway much the way he found it, divided and contentious.

Bibliography: G. Jones, *A History of the Vikings*, 1984; Snorri Sturluson, *The Saga of Harald Fairhair*, in *Heimskringla: History of the Kings of Norway*, trans. L. M. Hollander, 1964.

Joseph Carroll

HARALD III HARDRÅDE SIGURÐARSON OF NORWAY (C. 1015–1066).

King of Norway, called Hardruler, this tall, blond warrior with his numerous raids and campaigns, his service in the Varangian guards in Constantinople, his ambitious political aspirations, and his death in battle has been marked as the epitome of the Viking warrior and king.

While in his midteens Harald survived the battle of Stiklestad, where his half brother King *Óláfr II Haraldsson, later Saint Óláfr, was killed. He then fled to Russia where he served Prince Jaroslav of Kiev. From there, he ventured south to Constantinople where he joined the Varangian guard. Though later storytellers embellished his exploits in the service of the emperor, Harald's skill as a warrior and a leader must have been substantial. While in the emperor's service, he rose in prominence and gained much wealth in campaigns in the Mediterranean, especially Sicily, and in the East. In 1045, he returned to Norway with great wealth, from both his exploits in Byzantium and the dowry he received from marrying Jaroslav's daughter. He arranged a treaty with Óláfr's son, King Magnús the Good, which would allow them to rule jointly over Norway, though Harald would take a subordinate position. Magnus' subsequent death in the following year allowed Harald sole rule. Ever ambitious, he sought to expand his power but met with limited success in Denmark against *Sven Estridsen but was able to tighten his grip in the Hebrides, Orkneys, and Shetland. After the death of *Edward the Confessor in 1066, Harald made a claim on the English throne. He landed in Yorkshire with 300 ships and allied himself with Earl Tostig Godwinson. Harald was soon killed and his army defeated by the English and *Harold Godwinson at the battle of Stamford Bridge. Three weeks later, Harold Godwinson's army, weakened by the battle, was defeated by *William I the Conqueror at Hastings.

Aside from an illustrious military career, Harald was a strong and powerful leader of Norway. Though he had a reputation for the love of valuable possessions, he could be generous. He is credited with building churches, handpicking bishops, strengthening trading centers, introducing Norwegian coins as a method of payment, and founding the city of Oslo. He seemed to have been admired by his people despite the fact that his ruthless ways in politics and war earned him the name of Hardruler. With his death, many historians have marked the end of the Viking era. His two illegitimate sons, Magnús and Óláfr the Quiet, succeeded him to the throne.

The sources for Harald's life are as wide and varied as his career. He is remembered in skaldic poems and numerous Icelandic texts and sagas, the most famous being the one written by *Snorri Sturluson and appearing in his *Heimskringla*. Harald even appears in Greek texts where he is called Araltes.

Bibliography: H.R.E. Davidson, *The Viking Road to Byzantium*, 1976; G. Jones, *A History of the Vikings*, 1984; Snorri Sturluson, *Heimskringla: History of the Kings of Norway*, trans. L. M. Hollander, 1964.

Joseph Carroll

HARDING, STEPHEN, SAINT (D. 1134). Third abbot and one of the founders of Cîteaux, he shaped the administrative form of the Cistercian Order, emphasized strict observance of the Benedictine Rule, and provided reliable texts of key liturgical books.

The son of Anglo-Saxon nobility, Stephen entered Sherborne Abbey in Dorset, England, but after the Conquest he renounced his vows, traveled to Scotland, and studied in France. Returning from a pilgrimage to Rome, he entered the abbey of Molesme in the diocese of Langres, France, recently founded in an attempt to return to strict observance of the original Benedictine Rule, which had been adapted and relaxed over time. In 1098, seeking a still more austere life, Abbot Robert of Molesme led twenty-one monks, including Stephen, the abbot's secretary, to a remote site south of Dijon. They founded the "New Monastery" that became Cîteaux, the mother abbey of the Cistercian Order.

Stephen was elected prior under the second abbot, Alberic. He was elected abbot in 1109, and his administration saw many changes as the monastery's influence expanded. He enforced Cîteaux's freedom from secular responsibilities, even refusing noble supporters the customary privilege of holding court at the monastery. A system of granges (outlying farms) run by lay brothers (who followed an adapted rule with fewer liturgical responsibilities) took advantage of rapidly expanding land donations. The first daughter house at La Ferté was founded in 1113, shortly after the entry of *Bernard of Fontaines (later abbot of Clairvaux). By the time of Stephen's death, there were twenty daughter houses, including some of nuns. The regulations Stephen provided to deal with the growing order are the nucleus of the Charter of Charity, which regulates the relationships between Cîteaux and her daughters. The Charter safeguards the autonomy of individual abbeys, with a system of annual visitations and General

Chapters. It prescribes the behavior and treatment of visiting abbots, provides for replacement of abbots as necessary, arranges relief for houses that have fallen into severe poverty, and forbids monetary exactions from daughter houses.

Stephen was also concerned to provide appropriate, reliable books for the liturgy and study. In contrast to later austerity, the scriptorium at Cîteaux in Stephen's time produced richly illuminated manuscripts. His own texts are few. The "Monitum"(warning) that prefaces his manuscript of Jerome's Vulgate describes his consultation with Jewish scholars to establish the correct text and warns against adding back spurious passages, which Stephen removed. Of his correspondence, only an encyclical letter on the use of Ambrosian hymns and a letter to Sherborne, written late in his life, survive. Parts of the earliest Cistercian history, the "Little Exord," have been attributed to Stephen, but this has been disputed.

Stephen became blind and resigned his office about a year before his death in 1134. He was canonized in 1623. Some scholars contrast Stephen's legalistic insistence on the Benedictine Rule with Bernard's mysticism. This is unfair to both men. Stephen's attention to administration provided a solid base for later expansion of the Cistercian Order, while his love of the Benedictine Rule and his textual scholarship provided the springboard for later Cistercian spirituality.

Bibliography: J.-B. Van Damme, *The Three Founders of Cîteaux: Robert of Molesme, Alberic, Stephen Harding*, 1998.

Jill Averil Keen

HAROLD GODWINSON (C. 1020–1066). A skilled warrior and diplomat known for his intelligence and bravery, Harold Godwinson's fortune swung from exiled noble to the second most powerful man in England, which positioned him to assume the throne on 6 January 1066. Harold's short reign as the last of the Anglo-Saxon kings saw invasions by the other two claimants to the throne. *Harald III Hardråde of Norway, assisted by Harold's own brother Tostig, was defeated on 25 September at Stamford Bridge near York. That victory was quickly followed by the invasion of Duke *William of Normandy (thereafter William I of England), who defeated Harold weeks later on 14 October near Hastings in Kent. Harold was probably buried at Waltham Holy Cross, which he had rebuilt and where he established a college of canons.

Born the second son of Godwin, earl of Wessex, and his Danish wife Gytha, Harold was appointed earl of East Anglia around 1044–1045, due in large part to his father's influence and his sister Edith's marriage to King *Edward the Confessor. A series of family conflicts with the king, which first resulted in Edward's removal of Swein, Harold's older brother, from his earldom, eventually led to their family's exile in 1051. Godwin went to Flanders with his sons Swein, Tostig, and Gyrth, and Harold, with his brother Leofwine, sought refuge in Ireland with Diarmid, king of Leinster. That next year, the family harried England, forcing Edward to return Godwin and Harold to their former positions. When his father died in 1053, Harold became earl of Wessex.

Harold also gained the earldom of Hereford when the king's nephew, Ralph of Hereford, failed to defend his land against the Welsh. Harold kept the border under control through a series of negotiations and skirmishes before bringing north Wales under English control in 1063 with the help of his brother Tostig. During this period, as Leofwine, Tostig, and Gyrth became earls, the family gained control of southern England and part of Northumbria. Harold, now the wealthiest man in England, became Edward's right-hand man and oversaw much of the kingdom's administration. His skills as a diplomat, proven against the Welsh, were put to the test when Northumbria rebelled against Tostig, whom they replaced with Morcar, the brother of Edwin of Mercia. While Edward favored a military solution, Harold, likely fearing it would leave them open to a Norman invasion, convinced the king to recognize Morcar as earl.

With the question of heir unsettled, Edward grew ill in November of 1065. The king's heir, Edgar, son of Prince Edward and grandson of Edmund Ironside, was much too young to become king. As Harold knew, Duke William of Normandy was interested in the throne. In 1064 or 1065, for reasons not entirely clear, Harold traveled to the Continent and was captured by Count Guy of Ponthieu. William had Harold released and brought to Normandy. Pro-Norman sources state that Harold, during his stay, swore an oath to support William's claim to the English throne. Whether this oath was sworn, sworn freely, or sworn under duress is unknown. Whatever happened in Normandy, with Edward ill, Harold asked the English earls and archbishops to support his bid for the throne. Edward consented and died on 5 January 1066; the next day, Harold was crowned king of England.

Harold spent much of his nine months as king waiting for an invasion from Normandy. He spent four months with his fleet on the Isle of Wight while his infantry waited on the coast nearby. As the term of service for such an army was two months, on 8 September Harold had to disband the second host he had raised that summer. He returned to London, where he learned that his brother Tostig and Harald III Hardråde of Norway had entered the Humber with 300 ships. Harold rushed north and defeated them at Stamford Bridge on 25 September. Of the 300 Norwegian ships that had come to England, only 24 left with survivors. However, the success of this stunning and decisive victory was short-lived. Harold was still in York when William's fleet landed in the south of England three days later. Raising his fourth army of the summer, Harold marched to meet them. The two armies met on 14 October. After a long day of fighting, Harold died, and the English army broke.

Bibliography: I. W. Walker, *Harold: The Last Anglo-Saxon King*, 1997.

John Paul Walter

HARTMANN VON AUE (C. 1160–1220). An important poet of the German High Middle Ages and the first German poet to compose Arthurian romances, Hartmann adapted *Chrétien de Troyes' Erec et Enide* and *Yvain*, and an Old

French legend in verse, *La Vie de Saint Grégoire*, into German: *Erec, Iwein*, and *Gregorius*. He also authored *Die Klage (Büchein), Der arme Heinrich*, and numerous songs. Sources vary in listing the dates of his literary activity, but the years 1185 to 1205 are normally accepted.

Little is known about Hartmann and his life. Based upon his Alemannic dialect, scholars locate his origins in southwestern Germany, probably Schwaben, but the location of "Aue" is debated. He boasts that he is a "learned knight" who can read and a "ministerial vassal," possibly in the service of the dukes of Zähringen. His education must have included Latin, rhetoric, theology, and philosophy. Clearly, his knowledge of French must have been extensive.

A didactic purpose runs through all Hartmann's writings. The *Klage* is an allegorical dialogue between body and heart, mimicking Latin "laments" between the soul and the body. The heart demands denial of physical love in favor of a spiritual relationship between lover and beloved, a position to which the body is ultimately convinced. *Gregorius* teaches that no sin is unforgivable, even the sin of incest, when it is performed unintentionally and when the sinner properly repents and atones. The tale is a retelling of the Oedipus legend in medieval guise, but in this case there is not only a mother-son relationship but also a brother-sister one (Gregorius' parents). Through his penance, Gregorius is cleansed; eventually he is elevated to become pope and declares forgiveness of his mother's sin. In *Erec*, Hartmann portrays a knight who fails in his duty to others by passing too much time enjoying the embraces of his beautiful wife and by ruling her with a tyrannical hand. He passes through a number of increasingly intense dangers, *aventiure*, repeatedly rescued by Enite's transgression of his command for silence, eventually passing through a deathlike state. He emerges from this experience transformed, and through the benefits of Enite's selfless love the two become an exemplary ruling couple. This establishes the basis for their salvation in the world to come. *Der arme Heinrich* (Poor Henry) relates the tale of Sir Heinrich von Aue, who suffers from leprosy. He can only be cured by the willingness of a virgin, the daughter of his caregiver, to sacrifice her life for him, but he decides to suffer the vicissitudes of the disease rather than to be the cause of her death. He does recover as a result of their loving self-sacrifice. The two ultimately marry and earn eternal salvation. Like *Erec, Iwein* tells the story of a knight who neglects his duty to his people and to his wife. Contrary to Erec, however, Iwein loses honor because of his inordinate devotion to knightly adventures. Passing through a state of animallike nakedness and madness, which is analogous to Erec's passage through death, Iwein is cured by the administration of a healing balm by three women. He thereafter fights only in the service of the weak, and he and Laudine, like Erec and Enite, become a model ruling couple, serving their people and earning salvation in heaven. This meeting of God and the world is also evidenced in Hartmann's songs. He generally deals with a love thematic, finding unfulfilled love inadequate and criticizing and comparing the notion of courtly love to the love of God.

Hartmann espouses disciplined behavior, faithfulness, self-sacrifice, and duty to society. The good and successful life on earth, which includes the companionship and cooperative efforts of a correspondingly good man and woman, creates a model reigning couple and completes the recipe for eternal life. Hartmann combines sexual love with a spiritual relationship and dedication to the service of God's people, thus "pleasing God and the world," a medieval ideal.

Hartmann's contemporaries and immediate followers viewed his art as classic. His style was imitated widely, but his influence was also felt outside of literary circles. *Iwein* is commemorated in the Rodeneck and Hessenhof frescoes in Schmalkalden (Switzerland) and in the Malterer Tapestry (Freiburg im Breisgau). In modern times Thomas Mann adapted *Gregorius* to form the basis for *Der Erwählte* (The Chosen One). Hans Erich Pfitzner and Gerhard Hauptmann adapted *Der arme Heinrich* into opera and drama.

Bibliography: C. Cormeau and W. Störmer, *Hartmann von Aue: Epoche, Werk, Wirkung*, 1993; W. Hasty, *Adventures in Interpretation: The Works of Hartmann von Aue and Their Critical Reception*, 1996.

Kristine K. Sneeringer

HĀRŪN AL-RASHĪD (HĀRŪN IBN MUHAMMAD IBN ʿABDALLAH)

(763/766–809). The fifth caliph of the ʿAbbāsid dynasty, he ruled the Islamic Empire during the peak flowering of Arab-Persian civilization from 786 to 809. Much of the reputation of Hārūn derives from the fictitious stories of the *Arabian Nights*, which transformed Hārūn into an almost mythical figure. Muslim historical sources likewise have a tendency to embellish stories about Hārūn, oftentimes contrasting his orthodoxy with the heterodox positions of his immediate successors, thus overshadowing his historical personality. Hārūn's reign signifies a turning point in the history of the ʿAbbāsid dynasty. During his reign, the disintegration of the ʿAbbāsid Islamic Empire that began with the loss of the Iberian peninsula to the Umayyad intensified on different fronts. Hārūn's plans for his successorship, including the division of the administration of the empire among his sons, weakened the unity of the caliphate further and led to civil war among his sons.

Hārūn was born between 763 and 766 in al-Rayy, Iran, the third son of the third ʿAbbāsid caliph al-Mahdī (775–785); Hārūn's mother al-Khayzurān was a slave girl of Yemenite origin. Hārūn enjoyed a thorough education in the study of the Qur'an, philosophy, and law through special tutors, including Yahyā the Barmakid, who became Hārūn's main adviser and later his vizier. Hārūn led two expeditions against the Byzantine Empire at a young age, in 779–780 and 781–782. While Hārūn's participation did not play a decisive role in these military campaigns, their success, as well as the instigation of Hārūn's mother and his adviser Yahyā, led to his being appointed governor of the western provinces, as well as second in succession to the caliphate. Al-Mahdī's death under obscure circumstances brought Hārūn's brother al-Hādī to power in 785. Al-Hādī, attempting to alter the line of succession instituted by his father, incarcerated Hārūn and his adviser, Yahyā the Barmakid, but his own mysterious death in the following year ultimately brought Hārūn to power.

Hārūn ascended to the throne in 786 and appointed Yahyā the Barmakid as his vizier. In classical Muslim historical sources, Hārūn is generally depicted as a pious, religious ruler, unlike his immediate successors, who are portrayed as heterodox. Regular pilgrimages to Mecca and his personal participation in several military expeditions against the Byzantine Empire serve to illustrate Hārūn's orthodoxy, fulfilling his caliphal obligations. Successful expeditions against the Byzantine Empire led to Byzantine payments of tribute and the conclusion of peace treaties with Empress Irene (797–802) and Emperor Nicephorus (802–811).

Yet Hārūn was faced with frequent insurrections in different parts of his empire. Rebellions in Syria contributed to Hārūn's decision to move his residence to Raqqa, Syria, in 796. Instabilities in Ifriqiya gradually led to a loss of direct ʿAbbāsid power in parts of Northern Africa; frequent revolts in the eastern part of the empire, oftentimes tinged with religious fervor and worsened by the incompetence of successive governors, added to the disintegration of the unity of the empire.

Hārūn's removal in 803 of the Barmakids, who had been supporters of the ʿAbbāsid cause and had exerted influence on his predecessors as well as his early career, still puzzles historians. Hārūn's death sentence on Jaʿfar ibn Yahyā, and the incarceration of Jaʿfar's father Yahyā the Barmakid, who had been his tutor and adviser, is attributed in classical sources to a variety of motivations including jealousy on the part of Hārūn and heretical behavior or political ambitions on the part of the Barmakids, yet no single explanation is entirely convincing.

European medieval sources allege an exchange of embassies between Hārūn and *Charlemagne, including Hārūn's granting of the Holy Sepulchre in Jerusalem to Charlemagne. Arab sources are silent on diplomatic exchanges between Charlemagne and Hārūn, for which reason their historicity cannot be ascertained.

Hārūn died on a military campaign to the eastern province of Khurāsān in the city of Tūs (Iran), where he is buried, in the year 809. It is important to differentiate the legendary Hārūn al-Rashīd of the *Arabian Nights* from his historical personality. The former has developed into a mythical character often associated with a presumed despotism, decadence, and opulence of an imaginary world of the Orient; the historical Hārūn, as far as he can be separated from the embellishment of classical Muslim historiography, is a highly complex character struggling at the height of ʿAbbāsid achievement to halt the disintegration of the empire.

Bibliography: A. Clot, *Harun al-Rashid and the World of the Thousand and One Nights*, trans. John Howe, 1989; T. El-Hibri, *Reinterpreting Islamic Historiography: Hārūn al-Rashīd and the Narrative of the ʿAbbāsid Caliphate*, 1999.

Alfons Teipen

HAUTEVILLE, ROBERT DE. *See* ROBERT GUISCARD.

HEINRICH VON VELDEKE (C. 1150–1200). Known primarily for his *Eneasroman* but known also as the composer of a *St. Servatius* and several love lyrics, he is the father of German vernacular literature, serving as a stylistic and ideological forerunner and model for contemporary and subsequent poets.

Uncertainty prevails in our knowledge of Heinrich and of his works. He apparently was born in the first half of the twelfth century near Maastricht in Limburgian Belgium. Some successor poets bestowed upon him the title "Lord" or "Master," an indication that he was a member of the nobility and well educated. He may have served the counts of Loon and may have been related to this family. Heinrich purportedly finished about four-fifths of his *Eneide* between 1170 and 1175, when someone stole his manuscript. Through the intervention of Hermann, count of Thuringia, he regained access to it and completed it about 1185. Suggesting that he studied in a cathedral or monasterial school, his works evidence a familiarity with other authors and texts. He was well versed in the literatures of Germany, of France, and of antiquity. Over the course of time, both German and Dutch scholars have claimed him as their own, while his near-contemporary *Gottfried von Strassburg commends Heinrich as the first graft upon the stem of German literature.

Attempts to describe the circumstances of his life and creative activity are frustrating. Scholars have expended considerable effort concerning the question of whether or not the original language of Veldeke's *Eneasroman* was Old Limburgian or a more universal German literary language. Ludwig Ettmüller believed that the original had been composed in a lowland dialect but published his scholarly edition in 1882 based upon the Upper German majority in the textual tradition. About thirty years later, Otto Behagel reconstructed the *Eneasroman* in the old dialect, followed in the 1960s by Gabriele Schieb and Theodor Frings, who improved and revised the reconstruction. Specialists insist that these retranslations violate scholarly ethics because existing versions of the epic are exclusively Middle, Upper, or High German. Further, the work's distribution reached only to Upper German regions, no exemplar being found in the area around Maastricht. One of Veldeke's sources seems to have been the *Strassburg Alexander*, composed in an Upper German dialect (Alemannic), and the *Eneide* bears a close but problematic relationship to the German *Tristrant* of Eilhart von Oberge. The question of which language Veldeke employed is so consuming that it has been dubbed "The Veldeke Problem."

Beyond the question of language, the topics that develop in conjunction with the critical reasearch of the *Eneasroman* ultimately make the case for a German original even more convincing. Early investigations treat the love of Eneas for Dido and Lavinia. Though Virgil does not blame Aeneas for abandoning Dido in order to fulfill his destiny and submit to the will of the gods, the medieval authors cast doubt upon their hero's conduct. The Old French and Middle High German authors configure Dido's love without self-discipline, ridiculed by society, and unrequited by Eneas, as they expand the relationship of Virgil's Aeneas and Lavinia to comment on an ideal of love. In the critical literature, the love theme subsequently joins with and then yields to the notion of governing ("Herrschaft und Liebe"), modulating until discussions of peace and of rulership predominate. Critics have connected various portions of the text specifically to the reign of Emperor *Frederick I Barbarossa. However, these links are somewhat problematic, as at least one commentator believes the work was written initially (before it was stolen) in connection with *Henry the Lion, Barbarossa's powerful Welf rival. The motifs such as love and rule, which we find explicated in the secondary literature, generally expand from intratextual matters to compare the themes extratextually to the Old French and Virgilian versions.

Less interesting and important than the *Eneas* romance is Heinrich's *Servatius*, a work that is based on legends concerning the patron saint of Maastricht and that exists in its entirety only in a fifteenth-century New Limburgian manuscript. Of an Old Limburgian rendering only a fragment remains; an Upper German *Servatius* survives. As with the *Eneasroman*, text-critical problems plague the scholarship and prevent the development of a deeper understanding of this work. The transmission of Heinrich's love poems, imitated from French models, is completely Upper German, though the impurity of his rhymes points to less linguistic sophistication and to a greater proximity to his mother tongue than we find in his romance.

Bibliography: T. Klein, "Heinrich von Veldeke und die mitteldeutschen Literatursprachen. Untersuchungen zum Veldeke-Problem," in *Zwei Studien zu Veldeke und zum Strassburger Alexander*, 1985; J. Sinnema, *Hendrik van Veldeke*, 1972.

Kristine K. Sneeringer

HÉLOÏSE (C. 1100–1164). Scholar and abbess of Paraclete, she was best known as the wife of Peter *Abelard and as such was half of one of the most famous pair of star-crossed lovers in history.

Little is known of her parentage; however, she was the niece of Fulbert, a Parisian canon. Héloïse must have shown unusual scholarly ability. Her uncle encouraged her education, something rarely heard of, and asked Abelard, then the most popular and respected teacher in Paris, to tutor her. Abelard, some twenty years her senior, soon fell madly in love with her, and she eagerly returned his love. The couple unashamedly flaunted their love affair, and soon it was common knowledge to all but Fulbert. The couple became ever more daring until Fulbert caught them. By that time, Héloïse was pregnant. Abelard took her to his family home in Brittany. There a son, Astralabe, was born. Fulbert demanded that the couple marry. Abelard agreed to a secret marriage but not a public one, and Héloïse did not want to marry at all, for she believed the institution was disgraceful. They did, however, marry, and the marriage was kept secret. Abelard removed her from Fulbert's house and installed her at the convent at Argenteuil, where she had received her early education. Although he asked that she wear a postulant's habit, something certainly not necessary for her to stay at the convent, he continued to pay her conjugal visits there that are later described in their letters. Fulbert may have believed that Abelard was trying to rid himself of Héloïse, since he ordered his servants to break into Abelard's room while he was asleep and castrate him. After his castration, Abelard entered into the abbey of St. Denis and repented of his relationship with Héloïse. She stayed in the convent, eventually becoming abbess. However, she had little vocation and never regretted her affair with Abelard. She continued to communicate with Abelard via letters, which contain a brilliant exploration of sex, love, religion, and philosophy between two of the brightest minds of the Middle Ages. Upon the dispersal of the convent at Argenteuil, Abelard gave the property of the community of Paraclete to her and her nuns. Through her careful governing, Paraclete became one of the most respected convents in France, and six daughter communities were founded during her lifetime. Héloïse died in 1164. She was buried next to Abelard at Paraclete. In the nineteenth century, the pair were moved to the Père-Lachaise cemetery in Paris.

Although known mainly through her relationship with Abelard, Héloïse deserves recognition for her own accomplishments.

Bibliography: E. McLeod, *Héloïse. A Biography*, 2d ed., 1971; C. J. Mews, *The Lost Love Letters of Heloise and Abelard. Perceptions of Dialogue in Twelfth-Century France*, 1999.

Leah Larson

HENRY I OF ENGLAND (1068–1135). The last Norman king of England, Henry I successfully held both England and Normandy under his rule. His death, however, plunged his territories into civil war, as he was unable to secure the succession of his only surviving heir, the Empress *Matilda.

The youngest son of *William I the Conqueror and *Matilda of Flanders, Henry was entitled to only 5,000 pounds of silver upon his father's death. His eldest brother, Robert Curthose, received the family patrimony of Normandy, and William Rufus received the throne of England, a suitable portion for a second son, having been won through conquest. On 2 August 1100, William met his death in the New Forest, the victim of a hunting accident. Henry, present at the hunt, immediately rode to Winchester to assume control of the treasury. By 5 August, Henry was crowned at Westminster, as his heirless brother's successor. Henry married Eadgyth of Scotland, who upon the marriage changed her name to Matilda.

Curthose claimed the English throne, leading to several battles between him and Henry. An adroit commander and an incredibly persuasive individual, Henry soon had enough support throughout England and Normandy to threaten his brother Robert's hold on his patrimony. In 1105, Henry marched to Tinchebrai, where he crushed his brother's forces, then took Robert captive. Curthose remained imprisoned until his death in 1134. Like his father, Henry now claimed all of England and Normandy.

Despite his ruthlessness, Henry maintained a reputation for piety. In part, this was due to Henry's restitution of *Anselm, the former archbishop of Canterbury whom Rufus had forced into exile. Despite his early friendliness toward Anselm, Henry's insistence on his right to elect Church officials embittered their relationship, and Anselm once again left England for Rome in 1103. Entangled in his conflict with Curthose, however, Henry recognized his need for Church support. In the summer of 1105, he interrupted his campaign to meet with Anselm and renounced lay investiture.

After Curthose's incarceration, Henry's promise of free elections proved empty, as he maintained strict control of the English clergy. He held episcopal elections under his supervision and restricted travel of the clergy to Rome. Paradoxically, notwithstanding his despotic control of Church freedoms, Henry was a lavish patron of religious houses; he gave generously to monastic orders, particularly favoring Cluny.

Under Henry, England's financial and judicial administration began to take shape. Judicial matters were streamlined by the elaboration of the *writ* and the use of the *eyre* court, a system of peripatetic judges who made both royal justice available in the provinces and established Henry's authority. These innovations enhanced crown revenues, which remained particularly high.

Henry shared his wealth not only in pious giving but also by enriching his followers. He made use of the gentry and rewarded their loyalty with land and honors. Dependent on Henry alone for favor, these "made men" offered unstinting support to a suspicious king who feared being murdered in his bed. His generosity extended especially to Stephen of Blois (*Stephen of England), the son of his sister Adela. But enriching his nephew proved the undoing of his own progeny, for it was from this wealth that Stephen was able to mount his successful offensive against Henry's only surviving legitimate child, the Empress Matilda.

Henry's marriage produced only two children, Matilda and William. William drowned in a boating accident in 1120, leaving Henry without a male heir. A widower since 1118, Henry remarried Adeliza (Alice), daughter of Godfrey, duke of Brabant and count of Louvain, but the marriage was childless.

Empress Matilda, who had spent her adult life as wife to Holy Roman Emperor *Henry V, was now a widow. Henry, now desperate, called his daughter back to England to prepare her for the throne and present her to his barons. On 1 January 1127, they swore to uphold her claim. In 1128, Henry chose the sixteen-year-old Geoffrey of Anjou as her husband, without the approval of the English barons. Despite the difference in their ages and their antipathy toward each other, Geoffrey and Matilda produced a son, *Henry (II), and the barons again swore to uphold the family's claim.

Henry I left England in 1133 for Normandy, never to return. After Henry's arrival, Geoffrey demanded Matilda's dower castles and engaged him in battle. Embroiled in this conflict Henry died, reportedly from eating too many stewed lampreys. Matilda's unpopular marriage, and perhaps her gender, allowed Stephen of Blois to seize the throne of England. Thus England was ravaged by a fourteen-year civil war until Henry II gained the throne promised to his mother.

Bibliography: J. A. Green, *The Government of England under Henry I*, 1986.

Laura L. Gathagan

HENRY II OF ENGLAND (1133–1189).

Considered by many to be the greatest king of medieval England, Henry developed a government and judicial system in England that roughly prefigured the modern state. The most powerful man in Europe, Henry's family life was his only weakness; his four sons repeatedly rebelled against him, eventually joining forces with the king of France to deprive him of much of his French territory.

The eldest son of Geoffrey of Anjou and the Empress *Matilda, Henry II was influenced by his mother's unsuccessful battle for the English throne. His grandfather, *Henry I of England, designated Matilda as heir after the death of his only legitimate son. Though his barons swore oaths to uphold her claim, Henry I's sudden death in the midst of conflict with Geoffrey of Anjou allowed his wish to be overturned. Stephen of Blois (*Stephen of England), Henry's nephew and an extremely popular noble, moved swiftly to grasp the keys to the royal treasury on the strength of a tale that Henry's deathbed wish was that Stephen succeed him.

Over the following fifteen years, England experienced bloody civil war, as Matilda and Stephen vied for supporters, land, and authority. The oaths of the barons and Matilda's blood right could not prevail against a crowned king of England, however, and soon Matilda's battles were fought solely for the rights of her son Henry.

As a boy, Henry received an extensive education at the hands of such learned men as *Adelard of Bath and *William of Conches. It was on this foundation that Henry was to build a highly literate court and administration. At seventeen Henry inherited the duchy of Normandy, bequeathed to his mother, but hard won by his father. Shortly thereafter, in 1151, the death of Geoffrey made him count of Anjou and Maine. The English nobility waited expectantly for Henry to claim his birthright; his mother's life's work resulted in a collection of noble supporters eager to welcome a son of royal blood after Stephen's ineffectual reign.

Before gratifying these expectations, Henry surprised all of Europe by marrying *Eleanor, heiress to Aquitaine, the repudiated wife of *Louis VII of France. Acting with the conviction and speed that would come to characterize him, Henry intercepted her as she left France. Avoiding numerous other suitors' traps, Eleanor reached Poitou in safety and there was married to Henry in 1152. A month later, Henry was forced to defend Normandy from a furious Louis and handled him with such dispatch that his reputation improved further.

Henry crossed to England in the winter of 1153. Perhaps more than any other factor, the death of King Stephen's son Eustace worked to Henry's advantage.

After ten months of skirmishing, Stephen wearied of battle and agreed to treat with Henry. The Treaty of Winchester put an end to the civil war in England, and while it preserved Stephen's crown for his lifetime, it made Henry II heir to the English throne after his death.

Stephen died in 1154, and Henry took six weeks to restore order to England and begin building the administration, which was to be his greatest legacy. He introduced legal innovations such as possessory and grand assizes to adjudicate cases involving property and introduced the grand jury indictment to criminal courts. He made heavy use of the *eyre* court, a system of traveling judges that made royal justice available in the localities, and his reign saw a dramatic increase in jury trials.

The administration of crown revenues improved, following a general pattern of growing sophistication on all levels of government. Locally, corrupt sheriffs were rooted out, and even in higher positions, Henry relied on learned officials with bureaucratic experience, as opposed to men of noble blood.

Despite all of these accomplishments, however, Henry II has perhaps become most famous for his part in the murder of his archbishop, Thomas *Becket, whose martyrdom led to his canonization. Becket was a loyal supporter and friend as well as chancellor when Henry appointed him archbishop of Canterbury, a brilliant ploy to control Church affairs and the judicial activity of Church courts—if it had worked. However, in a surprising reversal, Becket became an outspoken champion of Church liberties and attempted to thwart Henry's Constitutions of Clarendon, a document giving secular courts adjudication over clergy found guilty in ecclesiastical courts. After a period of exile, Becket returned, only to be embroiled in the same struggle against Henry's demands. Henry's rage against Becket caused, albeit indirectly, his murder at the hands of royal soldiers, a crime that shocked England. The result was the eventual renunciation of many of Clarendon's provisions and a public penance performed by Henry himself.

His private life was stormy; his marital indiscretions enraged Eleanor, who encouraged her sons to rebel against their father. Henry eventually confined the queen at Salisbury, where she remained until after Henry's death. The surviving children of his marriage included four sons who proved to be Henry's undoing. The eldest, Henry, died in 1183, at which time *Richard, later called Lionheart, became the heir to the throne. His third son, Geoffrey, was betrothed to the heiress of Brittany; the youngest, *John (of England) was the king's favorite. Henry's penchant for exploiting his sons' insecurities for his own purposes resulted in disaster for these ambitious men, who invariably turned to Henry's rival *Philip II Augustus of France for support. When Richard requested Anjou, Maine, and Touraine from his father, Henry refused, touching off a rebellion that had been carefully fomented by Philip II, who hinted that his father had seduced Alice, Richard's intended bride.

In 1188, Richard did homage for these holdings to Philip II and took up arms against his father. By 1189, Henry was deserted by all but a few supporters and his illegitimate son and had to concede to Richard's demands. Not only was Richard made sole heir, but Philip II of France received Auvergne and Berry. Already ill, Henry learned that his favorite John had been active in the rebellion and died a week later, on 6 July 1189.

Bibliography: W. L. Warren, *Henry II*, 1977.

Laura L. Gathagan

HENRY III OF ENGLAND (1207–1272). Henry ascended the throne of England in 1216 at the age of nine. The government of the country was in the capable hands of deputies and advisers until Henry reached the age of his majority in 1227. There followed a period of bad government because Henry, despite some redeeming characteristics, was mostly an ineffectual leader who was unsuitable for such an office.

Henry, the son of King *John of England and Isabella of Angoulême, inherited not only the throne from his father but also the dissension that characterized his father's rule. However, as a young boy, Henry had no political enemies of his own, and under the protection of Pope *Honorius III, Henry enjoyed a relatively calm beginning to his reign. Under the guidance of the legate Cardinal Guala and *William Marshall, Henry's early years prospered. However, when Cardinal Guala went back to Rome in 1218 and William died in 1219, Henry was left to the machinations of Hubert de Burgh and Archbishop Stephen *Langton, two men who were more concerned with strengthening their own positions than with advising Henry.

Henry declared his majority in 1227 when he was nineteen. Even though he was not as ruthless as his father, Henry was plagued by many of the same problems that his father faced. He levied exorbitant taxes to pay for costly wars, and he filled his court with the French relatives of his wife, Eleanor of Provence. Because of this, he saw the same civil unrest that had culminated in the Magna Carta during John's reign. Henry, seeking to maintain the sovereignty held by his father and grandfather, *Henry II, lacked the forcefulness of personality and dominance needed to control the barons. The barons demanded that they be consulted on important matters of state and that they have more control over the governing offices of state, the Chancery, and Exchequer.

Although minor outbreaks of civil unrest cropped up throughout his reign, no serious political movement threatened Henry until 1264, when his sister's husband, Simon de *Montfort the Younger, mounted an insurrection that saw Henry and Prince *Edward (I) captured and imprisoned. This revolt did not result in Henry's deposition, however. Instead, Henry was summoned to a Parliament in which two knights from every shire and two burgesses from selected towns tried to impose a strict accounting on the king. De Montfort was ultimately defeated in 1265 when Prince Edward killed him at Evesham, but the Parliament initiated by him marked the beginnings of the House of Representatives.

Henry III, despite his failings as a leader, was a deeply pious man who was a patron of beauty and art. His contribution to English culture is found in the realm of architecture. He supported the remodeling of established churches and the construction of new, and it was during his reign that the simple, unadorned architectural style of the Normans gave way to the ornate style of Gothic architecture and many of England's most enduring cathedrals were built.

Bibliography: D. A. Carpenter, *The Reign of Henry III*, 1996.

Laura L. Gathagan

HENRY (HEINRICH) I OF GERMANY (876–936).

King of Germany from 919, the first in the Saxon dynasty, and father of Emperor *Otto the Great, Henry reestablished the power of the monarchy, recovered Lorraine, and reorganized the defense of Germany against Magyars, Slavs, and Vikings.

Henry, the grandson of *Liudolf of Saxony, became Saxon duke in 912 and was elected king by an assembly of Saxon and Franconian magnates in 919. Personally charismatic and a skilled politician, Henry had secured the deathbed recommendation of his predecessor and erstwhile enemy the Franconian Conrad I while appearing publicly reluctant to pursue the throne by going "birding" on one of his estates rather than attend the electoral assembly at Fritzlar. (The resulting nickname, "the Fowler," is not contemporary.) Henry then secured his position in Saxony by marrying Matilda, a direct descendant of the eighth-century Saxon leader Widukind, after persuading his first wife to enter a convent. Similarly, military campaigns to gain the allegiance of Swabia (920) and Bavaria (922) were made considerably easier by Henry's refusal to be consecrated, which did not imply an anticlerical attitude but rather signaled that he would permit the dukes to retain their regional power, especially over Church lands. Finally, from 920 to 926 Henry skillfully exploited the dispute between the last Carolingians in France and the emerging Capetian dynasty to secure the Lorraine. At the Diet at Worms in 926, King Rudolph of Upper Burgundy also acknowledged Henry as overlord.

To provide military security Henry built and repaired fortifications (*Burgen*), organized standing garrisons for them, and expanded his force of heavy cavalry. Henry did not, however, teach the Saxons to fight as heavy cavalry or introduce "feudalism"—they had been familiar with both since at least the mid-ninth century. From 927 to 928, Henry secured the eastern frontier against the Slavs; in 929 he forced the submission of Bohemia; and in 933 he defeated the Magyars at Riade. The next year Henry restored the river Schlei as Germany's border with Denmark. Henry financed this activity with the wealth his personal property (including the estates of both his wives) added to the royal fisc and used silver mines he owned at Goslar to provide a stable coinage. By the end of his reign he had increased the authority and prestige of the monarchy to such an extent that he could exercise in fact the power over the dukes and the Church that he had given up in theory at his election.

Henry's reputation is that of an innovative administrator, skillful war leader, and consummate diplomat. The institutions he founded served Germany and the empire well for centuries.

Bibliography: T. Reuter, *Germany in the Early Middle Ages c. 800–1056*, 1991.

Edward J. Schoenfeld

HENRY (HEINRICH) III (1017–1056). King of Germany, Burgundy, and Italy (1039–1056) and emperor from Christmas Day 1046, Henry expanded the power of the empire, promoted important social and economic changes, and supported the reform of the Church, especially the papacy.

The son of *Conrad II and second ruler in the Salian dynasty, Henry was crowned as heir apparent in 1028 and succeeded to power without difficulty after his father's death. In 1043, Henry secured his position as ruler of Burgundy by marrying Agnes, daughter of William V of Aquitaine and Poitou, forcing Henry (Henri) I of France to consent to the match. Henry III spent the early years of his reign consolidating his power along the eastern frontier of the empire. Military campaigns forced Bratislaw of Bohemia to acknowledge him as overlord in 1041, the Luitizi (Slavs living east of the Elbe river) submitted in 1045, and Boleslaw of Poland in 1046. In Hungary, Henry installed Peter (the Venetian nephew of Stephen I) as king after campaigns in 1043 and 1044, the latter concluding in a decisive German victory at Menfö. Peter's native Hungarian successor Andrew (Andras) continued to acknowledge Henry's suzerainty. Henry also secured oaths of allegiance from the Norman and Lombard princes in southern Italy.

Henry's domestic policies included the employment of *ministeriales*, a class of dependent lesser nobles who eventually became an important alternative to the Church as a source for administrators and also helped limit the influence of the territorial nobility. Toward the end of his reign, Henry was able to restrict the influence of the great nobles by installing members of his own family as dukes (except in Saxony and Lorraine). Henry supported the development of towns, promulgating the first charters establishing independent governments for towns north of the Alps and promoting commercial expansion of towns in Italy. Henry constructed fortifications (*burgen*) to protect the frontiers and control the countryside; one of his foundations later developed into the important city of Nuremberg.

In late 1046 problems in Rome required Henry to intervene in ecclesiastical affairs. Henry deposed the simoniac Gregory VI, removed local Roman factions from the papal election process, and supervised the selections of Clement II in 1046 and *Leo IX in 1048. Changes in papal elections were later secured by the establishment of the College of Cardinals and the expanded influence of canon law. Henry's devotion to Church reform was personal and sincere. He refused to accept payment (simony) for investing abbots and bishops, and in 1046, he permitted the newly elected archbishop of Lyons to omit a formal oath of allegiance to the crown in accord with the requirements of canon law.

Henry's reign marks the apogee of the empire established in the tenth century and thus represents a culmination of past trends. Henry's premature death in 1056 left the succession to a six-year-old child (*Henry IV), and the ensuing minority proved disastrous.

Bibliography: T. Reuter, *Germany in the Early Middle Ages c. 800–1056*, 1991.

Edward J. Schoenfeld

HENRY (HEINRICH) IV (1050–1106). Third Salian emperor, he came to the throne as a young child and found his authority weakened as a result. He tried to use episcopal appointments as a source of power and accordingly found himself in conflict with the pope. This was the Investiture Controversy.

As a result of the Cluniac reforms, the Church had founded the College of Cardinals to be independent of Rome and of temporal lords, enforced celibacy and prohibited simony, and now sought to control the appointments of its bishops, hitherto too often chosen by kings and emperors and only ratified by Rome. This was to be the major issue of the conflict between pope and emperor. Pope *Gregory VII was a most ambitious reformer, eager to make himself overlord, under God, over everyone else. His statement of principles, the *Dictatus Papae* (1075) stresses his absolutist vision of the papacy. This is only a sample:

#3	That he alone can depose or reinstate bishops
#9	That all princes shall kiss the feet of the pope and the pope only
#12	That he is allowed to depose emperors
#18	That his sentence can be annulled by no one and he alone can annul the sentences of all others
#19	That he should be judged by no one
#22	That the Roman Church has never erred, nor, as Scripture testifies, will ever err
#26	That one shall not be considered a Catholic who does not agree with the Roman Church
#27	That he can absolve subjects from their oaths of fidelity to iniquitous rulers

Considered against these more strident statements, it is surprising that the relatively minor one of episcopal investiture should have been the source of the conflict. But all attempts at thorough reforms would continue to be thwarted as long as the appointments of major ecclesiastical offices, including that of the pope, were dependent on temporal concerns and royal whims. In particular, the quarrel quickly became an attempt to wrest control of the German Church away from Henry IV.

Henry had no sympathy with religious reforms. His only desire was to rebuild the royal power lost during his minority. He won a decisive victory in Saxony in 1073, which made him too powerful for his princes' liking. But Henry felt he needed more support, looked to his bishops, and resented a foreign pope interfering with his choice of bishops. Henry persuaded the bishops to renounce obedience to the pope. Gregory promptly deposed Henry, releasing his subjects from their oaths of allegiance, and then excommunicated him in 1076. The princes saw this as a God-given opportunity for rebellion, and Henry found himself without support from his bishops, his temporal lords, or the pope. He was forced to give in to the pope's demands. These were that he meet the pope at Augsburg (1077), make a formal submission, and wait for a diet to decide whether he was fit to be reinstated as king. This would have left all the power in Gregory's hands. Henry short-circuited this by traveling to Canossa in December 1076 and presenting himself barefoot, as a penitent, confessing his sins and asking forgiveness. Henry thereby forced the pope's hand, and Gregory was obliged to forgive Henry. Gregory's only satisfaction lay in keeping Henry waiting for three days (barefoot in the snow, as legend has it), but the honors went to Henry in this exchange.

Forgiveness was a tactical blunder from Gregory's point of view: No longer excommunicated, Henry rebuilt a faction of supporters in Germany. His opponents felt that the pope had betrayed them and elected their own emperor: Rudolf. The diet at Augsburg never took place, and civil war wracked Germany for the next three years. Henry was excommunicated again in 1080, when Gregory decided to support Rudolf, but Henry killed his rival in the same year and turned to deal with the pope. He denounced Gregory as a usurper, set up an antipope, and invaded Italy. The antipope was set up in St. Peter's, Rome, while Gregory took refuge in the fortress of St. Angelo's, a few hundred yards away. Gregory called upon some Norman supporters, and as this army drew near Rome, the imperial forces left. The Normans looted Rome and took Gregory away, their captive. Gregory died in exile a few months later, thinking Henry had won.

But this was not so: Henry spent the rest of his reign fighting against his barons, and when he died, his son was actually leading a rebellion against him. He never did reestablish the power of his father and spent most of his life in strife and conflict.

Bibliography: K. Hampe, *Germany under the Salian and Hohenstaufen Emperors*, trans. R. Bennett, 1973; G. Tellenbach, *Church, State and Christian Society at the Time of the Investiture Contest*, trans. R. Bennett, 1991.

Andrea Schutz

HENRY (HEINRICH) V (1086–1125). Henry V was co-regent with his father in 1099, king of Germany in 1106, and emperor from 1111 to 1125 during whose time the Investiture Controversy was resolved.

Henry V was the last Salian emperor, youngest son of *Henry IV. He married *Matilda (Maud), daughter of *Henry I of England, in 1114 but had no legitimate offspring. The imperial line therefore shifted to the descendants of Henry's sister Agnes and her first husband, Frederick von Staufen, duke of Swabia. The princes did not endorse this shift and elected Lothar of Supplinburg, duke of Saxony, instead.

The Investiture Controversy was by no means resolved by the death of either Henry IV or Pope *Gregory VII. In 1111, Henry V occupied Rome with an imperial army, intending to create a solution to the contest before his coronation as emperor. Various solutions had been proposed over the last twenty-five years, some more extreme than others. Pope *Paschal II's idea was that the bishops accept temporal power (and obligations) from their kings, then surrender those powers, becoming no more than pastors of souls. This met with no one's approval. Henry took Paschal captive and away from Rome. Paschal soon thereafter gave Henry the right to invest his bishops with ring and staff, a solution that pleased Henry but not the cardinals. Nothing was resolved until after Paschal's death. The Concordat of Worms of 1122, between Henry V and Pope *Calixtus II, finally resolved the contest, with a solution similar to that practiced in England: The king accepted the bishops as feudal vassals after their election but prior to their consecration.

Bibliography: K. Hampe, *Germany under the Salian and Hohenstaufen Emperors*, trans. R. Bennett, 1973.

Andrea Schutz

HENRY (HEINRICH) VI (1165–1197). Henry VI was the second son of *Frederick I Barbarossa, king of Germany when his father died (drowned on the Third Crusade, 1190), king of Rome in 1169, and emperor in 1191. His chief competitor for the throne was *Henry the Lion.

Henry VI's reign was clouded by his conflicts with Henry the Lion and Pope Celestine III. The former, head of the Welf family and brother-in-law to *Richard the Lionheart of England, was busy stirring up trouble in Germany with the aid of English money. While Henry VI did not particularly care for his German kingdom (he was only there long enough to buy the captive Richard, whom he hated, from the impoverished duke of Austria and to arrange for and collect the first installment of Richard's ransom), his enmity with the pope caused him greater difficulties.

Henry VI was trying to become king of Sicily. His policy, in general, was governed by his desire to win and hold Sicily. King William II had died without legitimate issue, and the throne had gone to William's illegitimate cousin Tancred. Tancred's aunt Constance had a better claim, and she was Henry VI's wife. On the whole, the Sicilians did not want a German king, but a strong party favored Constance. Henry was victorious, and the empire now consisted of Germany, Burgundy, all Italy, and Sicily.

Still wanting more, Henry began to plan a conquest of Greece and a crusade to Palestine. To accomplish this, however, he needed the support of his princes and the pope and recognition for his heir *Frederick (II). Henry also wanted to make the German crown hereditary, as opposed to having the king elected. He tried to make a deal with his princes; their fiefs could be hereditary if the monarchy were. The bishops, who had hitherto controlled the election and coronation of kings, defeated this effort. They only agreed to crown Frederick next. Henry then tried to deal with the pope and offered him a large annual income from all churches in the empire in exchange for the papal lands of central Italy. But the pope, too frightened by the prospect of one man ruling everything but Rome, declined. These negotiations were interrupted by a fierce revolt in Sicily, which Henry suppressed savagely. He died almost immediately afterward. His younger brother Philip rushed to act as regent for the infant Frederick but when advised to take the throne did and so started another civil war.

Bibliography: K. Hampe, *Germany under the Salian and Hohenstaufen Emperors*, trans. R. Bennett, 1973.

Andrea Schutz

HENRY OF GHENT (C. 1240–1293). Henry of Ghent was the leading figure in the theological faculty in Paris from *Aquinas' death to the end of the century, referred to as the Solemn Doctor.

He was born at Ghent in Flanders (modern Belgium) before 1240. He received his early education at the cathedral school of Tournai, where he became archdeacon and was eventually appointed capitular canon; he always kept his residence there. While a student in Paris in 1264, he attended a sermon of Papal Legate Guy le Gros de Foulques (elected pope in 1265 with the name of Clement IV) concerning the privileges of the mendicant orders, a subject that became one of Henry's preoccupations. In 1275, he became master of theology in Paris and in Advent of 1276 he held his first disputation *de quolibet* at the Faculty of Theology. This particular kind of academic exercise was reserved for masters of theology and did not have predetermined topics. Before the celebration of Christmas and Easter, the master was to answer questions proposed by members of the audience on any kind of subject (*de quolibet* in Latin means "concerning anything"), either strictly doctrinal or concerning a controversial state of affairs, and to give his authoritative determination. Henry lectured regularly and successfully at the university until 1292, and in his hands the disputation *de quolibet* became an accomplished literary genre for the transmission and development of ideas and doctrines within the university community.

In 1277, Henry was appointed by Bishop of Paris Stephen *Tempier to be a member of the theological commission that composed the list of unorthodox and heretical propositions solemnly condemned in 1277. This syllabus, which was largely directed against the radical Averroistic movement in the Arts faculty, had a profound impact on the intellectual history of the Latin West. Henry appears to have been at the center of the more general anti-Aristotelian attitude in the Faculty of Theology, since he was also involved in the censure of Thomas Aquinas' teaching on the unicity of substantial form in man and the expulsion of the Augustinian Hermit *Giles of Rome from the university. He fought the Aristotelian views of his student, then colleague *Godfrey of Fontaines, although he probably donated his private library to him at the end of his career. Henry's polemical personality was not limited to doctrinal issues. With Aquinas, Aristotelism became a tendency embraced by many masters of the mendicant orders, and Henry, who was secular, directed his criticism also against the privileges of the friars. Indeed, his outspokenness on this matter earned him a reprimand by the future *Boniface VIII in 1290. On this occasion, the university rallied around him. Henry died on 29 June 1293.

Together with the fifteen collections of *Quodlibetal Questions*, which he carefully edited for publication, and which alone are already an impressive achievement, Henry's other major work is the even longer *Summa of Ordinary Questions*, which reflects his fifteen-years-long classroom teaching; it consists of sections on the nature of theology, on God and divine attributes, and on the Trinity. Another section on creatures was planned but never completed. Against the Aristotelian claim, Henry supports the Augustinian view that true knowledge is possible only with a special divine intervention, called illumination. Henry, however, was also influenced by *Avicenna's claim that being is the primary notion of the mind. As being is predicated of God and creatures analogously, Henry notes that this analogy depends upon the two distinct realities of divine being, which is cause, and created being, which is effect. Through analogy, man can attain a certain natural knowledge of God's nature, but only in a confused manner, which makes the terms of the analogy indistinct. *John Duns Scotus will later intensely elaborate on Henry's notion of univocity. God is the efficient cause of creatures in their actual existence in time and space, but He is primarily the exemplary cause of their essential reality (*esse essentiae*), which He knows through His ideas. Thus, the whole of creation, rationally considered, is the product of God's noetic activity. Referred to as the Solemn Doctor and praised for his intellectual sophistication, Henry of Ghent is frequently cited in fourteenth-century theological literature.

Bibliography: S. Marrone, *Truth and Scientific Knowledge in the Thought of Henry of Ghent*, 1985.

Roberto Plevano

HENRY THE LION (1129–1195). Henry was the duke of Saxony and Bavaria, head of the Welf family during *Frederick I Barbarossa's reign, and ultimately his chief adversary. Despite the conflicts between his house and the emperor, Henry was one of the emperor's greatly favored lords until his arrogance and ambition caused him to be dispossessed and exiled as an example to others.

Henry came into his inheritance at the age of ten. Upon attaining his majority, he was obliged to recover his lost patrimonies of Saxony and Bavaria. He regained Saxony through a compromise with Emperor Conrad III but had to negotiate for Bavaria with the next emperor, Frederick Barbarossa. The conflicts between the Welfs and Weiblingen (Guelphs and Ghibellines, in Italian) seemed to be coming to an end with the new emperor; despite being on opposite sides in the family feud, he and Henry the Lion were also first cousins, and their initial dealings appeared amicable. In 1152, Barbarossa returned Bavaria to his cousin, after making Austria (*Österreich*—the "Eastern realm" of Bavaria) an independent duchy to balance Henry's Bavaria. This was left to Henry's southern rival Henry Jasomirgott, who had previously held all of Bavaria from Conrad III. Henry's investiture did not take place until 1156, however.

Nonetheless, Henry the Lion gave Barbarossa loyalty for twenty years, but when Barbarossa's invasion of Italy and heavy-handed rule led to the rebellion of the Lombard League (1167) and then years of skirmishing, his conflicts with his cousin came to a head. Barbarossa asked for his cousin's support during this crisis and was refused. Henry had the right to refuse but the moral and political obligation to show the emperor some gratitude, especially since his reason for refusing was that Barbarossa refused to give him the important region of Goslar. Barbarossa was routed at the battle of Legnano (1176) and determined to crush Henry.

Henry, being ambitious and arrogant, had a habit of seizing church property and quarreling with bishops. Barbarossa had long tolerated these activities, but after Legnano, and largely in revenge, the emperor called his cousin to book as a vassal and deprived him of all but his allodial fiefs. Dispossessed and in disgrace, Henry the Lion fled to England and the court of his father-in-law, *Henry II. From there he and his son, *Otto IV, tried to thwart Staufen interests in Germany and throughout Europe.

Henry the Lion serves as an example of the limits of princely power in the empire, but to see him as a victim of fate would be too charitable. His family allegiances and pretensions were as much at fault for his downfall as his own arrogance. But he also stands as an example of the complications family ties brought to politics; his refuge with his English relations did nothing to ease the later tensions between his brother-in-law *Richard (the Lionheart) and *Henry VI.

Bibliography: K. Jordan, *Henry the Lion: A Biography*, trans. P. S. Falla, 1986.

Andrea Schutz

HERAKLIOS (HERACLIUS) I (575–641). As Byzantine emperor from 610, Heraklios distinguished himself as a spiritual leader and military hero. The previous emperor, Phokas, had presided over an insecure government ripe with corruption and repression. With the support of the army and navy (and his father, who was the governor of Carthage), Heraklios led a military coup to depose Phokas. Following Hellenistic tradition, Heraklios assumed the title *basileus*, which conferred a semidivine character on him.

Concerned about the tensions in the Eastern Church, Heraklios promulgated the *Ecthesis* in 638 in an effort to resolve doctrinal conflicts within the Church. This decree affirmed the doctrine of monothelitism, which claimed that the two natures of Christ, divine and human, were consolidated in one will. However, neither Rome nor the Eastern Churches approved of the *Ecthesis*, and between 638 and 680, it generated much controversy; Heraklios, himself, even changed his mind later. In 680, the Third Council of Constantinople officially recognized two wills in Christ, one human and one divine, and condemned monothelitism as a heresy.

However, Heraklios was also a military hero. Provoked by a Persian invasion of the empire, in 622 he gathered together a great Byzantine army to push the Persians back into their own realm. He was so successful that he not only repelled the invasion of the empire but invaded the Persians' own empire and defeated them at the battle of Nineveh on 12 December 627. The defeat provoked dissatisfaction with the Persian ruler Khusro and incited factions within the Persian court. Persia would never again be a major threat. Unfortunately, Heraklios focused on the eastern frontier of the empire to the detriment of the western one; by 612 imperial control of the Balkans had weakened, allowing invasion and conquest by the Avars and Slavs and creating sociopolitical unrest that would last for generations.

Bibliography: M. Whittow, *The Making of Byzantium, 600–1025*, 1996.

Alana Cain Scott

HERMANN OF REICHENAU (1013–1054).

Hermann of Reichenau, a Benedictine monk, was a brilliant scholar, poet-musician, astronomer-mathematician, and clock and instrument maker.

Also known as Hermannus Contractus (the Lame) because he was crippled from birth, Hermann began his studies at the age of seven under Abbot *Berno, a brilliant scholar himself, at the abbey of Reichenau. Despite his physical impairments, which severely limited his movement and caused him difficulties with speech, Hermann was a highly intelligent and gifted man. Not only an excellent scholar, he was also a respected teacher as well.

One of his important works, *Chronicon*, is a history of the Christian era from its beginnings up to 1054; it is a work that includes Hermann's own firsthand knowledge of the 1046–1056 reign of Emperor *Henry III. He may have composed *Salve Regina*, one of the best-known Church songs. His musical treatise *(De) Musica* formed the basis for medieval modal theory. It is a theoretical work based on *Boethius' musical theory and is a specialized and speculative treatment of the relationship of the musical categories that were used to classify the repertory of Gregorian chant.

But he is, perhaps, best known for introducing (or reintroducing) Arabic astronomical techniques and instruments into western Europe. He introduced the astrolabe, the chilinder (a portable sundial), and the quadrant with a cursor, an instrument used to measure the sun's altitude. He wrote two treatises on the construction and use of the astrolabe as well as others on the chilinder and quadrant. His scholarly work also includes brief treatises on arithmetic.

Bibliography: C. H. Haskins, *Studies in the History of Medieval Science*, 2nd ed., 1927; H. Oesch, *Berno und Hermann von Reichenau als Musiktheoretiker*, 1961.

Elaine Cullen

HERRAD OF HOHENBOURG (LANDSBERG) (C. 1130–1195).

Abbess of Hohenbourg (Sainte-Odile) in Alsace from approximately 1167 until her death around 1195, Herrad compiled the *Hortus deliciarum* (Garden of Delights) for the spiritual benefit of her nuns.

During Herrad's time as abbess, she founded a Premonstratensian priory to guarantee the presence of priests to say mass and built a compound that included a church and convent for the canons, a farm, a hospital for the poor, and a hospice for pilgrims. She also presided over a time of intellectual and cultural activity, the result of which is a collection of texts known as the *Hortus deliciarum*. While some poems of the *Hortus* were addressed to the women of Herrad's monastery, only a few of the texts can be attributed to her.

The *Hortus deliciarum*, written in Latin, sought to offer a comprehensive collection of teachings on faith, the Church, and nature in word, text, and music. The work contains more than 340 miniatures and approximately 1,200 textual extracts and poems, many accompanied by musical notation. The miniatures depict biblical events and Christian allegory as well as secular scenes. They belong to the most important sources for clothing, customs, and lifestyles of the High Middle Ages. In fact, one of the miniatures depicts a woman holding a writing instrument, indicating women's scribal activity at Hohenbourg. One of the most frequently reproduced miniatures depicts a ladder of virtues that illustrates the path toward God, each rung representing a religious or lay profession and its characteristic temptation.

Bibliography: M. W. Labarge, *A Small Sound of the Trumpet. Women in Medieval Life*, 1986; G. Webb, "The Person and the Place—V: Herrad and Her Garden of Delights," *Life of the Spirit* 16 (1961–1962): 475–481.

Alexandra Sterling-Hellenbrand

HILD (HILDA) OF WHITBY (C. 614–680).

The daughter of King Edwin's nephew Hereric, she was abbess of the double monastery of Whitby during the period of contention between the Roman and Celtic rites over the dating of Easter. Her life is chronicled in *Bede's Ecclesiastical History* and her death recorded in the *Anglo-Saxon Chronicle*.

She became a Christian, with Edwin, in 627 through the teaching of Paulinus, first bishop of Northumbria. Drawn to the monastic life, she first planned to enter the monastery at Chelles in Gaul, where her sister Hereswith was living. At the request of either Saint Aidan or King Oswiu, she became the first abbess of the Benedictine monastery then called Streanaeshealh, translated by Bede as "bay of the lighthouse." Hild was known particularly for her Rule's emphasis on scholarship, especially the study of Scripture, and its dedication to the performance of good works. Five of the monks in her establishment went on to become bishops. Her great holiness was prefigured, according to a dream her mother Breguswith had before the child's birth; unable to find her husband, then living in exile, she found instead a most precious necklace under her garment that spread a blaze of light, filling all Britain with its gracious splendor. As a prophecy, this fits well with Hild's accomplishments at what must have been one of the foremost intellectual establishments of her time.

The abbey's reputation, as well as its location, probably explains the location at Whitby of the synod convened in 664 to determine whether practices of the Celtic or the Roman rites would prevail. Although Hild supported the Celtic position, it was leading males, both secular and clerical, who had the deciding voice. Adherents of the Roman camp argued that Roman custom was followed throughout the world with the exception of these "two remotest islands of the Ocean." King Oswiu decided the issue in favor of Rome.

The monastery continued under Hild's leadership until her death in 680. It was destroyed in 687 during a Danish invasion.

Bibliography: S. Hollis, *Anglo-Saxon Women and the Church: Sharing a Common Fate,* 1992.

Patricia Silber

HILDEGARD OF BINGEN, SAINT (1098–1179). Author of three treatises revealing her divine visions, reference works in medicine and natural history, some saints' lives, and the first-known morality play, this Benedictine nun also founded two religious houses. She was a prolific letter writer, corresponding with some of the most important people of her time including several popes, Saint *Bernard of Clairvaux, and the emperor *Frederick I Barbarossa.

The tenth child of Mechthild and Hildebert of Bermersheim, a family of Rhenish nobility, Hildegard was dedicated by her parents to the religious life. At the age of eight she was offered as a companion to Jutta of Spanheim and accompanied Jutta to the newly founded monastery of St. Disibod when that holy woman was formally enclosed as a recluse on 1 November 1112. Jutta taught Hildegard to read and write Latin, and upon Jutta's death in 1136, Hildegard was elected magistra (teacher) of the dozen women then living at St. Disibod.

Hildegard apparently experienced visions throughout her life but did not record them until 1141, after hearing a voice say, "Cry out and write." At first refusing to obey, Hildegard began her first visionary treatise *Scivias* (an abbreviated Latin title for "Know the Ways of the Lord") after suffering a serious illness; she was assisted by the monk Volmar, acting as secretary, and the young nun Richardis of Stade, her closest friend. In *Scivias*, as in her subsequent visionary treatises, Hildegard uses concrete visual imagery (beautifully illustrated in illuminated manuscripts prepared at Rubertsberg). She adopts the role of "God's mouthpiece," thereby empowering herself, a "weak" woman, to speak out against the evils of her world. Her prophetic gift became known beyond the monastery, especially after Pope *Eugenius III, upon the urging of Bernard of Clairvaux, read and approved of a section of *Scivias* before the Synod of Trier (1147–1148).

In 1147, Hildegard claimed that God wanted her to establish a convent on the slope of Mt. Rupert. After convincing a reluctant abbot and finding a benefactress, Hildegard and her eighteen nuns moved into the Rupertsberg, equipped with running water and a scriptorium, in 1150. In spite of this victory, Hildegard suffered considerable emotional distress at the time because her friend Richardis had been appointed abbess at Bassum. Hildegard opposed the move and eventually persuaded Richardis to return, but before she could, Richardis became ill and died in 1152.

Hildegard was highly creative during the 1150s in spite of her sorrow. In 1151 she completed *Scivias* and also *Play of the Virtues*, her morality play. This musical drama allegorically depicts the plight of a human soul caught between a choir of virtues and the devil. The nuns may have performed *Virtues* in 1152 for the dedication of their church. Its text appears in the last version of *Scivias* and also in some manuscripts of the *Symphonia*, a collection of seventy-seven liturgical songs (hymns, sequences, antiphons, versicles, responsaries) composed by Hildegard. She probably wrote many during this decade because the nuns needed music for their new convent.

During the middle of the decade, Hildegard suffered from several bouts of illness. She began to compile information about medicine and natural history and later incorporated the information into reference works. She also found time to write the *Life of St. Rupert*, patron saint of her abbey, and began a strange work containing an invented language. In 1158, Hildegard undertook her first preaching tour and would make three more before her death. A woman preaching to mixed audiences was without precedent.

A staunch supporter of the Gregorian reform movement, Hildegard must have taken a dim view of the eighteen-year schism between the papacy and Frederick I that began in 1159. During these years, she wrote her last two visionary treatises. One, the *Book of Life's Merits*, was begun in 1159; in it Hildegard describes some thirty-five vices and opposing virtues and offers instruction about penance, confession, purgatory, and the fate of the soul after death. Then in 1163 she started the *Book of Divine Works*, her most mature visionary treatise. Claiming to be instructed by the "Living Light," Hildegard discusses a variety of theological topics ranging from cosmology to eschatology. During this time she also felt moved to establish a second religious community: The convent at Eibengen opened its doors in 1165, and Hildegard kept close watch over it until her death. In 1170 she completed the *Life of St. Disibod*, requested by her first monastic home, and also the "lives" of patron saints for some Trier monasteries. By this time, Hildegard had grown old, but her trials were not over.

Monk Volmar died in 1173, and Hildegard had to appeal to the pope before she received a successor, Godfrey of St. Disibod, who died in 1176. Godfrey did have the foresight to begin Hildegard's *Vita*. In 1177, Guibert of Gembloux became her secretary, so some of her problems were resolved. But soon she found herself in a new controversy.

In 1178, Hildegard permitted the burial of a once-excommunicated nobleman in the Rupertsberg churchyard after ascertaining that he had been reconciled with the Church before he died. The canons of Mainz believed otherwise and demanded that the corpse be removed. When Hildegard refused, they imposed an interdict on the Rupertsberg, which meant that the nuns could not receive communion or sing the divine office. (Some emotional letters indicate that Hildegard found the second restriction the most heartbreaking.) The interdict was lifted in March 1179, but it had taken its toll. Hildegard died on 17 September 1179.

Her friends prepared a case for canonization, but when it was finally heard in Rome nearly fifty years later, it was denied. In recent times an effort has been initiated to have Hildegard named a "doctor" in the Roman Catholic Church. Whether or not she ever receives such recognition, it must be acknowledged that Hildegard was without question the most influential woman in twelfth-century Western Christendom.

Bibliography: S. Flanagan, ed., *Secrets of God: Writings of Hildegard of Bingen*, 1996; B. Newman, ed., *Voice of the Living Light: Hildegard of Bingen and Her World*, 1998.

Deanna Evans

HINCMAR OF RHEIMS (806–882).

A prominent Carolingian theologian, he was a canon law specialist, historian, and archbishop of Rheims (845–882).

He was born in about 806 and educated at the abbey of St. Denis, under its abbot Hilduin. During the Norman raids on northeastern France in 822, he followed Hilduin to the court of the emperor *Louis the Pious. He joined Louis' court in 834 and, after the latter's death, became a staunch supporter of his son and successor *Charles II the Bald. Although their relationship was stormy at times, the trust Charles placed in him is made clear by the fact that he made Hincmar the executor of his will after his campaign in Italy in 878. In 845, with imperial support, he was elected to the archbishopric of Rheims, to fill the position left vacant by the death of Ebbo of Rheims. One of Charles' rivals, *Lothar II, attempted to remove him for alleged irregularities, but his election was confirmed by a council (Soisson, in 853) and by Pope *Nicholas I. Under Hincmar's rule, Rheims soon became a powerful ecclesiastical center.

Hincmar played a central role in the religious controversies generated by the teachings of *Gottschalk on election and predestination. He initially wrote a treatise to refute him, which was in turn condemned by Ratramnus of Corbie. Hincmar sought support from a number of his friends, including *Hrabanus Maurus, but when the latter pleaded old age as a reason to stay out of the controversy, Hincmar asked for and received support from *John Scottus Eriugena in the form of a treatise on predestination, which was not, however, well received. The controversy was continued at several councils: at Quiercy, called by Charles the Bald in 853 (supporting Hincmar); at Valences in 855, a meeting of the bishops of Lyon, Vienne, and Arles, which condemned Hincmar; and finally concluded at a meeting at Touzy in 860. Hincmar was later involved in yet another doctrinal struggle with Gottschalk, after he changed the words *trina deitas* in a hymn to *summa deitas* to eliminate what he considered to be a heresy, an act that caused much controversy and resulted in him writing yet another treatise defending his decision.

Hincmar also composed a treatise on canon law defending the divorce of the Emperor Lothar from his queen *Theutberga that effectively displays his command of the laws, wrote several treatises on the nature of kingship, and prepared a document defending ordinary people against the violence perpetrated against them by armed soldiers. In addition, he wrote a hagiographical life of his predecessor Saint Remigius of Rheims. Finally, from 861 to 882, he kept a chronicle, known as the continuation of the *Annales Bertinianii*, a valuable record of events in the Frankish Empire for the period. He died in 882 while fleeing from Norman attacks on Rheims.

Bibliography: J. Devisse, *Hincmar, Archévêque de Reims, 845–882*, 3 vols., 1975–1976; E. S. Duckett, *Carolingian Portraits: A Study in the Ninth Century*, 1962.

William Schipper

HONORIUS III, POPE (D. 1227, PONTIFICATE 1216–1227).

Cencio Savelli, cardinal-priest of SS. John and Paul, was elected pope on 18 July 1216, two days after the death of *Innocent III. Taking the name Honorius III, he worked to uphold the policies set forth by his predecessor, especially those concerning Holy Roman Emperor *Frederick II. He also promoted the Fifth Crusade (1217–1221), approved several monastic orders, vigorously attacked heresy, and compiled a portfolio of decretals.

Honorius was a capable administrator serving as chamberlain under Clement III and chancellor under Celestine III, where he compiled the *Liber censuum* to keep track of the money due the papacy. Honorius also put together a collection of decretals, the *Compilatio quinta* (1225), which became the first official book of canon law. He continued the program established by the Fourth Lateran Council (1215) by sending missionaries to the Baltics, attacking heresy, and crusading against the Moors in Spain. Along with Frederick and *Louis VII of France, Honorius attempted to eradicate heresy, focusing on the Albigensians in southern France.

The one area where cooperation proved futile was a crusade to the Holy Land. By an agreement in the Fourth Lateran Council, Frederick promised to lead a crusade, and Honorius pressured him to fulfill his agreement. Frederick continued to delay, however, and the crusade to Palestine failed without adequate leadership. The crusaders succeeded in capturing Damietta in Egypt but lost it two years later. Frederick had promised to join the crusade after his coronation by Honorius in 1220, but he failed to keep his word yet again. Honorius threatened Frederick continually with excommunication, while Frederick constantly delayed, pausing occasionally to reassert his rights in Lombardy, Sicily, and the Papal States.

Honorius also had to deal with the troubled monarchy of *John in England. Innocent had excommunicated John and placed an interdict upon his kingdom, throwing England into ecclesiastical confusion. After King John's death, Honorius restored Stephen *Langton and asserted papal authority over the Church of England and thus restored ecclesiastical government. Honorius also confirmed the orders of the Dominicans, Franciscans, and Carmelites during his pontificate, all of which aided in the struggle against heresy. Honorius has been credited with setting up the forerunner of the Inquisition with his relentless attack on heresy. Honorius, already elderly at his election, died on 18 March 1227, having served as pope for more than ten years.

Bibliography: R. P. McBrien, *Lives of the Popes*, 1997; J. Sayers, *Papal Government and England during the Pontificate of Honorius III (1216–1227)*, 1984.

Paul Miller

HRABANUS (RABANUS, RHABANUS) MAURUS (C. 780–856). Abbot of Fulda and archbishop of Mainz, he was a biblical commentator, poet, and encyclopedist.

Hrabanus was born near Mainz about 780 and at an early age was placed as an oblate in the Benedictine monastery of Fulda, where he received his early education. In the late 790s, he became a student of *Alcuin in Tours, who gave him his nickname "Maurus," after *Benedict of Nursia's favorite companion. He taught in the monastic school at Fulda until 822, when he was elected abbot of Fulda. In 842, he was forced into retirement during a conflict between *Louis the German over the succession to the imperial throne. In 847, he was recalled out of retirement to become archbishop of Mainz, where he remained until his death in 856.

Hrabanus was a prolific writer (complete works in *PL* 107–112; new editions in progress). Among his works are a "figured poem," *De laudibus sancti crucis*, originally planned as a poem in the form of a cross; commentaries on most books of the Bible; an instructional treatise for priests (*De clericorum institutione*); and an encyclopedia (*De rerum naturis*), based in part on *Isidore of Seville's *Etymologiae* but in an entirely different arrangement (Hrabanus' own) and with many allegorical interpretations added. Throughout his writings, he shows an abiding concern for the written traditions of the Church, and for that reason they appear at first glance to be mere compilations. He was also a prolific composer of poetry and hymns, most famously the *Veni creator spiritus*, although his authorship is disputed.

Hrabanus distilled a lot of early Church writings in his commentaries and his encyclopedia, and it is in this role that he made his contribution to early European intellectual culture. As a teacher at Fulda, he deeply influenced a number of students (such as Walahfrid *Strabo and *Gottschalk of Orbais, whose teachings he later denounced as heretical). His reputation as a teacher from an early time assured him the title of *praeceptor Germaniae* (teacher of Germany).

Bibliography: M. de Jong, "The Empire as *ecclesia*: Hrabanus Maurus and Biblical *historia* for Rulers," in *The Uses of the Past in the Early Middle Ages*, ed. Y. Hen and M. Innes, 2000; G. Schrimpf, ed., *Kloster Fulda in der Welt der Karolinger und Ottonen*, 1996.

William Schipper

HROTSVIT OF GANDERSHEIM (C. 935–C. 1001).

Hrotsvit was a canoness, dramatist, and author of legends and epics. At the crossroads of diverging cultures and literary tradition, Hrotsvit of Gandersheim capably amalgamated the rich literary and linguistic heritage of Roman antiquity, early Christian hagiography, and her native Saxon/Germanic traditions. In doing so, she left a complex and often quite exceptionally sophisticated corpus of Latin texts that bear eloquent testimony to the fledgling Latinate monastic literary culture of tenth-century Saxony.

Born in the fourth decade of the tenth century, Hrotsvit lived and wrote in the Gandersheim Abbey, in Saxony, during the abbey's golden age under Gerberga I's rule. Her name, *clamor validus Gandeshemensis*, "Strong Voice (or Testimony)," not only expresses her poetic mission, the glorification of Christian heroes both secular and religious, but it also links her to the patron saint of her foundation, John the Baptist, the *clamor/vox in deserto*, imbuing, thereby, her poetry with apocalyptic subtexts. The heroes of her works are the *Ottos (I, II, and III) and the whole *Liudolf dynasty and the saints and martyrs of Christianity, respectively. Writing in Latin, mostly in Leonine hexameters and rhymed, rhythmic prose, Hrotsvit chose hagiographic plots for her legends and plays and contemporary as well as near-contemporary events for her secular epics.

Her works are arranged in three books, organized generically and chronologically, and delineated as such by prefatory and dedicatory materials. Book One contains the eight legends ("Maria," "Ascensio," "Gongolf," "Pelagius," "Basilius," "Theophilus," "Dionysius," and "Agnes"); all but "Pelagius," which she claims to have composed based on an eyewitness report, are based on biblical, apocryphal, and hagiographic texts. "Maria" tells of the Virgin's life and begins the legend cycle quite appropriately upholding her example as the paradigm of monastic living. "Ascensio" depicts Christ's ascension to heaven and is the first of six narratives glorifying diverse male saints whose hagiographies are framed by examples of female sanctity. "Gongolf" is Hrotsvit's third poem, exulting a Frankish saint killed by his adulterous wife and her lover, and "Pelagius" narrates the story of a near-contemporary Spanish martyr. "Basilius" and "Theophilus" both depict pacts with the devil and laud Christ's mercy in the face of even the most heinous of sins. Both texts also insist on the limitless power of prayer and repentance. "Dionysius" is the tale of the first bishop of Paris grafted on the lore of Dionysius the Aeropagite, and "Agnes," concluding the legend cycle, relates the life and death of an early Roman virginal martyr.

Book Two, Hrotsvit's best-known and most controversial creation, contains the six dramas, based, as she claims, on Terentian comedy, for whose alluring but morally perilous mimetic powers she wished to substitute the glorious and morally beneficial ideals of militantly chaste Christianity. She chose the dramatic form, she argues, because the sweetness of Terence's style attracted many readers who, in turn, became corrupted by the wickedness of his subject matter. Of her six plays, two (*Dulcitius, Sapientia*) deal with the martyrdom of three allegorical virgins set during the persecution of Christians under Emperors Diocletian and Hadrian; two deal with the salvation of repentant harlots (*Abraham, Paphnutius*); and two (*Gallicanus, Callimachus*) are conversion plays. All six are generic hybrids, culling some spectacularly dramatic qualities from Roman, especially Terentian, drama and infusing them with the sacred spectacle of Christian martyrdom and miraculous conversions. Book Three contains her two extant epics. The first, the *Gesta Oddonis*, narrates the rise of the Ottonian dynasty, the second, *Primordia*, the foundation of Gandersheim Abbey.

Throughout all her works, Hrotsvit extols the ideal of monastic Christianity and exhorts her audience and readers to imitate and emulate her saintly models to the best of their abilities. In order to achieve this aim, Hrotsvit puts her poetic and intellectual arsenal to work and interpolates academic digressions in the form of lessons and elaborate dogmatic and cathecistic lectures; she punctuates her texts with homilectic prayers and reflective asides; she draws practical applications from dogmatic implications; and she ornaments her poetry and prose with a rich array of stylistic embellishments. Hers is, indeed, a strong voice, a strong testimony in the service of Christian monastic values bridging the millennium in its pristine strength of conviction and poetic grace.

Bibliography: *Hrotsvit of Gandersheim: A Florilegium of Her Works*, trans. K. M. Wilson, 1998.

Katharina M. Wilson

HUGH CAPET (939–996). Hugh Capet was founder of the Capetian dynasty. Upon the death of the last Carolingian king, Louis V, Hugh was elected and anointed the king of the western Franks, or West Francia, in July 987. He was the son of Hugh the Great, duke of Francia.

As the grandson of the Frankish king Robert I (r. 922–923), he had a blood connection to the throne, though the closest male heir was Louis V's uncle Charles (of Lotharingia), who was deemed unsuitable because he had married a commoner. Charles and his supporters tried to accuse Hugh of usurpation, but he had been elected and had royal blood, so their efforts failed. Hugh was married two times, first to a woman known only as "Mrs. Hugh" and second to

Adelaide of Aquitaine in c. 968. He had three children with his second wife, Robert (later Robert II) and two daughters named Hedwig and Giselle. Quiet and pious, he disliked pretensions and favored diplomacy over war. Otherwise, little is known about his personal life.

Like his son Robert II and grandson Henry I, Hugh fought to keep the royal Francia holdings together. Though nominally the king, Hugh realized the weakness of his position and spent his reign consolidating his family's power. Originally, Capetian territory was limited to the area around the modern Île-de-France, or Paris and the countryside directly surrounding it. Hugh had the support of the local lords around Paris but could not compete with the counts and dukes of Champagne, Blois, Chartres, Anjou, and others, for resources, wealth, and thus the loyalty of the people.

The Capetians successfully gained power through marriage alliances and a strong father-to-son succession, prompting the monarchy of France to be declared hereditary in 1223. Hugh assumed an innovative approach in assuring the succession. On 25 December 987, Hugh had his son Robert anointed deputy monarch and appointed the successor, only a few months after he himself had become king. Robert worked daily with his father, observing the machinations of government and his father's efforts to secure power for the Capetian family. He and his immediate descendants would follow this same policy.

Thus, Hugh deliberately secured the hereditary succession of the Capetian monarch. From this point to 1328 there were fourteen successive kings from the same family, all of whom were descended in a straight line from Hugh the Great. All later French kings shared blood ties to the Capetian family and Hugh Capet.

Bibliography: G. Duby, *France in the Middle Ages 987–1460: From Hugh Capet to Joan of Arc*, trans. J. Vale, 1993.

Alana Cain Scott

HUGH OF ST. CHER (C. 1190–1263). A Dominican scholar and author, he became a leading theologian at the University of Paris and later a cardinal during the pontificate of *Innocent IV.

Born around 1190 in the environs of Vienne, he completed his education at Paris, where by 1225 he was a Doctor of Canon and Civil Law and a bachelor in theology. In that year, or possibly the next, Hugh entered the Dominican Order, and the following year he was made the provincial general for France. By 1230, he qualified as a master of theology and succeeded Roland of Cremona, who had left to teach in Toulouse, in the Dominican chair in the faculty of theology. For the next six years, Hugh lectured in theology and led academic disputations. In 1236, he was once again appointed provincial general. His dealings with the papal court resulted in his being made a cardinal in 1244. From then on, he may have acted as an unofficial protector for his order. He at least defended the order as a member of the commission that investigated the anti-mendicant work, *De periculiis* of *William of St. Amour in 1255. Three years prior, while cardinal-legate to Germany, he had sanctioned the new feast, *Corpus Christi*, in the city of Liège (which would be universally celebrated by 1264).

Hugh is best known for two major works, which he wrote while teaching theology at Paris: the *Postilla super bibliam totam* (Commentary on the Whole Bible) and the *Scriptum super Sententias* (Commentary on the *Sentences* of *Peter Lombard). The first work began with his lectures in the Faculty of Theology, but their present form is the product of a team of scholars at the Dominican convent at Paris—under Hugh's direction. The *Postilla* was an attempt to update the *Ordinary Gloss*, a reference text for biblical exegesis, which contained extracts from the patristic sources linked to the each part of the biblical text. Hugh's team included additional patristic sources, dividing these sources into the various types of interpretation, from the literal to the three spiritual senses of Scripture. On occasion the authors introduced new literary theories drawn from their reading of Aristotle. Despite its impressive scholarship, the *Postilla* never superceded the *Ordinary Gloss*.

Hugh was solely responsible for the *Scriptum*. It was not strictly a commentary on Lombard's *Sentences*, as he introduced the method of resolving specific controversies, which were relevant to the context. This method would soon become the standard approach in all scholastic *Sentence* commentaries. There is a strong doctrinal connection between the *Scriptum* and his disputed questions, although these questions often broached material not included in the *Sentences*. His disputation on the nature of prophecy has been carefully studied, and it revealed Hugh as an excellent critic of his contemporaries as well as an original thinker.

In addition, Hugh wrote a commentary on *Peter Comestor's *Scholastic Histories*, a text that was just being abandoned by Hugh's generation. He also produced a biblical concordance and a *correctorium* of the Latin Vulgate. Works like these, while not always demonstrating original thinking, were of inestimable value to Hugh's order, as they furthered Bible study and were the necessary tools in sermon preparation.

Bibliography: R. E. Lerner, "Poverty, Preaching, and Eschatology in the Commentaries of Hugh of St.-Cher," in *The Bible in the Medieval World: Essays in Memory of Beryl Smalley*, ed. K. Walsh and D. Wood, 1985; W. H. Principe, *Hugh of St. Cher's Theology of the Hypostatic Union*, 1970.

James R. Ginther

HUGH OF ST. VICTOR (1096–1141). Extremely influential in the development of the medieval university, Hugh was a Canon Regular at the abbey school of St. Victor in Paris, joining in 1115 and becoming master of the school soon afterward. He has been called the second Augustine for his ascetic theology and was an expounder on the natural law ideas later developed by Thomas *Aquinas. Hugh was one of the first social thinkers to explore the idea of commerce in the emerging trade economy of Europe, which was gaining access to more and more distant markets in the East and in Africa during the twelfth century. Hugh was a strong advocate of this interaction with the world, and he was enthusiastic about all kinds of commerce, including international trade. He saw commerce as one solution to the dichotomy of individual goods and community welfare and taught that economic strength helped to prevent war, bolster peace, and reconcile cultural differences.

The abbey of St. Victor had been founded foremost as a school and secondarily as a house of canons regular. The canons regular were not monks but an order of religious who followed the Rule of Saint Augustine in idealizing the *via media*, or "middle way" of serving God, by combining prayer and charitable work. Hugh thus included in his philosophy and his religious vocation to pray and learn, an added element of community education and service to his neighbors, both immediate and further away. As a school, St. Victor's drew scholars who were not brothers in the house, and it also assisted hospitals, churches, and other schools in educating and maintaining the wider community of Hugh's progressively global vision.

More significant to him than his efforts with the larger community, however, were Hugh's ideas concerning philosophy and reason as ways of approaching God. His spirituality, though colored with mysticism, was fully grounded in mortal thought, trusting that God had made humans capable of seeking Him through the mental facilities with which He had endowed them. His system of spirituality was an idea of the integrated mind seeking truth not only by overtly "religious" doctrine but also by any mortal scientific knowledge that could be verified. He justified this by his appeal to the Incarnation; the integrated Christian life includes sources of two types, the first being lower, created or "natural" religion, and the second being based on the truth of the Incarnation, and "revealed" religion.

These two sources integrate with Hugh's three stages of spiritual growth to produce a fivefold schematic for spirituality: (1) *Reading*. By "reading" Hugh means the act of receiving the knowledge God sends, whether in texts or in the natural world. To read is first to look at symbolic marks and then to understand their meaning. Creation as an expression of divine thought is God's "book." (2) *Meditation*. The words of God's book mean more as they are contemplated. Hugh's meditation is less scholastically rigorous than many of his contemporaries' descriptions of meditation, having more in common with the emotive piety in the mysticism of medieval women. He calls again for an integration of intuitive and reasoned response to the stimulus being contemplated. Rejecting the almost Manichean prudery of antiaestheticism, he calls for both appreciation of beauty and openness to a revealing of God's purpose in creating the physical world beautiful. (3) *Christocentric prayer*. Jesus is the perfect and peerless "Word" in God's book. In *De sacramentis*, Hugh writes, "The word took flesh without losing the Divinity, and He offered himself to man like a book, written within and without: externally by humanity, and internally by Divinity, in order that he might be read, outwardly by imitation and inwardly by contemplation; outwardly in order to heal us and inwardly to lead us to happiness." (4) *Progress in Goodness*. This idea Hugh links again to Creation. The idea of sin itself is abstract, but to "embody" it is to give it a context that can be spiritually useful to all Christians. Creation is out of balance in envy and anger, since these both refuse to see the Creation as unified; pride is a rejection of creaturehood; covetousness misplaces the value of parts of the Creation. Progress in Goodness thus becomes a practical means of repenting of real sin. (5) *Contemplation*. Hugh's fifth stage is most comparable with the mystical union with God described by contemporary ecstatic mystics. As such it is attained by few but is the goal sought by all who begin their spiritual quest.

Bibliography: *Hugh of Saint-Victor: Selected Spiritual Writings*, with an introduction by A. Squire, 1962.

                                                                              Zina Petersen

HUGUCCIO OF PISA (C. 1140s–1210). After *Gratian, Huguccio is the best known of the professors of canon law of the twelfth century and a major figure in etymology and lexicography.

He was born in Pisa, taught canon law at the great University of Bologna, and served as bishop of Ferrara (c. 1190–1210), where he expired on 30 April 1210. His two best-known works are the *Summa decretorum* (the fullest and best-known commentary to the *Decretum* of Gratian) and *Liber derivationum* (or *Magnae derivationes*—a landmark in medieval lexicography); both await full critical editions.

We have contemporary references to Huguccio—whose name appears in a variety of spellings including Hugutio, Hugucchio, Uguicio, Ugwicio, and other forms of the diminutive of Ugo or Hugo—from *Salimbene (Adam) of Parma (who mentions the *Liber derivationum* but not the *Summa*) and Pope *Innocent III (who studied canon law at Bologna under Huguccio). He studied canon law at Bologna and later lectured there on the subject (archive records at Bologna mention an Ugo as *legum doctor*). We are not sure of his precise clerical status, though his background in the arts appears extensive and his studies at Bologna concentrated on canon law and theology. It is not unfair to say that Huguccio's great passion was philology. Most of his work involves detailed commentary, glossing, and explication; in his preface to the *Liber derivationum*, Huguccio makes a Greco-Latin etymological play upon his own name: *patria pisanus, nomine Hugutio, quasi Eugetio, id est, bona terra, . . . vel Hugutio, quasi Vigitio, id est, virens terra* ("a Pisan native, by the name Hugutio, Eugetio so to speak, that is, 'good land,' . . . or Hugutio, as it were Vigitio, that is, 'verdant land' ").

Huguccio's *Hagiographia* is a theological and philological work, containing etymological investigations of the names of saints in the liturgical calendar. He includes etymological information in his expositions of the Apostles' Creed (*Expositio symboli apostolorum*) and Lord's Prayer (*Expositio dominicae ora-*

tionis). He brought his interest in terminology to bear in his famous commentary on Gratian's *Decretum*, the *Summa decretorum*, nearly forty manuscripts of which survive. Huguccio's clear and detailed analysis follows *causa* by *causa*, question by question, chapter by chapter, even word by word, illuminating a variety of legal terms and influencing the work of later legalistic writers.

Huguccio's philological work proper includes the *Rosarium*, a treatise on verbs; the *De dubio accentu*, a brief tract on Latin pronunciation; a grammatical compendium evidently written after the *Summa decretorum* entitled *Summa artis grammaticae*; and the *Liber derivationum*. His *Liber derivationum* follows the medieval lexicographical model of grouping *derivationes*: locating a particular root and listing after it all supposed derivatives. It is an etymological dictionary in the main but is also a glossary (including many legal terms), grammatical treatise (there are a number of grammatical digressions or anecdotes culled from *Priscian), history of medieval Latin, and encyclopedia. His main sources were the *Etymologiae* of *Isidore of Seville, the *Elementarium* of Papias (c. 1041), and the *Panormia* of Osbern of Gloucester (mid-twelfth century). Huguccio arranged this voluminous lexicon into leaves of two columns; later copyists and lexicographers composed indices to aid in finding a particular word. Huguccio significantly influenced successors such as John Balbi (John Januensis de Balbi, who composed the *Catholicon* c. 1286) and Firmin Le Ver (c. 1370/1375–1444, who composed the bilingual Latin-French *Dictionarius*).

Bibliography: C. Leonardi, "La Vita e L'Opera di Uguccione da Pisa Decretista," *Studia Gratiana* 4 (1956–1957): 37–120; C. Riessner, *Die "Magnae Derivationes" des Uguccione da Pisa*, 1965; Uguccione da Pisa, *De dubio accentu, agiographia, expositio de symbolo apostolorum*, ed. G. Cremascoli, 1978.

Joseph McGowan

I

IDRĪSĪ, AL- (1100–C. 1165). Al-Idrīsī was a celebrated Islamic geographer, cartographer, royal adviser to the Norman king of Sicily *Roger II (r. 1130–1154), and author of one of the greatest geographic works of the medieval world.

Few facts are known about al-Idrīsī's life. A noble by birth, al-Idrīsī traced his lineage through a long line of important figures to the Prophet *Muhammad. A member of the Hammudid dynasty, he was born in Sabtah, modern Ceuta in Morocco, and spent much of his early life traveling in North Africa and Spain. Al-Idrīsī studied in Cordova for a number of years, and his travels took him to many parts of western Europe, including Portugal, northern Spain, the French Atlantic coast, southern England, and Asia Minor. In 1145, al-Idrīsī entered the service of King Roger II and spent the remainder of his life at Palermo. There is little scholarly agreement on al-Idrīsī's reasons for going to Sicily, and Muslim biographers seem to have taken little interest in him or his work, possibly because he was employed by a Christian king and thus would have been considered as something of a renegade. One fourteenth-century source informs us that he was invited by Roger to come to Palermo in order to make a map of the world for him. It is certain that Roger paid him handsomely for his services.

Although he had traveled extensively, it was not until al-Idrīsī came to Sicily that he established himself as a geographer and cartographer. During his career at Roger II's court, al-Idrīsī was responsible for the production of three important geographical works. The first of these, now lost, was a silver planisphere depicting a map of the world on one side and the zodiac and the constellations on the other. It is described as having been nearly six feet in diameter and weighing more than 450 pounds. The second was a series of world maps, on the Ptolemaic model, which divided the Earth north of the equator into seven climatic zones of equal width, each of which was further subdivided into ten portions by lines of longitude. These maps, a major feat in and of themselves, provided information more accurate on many areas than any maps produced theretofore. The third work, his most famous, was a book written as a key to the silver planisphere. This work of physical and descriptive geography, the *Book of Roger*, represented the most thorough and detailed work of its type up until that time.

The *Book of Roger*, completed shortly before Roger II's death in 1154, was compiled by combining material from Arabic and Greek geographic works with information obtained from firsthand observations and eyewitness reports of surveyors sent by Roger II to various regions. While the *Book of Roger* has been criticized on methodological grounds, such as al-Idrīsī's less-than-perfect mastery of the physical and mathematical aspects of geography and his failure to critically evaluate the Greek and Arabic sources upon which he depended so heavily, it remains a major work of medieval descriptive geography and is particularly valuable for the data it provides on the Mediterranean basin and the Balkans.

In addition to the *Book of Roger*, al-Idrīsī penned a number of other geographic works, including one, now lost, written for William I, Roger's son and successor (r. 1154–1166). This geographical encyclopedia is reported to have been larger than the *Book of Roger*. Geography was not the only area that interested al-Idrīsī, and he also wrote a book on medicine, the *Book of Simple Drugs*, a pharmacopoeia that lists the names of various medicinal plants and their pharmaceutical derivatives in multiple languages including Syriac, Greek, Latin, and Persian.

Al-Idrīsī's influence on European geographic thinking lies in the fact that portions of his works were included among Latin compendiums of various Arabic geographical works. An abridgement of the *Book of Roger* was published in Latin by the Medici press in Rome in 1592 and was translated into Italian eight years later. His maps seemed to have been of particular use, and there is evidence that they were copied wholesale for some 300 years after his death. As far as cartography is concerned, they were far superior to anything produced in Europe or the Islamic world for quite sometime thereafter.

Bibliography: I. Kratchkovsky, "Les géographes arabes des XI et XII siècles en Occident," trans. M. Canard, *Annales de l'Institut d' Études Orientales de l'Université d'Alger* XVIII–XIX (1960–1961): 1–72; G. Oman, "Al-Idrīsī," in *The Encyclopaedia of Islam*, ed. B. Lewis et al., new ed., vol. 3, 1971.

Erik S. Ohlander

ILDEFONSUS OF TOLEDO, SAINT (C. 607–667). The early medieval Spanish writer, bishop, and saint is known principally through his surviving writings and Julian of Toledo's *Elogium*; his treatise on the Blessed Virgin (*Liber de virginitate sanctae Mariae contra tres infideles*) is the best known and served to increase subsequent Marian devotion in Spain. Born in Toledo of a noble Visigothic family, Ildefonsus entered the monastery at Agali outside Toledo (later serving as its abbot) and served as bishop of his native city from 657 to 667.

Ildefonsus is perhaps even better known for the legends surrounding him such as the apparition of Saint Leocadia to him or the presentation of a chasuble to him by the Blessed Virgin Mary. Rubens painted the Ildefonsus altar in the church of St. Jacques de Candenburgh near Brussels, and the National Gallery of Art in Washington, D.C., houses El Greco's famous portrait of the saint. In 1508, the Colegio de San Ildefonso was founded in Alcalá.

Ildefonsus is not seen now as a particularly original writer but one well versed in Scripture and bearing the imprint of Augustine, *Gregory the Great, and *Isidore of Seville. His *De viris illustribus* (On Famous Men) contains fourteen lives, Spaniards all but for Gregory the Great and seven of them bishops of Toledo (Asturius, Aurasius, Eugene I, Eugene II, Helladius, Justus, Montanus). The book is an extension of a genre already undertaken by Jerome, Gennadius, and Isidore (who is described in Ildefonsus' portrait of him as *vir prudentissimus*), though Ildefonsus' collection is distinct in having a more local focus. His *Liber de cognitione baptismi*, a work in 142 chapters written while he was bishop of Toledo, is meant to prepare those about to receive the sacrament, while the *De itinere deserti* (On the Journey in the Desert) uses the experiences of the Israelites in the desert as an allegory for the life of a Christian after baptism. Two letters of his to Quiricus, bishop of Barcelona, survive (*PL* 96). His main work, the *Liber de virginitate sanctae Mariae contra tres infideles*, was written at the request of Quiricus during a period of relative decline in the Spanish Church. Ildefonsus sought, in his preface and twelve chapters, to counter arguments against and defamation of the virginity of Mary; the *tres infideles* mentioned in the treatise that Ildefonsus joins in debate are the heretics Jovinian (already attacked by Augustine), Helvidius, and Judaeus (apparently, the Jews of Spain). Some two dozen manuscripts of the treatise survive, attesting to the influence of Ildefonsus on the cult of the Virgin Mary in Spain.

Bibliography: Sr. A. Braegelmann, *The Life and Writings of Saint Ildefonsus of Toledo*, 1942.

Joseph McGowan

INE OF WESSEX (R. 688–726).

Ine, king of Wessex, was responsible for consolidating the military position and social cohesiveness of the kingdom during the late seventh and early eighth centuries.

Ine came to the throne following Cædwalla (685/686–688), one of the more militarily important rulers of Wessex, who had been responsible for extending West Saxon power eastward toward Kent. Ine held his own militarily against his immediate neighbors, Ceolred of Mercia, Geraint of Dumnonia, and the East Saxons, but was probably most successful at consolidating the gains of his predecessor. He was the first West Saxon king whom we know to have promulgated his own law code, which like all the Anglo-Saxon laws was written in the vernacular. It is important as it legislates for all Ine's subjects, both British and West Saxon, and may indicate some attempt on Ine's part to fuse the two populations together more thoroughly. He was also important for strengthening the Church's influence in Wessex, the first of whose rulers had only been converted in 635, by establishing a new diocese at Sherborne; his reign also saw the foundation of the first West Saxon nunneries. Ine's long reign was probably the single most successful in Wessex prior to that of *Alfred the Great.

Bibliography: B. Yorke, *Kings and Kingdoms of Early Anglo-Saxon England*, 1990.

David Day

INNOCENT III, POPE (C. 1160/1161–1216, PONTIFICATE 1198–1216).

An astute politician and pastoral leader, Innocent III was thoroughly involved in politics at the same time as he worked to consolidate the authority of the papacy and for ecclesiastical reform.

Innocent III was born as Lothar of Segni into a noble Italian family. He was educated at Paris, where he studied pastoral theology under Peter of Corbeil. It is unclear whether Lothar formally studied canon law, but his later judgments bear the indelible marks of the Bolognese school. By 1190, he had been appointed a cardinal-deacon, and he quickly became an integral part of the papal court. In 1198, the aged Celestine III died, and the College of Cardinals elected Lothar. At the age of thirty-eight, the youngest pope-elect and not yet a priest, he took the name Innocent III for his pontificate of eighteen years.

As pope, Innocent was both an astute politician and pastoral leader, and to him these were not mutually exclusive. If a general principle can be extrapolated from his reign, it was that centralized authority was the guarantor of pastoral ministry. To ameliorate papal authority was the optimum method for securing the pastoral efficacy of priests and bishops alike. Innocent argued that the papacy had been granted *plenitudo potestatis* (fullness of power), which in turn allowed all Church leaders to have *pars sollicitudinis* (sharing of responsibility). To safeguard the papacy was to protect the ministry of the Church as a whole. Innocent's outlook had significant implications for European politics, as well as an effect on the theory and practice of pastoral care.

With the death of Emperor *Henry VI in 1197, the political machinations began almost immediately. It was clear to all that Henry's infant son *Frederick (II) (whose regent was Innocent himself) would not take the throne, and so German princes began to seek a more realistic successor. They soon divided into two camps, the Hohenstaufens, who supported Philip of Swabia (Henry VI's brother), and the Welfs, who championed *Otto (IV) of Brunswick. In 1199 at Speyer, the Hohenstaufens issued an ultimatum to Innocent to cease and desist from his interference in imperial politics. Innocent was so concerned that he ordered his chancery to begin a new record of letters and documents, now known as the *Registrum super negotio Romani imperii* (Register Concerning the Affairs of the Roman Empire). Innocent chose the side that benefited the papal states.

In 1199, Otto offered full capitulation to Innocent's claims for the Italian territories, along with a commitment to respect the liberty of the German churches. Innocent held a secret meeting at Rome in 1201 and found in favor of Otto. This hardly guaranteed Otto the throne, and by 1205 it was apparent that the Welf candidate would never become emperor. The coronation of Philip took place in January 1206, and negotiations began to secure papal recognition. Approval was granted, but two years later Philip was murdered. Taking this as divine judgment, Innocent once again supported Otto, but it was short-lived. In 1210, Otto ordered his army into Italy to secure control of imperial territory, and thus Innocent soon favored Frederick as the legitimate imperial heir. Events moved well beyond Otto's control as the new emperor-elect signed a declaration similar to the one that Otto had made in 1199. Despite further protests made by the Welfs at the Fourth Lateran Council, Frederick was crowned emperor in July 1215.

In other political events, the ecclesiastical motivation was more apparent. In 1206, King *John of England refused to acknowledge Stephen *Langton as the new archbishop of Canterbury. Innocent replied with an interdict upon all of England in 1208. For two years, most of the leaders of the English Church sojourned in France, while the king of France prepared for an opportune time to invade England. In 1213, with no hope of winning the battle against Innocent, and with an imminent French invasion, John capitulated. The extent of his surrender surprised even Innocent, since John not only agreed to acknowledge Langton's election, but he also placed all royal lands and holdings under the overlordship of Innocent.

Perhaps the most damaging political event during Innocent's pontificate was the sack of Constantinople in 1204. Having called for another crusade, Innocent was pleased with the support the Byzantine emperor had promised the crusaders. However, the emperor quickly reneged, much to the anger of the Venetians who had financed the venture. The result was an attack on Constantinople, which included a tremendous amount of destruction and looting of Byzantine churches. While Innocent was incensed at the crusaders' behavior, rebuking their papal legate, he nonetheless took advantage of the situation to establish his ecclesiastical authority within Byzantine territory. That influence quickly waned, and the long-term effects of the Fourth Crusade would haunt the papacy as it pursued a policy of reunion later in the century.

Despite these pressing political affairs, Innocent devoted himself to ecclesiastical reform. His program emerged in canon law and an ecumenical council. Drawing upon his legal education, Innocent made careful deliberations of both cases argued before him and questions submitted to him. His written replies, or decretals, soon became authoritative legal texts. A number of attempts were made to produce a definitive collection, all of which Innocent himself spurned. In 1210, Innocent finally approved a collection completed under his supervision. It was reedited as part of the *Liber extra* in 1234, commissioned by Pope *Honorius III, who had been a trusted adviser to Innocent. While these decretals further developed the concept of precedence in legal argument, they also emphasized the universal authority of papal judgments. They were the implementation of the legal principle that "the will of the prince has the force of law"—in this case, the prince of the Church.

While the decretals spoke to concrete issues, the Fourth Lateran Council of 1215 proposed more general principles. The general call in 1213 announced that the council would consider how "to eradicate vices and to plant virtues, to correct faults and to reform morals, to remove heresies and to strengthen faith, to settle discords and to establish peace, to get rid of oppression and to foster liberty, to induce princes and Christian people to come to the aid and succor of the holy Land." The proceedings of the council have not survived (except a description of the liturgical commencement), and it is doubtful that there was much debate. Instead, it was an opportunity for Innocent to proclaim his vision of the Church. A broad vision it was, as the council addressed heresy, Church discipline, reform of clerical morals, elections and the administration of benefices, taxation, canonical suits, matrimony, tithes, simony, and the Jews. The council laid the groundwork for future pastoral theology by emphasizing the twin foundations of pastoral care, preaching and confession. Both duties were meant to prepare the laity for a life of virtue and proper reception of the Eucharist, which was to be received at least annually. Success of the reforms depended upon a clergy who were properly educated (which is why Innocent supported the establishment of universities) and committed to impeccable morals. The impact of the council was far reaching: Provincial councils throughout Europe echoed its canons, and it bolstered a new genre of pastoral literature in the universities.

Innocent's reforms were both repressive and innovative. He continued the oppression of heretical groups, such as the Waldensians (see Peter *Waldo) and the Cathars, and in 1209 approved of military action to be taken against the Albigensian Cathars. This "Crusade" depicts Innocent as a reactionary authoritarian, but it should be balanced with his approval of innovative movements. He endorsed the Franciscan movement in 1210 since this new order had acknowledged the central role of papal authority. Moreover, the Franciscans would further the role of preaching, so essential to Innocent's reform program.

Innocent completed a small corpus of writings during his lifetime, in addition to the large body of decretals. We have a record of seventy-eight sermons preached throughout his pontificate. He also wrote two popular works before his pontificate, both related to pastoral theology: *De missarum mysteriis* (On the Mysteries of the Mass) and *De miseria humanae conditionis* (On the Misery of the Human Condition). A commentary on the seven penitential psalms is also attributed to him, but its authorship has yet to be fully established.

Bibliography: J. Sayers, *Innocent III, Leader of Europe, 1198–1216*, 1994; H. Tillman, *Pope Innocent III*, trans. W. Sax, 1980.

James R. Ginther

INNOCENT IV, POPE (C. 1200–1254, PONTIFICATE 1243–1254). Sinibaldo Fieschi, a renowned canon lawyer, was elected pope on 25 June 1243 and took the name Innocent IV. He proved to be a challenge to Holy Roman Emperors *Frederick II and Conrad IV on several fronts, helped support the Seventh Crusade led by *Louis IX of France, and became involved in Sicilian politics.

Innocent believed in the supremacy of the papacy in all affairs and especially took a strong stance against the Holy Roman Empire, which he believed the papacy created. His election at Anagni was delayed for over a year because Frederick held two cardinals prisoner. The cardinals were released only because Frederick thought Innocent would be a friend to the empire. The two came close to an agreement at the outset, but imperial claims in Lombardy and Sicily prevented a truce.

Innocent fled to Lyons in 1245 and called a Church council to hear matters pertaining to Frederick. Spain, France, and England sent prelates to Lyons to discuss imperial problems as well as Church reform, liberation of Holy places, and an end to the East–West schism. Although Frederick sent his representative, Thaddeus of Suessa, to defend him, the council deposed him, and Frederick's excommunication was later renewed in 1248. Frederick and the papacy remained hostile toward each other for the remainder of Frederick's life.

The Church actively supported missionary efforts such as those in Prussia and the Baltic and followed a pro-French policy by supporting Louis' crusade to the Holy Land. The crusade failed in 1248, but the papacy continued to garner Louis' support against the empire. Relations between the papacy and empire grew worse, and the French king attempted to mediate but failed to bring the two sides together.

Frederick died in 1250, but Innocent continued to have problems with the empire. He wanted to prevent the new emperor, Conrad, from gaining control of Sicily and therefore gave it to Manfred, a bastard son of Frederick. Manfred, bribed by Muslims who feared a papal presence in Sicily, revolted against Innocent and defeated a papal army at Foggia on 2 December 1254. Innocent, who had moved to Naples, was ill at the time, and this crushing defeat certainly did not improve his health. Innocent died five days later on 7 December 1254. He had boldly challenged the Holy Roman Empire throughout his pontificate and strongly supported Church expansion and reform (to such an extent that he was the first to support torture in the Inquisition).

Bibliography: R. P. McBrien, *Lives of the Popes*, 1997; W. Ullmann, *A Short History of the Papacy in the Middle Ages*, 1972.

Paul Miller

ISIDORE OF SEVILLE, SAINT (C. 560–636). Archbishop of Seville, he is perhaps best known as an encyclopedist. In addition to his best-known work, however, he was also an indefatigable combatant of the Arian form of Christianity, and a voluminous and influential writer.

Isidore was born about 560 into a senatorial family, possibly at Carthagena in southeastern Spain or in Seville, in southwestern Spain. His father was Severianus, who may have been duke of Carthagena, although there is no direct contemporary evidence for this but only a later tradition. Little is known of the family, other than that the family left for Seville when Isidore was still very young, or perhaps even before he was born, after Carthagena was destroyed in Visigothic raids, and that both parents died while Isidore and his younger brother, Fulgentius, were still very young.

Certainly Leander, Isidore's older brother, was born at Carthagena and must have been considerably older than Isidore, since he became archbishop of Seville in 584, while the latter was a student at the cathedral school. Leander, himself a learned man who was friends with *Gregory the Great (whom he met while on an official embassy to Byzantium), was closely involved with Isidore's education in Seville and thereby exercised a profound influence on his younger brother. Isidore's older sister Florentina became a nun, and his younger brother eventually became bishop of Écija (fifty miles east of Seville).

Isidore succeeded Leander as archbishop of Seville in 601, after the latter's death. In 585, Hermengild, upon becoming king of the Visigoths, converted from Arian Christianity to Catholicism, and his brother Recared, who succeeded him the same year, likewise converted, setting the stage for making Seville the Catholic center of Spain. These conversions were confirmed at the Third Council of Toledo, presided over by Leander. Isidore himself presided over several provincial synods in Seville (in 619 and 625) and in 633 was in charge of the Fourth Council of Toledo, a national gathering of Spanish bishops that made some far-reaching decisions on liturgical matters, confirming Catholic Christianity and rituals. In addition, the council confirmed the anti-Jewish regulations of the Third Council of Toledo barring them from public office and having Christian slaves, for example, but also decreed that Jews could not be forced to convert to Christianity. Moreover, the council settled a serious political dispute concerning the succession to the Visigothic kingship and drew up regulations concerning the education of the clergy. The first and last of these are clearly a reflection of Isidore's own interests and convictions. Like his brother, he had worked consistently for the spread of Catholic Christianity in the area under his control and beyond; and he had himself founded a training school for young priests in Seville under the direction of a *magister doctrinae* (master of doctrine). He died in Seville on 4 April 636.

Not long after his death, his friend Braulio, the bishop of Saragossa to whom Isidore had dedicated his encyclopedia, added Isidore's name and a list of his accomplishments to Isidore's own book *De viris illustribus* (On Famous Men). In this entry, he praised Isidore for his eloquence, his knowledge, and his charity. He considered him to be the most learned man of his age, someone who had been appointed by God himself to preserve the documents and learning of the ancients and to rescue Spain from oblivion. Isidore's reputation was thus assured almost from the moment of his death.

But even without his friend's encomium, his fame would have spread. The work for which he continues to be known is his encyclopedia, variously known as *Etymologiarum Libri XX* (Twenty Books of Etymologies), *Originum Libri XX* (Twenty Books of Origins), or simply *Origines* (Origins). This work, intended as a dictionary to be consulted by scholars, distills into twenty books and is a phenomenal collection of knowledge on the natural world and on learning. Some of the work is based on the second-century Latin encyclopedia by Pliny the Younger, but he weaves into this much additional material drawn from a multitude of writers, organized into topics beginning with a discussion of language and the liberal arts. The work exercised a profound influence on European learning throughout the Middle Ages (as the survival of more than a thousand manuscript copies makes clear). Isidore also wrote doctrinal works, several philosophical treatises, a monastic rule, a history of the Goths, and biblical commentaries, but it his encyclopedia that has ensured him a lasting place in intellectual history.

Bibliography: M. C. Díaz y Díaz, "Introducción general" to *Etimologías, Edición Bilingüe*, by San Isidoro de Sevilla, ed. J. Oroz Reta and M.-A. Marcos Casquero, 1982; J. Fontaine, *Isidore de Seville et la culture classique dans l'Espagne wisigothique*, 2d ed., 3 vols., 1983; J. N. Hillgarth, "Isidorian Studies, 1976–1985," *Studi medievali* 31.2 (1990): 925–973.

William Schipper

IVO OF CHARTRES, SAINT (C. 1040–1115). Bishop of Chartres (1090–1115), saint, great scholar, teacher, and canonist, Ivo is perhaps best known for his role as an opponent of the divorce of King Philip I and his wife Bertha of Holland.

Ivo was born into a noble family in the region of Beauvais (just north of Paris). He went to study first in Paris, then later at Bec, in Normandy, where *Lanfranc was prior of the abbey there. He studied alongside *Anselm, who would later become archbishop of Canterbury. In 1080, he returned to Beauvais as the prior of the canons of St. Quentin. Ten years later, he was elected bishop of Chartres, a city that was famous for its schools.

Throughout his episcopacy, Ivo worked to defend the Church's right to judge in cases of marriage validity and incest and especially to break up potentially incestuous marriages before they could take place. He really came to the forefront in the divorce case of King Philip I (r. 1060–1108). Philip divorced his wife, Bertha of Holland, in 1092, after twenty years of marriage, because he was tired of her, she was too fat, and he wanted to marry Bertrade, the wife of the count of Anjou at the time. There were several reasons why the Church would have been opposed to this divorce and subsequent remarriage, but Ivo, who led the opposition, chose to focus on the fact that Philip and Bertrade, through her first husband, were too closely related to marry. Most of the bishops of France supported the king, but Ivo worked zealously to convince them and the pope to excommunicate the king. The king was excommunicated, and Ivo was even imprisoned for a short time by the king, but in the end the king won out, and was absolved by the pope. Despite this setback, Ivo continued his efforts, even against the marriage plans of another king, *Henry I of England, who was trying to arrange a marriage for one of his daughters, which Ivo knew would be incestuous.

Ivo also played a small but significant role in the Investiture Controversy, which was raging at this time mainly between the pope and the Holy Roman Emperor over the right to appoint bishops and control episcopal elections. Ivo took a position of compromise, and although his ideas were not accepted or popular during his lifetime, their influence is present in the final agreement between the two parties at the Concordat of Worms.

Ivo made his influence felt particularly through his writings, which were quite popular in the Middle Ages. His many letters provide important source material for the period and especially for Philip's marriage problems. His collection of decretals (papal letters), called the *Panormia*, was one of the most important collections of such documents before *Gratian compiled his definitive collection in 1140. The prologue to the *Panormia* was particularly influential in helping people find a way to settle disputes over discrepancies in the standard ecclesiastical authorities.

Bibliography: S. Kuttner, *Harmony from Dissonance: An Interpretation of Medieval Canon Law*, 1960.

Ryan P. Crisp

J

JACOBUS DE VORAGINE (C. 1230–1298). Archbishop of Genoa and hagiographer, he was the author of the *Legenda aurea*.

Jacobus (or James) was born in Varazze near Genoa. He entered the Dominican Order in 1244 and became provincial of the Dominicans in Lombardy. In 1288, Pope Nicholas IV sent him to Genoa, which was under a papal interdict for assisting the Sicilians in a revolt against the king of Naples. In 1292, with much reluctance, he accepted election to the post of archbishop of Genoa, which he had refused four years earlier. As archbishop, he worked to repair the city's decaying churches, endowed a number of hospitals, and became known for his care of the poor. He spent much of his time attempting to make peace between warring factions of Guelphs (papal supporters) and Ghibellines (imperial supporters) in the city and achieved a short-lived truce in 1295. For these peacemaking efforts, he was beatified in 1816 and is celebrated as a saint within the Dominican Order.

Besides numerous sermons, Jacobus wrote a chronicle of the city of Genoa and compiled a series of *Legenda sanctorum* (readings on the saints), now known as the *Legenda aurea* (Golden Legend). This collection, which appears to have been intended as an aid for preachers, presents popular stories from a variety of earlier saints' lives and biblical legends, arranged according to the Church calendar. It became one of the most widely copied and translated texts of the later Middle Ages. According to tradition, it was one of only two books available to Ignatius Loyola during the illness, which lead to his conversion. Jacobus' retellings of saints' lives often contradict the tone of his sources. He selected miracle stories designed to show the arbitrary power of God and his saints and to inspire awe and devotion to saints as people set apart from their communities. In this, he was very much a man of his time, but to later ages, the work seemed superstitious and unlikely to promote Christian behavior. During the Reformation, Protestants and Catholics alike attacked the *Golden Legend*.

For students of the late thirteenth through fifteenth centuries, however, the *Legend* provides insight into common devotional teaching. It is also useful for understanding the art and iconography of the late Middle Ages.

Bibliography: *The* Golden Legend: *Readings on the Saints*, trans. W. G. Ryan, 2d ed., 1993; S. Reames, *The* Legenda aurea: *A Reexamination of Its Paradoxical History*, 1985.

Jill Averil Keen

JACQUES DE VITRY (C. 1160/1170–1240). Bishop, cardinal, preacher, and historian, Jacques is best known for his *Life of Marie d'Oignies*, sermons, and his history of the crusades.

Jacques was born into a noble family in Rheims. He studied in Paris where he was connected with the canons of St. Victor. Attracted by the holiness of the Beguine Marie d'Oignies, he left his studies and joined the Augustinian canons at Oignies in Liège. In 1210, he was ordained. Marie inspired Jacques with an "apostolic zeal"; he served as her confessor and celebrated his first Mass in her presence. Moreover, she motivated him as a preacher. In 1213, the papal legate commissioned Jacques to preach the Crusade against the Albigensians in France and Germany. In 1214, again on commission, he preached the Fifth Crusade in France. In Perugia, in 1215, he was consecrated bishop of Acre in the Holy Land; he went to Jerusalem that same year and served there for the next nine years, involving himself in the European Church and politics. In 1225, he returned to Italy and resigned his office in 1228. In 1229, Pope *Gregory IX appointed him cardinal bishop of Tusculanum, and he remained a loyal member of the Curia until his death in 1240.

A prolific writer and preacher, his surviving works include the *Life of Marie d'Oignies*, the *Historia Hiersolomitana abbreviata*, seven letters, and around 450 sermons. The *Life* is the biography of Marie d'Oignies, possibly the first Beguine. He tried to promote the work of these holy women, of whom the mainstream Church disapproved. This work popularized the Beguine movement and is important for historians for what it reveals about early-thirteenth-century spirituality. The *Historia Hiersolomitana abbreviata* is a history of the crusades, but Jacques completed only the first two of three intended books: the *Historia orientalis* and the *Historia occidentalis*. The former, relying heavily on *William of Tyre's work, discusses the topography of the East and events up until 1179. The second is the more original; it is a religious and moral history of the West, which details the new movements (Beguines, Franciscans, for example) and their importance for the Church and the success of the crusades. His contemporaries complimented him for his skill as a preacher, and he was quite successful in convincing people to take up the Cross. His sermons, like the *Life*, make use of exempla because Jacques believed that examples were far more useful for converting laymen than precepts. He varied his sermons depending on his audience, always stressing the penitential nature of the pilgrim's journey, but included very practical advice on conduct and dress.

His works also reveal his primary influences. Jacques was influenced by *Bernard of Clairvaux and his followers in addition to the writings of the Victorines, especially *Richard of St. Victor. The *Life of Marie* may be an attempt to popularize Richard's teachings, drawing on two of his works: the *Twelve Patriarchs* and the *Mystical Ark*. Marie is Jacques' example of an ideal Victorine mystic. In the *Historia occidentalis*, he describes the life and work of canons but reserves his highest praise for the canons of St. Victor. Jacques was well read; he quotes Seneca and refers to Scylla and Charybdis in his sermons. He was also well schooled in the writings of the Church Fathers. For example, he refined their exploration of pilgrimage as a metaphor for a journey through life, as his sermons demonstrate.

Finally, Jacques was a keen observer and critic of his times. He believed that the Church bore the responsibility for preparing each and every person for pilgrimage, by providing help and guidance so the pilgrim would not stray from the road to the city of God, and did so in all of his writings.

Bibliography: D. J. Birch, "Jacques de Vitry and the Ideology of Pilgrimage," in *Pilgrimage Explored*, ed. J. Stopford, 1999; Jacques de Vitry, *Life of Marie d'Oignies*, trans. M. H. King, 1993.

Jana K. Schulman

JAMES I OF ARAGON (1208–1276). A man of both deeds and letters, he much expanded the territory of his western Iberian kingdom of Aragon through the reconquest of the Balearic Islands and Valencia and wrote, in vernacular Catalan, the first autobiography of a medieval king.

James I was born in Montpellier in 1208. His father, Peter II, promptly attempted to divorce his mother, Marie I of Montpellier, who was forced to leave her infant and travel to Rome to plead for papal protection of her son's legitimacy. Orphaned as a young child, James and his kingdom came under the protection of Pope *Innocent III, and James was schooled by the Knights Templars at Monzon castle. In 1221, he married Leonor, daughter of the king of Castile. This marriage was later annulled, and in 1235 he married Violante, daughter of King Andrew of Hungary. After her death, Teresa Gil de Viduare became James' third queen but not his last lover. James' legitimate unions produced six sons and three daughters, a total augmented by at least two illegitimate sons.

James began his career in arms at age ten. By his twelfth year, he had taken two castles by storm. In 1229, he successfully invaded the island of Majorca, bringing it and the other large Balearic Island, Minorca, under definitive Christian rule by 1232. From 1232 to 1245, he systematically expanded his kingdom southward into Islamic-controlled lands until he ruled the entire territory of Valencia all the way to the border of Murcia. Bellicose when necessary, James was often able to execute his conquests bloodlessly through a combination of strategic maneuvering, patient siege, and diplomatic negotiations. He prided himself on his knowledge of human nature and of Islamic culture; he used both to extract advantageous terms in any bargain. He was generous in his rule of the large Mudejar population of his newly conquered territories and granted them the right to continue to practice Islam. He also welcomed both Christian and Jewish settlers and managed to balance the interests of all three religious groups to create a remarkably pluralistic colonial society. While successful in expanding his kingdom on the Iberian Peninsula, James was not able to maintain his dynasty's position in southern France. However, by marrying his oldest son, Peter, to the Hohenstaufen heiress of Sicily, he set up his dynasty's eventual conquest of that island.

In the course of the Valencian conquest, James captured the center for Islamic paper production in Jativa and became the first European king to archive paper copies of official transactions. Also in Valencia, he published the first Roman law code in Europe, the Valencian *Furs*, and founded a university. In addition, he was instrumental in the reorganization and revitalization of the university at Montpellier. His greatest intellectual achievement, however, was the *Llibre dels feyts*, or *Book of Deeds*. Written in vernacular Catalan, James worked on this autobiography off and on throughout his life. It details his military exploits, political negotiations, and private moments from conception to death—the most complete surviving portrait of any medieval king. James I died in Valencia in 1276, completing one of the longest reigns in European history and leaving his sons a prosperous and much-expanded crown of Aragon.

Bibliography: T. N. Bisson, *The Medieval Crown of Aragon*, 1986.

Linda A. McMillin

JEAN DE JOINVILLE. *See* JOHN OF JOINVILLE.

JEAN DE MEUN (MEUNG) (C. 1240–C. 1305). French poet and translator, he was the author of the second, longer part of the *Roman de la Rose*, one of the most popular and influential medieval romances.

Little is known of Jean de Meun's life. His birth name was Clopinel (Chopinel), but he was later known by the name of his birthplace, Meung-sur-Loire. He may have been archdeacon of the Beauce, and he may have owned a home in Paris; however, there is no absolute proof. In addition to the *Roman de la Rose*, his surviving works include translations of Vegetius' *De re militari* (On Warfare), *Boethius' *De consolatione Philosophiae* (The Consolation of Philosophy), and the letters of Peter *Abelard and *Héloïse. Two poems, a *Testament* and a *Codicile*, are also thought to be written by him.

However, by far his most important contribution to history is his authorship of the second part of the *Roman de la Rose*, which begins at line 4,059 of the work begun some forty years earlier by *Guillaume de Lorris. Jean de Meun began work on the *Roman de la Rose* in 1269 and completed it in 1278. The tone of the poem shifts radically with Jean's authorship. Whereas Guillaume's poem centers on an exploration of courtly love, Jean's poem debates many of the moral and philosophical issues of the time. Those characters continued from Guillaume's sections of the poem become dark and cynical in Jean's hands. For example, the character of Friend, as written by Guillaume, is harmless. However, in Jean's section, this same character urges the Lover to sink to whatever depths of hypocrisy it takes for him to gain his purpose. Guillaume's treatment of courtly love, whether it is read as supportive or critical, is gentle. In contrast, Jean is harshly critical. He also displays an antifeminist slant throughout the poem that is especially evident in the indictment of marriage by the Jealous Husband quoted by Friend. Jean broadens the scope of the poem to include the major debates of his time. He creates the character of False Seeming, who many critics agree speaks for Jean himself. This character directly attacks the mendicant orders who were involved in a bitter dispute at the University of Paris with the secular university teachers. False Seeming depicts these friars as hideous and totally corrupt.

The *Roman de la Rose*, and especially Jean de Meun's contribution to the work, continued to inspire and spark debate for centuries to come. The most important author to be influenced by the work was Chaucer, who composed a Middle English translation, *The Romant of the Rose*. Chaucer also drew on Jean's work in the account of the chess game in *The Book of the Duchess*. Some scholars believe that Chaucer's Wife of Bath is based on the character of La Vielle in the *Roman de la Rose*. The work continued to cause controversy. Christine de Pizan (1364–1429) was involved in a literary debate over the depiction of women in the work. This debate inspired Christine to write *The Book of the City of Ladies* and *The Treasury of the City of Ladies*. Thus, although little is known about the life or person of Jean de Meun, his influence and his ability to inflame his opponents continued long after his death.

Bibliography: H. M. Arden, *The Romance of the Rose*, 1987.

Leah Larson

JOACHIM OF FIORE (1135–1202). Joachim was abbot of Corazzo, but he is best known for his vision of history as the manifestation of the Trinity. He reads Scripture throughout time, rather than toward an approaching apocalypse. His view of history is intricately numerological and symbolic, relying on the meanings of recurring numbers in Scripture: two, three, five, seven, and twelve.

The medieval mind tried to relate ordinary time to the eternal time of their faith. History's climax seemed to come midway through time, with Christ's incarnation; what was supposed to be happening now? A waiting period? Thinkers before Joachim saw history as a progressive revelation of the Trinity but still projected nothing into the last ages. Joachim solved the puzzle by seeing the Trinity as the key to the destiny of all men; in the history of mankind, there is the work of God the Father (the Old Testament), that of God the Son (the New Testament), and there must therefore be the work of God the Holy Spirit.

He called these three divisions *status*, intending not successive stages but spheres that are distinctive yet at work in each other, because the Trinity is three yet one: the Son proceeds from the Father, so the sources of his work lie there, but the Spirit moves from both Father and Son and so has a double root and double manifestation. Nonetheless, the culmination of history will come in the third *status*.

Joachim visualized history in two *diffinitiones: diffinito alpha*, a pattern of threes in which the Trinity was revealed and symbolized in the triangular shape of the letter alpha (A). But there are only two dispensations: two covenants, two testaments. This is the *diffinitio omega*, a pattern of twos represented by the circles of the letter ω, with the parallel streams each moving toward its own advent (the first and second comings). Joachim saw a third stream emerging from the middle stroke of the letter; history is fulfilled in two parts, but a third hovers over them, auguring a new quality of life rather than a new institution. The Roman Church will stand till the second coming, as the synagogue stood till the first, but in the third *status* the Church's quality of life will move from that of the *ecclesia activa* to *ecclesia contemplativa*. Twos represent authority, threes spirituality.

Twelve was the number for understanding the Bible and history: There were twelve patriarchs in the Old Testament and twelve apostles/churches in the New Testament; twelve married people, twelve clerics. These patterns must be followed by twelve monasteries and twelve monks/abbots (celibate people). But this number can be subdivided still further: Five of the patriarchs received their inheritances first, seven later. The five churches of Saint Peter were founded before the seven of Saint John. Five are the physical senses, seven the spiritual gifts. Five therefore is the number of things exterior, prior, material; seven is the number of things interior, posterior, spiritual. The twelve monasteries partake of the same division: Five are Cistercian monasteries, the other seven Joachim refused to name. The five tribes, churches, senses, and monasteries represent the uncompleted inheritance of the first and second *status*; the seven tribes, churches, and spiritual gifts represent the final inheritance of the third *status*. The threes of the earlier pattern can be superimposed on this pattern; the double movement of the Holy Spirit means that there are two other eremitical movements before the last: one with Elijah, Elisha, and the sons of the prophets, the second with Saint *Benedict and his disciples.

Joachim expected two new orders of spiritual men to lead the Church into the third *status*: one eremitical order to suffer for the Church on the mountain top; the other a preaching order to work in the world. It is in this regard that Joachim's influence was most felt. He resolutely refused to name these orders or the other monasteries, but his writings did allow others to "finish" interpreting history for him. Joachim had a profound effect on Dante and many other writers, as well as on many of the heretical sects operating in the thirteenth and fourteenth centuries. The debate about his orthodoxy has gone on ever since.

Bibliography: M. Reeves, *Joachim of Fiore and the Prophetic Future*, 1976; F. Robb, "The Fourth Lateran Council's Definition of Trinitarian Orthodoxy," *Journal of Ecclesiastical History* 48.1 (January 1997): 22–43.

Andrea Schutz

JOHN DUNS SCOTUS (1266–1308). Known also as the Subtle Doctor or the Marian Doctor, Scotus was one of the most influential medieval philosophers.

Scotus was born in Duns, Scotland, and attended a local grammar school. At a young age, probably twelve or thirteen, Scotus went with two Franciscans to Oxford. He entered the Franciscan Order there and began his studies in arts at the Franciscan house. It is likely that many of his commentaries on Aristotle's logical and psychological works (*Categories, Perihermenias, Sophistici Elenchi, De anima*) as well as his *Questions on Porphyry's Isagoge* date from this period.

After completing the equivalent of an arts degree, Scotus embarked on a doctorate in theology at Oxford, probably at the age of twenty-one. Our first certain date in his Oxford career is 17 March 1291 when he was ordained to the priesthood. Although some scholars have argued that Scotus spent part of the 1290s attending lectures and lecturing at the theological faculty at Paris, it seems that he continued his theological studies at Oxford throughout the decade, lecturing on *Peter Lombard's *Sentences* there throughout the latter half of the 1290s. By the summer of 1300, Scotus had begun to revise or "order" these lectures, thereby editing his first major theological work, the *Ordinatio*. Also in the summer of 1300, the English provincial Hugh of Hertilpole recommended that Scotus, along with twenty other Franciscans, be licensed to hear confessions. Although he was not one of the eight friars selected, this request would seem to indicate that Scotus intended to finish the theological program at Oxford. However, in 1302 he was selected, presumably by his provincial, to be sent to Paris for theological studies.

He started at Paris in fall 1302 and began his Parisian lectures on Lombard's *Sentences* while studying under the master Gonsalvus of Spain. Before he completed his first academic year there, the dispute between Pope *Boniface VIII and King Philip IV over the taxation of the clergy and Church property grew more heated. Throughout spring 1303, Philip and his chief minister Guillaume Nogaret attempted to publicize and win support for the view that Boniface was in fact an illegitimate pope who should be deposed. After an antipapal demonstration in Paris in June 1303, royal commissioners were sent to the Franciscan convent to determine which friars still sympathized with Boniface. As Scotus and Gonsalvus continued to side with Boniface, they were exiled from France. Scotus presumably went back to Oxford, although some scholars speculate that he might have gone to Cambridge.

Boniface suspended the University of Paris' right to grant degrees in theology and canon law in August 1303 but died in October of that year after being humiliated at Anagni by Nogaret. In April 1304, the following pope, Benedict

XI, lifted the ban on the university, and Scotus and Gonsalvus returned. Shortly thereafter, Gonsalvus was elected minister general of the Franciscan Order. In November 1304, Gonsalvus recommended that Scotus be promoted to regent master of theology at Paris.

Scotus incepted in theology in spring 1305, and he participated in ordinary and quodlibetal disputations as a regent theologian. In either Advent 1306 or Lent 1307 he participated in a solemn quodlibetal dispute. While master at Paris, Scotus also seems to have continued to revise his *Ordinatio*, his Parisian lectures on the *Sentences*, and his *Questions on Aristotle's Metaphysics*, which he presumably first wrote as an arts student at Oxford.

In summer 1307, Scotus was sent to teach at the Franciscan house at Cologne. Scholars have generally assumed that he was forced to leave Paris due to his controversial teachings on the theological issue of the Immaculate Conception of the Virgin Mary. Alternately, he may have been forced to flee due to his opposition to King Philip IV's planned policy to suppress the Order of Knights Templar. At any rate, he left Paris in a hurry, as he left all of his personal books there. He began teaching at Cologne in fall 1307; however, he died in the following year at the age of forty-two. The last record of his life is dated February 1308.

Despite his short life, Scotus was a prolific writer. Due to his unexpected death, none of his works were officially published, and many of them were left in an unfinished state. He wrote four commentaries on Lombard's *Sentences*: the *Lectura* (on books one and two of the *Sentences*) and the *Ordinatio* (both works at Oxford), his *Reportata parisiensia* (at Paris), and his *Lectura cantabrigiensis* (at Cambridge—although it is still unclear when he was at Cambridge). In addition to his commentaries on the *Sentences*, he also commented extensively on the Aristotelian corpus. All of his Aristotelian commentaries were probably completed at Oxford (although some may have been edited at Paris). His *Questions on Aristotle's Metaphysics* seems to have been comprised of two works: a literal commentary on Aristotle's *Metaphysics*, which no longer exists, and scholastic questions on themes raised throughout the *Metaphysics*. Scotus' *Questions* on this work, in their final form, were heavily edited and revised and probably did not take their final form until the 1300s, as they reveal much of his more mature metaphysical and theological points. He also wrote a *Treatise on the First Principle* (*Tractatus de primo principio*), which contains his proof for the existence of God, and his *Quodlibet*, published under the English title of *God and Creatures*. Many of the texts edited by Wadding in the seventeenth century and published as Scotus' *Opera omnia* are in fact not by the Subtle Doctor.

Scotus is equally remembered as a metaphysician and a theologian. His works combine an older Augustinian approach to theology with the newer Aristotelianism. He differed from Thomas *Aquinas on several points, namely, by placing primacy in the will rather than reason. Like Thomas, however, he agrees that reason does not contradict revelation. Unlike him, however, he holds that the principle of individuation is not inherent in matter but rather lies in a third principle superimposed on matter and form called *haecceitas*. The *Ordinatio* reveals great knowledge of the current philosophical and theological issues under debate and contains many implicit and explicit references to contemporary theologians such as *Henry of Ghent and *Godfrey of Fontaines.

After Scotus' death, his students edited his works and circulated them. The Scotistic synthesis later became the doctrinal basis of the Franciscan Order. Both in life and in death, however, Scotus had his critics, and the word *dunce* (derived from Duns) was later used to describe the labyrinthine system of argumentation he used and to denigrate his followers.

Bibliography: A. B. Wolter, "Reflections on the Life and Works of Scotus," *American Catholic Philosophical Quarterly* 67 (1993): 1–36.

Andrew G. Traver

JOHN OF ENGLAND (1167–1216). Unpopular king of England from 1199 to 1216, he lost most of the English lands in France and caused England to suffer a papal interdict; his unpopularity in England led to baronial revolt and his eventual signing of the Magna Carta.

John was the youngest son of King *Henry II and *Eleanor of Aquitaine. Because he was born after his father's first attempt to divide his domains among his sons, he acquired the nickname of "Lackland." Eventually, John was designated to receive Ireland, but he was no more satisfied by this than his brothers and joined in the last of their revolts, which resulted in their father's death in 1189. John's elder brother, *Richard I, then succeeded to all of their father's possessions. John held his lordship of Ireland and other estates from Richard. During Richard's crusade and captivity, John maneuvered to increase his power in England, but when Richard returned, the brothers were reconciled.

On Richard's death in 1199, there were two possible successors. John's rival was his brother Geoffrey's son Arthur, count of Brittany, a boy of twelve or thirteen. Geoffrey, who had died in 1186, was older than John. Many thought that his son should not be excluded merely because his father had died prematurely. England and Aquitaine preferred the adult to the child, but the northern French provinces chose Arthur. John, however, offered *Philip II of France a very large payment for the right to inherit all his brother's French lands, and Philip recognized him. By 1200, therefore, John had control of all his family's possessions.

John then made a tour of the French lands, especially Aquitaine, where he was not well known. On this journey, he attended the marriage of Isabella of Angoulême, daughter of a prominent Aquitainian lord, to another great lord, Hugh of Lusignan. John decided to marry Isabella himself. He did so without compensating Hugh, who complained to Philip II. Because Philip was John's lord for his French possessions, his court was the proper place for a complaint against John's conduct in France; however, John's dignity as king of England did not permit him to appear for judgment by the French king. When he did not come, Philip's court in 1202 declared John in contempt and confiscated all his French possessions. War followed. During it, in 1203, John captured Arthur, who was never seen again. Rumors soon spread that John had murdered him.

By 1204, John had lost most of the northern French possessions of his family. He retained only Aquitaine, and even that was reduced in size. This disaster was not popular with the barons of England, most of whom had Norman origins. Many had estates on both sides of the Channel. John's troubles grew worse after his mother, a steadying influence, died in 1204, and the archbishop of Canterbury, Hubert Walter, died the next year. A disputed election to the archbishopric led Pope *Innocent III to reject both candidates, one of whom John favored. Instead Innocent appointed Stephen *Langton, but John refused to accept him. In an attempt to coerce him, the pope placed an interdict on England in 1208 and excommunicated the king in 1209.

John's constant presence in England after 1204 led him to take an active role in governing the kingdom, but his high-handed and rapacious rule made him very unpopular. A plot to assassinate him came to nothing in 1212, perhaps because the barons still hoped that John would successfully recover the lands lost in 1204. About the same time, John began negotiations with the pope, which led to his acceptance of Langton and the end of the excommunication and the interdict. As part of the reconciliation, John surrendered England to the pope, receiving it back as a fief, and issued a charter granting various liberties to the Church in England.

Faced with invasions from France and the defeat of his allies at the battle of Bouvines in 1214, John retreated to England. This was, for many barons, the last straw, and they revolted. Although the rebels secured possession of London, enough lords continued to side with John so that a near stalemate occurred. The result in June 1215 was a negotiated settlement embodying various concessions by the king, soon nicknamed Magna Carta ("the great charter"). Within a few months, however, John got the pope to quash the charter. As a result the baronial revolt flared up again, worse than before, and the barons invited Philip II's son Louis to take the throne if he could. John's opponents had him on the run when he died on 19 October 1216. His nine-year old son *Henry III succeeded him.

Bibliography: J. C. Holt, *Magna Carta*, 2d ed., 1992; R. Turner, *King John*, 1994; W. L. Warren, *King John*, 2d ed., 1978.

Emily Tabuteau

JOHN OF GARLAND (C. 1195–C. 1272).

John of Garland was a medieval grammarian, rhetorician, and educator.

John was born in England around 1195. He studied at Oxford in the early thirteenth century, where he heard lectures on natural philosophy by John of London. In 1217 or 1218 he went to Paris and taught there for most of his life. He settled on the Left Bank in the *clos de Garlande*, from which he took his surname. In 1229, he was one of two grammarians chosen to teach at the new University of Toulouse. He then wrote an open letter praising the attractions of Toulouse, where students were allowed to read books by Aristotle on natural philosophy forbidden in Paris at the time. While in Toulouse, he witnessed the crusade that the Church was waging against the Albigensian heretics. He supported the suppression of heresy through polemical writings like *De triumphis ecclesiae* (The Triumph of the Church) (finished around 1252). When in 1231–1232 the count of Toulouse proved dilatory in paying his salary, Garland left Toulouse. He may have returned to England for a time to tutor the royal princes, but he was back in Paris by 1241. He may have lived until 1272.

During his lengthy teaching career, John of Garland wrote treatises on grammatical, logical, rhetorical, and moral topics, including the *Morale scholarium* (1241), a poetic work exhorting students to live up to the manners of the scholar, and *Stella maris* (before 1249), another poetic work on the Virgin Mary. The *Parisiana poetria* is perhaps his best-known work today (c. 1220, revised 1231–1235). It is a rhetorical work teaching students the mechanics of the *ars poetriae* (the art of poetry), one of the main divisions of medieval rhetoric. The art taught both poetry and prose composition and was part of the study of literature in many medieval universities. John's *Poetria* is similar to books by Matthew of Vendôme and Geoffrey of Vinsauf. All of John's works are marked by the deliberately ornate style that was so admired by his contemporaries.

Bibliography: T. Lawler, ed., *The* Parisiana poetria *of John of Garland*, 1974.

Kimberly Rivers

JOHN (JEAN) OF JOINVILLE (C. 1225–1317).

French nobleman and hereditary seneschal of Champagne, he accompanied King *Louis IX on crusade; he is the author of the *Life of St. Louis*, a biography of the king and an important document for the history of the Seventh Crusade.

Born in c. 1225, he joined the Seventh Crusade in 1248 where he became a close friend and comrade in arms of King Louis IX, Saint Louis. In the aftermath of serious illness, Saint Louis had vowed to recover Jerusalem but was never to arrive in the Holy City; rather, he engaged in subduing the Turks in Egypt. Joinville took part in the crusade to Egypt, where in 1250 he was taken prisoner with the king. After their release, Joinville served as royal steward at Acre (1250–1254) where he wrote a new explanation of the Creed, which contains information concerning his captivity. He returned to France with the king and queen in 1254. In later life, Joinville divided his time between the management of his estates and attending the royal court. However, in 1267, despite the urging of Saint Louis, he refused to participate in the Eighth Crusade to Tunis where Saint Louis died. In 1282, Joinville was one of the participants in the canonization process, and he erected an altar to the saint in his chapel at Joinville. He died in 1317 and was buried in Joinville.

Shortly after Saint Louis' death in 1272, Joinville began the first section of the *Life of St. Louis*, his prose account of the saint's life and career. Here he has collected illustrations of the king's piety and exemplary life, including his own reminiscences of shared conversations, with events of the king's early reign. He emphasizes important facets of the king's character: his just administration, his honorable dealing with subjects and equals, and his devotion to the Christian faith.

During 1298–1309, John undertook the second part of the *Life of St. Louis* at the request of Jeanne of Navarre, wife of Philip IV. John's close relationship with Saint Louis informs this section of his account. Rather than focusing solely on political or military events, John relates discrete episodes that illustrate the king's fortitude during illness, his courage during war and captivity, and his warmth to his close associates. The portrait he provides shows Saint Louis as a good Christian but also a good king and friend. Nonetheless, Joinville provides at times a more critical view than others of Saint Louis' contemporary biographers. He does not always approve of the king's approach to political problems. Joinville's first-person narrative provides his observations, and examples from their conversations provide a vivid picture of their shared experiences. He also provides a number of vignettes of the cultural practices he observed while on crusade. Joinville's intellectual curiosity and direct approach to biography makes it one of the most valuable accounts of the social and military life of his age.

Bibliography: M. K. Billson III, "Joinville's *Histoire de Saint-Louis*: Hagiography, History, and Memoir," *American Benedictine Review* 31 (1980): 418–442. John of Joinville, *Life of Saint Louis*, in *Chronicles of the Crusades*, ed. M.R.B. Shaw, 1963.

Patricia Price

JOHN OF PLANO CARPINI (GIOVANNI DE PLANO CARPINI) (1180–1252).

John of Plano Carpini, a Franciscan friar, conducted a diplomatic mission for Pope *Innocent IV to the court of the Mongol khan during 1245 and 1247 and wrote the first European account of the Mongols.

Between 1237 and 1242, the armies of the hitherto unknown Mongols devastated Russia and eastern Europe, and only the death of their Great Khan Ogadai in 1241 brought the carnage to an end. Mongol forces withdrew to the East to participate in determining the succession. Meanwhile, the papacy and various European rulers were panic-stricken by the new threat posed by the Mongols, or Tartars as the medieval Europeans called them. Europe's rulers desperately needed accurate information about Mongol intentions and to open up diplomatic relations.

On Easter 1245, Pope Innocent IV ordered the first of the so-called Mongol missions and sent the Franciscan friar John of Plano Carpini as an envoy to the Mongol khan. Carpini, a native of the region around Perugia in Italy, was an excellent choice for such a sensitive and dangerous assignment. As a Franciscan, he belonged to a new religious order that still possessed the full fervor and commitment of youth. Carpini had been one of Saint *Francis' early disciples. From 1222 onward, he had played a significant role in the establishment of the Franciscan Order in Germany, the lands of Scandinavia, and eastern Europe. In addition to these experiences, the order's strong emphasis on poverty and asceticism gave him the discipline and stamina needed to survive the long, difficult, and potentially deadly journey to and from the Mongol Empire's heartland.

On 16 April 1245, the sixty-five-year old, portly John departed from Lyon and reached the Mongol great camp on 22 July just in time to witness the election of Guyuk as Great Khan. Much of Carpini's successful traveling was due to his being able to utilize the Mongol post horse system called *Yams*. This circumstance allowed Carpini to travel across central Asia on horseback with access to frequent remounts. In two and a half years, he traveled over 15,000 miles. It was a taxing ordeal involving hunger, thirst, cold, heat, injury, and possibly hostile natives. Returning to the pope in November 1247, Carpini's mission accomplished little diplomatically. Mongol rulers were only interested in submissive vassals, not allies.

After he returned home, Carpini wrote an account of his journey titled *Historia Mongolorum* (History of the Mongols), which provided much valuable information and was the first European description of Mongolia and China. While Carpini never achieved the fame of his near-contemporary Marco *Polo, the information about Asia that he brought back to Europe made its way into various encyclopedic works of history and geography, particularly *Vincent of Beauvais' widely read *Speculum historiale*, which largely copied Carpini's *Historia*. Roger *Bacon also used Carpini in the writing of the geographical section of his great survey of human knowledge, the *Opus Maius*. Because Europe lost contact with the Far East when the Ming dynasty ousted the Mongols from China in 1368, European knowledge of China remained static and increasingly obsolete. Columbus and other European explorers expected to reach the Cathay and Tartary of Carpini and Marco Polo, not the China of the Mings in the sixteenth century.

Bibliography: J.R.S. Phillips, *The Medieval Expansion of Europe*, 2d ed., 1998.

Ronald H. Fritze

JOHN OF SALISBURY (C. 1115/1120–1180). Certainly a skilled diplomat, gifted teacher, and noted ecclesiastic, John of Salisbury's primary importance is as the author of a number of Latin philosophical and historical works. His two major books, the *Metalogicon*, on Aristotelian logic, and the political treatise *Policratus* especially mark him as a great man of learning and a humanist whose eloquent literary Latin stands out in the renaissance of the twelfth century.

John was born in Old Sarum (near Salisbury), England, and very little is known of his early life. In 1136, he went to Paris to undertake university study, and it was there that he began his association with some of the greatest figures of his time. His first teacher was the scholastic philosopher Peter *Abelard, and he later studied under Robert of Melun, *William of Conches in Chartres, and possibly *Gilbert of Poitiers. With these men, John studied the trivium (grammar, rhetoric, and dialectic) as well as some of the more advanced sciences of the quadrivium (arithmetic, astronomy, music, and geometry). Supporting himself by teaching, and with some patronage of men like his student and friend Peter of Celle, John studied in Paris and Chartres for twelve years before, according to his own account of ecclesiastic events, the *Historia Pontificalis*, he joined the papal court of *Eugenius III in 1148, attending the Synod of Rheims.

John's six years with the papal court in Rome were valuable experience that put him at the center of Church matters and politics, as well as allowed him access to some of the faith's most important leaders. His service so impressed *Bernard of Clairvaux that he wrote John a letter of recommendation to Theobald, archbishop of Canterbury, to whom John became secretary in 1154. John's return to England brought him home and into the mounting tensions between the primate of England and King *Henry II of England, which later came to a head while he served Theobald's successor, Thomas *Becket.

Under Theobald, John was sent on three diplomatic missions to the papal court. In 1155–1156, he successfully appealed to his countryman Nicholas Breakspear, who had ascended as Pope *Hadrian IV, for Henry II's investiture with Ireland. He made two other visits to the court in Rome: in 1156–1157 and in 1158–1159 on a mission to mitigate some disfavor toward Theobald held by some Roman cardinals. John's conduct on this latter mission was reported to Henry II as damaging to the king; this, coupled with John's support of ecclesiastical rights, gave rise to problems between John and the monarch.

In 1162, when Thomas Becket succeeded Theobald, these tensions were exacerbated. Becket had served the king as chancellor, but upon his ascendance to the archbishopric, he began a campaign to reclaim lands and rights from the crown. After numerous bitter conflicts with Henry II, Becket was driven to exile in France where he joined John, already in exile there. Six years later, when a degree of reconciliation was achieved between Henry and Becket, they returned from France, and thus John was present in Canterbury when Thomas was murdered in the cathedral on 29 December 1170. John had always preached moderation to Becket, and thus he was allowed to stay on as secretary to Becket's successor Archbishop Richard. In 1176, the French King *Louis VII summoned John to become bishop of Chartres, and it is there that John finished his career and died in 1180.

John's two most important works, the *Metalogicon* and the *Policratus*, were composed in the years of Henry II's disfavor. These two works are as much the rich products of the revival of classical learning as the political and cultural tensions John experienced. While the *Metalogicon* preserves not only a consideration of the trivium and especially Aristotelian logic, it also is a personal memoir of the teachers John worked with in his youth.

The *Metalogicon* is a defense of the trivium and one of the first European commentaries on the lately rediscovered (to the Latin West) *Organon* of Aristotle. Though the work is wide-ranging and encyclopedic, John's aims are clear: He attacks those who detract from the study of the trivium (calling them Cornifucians) and then proceeds to elucidate notions of Aristotelian genera and species. Genera and species, he claims, are not things but forms of things that are compared, abstracted, and unified in universals by the mind, and thus they are fictions and do not correspond to extramental reality. The real can only be grasped through the eloquence, learning, and dialectic of the trivium. As John covers his materials, he also reflects upon the twelfth-century masters of his youth in Paris and Chartres and thus has left not only an explication of logic and its place in the trivium but also memorable portraits of his teachers.

John addressed his *Policratus* (statesmen's book) to Thomas Becket while Becket was still chancellor to Henry II. While largely mined for its political theory, it ranges over many topics including dreams, literature, hunting, gambling, court, music, books, and social well-being. However, it was John's political contemplation on the king and the law, including a justification of tyrannicide, that had the most influence in the following centuries. John insisted that the ruler was not above natural law, and envisioning the state as a body with the monarch at its head and the Church as its heart, he claims that the head must rule the body sanely and moderately. If the head is corrupting or destructive to its body in violation of natural or fitting law, he must be removed by God or God's agent: justifiable tyrranicide. The *Policratus* is not intended to be radical or revolutionary but rather moderate, as John was throughout his active life, and to reinforce the rights of the Church in England.

While these two works are John of Salisbury's major contributions, he wrote a number of other shorter works, including the memoir of his time in the papal court, the *Historia Pontificalis*, numerous letters, and two hagiographical works: lives of *Anselm of Canterbury and his own master and friend Thomas Becket. John's learning, perceptions, and eloquent Latinity reveal him as a renaissance man and humanist of his age.

Bibliography: John of Salisbury, *Policratus*, ed. and trans. C. J. Nederman, 1990; C. C. Webb, *John of Salisbury*, 1932; M. Wilks, ed., *The World of John of Salisbury*, 1984.

Matthew Hussey

JOHN SCOTTUS ERIUGENA (ERIGENA) (FL. 850–870; D. C. 877–879).

Translator, exegete, poet, and philosopher, John Scottus Eriugena was a highly original thinker and man of letters in a period generally marked by little original philosophical speculation.

The philosopher's name simply translates as "John of Ireland," "Scottus" meaning "Irish" in the ninth century, and "Eriugena" translating as "of Irish birth." Eriugena was probably educated in an Irish monastery, and though the extent of Irish scholarship and learning in the eighth and ninth centuries has been somewhat exaggerated, Eriugena was certainly a highly learned man, with admirable command of Greek—a not uncommon feature of Irish learning in the period. Whether he was a cleric or layman is not known.

For reasons that have not come down to us, Eriugena chose to leave Ireland and immigrate to the Carolingian domain of *Charles II the Bald, the grandson of *Charlemagne. Charles had a vigorous interest in learning and the arts, and Eriugena first appears in the historical record as a teacher at Charles' "palace school" in 850 or 851. The exact nature and location of this school are a matter of dispute; it was perhaps associated in some way with the cathedral school at Laon, where a number of learned Irish émigrés, including Sedulius Scottus, formed a community.

Eriugena's works belong mostly to the 860s. His early work included glosses and a commentary on the *De nuptiis Philologiae et Mercurii* of Martianus Capella that demonstrate his Neoplatonic leanings. He was invited by *Hincmar of Rheims to participate in a theological dispute over predestination; the result was Eriugena's *De praedestinatione* (850–851), a treatise that did not please any of the participants in the controversy. In its originality of approach and thought, the work's speculative and rational tone initiated the reputation of Eriugena as a borderline heretical thinker.

In 858, he began to translate the works of *Pseudo-Dionysius the Areopagite from Greek to Latin; Pseudo-Dionysius' works had been given to *Louis the Pious by the Byzantine Emperor Michael Balbus in 827 and thence passed into the hands of Charles the Bald, who commissioned Eriugena to the task. Eriugena not only translated the fifth-century eastern philosopher's works, but he also composed a commentary on them. From his acquaintance with Pseudo-Dionysius, Eriugena absorbed the concepts of Neoplatonic procession and return, and the preference for negative (apophatic) over positive (cataphatic) theology so fundamental to his own philosophy. His other translations included the *Ambigua ad Johannem* and *Quaestiones ad Thalassium* of Maximus the Confessor and the *De imagine* of Gregory of Nyssa. Eriugena also composed a homily on the prologue to the Gospel of John and an unfinished commentary on the Gospel of John proper. He wrote poetry, marked by the use of Greek vocabulary, on religious topics such as the passion and incarnation of Christ, Saint Denis, and panegyric verses to Charles and his queen. Only a few of Eriugena's poems are personal in nature.

The *De divisione naturae* (or *Periphyseon*) was composed between 862 and 866. It is his most important work, an entire complex philosophical system in five books, cast in dialogue form between a "Master" and "Pupil." In the work, Eriugena endeavors to explain the workings of the entire universe by breaking down Nature into four categories. In his analysis he shows the influence of Neoplatonic thought, the *via negativa* of Pseudo-Dionysius, as well as of Western thinkers such as Augustine. To an extent, Eriugena sought to reconcile the insights of Pseudo-Dionysius within an overall framework of Augustinian theology.

In the *De divisione naturae*, "Nature" refers to all of reality, including God and, literally, things "supernatural": that which is and also that which is not. There are four categories of Nature:

1. *Nature which creates and is not created.* This refers to God, who creates but is Himself without cause. God is the Beginning, the First Cause. To understand God, one can utilize the *via negativa* or the *via affirmativa*, that is, respectively, apophatic and cataphatic theology. Within the terms of positive theology, one can begin to understand God by describing what he is; within the terms of negative theology, one can understand God by declaring what he is not. In his discussion of Nature, which creates and is not created, Eriugena stresses the essential unity of God, even in differentiation. God supersedes all; there is nothing outside of Him or beyond Him. God resides in all things, giving us the basis for the second and third types of Nature.

2. *Nature which is created and creates.* This division refers to the primordial causes, through which the First Cause (God) proceeds out to all creatures, into the various forms of Nature. All creatures participate in the procession of the First Cause (God) through the primordial causes. Yet these primordial causes remain part of God the Father through His aspect as the Word (Jesus), or divine wisdom, through which all things are conceived.

3. *Nature which is created and does not create.* These are the creatures of Nature in the usual sense; they participate in the primordial causes just as the primordial causes participate in God. Here we can see the influence of the hierarchical notions of Pseudo-Dionysius. Eriugena thus argues that through this process of participation created Nature is within God, so to speak, co-eternal with God, and not in any way external to Him. Man falls into this category.

4. *Nature which neither creates nor is created.* This division comprises God alone; God as the End. Here God is the site of the return of the Neoplatonic procession into Nature. This is the home of the soul after death, as it longs to return to the site of its original procession.

Although Eriugena's immediate impact after his death was rather minimal, he did exert a certain influence upon thinkers in the twelfth century such as *Alan of Lille and Honorius of Autun. However, Eriugena's perceived tendency toward pantheism, and the great importance he placed upon rational inquiry, as opposed to authority, made his work a bit suspect. Through its use by the Albigensians, and Amalric of Bena, the *De divisione naturae* was condemned by Pope *Honorius III in 1225 and all copies ordered to be incinerated. Eriugena's translation and commentary of Pseudo-Dionysius exerted a greater influence, finding its way into the work of Thomas *Aquinas and Meister Eckhart.

Bibliography: Iohannis Scotti Eriugenae, *Carmina*, ed. M. W. Herren, 1993; J. J. O'Meara, *Eriugena*, 1988.

Andrew Scheil

JORDANES (WROTE C. 554). Jordanes was a historian at Constantinople whose short history of the Goths has been seminal in shaping modern accounts of Germanic history and prehistory.

Known only from his own writings, Jordanes states that his grandfather had served as a secretary to a barbarian leader and that he himself had been secretary to a Gothic general in the eastern Roman army. His father and possibly grandfather had barbarian names, suggesting descent from either Alans or Goths. Jordanes makes a comment often assumed to state that he himself was a Goth, but the wording is ambiguous. After some form of religious conversion, he wrote two historical works, almost simultaneously, at the request of friends: a short epitome of Roman history, in the dry style of the historical breviaries produced in the fourth century by Eutropius; and a short *Origin and Deeds of the Getae* (often called *Getica*; the Getae were an ancient tribe assimilated with the Goths by late antique writers). The latter, in its often extravagant account, is quite different from the Roman history. Jordanes states that he loosely paraphrased the lost Gothic history of *Cassiodorus, a court servant of *Theodoric; the extent of his dependence has been much debated, with some scholars wishing to see the extant *Getica* as an accurate abridgement of a propagandistic work produced for the Gothic kings of Italy, others seeing Jordanes as exploiting many earlier histories to produce a work with its own agenda. Though Jordanes praises the Goths in the *Getica*, the work is not pro-Gothic propaganda; like the Roman history, the *Getica* concludes with the celebration of the destruction of the Gothic kingdom in Italy by the armies of *Justinian, which was being completed at the time Jordanes wrote.

Jordanes' Gothic history was used throughout the Middle Ages into the Renaissance, especially for histories of kingdoms wishing to claim the Goths as forebears, including Spain (for instance, the thirteenth-century history by Bishop Rodrigo Ximenius of Rada), Sweden, and Austria. It was from the sixteenth century, however, that the *Getica* became a crucial text. Northern European scholars, such as the brothers Johannes and Olaus Magnus (published 1554, 1555), sought to lay claim to an alternative Germanic antiquity rivaling that of the Greco-Roman past. Jordanes' *Getica*, together with the *Germania* of Tacitus and the newly discovered Gothic translation of the Bible by Ufilas, was used to show the alleged antiquity of Germanic cultural continuity. It propagated the terms "Visigoth" and "Ostrogoth," not in fact used as ethnic identifiers by the Goths themselves. Jordanes' mention of Decineus, whom he claimed had taught philosophy to the Goths in antiquity (the story was ultimately derived from Herodotus, concerning much earlier barbarians) suggested cultural parity of the early Germanic tribes with the ancient Mediterranean world, and his account of the early Goths' migration from "Scandza" in the cold north was used to argue for the historical unity of northern European peoples including the Scandinavians. Such claims remain very influential on Germanic studies today.

Bibliography: W. Goffart, *Narrators of Barbarian History* (A.D. *550–800): Jordanes, Gregory of Tours, Bede, and Paul the Deacon*, 1988.

Andrew Gillett

JUSTINIAN I (C. 482–565, R. 527–565).

(Eastern) Roman emperor, Justinian reconquered the Western Roman Empire, had the church of Santa Sophia rebuilt, and codified Roman law.

Born about 482 possibly near modern Nish in Serbia, Petrus Sabbatius Justinianus was adopted by his Uncle Justin, who gave him an excellent education in Constantinople. In 518, Justin became emperor as Justin I, and his nephew eventually officially shared power as co-emperor until becoming emperor in his turn in 527. He married, in 525, his only wife *Theodora, who had herself been a performer. He also met in the 520s many of the men who were to be his associates and generals through much of his life: the treasurer John of Cappadocia, the military genius Belisarius, the legal expert Tribonian, the eunuch Narses. His life and achievements are especially closely linked with the characters and accomplishments of Theodora and Belisarius.

The early part of his reign was marked by successes; he quelled the Nika riots of 532, when it seemed for a time that his throne was in jeopardy. According to *Procopius, his biographer, it was the Empress Theodora who stiffened his resolve by saying that "the purple is the noblest shroud." He gave to the mathematician and architect Anthemius of Tralles the task of rebuilding the church of Santa Sophia (Hagia Sophia), burned during these disturbances. This enormous domed church, now converted into a mosque, still stands today. His most notable contribution to world civilization was also largely completed during the first years of his reign; he assembled a team of distinguished jurists under the chairmanship of Tribonian to codify the Roman law as the *Corpus iuris civilis*, published in 529–533. This enormous work was to be rediscovered in the West in the late eleventh century and has since then never ceased to dominate legal thinking in the "civil law" countries (most of western Europe and its colonies). Roman law gradually infiltrated and often replaced local customary law during the twelfth and thirteenth centuries and was taught in the schools.

The (Eastern) Roman Empire of Justinian's time was the site of some religious controversy. In the previous century, the Nestorians, who believed that Christ was in the fullest sense a man, on whom the divine nature had been superimposed, had been condemned in Church councils, as had the Monophysites, of whom the Empress Theodora may have been one. They believed that Christ was essentially divine and that there was no conflict in him between a human and a divine nature. The Nestorians survived in central Asia, where missionaries still found them as late as the fourteenth century. If much of the empire was orthodox, Egypt and Syria were strongly Monophysite, and some accommodations had to be made for these religious differences.

Justinian's great project, however, was to reconquer the Western Roman Empire that had been overrun by mostly Germanic tribes in the previous century. Thanks largely to the military genius of his generals Belisarius and Narses, he was successful in retaking western North Africa (modern Tunisia) from the Vandals and in reclaiming Italy from the Ostrogoths. He even established a foothold in Spain. These gains were, of course, wiped out in the seventh century by the Lombards (Italy) and the armies of Islam (Africa and Spain) in the seventh and eighth centuries.

Justinian's conquests often depended on considerable sea power, and his war galleys and troop transports were often used to good effect in the African and Italian campaigns. His armies consisted of cavalry and infantry, and his generals, especially Belisarius, often had at their command a special body of soldiers who were highly trained and loyal: the comitatus. These men fought in armor on horseback, with spear, sword, and above all, the bow. Also traveling with the Roman army were auxiliaries such as Isaurians, Saracens, and especially Huns.

Toward the end of his reign, Justinian fared less well. The 532 peace with the Persian Empire was breached in the early 540s, and King Khusro made raids into Palestine, including the capture and sack of Antioch. An outbreak of the bubonic plague occurred in 542–543, which killed a large proportion of the population and ruined the economy. Justinian himself contracted the disease. Theodora died in 548, and the last years of Justinian's reign were marked by other disasters, such as the collapse of the dome of Santa Sophia, a war in Lazica, and incursions by Slavs and Huns. It was in these years that Justinian, according to Procopius, took to walking the palace at all hours of the night, even, it was rumored, without his head. When he died in 565, he had outlived all his associates except Narses.

Bibliography: R. Browning, *Justinian and Theodora*, 1971; J. B. Bury, *A History of the Later Roman Empire from the Death of Theodosius to the Death of Justinian*, 2 vols., 1923; Procopius, *Works*, trans. H. B. Dewing and G. Downey, 7 vols., 1914–1940.

F.R.P. Akehurst

K

KHAYYĀM, 'UMAR. *See* 'UMAR KHAYYĀM.

KILWARDBY, ROBERT (C. 1215–1279). English scholar and prelate, Robert Kilwardby was born c. 1215, perhaps in Yorkshire. He studied in Paris around the years 1231–1237 and taught at the faculty of Arts until 1245; Roger *Bacon was probably one of his students. Several didactic works of logic, grammar, and ethics belong to this period; they provide an insight on the teaching curriculum and methodology in the arts faculty. Having returned to England, he entered the Dominican Order and studied theology at Oxford until 1256, when he became regent master in theology at Blackfriars, the Dominican house in Oxford. Among the writings he composed there, *De ortu scientiarum* was one of the first expositions in the West of the Aristotelian division of sciences and had great notoriety. Kilwardby's *Questions* on the four books of *Peter Lombard's *Sentences* show a general Augustinian inspiration, even when presenting Aristotelian doctrines.

Kilwardby rose to considerable prominence inside the Dominican Order and the English Church. He was elected prior provincial in England in 1261 and a second time in 1272. In the same year, Pope Gregory X named him archbishop of Canterbury, the highest ecclesiastical position in England. The duties of this office included supervision of university life. In 1277, he prompted the Oxford masters of theology to issue a condemnation of thirty propositions of grammar, logic, and natural philosophy, the last targeting the doctrine of the unicity of substantial form in substances.

A respected theologian himself, Kilwardby reacted against the Aristotelism of Thomas *Aquinas within the university and the Dominican Order. After the death of *Henry III of England, Kilwardby emerged as a supporter of political stability; he proclaimed *Edward (I) the new king of England and solemnly crowned him two years later. He died in Viterbo on 10 September 1279, one year after his appointment as cardinal bishop of Porto.

Bibliography: A. G. Judy, ed., *De ortu scientiarum*, 1976.

Roberto Plevano

KOMNENA, ANNA. *See* ANNA COMNENA.

KOMNENUS, ALEXIUS. *See* ALEXIUS I COMNENUS.

L

LANFRANC OF BEC (C. 1005–1089). Archbishop of Canterbury (1070–1089), Lanfranc served as an adviser and then justiciar to *William, duke of Normandy and later king of England.

An Italian by birth, Lanfranc studied and practiced law before migrating to Avranches, France, where he pursued theology and the Bible; he later established a school there. In 1042, Lanfranc left Avranches and entered the Benedictine monastery at Bec. He founded another school at Bec where he trained future Pope Alexander II and *Anselm, who later followed him at Bec and Canterbury. Beginning in 1050, Lanfranc defended the doctrine of transubstantiation against the views of *Berengar of Tours, who denied the physical change of the elements.

In 1070, Lanfranc was nominated to the see of Canterbury, where he reorganized the English ecclesiastical establishment, replacing most of the Saxon abbots and bishops with Normans and reaffirming the canon of clerical celibacy at the Winchester Council of 1076. While remaining faithful to Rome, Lanfranc sought to bolster English Church practice, bringing it more into the European mainstream, and to maintain its independence in the face of William's program of political consolidation in the years following the Conquest.

Bibliography: M. T. Gibson, *Lanfranc of Bec*, 1978.

Daniel Kline

LANGTON, STEPHEN (C. 1155–1228). Scholar and theologian, professor at the University of Paris, cardinal and archbishop of Canterbury, Stephen Langton spent several years in exile before taking up his duties as archbishop; he also played an important role in the composition of the Magna Carta.

Langton was born at Langton in Lincolnshire, England, perhaps about 1155, into a family of moderate local importance. Nothing is known of his early life.

He studied at Paris, probably under Peter the Chanter, and became a professor at the university. In 1206, Pope *Innocent III, with whom he had been friends while Innocent was also at the University of Paris, made Langton cardinal-priest of St. Chrysogonus. Langton joined the papal court at Rome, where he may have continued teaching. In December of that year, however, in the pope's presence, the monks of Canterbury cathedral elected him archbishop of Canterbury. This was Innocent's solution to the disputed election to the archbishopric, which had occurred the previous year. King *John of England, who favored one of the candidates whom Innocent rejected, refused to accept Langton's election, and he spent more than six years in exile, a good deal of it at the Cistercian abbey of Pontigny. Only in 1213, after the imposition of an interdict on England in 1208 and the excommunication of John in 1209 had forced the king to give up his opposition, was Langton able to take up his position in England.

Langton arrived in England in July 1213. By then unrest was rife. Within a year, it would lead to the civil war between King John and many of his dissatisfied barons. This conflict was temporarily resolved by the issuance of the Magna Carta in June 1215. Langton undoubtedly played a considerable part in the genesis of the Magna Carta, though different historians have interpreted the exact nature of his role differently. At the least, he served as a mediator between the king and the rebel barons. Possibly it was he who suggested to the barons that the coronation charter of *Henry I of England could serve as a model for the concessions they wanted from the king. He and the other prelates of England are mentioned in the preamble of the document as councilors to the king; and Chapter 55 adds him by name to the board of twenty-five barons who were to oversee the enforcement of the charter, for the specific purpose of deciding on the fairness of fines and amercements.

When Innocent annulled the charter at John's request and ordered Langton to promulgate his sentence of excommunication of the barons who had opposed John, Langton refused. As a result, he was suspended from his functions as archbishop and went into exile from England. While in exile, he attended the Fourth Lateran Council. He did not return to England until the spring of 1218, by which time John was dead and his son *Henry III of England was accepted as king.

The last ten years of Langton's life were devoted to competent, undramatic rule over the English Church. The canons of the Council of Osney, which he held in 1222, applied the decrees of the Fourth Lateran Council in England. After the withdrawal of the pope's personal representative in 1221, Langton also functioned as the king's principal ecclesiastical adviser. He had presided over the young king's solemn coronation in 1220. He headed the English delegation to the French court after the death of *Philip II in 1223, which attempted unsuccessfully to secure the restoration of Normandy to Henry III. He worked to prevent the outbreak of civil war during Henry's minority and had much to do with the king's solemn reissue of the Magna Carta in 1225. He died on 9 July 1228.

While he was at Paris, Langton produced lectures on morality and theology, commentaries on Scripture, and sermons. At the time of his departure from the university, he certainly ranked among its most prominent theologians, though his theological works did not have much influence in later times. His biblical commentaries had more influence on later writers. One of his enduring monuments is the division of the Bible into the chapters still used today, and he may also have been responsible for a slight rearrangement of the order of books in the Vulgate Old Testament. He continued to produce sermons throughout his career. He is almost certainly the author of the Latin hymn "Veni, Sancti Spiritus."

Bibliography: F. M. Powicke, *Stephen Langton*, 1928; P. B. Roberts, *Studies in the Sermons of Stephen Langton*, 1968; J. F. Veal, *The Sacramental Theology of Stephen Langton and the Influence upon Him of Peter the Chanter*, 1955.

Emily Tabuteau

LATINI, BRUNETTO (C. 1220–1294). A Florentine poet, politician, and notary of great distinction, Latini's accomplishments have been overshadowed by his notorious appearance among the Sodomites in Canto 15.22–124 of Dante's *Inferno*. Thanks to this passage, Latini has been known principally as Dante's (and Guido Cavalcante's) teacher; the most likely explanation for this identification is that Dante and Guido trained as notaries under Latini. Nonetheless, Latini was also a major figure in the cultural and political developments of Florence during the second half of the thirteenth century. Latini produced three important literary works in this period along with many shorter works; his services as a notary also left a number of surviving political documents (produced, and occasionally signed, by Latini) that testify to his importance in the councils of empires and independent city–states.

Latini's literary and political careers emerged during a tumultuous phase in Florentine history, a phase dominated by the factional conflicts between Guelph and Ghibelline forces in northern Italy. Crucial to Latini's identity in all his many roles is his training as a notary, a distinguished profession of the governing classes that demanded political and literary skills along with elaborate scribal craftsmanship. He was born to the notary Bonaccorso Latini around 1220. Latini was himself married and had at least one daughter (married in 1248) and two sons. Although little is known of his early life, Latini was a distinguished notary and a member of the Guelph faction by the time he was made syndic of the commune of Montevarchi in February 1260. A few months later he was sent as an envoy, to *Alfonso X the Wise of Castile, to seek Alfonso's support for the Florentine Guelph cause. On 4 September of that year, however, the Guelphs were defeated in the battle of Montaperti by Ghibelline forces commanded by Farinata degli Uberti and supported by King Manfred of Sicily. Latini reports in the *Tesoretto* that he heard this news, from a Bolognese student in the pass of Roncesvalles, on his way back to Florence. Latini consequently detoured to

Montpellier, then settled into exile in France for six years. Surviving letters place him in Arras and Paris in 1263 and Bar sur l'Aube in 1265. During these years Latini wrote a massive encyclopedic work in French, the *Livre dou Trésor*.

On 28 February 1266, Guelph forces supported by *Charles I of Anjou defeated the Ghibellines (and killed King Manfred) in the battle of Benevento; Latini returned to Florence and held a series of important positions in the Florentine commune, including chancellor (1272–1274) and prior (1287). In the first years of his return, Latini also maintained an important political role that may have come from his contacts with the Angevin court during his exile in France. Records show that he served as an Angevin notary in 1271. After Latini's return, he (or members of his circle) translated the *Trésor* into an Italian text known as the *Tesoro*. The *Tesoretto* (Little Treasure) is a separate work, a dream-vision poem quite different from his other "treasures." Once dated to the years of Latini's exile, scholars now place this poem in the later 1280s, along with the *Favolello*. After his death in 1294, Latini was widely eulogized as a master of rhetoric and leader of the Florentine commune.

Latini's interest in the relationship between classical learning and politics reveals his founding role in the Florentine humanism of later centuries. Latini's encyclopedic prose work the *Trésor* consists of three books on philosophy, ethics, and rhetoric, respectively. Each book relies on a compilation of texts from a wide range of sources, from the Bible to Cicero to medieval scholar *Isidore of Seville. Such collections were well known in western Europe, but most early examples were in Latin. Latini's *Trésor* is a particularly rich collection of such texts translated into the vernacular for the benefit of secular governors not trained in Latin as the clergy were. The first book treats a wide variety of topics, covering scholastic philosophy, Church doctrine, and European history, among other points of academic interest. The second book takes up the issues of ethics and economics as they apply to the civic sphere, drawing on Aristotle's *Nichomachean Ethics* and a text by the twelfth-century scholastic *William of Conches. Rhetoric and its uses in politics are favorite topics for Latini, and his third book adapts the *De inventione* by Cicero to instruct governors in the political uses of oratory and writing. A separate work, Latini's *Rettorica*, also builds on his translation of the same Ciceronian text and is part of a series of translations Latini made from Cicero. Some are direct renderings into Italian of famous speeches by Cicero, which had circulated in Latin manuscripts for centuries as rhetorical models. Others are inspired transformations of the original: Latini's *Favolello* is a version of Cicero's *De amicitia* but not a direct translation. Although some of Latini's writing may have originated in the context of Angevin patronage during his exile, all these works finally served the interests of enlightened citizenship in the communal city–state to which Latini devoted his life.

The *Tesoretto* is different from Latini's translations and compilations. This narrative poem is constructed as a dream-vision, patterned on the widely read allegories of *Alan of Lille. However, it also uses "Ser Brunetto" as the dreamer whose waking reality is that of Latini trying to return to Florence from the court of Alfonso the Wise. Latini's fictional alter ego responds to the news of the Guelph defeat at Montaperti by going on a pilgrimage from the Garden of Love through Penitence to a final Cosmic Vision on a mountaintop; the trip is punctuated by dialogues with Nature, the Virtues, Ovid, and Ptolemy. Abstract and authorial personifications mingle suggestively in Latini's vision, as do pilgrimage and the particular concerns of a mature life on the public stages of Florentine politics and power.

Most critical attention to Latini in recent years takes up the question of his fictional encounter with Dante the pilgrim in *Inferno* 15, debating the meaning of sodomy in that context or the basis for such an accusation by a student against his teacher. No factual basis for the charge has ever been discovered, and critics have suggested a variety of allegorical meanings. Dante does attack Latini as a writer: directly in *De vulgari eloquentia* I.13.1 as a mere "municipal" poet and allusively in *Convivio* I.11 as one of the Italian "traitors" who do not write in their native language. Still, Dante's opening for the *Inferno* echoes Latini's *Tesoretto*, and several other points of influence between the two poets have led some Dante scholars to argue that Latini was an important figure in Dante's literary development. Yet Latini's reach was not limited to his most famous student. For centuries after his death, Latini's prose and poetry were widely circulated and regularly imitated in northern Italy. His *Trésor* became a major source for John Gower's *Confessio Amantis*, among other learned works in England and France. Latini did not suit the "new style" of his students, but many other readers admired his work.

Bibliography: J. B. Holloway, *Twice-Told Tales: Brunetto Latino and Dante Alighieri*, 1993; B. Latini, *Li Livre dou trésor*, ed. F. J. Carmody, 1948; B. Latini, *Il Tesoretto*, trans. J. B. Holloway, 1981.

Joel Fredell

LEO III, EMPEROR (C. 680–741).

Byzantine emperor and founder of the Isaurian dynasty, Leo rose through the imperial ranks by means of his military prowess and administrative abilities. He fought off the Arab attack and siege of Constantinople (c. 717–718), reorganized the military administrative units, revised Justinianic law in the legal manual the *Ecloga*, and initiated imperial support for iconoclasm.

Originating in Germanikeia in northern Syria, Leo and his parents were transferred to Thrace as a result of Justinian II's resettlement policy. Offering his services to Justinian II, he served in the Caucasus and later under Anastasios II became military commander (*strategos*) of the Anatolian theme, the largest and most important Byzantine province. He used his powerful position to revolt against Theodosios III, capping a series of seven violent and successful revolts that had lasted twenty years. Defending Constantinople against the second Arab siege in forty years, he used Greek fire to torch the Arab fleet and witnessed how famine and sickness broke the Arab resolve. Arab attacks, however, continued in Asia Minor, although the very existence of the Byzantine Empire would not again be threatened by Arab invaders.

Internal threats of usurpation led Leo to carve the Anatolian theme into semi-independent divisions under military commanders, limiting the power of a single powerful *strategos* but also lending flexibility and strength enough to respond to local threats. He created the Thrakesion, which was the western portion of the Anatolian district, the Kibyrrhaiot theme, which was made up of southern Asia Minor and neighboring islands, as well as the Droungariot of the Aegean islands.

He published the legal manual the *Ecloga* in c. 741 in his name and in the name of his son Constantine V. The *Ecloga* became a significant document in the formation of Byzantine law as well as very influential in the development of law in the Slavic countries. The point of the revised legal manual was to provide judges with an accessible legal manual that reflected the practical needs and customary practices of the day. Developments include replacing capital punishment with various levels of mutilation, a change interpreted as reflecting the absorption of Christian ethics as well as Eastern influences.

Bibliography: S. Gero, *Byzantine Iconoclasm during the Reign of Leo III*, 1973.

Tom Papademetriou

LEO III, POPE (PONTIFICATE 795–816).

A largely self-serving figure who aroused intense opposition resulting in two separate assassination plots, he became the first and only pope to recognize a Western ruler's sovereignty over the papal see when he crowned *Charlemagne Holy Roman Emperor before St. Peter's tomb at the Christmas Mass in 800.

Upon the death of Hadrian I in 795, Leo was unanimously elected pope; however, he had to contend with Hadrian's ambitious relatives from the outset. These opponents viciously attacked him during the procession on St. Mark's Day in 799, and they attempted to cut out his eyes and tongue, which, some contemporaries say, were miraculously restored by God. After a formal deposition, he was exiled to a monastery where he recovered from his wounds. With the aid of friends, Leo was able to make his way to the court of Charlemagne, king of the Franks, to whom Leo III had presented the keys of St. Peter's confessio in 795 in recognition of Charlemagne's suzerainty over Rome. Charlemagne, refusing to acknowledge the deposition, offered Leo protection but also listened to formal charges of perjury and adultery leveled at Leo by his opponents. It was a volatile situation, for many believed the charges to be well founded. After consulting his chief adviser, *Alcuin, who supported the pope's divinely ordained sovereignty on earth, Charlemagne provided an escort for Leo III's return to Rome in late November. Charlemagne followed Leo to Rome in December, ostensibly to investigate the charges himself, but Leo III took an oath of purgation and cleared himself of all charges. Two days later at Christmas Mass, Leo III crowned Charlemagne Holy Roman Emperor.

For the remainder of Charlemagne's life, Leo maintained his allegiance to the

Frankish throne. His only serious deviation from the policies and practices set forth by Charlemagne was his resistance in 810 to inserting the *Filioque* (meaning "and from the Son") into the Nicene Creed, which had been established in 381 at the Council of Constantinople as the definitive statement of belief for the Church. The *Filioque* had become popular in the West and was part of the Frankish Creed. Although Leo personally approved of the doctrine, he did not want to offend the Greeks. He was able to sidestep the issue because the Church in Rome used an ancient form of the Mass that did not include the creed. Leo III was also responsible for maintaining relations among factions within the English Church and helped to settle political disputes in England. He also established himself as a capable administrator of Church funds and worked to refurbish many churches. After Charlemagne's death in 814, Leo III again came under attack, and he had to suppress a second conspiracy and deal with revolts in Campania. He died in 816, but he was not canonized until 1673. His feast day (now suppressed) was celebrated on 12 June.

Bibliography: R. Davis, trans., *The Lives of the Eighth-Century Popes* (Liber Pontificalis): *The Ancient Biographies of Nine Popes from AD 715 to AD 817*, 1992.

Clinton Atchley

LEO IX, POPE (C. 1002–1054, PONTIFICATE 1049–1054). The Holy Roman Emperor *Henry III, nominated his cousin Bruno, bishop of Toul, to become pope after the short reign of Damasus II. As Leo IX, he strengthened his reputation as a renowned reformer and brought some of the leading minds with him to Rome, thus ushering in a period of remarkable papal reform. Leo also led a futile campaign against the Normans in Sicily and became involved in the formal beginning of the East-West schism that lasts to this day.

Although the nomination by the emperor secured his position, Leo wanted to be accepted by the clergy and Roman people and therefore crossed the Alps dressed as a pilgrim. He was formally elected on 12 February 1049 and, true to the Cluniac movement to which he belonged, stressed the need to clean up the Church, especially simony and clerical marriage. Leo brought some of the leading reformers with him, such as Hildebrand (later *Gregory VII), Humbert, Frederick of Liège, Hugh the White, and *Peter Damian. These leading minds began a process of change within the Church system that increased papal supremacy and brought more respect to the papacy. Leo did his part by traveling throughout much of Europe holding synods in such places as Pavia, Rheims, Mainz, Vercelli, Mantua, Salerno, and Rome. Leo also used the legatine system to a great extent. The "apostolic pilgrim," as Leo was known, brought the papacy into view of the people. It was no longer just heard but now seen as well, which greatly increased papal authority and respect.

Problems began for Leo in 1053, however, as he led a campaign against the troublesome Normans in southern Italy. The papal army was defeated, and Leo was captured and held for nine months. Michael Cerularius, the anti-Western patriarch of Constantinople, did not appreciate Leo's attempt to subdue southern Italy, an area in which he claimed jurisdiction, and made an excuse to close Latin churches over the use of unleavened bread. Leo sent Humbert at the head of a delegation to reconcile matters, but negotiations failed. On 16 July 1054, Humbert placed the papal decree of excommunication of Michael on the high altar at St. Sophia, which prompted Michael to excommunicate the legates. The schism between East and West now became public as the papacy battled with Constantinople for religious superiority.

Leo unfortunately did not witness the war of words between Michael and the legates as he died on 19 April 1054, a month after returning from captivity. The great reformer who initiated the process of improving the Church system was soon canonized, becoming the first pope since Hadrian III to become a saint.

Bibliography: R. P. McBrien, *Lives of the Popes*, 1997; W. Ullmann, *A Short History of the Papacy in the Middle Ages*, 1972.

Paul Miller

LEOBA (LEOBGYTHA, LEOFGYTH) (D. C. 780). Leoba, an eighth-century Anglo-Saxon nun, was a follower of her kinsman Saint *Boniface, apostle to the Germans. Daughter of an otherwise unknown nobleman Dynno and his wife Aebba, born in their old age, she was presented to the Church as an oblate at the double monastery of Wimborne in Wessex (Dorset). Shortly after 732, she wrote to Boniface, reminding him of their relationship, enclosing a poem she had composed, and asking him for his prayers and for instruction in Latin composition.

Sometime in the mid-eighth century, Boniface, drawing on a strong English tradition of female religious leaders, called a group of nuns from England to assist him in missionary work in Germany. Leoba became among the most influential of them. She was appointed abbess of the convent of Tauberbischofsheim, where she was active in teaching the nuns under her rule and ministering to the villagers living near the convent. She frequently traveled about, supervising other convents. *Charlemagne's wife, Queen Hildegard, held Leoba in great respect and frequently requested her attendance at court. Although the nun recognized the importance of royal support of the missionary effort, she went to court and stayed no more than necessary.

Despite apparent homesickness, Leoba remained in Germany, continuing the work Boniface had set for her and maintaining a close relationship with Lull and the monks of Boniface's foundation at Fulda. When she died c. 780, her body was carried to Fulda in a cortege and buried beside the altar there, rather than in Boniface's tomb as he had wished.

Bibliography: Rudolph of Fulda, "The Life of Saint Leoba," trans. C. H. Talbot, in *Soldiers of Christ: Saints and Saints' Lives from Late Antiquity and the Early Middle Ages*, ed. T.F.X. Noble and T. Head, 1995.

Janice R. Norris

LEONINUS (LEONIUS, LÉONIN) (C. 1135–1201). French composer, musician, and poet, Leoninus is the first composer of polyphonic music whose fame spread during his lifetime.

Although Leoninus' surviving compositions are many, little is known of his life. Extrapolating from what is known about composers of church music, it is likely that he was an ecclesiastic, a member of the secular, nonmonastic clergy. He must have been well educated and versatile. What is known about Leoninus comes from several documents and a treatise written in the late thirteenth century. The documents indicate that he was a master and had studied at Paris; he was an administrator of St. Benoit, a member of the community of St. Victor by 1187, and later a canon at the cathedral of Notre Dame. The author of the treatise, an Englishman, states that a Magister Leoninus was the best composer of organum—music with a sustained-note tenor and a more mobile upper part or parts—and that he wrote an extensive book of organum, the *Magnus liber organi de Gradali et Antiphonario*, for the Mass and to increase the divine service.

He worked at the cathedral of Paris, a center of musical composition, during the second half of the twelfth century. Influenced by the school of organum at St. Martial at Limoges, Leoninus created new styles and new forms that, then, became the defining characteristics of a new age. He composed for two voices like those who preceded him did, but he extended the range of the melody. He developed a consistent system of rhythm and a method of musical notation, which provides the basis for modern notation.

Although better known for his musical compositions today, especially among English speakers, his poetry is still included in histories of French literature. Leoninus composed his principal work the *Hystorie sacre gestas ab origine mundi* (Acts of Sacred History) at the urging of the abbot of St. Victor. This poem retells the stories of the first eight books of the Old Testament in 14,000 hexameter lines. His purpose, he announces in both the prologue and epilogue, is to encourage his listeners to love God. His other poems, of which eight survive, are shorter; four are religious texts that convey moral lessons; the other four are letters to important people, like Popes *Hadrian IV and *Innocent III.

His poetry did not meet with the same success his music did. His compositions were so artistic, so beautiful, that they were copied and performed in France, England, Spain, Italy, and Germany; in fact, they were still being copied and performed in the beginning of the fourteenth century.

Bibliography: C. Wright, "Leoninus, Poet and Musician," *Journal of the American Musicological Society* 39 (1986): 1–35.

Jana K. Schulman

LIUDOLF OF SAXONY (D. 866). Duke or count of Eastern Saxony c. 850–866 and ancestor of the Saxon dynasty of German kings, Liudolf established the influence of his family in imperial affairs and founded the important canonry at Gandersheim.

While authors writing during the reigns of his descendants emphasized Liudolf's wealth and authority by referring to him as a duke, his position originally was more likely that of a count or margrave—a rank more in keeping with the fact that his estates were mainly limited to southeastern Saxony and northern Thuringia. Despite the lack of any references to him in contemporary annals, Liudolf likely participated in military campaigns against the Danes, Slavs, and Bohemians, since such service was required of all capable men in Saxony. He married Oda, a member of the Frankish branch of the noble Billung family, who died in 913 at the reputed age of 107.

Liudolf founded Gandersheim in order to house relics of Pope Innocent II, which he had obtained during a pilgrimage to Rome just after taking office as count. The first three abbesses were Liudolf's daughters Hathumoda (852–874), Gerberga (874–897), and Christina (897–920); and Gandersheim thus fulfilled the common function of preserving a portion of Liudolf's property for the use of his descendants, especially unmarried females. *Hrotsvit of Gandersheim's *Primordia coenobii Gandeshemensis* records the history of Gandersheim. The marriage (probably in 874) of Liudolf's eldest daughter, Liutgard, to Louis the III (called the Younger), king of East Francia (876–882), marked the beginning of Liudolf's family's rise from the regional to the imperial aristocracy.

Bibliography: T. Reuter, *Germany in the Early Middle Ages c. 800–1056*, 1991.

Edward J. Schoenfeld

LIUTPRAND OF CREMONA (C. 920–C. 972).
Bishop of Cremona, diplomat, and author, Liutprand served at the courts of Hugh of Provence, Berengar II, and *Otto I. For the latter two, he went on diplomatic missions to the Byzantine emperor in Constantinople. His writings have provided historians with a colorful, quasi-narrative, and semiautobiographical history of those parts of Europe in which he lived and served.

Liutprand was born in or near Pavia into an aristocratic Lombard family. Both his father (who died when he was seven) and stepfather served at the court of Hugh of Provence, king of Italy, and both made diplomatic missions to Constantinople for their ruler. Probably on account of these close familial contacts with the king, Liutprand was taken into the royal court at Pavia where he received a classical education and, by his own account, impressed his ruler with his singing ability. Possibly with an eye to diplomatic service, Liutprand entered the clergy, and he became a deacon in Pavia.

In 945, Hugh was forced from Italy by Berengar II of Ivrea. At great expense, Liutprand's stepfather bought him a secretarial position at the new ruler's court. In 949, Berengar chose Liutprand to go on a diplomatic mission to Constantinople, a mission that the tight-fisted king forced Liutprand's stepfather to finance. What the goal of the mission was is not known, but the young diplomat appears to have gotten along well with Byzantine Emperor Constantine Porphrogenitus. Sometime after his return in 950, Liutprand fled Berengar's service in disgust at the ruler's depravities and went into what he describes as "exile" at the court of the Saxon ruler of Germany, Otto I. In 961, Otto, accompanied by Liutprand, brought an army into Italy, overthrew Berengar, and made Liutprand bishop of Cremona. As such, Liutprand served his master (who became emperor in 962) in many capacities. Among these was his service as translator of Otto's Saxon into Latin at the Church synod, which deposed Pope John XII in 963. In 968, Otto sent Liutprand on his second mission to Constantinople to secure a Byzantine princess for his son and heir *Otto II. Liutprand failed utterly to achieve this goal. He may have returned to Constantinople in 971 on the delegation that brought back the Greek *Theophano as bride for Otto II. Liutprand probably died in 972.

Liutprand wrote three works, which have come down to us, all composed during his time of service to Otto I. The *Antapodosis* (Retribution) provides a six-book history of the complicated political struggle for sovereignty in Italy during the period from about 886 to 950, along with hefty doses of the history of Germany and Byzantium. Liutprand waits until book three to explain his title (which his English translator F. A. Wright has rendered *Tit for Tat*), namely, that by revealing the disgusting behavior of Berengar II and his wife Willa Liutprand would gain retribution for his mistreatment at their hands before he fled to Germany in 950. The *Antapodosis*, however, ranges far afield from Berengar and Willa, who receive little of the promised vituperation. It also stops in the middle of Liutprand's description of his first mission to Constantinople, that is, before he went to Germany, and so does not get as far as Berengar's fall from power. This indicates that Liutprand never got around to finishing this highly anecdotal work, which appears to wander according to its author's whims.

The *Liber de Ottone rege* (Book about King Otto) is the least autobiographical of Liutprand's works. Dedicated to Otto I, his wife *Adelaide, and their son Otto II, it tells the story of Otto I's deposition of Pope John XII, the sorriest of all pontiffs, on grounds of sacrilege and adultery. Finally, Liutprand wrote the *Legatio*, which is a marvelously acerbic account of his second trip to Constantinople and his mistreatment at the hands of Emperor Nicephorus Phokas. Liutprand wastes not a word in showing his contempt for the Greeks and their ruler.

All three works can, perhaps, be best understood in the context of the rise of the ducal house of Saxony to the German and the Western imperial thrones. The Saxon or Ottonian dynasty had only begun relatively recently with Otto I's father, *Henry I of Germany, and so sought recognition and legitimization. The Ottonians were Liutprand's masters, and his writings have a propagandistic quality of defending their claims against Italians, Byzantines, and popes. Urbane, witty, well educated, and loving to show off his learning with pyrotechnics of classical quotes, Liutprand remains a lively guide to the tenth century.

Bibliography: P. Buc, "Italian Hussies and German Matrons: Liutprand of Cremona on Dynastic Legitimacy," *Frühmittelalterliche Studien* 29 (1995): 207–225.

Jay T. Lees

LLULL, RAMON (RAYMOND LULL) (C. 1232–1315). A philosopher and mystic of thirteenth-century Spain, Llull devoted his life to advancing missionary work among the Jews and Muslims of Spain and Northern Africa. His extensive writings in vernacular Catalan are instrumental in the shaping of that language.

Llull was born on Majorca, the son of an affluent father who had participated in the Christian reconquest of the island. He spent the early part of his adult life attached to the court of *James I, where he traveled, wrote troubadour poetry, married, had two children, and became seneschal for the future James II of Majorca. At age thirty, he had a conversion experience that led him to renounce wealth and family, embrace a mendicant lifestyle, and aspire to become a missionary. He undertook a series of pilgrimages followed by a nine-year stint devoted to studying philosophy and theology and learning Arabic from a Muslim slave he had purchased as a tutor. In 1274, he had a mystical vision on Mount Ronda in Majorca, a definitive moment for his philosophical thought. He founded a monastery at Miramar in Majorca in 1276. He spent the latter part of his life engaged in writing, teaching, preaching, and fund-raising. He spent several terms at the University of Paris where he was an outspoken critic of the Averroists. He also taught at the Universities of Montpellier and Naples. He visited both papal and secular courts to secure support and funding for new language schools and for chairs of Hebrew and Arabic at existing universities. He undertook preaching tours in the synagogues and mosques of the crown of Aragon and missionary trips to North Africa. Llull's missionary zeal had much in common with the Dominicans of his day, and he almost joined this order in 1293. However, his spirituality had greater ties to Franciscan sensibilities, and he became a Franciscan tertiary late in life. He died in Majorca in 1315 and was beatified in 1858.

Llull was a major contributor to early Catalan literature. His some 265 works included poetry and narrative fiction, mystical treatises, philosophical and theological works, scientific discussions, and an autobiography. One of his most famous works is the *Book of the Lover and the Beloved*, a mystical text that incorporated Muslim Sufism. The first prose novels written in Europe on contemporary themes, *Blanquerna* and *Felix*, are a part of his corpus, as are the *Book of the Gentile and the Three Wise Men*, an apologetic work, and the *Book of Beasts*, a political satire. His unique philosophical thought is represented in various renditions of the *Art*. In it, Llull constructed an ontological matrix that incorporated a set of divine attributes common to Christian, Muslim, and Jewish theology, which are then represented by letters and figures and manipulated by algebraic logic. He developed this method in order to demonstrate the philosophical logic of conversion to non-Christians. He also applied the *Art* more generally to attempt a classification of all knowledge in *The Tree of Science*. While not as useful in proselytizing as he might have hoped, Llull's *Art* remained influential in European philosophical thinking into the seventeenth century.

Bibliography: J. N. Hillgarth, *Ramon Lull and Lullism in Fourteenth-Century France*, 1971.

Linda A. McMillin

LOMBARD, PETER. *See* PETER LOMBARD.

LORRIS, GUILLAUME DE. *See* GUILLAUME DE LORRIS.

LOTHAR II OF LOTHARINGIA (C. 838–869). King of Lotharingia, Lothar II was the second son of Emperor Lothar I and his wife Ermengard, daughter of Hugh count of Tours, an influential noble in Alsace who strategically married his three daughters into dominant Carolingian noble houses. A great-grandson of *Charlemagne through *Louis the Pious, Lothar II was heir to a remnant of that vast empire after it had been divided and subdivided by generations of Carolingian princes. His middle Frankish kingdom of Lotharingia, with the capital at Aachen, took its name from his.

He became king in 855 at the age of seventeen and for political reasons quickly married *Theutberga of the powerful Bosonid family. Lothar's reign of fourteen years was characterized by continuing struggles with his uncles *Charles II the Bald and *Louis the German and by escalating pressure from Vikings entrenched in Frisia. However, from 858 most of his energies went into attempts to divorce the barren Theutberga in order to marry *Waldrada, his longtime concubine and mother of his four children. Although he was eventually granted a divorce by Lotharingian bishops and married Waldrada, he was opposed by *Hincmar of Rheims and a succession of popes for whom the issue at stake was ecclesiastical control of marriage.

Lothar died in 869, having failed to secure papal recognition of his marriage to Waldrada. His only son Hugh failed to inherit Lotharingia and in 885 was blinded to ensure his fate before being imprisoned in the monastery of Prüm. Lotharingia was rapidly dismantled by his uncles and ceased to exist as an independent kingdom.

Bibliography: P. Riché, *The Carolingians: A Family Who Forged Europe*, trans. M. I. Allen, 1993.

Janice R. Norris

LOUIS VI (THE FAT) OF FRANCE (1081–1137). King of France from 1108 to 1137, Louis VI is credited with bolstering royal authority by securing the Île-de-France as the center of the French royal domain and by gaining control over royal government. He gained his nickname because, in his later years, his corpulence was so great that he was no longer able to ride.

Son of Philip I Capet and Berthe of Holland, Louis was educated in the royal abbey of St. Denis, north of Paris. Louis is better known to historians than his predecessors because his biography, *The Deeds of Louis VI*, was written by

Abbot *Suger of St. Denis. While this was not the first biography written of a French king, Suger's work attained great popularity as a narrative account, rather than a hagiographical or strictly biographical work. Because Suger's life was so entwined with that of his monarch, *The Deeds of Louis VI* is an eyewitness account of the turbulent period of Louis' reign.

Louis' stepmother Bertrada, countess of Anjou, who married his father Philip I after his repudiation of Berthe in 1097, contested Louis' accession to the throne of France. Bertrada was thought to have attempted to have Louis violently assassinated and later poisoned so that the crown would go to her own sons. However, in 1098, Louis was knighted and in 1108 became king of France. Adelaide of Savoy became his wife in 1115, and they had six sons and one daughter. His career was one of constant warfare against the powerful feudal nobility; he attacked the strongholds of lords such as Hugh de Puiset, the Montlhéri, and Thomas de Marle. While he was successful in diminishing the power of these lords whose lands were in close proximity to the Île-de-France, he was less successful in his wars with Blois-Champagne, Flanders, and Normandy. He fought two unsuccessful wars against *Henry I of England, who was able to claim the ancestral duchy of Normandy in 1106, ending the claims of William Clito, son of Henry's brother Robert, duke of Normandy.

To counter the power of the nobility, Louis granted royal charters to support the growth of towns and worked to gain the goodwill of the ecclesiastical authorities, although he was not a great supporter of Church reform. As befitting a king brought up at the abbey of St. Denis, he declared Saint Denis the patron saint of France on his accession in 1108 and in 1124 gave the monastery jurisdiction over the county of the Vexin. His greatest coup in improving the prestige of the monarchy was the arrangement of the marriage of his son later *Louis VII to *Eleanor of Aquitaine, the greatest heiress of the day. Louis VI died in 1137, soon after his son left for Aquitaine to celebrate his marriage to Eleanor.

Bibliography: J. Delperrié de Bayac, *Louis VI: La naissance de la France*, 1983; Suger, Abbot of St. Denis, *The Deeds of Louis the Fat*, trans. R. Cusimano and J. Moorhead, 1992.

Sharon Michalove

LOUIS VII OF FRANCE (1120–1180).

Louis VII was king of France. The second son of *Louis VI and Adelaide of Savoy, Louis was originally destined for a career in the Church, but on the death of his older brother Philip in 1131, Louis became the royal heir. He was crowned king in 1137. He continued his father's expansion of royal power, extending it beyond the Île-de-France, encouraged trade and the expansion of urban liberties, and negotiated successful alliances with the Church and with local magnates. Despite a failed marriage and a disastrous crusade, by the end of his long reign Louis had decisively established the prestige of the French monarchy.

Louis had not been trained to be king; he had neither the physical stamina nor the tough-mindedness to engage men brutalized from childhood by military and political training. Nevertheless, at seventeen, newly married to *Eleanor of Aquitaine, he found himself in nominal control of all of the territory encompassed by Aquitaine—from Bourges to the Pyrenees, and from the mouth of the Loire to the Cévennes—as well as the domain lands of the Capetians. This placed him in a better position than any of his predecessors, but he was unable to take advantage of its potential. Furthermore, his devotion to his wife led him into ill-advised military conflicts in Poitou and in Toulouse, as well as into political conflicts with the count of Champagne and with *Bernard, the powerful abbot of Clairvaux, who criticized the power Eleanor had over Louis. However, Eleanor is rumored to have dallied when she accompanied Louis on the disastrous Second Crusade (1147–1149) and despite papal attempts to keep them together, Louis and Eleanor secured an annulment on the grounds of consanguinity (they were cousins within the fourth degree) in 1152 after fifteen years of marriage and two daughters.

Eleanor rushed into marriage with Henry Plantagenet, count of Anjou, that same year, bringing Aquitaine with her. Henry was already duke of Normandy and by 1154 would also become king of England (*Henry II). Consequently, Louis had not only lost Aquitaine, but his greatest vassal now proved to be the most dangerous threat to the royal domain. Although French scholars have criticized Louis for losing Aquitaine by dissolving his marriage and thus putting at risk the monarchy his father had struggled so hard to build, it is clear that Louis, and indeed the monarchy itself, was not yet strong enough to control the magnates of Aquitaine and to attempt it would have exhausted Capetian resources.

Despite this shaky beginning, Louis grew into his role. He sought, as had his father, the counsel of *Suger, abbot of St. Denis, whom he made regent when he embarked on the Second Crusade. Louis supported the growing commercial activities in the rising towns of France, particularly Paris. He was also the first king to grant craft guilds privileges that had customarily only been held by merchant guilds, such as the right to compel all practitioners to become guild members.

From 1152 until his death in 1180, Louis' command of his kingdom grew steadily stronger. He led successful military expeditions against rebellious magnates, such as Geoffrey de Donzy in 1153, Etienne De Sancerre in 1157, and Nevelon de Pierrefonds in 1160, which reinforced submission to the Capetians and the growing central authority of the monarchy. After a brief marriage to Constance of Castile in 1154 (she died in childbirth after bearing him two daughters), he formed a powerful alliance with the counts of Blois and Champagne by marrying Adèle of Champagne in 1160. It was Adèle who bore him his son and heir *Philip II Augustus.

The difficulties Louis experienced during his reign have often been underrated. The danger represented by the Angevins was unprecedented, yet Louis was able to make use of Henry's internal problems and to exploit his own prestige as anointed king and his position as feudal suzerain—a position that

Henry chose not to challenge. From his earliest years as a student at the monastery of St. Denis, Louis was a friend of the Church, yet he never hesitated to protect royal rights or use his alliance with the papacy to further his own goals. His lifelong reputation for piety served him well, as did the general weakening of resistance to centralized authority and government that characterized the second half of the twelfth century. Louis was, in the end, a successful king who passed on a monarchy stronger than the one he had himself inherited.

Bibliography: E. M. Hallam, *Capetian France, 987–1328*, 1990; M. Pacaut, *Louis VII et son royaume*, 1964.

Marguerite Ragnow

LOUIS IX OF FRANCE, SAINT (1215–1270). King of France, crusader, and saint, Louis was born at Poissy to Louis *VIII and *Blanche, daughter of Alphonse of Castile and granddaughter of *Henry II of England; he came unexpectedly to the throne at the age of eleven upon the early death of his father in 1226. First through the regency of his mother, and then through his own efforts, the prestige of the medieval French monarchy reached its zenith under Louis; his work to peacefully consolidate royal territory and power, to create an effective administration, and to protect the rights of all of his subjects while losing none of his own made him a popular as well as successful monarch. In France, he is considered the patron of the monarchy, and his policy of pursuing peace at home while aggressively devoting every resource to crusading against the Muslims (the Seventh and Eighth Crusades) has led some to consider him the model medieval Christian king.

When Louis came of age in 1234, the monarchy was as strong as it had been at the death of his father eight years earlier. Blanche of Castile's regency (1226–1236) was marked by several victories over rebellious barons, particularly Raymond VII in Languedoc, Peter Mauclerc in Brittany, and Philip Hurepel in the Île-de-France, as well as by indecisive struggles against *Henry III of England. In these disputes, Blanche was supported by the royal household and most of the towns; the papacy, particularly in the person of the legate Frangipani, was also a helpful ally. Most important, however, was the lack of organization among her enemies. The French barons were never able to unite in the kind of alliance that the English barons had achieved in forcing the Magna Carta on *John of England in 1215.

Louis' reign, once he came of age, can be charted along two major tracks: Crusades against the Muslims in the Holy Land and the just treatment of his people at home, two concerns that often coincided. Inspired by a serious illness, Louis took the crusader's vow in 1244. He spent four years in preparation, collecting revenues and building support for his venture. He also enlarged and refortified the port of Aigues-Mortes, from which he planned to sail with his crusading army. It was during this period that Louis commissioned *enquêteurs*, or special investigators, to identify abuses and injustices within his government.

Armed with this intelligence, Louis improved government administration and expanded both the judicial system and the tax base, which enabled him to raise funds for his crusade.

In 1248, accompanied by his wife Marguerite of Provence, whom he married in 1234, Louis embarked on his first crusade (the Seventh Crusade), leaving his mother Blanche as regent once again. After wintering in Cyprus, Louis and his army took the coastal city of Damietta in the spring of 1249; later that year they pushed further into the Egyptian interior, only to be decisively defeated and captured in April 1250 at Al-Mansurā. Louis negotiated his release and that of his army by surrendering Damietta and paying a large ransom. His two surviving brothers, *Charles I of Anjou and Alphonse of Poitiers, sailed home with most of the remaining troops, while Louis and a small band traveled to the Holy Land, where they visited shrines and helped to fortify the Christian states. His mother Blanche died in 1252, but it was only after Louis became convinced that things were deteriorating at home that he returned to France in 1254.

Many historians consider Louis' failure on this crusade to have been a personal turning point. Convinced that his personal sinfulness was to blame for his failure to defeat the Muslims, he dedicated himself to the reform of his government, reinstating the *enquêteurs*, restraining the excesses of the Inquisition, opening the royal courts to all freemen, and establishing a new gold coinage of high standard. He sponsored charitable works on an unprecedented scale, founding many hospitals and houses, including a convent for the Beguines and a 300-bed hospice for blind men, the Quinze-Vingt. His biographer *John of Joinville reports that Louis personally fed and ate with the sick, and according to another source, once a week he washed the feet of the destitute with his own hands and gave them alms. Louis also did his best to protect his Jewish subjects against abuse, all the while promoting efforts to convert them to Christianity.

Medieval culture also blossomed during Louis' reign. Towns and commerce flourished, and numerous monuments to Gothic architecture rose up throughout the country, including Louis' own palace chapel in Paris, La Sainte Chapelle. The prestige and reputation of the University of Paris also increased. Louis' own patronage was instrumental in the foundation of the College of the Sorbonne, which became the seat of the theological faculty. Its founder, *Robert of Sorbon, numbered among Louis' friends, and Thomas *Aquinas was Louis' frequent guest.

Louis' reputation for peace and justice extended beyond his own subjects. He also sought peaceful settlement of disputes with other monarchs. He spent five years negotiating the Treaty of Paris (1259) with his cousin and brother-in-law Henry III of England, who renounced all claims to the former Plantagenet provinces lost by John (Normandy, Maine, Anjou, and Poitou) and became Louis' vassal in Aquitaine. Although criticized for giving up disputed territory on the borders of Gascony and confirming Henry's possession of Aquitaine, Louis increased the power and prestige of the French monarchy through this treaty and the Treaty of Corbeil (1258), which settled territorial disputes with the crown of Aragon.

In a *parlement* at Paris in 1267, amidst much controversy and anti-crusading sentiment, Louis, wracked by illness, once again took the crusader's cross. After making considerable preparations, Louis departed Aigues-Morte for Sardinia in 1270. Stopping there only briefly, he invaded Tunisia on 18 July (the Eighth Crusade). During the siege of Tunis, on 25 August 1270, Louis died, not from wounds but from disease. His son Philip III succeeded him. According to the sources, Louis' heart was given as a relic to his brother Charles of Anjou, who brought it to Sicily; his flesh was interred with the other bodies of crusaders who had died at Tunis, and his bones were sent to Paris, where they were buried in the royal abbey of St. Denis. It was on this journey that miracles were first reported in connection with the bones. Saint Louis' canonization was proclaimed at Orvieto in 1297 by Pope *Boniface VIII.

The *Enseignements*, written instructions Louis left to his son Philip and his daughter Isabel, outlined his principles of good governance: Never deny justice to anyone for any reason, always support the poor against the rich until the truth is made clear, do justice, do not privilege your own interests at the expense of fairness, surrender what you find you hold unjustly, seek the advice of honest men, and encourage them to be truthful. Louis lived by these principles and was venerated for it. By the end of his reign, not only was royal power higher than ever before, but the monarchy was both respected and popular.

Louis was pious and ascetic, an ardent prosecutor of heretics but also a conscientious king who exercised justice and fairness in his dealings with his subjects. He admitted the legitimacy of the nobility's claims to share in the power and authority of the kingdom, just as he admitted the spiritual dominion of the Church, but he did not allow encroachments into the rights, prerogatives, and authority of the monarchy.

Bibliography: John of Joinville, *Life of Saint Louis*, in *Chronicles of the Crusades*, ed. M.R.B. Shaw, 1963; W. C. Jordan, *Louis IX and the Challenge of the Crusade: A Study in Rulership*, 1996; J. Richard, *Saint Louis: Crusader King of France*, ed. S. Lloyd, trans. J. Birrell, 1992.

Marguerite Ragnow

LOUIS THE GERMAN (C. 804–876). One of the sons of *Louis the Pious, Louis later became king of East Francia. While he was still a child, he was awarded Bavaria in a partition of the Frankish Empire known as the *ordinatio imperii* of 817. He did not, however, take up his chief residence in Regensburg until 829. An ambitious king, he eventually acquired more territory from his father and moved his residence to Frankfurt.

Louis the German could be considered the first emperor of what eventually developed into German territory. In February 842, Louis met his brother *Charles II the Bald (who at the time ruled West Francia) in Strasbourg on what would become a linguistically and historically important occasion. Louis and Charles agreed to unite against their brother Lothar, emperor and king of Italy. Their oaths of mutual support are recorded in *Nithard's *Histories* and serve philologists as evidence that the Franks had, by the mid-ninth century, developed different languages in the eastern and western parts of the realm; the native language of the East is *teudisca lingua* (the German tongue), whereas the language of the West is differentiated from it as the *romana lingua* (the Romance tongue). Each emperor took the oath in the language of the other, in order to be understood clearly by the opposing soldiers.

Although the significance of the oaths cannot be denied, Louis and his brothers continued to fight over their father's lands. The Treaty of Verdun (843) ended, albeit temporarily, the civil war between them and divided the territory among the brothers. Louis received much of what is now modern Germany. Unfortunately, just as his and his brothers' disputes over land reduced the empire, so too did the quarrels of Louis' own sons; while Louis pacified them by granting them fiefs, their revolts helped speed up the decline of Carolingian power in the East.

Bibliography: B. Arnold, *Medieval Germany, 500–1300. A Political Interpretation*, 1997.

Alexandra Sterling-Hellenbrand

LOUIS THE PIOUS (778–840). Louis the Pious was the son and, after the deaths of brothers Pepin and Charles, sole heir of *Charlemagne. Crowned emperor at Aachen in 813, shortly before the death of his father, and recrowned as Holy Roman Emperor at Rheims in 816 by Pope Stephen IV, Louis reigned from 814 until 840.

Louis is perhaps best remembered for the great turmoil he himself brought about in his plans for his own successors. He had three sons by his first wife, the eldest of whom (Lothar) was designated Louis' heir as emperor by the *ordinatio imperii* of 817. Younger sons *Louis the German and Pepin received Bavaria and Aquitaine, respectively. Louis overturned the *ordinatio* in order to make provisions for his fourth and youngest son, *Charles II the Bald (son of Louis by his second wife Judith). In his attempts to reallocate his lands, Louis disrupted the peace he had tried to maintain and laid the groundwork for civil war. Louis' reputation has also suffered because of the conflicts created by his own sons and the enmity over the breakup of his empire following his death. In 843, the Treaty of Verdun finally divided the empire among Louis' three surviving sons (Lothar, Louis the German, and Charles the Bald).

Raised at Aquitaine to become its king, Louis is reported to have had a certain affinity for the monastic life; indeed, few of his contemporaries had anticipated that he would be Charlemagne's only surviving son and heir. Louis was considered devout and religious by his contemporaries, and he did not appear to support secular learning as enthusiastically as Charlemagne had done. Two Latin prose lives of Louis the Pious, one written during Louis' lifetime and the other after his death, support this perception. The author of the first, Thegan, was a cleric from Trier; the author of the second is anonymous, known only as the Astronomer (based on the knowledge he displays in his work). Thegan, in particular, portrays a man well versed in the interpretation of the Scriptures who (unlike his father Charlemagne) would have had little to do with non-Christian poetry. *Hrabanus Maurus, a pupil of *Alcuin, influenced Louis' educational policies, which emphasized Christian theology. Alcuin had described the dominant aesthetic of the time when he asked what Ingeld a (Germanic heroic figure) had to do with Christ. Literature in Latin in the context of the Church continued to flourish under Louis the Pious and throughout the ninth century in the Frankish realm.

Despite the Synod of Frankfurt (794) that proclaimed every language pleasing to God, there are few original Old High German texts from the early ninth century. Scholarship has tended to explain this as an effect of Louis' piety and has therefore focused primarily on recovering pieces of pre-Christian Germanic literature that survived the reign of Louis the Pious, which inaugurated a long period of vernacular silence. Evidence shows that the early vernacular maintained a covert presence, however. Two verse poems survive that date from opposite ends of Louis' reign: The *Wessobrunn Prayer*, a description of the void before Creation, dates from around 790–813; the *Muspilli*, an account of the terrors of the Last Judgement, dates from around 850. There is evidence of some glosses and translations; however, it is clear that the monastic community regarded the vernacular with suspicion because of its connection to pagan content and used it reluctantly to educate both religious and laymen.

Entrusted with the preservation of the Carolingian heritage, Louis the Pious understood Frankish society as tightly held within a Christian framework. He continued to support an active intellectual culture that, though predominantly clerical, attempted in its own context to carry on the Carolingian reforms of Louis' predecessors. It is for this reason that Louis' contemporary biographers considered him the equal of his father.

Bibliography: A. Cabaniss, trans., *Son of Charlemagne: A Contemporary Life of Louis the Pious*, 1961; R. McKitterick, *The Frankish Church and the Carolingian Reforms, 789–895*, 1977; T.F.X. Noble, "Louis the Pious and the Frontiers of the Frankish Realms," in *Charlemagne's Heir. New Perspectives on the Reign of Louis the Pious*, ed. P. Godman and R. Collins, 1990.

Alexandra Sterling-Hellenbrand

M

MACBETH OF SCOTLAND (R. 1040–1057). *Mormaer* (ruler) of the Scottish province of Moray, Macbeth seized the throne of Scotland from Duncan, son of Malcolm II Mackennath, in 1040 and ruled until 1057.

Despite Shakespeare's treatment of Macbeth, it is clear that most near-contemporary chroniclers considered him the rightful king whose seizure of the throne by force was not unusual in Scottish political practice. He was a representative of a junior branch of the Scottish royal house (the "line of Loarn" as opposed to the "line of Fergus," the two sons of Erc, the traditional ancestor of the Dalriadan royal house) and took the throne from Duncan after killing him in battle. He then ruled strongly for nearly fifteen years before being driven from the throne in turn by Duncan's son Malcolm III Canmore, who in 1054 defeated him in battle at Dunsinnan Hill with the military assistance of *Edward the Confessor. He was finally killed at Lumphanan on 15 August 1057.

Macbeth was one of three strong kings who dominated eleventh-century Scotland, along with Malcolm II Mackennath (r. 1005–1034) and Malcolm Canmore (r. 1057–1093). All three helped consolidate Gaelic-Pictish Scotland by establishing Scotland's political heartland in the area between Perth and Edinburgh in the face of Scandinavian and English interference and gradually moving toward a system of royal succession in which eldest sons inherited from fathers.

Bibliography: G.W.S. Barrow, *Kingship and Unity: Scotland 1000–1306*, 1981.

David Day

MAGNÚS HÁKONARSON (1238–1280, R. 1263–1280). King of Norway, he earned for himself the nickname "Law-Amender" because of his interest in revising the laws of his country.

Magnús, born in 1238, was the third son of King *Hákon Hákonarson. After his surviving brother died in 1257, Magnús was acclaimed king. He received the crown in 1261 and began his reign as sole king after his father's death in 1263. While we know little of Magnús' education, a Scottish chronicler reports that Magnús attended lectures in theology at the Franciscan house in Bergen. He was well disposed to the Church, granting it concessions; he acceded to the request that he leave the revision of Church law to the Church, even though the king had always legislated for the Church, with the advice of the bishops, before.

During Magnús' reign Norway's economic growth peaked: The centralization of trade in the cities took place, an organized and wealthy merchant class developed, and trade with Iceland, Greenland, England, Flanders, and other areas flourished. Norwegian merchants exported timber, herring, dried codfish, furs, and falcons to England and imported grain, malt, cloth, lead, spices, ales, beans, and honey. Trade with the Germans was also extensive, and Magnús granted merchants in Lübeck their first charter in Norway in 1278 and merchants in Bremen one in 1279. Magnús seems to have favored diplomacy and peace in foreign affairs, making peace with the Scots in 1266, perhaps so that he could concentrate his efforts on legal and administrative reforms at home.

Magnús earned for himself the epithet *lagabœtir*, or Law-Amender, as he involved himself far more in legislative activity than his predecessors. He focused first on the law of the Gulathing, completing that revision in 1267. In 1269, he finished revising the law of the Frostathing. Then, wishing to bring Iceland, which the Norwegian crown had acquired in 1262, and Icelandic administration into closer harmony with that of Norway, he had a new code of laws compiled for Iceland. In 1271, he sent to Iceland *Járnsíða*, the first of the two Norwegian-based legal codices for Iceland.

After King Magnús sent *Járnsíða* to Iceland, he returned to his revision of the Norwegian laws. In 1273, he published a new law regulating the succession to the throne. Between 1271 and 1274, he concentrated on reconciling the secular laws from the four provinces so that one law would obtain for the entire country. He and his advisers called this law *Nyere Landslov*, or the *New Law of the Realm*; this law applied to the four ancient law provinces and also to Jämtland, Härjedalen, the Faroe Islands, Shetland, the Orkneys, and probably Greenland. In addition, this law formed the basis for the second Norwegian-based legal code intended for Iceland, called *Jónsbók*, which the Icelanders adopted in 1281.

The *New Law of the Realm* reflects an awareness of a need for change; social conditions had changed significantly in Norway and other parts of Magnús' realm; as the yeoman class rose in status, they needed the safeguards of the law. One change in Norwegian jurisprudence involved redefining the conception of crime and punishment. No longer was crime a private matter to be redressed by the victim's family but a violation of law and an offense against the state. Fines were assessed against the malefactor and paid to the injured party (as traditional) and the king (an innovation).

The king saw an increase not only in his revenues but also in his power and dignity. The *New Law of the Realm* demonstrates that laws and justice emanated from the king who was the head of the state, who had inherited the throne by right, with the people's consent, and who, because he was God's anointed, ruled by divine right. All of this furthered the idea of kingship that Magnús' father Hákon and his predecessors had initiated earlier. Magnús died in 1280 and was succeeded by his second son, Eirik Magnússon, in 1280.

Bibliography: K. Gjerset, *History of the Norwegian People*, 1915; M. Rindal and K. Berg, *King Magnus Hákonarson's Laws of Norway and Other Legal Texts*, vol. 7, 1983.

Jana K. Schulman

MAIMONIDES, MOSES (ALSO KNOWN AS RAMBAM—RABBI MOSES BEN MAIMON) (1135–1204).

A rabbinic authority and codifier of Jewish law, philosopher, and court physician, Maimonides became one of the most influential and studied figures in the post-Talmudic period.

Maimonides was born in 1135 in Cordova, Spain, and was first educated by his father, Rabbi Maimon ben Joseph, who taught him the fundamentals of the rabbinic tradition and introduced him to the sciences and mathematics. By virtue of living in the south of Spain, Maimonides benefited from contact with Arab philosophy, in particular the philosophy of *Avicenna, and became familiar with the Arabic philosophical vocabulary and approach.

At the age of thirteen, Maimonides was forced to flee with his family after the Almohad dynasty had conquered Cordova in 1148 and began to force non-Muslims to convert to Islam. After wandering for the next twelve years, his family settled in Fez, Morocco, in 1160. Muslim authorities comment that the family had converted to Islam to avoid persecution. However, it is more likely that they immigrated to Fez because the Almohad ruler was more lenient toward the Jews living there. Not deterred by his wandering, Maimonides began work on his commentary of the Mishnah and produced shorter treatises such as that on the Jewish calendar, on the principles of logic, as well as his study of the *halakhah* in the Jewish Talmud.

In Fez, Maimonides studied with the famous rabbi Judah ha-Kohen ibn Susan. It was during his time in Fez that he studied medicine, largely from the Arabic sources, as well as became engaged with the challenges of being a Jew in Fez. In reaction to the forced conversions that continued to take place, he wrote the famous *Iggeret ha-Shemad* (Letter on Forced Conversion), stating that Jews who were being forced to transgress Jewish law should leave the country of their persecution. Following the principles he himself laid out, he and his family left Fez in 1165 and traveled to Palestine, which was then under the control of the Christian crusaders. He took advantage of the safe conditions to visit the numerous Jewish historical places in Jerusalem and Hebron before leaving with his family for al-Fustat (Old Cairo), in Egypt.

After the death of his father, his brother, who was a jewel merchant, supported Maimonides' family. When his brother drowned during a sea voyage to the East, Maimonides became despondent but later decided to become a physician;

he gained fame as physician to the vizier of *Saladin. Subsequently, he also became the head of the Jewish community. During this period, Maimonides was charged with many community responsibilities in addition to his professional responsibilities and continued to write extensively. In 1180, he produced the full version of his commentary on the Mishnah, the *Mishneh Torah*, and in 1190, the *Guide of the Perplexed*. He was also a prolific letter writer and corresponded with scholars and individuals from throughout Europe. Maimonides died in al-Fustat in 1204 and was buried in Tiberias in Galilee in the land of Palestine.

Maimonides was considered by contemporaries to be an extremely learned and experienced physician. Not only did he have practical experience, but he also wrote commentaries in Arabic on the teachings of Hippocrates and Galen and medical treatises dealing with preventative measures, diagnosis, and medicines, as well as more specific topics such as his "Treatise on Asthma." Maimonides relied heavily on reason and scientific observation and synthesized this scientific knowledge with spiritual principles to establish the principles of health.

His skill as an astronomer was also well proven. His familiarity with the Ptolemaic system and its failures was demonstrated in various works such as his treatise on the calendar and the *Guide of the Perplexed*. He was, however, strongly opposed to astrology, going against the popular trend among medieval Jewish scholars.

In the *Mishneh Torah*, which was organized and classified according to subject matter, Maimonides attempted for the first time to codify the whole of Jewish law in an objective and systematic manner. He wrote the work in Hebrew and divided it into fourteen books to correspond with the distinct categories in *halakhah*. As an interpreter of *halakhah*, he wished to compose a handbook that was logically arranged, that could be used as an easy reference manual to be used in conjunction with the Torah, and that could guide Jews in how to live their lives. He wished to relieve them of the burden of studying the Talmud but managed, rather, to alienate those traditional Jews who feared the abandonment and atrophying of Talmudic study. Despite these fears, the *Mishneh Torah* was itself the focus of hundreds of studies and commentaries, disproving the fears of his critics.

His practical application of *halakhah* can be seen in his collection *Responsa*, which contains questions and answers concerning practical and legal matters; Maimonides is visible as the concerned leader of the community and as one who rendered *halakhic* decisions preserving the fundamental doctrines of Judaism. The questions and their answers are excellent sources to understand the role Maimonides played in his community and how he was perceived by his contemporaries.

Maimonides' most important work was the *Guide of the Perplexed*, a philosophical treatise that he wrote in Arabic (*Dalālat al-Ha'irin*), which was quickly translated into Hebrew. Having been influenced by Aristotelian philosophy as it had been mediated through the work of Hellenistic philosophers and contemporary Islamic commentators, Aristotelianism became a fundamental part of his own philosophical system. In trying to reconcile faith and reason, he believed that the tools of philosophical inquiry could support the statements of the Jewish faith. Maimonides intended for the *Guide of the Perplexed* to explain the spiritual meaning of the difficult biblical terms and passages like those that referred to God in anthropomorphic terms. He first dealt with the most difficult topic of all, that is, God. In exploring the question of the "image of God" (*zelem Elohim*) Maimonides explained that this "image" was the spiritual essence of God, which in man is equated with reason. In exploring the attributes of God, Maimonides followed the reasoning of Avicenna, who concluded that essential attributes emanate from the essence. Maimonides continued his inquiry by demonstrating God's existence using metaphysics and physics. He discussed the creation of the world, corporeal and incorporeal beings (angels), the legitimacy of prophecy, the nature of evil, the laws of nature and divine providence, the nature of man and moral virtue, as well as the law of Moses and the principles of Jewish eschatology.

During his own lifetime, Maimonides faced rigorous objections to his philosophical perspective as well as to his attempts to bypass the burden of Talmudic study. These objections formed the cornerstone of a controversy that became known as the Maimonidean Controversy. Questions were raised concerning Maimonides' description of the relationship of reason and philosophy to faith and tradition, as well as to concepts like the resurrection of the body, and his explanations for biblical anthropomorphic references to God. Part of the conflict also stemmed from Maimonides' critique of what he perceived to be the corruption of the Jewish leadership and teachers, the *geonim*. He criticized in particular their practice of charging fees for teaching the Torah and Talmud. The clash was to manifest itself during his lifetime in 1180, again in 1230–1232 and in 1300–1306. The issues at the heart of the Maimonidean Controversy would continue to circulate and rise up even in much later times.

Maimonides continued to be one of the most studied medieval Jewish scholars, and whether he was appreciated or vilified, he made an enormous impact on the development of Jewish scholarship.

Bibliography: O. Leaman, *Moses Maimonides*, 1990; M. Maimonides, *The Guide of the Perplexed*, trans. S. Pines, 1963.

Tom Papademetriou

MĀLIK IBN ANAS (708/716–796).

He is best known as the collector/editor of the *Muwatta'* (The Leveled Way), one of the first extant anthologies of *hadith*, which is of great historical value as evidence of the Medinese Muslim law of the early-second-century Muslim community. The *Muwatta'* is considered an important stepping stone in the development of Islamic law, which grows out of a combination of both local traditions and practices and examples of the actions and sayings of the prophet *Muhammad. One of the four surviving Sunni schools of Islamic law, the *Mālikiyya*, dominant in the Islamic West, is named after Mālik.

Abū ʿAbd Allāh Mālik ibn Anas ibn Mālik ibn Abī ʿĀmir, affiliated with the tribe of the Banū Taym ibn Murra, was born between 708 and 716. Little reliable historical information is available about Mālik; apart from his date of death in 796, his role as a collector of *hadith* (reports about the actions and sayings of the prophet Muhammad) and his temporary opposition to the early ʿAbbāsids, for which he was flogged in 762, not much can be said about Mālik with certainty. Of legendary character is a tradition recorded by al-Tirmidhī that the coming of Mālik was already prophesied by Muhammad, as is the claim that the duration of Mālik's mother's pregnancy extended to three full years. The number of teachers from which Mālik learned traditions is also greatly exaggerated; later texts speak of 900 teachers, out of which 300 were Muslims of the generation immediately succeeding the companions of the Prophet Muhammad. Among Mālik's more famous teachers are reportedly counted Ja'far al-Sadiq, the famous sixth imam of Shiite Islam, and Sahl ibn Saʿd, one of the last surviving companions of the Prophet. Mālik also knew Abū Hanīfah, the famous founder of the Hanīfi school of law, and Muhammad ibn Ishaq, author of the first extant biography of Muhammad. His relationship to the latter was strained, each scholar accusing the other of untrustworthiness.

Mālik's paternal uncle and grandfather are reported to have been collectors of *hadith*; a few traditions relate that Mālik intended to become a singer at first but was kept from that career due to his unattractive outward appearance. Mālik's attitude toward the ʿAbbāsid political powers of the day is ambivalent; after reportedly issuing a *fatwā* (decision regarding religious law) in connection with an uprising led by the proto Shiite Muhammad al-Nafs al-Zakkiyyā in 762, that the oath of allegiance paid toward the ʿAbbāsid caliph al-Mansūr could be considered nonbinding since it had been given under duress, Mālik was punished for this offense with flogging by the ʿAbbāsid governor of Medina. Relations with the ʿAbbāsids normalized after this incident; indeed, al-Mansūr himself and two later ʿAbbāsid caliphs, al-Mahdī and *Hārūn al-Rashīd are reported to have consulted Mālik on religious matters. Mālik's death date of 796 is fairly well established; he is reported to have died after a brief illness and is buried in the famous Medinese cementery al-Baqiʿ.

Mālik's influence on Islamic law lies in his edition of the first extant manual of Islamic law and collection of *hadith*, the *Muwatta'*. Mālik's motivation for composing this work cannot be reliably reconstructed. A few traditions indicate that ʿAbbāsid Caliph al-Mansūr, upon visiting Mālik in connection with his pilgrimage to Mecca in 769, asked Mālik to compose a work on Islamic law that would help to overcome differences in legal practice between Medina and Iraq. According to other authorities, al-Mansūr asked not for the composition but rather the publication of a work Mālik already had composed. In either case, Mālik appears to have been somewhat reluctant to impose uniformity on the existing diversity of Islamic law.

The *Muwatta'* is a collection of traditions that are not explicitly attributed to the Prophet Muhammad, as is the case with later, orthodox collections of *hadith*. Rather, material presented in the *Muwatta'* is oftentimes prefaced with the common formula: "The generally agreed on way of doing things among us . . . is . . ."; other material in the *Muwatta'* relates the practices and opinions of companions of the Prophet, or those of later Muslims, or Mālik's own opinion. The *Muwatta'* thus is understood by Western scholars as a stepping stone in the development of Muslim law. Whereas early legal practice was based on a variety of sources, including local practice and tradition, the opinion (ray) of a certain scholar, or the example of either Muhammad or his companions, only in the early ninth century did Islamic scholars develop an insistence that Islamic law be founded on the example (Sunna) of the Prophet to the exclusion of local practices and traditions.

Bibliography: Mālik ibn Anas, *Al-Muwatta*, trans 'A'. ʿAbdarahman and Y. Johnson, 1982.

Alfons Teipen

MAʾMŪN, ABU ʾL-ʿABBAS ʿABD ALLĀH IBN HĀRŪN AL-RASHĪD, AL- (786–833).

Al-Maʾmūn, son of the famous caliph *Hārūn al-Rashīd of the 1001 Arabian Nights, was the seventh caliph of the ʿAbbāsid dynasty who reigned from 813 to 833. Renowned for his active support of the translation movement that enabled much of ancient Greek philosophy, astronomy, medicine, and mathematics to be passed on via the Muslim world to medieval Europe, al-Maʾmūn is sometimes credited with the founding of the *Bayt al-hikma* (House of Wisdom) in Baghdad to further the translation and study of ancient texts.

Al-Maʾmūn was born on 14 September 786, the same day that his father Hārūn al-Rashīd became caliph, as eldest of eleven sons. Al-Maʾmūn's mother, Marājil, possibly the granddaughter of a Persian rebel against the Caliph al-Mansūr, was a concubine of Hārūn. After the death of al-Maʾmūn's mother, Hārūn's wife Zubayda, granddaughter of Caliph al-Mansūr, and thus herself of ʿAbbāsid lineage, raised the boy. Al-Maʾmūn's younger half brother Muhammad (al-Amīn), son of Hārūn and Zubayda, was designated by his father as the primary successor to the caliphate. In 799, al-Rashīd divided the future administration of the empire between his three sons: al-Amīn, al-Muʾtamin, and al-Maʾmūn; the latter was appointed as the governor of the Eastern Empire, including the important province of Khurāsān. The agreement between al-Rashīd and his sons also designated al-Maʾmūn as secondary successor to the caliphate and was sealed by sacred oath and proclaimed in Mecca during the pilgrimage of the year 802. In 804, al-Maʾmūn married his cousin, Umm ʿIsā bint Mūsā al-Hādī, who bore him two sons.

Upon the death of Hārūn al-Rashīd in 809, al-Amīn, in violation of the sacred oath undertaken with both father and half brother, designated his own son Mūsā as successor to the caliphate. Challenging al-Amīn's decision, al-Maʾmūn inaugurated a civil war, out of which he emerged victorious in the year 813. Al-Amīn was executed by a general of al-Ma'mūn's army; this killing constituted the first regicide in 'Abbāsid history and created problems of legitimization for al-Ma'mūn's caliphate. In 817, al-Ma'mūn declared 'Alī ibn Mūsā al-Ridā, recognized by Shiite factions as the eighth imam (religious-political leader), as his successor to the caliphate, passing over his brother al-Mu'tamin. This move, interpreted by historians as an attempt to reconcile 'Abbāsid and Shiite claims to political and religious leadership, failed when 'Alī ibn Mūsā died in 818. Shiite support for al-Ma'mūn was waning when accusations were brought forth that 'Ali had been poisoned by al-Ma'mūn.

Al-Ma'mūn, having stayed in the Marw, the provincial capital of Khurāsān, moved his administration, court, and army to Baghdad in the year 819. Having pacified the empire after the civil war as well as several independent insurrections, al-Ma'mūn declared Mu'tazilism the official doctrine of the empire in 827. The tenets of Mu'tazilism include a belief in the unity of God, in divine justice and human free will, in promise and threat on the Last Day and the Day of Judgment, and in spreading the message of Islam. Regarding himself as the ultimate arbiter in religion and politics, al-Ma'mūn introduced the inquisition (*mihna*) both to assert his own authority and to undermine the religious authority of the religious scholars (*'ulama*) who based their authority on Holy Scripture (Qur'an). In his insistence that the Qur'an was created, and not the eternal word of God, al-Ma'mūn attempted to lessen the authority of the interpreters of the Qur'an and their ideological claims. According to some traditions, al-Ma'mūn founded the House of Wisdom (*Bayt al-hikma*) during one of the last years of his reign, furthering the study and translation of ancient Greek philosophy and sciences. Shortly after the institution of the *mihna*, al-Ma'mūn died en route to a campaign against the Byzantines in 833 after a brief illness and was buried in the city of Tarsus (in modern-day Turkey).

Al-Ma'mūn's significance lies in his adoption of Mu'tazilite doctrine, his institution of the *mihna*, and his support for the translation movement. Although the movement itself predates al-Ma'mūn by more than a half century, he is traditionally regarded as one of its most important supporters. He also is reported to have held disputations with theologians and philosophers of different religious traditions in his Baghdad court. Al-Ma'mūn's motivation to institute the *mihna*, however, is subject to controversy. While some scholars understand the *mihna* as an outcome of political motivations, emphasizing a pre-Islamic Sasanid-Persian influence on al-Ma'mūn's understanding of authority that combines religious and political authority, other scholars interpret al-Ma'mūn's inauguration of the *mihna* as a result of his commitment to rationalist, Mu'tazilite theology.

Bibliography: M. Cooperson, *Classical Arabic Biography. The Heirs of the Prophets in the Age of al-Ma'mūn*, 2000; T. El-Hibri, "The Reign of the 'Abbasid Caliph al-Ma'mūn (811–833): The Quest for Power and the Crisis of Legitimacy," 1994.

Alfons Teipen

MAP, WALTER (C. 1130/1135–C. 1210). A secular clerk and author of *De nugis curialium* (Courtiers' Trifles), Walter Map served in the court of King *Henry II of England and later became archdeacon of Oxford.

Little is known about Map. Most likely he was of Welsh descent and born between 1130 and 1135. He spent most of his adult life in Herefordshire. Nothing is known about his early education, but by 1154 he was sitting at the lectures of Gerard la Pucelle in Paris. Map won the patronage of Gilbert Foliot, bishop of Hereford and later of London, and also of Henry II. In 1173, Map was made a canon at St. Paul's and was given the prebend of Mapesbury. That same year he was appointed a royal clerk and acted as a royal justice in London. A high point of his career was to attend the Third Lateran Council in 1179 as Henry's representative; there he engaged in a fierce debate with the Waldensians and believed himself the victor. Throughout the 1170s, Map acquired many churches, prebends, and other forms of financial support. He succeeded Geoffrey Plantagenet, Henry II's illegitimate son, in his London prebend and was further rewarded by Henry with the living of Ashwell in Hertfordshire. Thus Map was able to maintain an expensive household.

In 1189 Henry II died, and Map's career at court ended. But his ecclesiastical career continued to flourish. Earlier Map had been appointed a canon at Lincoln, then the chancellor of its cathedral school. After Henry's death, he became its precentor. In 1196 or 1197, Map was moved to the archdeaconry of Oxford and held that position when he died on 1 April 1209 or 1210.

Until the nineteenth century, Map was believed the author of scurrilous Latin verse and French romances. Currently his literary fame rests solely on *Courtiers' Trifles*, an entertaining collection of personal anecdotes and tales written in Latin and surviving in a single manuscript of the late fourteenth century. The tales all serve a moral purpose but reveal Map as an excellent raconteur. The autobiographical anecdotes bring to life the court of Henry II. Throughout the work, Map displays a sophisticated wit and considerable verbal skill; however, he also reveals himself as arrogant, opinionated, and prejudiced. This charge is substantiated by the report of *Gerald of Wales, who notes that when named a royal justice, Map quipped that he would do justice to everyone except Cistercians and Jews. Map also disliked Waldensians and women. He describes *Eleanor of Aquitaine as having cast "unchaste" eyes at Henry and then contriving an "unrighteous" annulment from *Louis VII of France. Map's misogyny is most apparent in "The Letter of Valerius to Ruffinus, against Marriage." Although he wrote this antimatrimonial satire separately from *Trifles*, he incorporates it into the extant text to assert his authorship. This fictional letter had some influence on the authors of later vernacular literature including Geoffrey Chaucer, who alludes to it as *Valerie* in the Wife of Bath's Prologue.

Bibliography: Walter Map, De nugis curialium: *Courtiers' Trifles*, ed. and trans. M. R. James, rev. C.N.L. Brooke and R.A.B. Mynors, 1983.

Deanna Evans

MARBOD (MARBODUS) OF RENNES (C. 1035–1123). Bishop and teacher, Marbod was also a poet of renown.

Known in literature both as "of Angers" and "of Rennes," Marbod studied with Rainald, himself a student of *Fulbert of Chartres. In 1067, Bishop Eusebius Bruno appointed Marbod master. He was later made archdeacon. In 1096, he was appointed bishop of Rennes by Pope *Urban II. He served with such distinction that despite his advanced age he administered the diocese of Angers in tandem with Rennes in 1109. At the age of eighty-eight, Marbod resigned his bishopric and retired to the Benedictine monastery of St. Aubin in his native Angers, where he died. Angers may be said never to have forgotten him; the main edition of his works was printed there in 1524, and his biography was published there in 1889. His complete works are printed in *PL* 171.

Best known to modern scholarship for his love poetry, he was equally celebrated in the central Middle Ages for his versified saints' lives and hymns. Marbod's position as the leading teacher in Angers brought him into contact with the young women of the convent of Le Ronceray at Angers, many of whom were resident in the convent to be educated before leaving for marriage. The poetry, which emanated from these relationships, is part of a long-standing tradition of literary correspondence between scholar–poets and learned women. With their combination of instruction and mutual esteem, at times moving into literary flirtation and sometimes more, at once formalizing and liberating genuine human relationships through the authorization of poetry, they are examples of a poetry that survives from similar milieus across western Europe. The bisexual motif of at least one poem (see *PL* 140) may be a literary exercise or written out of real-life experience. Whether to men or to women, or when turning from both at last to the episcopal duties that appear to have profoundly engaged him, there is a warmth and humanity that preclude both heartless sensuality and equally heartless austerity.

Horace was his model, a rare choice for his time and place but one easily understood. "Oscula dum sperno, spernens tamen oscula cerno" (When I spurn kisses, I, nevertheless, must think of kisses) is as neat a tag as learning and experience can produce. To reduce his observation that the word death (*mors*) sounds sharp and uncultivated while the word life (*vita*) is easy and cheerful simply to a reflection of a theory of language is to miss the point of the playfulness of early medieval scholarship. Perhaps his two most influential works are the poem on precious stones (the *Liber lapidum*) and the third and fourth chapters of the *Liber decem capitulorum*, "De meretrice" (On the Prostitute) and "De matrona," the first a checklist of medieval misogyny, the second a celebration of the good woman who is God's greatest gift to a man.

Marbod may also have been alive to the rising power and subject matter of vernacular verse. Dronke calls attention to his poem "Ad sonitum cithare solitus sum me recreare." Within the framing device of listening to a young boy singing of a lady who finds her beloved dying of a spear thrust, he paints a scene comparable, if not necessarily identical, to Thomas of Britain's *Tristan*. Marbod's poetry was copied and recopied in the verse miscellanies of the twelfth and thirteenth centuries.

Bibliography: P. Dronke, *Medieval Latin and the Rise of the European Love Lyric*, 2d ed., 2 vols., 1968; Marbodi, *Liber decem capitulorum*, ed. R. Leotta, 1984.

Helen Conrad-O'Briain

MARCO POLO. *See* POLO, MARCO.

MARGUERITE PORETE. *See* PORETE, MARGUERITE.

MARIE DE CHAMPAGNE (1145–1198). Best known for her patronage of the arts, Marie de Champagne was the daughter of *Eleanor of Aquitaine and *Louis VII of France.

After the divorce of her royal parents, Marie spent her early childhood in Paris. Betrothed to Henry I (the Liberal) of Champagne in 1153, she was sent to the Benedictine convent of Avenay to be educated under the direction of Abbess Alice of Mareuil. There she would have learned to read Latin as well as French, and eventually she acquired a personal library. In 1164, she was married to Henry, with whom she had two daughters, Scholastique and Marie, and two sons, Henry II and Thibaut III. She is said to have spent some time at Eleanor's court in Poitiers in the early 1170s.

Count Henry died in 1181. Prior to this time, Marie had not participated in political life; Henry had been twenty-two years older than she and had already selected the officers of his demesne when she arrived at Troyes. At the age of thirty-four, she took up the duties of the regency during her sons' minorities and exercised considerable freedom and power from 1181 until the majority of her son Henry II. She had had some preparation for regency through her relationships with both the Capet and the Plantagenet dynasties, her years of convent education, and her experience as consort to her husband, and it appears that her court was well run. After Henry's accession in 1187, she retired briefly, but when he left to join the Third Crusade in 1190 (he died in 1197), she resumed her regency, which lasted until her death in 1198.

Despite fifteen years of relatively independent rule over a major economic region and urban center, Marie is famous only for her patronage of artists at Henry's court in Troyes. Certainly, under her regency she encouraged the romance writer *Chrétien de Troyes and his continuators. Chrétien's best-known work, *Le Chevalier de la Charette* (The Knight of the Cart), was written at her direction; he states in his introduction that she furnished him with both the subject and its treatment. Marie also patronized the poets Conon de Béthune, Gace Brulé, and perhaps Huon d'Oissy; Gautier d'Arras composed a romance for her. Later in the 1180s, she commissioned a paraphrase of the psalm "Eructavit" as well as a translation of Genesis. Undoubtedly the best-known result of her patronage is the work of her court chaplain Andreas *Capellanus, *De arte honeste amandi* (The Art of Courtly Love), which defined love and various ways of obtaining and retaining (Books I and II) or rejecting it (Book III). Possibly influenced by his observations of Marie, Queen Eleanor, and other aristocratic women at the court of Poitiers a decade or so earlier, Andreas described gatherings in which women heard and rendered decisions on questions of proper behavior for lovers at court. (The actual existence of these "courts of love" has been vigorously contested and now appears dubious.)

Bibliography: J. F. Benton, "Collaborative Approaches to Fantasy and Reality in the Literature of Champagne," in *Culture, Power and Personality in Medieval France*, ed. T. Bisson, 1991; T. Evergates, ed., *Aristocratic Women in Medieval France*, 1999; J.H.M. McCash, "Marie de Champagne and Eleanor of Aquitaine: A Relationship Reexamined," *Speculum* 54 (1979): 698–711.

Judith Davis

MARIE DE FRANCE (FL. 1165–1190). Marie de France was the first major female writer in Europe. Of her life almost nothing is known; she is supposed to have lived in France and perhaps in England during the second half of the twelfth century. Her identity has been the subject of extensive speculation: She is said to have been, variously, the illegitimate daughter of Geoffrey IV of Anjou, the abbess of Shaftesbury, and a daughter of King *Stephen of England; however, none of these theories has proved conclusive.

Evidently both well educated and well read in Latin and French as well as English, she was conversant with both classical and contemporary literary works, which influenced her own choice of subjects and motifs. Her work comprises a book of *lais* or short story-poems, dated between 1160 and 1170; a collection of fables, *Isopet*, written between 1167 and 1189; and a retelling of the Saint Patrick legend, *L'Espurgatoire Saint Patriz*, written after 1189 and possibly as late as 1215. She identifies herself in each work; at the end of the fables, she states clearly that Marie of France has written the work: She does not want a lot of clerks claiming it for themselves.

The *Lais*, collected in five manuscripts, including the prominent Harley 978, constitute Marie's best-known work, considered one of the best in early French literature. It is evident that she was familiar with the geographical regions in which she situated her tales: Brittany, Normandy, Nantes, and the south of Britain. She is known for her accurate depictions of twelfth-century court life as well as her treatment of the crises and suffering associated with love. Sources of her tales include Irish and Breton legends, as evidenced in motifs of marvelous adventure and shape-shifting; she also drew upon Ovid and other classical authors. Her subjects include a feckless knight and his fairy love ("Lanval"); the metamorphosis of one knight ("Yonec") into a hawk and another ("Bisclavret") into a werewolf; the self-sacrifice of a wife ("Eliduc") or a maiden ("Fraisne") for her love; the secret meeting of Tristan and Iseult ("Chèvrefeuille"), and tragic love ("Les Deus Amanz," "Laüstic," and "Chaitivel"). Scholars have remarked on the strength of her female characters; her accurate depiction of human love; and the importance of symbolism and the supernatural to the success of her stories.

Marie's collection of 102 fables appears in twenty-three manuscripts, attesting to its popularity. Like their Greek archetypes, these tales employ animals to condemn pride, oppression, and greed and to extol the virtues of the simple life. Several incorporate feudal themes such as the importance of loyalty to one's lord, the necessity of choosing an honest seneschal, and the importance of honor to the vassal-lord relationship.

The unique manuscript of *Saint Patrick's Purgatory*, Marie's translation from the Latin of Henry of Saltrey, recounts the journey through purgatory of an Irish knight, Owein, his pilgrimage made possible by Saint Patrick to strengthen the laity's belief in an afterlife. Owein battles temptation and returns to recount his experiences. The didactic *Espurgatoire* is one of the oldest European vernacular works to present a picture of life after death.

Bibliography: G. S. Burgess, *Marie de France: An Analytical Bibliography*, Supplement no. 2, 1997; *The lais of Marie de France*, trans. R. W. Hanning and J. Ferrante, 1978; Marie de France, *Les fables*, ed. and trans. C. Brucker, 1991.

Judith Davis

MARSH, ADAM (ADAM DE MARISCO) (D. 1258).

Adam was a Franciscan theologian at Oxford and, along with Robert *Grosseteste, the founder of the Franciscan school there.

Adam was probably from Somerset. He was educated at Oxford and had become a master of arts by 1226. In 1232–1233 he entered the Franciscan Order at Worcester, and according to *Matthew Paris, he gave up a large income and a worldly position to do so. After 1233, he was sent back to Oxford to study theology and matriculated there in fall 1244.

In 1245, he accompanied Grosseteste to the Council of Lyons. Grosseteste reported that the Franciscans at the University of Paris wanted Adam to stay there and teach, due to the recent deaths of their masters *Alexander of Hales and John of La Rochelle. Nevertheless, Adam returned to Oxford and taught there until 1250. Although he continued to live at Oxford after 1250, his career after that point was occupied by public life. He accompanied Boniface, archbishop of Canterbury, on his metropolitan visitations. King *Henry III of England frequently summoned him to the royal court and on two occasions, in 1247 and 1257, selected him for diplomatic missions. In the latter year, Adam was one of the royal delegates sent to France to negotiate a peace with King *Louis IX. Adam was also a spiritual counselor to Simon de *Montfort the Younger and his family. Both King Henry and Archbishop Boniface tried to obtain the bishopric of Ely for Adam, but their efforts were unsuccessful.

Adam was a prolific letter writer. His scriptural commentaries have not yet been edited or studied. He probably wrote a treatise on tides, *De fluxu et reflexu maris*, which has traditionally been ascribed to Grosseteste. He was known by the title "Doctor Illustris" and was praised by Roger *Bacon.

Bibliography: C. H. Lawrence, "The Letters of Adam Marsh and the Franciscan School at Oxford," *Journal of Ecclesiastical History* 42.2 (April 1991): 218–238; A. G. Little, "The Franciscan School at Oxford in the Thirteenth Century," *Archivum Franciscanum Historicum* 19 (1926): 803–874.

Andrew G. Traver

MATILDA, EMPRESS (1102–1167).

The only surviving child of *Henry I of England, Matilda was widow of Holy Roman Emperor *Henry V and heiress to the English throne. Robbed of her birthright by her cousin Stephen of Blois (who became *Stephen of England), Matilda nevertheless prevailed to see her son crowned *Henry II of England after Stephen's death.

Matilda married Henry V at age sixteen and played an active role in imperial politics. Subsequent to the death of her brother William in the "Whiteship disaster" of 1120 and the death of her husband in 1125, Matilda was called back to England by Henry I. Unsuccessful in his attempts to sire another heir, he began grooming Matilda for the accession. The barons of the kingdom swore to uphold her rights, but Henry chose Geoffrey of Anjou for Matilda's second husband without their approval. After the birth of Matilda's first son, Henry, the English nobles were again required to swear to uphold her claims and those of her infant son.

The death of Henry I in 1135 caught Matilda unaware. Residing in Anjou, she was far from his deathbed, so Stephen of Blois, nephew of Henry I, was able to declare himself king of England on the basis of Henry's supposed last wishes. Acting with amazing rapidity and the help of his brother Henry, bishop of Winchester, Stephen crossed quickly from Boulogne to London. The archbishop of Canterbury was persuaded to crown Stephen, and the keys to the treasury were placed into his hands.

Regardless of Stephen's preemptory strike, Matilda claimed both England and Normandy as her father's designated heir. Arriving in England in 1139, the empress attempted to regain her lost patrimony, supported by her uncle King David of Scotland, her half brother Robert Earl of Gloucester, Brian FitzCount, and many others. Thus began eight years of civil war when, according to one contemporary, "God and his saints slept." The English nobility shifted sides repeatedly as Stephen and Matilda vied for their support, promised lands and honors, and besieged one another as the countryside was rapaciously plundered. Stephen's weakness as a ruler allowed Matilda to gain political ground, but when her supporters finally captured him, Matilda was unable to depose an anointed king of England. Her inability to personally lead armed forces proved a disadvantage. When Robert of Gloucester was captured in battle, Matilda was forced to trade her royal prisoner Stephen to secure his release.

After 1141, Matilda involved her son Henry in her struggles and tirelessly worked toward his future, abandoning her own hopes for the throne. She left England in 1148 and returned to Normandy. She gained favor with the papacy, while Stephen turned Pope *Eugenius III against his cause by interfering with episcopal elections and papal councils. After the death of Stephen's eldest son in 1153, he finally treated with Matilda and Henry. Stephen would live out the rest of his life as king, but on his death the crown would pass to Matilda's line as Henry II became the first Angevin king of England.

After Stephen's death, she ruled Normandy jointly with Henry or in his name and advised him until her death. A courageous and determined leader, the Empress Matilda was, nevertheless, unable to prevail against English twelfth-century mores that considered women unfit to hold ultimate political power.

Bibliography: M. Chibnall, *The Empress Matilda: Queen Consort, Queen Mother and Lady of the English*, 1991.

Laura L. Gathagan

MATILDA OF FLANDERS, DUCHESS OF NORMANDY (MATILDA I)
(1031–1083). The first Norman queen of England and the formidable wife of *William I the Conqueror, Matilda participated in the Norman Conquest and was mother of seven children including two kings of England: William Rufus and *Henry I.

The daughter of Baldwin V of Flanders and Adela, sister of the king of France, Matilda married William of Normandy, providing the blood through which her children would claim royal rights. Because of papal disapproval regarding their marriage, the pair later founded dual monasteries in Normandy to legitimize their union—a fitting gesture for Matilda who, as duchess of Normandy, endowed over a dozen monastic houses. In 1066, Matilda supplied ships and men for the Norman Conquest of England, while acting as regent in Normandy during William's absence. After their victory, she was crowned in 1068 at Winchester, her coronation setting the stage for her active political role.

One of the greatest lay landholders in the Domesday Book, Matilda acted as regent in England, signed hundreds of charters, adjudicated court cases, dispensed royal justice, and traveled tirelessly throughout her career in support of Norman political policy. Continuing the work she began as duchess, Queen Matilda enriched and founded English monasteries, not only as an expression of piety but to enhance her prestige and reverse negative public opinion of her predatory activity.

A fearless champion of her children, she supported her first son Robert Curthose in his rebellion against her own husband, then later presided over their reconciliation. After her death on 2 November 1083, she was entombed at her monastic foundation in Caen, Normandy, where her body resides today.

Bibliography: L. L. Gathagan, "The Coronation of Matilda of Flanders," *Haskins Society Journal* X (forthcoming).

Laura L. Gathagan

MATILDA OF TUSCANY (1046–1115).
The daughter of Boniface of Canossa, marquis of Tuscany, and Beatrice of Lorraine, heiress to large possessions

in northern Italy, and a talented military commander, Matilda was a central actor in the Investiture Controversy that pitted Pope *Gregory VII against the Holy Roman Emperor *Henry IV.

As a child, Matilda accompanied her mother and stepfather Godfrey of Lorraine (the Bearded) on military campaigns, doubtless learning the skills that would make her later endeavors successful. She was a skilled horsewoman. The leading military power behind Gregory from 1074 until his death, Matilda's support began when negotiations with her kinsman Henry IV, concerning the investiture of bishops, failed. After Henry attempted to depose the pope, she and her army escorted Gregory across Germany to her fortress in Canossa where, in perhaps the most famous episode of the century, Henry appeared before the pope outside the snowy gates as a penitent. When relations between Henry and Gregory once again deteriorated, Matilda led her troops against the emperor for the first time in 1080.

Through the close of the century, Matilda saw her military and economic fortunes fluctuate as she continued to battle Henry; after Gregory's death in 1085, she supported his successors, especially Pope *Urban II. Henry's final defeat at her hands occurred in 1092, as Matilda's troops captured the imperial standard as they attacked Canossa.

Critical to the political success of reform, Matilda not only supported the Church in war, but she provided a court atmosphere friendly to canon lawyers and cutting-edge political theory.

Bibliography: M. Huddy, *Matilda, Countess of Tuscany*, 1910.

Laura L. Gathagan

MATTHEW OF AQUASPARTA (C. 1238–1302). A Franciscan cardinal and theologian, he was born in Aquasparta in the diocese of Todi about 1238. He held the post of minister general of the Franciscan Order from 1287 to 1289 and became cardinal bishop of Porto and St. Rufina in 1291. A disciple of *Bonaventure, Matthew's *Questiones disputatae de cognitione* defended his theory of cognition and upheld the Augustinian theory of divine illumination. He died on 29 October 1302 in Rome.

A descendant of the Bentivenghi family, Matthew joined the Friars Minor at St. Fortunat in Todi around 1254. By 1268, Matthew had become a lecturer on the Bible (*baccalarius biblicus*) at the University of Paris, and he spent from 1270 to 1273 commenting on the *Sentences* of *Peter Lombard. Around 1276, Matthew was master of theology, and he became regent master of the Franciscan Studium from 1277 to 1279, holding the chair of philosophy at Paris. Matthew also spent some time during his early career teaching at Bologna, but the dates of his stay there are a matter of some debate.

Matthew replaced his teacher *John Peckham as the lector of the Sacred Palace (*Lector sacri palatii*) in Rome in 1278. In this position, Matthew served as official theologian to the pope and the Roman Curia. In 1282 Matthew was elected provincial of Umbria, then general minister of the Franciscan Order in 1287. He proved himself an able moderator as he reinstated *Peter John Olivi and John of Parma. Matthew held this position until the next general chapter in 1289.

Pope Nicholas IV (1288–1292), himself a former general of the Franciscan Order, appointed Matthew cardinal priest on 16 May 1288, and in 1289 Matthew was made director of the Sacred Apostolic Penitentiary. In 1291, he rose to the position of cardinal bishop of Porto and St. Rufina. In this faculty, Matthew was loyal to Pope *Boniface VIII, supporting and expounding the idea of *plentitudo potestatis* (belief in the pope's ultimate authority). He may have helped to draw up *Unam Sanctum*, the famous bull of 1302. Boniface appointed Matthew pontifical legate to Lombardy, Romagna, and Florence in 1297 and 1300, and Matthew assisted the pope in his conflict with Philip IV of France (1285–1314).

Matthew's voluminous writings reflect his historical positioning between Bonaventure and *John Duns Scotus, and he is often noted for his clarity. His theological writings place him in what is termed the old Franciscan School; he defended the tenets of Augustine and Bonaventure against newer Thomistic and Aristotelian theories. Matthew maintained that divine illumination is necessary to explain knowledge. Although he wrote over 200 sermons, a massive commentary on the *Sentences* of Peter Lombard, various biblical exegeses, *Questiones disputatae*, and *quodlibets*, these pieces had little circulation, and Matthew seems to have had little influence on later thinkers.

Bibliography: H. M. Beha, "Matthew of Aquasparta's Theory of Cognition," *Franciscan Studies*, 2d ser., 20 (1960): 161–204; 21 (1961): 1–79, 383–465.

Karolyn Kinane

MATTHEW PARIS (C. 1200–1259). English historical writer, hagiographer, and artist, Matthew Paris' *Chronicon* covered world history from Creation to his own period. He reported extensively on the activities and relationships between King *Louis IX of France, the Hohenstaufen *Frederick II, King *Henry III of England, and the papacy.

Matthew was a Benedictine monk who lived and worked in the abbey of St. Albans in Hertfordshire. He became the abbey chronicler upon the death of Roger of Wendover, continuing and revising the latter's *Flores historiarum*. By the time of his death in 1259, he had produced five historical works in Latin, the greatest of which was his *Chronica majora*—the continuation of Roger's work—that began with the Creation and continued to his own day. In this chronicle, and its supplement, the *Liber additiamentorum*, which contained a collection of documents to which he was privy, Matthew provided reliable information on the tensions between Henry III and his magnates, and between the empire and the papacy. Matthew reported events as a direct commentator on current events of his day. At one point, he admits that he even participated in them.

For instance, King *Hákon IV of Norway requested his help in 1246 for a problem concerning a Benedictine abbey in Norway. In 1248, Matthew even went to Norway to reform that abbey. At that time, he brought letters from King Louis IX asking for King Hákon's support of the Seventh Crusade. He was familiar with the royal household of Louis IX and provided many useful insights into Louis IX's commitment and preparation for his crusade to the Holy Land; the *Great Chronicle* includes extensive commentary on Louis and the crusades. His criticism of the papacy after the dissolution of the monasteries is balanced by criticism of Louis IX for his moral failure in plundering the Church for the purpose of the crusade.

In addition to the historical works in Latin, Matthew produced four hagiographies in French verse: *La vie de St. Auban* (Saint Alban), *La estoire de St. Aedward le rei* (*Edward the Confessor), *La vie de St. Edmond*, and *La vie de St. Thomas de Canterbéry* (Saint Thomas *Becket). He accompanied these texts, as well as the historical ones, with illustrations, diagrams, and maps that he himself drew. His maps of Britain and the Holy Land contributed much to medieval cartography.

Matthew remains a controversial source because it has been proven that he was not above reporting invented material and rumor as fact. His strong prejudices and possible distortions require historians to corroborate his account as much as possible. Yet the whole of his corpus remains a valuable source for understanding the prevailing values and attitudes of a person of his position, in his own day.

Bibliography: R. Vaughn, ed. and trans., *The Chronicles of Matthew Paris: Monastic Life in the Thirteenth Century*, 1984.

Tom Papademetriou

MECHTHILD OF HACKEBORN (C. 1241–1298).

Younger sister of abbess Gertrude of Hackeborn and mentor of *Gertrude the Great, Mechthild of Hackeborn entered the convent at Helfta at the age of seven. She had apparently come to the abbey to visit her older sister and reportedly went to each nun, begging to stay. Mechthild's visionary experience is recorded in the *Liber specialis gratiae* (The Book of Special Grace), written down around 1291.

Mechthild's *Liber specialis gratiae* states (book 5) that two persons wrote the work; Gertrude the Great is believed to be the chief compiler. Evidence of Gertrude's authorship includes the quality of the Latin and passages that recount episodes also recorded in Gertrude's *Legatus*. The *Liber specialis gratiae* has seven sections: the Annunciation and various feast days (book 1), Mechthild's own mystical experiences (book 2), convent life (books 3 and 4), the afterlife (book 5), the heavenly rewards granted the abbess Gertrude and her sister Mechthild (books 6 and 7). In her *Liber*, Mechthild displays vivid nature imagery (trees and animals) and rich colors.

Music also figures prominently in Mechthild's spirituality, in keeping with

Mechthild's position as choir mistress (the *Liber* identifies her as *domna cantrix*). Like Gertrude the Great, Mechthild served as counselor and spiritual adviser to convent sisters as well as outside laity and clergy seeking information about what practices Christ wished performed and the state of souls in the afterlife.

Bibliography: M. J. Finnegan. *The Women of Helfta: Scholars and Mystics,* 1991.

Alexandra Sterling-Hellenbrand

MECHTHILD OF MAGDEBURG (C. 1207–C. 1282/1297).

A celebrated medieval mystic and author, Mechthild first lived as a Beguine and then retired to Helfta.

Mechthild was born in Magdeburg, Thuringia, in Lower Saxony. She was probably from an aristocratic family because her work reveals a familiarity with court society and conventions, and she uses Latin easily. Her first mystical experience occurred when she was twelve years old, and she had such episodes daily for the next thirty years. Her spiritual yearnings prompted her to leave her home to join a local group of Beguines in 1230. In 1270, she retired to a Benedictine convent at Helfta, which had gained popularity as a center for mysticism. Her most famous work, written in Low German, is entitled *The Flowing Light of the Godhead,* chiefly composed and in circulation by the time she arrived in Helfta. Mechthild's spiritual adviser, the Dominican theologian Henry of Halle, collected her writings and assembled them into their present form.

Mechthild's work includes a variety of styles and techniques, though the theme of God's abiding love remains constant. Her writings contain poetry, prose, and dialogue and provide an autobiographical account of spiritual experiences. *The Flowing Light of the Godhead* presents God as a font of grace and love from which all Christians must partake. She portrays the center of Christ as a fiery love capable of producing sparks of love in those people who believed. Many of her works use allegorical imagery—in one case, a personified Love asks Mechthild to dance and during the dance she comes to understand and commune with Love. Christ is once described as a young courtier in the medieval chivalric framework. Sometimes Mechthild's work is examined within the context of Helfta's role as a mystical center, where other mystics such as *Gertrude the Great also settled and gained spiritual influence, yet Mechthild actually stimulated the work that went on there. Gertrude, for instance, did not begin her autobiography until after Mechthild's arrival.

Beguines were laywomen who dedicated themselves in service to the needy. Organized in communities, many Beguines continued to live at home, though in some cases they would gather and live in Beguinages or religious houses. They did not take orders and therefore did not live in cloisters or wear habits. During Mechthild's life, the Beguines suffered from some persecution, not only because the groups were led by women but also because they did not tolerate clerical authority. For example, they refused to turn over any resources they collected such as money and gifts to the local church but used them to help the needy.

In fact, many Beguines became critical of clerical abuses and spoke out against them. Mechthild herself regularly disparaged the corruption in the Church, calling the Church a maiden with filthy skin, and this made her unpopular with ecclesiastical authorities. Seeking asylum at Helfta, she spent the rest of her life there. Though she suffered from blindness, she completed the last book of *The Flowing Light of the Godhead* to honor the women who had provided her with shelter.

Bibliography: E. A. Petroff, *Medieval Women's Visionary Literature*, 1986.

Alana Cain Scott

METHODIUS. *See* CYRIL AND METHODIUS, SAINTS.

MICHAEL PSELLOS. *See* PSELLOS, MICHAEL.

MICHAEL SCOT (B. BEFORE 1200–D. C. 1235). A cleric, scientist, scientific writer, and supposed astrologer to Emperor *Frederick II, Michael Scot translated Arabic philosophical treatises and introduced the commentaries of *Averroës on Aristotle to Western scholars.

Few facts about Michael's life can be confirmed. His birth is projected to have been prior to 1200, and he appears in Toledo in 1217, where he acquired a rudimentary knowledge of Arabic. It was in Toledo that he began his first translation of a work by al-Bitrûji, *Kitâb fi 'l-Hay'a* (called *In astrologia* as well as other titles in Latin), from Arabic into Latin; he was assisted in this project by Abuteus (Andreas) Levita, a Jew who later converted to Christianity. His dependence on Abuteus, and on the preexisting translations of *Gerard of Cremona, made the translation of al-Bitrûji's treatise rather uneven and even inaccurate. This translation, however, was significant in that it was one of the first to introduce Spanish-Arabic astronomy and mathematical methods to Western scholars.

In the same period, in 1220, Michael translated from the Arabic two works on animals: a work by *Avicenna based on Aristotle's work and Aristotle's works themselves. This latter translation was to make a major impact on scientific thinking, as it was heavily relied upon by *Albertus Magnus, who commented upon the treatise. By 1224, Michael was already a priest and had resigned from an appointment to become archbishop of Cashel, Ireland, made by Pope *Honorius III because he did not know Irish. He was still granted benefices, however, in Scotland and England by the pope.

Michael projected himself as a scientific companion to the Holy Roman Emperor Frederick II. Toward the end of his life, he did, in fact, receive the patronage of Frederick II. It is not clear whether he served in the capacity of court astrologer, but certainly he would have been highly regarded and valued by

Frederick II for his scientific knowledge. Earlier, however, he had dedicated three works on various scientific subjects to the emperor, ranging in subjects from astronomy and astrology to human reproduction and physiognomy. The works are *Liber introductorius*, *Liber particularis*, and *De secretis naturae*. Dedicated and presented to Frederick II in 1228, they are likely to have been commissioned, at least in part, by the emperor.

The *Liber introductorius* was meant to combine the popular science of astrology with other scientific information about planetary movement, geography, meteorology, tides, medicine, and even theology culled from a wide variety of popular and scholarly sources, all organized and introduced by Michael. The *Liber particularis* was likely the result of direct questioning by Frederick II to Michael Scot covering spiritual matters like the topics of heaven and hell and the abode of God. *De secretis naturae* dealt with the subject of human beings, their anatomy, physiology, sexuality, and conception and included detailed descriptions of the development of the fetus during pregnancy.

Michael's greatest contribution to the history of philosophy was his effort to introduce the great Arabian commentator Averroës to Western scholars. Providing translations that were less literal than Gerard of Cremona's and seeking to convey the true sense of Averroës and Aristotle, he provided Western scholars with fresh, objective, and methodical commentaries. The most important of these works that Michael translated were Averroës' *Great Commentary on the De Caelo*, the *Great Commentary on the De Anima*, and the *Great Commentary on the Physics*. These all included the full texts of Aristotle's treatises, as well as paragraph-by-paragraph expositions and commentaries on the texts by Averroës.

The large numbers of extant manuscripts attest to the importance of Michael's work. While later scholars like Roger *Bacon and Albertus Magnus criticized Michael for his inaccuracy in translating and interpreting, they and many others relied heavily upon his works.

Bibliography: L. Thorndike, *Michael Scot*, 1965.

Tom Papademetriou

MONTFORT, SIMON DE, THE ELDER (C. 1160–1218).

Also known as Simon the Crusader, de Montfort proved himself a true son of the Church as a participant in the Fourth Crusade and, later, as the leader of the Albigensian Crusade. He also provided a strong foundation of power and fortune that eventually allowed his son, Simon de *Montfort the Younger, to control, however briefly, the throne of England.

The de Montfort family held significant lands in France, particularly in Normandy, to which Simon succeeded as lord of Montfort in 1188; he also inherited a claim to the earldom of Leicester in England through his mother. Always devout, Simon responded to the call by Pope *Innocent III to participate in the Fourth Crusade; *Saladin's death had led to a crumbling of the Muslim Empire, and Innocent saw an opportunity for his crusaders to regain the Holy Land.

Simon joined other French nobles in Venice in late 1202, where the crusaders were forced to pay the Venetians exorbitant prices for the ships they needed to carry them across the sea. In partial payment, the crusaders chose to acquiesce to a Venetian proposal to attack the Christian city of Zara on the Dalmation coast, a city Venice wanted to control. Upon reaching Zara, Simon refused to join in the siege, citing the pope's admonition against the attack on pain of excommunication. The French nobles, spurning the papal injunction, took the city and destroyed it. Simon disavowed the French action and, in 1203, left to pursue a solitary journey to the Holy Land, where he distinguished himself in battle against the Muslims; he returned to France in 1206.

He traveled to England that same year to claim his Leicester inheritance, but King *John of England's loss of Normandy to *Philip II Augustus of France in 1204 had led John to forbid his vassals who continued in their loyalty to the French king to take possession of their English estates. In accord with this decision, Simon's lands in England were put in the hands of "keepers," and the revenues proceeding from them were given to the king, though Simon styled himself henceforth as count of Leicester.

Simon's religious devotion was apparent in his family's ties to religious houses near his French estates and in his personal relationship with the future Saint *Dominic, whose work Simon supported through donations and military protection. Despite his piety, Simon was willing to stand up against the Church when he felt he had been wronged or when papal wishes contravened his own. This attitude was clearly revealed in his overt resistance to Innocent's directives concerning the acquisition of the lands of Raymond VI, count of Toulouse. The continuing battle between Simon and Raymond served as a backdrop to Simon's actions in the Albigensian Crusade.

This Crusade began in the summer of 1209, when Innocent determined to make a last attempt at rooting out the Cathari, or Albigensian heresy. The Albigensians believed that all matter (and flesh) was wicked and that God could not possibly have chosen to send his son to earth in the form of a human being. Thus, the Albigensians denied the divinity of Christ and the materialistic institution of the Church and, by extension, its authority. Having failed to dissuade the Albigensians from their heresy through a preaching campaign, Innocent began to excommunicate those lords who, like Raymond of Toulouse, provided support to these heretics.

The call for a crusade against the Albigensians brought Simon to the attention of the pope, who named him as the general of the papal armies. Fiercely opposed to heresy, Simon rooted out the Albigensians with fire and sword; his name soon came to be associated with fear and hate across southern France. Simon was able to win control of Toulouse and Narbonne, and though much of his military strategy was defensive, he was never defeated. He oversaw the slaughter of thousands of the Cathari and became a great French lord in the process. Innocent even saw to it that Simon's Leicester lands were placed in family hands.

By 1218, Simon's star was on the rise, but on 25 June, he was struck in the head by a stone launched in a siege and died on the spot. The reportage of his death revealed his importance in European affairs; indeed, even King John believed Simon might have been capable of displacing him from the throne of England. In fact, John's successor, *Henry III of England, was to be the target of the de Montforts' ambition, a legacy that passed from father to son.

Bibliography: Peter of les Vaux-de-Cernay, *The History of the Albigensian Crusade*, trans. W. A. Sibly and M. D. Sibly, 1998; J. R. Strayer, *The Albigensian Crusades*, 1992.

Connie Evans

MONTFORT, SIMON DE, THE YOUNGER (1208–1265).

Son of Simon de *Montfort the Elder, he was the leader of the short-lived Barons' Revolt, which temporarily displaced *Henry III of England, and established the principle of advisory parliaments before his deposition from power.

A French noble, de Montfort was heir to the earldom of Leicester, and in 1231, Henry III granted him the title; the negotiations that were involved honed de Montfort's skills as a politician and negotiator. De Montfort, caught up in the factionalism of Henry's reign, improved his fortunes considerably when he married Eleanor, Henry's sister, in 1238.

With his earldom confirmed, de Montfort became Henry's confidant, though he ran up debts with other magnates, which angered the king. De Montfort and his wife fled to France and were shortly reconciled to Henry, but they remained on the Continent, and the earl spent several years on crusade. Henry, meanwhile, was facing demands from his heavily taxed barons, who wanted a voice in government.

De Montfort served as Henry's lieutenant in Gascony in the late 1240s, but his conduct there was called into question by the Gascons, who demanded that the earl answer charges in 1252. The magnates took de Montfort's side against Henry and the Gascons; de Montfort was vindicated after a fashion, and his relationship with Henry stabilized until 1258.

By the late 1250s, Henry was making exorbitant financial demands on his magnates, whose advice he failed to take. They, along with de Montfort, felt it was time to make the king adhere to their counsel; as well, de Montfort was also nursing his own old grievances. Under the leadership of de Montfort and others, the barons in 1258 met in council at Oxford and drew up a reform program called the Provisions of Oxford. Among other things, the Provisions created a Great Council, now a Parliament, which was to meet three times a year, but factionalism among the barons made the Provisions difficult to enforce.

In 1261, Henry took advantage of the baronial factionalism and restored a royalist court centered on barons who opposed de Montfort. Angry that Henry had reneged on the Provisions, de Montfort became a focus of the reform movement once again and was exiled to France in late 1261. By 1263, English knights, angry at the granting of offices and lands to foreigners, aligned with the disgruntled barons and summoned de Montfort to return to England.

The dispute was submitted for arbitration to *Louis IX of France, and when Louis declared for Henry in the Mise of Amiens in early 1264, de Montfort and his supporters rejected the decision; they insisted on adherence to the Provisions, and by March, civil war had begun. The first battle at Lewes in May 1264 was a decisive victory for the barons, who captured Prince *Edward of England, holding him hostage to his father's promise to restore the Provisions.

De Montfort now wanted his authority over the king validated and called meetings of the Great Council for the purpose of governance. These parliaments, particularly that of June 1264, made de Montfort's government legitimate, based on a broad constituency. Through March of 1265, de Montfort enjoyed his greatest power, taking the opportunity to acquire wealth and build up his military force. Not surprisingly, many of his supporters began to turn against him.

Prince Edward escaped from custody in May 1265 and vowed revenge upon de Montfort, who was forced to sign a treaty with the Welsh for support against Edward's army. De Montfort found himself surrounded by Edward's army at Evesham on 4 August 1265. The superiority of the prince's forces made defeat inevitable. Edward rescued his father, and de Montfort suffered a horrible death and was subsequently hacked into pieces by Edward's troops, who paraded his severed head around the battlefield on a pike.

De Montfort was defeated by a number of factors, including the loss of chief allies and his son's failure to provide support. Henry was restored to his throne to rule until 1272, but his son, Edward I, learned from the mistakes of his father and de Montfort's example: He called advising parliaments throughout his reign to keep abreast of his subjects' opinions. These meetings eventually evolved into the institution of Parliament, which is de Montfort's most important and enduring legacy.

Bibliography: M. W. Labarge, *Simon de Montfort*, 1962; J. R. Maddicott, *Simon de Montfort*, 1994.

Connie Evans

MOSES MAIMONIDES. *See* MAIMONIDES, MOSES.

MUHAMMAD (MOHAMMED) (570–632). According to Islamic belief, Muhammad is the last prophet sent to humankind to convey revelation from God contained in the Qur'an. Muslims believe that this revelation derives from the same God that is worshiped by Jews and Christians; whereas the revelation of the latter or its interpretation has been tampered with and no longer is extant in its original form, Muhammad has brought that same revelation in its pristine form.

Muhammad ibn 'Abd Allāh ibn 'Abd al-Muttalib ibn Hāshim was born— according to Muslim tradition—in the year 570 in the Arabian city of Mecca, a member of the Meccan tribe of the Quraysh. Muhammad's father, 'Abd Allāh, had died even before Muhammad was born; his mother Amina died in his early childhood, after which date first Muhammad's paternal grandfather and later Muhammad's paternal uncle Abū Tālib raised the boy. Muslim tradition relates several stories in which Muhammad's extraordinary career as a prophet is already apparent in his early childhood. One such tradition relates how a Christian hermit named Bahira, whom the young Muhammad meets on his travel to Syria, recognizes signs of prophethood in the young boy.

Muhammad is described in Muslim tradition as a trustworthy and honest person even before his call to prophethood. His place of honor within pre-Islamic Mecca is recognized in a tradition that describes the rebuilding of the sacred shrine of Mecca, the Ka'ba. After the shrine has been demolished and rebuilding has started, Muhammad is chosen to place the black stone, a rock of religious significance (possibly of meteorite origin), into the wall of the Ka'ba.

As a youth, Muhammad began working for a wealthy trade woman, Khadījah bint Khuwaylid, and earned the respect and admiration of his employer, who in the year 595 offered herself in marriage to him. Muhammad's acceptance of the proposal ushered in for him a period of prosperity that enabled him to devote more time to his interest in religious matters. Muslim tradition identifies Muhammad as a *hanif*, a nondenominational, proto-monotheist religious seeker who traced his religion back to the patriarch Abraham. In regular intervals, Muhammad retreated into a cave located on Mount Hira, a hill close to the city of Mecca. During one of these meditative retreats, Muslim tradition tells us, Muhammad encountered a voice (later identified as the voice of Archangel Gabriel) that commanded him to recite. This experience, in the month of Ramadan in the year 610, ushered in the first of many revelatory experiences that ended only in 632 with the death of Muhammad. The collection of these revelations will become the central holy scripture for Muslims, the Qur'an (literally: The Recitation).

The message received in these revelations is to a large extent congruent with revelations of Judeo–Christian vintage; its insistence on radical monotheism, however, paved the way for enmity and opposition from the polytheist Meccan establishment. Such enmity developed in Mecca soon after Muhammad began preaching the oneness of God to the Meccan public. Religious persecution ensued in Mecca, and the young Muslim community was in grave danger. When the persecution of the Muslim community produced the first martyrs of Islam, a group of Muslims emigrated to Abyssinia (Ethiopia) where they dwelled for a number of years under the protection of a Christian ruler, known in Muslim tradition as al-Najjash.

Muhammad himself and a large number of his followers remained in Mecca. Muhammad's situation grew precarious after the year 619 (the "Year of Sadness") when both his wife Khadījah and his Uncle Abū Tālib died. No longer able to rely on the protection of his own family and clan, Muhammad began exploring the possibility of preaching his message in other cities. Beginning with the year 620, Muhammad established contacts with the city of Yathrib, some 250 miles north of Mecca. Over the next two years, seventy-three men and two women from Yathrib converted to Islam. In 622, Muhammad and his followers were invited to move to the oasis of Yathrib, now to be renamed madīnat al-nabī (the City of the Prophet), that is, Medina.

The majority of Muslims immigrated in the year 622 to the oasis of Yathrib/ Medina. This emigration, called the *hijra*, enabled the Muslims, now free from religious persecution, to establish a religiopolitical Muslim community (the *ummah*). In a series of raids and battles against their Meccan persecutors, the Muslim community of Medina gradually grew in strength; in 630, the city of Mecca fell to the Muslim army without major bloodshed. Mecca's central shrine, the Kaʿba, was cleansed of its idols and rededicated to its original state of purity, to serve as the house of worship of the one true God. Muhammad remained stationed in Medina, where he died and was buried in 632.

Of special significance to Muslims is an event that Muslim tradition places in the year 620. During one night in the month of Ramadan, Muhammad reportedly was carried from Mecca to the Temple Mount in Jerusalem and from there ascended into the seven heavens. Muslim tradition is not unanimous on the physicality of this experience; its significance for Islam is, however, beyond question. Muhammad received in this experience the injunction to pray five times a day.

Muhammad's multiple marriages have been an issue of controversy. While Muhammad lived a monogamous life as long as his first wife Khadījah was alive, after her death in 619, Muhammad married a number of women. Whereas some Western Orientalists read these multiple marriages as an indication of Muhammad's moral decadence, Muslim apologists insist that the vast majority of these later marriages were motivated by social and political factors.

Misunderstandings have governed Western understanding and appreciation of Islam for a long time and have unduly strained Christian–Muslim relations. Early descriptions of Muhammad and Islam are ill-informed or even outright forgeries; the medieval song of Roland, for example, mistakenly represents Islam as a religion that bows to the statues of different deities.

Muhammad's significance for Islam has often been wrongly seen as parallel-ing that of Jesus for Christianity; indeed, Islam has often been seen as an aberration and heresy deriving from Christianity. Such misconceptions of Islam have led to the charge that a polygynous, supposedly violent Muhammad falls far short of the ideal, celibate, and peaceful Jesus. Indeed, some medieval theologians concluded that Muhammad must be the Antichrist. Later European Orientalists, working under similarly mistaken premises, have often termed Islam as "Mohammedanism." Such interpretation misses the significance of Muhammad entirely. The center of Islam lies not in Muhammad but rather in revelation and community. Neither does the Islamic era commence with Muhammad's birth or death date, nor does Islamic tradition claim that he was more than an ordinary human being. Indeed, not Muhammad but the Qur'an has been suggested as a point of comparison to Jesus: Both the Qur'an and Jesus constitute the centers for their respective religious traditions; in later Sunni Muslim orthodox theology, the Qur'an is celebrated as the eternal word of God that resided with God before all time in sense and essence, only to be revealed and created in history in sound and form.

Muhammad is esteemed highly as a Prophet and a leader of his community; Islamic tradition portrays him as an extraordinary person blessed by God, sinless from his birth, whose heart has been washed white by angels, to whom his companions pay the utmost respect. In spite of such reverence, Islamic tradition and the Qur'an insist that Muhammad remains a mere human being.

Bibliography: M. Lings, *Muhammad: His Life Based on the Earliest Sources*, 1983; W. M. Watt, *Muhammad at Mecca*, 1953; W. M. Watt, *Muhammad at Medina*, 1956.

Alfons Teipen

N

NECKHAM, ALEXANDER (OR NEQUAM) (1157–1217). Alexander was abbot of Cirencester, a scholastic theologian, and a poet.

Alexander was born in St. Albans in England where he received his basic education. His mother, Hodierna, whose elegy he included in the *Suppletio* (supplement) to the poem *Laus sapiente divine* (Praise of Divine Wisdom), was *Richard the Lionheart's nurse. Around 1175, he went to Paris where he studied theology, medicine, and law in the school of Adam of Petit Pont, *John of Salisbury's teacher. While there, he wrote *De nominibus utensilium* (The Names of Objects), a vocabulary book for beginning Latin students, which describes items needed for traveling, farming, and running a large household. This work includes the earliest reference to a magnetic compass outside of China. By 1182, Alexander was a schoolmaster at Dunstable and a year later moved to the same post at St. Albans. From there, he went to Oxford where he became a master of theology and was teaching by 1190. His works from this period include sermons and scholastic disputations. He became a supporter of the recently introduced Feast of the Immaculate Conception after repeatedly being struck ill when he ignored the feast and attempted to lecture as if it were an ordinary day. Sometime between 1197 and 1202, he became an Augustinian canon in Cirencester where he was elected abbot in 1213. In 1215, he attended the Fourth Lateran Council. He died in 1217 and is buried in Worcester Cathedral.

Although Alexander was not a particularly original thinker, his works, most written at Cirencester, provide our leading evidence for trends of scientific and philosophical thought in the late twelfth and early thirteenth centuries. He was enthusiastic about Aristotle, several of whose works he placed on his list of books every student should read. He wrote biblical commentaries and hymns, many to the Virgin and Mary Magdalene, who also feature prominently in *Super mulierem fortem* (About the Brave Woman), a commentary on Proverbs 31: 10–31. His major theological work, *Speculum speculationum* (Mirror of Speculation), which survives only in one incomplete manuscript, shows the encyclopedic nature of his thought. In four books it covers doctrines of God and the Trinity, Creation, the angels, the nature of the soul and its faculties, free will, and grace. Among Alexander's contemporaries, his most popular work (to judge by surviving manuscripts) was *Corrogationes Promethei* (Questions of Prometheus), which combines a study of difficult words and passages in the Bible.

Today, however, he is best known for his works of natural philosophy. *De naturis rerum* describes the planets and various natural phenomena including spots on the moon and vacuums; wild animals, created before the Fall who are only enemies to humankind because of it; and domestic ones, given to humankind after the Fall to show God's compassion. The second part is a commentary on Ecclesiastes. Many stories and morals from this work find their way into later sermons and preaching collections. *Laus sapiente divine* repeats much of the same information in a more organized and less digressive way, covering the stars, the rivers of Europe, the elements, gems, herbs, trees, and the liberal arts. Although much of his natural history is borrowed from earlier bestiaries, there are also sections that could only have come from Alexander's own observations.

Bibliography: R. W. Hunt, *The Schools and the Cloister: The Life and Writings of Alexander Nequam (1157–1217)*, ed. M. Gibson, 1984.

Jill Averil Keen

NICHOLAS I, POPE (C. 820–867, PONTIFICATE 858–867).

With the election of Nicholas on 24 April 858, the papacy began its rise in stature, which peaked during the pontificate of *Innocent III. Nicholas believed his position gave him more power than any secular or nonsecular authority and thus clashed with many rulers and bishops. Nicholas meddled in such affairs as the disputed marriage of *Lothar II, king of Lotharingia, and the conflict between the patriarch of Constantinople and the Byzantine emperor. He also produced numerous decrees that later became canon law.

Nicholas became involved in Carolingian politics initially by supporting *Charles II the Bald when his sons revolted. He did not see this as a political move but rather just intervention over a question of broken father-son obligations. It was not surprising, therefore, when Nicholas intervened in the marriage dispute of Lothar II of Lotharingia. Prior to becoming king, Lothar had taken *Waldrada as his concubine and had three children. After becoming king, Lothar left Waldrada and entered into a Christian marriage with *Theutberga, but they had no children. Lothar, therefore, wanted to return to Waldrada and elevate the status of the relationship. The archbishops of Cologne and Trier supported Lothar, but the pope and *Hincmar, archbishop of Rheims, supported the second marriage. Nicholas deposed the two archbishops and summoned them to Rome. Lothar gathered an army but eventually backed down. Nicholas not only disavowed the legitimacy of old Germanic law but also displayed the power of the papacy. Nicholas also successfully reduced the power of bishops and metropolitans by excommunicating those who ignored papal authority, such as the archbishops of Rheims and Ravenna.

Affairs in Constantinople also attracted Nicholas' attention. The patriarch of Constantinople, Ignatius, was deposed in 858 by the emperor, Michael III, for meddling in imperial politics. The very learned statesman Photius replaced him. Nicholas believed he had the right to investigate the matter, citing Matthean passages and the Council of Sardica, and thus sent papal legates. The legates found in favor of Michael's deposition of Ignatius in 863, but Nicholas decided to dismiss the legates and restore Ignatius. Photius and Nicholas defended their respective positions fiercely, which made an agreement difficult. Adding to the dispute was Bulgaria's appeal to Rome rather than Constantinople for recognition. Nicholas eagerly sent missionaries and a detailed epistle, but Photius argued that Rome was operating outside its jurisdiction. Relations worsened, and the Photian schism was never reconciled. Nicholas died on 13 November 867, defending the supremacy of the papacy in all affairs, and he was later canonized for his ecclesiastical achievements.

Bibliography: R. P. McBrien, *Lives of the Popes*, 1997; W. Ullmann, *A Short History of the Papacy in the Middle Ages*, 1972.

Paul Miller

NICHOLAS II, POPE (1010–1061, PONTIFICATE 1059–1061). Reformer pope, Nicholas II issued the decree that created the College of Cardinals.

Though not much is known about the early life of this Frenchman named Gerhard (Gerard), he was bishop of Florence when elected to the papacy on 6 December 1058. He was not listed as pope until 24 January 1059 because he had to subdue opposition. Upon the death of the previous pope, Stephen IX (X), the reformist faction of the Roman clergy chose Nicholas, and the antireformist faction chose John, bishop of Velletri, who became Benedict X. After convening a church council in Sutri to condemn Benedict, Nicholas marched into Rome and supplanted him with help from supporters' troops.

Nicholas II saw himself as a papal reformer and should be placed in the category of other leaders such as Pope *Gregory VII. He promulgated the famous decree that created the College of Cardinals, intended to elect the new pope when the papal office became vacant. By the creation of this body, Nicholas and other reformers hoped they would limit political influence, along with abuses such as simony, in the election of a new pope. The decree included a multitude of other directives, allowing for non-Italian papal candidates and for papal elections outside of Rome. It also prohibited clerical marriage and concubinage and formally rejected lay investiture.

Nicholas also allied with the Normans and reconciled with the Lombards in northern Italy. Though this secured papal power in Italy, it upset imperial powers such as the German hierarchy and laid the groundwork for future tensions between the papacy and the Holy Roman Empire.

Bibliography: R. P. McBrien, *Lives of the Popes*, 1997.

Alana Cain Scott

NITHARD, ABBOT OF ST. RIQUIER (C. 790–844).

Nithard was official historian of *Charles II the Bald and illegitimate grandson of *Charlemagne.

Born sometime before 800, Nithard was the illegitimate son of Charlemagne's daughter Berthe and Charlemagne's minister of state, court poet, and abbot of St. Riquier Angilbert. Nithard would follow his father in this last position, probably in 842. As a student at Charlemagne's palace school, Nithard was educated in science and letters for his career as a churchman. However, he was not only a cleric but a soldier and diplomat as well, serving in Charles' army at the battle of Fonetnoy in 841 and acting as an emissary with Count Adalgar to make peace with Charles' brother Lothar in 840. He was also chosen as one of twenty-four magnates, half from the Western Empire and half from the Eastern Empire, to discuss the division of the empire between Louis and Charles. He probably died near Angoulême in 844 during a battle between Charles the Bald and Pepin II of Aquitaine, although some historians, following the epitaph written by Mico, deacon of St. Riquier, believe that he may have died in battle at Ponthieu against the Normans in 845.

His history of the sons of *Louis the Pious was written from personal memories, manuscripts, and official documents. Written primarily as a propaganda piece to validate the actions of Charles the Bald, the four volumes of the *Historiarum libri quattuor* cover the period from the death of Charlemagne in 814 to the Treaty of Verdun in 843. Unlike most historians of the time, Nithard did not start his work with a recounting of the history of antiquity, copying earlier authors and then adding the history of his own time as a short update at the end. Instead, Nithard's purpose was to detail the history of his own time, from the point of view of a witness. While the most important source of information about the sons of Louis the Pious and the conflicts among them, it has long been considered an unpolished and somewhat inaccurate account. However, critical opinion is now changing and a recent author declared that the writing was clear and correct, much in the style of *Alcuin and *Einhard. Janet Nelson argues that in fact Nithard's history is complicated, and in true historian's fashion, he is selective in the selection and presentation of his materials, shaping his history as a work of art. It was not, however, a highly disseminated work and only one contemporary manuscript copy exists. This manuscript was written at the abbey of St. Médard in Soissons and is now in the Bibliothéque Nationale (BN lat. 9768).

Bibliography: J. L. Nelson, "Public *Histories* and Private History in the Work of Nithard," *Speculum* 60.2 (April 1985): 251–293; Nithard, *Histoire des Fils de Louis le*

Pieux, ed. and trans. P. Lauer, 1926; B. W. Schoz and B. Rogers, trans., *Carolingian Chronicles: Royal Frankish Annals and Nithard's Histories*, 1970.

Sharon Michalove

NORBERT OF XANTEN (C. 1080–1134). A twelfth-century religious reformer, Norbert advised popes and rulers, founded the Premonstratensian Order of Canons Regular, and served as archbishop of Magdeburg.

Norbert was born into a noble family in Lorraine. As a young man, he went to the court of the German ruler *Henry V who was fighting with the papacy over the control of the clergy (the Investiture Controversy). In 1111, Norbert accompanied Henry to Rome and witnessed his ruler humiliate Pope *Paschal II. Some years later, Norbert had a conversion experience (the story is that he was narrowly missed by a bolt of lightning). He experimented with different forms of devotion, those of the monk, the canon regular, and the hermit, but ultimately committed himself to the life of the itinerant preacher. His activities provoked a Church council in 1118, which condemned him for preaching without authorization. Norbert circumvented the council by going to Pope Gelasius II and getting a license to preach. In 1121, the bishop of Laon persuaded him to establish a religious community in Prémontré. Norbert chose the Rule of Saint Augustine for canons regular, clergymen who chose to live according to a Rule like monks but could also serve as active clergy. Norbert spent little time in Prémontré. He continued to travel and preach, sending those who wanted to follow him back to Prémontré. His greatest success came in 1124 in Antwerp, when he defeated the followers of Tanchelm (d. 1115), a former priest who had castigated the clergy and been declared a heretic.

In 1126, King Lothar III appointed Norbert as archbishop of Magdeburg, located on the eastern frontier of Saxony. Norbert's decision to accept this position caused what some have seen as a split in his order. The followers in Prémontré modeled themselves on the Cistercians and lived a monastic life of withdrawal, whereas those in Magdeburg often served actively as clergy. Lothar probably chose Norbert to further missionary efforts to expand Christianity among the Slavic peoples across the Elbe River. This was, however, not to be. Norbert faced revolts in Magdeburg and spent most of his time at Lothar's court. There he helped persuade his ruler to take the side of Pope Innocent II against the claims of Anacletus II in the papal schism of 1130. Norbert accompanied the ruler to Rome in 1133 and was instrumental in keeping the alliance between Lothar and Innocent together. In 1134, Norbert died in Magdeburg.

Norbert's foundation of Prémontré is representative of attempts to reform the monastic life that swept western Christendom from about 1050 to 1150. Particularly noteworthy is the effort he made to open his order to women. Prémontré itself was a double-monastery with a place for women guided by a prioress, and Norbert and his followers established female convents in Flanders, France, and Germany.

While monastic reform may have been a motivating factor for Norbert, his personal commitment to preaching, acceptance of the position of archbishop, and use of his followers in Magdeburg as active clergy are symptomatic of a changing world in which the idea that monastic withdrawal was the pinnacle of spiritual commitment was being rivaled by devotion to clerical service. This active engagement with the world places Norbert on a line of development, which would culminate with *Francis, *Dominic, and the mendicant orders of the thirteenth century.

Bibliography: J. T. Lees, *Anselm of Havelberg: Deeds into Words in the Twelfth Century*, 1998.

Jay T. Lees

NOTKER BALBULUS (THE STAMMERER) (C. 840–912). One of the chief figures in the early history of the celebrated Benedictine abbey of St. Gall, Switzerland, Notker came from a noble Alemannic or Swiss family and spent most of his life at St. Gall as student, monk, teacher, librarian (in 890), poet, chronicler, and sequence writer. His contributions to the development of early medieval liturgy and his popular life of *Charlemagne (*Gesta Karoli Magni imperatoris*) place him as a significant figure in the Western Church.

Notker was born into a wealthy landholding family from Jonschwil in Thurgau, near St. Gall. He was schooled at the abbey at St. Gall, the Irishman Moengal (or Marcellus, the name by which Notker refers to him) and Swiss Iso among his teachers. Despite his speech defect (whence the epithet *balbulus*, "stammerer"), Notker became a famous teacher of the abbey school. He was one of the teachers of Salomo whose abbacy (890–920) set the standard at St. Gall. His major works include his hymns (four on Saint Stephen and the Sequence, the *Liber hymnorum*), "Deeds of Charlemagne," and *Martyrology*. He also wrote a prosimetric *Vita sancti Galli* (Life of Saint Gall, only fragments of which survive), a continuation of Erchanbert's chronicle of the Frankish kings (*Breviarium regum Francorum*), and a "Formelbuch" (a collection of sample letters, including letters to students Salomo and his brother Waldo).

The *Liber hymnorum* has secured Notker's fame in liturgical history. Ekkehard IV's *Casus sancti Galli* (his chronicle of the abbey) tells us Notker wrote a sequence of some fifty hymns; some forty or so are believed actually to be by Notker, as well as some of the melodies. To be sung after the Alleluia in mass, Notker's hymns drew on and adapted the existing sequence of Ado of Vienne. Notker explains in his preface to the *Liber hymnorum* that a monk from the West Frankish monastery of Jumièges (recently devastated by Normans) brought an antiphonary to St. Gall in 862 with text set to the *jubilus* or Alleluia melody. Notker saw the mnemonic potential of this device and expanded upon it, his sequence employing half strophes, with one syllable to a note; he says he showed his work to his teacher Iso, who praised its ingenuity and suggested some emendations. Among the more celebrated of the hymns is *Scalam ad caelos subrectam, tormentis cinctam* (A Ladder Raised Up to the Heavens, Girt with Torments) for the Feast of Holy Women (*In natale sanctarum feminarum*); the hymn adapts details from the Passion of Perpetua to praise holy women from all walks of life. The completed sequence for the liturgical year is dedicated c. 887 to Liutward, bishop of Vercelli, chancellor of Charles III the Fat (who visited St. Gall during Notker's residence). Notker's sequence marked him as a liturgical innovator and a first German liturgical musician of note; the sequence remained in use into the twelfth century.

Bibliography: P. Godman, *Poetry of the Carolingian Renaissance*, 1985; W. von den Steinen, *Notker der Dichter und seine Geistige Welt*, 2 vols., 1948, 2d ed. 1978.

Joseph McGowan

NOTKER LABEO (NOTKER THE GERMAN OR TEUTONICUS) (C. 950–1022).

Notker was a monk of the Benedictine abbey at St. Gall particularly noted for his works in late Old High German (OHG), including his Psalter (manuscripts of which have allowed linguists to observe some of the changes that occurred between OHG and early Middle High German). Notker was a prolific translator and commentator, one of the great scholars of St. Gall, and of particular importance to the development of the German language.

Notker came from an old noble family in the region of Wil in Thurgau, just north of St. Gall. He entered the Benedictine abbey at St. Gall where his uncle *Ekkehard I was an important figure (in all, four of Ekkehard's nephews entered his monastery). Notker would have a lifelong association with the monastery; he would become director of the abbey school, and among his pupils was Ekkehard IV (whose continuation of the St. Gall abbey history, the *Casus sancti Galli* begun by Ratpert, covered Notker's career). Besides the details Ekkehard IV gives us of Notker's life, we have autobiographical information from a letter Notker wrote to Hugo II, bishop of Sitten. In it, Notker describes his duties as teacher (the trivium, quadrivium, and theology), explains his method (grammar and the other arts are indispensable to an understanding of theology), and lists his works.

Notker's surviving works bear out his method: translations with commentarial matter of *Boethius' De consolatione Philosophiae* (Consolation of Philosophy), Martianus Capella's *De nuptiis Philologiae et Mercurii* (The Wedding of Philology to Mercury), and Boethius' versions of Aristotle's *Categoriae* (Categories) and *De interpretatione* (On Interpretation); the brief Latin logical treatises *De syllogismis* (On Syllogisms) and *De partibus logicae* (On the Parts of Logic) and perhaps also *De definitione*; the *De arte rhetorica* (On the Rhetorical Art); the *De musica* (On Music), which is mostly in OHG; his *Computus*; and a translation of the complete book of Psalms. His letter to Bishop Hugo mentions planned translations of the *Disticha Catonis* (The Distichs of Cato), Terence's *Andria* (The Girl from Andros), and Virgil's *Bucolica* (Bucolics); they do not at any rate survive, nor do his versions of Boethius' *De sancta trinitate* (On the Holy Trinity), Book of Job (based on Pope *Gregory the Great's *Moralia in Iob*), and *Principia arithmeticae* (based probably on Boethius).

Notker's Psalter is his longest work of translation, including all 150 Psalms along with OHG (in the "Alemmanic" dialect of St. Gall) versions of the Lord's Prayer, Apostles' Creed, and Athanasian Creed. It survives in whole in only one manuscript (St. Gall, Stiftsbibliothek MS 21, of the twelfth century) and roughly a score of fragments. Notker's translation work is often praised for its clear style and is said to serve as a first example of scholarly prose in German. Notker was also something of an early medieval linguist; historians of the German language refer to the pattern Notker observed in his spelling of initial consonants as "Notker's initial sound law." Notker also employed for German writing a system of diacritics that differentiated between short and long vowels as well as diphthongs. This attention to linguistic details is characteristic of Notker's overall educational program at the St. Gall school.

Bibliography: J. K. Bostock, *A Handbook on Old High German Literature*, 2d ed. rev., 1976; J. C. King and P. W. Tax, eds., *Die Werke Notkers des Deutschen* (series), 1972–1996.

Joseph McGowan

O

ODILO OF CLUNY, SAINT (C. 962–1049). The fifth abbot of Cluny, one of the most influential monasteries of any time period, Odilo was an abbot of tremendous administrative ability who saw the number of Cluniac houses increase from thirty-seven to sixty-five. Saint Odilo is also responsible for introducing the commemoration of All Souls' Day (2 November) into the liturgy.

Odilo joined the monastery at Cluny at an early age and worked closely with his predecessor, Abbot Majolus. In 991 at the age of twenty-nine, he became coadjutor to assist Majolus in his duties, and upon the death of Majolus three years later, he assumed the abbacy. Although the reformation of monasteries in southern France and Italy after the model of Cluny had truly begun during the abbacy of Saint *Odo of Cluny, it was not until Odilo's abbacy that any administrative effort was made toward centralizing these monasteries under the auspices of Cluny. Odilo was able to increase the number of abbeys devoted to Cluniac principles and increase their supervision, which resulted in greater dependency of these subordinate monasteries on Cluny. From this position, Cluny extended its influence over several centuries. Odilo was also known for his generosity. During the famines from 1028 to 1033, he melted sacred vessels and ornaments to sell in order to support the poor. He was responsible for establishing the "Truce of God" among independent warring factions and introduced the concept of the Church as a sanctuary that could not be violated.

Bibliography: J. Evans, *Monastic Life at Cluny, 910–1157*, 1931.

Clinton Atchley

ODO OF CLUNY, SAINT (879–942). Abbot of Cluny and a prolific writer, Odo was instrumental in elevating the monastery at Cluny to the position of preeminence that it enjoyed throughout much of the Middle Ages. He was also a great reformer of monasteries to Cluniac principles. He wrote several books of moral essays, sermons, hymns, and choral antiphons.

Odo was born into a wealthy Frankish family and was raised in the household of William, duke of Aquitaine. When he was nineteen, he received a canonry at St. Martin's Church at Tours. He later spent several years studying dialectic and music in Paris under the tutelage of Remigius of Auxerre. He soon relinquished his canonry after being profoundly affected by his reading of the Rule of St. *Benedict. He was determined to become a monk, and at the age of thirty, he went to Baume-les-Messieurs, where he joined the monastery headed by Berno. When William, duke of Aquitaine, founded a monastery at Cluny in 909, he selected Berno to establish the order. Odo was appointed director of the monastery school at Baume and later became abbot of Baume in 924. Three years later, he succeeded Berno as abbot of Cluny. Under Odo's abbacy, Cluny returned to a strict adherence of the Benedictine Rule and became a model for monastery reform in France and Italy.

Bibliography: G. Sitwell, ed. and trans., *St. Odo of Cluny, Being the Life of St. Odo of Cluny by John of Salerno and the Life of St. Gerald of Aurillac by St. Odo*, 1958.

Clinton Atchley

ODO RIGALDUS. *See* EUDES RIGAUD.

OFFA OF MERCIA (R. 757–796). Perhaps the most underrated early medieval ruler, Offa was the greatest Anglo-Saxon king prior to *Alfred the Great, ruling much of middle and southern England and assuming the title *rex Anglorum* (king of the English); however, he is little known outside the small circle of scholars specializing in that period.

Offa's obscurity is due to paucity of sources: He had no biographer as *Charlemagne had in *Einhard or Alfred the Great in *Asser; there are no annals for Mercia like those for Northumbria and Wessex; the *Anglo-Saxon Chronicle* makes no mention of him before 776 and references thereafter are scanty; evidence from charters and the letters of *Alcuin of York and Charlemagne is sporadic; and that from coin hoards is controversial. Nevertheless, what survives is impressive. Offa, son of Thingfrith, claimed a genealogy that included Eawa, brother of the mighty seventh-century Mercian king Penda; the legendary fourth-century ruler Offa of Angel; and ultimately (like most Germanic kings) the pagan god Woden. His birthdate is unknown, but given the duration of his reign, he must have been young when he came to the throne. Offa's powerful cousin Æthelbald (716–757) ruled Mercia (in central England) and enough additional territory to be styled *rex Suutanglorum* (king of the southern English) and *rex Britanniae* (king of Britain).

At his death, Offa quickly defeated a rival Beornred, and during the period 757–776, he consolidated his position in Mercia and attempted to reconstruct Æthelbald's empire. He strengthened his hold over Sussex with a successful military campaign in 771. Early on, he extended his power to Kent, but after losing the battle of Otford in 776, he was unable to regain that kingdom until

784. By then, he controlled East Anglia, Essex, Lindsey, London, and more. This reduced the number of kingdoms in present-day England to Mercia, Northumbria, and Wessex. Offa exercised no authority over Northumbria, though he did establish a marriage alliance with its king, Æthelred. In 779, he defeated Cynewulf of Wessex in battle, and after Beohrtric succeeded to the throne in 786, Offa helped drive out his rival Egbert and in 789 entered into a marriage alliance with him. The uncertain boundary with Wales led to fighting early in Offa's reign, but he achieved peace there by 784. With his borders secure and allies in neighboring kingdoms, Offa was able to turn to other projects.

Several aspects of Offa's reign reveal the extent of his power. The most enduring of his achievements is Offa's Dyke, a 130-mile-long earthen wall on the Welsh border from the mouth of the Dee River to the mouth of the Wye, once twenty-five feet high and sixty feet wide, possibly topped by a wooden or stone wall, and with a parallel ditch on the western side. Twice as long as Hadrian's Wall in the north, it is a stunning feat of engineering skill and political organization. Offa also strengthened his relationship with Northumbria and Wessex by patronizing building projects there. During the latter part of his reign, Offa frequently concerned himself with foreign affairs, daring to claim that he was Charlemagne's equal. Though the Carolingian Empire obviously dwarfed even the expanded Mercia, Charlemagne did treat Offa with great respect, though around 789 a rift between the two over a proposed marriage alliance had to be healed by Alcuin and Gerwold of St. Wandrille. There was extensive trade between the two kingdoms, and Offa—who had several mints—produced silver pennies similar to new Frankish coins. Perhaps in imitation of Charlemagne, he had his son Ecgfrith crowned during his own lifetime.

Offa, who owned a copy of *Bede's *Ecclesiastical History*, supported the Church and religious reform, and in 787 Pope Hadrian I granted his request for a third Anglo-Saxon archbishopric at Lichfield to rival the uncooperative Archbishop Jaenberht of Canterbury. He even had contacts with the Islamic caliph al-Mansūr, though suggestions that he became a Muslim need not be taken seriously. More plausible, though controversial, is the claim that the epic *Beowulf* was first written down at Offa's court and that references to his possible ancestor, Offa of Angel, were intended to flatter him. Offa also produced dooms (laws) that were a model for those that came later. He also patronized some monasteries and founded others, like St. Albans Abbey.

Offa died at the peak of his power but within a century was eclipsed by the West Saxon Alfred. Yet he had done much to prepare the way for the latter's successes in consolidating smaller kingdoms, in law, in relations with the Church, in foreign affairs, and perhaps in other ways that a dearth of knowledge prevents us from seeing.

Bibliography: Frank Stenton, *Anglo-Saxon England*, 3d ed., 1971; J. M. Wallace-Hadrill, *Early Germanic Kingship in England and on the Continent*, 1971.

William B. Robison

ÓLÁFR I TRYGGVASON OF NORWAY (D. 1000). Great-grandson of
*Harald I Fairhair, Viking raider of the British Isles, he became king of Norway
in 995. He made great progress in the Christianization of his kingdom and was
influential in the conversions of the Faroe Islands, the Orkneys, Shetland, Iceland, and Greenland. Like many early Norwegian kings, what is known of
Óláfr's life is an unclear mixture of legend and history based on bits of skaldic
verse written to commemorate him or sagas, the best known written by *Snorri
Sturluson some two centuries after the king's death.

Óláfr went on Viking expeditions early in his life, perhaps in the Baltic. By
the year 991, the *Anglo-Saxon Chronicle* records his presence in the eastern and
southern coasts of England and possibly as the leader for the Vikings at the
battle of Maldon, made famous by the well-known Old English poem of the
same name. Shortly thereafter, the English king *Æthelred the Unready bought
peace from him by payment of the Danegeld. It is also believed that while
abroad, most likely in England, Óláfr converted to Christianity.

Upon his return to Norway, Óláfr found a country dissatisfied with its current
ruler, the powerful Earl Hákon, whose flight and subsequent death proved to be
quite an opportunity for an ambitious warrior. After winning the favor of the
people of Trondheim in 995, Óláfr was proclaimed king and then traveled
throughout the country, gathering support. Soon he began the work of converting
Norway to Christianity. Though King Hákon the Good and earlier missionaries
had made some inroads to conversion, the new king met with much resistance,
which he countered with brutal threats of torture and execution. In addition, he
charged missionaries with the conversion of numerous Scandinavian settlements—the most notable being Iceland.

Although a powerful king, Óláfr's reign was not to last long, especially
against the ambitions of the king of Denmark, *Sven I Haraldsson (Forkbeard),
Óláfr Skotkonung, king of Sweden, and Eiríkr, son of Earl Hákon, the previous
ruler of Norway. These three formed an alliance, and in the year 1000 Óláfr with
only eleven ships met their overpowering forces in a pitched sea battle near the
island of Svoldr. According to Snorri's account in *Heimskringla, Óláfs saga
Tryggvasonar*, which glorifies Óláfr, Óláfr managed to turn back the kings of
Denmark and Sweden, despite overwhelming odds, but against Eiríkr Hákonarson he soon found himself cornered on his royal ship the *Long Serpent*. Rather
than be taken prisoner, Óláfr jumped overboard to a watery death. Rumors of his
survival persisted, some claiming that he made a journey to the Holy Land.

During his five-year reign, Óláfr strengthened the power of the king over the
various territories and implemented changes in the internal structure of the kingdom. Despite his aggressive policies aimed at spreading Christianity, at his death
in the year 1000 many pockets in Norway and abroad hung tenaciously to their
pagan beliefs.

Bibliography: G. Jones, *A History of the Vikings*, 1984.

                                                                    Joseph Carroll

ÓLÁFR II HARALDSSON OF NORWAY, SAINT (C. 995–1030).

King of Norway and later saint, Óláfr Haraldsson, also known as Óláfr the Stout, thoroughly Christianized Norway, moving it from its pagan past and into the larger Christian world of medieval Europe. Though violence and martial responses to Danish threats marked his life and reign, his death on the battlefield at Stiklestad was hailed by many Norwegians as a martyrdom, and a cult of sainthood grew quickly.

Reputed to be a descendant of *Harald I Fairhair, Óláfr was born a pagan and in his early teens began the career of a Viking. From Finland, Sweden, Denmark, and Gotland to the British Isles, France, and perhaps even Spain, Óláfr made raids and fought in numerous battles. Around 1013, while fighting as a mercenary of Duke Richard II of Normandy and later for *Æthelred the Unready of England, it is believed that Óláfr was baptized. By 1015, the ambitious Viking returned to his homeland and quickly took advantage of unstable political conditions, winning the crown for himself.

Óláfr's central seat of power was in Nidaros, from which he could keep a watchful eye on his northern subjects who were somewhat resistant to his kingship. It is from Nidaros that he also continued his predecessors' mission of Christianizing Norway. He laid the foundations of churches there and elsewhere, and with the help of missionaries, some from England, he began to convert his pagan subjects. By 1024, he laid the political foundations for a religious state when he, with the aid of Bishop Grimkell and other ecclesiastics, worked out the code of Church law at Moster.

On the foreign front, Óláfr worked to end the antagonism between Norway and Sweden, and the two countries eventually formed an alliance against the encroachment of *Cnut, king of Denmark and England. Eventually Cnut, however, managed to win the favor of powerful Norwegian chieftains. By 1028, they drove Óláfr and his Swedish wife Astrid into exile to Russia where they stayed with her relatives at Kiev. In 1030, Óláfr returned to reconquer his kingdom, but his small army, reinforced with assistance from his half brother *Harald III Hardråde and Onund of Sweden, was soundly defeated at Stiklestad by a superior force of combined Norwegian peasants and chieftains and Danes, and he was killed there.

The character of King Óláfr's reign is marked by the cult of sainthood that arose quickly and spread throughout Europe after his death. Numerous hagiographic narratives and sagas have shrouded the figure in legend that is often difficult to separate from history. His extensive conversion of Norway, which built upon the proselytizing done by his predecessors *Óláfr Tryggvason and Hákon the Good, was extremely successful in part because it was so brutal. For the convert Óláfr gave his friendship; for the stubborn pagan, there was blinding, maiming, despoiling of goods, and even execution. Though hard and merciless to his adversaries, in general Óláfr was thought to be a good king. He acquired quite a reputation as lawgiver and an honest man. However, it was his sainthood that earned him the title of the "Perpetual King of Norway."

Bibliography: G. Jones, *A History of the Vikings*, 1984; Snorri Sturluson, *Saint Olaf's Saga*, in *Heimskringla: History of the Kings of Norway*, trans. L. M. Hollander, 1964.

Joseph Carroll

ORDERIC VITALIS (1075–C. 1142/1143).

The greatest of the historians of the Anglo-Norman kingdom, Orderic wrote in the late eleventh and twelfth centuries.

He was born in England in 1075, son of Odelerius of Orléans, a cleric in the household of Roger of Montgomery. His mother was Anglo-Saxon. He was named Orderic at birth, but when his father brought him to the Norman abbey of St. Évroul, at the age of ten, the monks found this name odd-sounding and called him Vitalis instead. Orderic spent the rest of his life as a monk of St. Évroul, but he always retained his sense of being an English alien in the Norman world.

Orderic wrote two works, both focused on the history of Normandy. His first effort was a series of interpolations to and a continuation of the history of Normandy that *William of Jumièges had written in the 1060s, which was itself an extension of the work of the first historian of the dukes of Normandy, Dudo of St. Quentin. These interpolations were begun before 1109. A few years later, Orderic began his independent history of the Normans, to which he gave the title of *The Ecclesiastical History of England and Normandy*. This is a massive work, in thirteen books, and most of it still survives in the manuscript that Orderic himself wrote. The abbot of St. Évroul commissioned it as a history of that abbey, but Orderic extended the work into an eclectic chronicle, beginning with the life of Jesus, moving rapidly through Christian history up to the tenth century, and then developing in great detail the history of the Normans both in Normandy and in other parts of the world in which they were active: Italy, the Holy Land, and especially, England.

His account is especially full from the reign of *William I the Conqueror both as duke of Normandy and as king of England through 1141; however, the work ends in 1142 in a discouraged tone with the latest news about the civil war between the rival claimants to England and Normandy, *Stephen of Blois (later Stephen of England) and Empress *Matilda. In the course of his narrative, Orderic includes not only the sort of political and institutional history that one might expect but also a history of the First Crusade, a detailed history of the spread of monasticism in Normandy, an equally detailed discussion of the great families of Normandy, especially those that had a connection with St. Évroul, and many digressions on matters more or less closely connected to his principal subject.

Bibliography: M. Chibnall, ed. and trans., *The Ecclesiastical History of Orderic Vitalis*, 6 vols., 1969–1980; L. Shopkow, *History and Community: Norman Historical Writing in the Eleventh and Twelfth Century*, 1997.

Emily Tabuteau

OSWALD OF NORTHUMBRIA, SAINT (D. 642). As the third king of Northumbria, Oswald reunified the kingdom, actively supported the Church, sought the conversion of his kingdom to Christianity, gave the island of Lindisfarne to Bishop Aidan, was powerful enough to wield influence in Kent, and resisted Mercian expansion until his death in battle against the Mercian king Penda. Oswald, the first Anglo-Saxon royal saint, was so popular he was venerated on the Continent as well as in England.

Oswald was the son of King Æthelfrith of Bernicia and Acha, the daughter of King Ælle of Deira. When his uncle, Edwin of Deira, succeeded Æthelfrith, Oswald went into exile among the Scots of Dal Riada, where he was baptized. With Edwin's death in 633, Northumbria split back into the kingdoms of Bernicia and Deira. Cadwallon of Gwynedd killed the kings of both places and was, in turn, killed in 634 by Oswald at the battle of Heavenfield. As rightful heir to both kingdoms, Oswald reunited the Northumbrian kingdom. He was a powerful king who also ruled over the kingdom of Lindsey and the South Saxons and wielded influence in Kent. He also sponsored the baptism of the West Saxon king Cynegisl and later married Cynegisl's daughter. These alliances, it is believed, were made in order to oppose the power of King Penda of Mercia.

Shortly after taking the throne, Oswald sought help in Christianizing his kingdom from the monastery of Iona. The monastery sent Bishop Aidan to him, and Oswald later gave him the island of Lindisfarne. Oswald also took an active role in supporting the Church by donating royal lands for monasteries and acting as interpreter to his thanes for Bishop Aidan.

In 642, Oswald died at the battle of Maserfeld, suggested to be Oswestry, fighting against King Penda of Mercia. Immediately, people began attributing miracles to him, and his cult was established at the monastery of Bardney in Lincolnshire.

Bibliography: C. Stancliffe and E. Cambridge, eds., *Oswald: Northumbrian King to European Saint*, 1995.

John Paul Walter

OTFRIED OF WEISSENBURG (C. 800–C. 870). A monk, priest, and teacher, Otfried also is the author of a life of Jesus, the *Evangelienbuch*, the first Christian text to use German instead of Latin.

Otfried of Weissenburg can be considered the last product of the Carolingian Renaissance. Having resided for a time at the monastery in Fulda, Otfried had the opportunity to study with *Hrabanus Maurus, standing thus in a direct intellectual line from *Charlemagne and *Alcuin, who was the teacher of Hrabanus Maurus. Aside from his study time at Fulda, all that is known of Otfried is that he was a monk, priest, and schoolmaster at Weissenburg. His enduring contribution to German history and literature is his life of Jesus, or *Liber evangeliorum domini gratia Theotisce conscriptus* (*Evangenlienbuch*). This *Liber evangeliorum* was probably written between 863 and 871. The dates derive from the work's four dedications: to the worldly king *Louis the German; to Archbishop Liutbert of Mainz (the successor of Hrabanus Maurus); to one of Otfried's teachers, Bishop Salomo of Constance; and to two fellow monks, Hartmut and Werinbert, from the monastery at St. Gall.

The *Liber evangeliorum* is a poetic depiction of the life of Jesus. In five books, the work combines texts from the four Gospels with commentaries, patristic writings, and collections of sermons. The first book treats the prophecies of the Old Testament and the birth of Christ. The second book discusses the first miracles, chief among them the wedding at Cana. The earthly life of Christ and his teachings remain the focus of books three and four, while book five deals with the Resurrection. Writing primarily for a clerical audience and the educated nobility, Otfried is above all a theologian and teacher who places great importance on the task of exegesis. Thus, he instructs his audience with commentary in three categories that follow each chapter; Otfried refers to these successive sections of commentary as "mystice," "spiritualiter," and "moraliter."

Otfried's *Liber evangeliorum* is remarkable in the history of German language and literature for two reasons: He wrote in German and was the first poet to use end rhyme in the vernacular. Otfried used Christianity to give legitimacy to his use of the vernacular, a Rhine-Frankish dialect. And Otfried goes to great lengths to justify his use of German. He offers two justifications, one in a letter in Latin (*Ad Liutbertum*) to Liutbert of Mainz and another in the German introduction to the work. In the former, in highly rhetorical Latin, Otfried cites both pagan (Virgil and Ovid) and Christian (Juvencus and Prudentius) models who praised the deeds of their respective peoples. In the German introduction to his text, Otfried goes on to emphasize the same in the vernacular, placing it on an equal footing with classical languages of poetry such as Hebrew, Greek, and Latin. Otfried wishes to give the German vernacular the chance to emulate the poetic art of its Latin forebears.

The *Liber evangeliorum* also shows the first evidence of end rhyme (even if not consistently applied) in a text written in the German vernacular. Old High German epic works were written exclusively in alliterative verse according to Germanic vernacular tradition. Otfried's verse consists of long lines divided into two half-lines with a caesura. The end rhyme can be found in the last syllables of the two shorter half-lines that make one single long line of verse. Traces of the older epic alliterative tradition also remain visible in these long lines. Otfried does not appear, however, to apply a uniform style throughout the *Liber evangeliorum*. Indeed, because of some stylistic inconsistencies in his work, Otfried has been unfavorably compared to the poet of the Old Saxon biblical epic known as the "Heliand."

There is evidence that Otfried's *Liber evangeliorum* was known in such diverse places across the southern German-speaking areas as Mainz, Freising, Constance, and St. Gall. Four main manuscripts survive, two of these in Vienna and Heidelberg. One of the best-preserved manuscripts, though copied with little attention to accuracy, is the one known as "the Freisinger Otfried," written as a commission by Waldo of Freising (884–906). Otfried's influence has also been seen by some scholars in the strophes of the "Ludwigslied," written in praise of Louis III around 881.

Bibliography: J. K. Bostock, *A Handbook on Old High German Literature*, 2d ed. rev., 1976; W. Kleiber, ed., *Otfrid von Weissenburg*, 1978.

Alexandra Sterling-Hellenbrand

OTTO I (THE GREAT) (912–973). Otto I was the first German king to intervene in Italy and be crowned emperor (in 962).

Son of *Henry I of Germany and his second wife Matilda, Otto's first wife was Edith (d. 746), daughter of Edward the Elder, mother of Liudolf. His second was *Adelaide, dowager queen of Italy, mother of *Otto II. Henry designated Otto his successor on his deathbed. An older half brother, Thankmar, was excluded since his mother Hatheburg had vowed to become a nun after her first husband's death, invalidating any subsequent marriage. Unlike his father who refused consecration, Otto accepted both chrism and regalia from Hildibert of Mainz and Wikfried of Cologne at Aachen. The great German nobles vowed fealty; the crowd sealed the princely election by their acclamation. At the coronation banquet, he was served by the dukes of Lotharingia, Franconia, Swabia, and Bavaria, symbolizing their fealty and access (and by extension, that of their people) to the king.

Nevertheless, when Arnulf of Bavaria died in 937, his sons refused to honor their father's promise of fealty. Otto put down the revolt, although he later made one son, Arnulf, count palatine responsible for royal interests in Bavaria, in a characteristic act of forgiveness. Hermann Billung and Count Gero maintained Otto's authority in the lands between the Elbe and the Oder, allowing Otto to concentrate on centralizing his government and later to add the overlordship of Italy and imperial title. However, Thankmar had expected to be assigned authority in the East. In reaction, he joined Eberhard of Franconia, brother of Conrad I, in revolt in 938. They took Otto's brother Henry prisoner; before he was rescued, Henry had entered the alliance against Otto in return for the throne. Captured, Thankmar was executed and Eberhard briefly imprisoned. In 939 Giselbert of Lotharingia joined the rebellion. Otto won a stunning victory against the rebels at Birthen on the Rhine, but the fighting continued, and Louis d'Outremer, the French king, hoping to regain Lotharingia for the French, joined the rebels. Louis, however, was on such bad terms with his own nobility that many of them supported Otto. Archbishop Frederick of Mainz came out against the king, and even Saxony appeared on the verge of rebellion. Then Eberhard was killed in battle and Giselbert drowned. The rebellion, robbed of its leaders, collapsed. Their deaths allowed Otto to join their lands more closely to the crown. Henry was pardoned, although by 941 he was conniving at his brother's murder, only to be forgiven again.

Otto kept the government of Franconia, which, lying at the heart of Ottonian

Germany athwart the main north-south routes, became the fulcrum of the crown lands. There followed a series of marriages designed to strengthen royal control of the duchies—Otto's daughter Liutgard to Conrad of Lotharingia, Henry to the daughter of Arnulf of Bavaria, and Liudolf to the daughter of Herman of Swabia. The extension of royal power is clearly apparent in the royal diplomas; up to 942 they were issued only from Saxony and Franconia. In that year, they are also issued from Lotharingia, in 952 from Swabia, and finally from Bavaria in 953.

At Easter 951, Otto decided to go to Italy. The power vacuum in Italy after the death of Lothar, king of Lombardy, in 950 and the attempts of Berengar II of Ivrea to force a marriage between his son and Lothar's young widow Adelaide naturally drew in Liudolf of Swabia and Henry of Bavaria, whose gains in Italy would have been disastrous for Otto's policies. Otto entered Pavia, was crowned king of Lombardy, and married Adelaide. This marriage was the catalyst for a revolt led by Liudolf, who feared that his place in the succession would be lost to the children of his father's second marriage. He was joined by Conrad of Lotharingia and Archbishop Frederick of Mainz. In 953–954, all the duchies were in revolt, but the revolt was unpopular and failed partially because the conspirators attempted to involve the Hungarians. They invaded again, and Otto defeated the Hungarians at Lechfeld near Augsburg on 10 August 955. Liudolf was forgiven and was fighting in Italy successfully on his father's behalf when he died in 957. By the end of the decade, Otto had finally consolidated his position, with his borders secure and the Church attached to his service.

In 960, Pope John XII called on Otto to rescue the papacy from the threat of Berengar. Otto issued the *Ottonianum*, a diploma binding himself to protect the papacy. In return, the Romans promised that they would not elect a pope until the emperor had been notified and that the papal candidate must swear an oath to the emperor's son or legate. For the next five years, Otto had to deal with the reluctance of the Romans to abide by their undertakings. During this decade, too, Otto moved to secure the succession in Germany and in Italy, crowning his son Otto in 967 and opening up a diplomatic initiative to secure a Byzantine bride for him, a marriage that took place before his death in 973.

Throughout Otto's reign, he centralized authority with the tools available to him, alienating power from the duchies, using royal counts and the Church as the instrument of administration. The Church was an attractive tool since there was no chance of hereditary succession, which tended to turn offices into property, administered for the benefit of the holder and his family. Furthermore, it offered a pool of potential administrators who by their training and organization were inclined to identify with a centralizing power, which offered a realistic chance of order, justice, and the promotion of Christian values. His move into Italy was an example of real politik. No centralizing power in Germany could allow Bavaria, Swabia, or Lotharingia to absorb Lombardy, thus forming a second focus of state formation. Finally, there was no available paradigm of a nation–state. The imperial title and model could attract men's loyalties, pride, and energies in a way that mere kingship could not. An emperor could not be mistaken for a first among equals.

Bibliography: G. Barraclough, *The Origins of Modern Germany*, 1963; B. H. Hill, Jr., *Medieval Monarchy in Action: The German Empire from Henry I to Henry IV*, 1972.

Helen Conrad-O'Briain

OTTO II (955–983). Son of Emperor *Otto I, he continued his father's policies. Crowned King at Christmas 967, ensuring a smooth transition on his father's death, he married *Theophano in 972, the marriage sealing Byzantine recognition of the Saxon emperors. Theophano's dowry was supposedly the Byzantine lands in Italy; Otto received Capua-Benevento and relinquished claims to Apulia and Calabria. For seven years, he contended with rebellion in Lotharingia and in Bavaria, where his cousin Henry the Wrangler had allied with Poland and Bohemia. In 975, Otto concluded a truce with *Harald Bluetooth Gormsson. In 976, he deprived Henry of Bavaria of his duchy. In 977, Otto entered Lotharingia to end the revolt and protect it from France. In 978, Otto defeated Boleslav of Bohemia and received his homage. By 980, Otto could turn to Italy to drive the Saracens from Calabria and Apulia, as well as the Byzantines. However, Otto's luck ran out in Italy. The Slav and Danish borders rose, and his Italian campaigns ended with a massacre of German troops. Rescued by a Greek vessel, he rejoined Theophano at Rossano, swimming ashore rather than trust wife and treasure to the captain. He did not take the field again but fell ill in Pavia and died in Rome.

Like other Saxon kings, he has been accused of depleting the royal fisc, but he needed the loyalty of the bishops and was willing to pay for it. The attempted annexation of southern Italy probably involved a desire to enrich the royal treasury as much as to revive the empire.

Bibliography: G. Barraclough, *The Origins of Modern Germany*, 1963; B. H. Hill, Jr., *Medieval Monarchy in Action: The German Empire from Henry I to Henry IV*, 1972.

Helen Conrad-O'Briain

OTTO III (980–1002). Last of the Saxon kings and third to be emperor in the West, a long minority and an early death left Otto III with only the beginnings of a reign.

The son of *Otto II and *Theophano, he was only three when his father died. When news of his father's death arrived, his father's first cousin, Henry the Wrangler, immediately moved to take custody of the three-year-old, apparently with the intention of turning this regency into kingship. Despite Henry's partially successful approach to the German bishops, when he had himself proclaimed at Easter 984, he failed to win support. In June 984, *Gerbert of Aurillac, the greatest scholar of his day and a gifted administrator, was canvassing support for Theophano's regency with apparent success. Without a base in Swabia, Lotharingia, or even Bavaria, Henry appealed for consideration to a diet of the

German magnates, only to be faced with a unanimous decision in favor of Otto. In 985, Henry agreed to withdraw his claim in exchange for the return of his former duchy of Bavaria; the regency was awarded jointly to Theophano and Otto's grandmother, *Adelaide. Theophano managed to maintain her superiority over her mother-in-law until her early death in 991.

His mother, despite her early death, had made a strong impression on her son, although his overtures to Constantinople for a bride and interest in things Greek were characteristic of his dynasty, and his interest in Italy would undoubtedly have been fostered as well by his grandmother who had been queen of Lombardy. Despite his interest in Italy, it can be argued that there is ample proof of his recognition of Germany as the heart of his domains. His pious opening of the tomb of *Charlemagne in Aachen is suggestive of his desire to renovate the Roman Empire, but his policy on Germany's eastern borders is an even better indication of the paramount importance he placed on the German lands. In 1000, he actively opened the Slavic lands to German influence, using the Church much as his parents had before him. In May 996, Otto was crowned emperor by Gregory V, his cousin and nominee. In his plans to renew the empire, now Otto attempted to take his father's and grandfather's policies to their next logical step, his methods directed by his own excellent education and choice of counselors. These methods were designed to limit feudalization and to develop direct imperial rule in both Germany and Italy. His intentions were by no means to neglect his German lands in favor of the Italian. Unfortunately, his death at the age of twenty-two prevented him from carrying out his plans.

Bibliography: G. Barraclough, *The Origins of Modern Germany*, 1963; B. H. Hill, Jr., *Medieval Monarchy in Action: The German Empire from Henry I to Henry IV*, 1972.

Helen Conrad-O'Briain

OTTO IV (C. 1174–1218). Son of *Henry the Lion, his career is mostly to be seen in the context of those of others: *Frederick I Barbarossa, *Henry VI and his wife Constance, their son *Frederick (II), and Frederick's uncle Philip. Otto became emperor with the support of the pope, not because of his virtues but because of the territorial expansion under Barbarossa and his son Henry VI.

Barbarossa's expansion into Italy had moved steadily closer to papal lands. The marriage between Henry VI and Constance, heiress of Sicily, threatened actual encirclement of Rome, and the birth of their son Frederick meant that everything possible had to be done to prevent the realization of his joint succession. Pope *Innocent III not only wanted to get Sicily away from the empire; he also wanted to recover some of the lost papal lands. Accordingly, in 1200, Innocent explained to the cardinals that the princes of Germany could nominate a king, but the pope had to examine the candidate's suitability before making him emperor. Although he protected the infant Frederick, and upheld the boy's right to Sicily, he actually supported Otto's claim to the imperial throne. Otto was busy in Germany, fighting a civil war with Frederick's uncle Philip, who had been persuaded to take the German crown. But Philip was murdered in 1208, and Otto got control of Germany. This was exactly the solution Innocent desired and, on Otto's promising to restore the papal lands, he crowned him emperor in 1209. Otto, however, did not keep his promise. The pope was exceedingly disillusioned, all the more when Otto prepared to invade Sicily. Innocent excommunicated Otto and deposed him as emperor. Furthermore, while assisting his uncle *John of England, Otto was utterly defeated by *Philip II Augustus at the battle of Bouvines in 1214.

Otto lost the imperial race; Frederick became master of Germany and managed to keep both Sicily and Germany, even after Innocent's death.

Bibliography: K. Hampe, *Germany under the Salian and Hohenstaufen Emperors*, trans. R. Bennett, 1973.

Andrea Schutz

OTTO OF FREISING (1109/1114–1158). One of the greatest historians of the Middle Ages, Otto of Freising attempted to construct a philosophy of history that would explain past, present, and future. Also a public figure, Otto served as bishop of Freising and accompanied Conrad III on the Second Crusade.

Otto was born into the highest echelon of the German nobility. His mother was the daughter of Emperor *Henry IV; his Babenberg father was the duke of Austria; his Hohenstaufen half brother ruled Germany as Conrad III; and he was an uncle of Emperor *Frederick I Barbarossa. He received the finest of educations in Paris, the center of scholastic learning. He probably studied with *Hugh of St. Victor and was acquainted with Peter *Abelard. Upon leaving Paris in 1133, he joined the Cistercians. Around 1137, he was chosen as abbot of his monastery at Morimund but quickly left for Germany to become bishop of Freising. Freising was in the middle of a war zone of squabbling Babenbergers and Hohenstaufen. The bishop, with relatives on both sides of the fight, worked hard to maintain Freising's neutrality and rebuild the dilapidated diocese. So successful was Otto that by the end of his life Freising itself had gained a reputation as a center of learning.

In 1147, Otto joined King Conrad on the ill-fated Second Crusade. In the Holy Land, he was given command of part of the German army, only to be ambushed by the Turks. Otto barely escaped, losing even his shoes in the flight. In 1152, Conrad died. His successor was Frederick I Barbarossa, a man bent on regaining the power and prestige attained by German rulers before the Investiture Controversy. Frederick wanted a written account of his reign, which would promote this cause. Impressed by his uncle's grasp of history, he chose Otto to produce such a work. Otto devoted himself to this task until his death in 1158.

Otto of Freising wrote two works of history, the *Cronica sive Historia de duabus civitatibus* (The Chronicle or History of the Two Cities) and the *Gesta Friderici I. imperatoris* (The Deeds of Emperor Frederick I), both of which have been translated into English by C. C. Mierow. In the *Cronica*, Otto attempts to interpret the course of history from the creation of the world until 1146 (the date of the work's completion). Moreover, he uses this interpretation to prophesy the future. Confronted by the apparent tangle of historical events, which he likens to the confusion of a Babylonian Captivity, Otto says he will scrutinize history through the lense of God's eternal and orderly plan for the world. Thus Otto's *Cronica* is more than a chronicle. It is the application of theology to history to give the latter meaning. Otto finds the model for his history in Augustine's *City of God*, namely, that of a struggle between the cities of God and man. Within this model, Otto uses various schemes of dividing time and space to show meaningful historical development.

Most important for him is a four-part division of time derived from a prophecy in the Book of Daniel (2:31–45) as interpreted by Orosius, a follower of Augustine. This prophecy tells of four empires stretching one after the other in time until God replaces them with his own kingdom. Otto identifies the empires as those of the Babylonians, the Persians and the Medes, the Greeks, and the Romans and thus discerns a geographical movement from east to west. Otto sees the final empire, Rome, as still existing in the twelfth century. Its crown had gone from Rome to Constantinople, then to the Franks, and finally to the Germans. The story of the Roman Empire was also the story of the Christian Church and its merger with the empire to form a mixed city. However, recent events, particularly the great clash of Church and empire in the Investiture Controversy, convinced Otto that the mixed city was unraveling and that God's plan for the world was moving inexorably to its close.

In the *Gesta Friderici*, Otto focuses on events from the latter part of the eleventh century through the early years of Barbarossa's reign. Here he departs from the *Cronica*'s concern for the world's end and emphasizes the contemporary reign of Barbarossa as a conclusion to the bitter quarrel between Church and state with laughter and peace replacing tears and war. Otto also discusses scholastic theology and *Bernard of Clairvaux's attacks on some of its proponents, including Peter Abelard and *Gilbert of Poitiers. Otto's account of Frederick ends in 1156. His secretary Rahewin extended the history to 1160 and in outline form to 1169.

Bibliography: Sverre Bagge, "Ideas and Narrative in Otto of Freising's *Gesta Friderici*," *Journal of Medieval History* 22 (1996): 345–377.

Jay T. Lees

OTTOCAR II (PREMYSL OTAKAR II) OF BOHEMIA (1230–1278).

King of Bohemia from 1253 and duke of Austria from 1251 to 1274, Ottocar was the greatest ruler of the Premyslid dynasty and made Bohemia the most powerful state within the Holy Roman Empire.

Ottocar's reign saw the culmination of efforts to strengthen Bohemia and extend the Premyslid domains beyond it. In 1251, Ottocar's father Wenceslas (Vladislaw) I (1230–1253) succeeded in making Ottocar duke of Austria by having him marry Margaret, the heiress of the last Babenberg duke Frederick II the Warlike. Succeeding to the throne of Bohemia in 1253, Ottocar neutralized the opposition of Béla IV, king of Hungary, to Ottocar's position in Austria by agreeing to let the Hungarian king take control of Styria. Ottocar then exploited disputes between Béla IV and the Styrian nobility to add Styria to the Premyslid domains in 1261. Ottocar next added Carinthia and Carniola in 1269, making an arrangement with their nobility that was formalized in the will of the previous duke, Ulrich of Spannheim. In 1271, Ottocar intervened in the succession to the Hungarian throne, with an eye to adding Slovakia to his possessions, but was defeated by Béla IV's successor Stephen V at the battle of Mosony. To the north, Ottocar supported the Teutonic Knights, who named their city of Königsberg (now Kaliningrad) in his honor.

Ottocar's territorial ambitions were matched by his involvement in the politics of the Holy Roman Empire. In 1254, Ottocar conspired with the archbishop of Cologne to depose the German king William of Holland, but Pope Alexander IV thwarted Ottocar's plans. When William died in 1256, Ottocar ensured that there would be no effective successor by first supporting the election of Richard of Cornwall and then switching his support to *Alfonso X of Castile just three months later (both candidates were elected by a majority of four out of the seven electors). The resulting continuation of the so-called Great Interregnum placed the balance of power within the empire firmly in the hands of the territorial princes such as Ottocar, who eventually returned his support to Richard in exchange for confirmation of Ottocar's territorial gains in Austria and Styria. After Richard of Cornwall died in 1272, Ottocar once again tried to become emperor, but the other electors chose the relatively weak Rudolf of Habsburg before Ottocar could reach Germany.

Rudolf's election proved disastrous for Ottocar, because the new emperor declared that Richard's grant of Austria to Ottocar had been fraudulent and that the lands of Austria, Styria, Carinthia, and Carniola should return to the imperial crown. Ottocar fled to Bohemia to organize opposition, but his attempt to restore his position militarily was defeated by the combined armies of the Hapsburgs and Hungarians at the battle of Dornkrut (also called the battle of Marchfeld) in 1278. Ottocar died of wounds received in the battle.

Domestically, Ottocar continued policies established by his grandfather Ottocar I (king of Bohemia, 1198–1230), emphasizing the internal development of the kingdom. Ottocar II encouraged immigration from Germany and the founding of numerous cities, the most famous of which, České Budějowice (Budweis), eventually lent its name to several internationally known brands of beer. Ottocar gave special attention to the architectural and economic development of Prague and attracted a considerable number of artists and intellectuals to his court there. In a very real way, Ottocar's reign laid the foundation for the position Prague would take as one of the premier intellectual centers of northern Europe during the reign of Emperor Charles IV in the fourteenth century.

Ottocar's status is thus an ambiguous one. From the point of view of western

Europe, he was an ambitious princeling of the sort whose personal agendas spelled the ruin of the Holy Roman Empire as a political force. From the point of view of central and eastern Europe, he was an ambitious state builder whose efforts foreshadowed the later supranational states established by the Jagiellonians and Hapsburgs; indeed, it was Ottocar's unification of the Austrian lands that provided the core of the later Habsburg monarchy. From the point of view of the Czech Republic, he was in many ways a national hero, responsible for completing the development of Bohemia as a state and the first ruler to effectively project Czech national power within the community of European nations. It will come as no surprise that this ambitious character has been the subject of plays and other literary treatments down to recent times.

Bibliography: F. Grillparzer, *King Ottocar, His Rise and Fall, a Tragedy in Five Acts*, trans. H. H. Stevens, 1938; J. K. Hoensch, *Premysl Otakar II von Böhmen, der goldene König*, 1989; J. Kuthan, *Premysl Otakar II: König, Bauherr und Mäzen, höfische Kunst im 13 Jahrhundert*, 1996.

Edward J. Schoenfeld

P

PASCHAL II, POPE (C. 1050–1118, PONTIFICATE 1099–1118). Although he was a timid Benedictine monk who sustained the first successful crusade and dedicated many churches, Paschal's reputation is colored by the Investiture Controversy and the disastrous Concordat of Sutri. In his desire to increase the Church's freedom from secular power, Paschal tried to prohibit lay investitures and called for bishops to relinquish many temporal powers, a stand that embroiled him in conflict with Emperor *Henry IV and caused Emperor *Henry V to take him prisoner. Paschal died without resolving the struggle.

Little is known of Paschal's early life. He was born Rainerius in central Italy around 1050. As a youth, he entered a Benedictine monastery and became cardinal priest of San Clemente in Rome under Pope *Gregory VII. Under Pope *Urban II, he first served as legate in Spain and was afterward appointed abbot of St. Paul's Outside-the-Walls in Rome. He was unanimously elected to succeed Urban II, though he himself protested.

Although the antipopes were not a major issue for Paschal during the reign of Henry IV, Church and empire could not resolve their conflict over the right of investiture. In 1102, Paschal excommunicated Henry IV and denounced lay investitures. He supported the revolt of the future Henry V, but the son would no more relinquish the power of investiture than his father. Paschal attacked Henry V at several synods, including Guastalla in 1106 and Troyes in 1107. Paschal's successful negotiations with England and France in 1107 seemed to have little immediate effect on relations with Henry V, but those settlements would pave the way for the Concordat of Worms in 1122, four years after Paschal's death.

During discussions at Rome and Sutri in February 1111, it was determined that Henry V would receive coronation in exchange for his oath of obedience and that lay investiture of bishops would be stopped. In an evident desire to insulate further the Church from the power of the crown, Paschal decided that upon Henry's coronation the bishops would relinquish all temporal rights and privileges acquired since *Charlemagne. These decisions, known as the Concordat of Sutri, caused great disturbances, particularly among German bishops loath to lose power. Paschal was taken prisoner, and German troops descended upon clergy and congregation at St. Peter's.

For sixty-one days Paschal was held captive until, at Ponte Mammolo, he agreed to grant investiture and to allow the bishops to retain their temporal regalia. Two days later, Paschal crowned Henry emperor, on 13 April 1111. The forced treaty was dissolved in 1112 at the Lateran council, and in 1116, Paschal formally condemned the grant. The pope fled to Benevento in 1117 and died at Rome a year later.

In his struggles with temporal powers, Paschal has been assessed both as a visionary and as a weakling. He has also received harsh criticism for his sanctioning of *Bohemond of Antioch's attack (1107–1108) on Byzantine Emperor *Alexius I, which exacerbated problems between the Latin and Greek churches.

Bibliography: U.-R. Blumenthal, *The Early Councils of Pope Paschal II, 1100–1110,* 1978.

Karolyn Kinane

PASCHASIUS RADBERTUS. *See* RADBERTUS, PASCHASIUS, SAINT.

PAUL THE DEACON (PAULUS DIACONUS) (C. 725–C. 799). Paul the Deacon was a Benedictine monk whose *Historia Langobardorum* (History of the Lombards) best records the histories and traditions of the Germanic tribe that invaded and settled much of Italy.

Born in Friulu (extreme northeast Italy) to prominent Lombard parents, Paul received instruction from the grammarian Flavianus. He knew the Latin classics and had a certain command of Greek, unusual for the time. He enjoyed patronage early on from the Lombard court, first under King Liutprand (r. 712–744) and later under King Desiderius (c. 744–774). He probably performed several official duties at court and was tutor to Desiderius' daughter Adelperga. Paul spent time at the courts in both Pavia and Benevento. When the Lombard kingdom fell to *Charlemagne's armies in 774, Paul took to the Benedictine monastery at Monte Cassino, possibly against his will. Two years later, after participating in a failed revolt undertaken by the Lombard nobles, his brother was taken captive by Charlemagne's forces. In 782, Paul wrote Charlemagne personally asking release from the monastery to plead his brother's case, a suit in which he was ultimately successful. His impassioned missive brought him to Charlemagne's attention; he invited him to join his court.

In 783, Paul left Monte Cassino and went to Charlemagne's court, where he spent the next five years, acting at one point as Greek tutor to Charlemagne's daughter Rotrund (then betrothed to Constantine VI of Constantinople). At court, Paul would certainly have come into contact with the other intellectuals Charlemagne had invited there, such as Peter of Pisa, Paulinus of Aquileia, *Alcuin, Theodulf the Visigoth, and Dicuil from Ireland. Between 785 and 787, Paul returned to Monte Cassino, where he spent the rest of his life studying, writing, and working on his *Historia Langobardorum*. He died at Monte Cassino around 799.

Paul was a prolific writer, and his writing reflects the high level of literacy of his times. Eighth-century Italy enjoyed an advanced intellectual atmosphere that had survived from classical educational practices and cultural legacies, and King Liutprand, who had centralized royal power, favored both lay and religious scholars. Paul's poetry shows a solid understanding of classical rules, yet it also reflects an acceptance of new poetic practices that take a step toward freeing medieval Latin from the rigid classical norms of genre, meter, and diction. His early historical work the *Historia Romana* was a continuation of Eutropius' *Breviarium*.

While at Charlemagne's court, he wrote a history of the bishops of Metz at the request of Angilram, bishop of Metz and archchaplain of the court. He wrote an abridgment of Festus' epitome *De verborum significatu* (originally by Verrius Flaccus), as well as making an edition of Pope *Gregory the Great's letters for his friend Adalhard, abbot of Corbie. Paul also composed a *Vita* of Gregory and an influential commentary on the Rule of St. *Benedict. Moreover, Charlemagne recommended Paul's homilies to his own clergy. Paul left his final and most important work, his *Historia Langobardorum*, unfinished at the time of his death.

Paul wrote his *Historia Langobardorum* at the end of a life during which radical changes in Western civilization had taken place. The flourishing Lombard kingdom had reached its zenith and fallen, the Byzantine East had lost its hold over Italy, and another great power from the north, Charlemagne, had conquered and absorbed the Lombard civilization. Paul's *Historia Langobardorum* enjoyed an exceptional popularity in the Middle Ages and still serves as one of the oldest sources of the history of Italy. In the *Historia*, Paul recounts the oral traditions of the Langobards, transforming their legends and tales into a coherent account of this Germanic tribe and explaining its place in a new, Christian world order. Paul invests the old tales with Christian morality, taking as his focal point for the entire work the Christianization of the Langobards.

Bibliography: W. Goffart, *Narrators of Barbarian History* (A.D. *550–800): Jordanes, Gregory of Tours, Bede, and Paul the Deacon*, 1988.

Paul B. Nelson

PECKHAM (PECHAM), JOHN (C. 1230–1292).

Prolific writer on subjects ranging from theology to optics, physics, mathematics, and poetry, John Peckham served as archbishop of Canterbury from 1279 on.

Peckham was one of the earliest and most vocal of the English reformers. He studied arts in both Oxford and Paris and was a reader in Divinity at Oxford.

He joined the Franciscans in the late 1250s, and he became a master of theology in Paris in 1269. From 1272 until 1275, Peckham was master at Oxford. In 1275, he became minister provincial of the English province. Peckham was lector for the papal curia from 1277 to 1279, at which time he was elected archbishop of Canterbury, succeeding Robert *Kilwardby.

He was a staunch enemy of pluralism (the existence and tolerance of disagreement or moral relativism in religious method or content), which he saw encroaching on the Church in alarming ways. Austere in his own practice (he was rumored to have kept seven Lents a year), he was adamant in his defense of orthodoxy, condemning even his fellow Franciscans if he perceived them to be stepping over doctrinal lines. In 1286, the Averroist heresy (belief in a universal mind, and the superiority of philosophy to religion) threatened the schools, and Peckham reacted to it by declaring all Dominicans Averroists and accusing no less than Thomas *Aquinas of harboring the heresy because of Aquinas' efforts to reconcile Church doctrine with Aristotelian logic.

Peckham's determination and zeal in reform seem extreme but they were largely due to the sad reality of the priestly illiteracy, ignorance, and corruption that were widespread in the time Peckham lived and preached. The sorry condition of the education and discipline of the secular clergy was seen as the root of all social ills, since the laity could not be expected to teach or minister to themselves in the ways of the Church. To counter this decay, Peckham convened the Council of Lambeth from 7 October to 10 October 1281. The resulting "Canons of Lambeth" include Peckham's intentions to remedy present ills, directing that, four times a year, each priest must explain clearly to his flock the minimum of the following tenets of Christianity: the Creed; the Ten Commandments; the two precepts of the Gospel (i.e., love of God and love of fellow man); the seven works of mercy; the seven deadly sins; the seven cardinal virtues; and the seven sacraments of grace. Provision is given that should a priest claim ignorance of these concepts himself, the archbishop must explain it to him.

Peckham wrote prolifically all his life. His concern with pastoral care and clerical rigor, though different in intent from later reformers, was no less influential in the maintenance of the Christian faith in England.

Bibliography: D. Douie, *Archbishop Peckham*, 1952.

Zina Petersen

PEPIN (PIPPIN) III, THE SHORT (714–768). Son of *Charles Martel and father of *Charlemagne, Pepin became king of the Franks in 751 and is the father of the Carolingian dynasty. During his reign, he consolidated and expanded Frankish power, allied with the papacy, reformed the Church, and renewed relations with the East.

The younger son of Charles Martel, he inherited Burgundy, Neustrasia, Provence, and the "Mosel Duchy," including Metz and Trier, from his father. He and his brother Carloman, while still mayors of the palace, fought against the Aquitainians and took Bourges and the duchy near Poitiers. After Carloman withdrew from the world and went to Rome in 747, Pepin became sole master of all the Frankish lands. In 748, he defeated the Saxons and forced the Bavarians to recognize one of his men, Tassilo III, as their duke. Having expanded the realm, Pepin then prepared to have himself proclaimed king of the Franks. He was no longer satisfied with ruling in name only—as mayor of the palace.

However, it was not possible to simply announce himself as king because he had to negotiate the delicate task of removing the last Merovingian puppet king. Pepin's propagandists began to sow the seeds, stressing the need for an active king who embodied political and moral qualities. Fulrad, the abbot of St. Denis, helped; among other things, he went to Rome to sound out Pope Zacharias. The pope supported Pepin's cause, and in 751, Pepin had himself elected king of the Franks. In addition, Pepin had himself anointed by the bishops, perhaps even by Saint *Boniface, who represented the pope in France, to emphasize papal approval of his rule and to seal the alliance between the monarchy and the Church. Power to rule came from God, but anointing made Pepin the elect of God. Pope *Stephen II (III) anointed Pepin's two sons and reanointed Pepin in 754.

This alliance between Pepin and the pope brought him to the aid of Pope Stephen II. Aistulf, king of the Lombards, had seized Ravenna, thereby ending Byzantine rule in northern Italy. He then sought to capture Rome, and the pope asked Pepin for help. Pepin agreed to restore to the pope the lands taken by the Lombards. In 755, Pepin entered Italy, captured Pavia, and forced Aistulf to promise the return of Ravenna. However, as soon as Pepin left, Aistulf reneged on his promise and renewed his efforts to take Rome. Stephen sent new letters to Pepin, and Pepin besieged Pavia again, defeating Aistulf, who died in late 756.

While Aistulf's death temporarily slowed down the Lombards, it did not stop their attempts against Rome. However, Pepin could no longer help the pope; the Aquitainians challenged him. His adversary Waifer fought for over ten years. Pepin thus built up his own army and reinforced and multiplied the ties of vassalage with nobles who could help him. By 760, he had taken Septimania from the Arabs. After 760, Pepin led a campaign against the Aquitainians every year. Gradually, he advanced across Auvergne, Berry, Limousin, and Quiercy. He captured towns and, against custom, wintered in hostile territory. One of his men killed Waifer. Eventually, Pepin took Aquitaine but at a cost: Aquitaine lay in ruins.

Pepin is known to history as a "warrior prince," but he involved himself in more than war. Pepin and his brother Carloman reformed the Frankish Church. In 743, corruption was abundant in the Frankish Church; few could read, and the bishops drank and caroused. Carloman, and Pepin to a lesser degree, worked with Boniface to improve matters. They reformed the clerical life—clerics could no longer hunt or accompany an army into battle except as chaplains—and took the Rule of St. *Benedict as the guide to monastic life. They reestablished canons (laws) that restored authority to the bishops and condemned popular superstition and pagan rituals. After Carloman withdrew, Pepin looked to Chrodegang of Metz to continue the reform process. Chrodegang undertook the romanization of liturgical forms and centralized worship. He set up a school in Rouen to train the local clergy in Roman chant in order to unite the Church and the kingdom by common forms of prayer.

Pepin was the first Western ruler to treat with the Muslim princes of the East. He and the caliph of Baghdad sent embassies to each other, which, among other things, brought Greek manuscripts into Gaul where they were translated into Latin. In 751, Pepin instituted a chancellor to direct royal administration. The use of clerics in this role resulted in several significant improvements: The script of documents became more regular; the layout became clearer; and the language improved—Latin spelling and grammar became much better. Pepin revitalized the law and written expression.

By the time of his death in 768, Pepin had accomplished much: He and his heirs could claim the title of kings of the Franks; he had expanded the realm, reformed the Church, improved the government, and paved the way for his son Charlemagne's further accomplishments and successes.

Bibliography: P. Riché, *The Carolingians: A Family Who Forged Europe*, trans. M. I. Allen, 1993.

Jana K. Schulman

PETER COMESTOR (PETER MANDUCATOR) (C. 1100–1178).

Peter was a theologian, a chancellor of the cathedral school at Paris, and the author of the influential *Historia scholastica* (Scholastic Histories).

Peter was born around Troyes c. 1100. Little is known of his early life; he was a canon of the Augustinian abbey of Saint-Loup in Troyes and in 1147 was selected dean of the cathedral of Troyes. Peter was the student of a Master John of Tours, a pupil of *Anselm of Laon, and may have heard lectures by Peter *Abelard. By the 1150s, he had settled in Paris, where he studied under *Peter Lombard. He taught theology there but then resigned to become chancellor of the cathedral school of Notre-Dame; Peter held the office of chancellor from 1168 to 1178. He retired to the abbey of St. Victor c. 1178 and subsequently died there.

Peter's chief claim to fame lies in his influential *Scholastic Histories* (finished 1169–1173). This work fulfilled what *Hugh of St. Victor had outlined in his *Didascalicon* as prerequisite for training in theology, namely, a thorough grounding in biblical history. As such, Peter wrote a chronological handbook of biblical history from Genesis through the Gospels. Not only did Peter quote the standard Patristic sources for biblical interpretation; he also cited contemporaries, such as Andrew of St. Victor, and classical sources such as Josephus. He earned the nickname "Manducator" (the Eater) by the observation that he had eaten and digested all of the Scriptures in this work. The *Scholastic Histories* rapidly became a standard textbook for theology in the schools; it was also translated into the vernaculars and versified and became a popular introduction to biblical history for much of the medieval period.

Peter also preached sermons (about 150 of which are still extant) and wrote the *Sententiae de sacramentis*, a work on sacramental theology that provides a valuable witness to the oral teachings of Peter Lombard. Peter's lectures on the Gospels remain unedited.

Bibliography: I. Brady, "Petrus Manducator and the Oral Teachings of Peter Lombard," *Antonianum* 40 (1966): 454–490; B. Smalley, *The Gospels in the Schools c. 1100–1280*, 1985.

Andrew G. Traver

PETER DAMIAN, SAINT (C. 988/1007–1072). An eleventh-century reformer who wrote against greed and sexual immorality within the Church, Peter preferred to be a simple monk, although he did serve as an abbot, a cardinal-bishop, and a papal legate.

Peter was born at Ravenna in 988 or 1007; the date of his birth is disputed. He was orphaned young. One tradition states that he was raised by an older brother who mistreated him; recently uncovered evidence suggests that he was raised by a kind and loving older sister who was like a second mother to him. In either case, another older brother, an archpriest of Ravenna named Damian, recognized the boy's potential and sponsored his education, including advanced study in the liberal arts. His writings show that he learned not only the usual trivium and quadrivium but also civil law, canon law, and the writings of ancient Latin authors. In gratitude, Peter adopted his brother Damian's name as his own surname.

Peter did well at school, becoming a master and professor. Although he was living a secular life at this point, he prayed, fasted, wore a hairshirt, gave alms, and served food to the poor with his own hands at his own table. About 1035, two Benedictine monks visited him and inspired him to join their order. He was received into a Benedictine hermitage, Fonte-Avellana in Umbria, where he prayed, fasted, and channeled his intellectual gifts into the study of Scripture, becoming as much an expert on Scripture as he had previously been on classical authors. Having acquired a reputation for virtue and learning, he was often called upon to visit other monasteries and instruct their monks. At the death of the abbot of Fonte-Avellana in 1041, Peter was appointed head of the community, an honor that he reluctantly accepted. He went on to found at least five other hermitages.

He wrote a *Life of St. Romuald* about 1042. This hagiography showed a remarkable sense of integrity on the part of its author; it was customary at this time to embellish lives of saints with fabricated miracles, but Peter insisted on sticking with verifiable facts. In 1045, he composed a written Rule for the monks under his care, based on the Rule of St. *Benedict and augmented with ascetic practices suited to the hermitage.

In Peter's time, the Church suffered from the clerical sins of sexual immorality and simony (the buying and selling, whether for money or other temporal rewards, of spiritual objects such as the sacraments). A movement toward personal sanctity was gathering momentum as a remedy for these ills. Peter strove to promote reform within the context of this spiritual movement. His writings demonstrate his intensely contemplative interior life as well as his practical efforts to redeem himself by resisting worldly temptations. He wrote copiously, laboring to encourage the strict observance of morality and discipline among clergy and religious. He once rebuked the bishop of Florence for playing chess, imposing a strict penance that the bishop meekly accepted. He argued that monks should forego travel, since solitude and retirement were part of their essential condition; he also discouraged the common practice of finding surreptitious ways for clergy and religious to enjoy luxuries despite their vows of poverty. He suggested mortification of the flesh (such as whippings) as an alternative to fasting but warned against excess in any such practice.

His most famous writings are two treatises on clerical morality addressed to Pope *Leo IX. The *Liber Gomorrhianus* of 1049 or 1050 was a devastating attack on the sexual immorality rampant among the clergy, describing sexual sins with alarming frankness and arguing in favor of severe punishments. He coined the term "sodomy" (by analogy to "blasphemy") to describe sexual acts between persons of the same sex. The *Liber Gratissimus* of 1052, the most influential of his writings at the time, featured equally biting invective against clerical simony. Peter castigated those who traded spiritual favors for political advancement, stating that this practice was just as simoniacal and disgraceful as selling sacraments for money. Although he did not favor a complete separation of Church and state, he was uncomfortable with the close relationship between temporal and spiritual authorities in his time. Peter felt that spiritual interests should be preferred to earthly pursuits, a valuation that was not always reflected in Church-state interaction.

Pope Stephen IX (X) made Peter cardinal-bishop of Ostia in 1057, a position that he accepted only when reminded of his vow of obedience and threatened with excommunication. In this role, Peter helped persuade the antipopes John of Veletri (1058) and Cadolaus of Parma (1062) to step down. Nevertheless, Peter pleaded with subsequent popes to let him return to the hermitage; *Nicholas II refused, but in 1062 Alexander II agreed, provided that he remain on call to help the Church if needed. Peter returned to Fonte-Avellana and resumed the life of a simple monk but responded as promised to Alexander's requests. In 1069, he presided as papal legate over a synod summoned to consider an application for divorce by *Henry IV of Germany; he also acted as papal legate in 1072 to settle a dispute concerning the excommunication of Henry, archbishop of Ravenna. He died on 22 February 1072.

Peter was an important contributor to the spirit of reform that swept the eleventh-century Church, speaking out boldly against the greedy and licentious behavior of the clergy and the religious. In his own time, the *Liber Gratissimus* was particularly influential. The *Liber Gomorrhianus* is now especially valued by scholars who focus on the history of sexuality; in the course of its antihomosexual diatribe, it furnishes the most complete description available of male homosexual behavior in the Middle Ages. Peter's intense personal devotion to the ideals he promoted won him the enthusiasm of his subordinates, the confidence of his superiors, and even grudging admiration from his enemies.

Bibliography: O. J. Blum, *St. Peter Damian: His Teaching on the Spiritual Life*, 1947.

Anne Collins Smith and Owen M. Smith

PETER JOHN OLIVI (1248–1298). Franciscan philosopher and theologian, Olivi's position and his writings on Franciscan poverty caused controversy and raised questions about his theological orthodoxy.

Olivi was born in 1248 at Serignan, near the town of Béziers in Languedoc (southern France). A Franciscan novice by the age of twelve, he was sent to Paris to study theology under the masters of the order John *Peckham, *Matthew of Aquasparta, and *Bonaventure and appointed a teacher of theology in the Franciscan houses of Narbonne and Montpellier by 1274. In that capacity he produced a consistent literary output, and his reputation quickly grew within the order. In 1279, he contributed to the preparatory works for the papal bull *Exiit qui seminat* with a definition of Franciscan poverty.

Olivi's ambition of becoming a university master of theology was nevertheless frustrated shortly after by growing suspicions about his theological orthodoxy and by his own stand in the controversy about Franciscan poverty. This was the result of the fact that Olivi put much emphasis—in such writings as the seventeen *Questions on Evangelical Perfection*, the *Commentary on Matthew*, and the *Treatise on Usus Pauper*—on material restraint in the Franciscans' style of life. He held that the members of the order were bound by their vow to have neither ownership nor free use of the goods at their disposal but only a restricted use (*usus pauper*), appropriate to evangelical poverty. This latter determination of the vow of poverty was a very sensitive issue inside the Franciscan Order, which was shaken at that time by the internal conflict between Spirituals and Conventuals over the interpretation of St. *Francis' Rule. For Olivi, evangelical poverty, which leads to the achievement of desirable moral and social ends, is the sign of the spiritual character of Christ's messianic mission and is the basis for a radical renewal of the Church in his time. This last opinion puts Olivi within the tradition of Joachimism (see *Joachim of Fiore) and thirteenth-century apocalyptic literature, although he did not share the extreme view of some Spirituals of identifying the Antichrist with the pope and the Church.

In 1283, by order of the Franciscan minister general, a commission of professors and bachelors of theology of the order examined Olivi's writings and censured as heretical or erroneous many theological, philosophical, and moral propositions; moreover, his works were banned from all Franciscan houses. Olivi complained that he could not have access to the commission's documents and defend himself accordingly. Later in the year, Olivi was ordered to assent to the conclusions of the Parisian commission by the minister general, to whom he was obedient. The censure against Olivi's writings remained in place. In 1285, he could finally prepare an explanatory defense and sent the Parisian commission an articulated apology. Summoned by the minister general to Paris, Olivi had the chance to defend his doctrines. In 1287, he attended the general chapter meeting of the order at Montpellier and finally clarified with the new minister general, Matthew of Aquasparta, his position on the issue of Franciscan poverty. The ban on his writings was lifted, and he was rehabilitated and reinstated as theology teacher, this time in the convent of Santa Croce in Florence, where he taught Ubertino of Casale, who was to become a leading spokesman for the Spirituals. In 1289 Olivi was transferred to Montpellier and taught and worked in Franciscan houses of southern France until his death in 1298 at Narbonne.

While the controversy over poverty continued to grow within the order, and Olivi's writings were championed by the Spirituals, Olivi himself always maintained a moderate position, was of irreproachable moral conduct, and had many followers among friars and laymen. His tomb in Narbonne quickly became a site of popular devotion. After his death, Olivi's name was entangled in the crackdown against the Spirituals; his writings were again condemned and prohibited in 1299, with harsh penalties for any friar found to have read them. Pope John XXII later reiterated the condemnation, and the Conventuals dispersed Olivi's remains and defaced his tomb.

Bibliography: D. Burr, *Olivi and Franciscan Poverty. The Origins of the Usus Pauper Controversy*, 1989; D. Flood, "The Theology of Peter John Olivi. A Search for a Theology and Anthropology of the Synoptic Gospels," in *The History of Franciscan Theology*, ed. K. B. Osborne, 1994.

Roberto Plevano

PETER LOMBARD (C. 1100–1160). Theologian, teacher, bishop of Paris, and author, Peter Lombard's biblical commentaries and his *Four Books of Sentences* were extremely influential and remained standard resources and textbooks well into the sixteenth century.

Peter Lombard, often referred to simply as "The Lombard," was born in the region of Novara in Lombardy. Virtually nothing is known about the first thirty years of his life, although a number of legends and speculations have survived to this day. He studied for a time at the cathedral school of Rheims, until about 1136 when he transferred to Paris. It is unclear whether he studied in the Victorine school or attached himself to one of the masters connected with Notre Dame. By 1142, he was recognized as a teacher and writer in his own right, and it is probably one of the reasons he was invited to join the cathedral chapter in 1144. In addition to his teaching responsibilities, Lombard progressed through the ecclesiastical ranks from subdeacon (by 1147), to deacon (1150), to archdeacon of Paris (by 1156). Three years later, the canons elected him as bishop of Paris, choosing him over another archdeacon of Paris, Philip, who was also the brother of the French king. Lombard died a year later on 21–22 July.

Peter Lombard's influence on medieval thought was substantial. While teaching at Paris, Lombard lectured on the whole Bible, although only his commentaries on the Psalms and the Pauline epistles survived. Much of these two commentaries consist of compilations of extracts from patristic writers. These two collections soon became known at the *glossa magna* (the Great Gloss), exceeding in popularity the similar works of *Anselm of Laon and *Gilbert of Poitiers. By the end of the twelfth century, Lombard's glosses were the standard resources for medieval exegetes and remained so well into the sixteenth century. While collections of patristic citations may seem derivative, it is Lombard's skillful colligation that won him so much esteem among his successors.

Even more popular than his biblical commentaries was his *Four Books of Sentences*. This work reflected over two decades of teaching theology, and it is one of the finest-structured texts from the period. The text covered the whole gamut of theology, from God himself (Book I), to Creation and especially the nature of humanity (II), the Incarnation and the virtues of the Christian life (III), and the seven sacraments and the end of history (IV). Like his biblical commentaries, the *Sentences* are awash with citations from the Fathers, but Lombard's voice can also be heard. Although this book was part of a trend in twelfth-century theology to systematize theological thought, it was the only one to attract commentators, almost from the date of its publication. Major thinkers like Peter of Poiters, Stephen *Langton, and *Alexander of Hales all published commentaries, some of them using it as a textbook for their lectures. Others, such as *William of Auvergne, used the *Sentences* as a model to write their own theology texts. By 1240, lecturing publicly on the *Sentences* became a requirement to complete the degree in theology at Paris, and a few years later the first *Sentences* lectures, by Richard Fishacre, took place at Oxford. It remained the main textbook for theological education in Europe until the sixteenth century and in some parts of Catholic Europe until the seventeenth century.

Bibliography: M. L. Colish, *Peter Lombard*, 2 vols., 1994; E. F. Rogers, *Peter Lombard and the Sacramental System*, 1917, reprint 1976.

James R. Ginther

PETER OF BLOIS (C. 1135–C. 1212). The twelfth-century humanist and political thinker Peter of Blois was the son of a minor noble. He was educated at Tours, where he studied poetry and classics, at Bologna, where he studied law, and Paris, where he studied theology. Broadly educated and ambitious, Peter led a peripatetic career, serving first as the tutor of the Sicilian king William II, then moving on to a benefice at Bath, where he was made archdeacon

c. 1175. A skillful secretary and ambassador, and a capable administrator in the developing royal and ecclesiastical arms of government, he was active in various areas of English political affairs from 1195 until late in his career, when he returned to seek benefices in France. He served as an adviser and secretary to Archbishops Richard and Baldwin of Canterbury. He undertook several missions for *Henry II of England and upon the king's death served *Eleanor from 1191 to 1195. In 1202, he was made archdeacon of London and ordained. At the end of his life, Peter suffered a number of political and personal setbacks, including poverty and difficulties concerning his benefices.

Peter of Blois' literary output was prolific. Perhaps his most notable contribution to an understanding of the life of an ambitious man of letters in the late twelfth and early thirteenth centuries is his voluminous correspondence. Collections of his letters were popular, numbering fifty-seven manuscripts in England alone. Many of his later letters arose in response to theological questions posed by contemporary English clerics. Peter's letters continued to be reproduced into the 1600s. A student of *John of Salisbury, he acquired a rich and varied education and wrote widely on topics of contemporary interest including politics, administration, and theology. Peter has been credited as the first author to use case studies in medicine. His name has also been associated with a rhetoric of prose composition, the earliest in England. He wrote in a number of genres: poetry, sermons, satires, political treatises, canon and civil law, theology, and history.

Bibliography: L. Wahlgren, *The Letter Collections of Peter of Blois: Studies in the Manuscript Tradition*, 1993.

Patricia Price

PETER THE HERMIT (C. 1050–C. 1112).
Peter the Hermit was an evangelical monk whose preaching inspired the People's Crusade.

Little is known of Peter's life before his involvement with crusading in the late eleventh century. Born near Amiens, he was presumed to be of humble origin. His contemporaries referred to him as "Little Peter," and he gained fame through his inspirational sermons, which urged people to abandon all and walk to Jerusalem. His charismatic speaking voice entranced his listeners, even those who did not understand his language.

His obsession with a pilgrimage grew after Pope *Urban II called the First Crusade, and he attracted many followers, many of whom regarded him as divinely inspired. In the spring of 1096, Peter, along with Walter the Penniless, began to lead groups of urban and rural poor toward the Holy Land; these groups collectively came to be known as the People's Crusade. Their lack of organization and supplies, along with little or no discipline, alarmed the residents of the areas through which they passed. In addition, their fierce anti-Semitism—they saw the Jews as Christ's enemies at home—led to attacks on the Jews as they traveled.

Walter's group arrived in Constantinople in July 1096 with an imperial escort, but Peter's group had attacked the Hungarians and sacked Belgrade; the emperor's forces in turn decimated about a quarter of the pilgrims in retaliation. When the remainder of Peter's group reached Constantinople in August 1096, the emperor, fearing an attack on the city, arranged to ship them over the Bosphorous into Asia within a matter of days. Upon their arrival, the disorganization and poor leadership led to random killings, mostly of Christians. When they took a castle near Nicaea, the Turks surrounded them, and most of the pilgrims in Peter's group were massacred. When the other crusaders set out for revenge, they were attacked and slaughtered as well, virtually wiping out the People's Crusade.

Peter and the survivors returned to Constantinople, where they joined up with the First Crusade. Discouraged with the prospects of the crusade, Peter deserted but was forced back. The crusaders eventually took Antioch in a bloody battle and opened up the road to Jerusalem. Reaching Jerusalem, Peter addressed the crusaders and inspired them to attack in July 1099. They entered the city on 15 July 1099 and killed all the Muslims still in the city, and Peter began to be seen as a prophet of the cause. Peter was present at the final battle of the Crusade at Askalon, where he led the clergy in prayers for its success. The Crusade having concluded, Peter retired to a monastery in northeastern France, where he died.

Bibliography: D. A. Goodsell, *Peter the Hermit: A Story of Enthusiasm*, 1906; S. Runciman, *A History of the Crusades. Vol. 1.: The First Crusade and the Foundation of the Kingdom of Jerusalem*, 1968.

Connie Evans

PETER THE VENERABLE (C. 1092–1156). A powerful and influential twelfth-century abbot of Cluny, the leading Benedictine monastery, Peter worked to reform the Cluniac abbeys, sponsored a translation of the Qur'an into Latin, and was a prolific writer.

Peter was born around 1092 in Auvergne or Montboissier, France, the son of Maurice de Montboissier and his wife Raingarde, who were both very devout. Peter was placed in the monastery of Sauxillanges to be educated as a young child, where his masters instilled in him not only a love of learning but also a desire for God. Abbot Hugh of Semur heard his profession of monastic vows at Cluny, a Benedictine abbey in Burgundy, France, in 1109. Peter was made prior of a Cluniac house, Vezelay, in 1112 or 1116 and prior of another house, Domene, shortly thereafter.

Peter was unanimously elected abbot of Cluny on 22 August 1122, undertaking the government of Cluny itself, which housed 300 to 400 monks, as well as 2,000 Cluniac houses throughout Europe. On his accession to the abbacy, Peter observed a number of abuses involving both the practical and moral rules of the Benedictine Order and promptly undertook to correct them. Throughout his term as abbot, Peter strove to bring the life of the Cluniac monks into accord with the Rule of St. *Benedict. He traveled extensively, visiting the monasteries, enforcing his reforms, consolidating the order, and affirming the headship of Cluny. He documented the reforms he brought about in a work called *Statuta*, published in 1146–1147.

The early years of Peter's abbacy were not without excitement. Pope *Calixtus II had asked the previous abbot of Cluny, Pontius of Melgueil, to resign because his poor leadership had led to dissension and turmoil. In 1125, when Peter was visiting Rome, Pontius took advantage of Peter's absence to seize Cluny with a small army of followers. Pope Honorius II ordered Pontius to be forcibly removed and imprisoned.

Even as Peter strove to reform the abbeys internally, he defended them from external criticism. *Bernard of Clairvaux, a powerful Cistercian, attacked the Cluniac monasteries for their laxity. In a famous letter composed around 1127, Peter refuted Bernard's criticisms systematically, thoughtfully, and firmly. Although addressed to Bernard, this letter was circulated as a directive to the Cluniac houses as well.

Peter sponsored the first translation of the Qur'an into Latin in 1143, as part of a text entitled *Contra Sarracenos* (Against the Saracens). Scholars used to believe that he wanted to alter the mission of the crusades from military conquest to peaceful conversion. Recent scholarship, based on careful examination of Peter's letters and other texts, has instead shown that he did support the military mission of the crusades. Nonetheless, he favored entering into religious dialogue with the Islamic inhabitants of the Holy Land, and he discouraged the participation of clergy and other religious in military activities.

Peter figured prominently in the resolution of Church disputes. Along with Bernard of Clairvaux, he supported Pope Innocent II against the antipope Anacletus II. He and Bernard guided the General Council of Pisa in 1134 as well. He also participated in the Council of Rheims in 1130. He took in the controversial philosopher Peter *Abelard at Cluny after Abelard's teachings had been condemned at the Council of Sens in 1140, eventually reconciling him with Bernard of Clairvaux and with the pope.

In addition to a number of sermons and theological treatises, about 200 of Peter's letters have been preserved. His writings address doctrinal issues, such as the divinity of Christ and the real presence of Christ in the Eucharist, as well as practical issues, such as the statutes and privileges of the Benedictine Order. He also wrote polemical works against the Jews and Muslims. He died on 25 December 1156 at Cluny.

Peter the Venerable was a gifted leader and a passionate reformer who was successful in reforming his own order and in ameliorating some of the bitter personality conflicts that hampered the Church in his day. Under his guidance, the abbey of Cluny reached the height of its importance in the Christian world.

Bibliography: J. Kritzeck, *Peter the Venerable and Islam*, 1964; J.-P. Torrell, *Pierre le Venerable et sa vision du monde, sa vie, son ouevre, l'homme, et le démon*, 1986.

                                                   Anne Collins Smith and Owen M. Smith

PETER WALDO. *See* WALDO, PETER.

PHILIP II AUGUSTUS OF FRANCE (1165–1223). Capetian king of France, Philip is credited with establishing the political foundations for early modern France and was instrumental in breaking up the English Angevin Empire.

Philip did not enjoy much of a childhood, becoming king in 1180. Philip moved cautiously in his relations with the French magnates and slowly increased the size of the royal demesne. He enjoyed a close relationship with the Church, and to prove his zeal he expelled the Jews from his country in 1182, though he was eventually forced to recall them for reasons of finance. The need for a sound financial base was underscored by growing tensions with the French magnates and also with his uncle by marriage, the count of Flanders.

Seeking to limit the English influence in France, Philip reached an agreement with *Henry II of England in 1180 but secretly encouraged discord between Henry and his ambitious sons. He began to make forays into Angevin territory, and Henry responded by attacking France in 1188. *Richard the Lionheart, Henry's heir, brought the conflict to an end by pledging the French lands as a vassal to Philip and joined in the war against his father, and the aging king was forced to accept a humiliating peace.

Philip also oversaw the rise of Paris as his capital city and spent a great deal of money to modernize it, even enclosing it inside a new wall. Since his father had been a major figure in the Second Crusade, Philip was imbued with the same spirit and used the defeat of the Latin kingdom in Jerusalem in 1187 by the Muslim leader *Saladin as his call to embark on the Third Crusade. *Frederick I Barbarossa, who drowned on the trip, and Richard I also took up the Cross.

Neither Philip nor Richard reached the Holy Land until 1191, where ill feelings between the two monarchs led to constant competition between them. After taking the city of Acre and suffering a severe bout of illness, Philip returned home by the end of the year, though Richard remained behind. The Third Crusade culminated in a short-term agreement with Saladin, and Richard was captured and held for ransom by the Holy Roman Emperor on his return home.

Philip encouraged his nobles to participate in the Fourth Crusade, which had mixed results for the Church but allowed Philip time to consolidate his domestic power free from the influence of the French magnates. He used Richard's kidnapping to continue dismantling the Angevin Empire in France and struck a bargain with Richard's brother *John (of England) to recognize him as heir to the Angevin lands; John subsequently made homage to Philip as his vassal for the lands. Philip also invaded and took over Normandy, a significant part of the Angevin Empire.

On Richard's release, he went to war with Philip in 1194 and continued fighting until his death in battle in 1199. The cost of the war angered the English nobles and left Richard's successor John in a weakened political position. John proved to be a very ineffective king, and the succession was challenged by his nephew, Arthur of Brittany. Philip supported Arthur as a way to split the Angevin Empire but eventually signed an agreement with John to end the war.

In pursuing Isabella of Angoulême for his second wife, John ran afoul of the Lusignans, one of whom was engaged to Isabella. As overlord of both John and the Lusignans, Philip summoned John to a manorial court to answer charges. John refused to appear, and Philip, in the guise of overlord, took over the Angevin lands in France; when the dust settled in 1206, John was left with only Gascony and part of Poitou. With the rest of the Angevin Empire in Philip's hands, the wealth and prestige of the French monarchy was greatly enhanced.

Philip himself ran afoul of the papacy in regard to his own marital problems. After the death of his first wife in 1190, Philip took for his second bride the Danish princess Ingeborg, sister of King Cnut VI, in 1193. Philip repudiated her immediately after the ceremony on the grounds of consanguinity and almost immediately embarked on another relationship with Agnes of Meran; he sought a divorce from Ingeborg, which was granted by the French clergy but reversed by the pope. In 1198, the pope, now *Innocent III, went further and issued an interdict against France because Philip had married Agnes. In 1200, Philip made a false promise to repudiate Agnes in order to get the interdict lifted, but nothing changed. A Church council was called in 1201 to deal with the situation, but the impasse was only resolved when Agnes died later that year, after which Ingeborg took up the queen's duties.

Innocent was a skilled political creature but was not able to push Philip too far, as he needed French support. Philip generally went along with the pope in spiritual matters but resented his influence in wholly secular affairs, though he welcomed the pope's tacit approval of his takeover of the Angevin lands. Philip even planned to invade England, but John's submission to the pope in 1213 put an end to that scheme.

Philip encouraged reform in the Gallican Church, along with monasticism, and vigorously suppressed heresy in his lands, as shown by his pursuit of the Albigensians. He maintained a good relationship with the French clergy, who took his side in disputes with the pope; many of them served the king ably in governmental and administrative posts. He also engendered a new and significant respect for the monarchy in France and made many reforms in administration, finance, and the law that supported the authority of the king. A moderate in most things, Philip sought the advice of learned men for his decisions and was able to keep an eye on daily life in the provinces through the reports of the *baillis*, his chief representatives in the localities. He encouraged the rise of communal associations in the towns and cities, as such associations kept careful records that Philip could then use as sources of information. Preferring diplomacy to war, he nevertheless made sure that his country had adequate defenses; he fortified the major towns and oversaw the construction of the first French naval fleet.

Philip's dominance in Europe was ensured with his victory in the battle of

Bouvines in 1214, which pitted him for the final time against John of England, whose coalition forces under *Otto IV, the German king, and the count of Flanders were completely routed. As a result, *Frederick II was restored to the German throne, Flanders and Boulogne were forced into submission, and the Angevin Empire in France was firmly placed in Philip's hands. John died in 1216, and England would not again be a threat to France for many years.

He approved his son Louis' plan to invade England in 1216 to take advantage of the chaos after John's death, but the English barons united to defeat him. Louis had better success against the Albigensians in France, a crusade which began the process that culminated in the southern part of France coming under Capetian rule.

His kingdom secure and the succession ensured, Philip died in 1223; his magnificent funeral at St. Denis reflected the greatness he had brought to France, now irrevocably one of the most dominant states of Europe, with the strongest monarchy on the Continent.

Bibliography: J. W. Baldwin, *The Government of Philip Augustus: Foundations of French Power in the Middle Ages*, 1986; J. Bradbury, *Philip Augustus, King of France 1180–1223*, 1998.

Connie Evans

PHILIP THE CHANCELLOR (C. 1160/1185–1236). Theologian, philosopher, administrator, and poet, Philip was one of the most influential clerics of the church of Paris in the thirteenth century and chancellor of the University of Paris.

Incorrectly known as Philip de Grève, he was born into a noble Parisian family related to the royal families of *Philip II Augustus and *Louis VII. His father, also called Philip, had been archdeacon of Paris (c. 1175–1184/1185), which has led to some confusion about his own chronology. With his father being well placed in the political circles of Paris, Philip had the opportunity to pursue an ecclesiastical career. By 1202, he was archdeacon of Noyen, a position he retained until his death. He probably studied both the arts and theology at the University of Paris and was a master of theology before 1217. In 1218, Philip became chancellor of Notre Dame, Paris—a post that required not only administrative acumen but also political courage and insight. Philip was responsible for the management of the cathedral and its congregation of canons and, in effect, the leading official of the University of Paris.

That Philip was a fastidious chancellor became immediately clear to all when he began to excommunicate and imprison erring students. His based his actions on two papal sanctions: that university students were under his judicial care and that he was the only university official who could maintain a prison. Pope *Honorius III resolved the legal contradiction in 1221 when he decreed that the chancellor could neither excommunicate nor imprison students without explicit papal permission. Even though it was the corporation of masters that brought the suit against Philip, there was no rift between chancellor and master, for in the end he became one of their most powerful allies. In 1229, when the university went on strike and masters and students began to vacate the city, Philip found himself caught between the concerns of his fellow masters and the condemnation of his bishop, *William of Auvergne. He quickly distanced himself from the bishop and began to plead with the masters to return to Paris. While others like *Alexander of Hales negotiated the means of ending the strike, Philip instead traveled to places like Orléans, where many of the masters had congregated. There he preached an impassioned sermon in which he promised he would champion the rights of his "gentle sons."

In addition to being the defender of the secular masters' cause during the strike, Philip also gained the admiration of the Dominican and Franciscan theologians. Despite the fact that he had multiple benefices (a status that the mendicants publicly condemned), these masters were grateful to Philip as he had ensured that the mendicants presented as magisterial candidates received the license to teach. It is not surprising then that when he died on 23 December 1236 he was interred in the Franciscan cemetery in Paris.

Philip was also a highly regarded theologian. Many of his theological disputations survive, and they became the basis of his major work, the *Summa de bono*, written sometime between 1225 and 1228. This exhaustive summary covers virtually every topic of importance to scholastic theology. In addition, he was a voluminous author of sermons, and we have over 400 in his name, including a very popular collection of sermons on the Psalms. Philip was a well-respected preacher and was called upon to preach in many places outside of Paris for special occasions. His eloquence also emerged in his poetry, as he wrote a number of hymns for worship.

Bibliography: P. Dronke, "The Lyrical Compositions of Philip the Chancellor," *Studi Medievali* 28 (1987): 563–592; W. H. Principe, *Philip the Chancellor's Theology of the Hypostatic Union*, 1975; N. Wicki, ed., *Philippi Cancellarii Parisiensis Summa de bono*, 2 vols., 1985.

James R. Ginther

PIPPIN III. *See* PEPIN III, THE SHORT.

POLO, MARCO (C. 1254–1324). A Venetian merchant, Marco Polo traveled to and within the China of Kublai Khan between 1271 and 1295. His book about his travels in the East has made him the most famous Western traveler of all time and exercised a great influence on the expectations of European explorers during the so-called early modern Age of Discovery.

Marco Polo was born in Venice about 1254 into a family of merchants of merely modest means. Little is known for certain about his life. Between 1260 and 1269, his father Nicolo and his uncle Maffeo visited the China of Kublai Khan (1260–1291). Kublai Khan wanted to establish relations with the pope and employed the Polos as his emissaries. In 1271, they returned to China along with the young Marco Polo, carrying greetings from Pope Gregory X. After traveling three and a half years, they finally reached Kublai Khan's summer palace at Shangtu where the khan greeted them joyfully. The young Marco soon proved to be an adept student of foreign cultures, and his abilities attracted the favorable notice of Kublai Khan. As a result, the great khan entrusted Marco with many missions and offices over a period of seventeen years. During that time, he traveled throughout much of Asia and increased his knowledge of its lands and peoples.

Their many years in China, however, caused the Polos to grow homesick for Venice. After securing the permission of Kublai Khan, they journeyed home to Venice during 1292–1295, much richer than when they had left. Soon after, Marco was taken prisoner in a war with Genoa. He shared his captivity with a writer named Rusticello of Pisa, and the two began to collaborate on writing a book about Marco's travels. Meanwhile, in 1299, Venice and Genoa made peace and Marco was able to return home, where he married and raised a large family. He died in 1324 at the age of seventy.

Marco Polo's book is his great legacy to the history of travel, exploration, and geography. The book was probably written from memory without benefit of notes. Just how much Rusticello embellished the account cannot be determined, but he obviously did some enhancing. Others did the same thing, as the many variant manuscript copies of Marco's travels indicate. Contemporaries found his stories of China and other Asian lands to be interesting but sometimes unbelievable. Still, Marco's book proved to be quite popular. Originally composed in a hybrid French-Italian dialect, it was soon translated into Latin and various European languages and dialects, with between 143 and 150 different manuscripts or printed editions surviving in seven basic versions.

Most people assume that Marco Polo's book is a travelogue describing his itinerary and the adventures that befell him. Instead, *The Travels* begins with a brief prologue in the form of an itinerary, while the main body of the book is a country-by-country or region-by-region description of the lands and peoples of Asia. Marco Polo visited some of the places that he described, but in other cases, such as Japan, he was merely reporting stories that he had heard. Fact and fantasy are intermingled. He provided recognizable descriptions of coal and paper money but also included standard European legends about Asian geography and ethnography such as that of Prester John. Still, *The Travels of Marco Polo* supplied a relatively accurate survey of the many lands and peoples of Asia and was far superior to what had been available to medieval Europeans.

It is interesting that some of Marco Polo's contemporaries went so far as to claim that he had never even made the long journey to China. Some modern scholars have echoed that opinion. They suggest that he largely compiled his book of travels from preexisting Arabic and Persian sources. Most scholars, however, still continue to credit Marco Polo with making a great journey to China that places him as the greatest or among the greatest of the medieval

European travelers. Certainly his book exercised a considerable influence on Christopher Columbus and his expectations of what he would find when he sailed west across the Atlantic Ocean to reach Asia in 1492.

Bibliography: M. B. Campbell, *The Witness and the Other World: Exotic European Travel Writing, 400–1600*, 1988; J.R.S. Phillips, *The Medieval Expansion of Europe*, 2d ed., 1988; F. Wood, *Did Marco Polo Go to China*, 1995; H. Yule and H. Cordier, eds., *The Travels of Marco Polo: The Complete Yule-Cordier Edition*, 2 vols., 1903, reprint 1993.

Ronald H. Fritze

PORETE, MARGUERITE (D. 1310). Marguerite Porete was the author of *The Mirror of Simple Souls*, a book condemned by the Inquisition and associated with the heresy of the Free Spirit, the freedom from sin of the soul joined to God while still on earth. She was burned at the stake on 1 June 1310 at the Place de Grève in Paris.

Marguerite was born at Hainaut and became a Beguine. The ideas in her book reflect those shared by other Beguines and are associated with Cistercian spirituality. They are, in fact, not unlike *Hildegard of Bingen's perceptions of the divine. The key difference from those of Hildegard is that Marguerite represented them as her own, not as received from above. This is probably why the Inquisition burned her book in 1306 after she refused to testify; she was subsequently imprisoned. Although she had submitted her text to three noted scholars, who approved it, the Inquisitor took parts of the book out of context for appraisal by the theological regents of the University of Paris. On their declaration that it was heretical, she was condemned to execution.

The book was translated into Latin, Italian, and Middle English and widely circulated. Written in Old French, it takes the form of a dialogue between Love and Reason about the conduct of the Soul. The prose dialogue is frequently marked by allegory, exempla, and verse commentary. The bridal imagery found throughout indicates familiarity with *minnemystik*. She perceived the *souls* of her title as forming an invisible ideal community that would guide the earthly church, *Ste. Eglise la Petite*. Some contemporary commentators believe that she was a heretic.

Bibliography: E. L. Babinsky, trans., *The Mirror of Simple Souls*, 1993.

Patricia Silber

PRISCIAN (PRISCIANUS CAESARIENSIS) (LATE FIFTH–EARLY SIXTH CENTURY). One of the most important of the late Latin grammarians, Priscian was born in Caesarea in North Africa, and after studying under Theoctistus, he became a teacher of Latin in Constantinople. Along with the *artes* (the *minor* and *maior*) of Donatus (fl. fourth century), Priscian's work established a grammatical educational tradition that would last through the medieval period.

Priscian's surviving works include the *Institutiones grammaticae* in eighteen books; the *Institutio de nomine et pronomine et verbo* (in essence a core epitome of the *Institutiones*); the panegyric *De laude Anastasii imperatoris* (written for his Byzantine patron Emperor Anastasius); three works for patrons from Ostrogothic Rome—the *Praeexcercitamina* (a school-text of exercises utilizing the opening lines of the twelve books of Virgil's *Aeneid* and based on the *progymnasmata* attributed to Hermogenes of Tarsus), the *De figuris numerorum* (on the Greek influence on the Roman system of weights and measures), and *De metris fabularum Terentii* (On the Meters of Terence's Plays; an investigation of the influence of Greek meters on Roman prosody); a translation of the *Periegesis* of Dionysius "the Guide" (*Periegetes*; a geographical description in 1,185 hexameters drawing on the work of Eratosthenes).

Priscian's fame today and in the medieval period is based upon the *Institutiones*, a work originally planned to aid Greek-speaking students in their study of Latin and written at the request of the Roman consul Julian. It treats in the first sixteen books each part of speech in great detail; books 17–18 treat syntax. Priscian's description of Latin syntax, based on the *Syntax* of Apollonius Dyscolus of Alexandria, is the earliest surviving one in any detail to survive. The *Institutiones* became part of the core curriculum of a medieval West united by Latin as an ecclesiastical and intellectual *lingua franca*. The work drew about it a diverse and enduring appendix of commentaries and glosses (especially to his grammatical terminology).

Priscian was of no small influence to and often generated commentarial matter by Insular grammarians (Tatwine and [Saint] *Boniface of Anglo-Saxon England and the Irishmen Virgilius Maro Grammaticus, Murethach, and Sedulius Scottus; Old Irish Priscian glosses occur in manuscripts at St. Gall, Karlsruhe, Leiden, and Milan) and scholars of the Carolingian Renaissance (*Alcuin, *Hrabanus Maurus, and his student Walahfrid *Strabo). If surviving glosses are any indication, Priscian served as a valuable guide to Greek and Latin grammatical terminology; his works were drawn on by later glossographers such as Papias (his *Elementarium* of c. 1041). The *Institutiones*, in explaining grammar and syntax, drew on many and sometimes extensive quotations of classical authors; at times Priscian serves as an important witness to their words for medieval and even modern readers (Cicero's *Aratea*, for example). In analyzing nouns as being of two classes, *principalis* and *derivativa*, Priscian influenced later lexicographers who penned treatises under the name *Derivationes*.

Bibliography: C. H. Haskins, *Renaissance of the Twelfth Century*, 1927; H. Keil, *Grammatici latini*, 8 vols., 1855–1880; V. Law, "Grammar," in *Medieval Latin: An Introduction and Bibliographical Guide*, ed. F.A.C. Mantello and A. G. Rigg, 1996.

Joseph McGowan

PROCOPIUS (WROTE C. 544–555). Procopius was the Greek author of three extant works concerning the time of *Justinian: the *Wars*, a lengthy history in classical style, describing Justinian's wars against the Persians, the Vandals in North Africa, and the Goths of Italy; the *Anecdota* (or Secret History), a vicious invective against Justinian and *Theodora; and the *Buildings*, a panegyrical description of Justinian's public constructions.

Procopius came from Caesarea in Palestine and received a legal education. In 527, the general Belisarius appointed him as *assessor* (judicial adviser). Procopius accompanied Belisarius on campaign along the eastern Roman frontier with Persia (529–531) in North Africa, against the Vandals (533–534), and in Italy during the first stage of the protracted war against the Gothic successors of *Theodoric (535–552). In 542, Belisarius was recalled to Constantinople, temporarily in disgrace. Procopius appears to have left his service at this time, if not before, and thereafter to have remained in Constantinople. His experience equipped him well to write military and political history, the main subjects of the classicizing style in which he chose to write the *Wars*. By his time, other forms of historical narrative, including the genres of both ecclesiastical history and of chronicle propagated by Eusebius, were well established. Nevertheless, a tradition of classicizing history in the style of Thucydides, comfortably absorbed into Christian literary culture, was maintained in the East from Ammianus Marcellinus in the late fourth century until Theophylact Simocatta in the early seventh. Procopius' own *Wars* were continued, perhaps after his death, by the poet and historian Agathias.

Living in Constantinople supplied Procopius with the rumors to write the ferocious invective of the *Anecdota* (presumably published posthumously) but probably also provided him with the motives to write the panegyrical *Buildings*, as the purpose of eulogistic works such as the latter was usually to elicit or repay some act of generosity from the honorand. The wildly differing attitudes toward Justinian in Procopius' three works are disconcerting, but common authorship, once queried, is now accepted, and it is even clear that Procopius was writing the latter books of the *Wars* and the *Anecdota* simultaneously, c. 550 (he began the *Buildings* after 553). Even the *Wars*, the lengthiest work (in eight books), shows marked changes in attitude over the long period of composition (c. 544–553) (for instance, he describes the victory over the Vandals in 534 enthusiastically but is sympathetic to the Goths by the latter stages of the war in Italy, c. 552).

Procopius' works are our most detailed sources for the politics and military events of Justinian's reign and contain many administrative and social data. The classicizing *Wars*, together with Justinian's vast codification of Roman law, have traditionally formed the basis for interpretations of Justinian's reign as an enlightened period of restoration, whereas the *Anecdota* and *Buildings* have been regarded uncomfortably. More recent views suggest that other sources (for instance, the strongly Christian chronicle of Malalas) may give a truer picture of Justinian's regime—as repressive, autocratic, and characterized more by religious intolerance than by classical learning.

Bibliography: A. Cameron, *Procopius and the Sixth Century*, 1985.

Andrew Gillett

PSELLOS, MICHAEL (1018–C. 1081).

A Byzantine intellectual, imperial statesman, and writer, Psellos produced historical, philosophical, rhetorical, theological, and legal works, was an influential imperial counselor and state minister, and staunchly promoted privileges of the Byzantine civil aristocracy.

Psellos was born into a family of modest position and received an intensive education that prepared him for the civil imperial administration. A recipient of a classical liberal arts education, he studied Plato and the Neoplatonists and is considered to have been one of the greatest Byzantine philosophers and humanists.

During his early career as a bureaucrat, feudal magnates were reversing *Basil II's fiscal policies that protected the small landholders and were acquiring land from peasant and military holdings, thus turning their occupants into dependents. With rulers that were unable or unwilling to oppose the wealthy landed nobility, the foundations of Byzantine fiscal strength were quickly eroding. Psellos went to work as an imperial secretary during the period when imperial centralized authority was suffering from the capricious rule of the Empresses Zoe and Theodora. Rightful heirs of the Macedonian dynasty, the princesses maintained the legitimacy of the purple even through a number of failed marriages by Zoe. However, Zoe's last marriage to Constantine IX Monomachus, an ineffectual ruler who was a member of the Byzantine civil aristocracy, did create an atmosphere during which culture and education bloomed and allowed men of great learning to exercise substantial political power. Gaining considerable stature and social prestige, Psellos and his young colleagues John Xiphilinos and Constantine Leichoudes became imperial counselors and leading ministers of the state.

In 1045, these men played a leading role in establishing the University of Constantinople, including faculties of philosophy and law. The philosophy curriculum was based on the trivium and quadrivium. Psellos became the "consul of philosophers" (*hypatus*), while his colleague Xiphilinos was the "guardian of the law" (*nomophylax*). The new university served to train individuals to join the cadre of those in the civil bureaucracy.

The inability of the empire to maintain financial order, however, had allowed the army to atrophy in the face of external threats. Seljuk Turks moved east, the Pechenegs and Cumans moved south from the northern steppes, and the Normans moved east, forcing the Byzantines to make creative alliances and pay their enemies for peace. In addition, toward the end of Constantine IX's life, in 1054, the great schism between the Roman and Constantinopolitan churches occurred. This event that symbolically represents the rupture between East and West was partly driven by doctrinal issues but can mostly be attributed to the inability of Emperor Constantine IX to control raging forces that included a powerful and independent papacy and an equally strong patriarchate with popular appeal in Constantinople.

After Constantine IX's death, Psellos' circle temporarily lost power. Deeming it prudent to leave court, Psellos retired to a monastery on Mt. Olympos, where he stayed for a time and changed his name from Constantine to Michael. He was, however, quickly rehabilitated, and he joined the service of Isaac Comnenus, the first ruler of the Comnenian dynasty who belonged to the military aristocracy. The latter had achieved popular support, as well as the support of the Church, until he attempted to alienate Church properties to strengthen the imperial treasury. He could not withstand the pressure from the civil aristocracy and resigned his throne on the advice of Psellos and retired to a monastery.

Psellos' claims about the crucial role he played in the imperial politics under the reigns of Constantine X Ducas, Romanos IV Diogenes, and Michael VII Ducas may be quite exaggerated. He claimed that the abdication of Isaac Comnenus and accession of Constantine X Ducas were the result of his own work. He did, however, become an adviser of the emperor as well as the tutor of the emperor's son and heir. External threats again led to a situation where the military aristocracy asserted itself with the accession of Romanos IV Diogenes, who was ultimately defeated and captured by the Seljuks at Manzikert in 1071, ransomed, blinded, and deposed upon his return to Constantinople. Psellos' pupil Michael VII was raised to power, but soon thereafter Psellos fades from the scene.

Of Psellos' compositions, the *Chronographia* is perhaps his most famous; it begins with the reign of Basil II and chronicles the events from the years 976 to 1078, much of which he had witnessed personally. Rather than presenting a stream of events with definite judgments, he provides images and impressions made up of complex and even contradictory descriptions of his subjects. He considered the role of Nature (*physis*) with its own set of laws as determining the course of events, rather than the intervention of God's miraculous power. The *Chronographia*, entertaining as it is, is also a valuable source for the political and intellectual history of eleventh century Byzantium.

Bibliography: M. Angold, *The Byzantine Empire, 1025–1204*, 2d ed., 1997; A. Kaldellis, *The Argument of Psellos'* Chronographia, 1999.

Tom Papademetriou

PSEUDO-DIONYSIUS THE AREOPAGITE (FL. C. 500). The author of a number of Greek philosophical treatises dated to the sixth century, Pseudo-Dionysius was thought throughout the Middle Ages to be the authentic Dionysius the Areopagite, an Athenian converted by Paul in Acts 17:34. Uncovered as spurious only in 1895, we know nothing of the specific author except that he betrays a certain Neoplatonic influence and probably was of Eastern origin.

Pseudo-Dionysius wrote four works—*The Celestial Hierarchy*, *The Ecclesiastical Hierarchy, The Divine Names* (his most important), *The Mystical Theology*—and a number of letters. Pseudo-Dionysius was clearly influenced by Neoplatonism, especially in his application of the doctrine of procession and return, and he was a major conduit of the apophatic, or negative, theology prevalent in Greek Orthodox Christianity into the Latin West. The *via negativa* sees God as fundamentally unknowable, and through a recognition of this inscrutability the believer is lifted closer to God. Pseudo-Dionysius thus plays an important part in the history of medieval mysticism.

The Mystical Theology and Pseudo-Dionysius' letters constitute short explications of the basic themes and approaches developed in his longer works. In *The Celestial Hierarchy*, Pseudo-Dionysius expounds the nature of symbolism and hierarchy and goes on to explain the heavenly hierarchy of angels. The work thus was an important source of "angelology" in the West. Angels are arranged in a hierarchy, in three ranks of three. In the first rank, seraphim, cherubim, and thrones all "stand" closest to God; the second rank consists of the dominions, powers, and authorities; in the third rank, closest to humanity, reside the principalities, archangels, and angels. These ranks mediate between God and man; they enable God to proceed "out" from his unitary perfection, passing on his divine light to humanity. In his treatise *The Ecclesiastical Hierarchy*, Pseudo-Dionysius provides an analysis of the earthly counterpart to the celestial hierarchy. The work delves into the liturgical symbols behind the sacraments: baptism, eucharist, consecration, and ordination, for example. Pseudo-Dionysius also explains the workings of the earthly church hierarchy as an image of the heavenly hierarchy, especially in its tripartite structure.

His major work, however, is *The Divine Names*, a work that purports to explain a very simple thing—the various names applied to God—but does so in an exceedingly complex way. By means of apophatic theology, Dionysius leads the reader through various names applied to God in the Bible—"God," "being," "life," "wisdom," "mind," "word," "truth," "faith," "power," "righteousness," "salvation," "redemption"—always with an eye to showing the essential unity of God, a unity that yet always resides in differentiation.

Pseudo-Dionysius exerted great influence in the Byzantine Empire, and his philosophy entered Western thought mainly through *John Scottus Eriugena. Through Eriugena's translation and commentary, Pseudo-Dionysius' angelology and theories of symbolism and hierarchy influenced the theology and philosophy of Thomas *Aquinas and Saint *Bonaventure, as well as Gothic art and aesthetics.

Bibliography: P. Rorem, *Pseudo-Dionysius: A Commentary on the Texts and an Introduction to Their Influence*, 1993.

Andrew Scheil

R

RADBERTUS, PASCHASIUS, SAINT (C. 785/795–C. 860/865). A Benedictine monk and theologian of the Carolingian Empire, Paschasius Radbertus of Corbie was a prolific author of theological tracts, exegetical commentaries, saints' lives, and homilies.

He was born sometime between 785 and 795 near Soissons. Initially he was raised by the nuns of the convent of St. Mary's at Soissons. He took his vows and entered the monastery at Corbie sometime before 820. The details of his life between his childhood and his monastic vows are unknown. Radbertus never advanced beyond the rank of deacon.

At Corbie, he was presumably involved in the teaching of young monks and the study of letters both sacred and secular. His abbot was Adalard the Elder; Radbertus would write *Vitae* of Adalard and of Adalard's brother Wala (also an abbot of Corbie) as a tribute to his esteemed mentors. These texts contain valuable historical information about the life of Radbertus and his contemporaries, as well as the politics and controversies of his day. In 822, Radbertus assisted in the founding of the abbey at New Corvey. He also attended the Synod of Paris in 847 and the Synod of Quiercy in 849. He was proclaimed the abbot of Corbie itself, c. 843–844. At some point between 849 and 852, he relinquished his seat due to internal disputes and retired to St. Riquier. He did, however, return to Corbie before he died c. 860–865.

Radbertus was a prolific author. His extant works include treatises on the Virgin Mary: *De partu Virginis* (a defense and explanation of the virginity of Mary in two books) and a tract on the life of Mary (*De nativitate sanctae Mariae*); and it is also accepted now that he wrote "Cogitis me," on the Assumption of the Virgin Mary (formerly known as "Epistle IX" of Pseudo-Jerome). He also wrote a treatise on faith, hope, and charity (*De fide, spe, et caritate*). Radbertus composed saints' lives: the *Vita sancti Adalhardi* (Life of St. Adalard) and the *Vita Walae* (Life of Wala), also known as the

Epitaphium Arsenii. The *Vita sancti Adalhardi* clearly falls into the traditional genre of the saint's life, while the *Life of Wala* is a rather more secular biography, like *Einhard's *Life of Charlemagne*. Both works provide fascinating details of ninth-century monastic life, as do many of Radbertus' works. Radbertus also composed, or possibly just revised, a work on the deaths of Saint Rufinus and Saint Valerius, the *Passio Rufini et Valerii*. Radbertus' commentary on the Gospel of Matthew is a very large commentary in twelve books written over a number of years from c. 826 to 851. He also authored a commentary on Psalm 44 in three books and a commentary on Lamentations in five books, as well as assorted poems and letters.

Radbertus' most famous work is *De corpore et sanguine Domini* (On the Body and Blood of the Lord). This treatise was written for his student Placidus, of the abbey at Corvey; it was revised in 844 at the request of *Charles the Bald and presented to him as a gift. Radbertus' work is the first concentrated theological investigation into the nature of the Eucharist and the doctrine of transubstantiation. In it, he emphasized the true physicality of the Real Presence: In the sacrament of the Eucharist the bread and wine were literally transformed into the actual, physical body and blood of Christ. This flesh of Christ was the very same born of the Virgin Mary. By partaking of Christ's body and blood, the believer was absorbed into the mystical body of the Church.

Radbertus' position provoked opposition from his fellow monk at Corbie, Ratramnus, as well as from *Hrabanus Maurus; this was the so-called First Eucharistic Controversy. This debate has been somewhat exaggerated in terms of its importance, vehemence, and wide-ranging implications: It was more or less an internal dispute at Corbie. In opposition to Radbertus, Ratramnus took a position in his treatise (also titled *De corpore et sanguine Domini*) that the body and blood of Christ were present in the physical bread and wine in a spiritual sense, not in a direct, physical manifestation. Radbertus would later return to this controversy in his letter to Frudegard, a monk at Corvey. Radbertus is best known for his work on the Eucharist, and his extant corpus is an important source for the study of ninth-century theology.

Bibliography: P. Radbertus, *Charlemagne's Cousins: Contemporary Lives of Adalard and Wala*, trans. A. Cabaniss, 1967.

Andrew Scheil

RADEGUNDE OF POITIERS (C. 525–587).

Reluctant wife of Clothar I, Radegunde left him and became a deaconess, living as a nun at the convent of Poitiers but still involved in politics.

A Thuringian princess and daughter of Berthar, she was seized by the Frankish king Clothar I in 531 when he and his half brother Theuderic invaded and destroyed Thuringia. For ten years, she was raised and educated to be Clothar's future wife at his villa of Athies. He probably had at least one other wife when he married Radegunde at Soissons c. 540, and later he took others. Around 550,

Clothar ordered the murder of Radegunde's sole surviving brother, and she, already living an ascetic life while queen, left him.

Medard, bishop of Noyon, ordained Radegunde deaconess (rather than nun). She then journeyed toward Poitiers, depositing her jewelry and royal regalia at various monasteries on her way. Initially, she lived in a villa near Poitiers that Clothar had given her, perhaps as a morning gift, but later he endowed a convent for her dedicated to the Virgin Mary. She appointed her spiritual daughter, the virgin Agnes, as its abbess while she lived there as a simple nun. The convent followed the Rule for nuns written by *Caesarius of Arles that Radegunde had requested from the abbess Caesaria II. Although this Rule required strict claustration, Radegunde never ceased to be involved in secular politics of the Frankish kingdoms. Her convent housed the daughters of Frankish kings; she wrote frequently to kings and bishops, and they visited her at Poitiers.

At Radegunde's request, Byzantine Emperor *Justinian sent a piece of wood from "the true cross" housed in a reliquary of bejeweled gold. By this time, there was some ill will between the convent and the local bishop Maroveus. He refused to celebrate the installation of the relic, and King Sigibert of Austrasia had to request that Eufronius, bishop of Tours, perform the ceremony in 569. Radegunde and her convent were a source of spiritual and secular power at Poitiers, and perhaps the bishop felt competition.

The Italian Venantius *Fortunatus, poet and later bishop of Poitiers, composed many of his most important works for Radegunde during her lifetime, some describing life at the convent and others to be used in the liturgy. He also, after her death, wrote a biography that some historians believe set a new paradigm of piety for royal women: It was one of the most widely read *vitae* of its time. A second, supplementary life was written in the seventh century by the nun *Baudonivia.

Radegunde died 13 August 587 at the convent of the Holy Cross, later renamed St. Radegunde's at Poitiers, and three days later was buried in the church of St. Mary as she had requested and where members of the convent were usually interred. *Gregory, bishop of Tours, officiated at her funeral as Maroveus of Poitiers was, perhaps deliberately, absent. The citizens of Poitiers and local magnates attended while the nuns watched the procession from the top of the convent wall. Even before her death, there were miracles associated with Radegunde, and they multiplied at her death when she was popularly declared a saint.

Bibliography: J. A. McNamara, J. E. Halborg, and E. G. Whately, "Radegund, Queen of the Franks and Abbess of Poitiers (ca. 525–587)," in *Sainted Women of the Dark Ages*, ed. and trans. J. A. McNamara, J. E. Halborg, and E. G. Whately, 1992.

Janice R. Norris

RADULPHUS GLABER. *See* GLABER, RADULPHUS.

RAMON BERENGUER IV (C. 1113–1162). Son of Ramon Berenguer III and Dolca of Provence, Ramon Berenguer IV became count of Barcelona upon the death of his father in 1131. He inherited sovereignty over the counties of Barcelona, Gerona, Vic, Besalu, and Cerdagne. Three years later he was betrothed to Petronella, the infant heiress to the kingdom of Aragon, and married her in 1150. He successfully negotiated with the Knights of the Hospital, of the Temple, and of the Holy Sepulcher to secure his wife's inheritance so that their union created a united eastern Iberian kingdom, the crown of Aragon, for their heirs.

Ramon extended his reign southward into Islamic territories with the conquests of Tortosa, Lerida, and Fraga. He also defended his younger brother's inheritance in Provence through diplomatic negotiations with *Frederick I Barbarossa. His support for the rulers of Montpellier further extended his dynasty's influence into southern France. His reign saw the creation of the *Usatges of Barcelona*, a code of customary law that redefined the political structures of both new and old Catalonia. His 1151 survey of his lands began the regular territorial administration of these territories and placed his Catalan domains on firmer fiscal footing. He remained a "prince-count" to his death in 1162, leaving the title "king" to his eldest son, Alfonso II. Nevertheless, he was the most effective ruler of Spain in the mid-twelfth century.

Bibliography: T. N. Bisson, *The Medieval Crown of Aragon*, 1986.

Linda A. McMillin

RAMON LULL (OR LLUL). *See* LLULL, RAMON.

RAMON OF PEÑAFORT (RAYMOND OF PENNAFORT), SAINT (C. 1180/1185–1275).

Canonist and Dominican, he worked as a missionary among the Jews and Muslims of Spain and Northern Africa.

Born in Catalonia at the tower of Peñafort near Vilafranca del Penedes in the early 1180s, Ramon was educated in law at the University of Bologna and held a post there as master. In 1219, he returned to Barcelona and became an official in the cathedral chapter. By the early 1220s, he joined the Dominican Order. Ten years later he became papal confessor, chaplain, and penitentiary to Pope *Gregory IX. In this position in 1234, he compiled the book of decretals, a document central to Roman Catholic canon law until 1917. He also established a papal inquisition in Aragon in 1232. He became master general of the Dominicans in 1238 and oversaw the redaction of the order's constitutions.

He remained in this office for only two years, after which time he stepped down to devote himself to missionary activities among the Jews and Muslims of Spain and Northern Africa. He was instrumental in the foundation of a network of schools of Arabic and Hebrew for the training of Dominican friars, and it was at his request that Thomas *Aquinas wrote the *Summa contra gentiles*. He also played a role in the foundation of the Mercedarians. A prolific writer, his most important works include *Raymundina* (a guide for confessors), *Summa* *iuris canonici, Summa pastoralis,* and *Dubitabilia cum responsionibus.* He died in 1275 and was canonized in 1601.

Bibliography: V. F. Comins, *San Ramón de Penyafort: Biografía,* 1994; T. M. Schwertner, *St. Raymond of Pennafort,* ed. C. M. Antony, 1935.

Linda A. McMillin

RASHI (SOLOMON BEN ISAAC) (1040–1105). Rashi, an acronym of Rabbi Shlomo Yitzhaqi, is the celebrated Jewish commentator on the Bible and the Talmud. Rashi's work had a marked influence on medieval Christian Bible commentary and still serves among Jews as one of the most authoritative introductions to the two texts.

Rashi was born at Troyes, the capital of Champagne in northern France. Little is known of his early life, save that he was born into a family of scholarly reputation. After his initial education in Troyes, Rashi went to study in the Rhenish academies of Jewish learning in Worms and Mainz. Here, he was introduced to the influential methods, teachings, and traditions of Rabbi Gershom ben Judah (d. c. 1040). Around 1065, Rashi returned to his boyhood home, started his own academy, and was appointed rabbinic judge of Troyes' small Jewish community. Like other rabbis and teachers of the time, he did not receive remuneration for his work and thus earned his livelihood as a vintner. His free time, however, was fully devoted to study and teaching, and his small academy quickly gained a reputation as a center of rabbinic learning. Rashi died at Troyes in 1105.

Rashi's great Bible commentary represents a masterful reconciliation of the two basic methods of interpretation: literal and homilectical. Methodologically, Rashi's commentary begins with a careful philological examination of the literal meaning, taking into account both text and context. When presented with a difficult word or phrase, Rashi would frequently resort to simple explanations of his own by giving an alternative Hebrew word where he thought the biblical word might not be understood. In especially difficult passages, he would often resort to translating words into the vernacular, in his case, medieval French. He was also something of a grammarian, and his commentaries occasionally digress into remarks on syntax and morphology. If he deemed it necessary, he would then supplement this with the use of Aggadic material such as allegory, parable, and homily. While his main exegetical objective was to establish the plain meaning of the text, he was not averse to including such Mishnaic material and thus found detractors among later critics. Nevertheless, Rashi's commentary excelled all others before or after because of its lucidity and precision.

Rashi's commentary on the Talmud, drawn from generations of Franco-German scholarship, also represents a grand achievement in the art of interpretation. Whereas the Bible commentary was intended as a popular work, Rashi's commentary on the Talmud was obviously intended for the serious student. Be this as it may, Rashi's commentary was anything but dry and lexical. In striving to help the student make sense of the text, Rashi's explanations are often colorful and imaginative. He not only provides a solid commentary on the text but also attempts to explain the social backgrounds to Talmudic times. Like an oral exchange between student and teacher, Rashi interjects his commentary into the text, identifying and explaining statement and question, word and phrase, argument and reference, all in an attempt to elucidate the intricacies of a notoriously difficult work.

Rashi's Talmud commentary circulated rapidly and by the beginning of the thirteenth century became a standard reference of every Talmudic scholar. His interpretations of Talmudic passages quickly became influential in determining juridical decisions, and it is often said that if it were not for his commentary, the Talmud would have all but disappeared. His work as Talmud commentator was continued by a group of writers known as tosafists, or supplementers, who for about 200 years after Rashi continued to add commentaries to the Talmudic text, composed glosses, and refined or expanded Rashi's own interpretations and arguments.

Rashi's commentaries had a much wider appeal than those that came before him, and their influence extended beyond the relatively closed scholarly establishment. Typeset in a special script that came to be known as Rashi Script, his Bible commentary was the first dated printed Hebrew book (1475) and had a profound influence on both Jew and Gentile. Shortly after Rashi's death, a number of Christian scholars, like the so-called Victorines, made use of his work; his Bible commentary had a significant influence on Christian Bible study, especially on the Franciscan scholar Nicholas de Lyra (d. 1349), who, in turn, influenced Martin Luther's work on a German version of the Bible. Rashi's customary use of a vernacular gloss to clarify the exact meaning of difficult words and phrases also makes his commentary an important source for the study of Old French.

Bibliography: M. Liber, *Rashi*, trans. A. Szold, 1948; C. Pearl, *Rashi*, 1988.

Erik S. Ohlander

RAYMOND IV OF TOULOUSE (C. 1041–1105). The count of Toulouse, Raymond IV was one of the leaders of the First Crusade. After helping to conquer Jerusalem, he made himself the count of Tripoli.

Raymond spent most of his life bringing all the familial lands that had been dispersed over generations back into his possession. By the time he left on crusade in 1096, he was master of thirteen counties in southern France, as well as the marquis of Provence and duke of Narbonne. In this effort, he had proven himself a good soldier and general, and it is also thought that he may have even fought for a brief time in Spain against the Muslims. He also proved himself to be a supporter of Church reform. This made him the ideal candidate to lead the First Crusade, and Pope *Urban II chose him to do so, along with Bishop *Adhémar of Le Puy, Urban's legate. He and Urban met together to discuss this adventure before the famous Council of Clermont, where the pope called upon the knights of Christendom to recover Jerusalem from the Muslims. As Raymond prepared to leave on crusade, he left his counties to his son and heir Bertrand, but he took his wife. One chronicle even suggests that he made a vow never to return to France.

Although Raymond was the richest of the leaders of the crusade, he was also the oldest, and he was chronically ill. When his army arrived at Constantinople, Raymond refused to become a vassal of the Byzantine emperor as the other leaders did, but he did swear to respect the property of the emperor. When the crusaders took the city of Antioch, only Raymond stood against *Bohemond's efforts to keep it for himself, reminding the others of their oaths to the emperor. Despite his efforts, spurred partly by a desire to have Antioch for himself, he was forced to give way to Bohemond and to continue on to Jerusalem. Raymond now became at odds with Godfrey of Bouillon. Raymond took up his position to the south of Jerusalem, Godfrey to the east. Although Godfrey's men were first to take Jerusalem, Raymond was able to take the Tower of David, a vital stronghold in the city.

According to several chroniclers, Raymond was offered the kingship of Jerusalem first but declined it; he may have been outmaneuvered by Godfrey, who tricked him out of control of the Tower and agreed to be the ruler in Jerusalem rather than the king. Raymond thus decided to find another city to make his own, and he decided to create his own county based on the city of Tripoli. However, when Raymond died on 28 February 1105, he had not yet fully taken the city of Tripoli. His nephew William-Jordan succeeded him and continued Raymond's conquests. A few years later, Raymond's son Bertrand showed up to successfully challenge his cousin's claims to his father's lands.

Bibliography: J. H. Hill and L. L. Hill, *Raymond IV Count of Toulouse*, 1962.

Ryan P. Crisp

RAYMOND LLULL. *See* LLULL, RAMON.

RAYMOND OF PEÑAFORT. *See* RAMON OF PEÑAFORT, SAINT.

REGINO OF PRÜM (C. 845–915). Born near Speyer, Germany, Regino (sometimes spelled Reginon) served as abbot of Prüm from 892 to 899 and then of St. Martin's monastery in Trier until his death in 915. He is the author of important works on Church administration, musicology, and history.

Regino became abbot of Prüm after Northmen sacked it in 892. While abbot of Prüm, Regino participated in the Synod of Tribur (895), which established guidelines distinguishing between lay and ecclesiastical jurisdictions. His later work on a related topic, *Libri duo de synodalibus causis et disciplinis ecclesiasticus* (Two Books on Synodal Cases and Ecclesiastical Discipline), a handbook on canon law, was used in Germany as a manual for visiting bishops for about a century after Regino's death. Much of its content was incorporated into its eventual replacement, *Burchard of Worms' *Decretorum Libri XX*, which in turn became one of the sources used in *Gratian. Ironically, his resistance to political pressure from local lay lords gave his opponents within the monastery the excuse to depose him in 899.

After his deposition, Regino moved to Trier, where Archbishop Ratbod appointed him abbot of St. Martin's. Regino's earliest published work, a treatise on musicology titled "De Armonica Institutione," written in the form of a letter, was dedicated to Archbishop Ratbod and probably intended to secure the archbishop's support. Along with his "Tonarius," a collection of chants, "De Armonica Institutione" is still used by enthusiasts of early music, and the two musicological treatises are the only works by Regino that have been translated into English.

Regino's most influential work is his *Chronicle*, which is divided into two books, the first covering the period from the birth of Christ to the death of *Charles Martel and the second proceeding from that date until 908. Even in the highly derivative first book, Regino made a significant innovation, becoming the first historian to reject outright Dionysus Exiguus' mistaken dating of the Incarnation to 753 A.U.C. (years after the traditional date for the foundation of Rome). On the basis that Herod the Great had died in 750 A.U.C., Regino placed the birth of Christ in 749 A.U.C. (4 B.C), a correction that eventually gained wide acceptance and is still the most prevalent date used in modern times. Despite his careful work with regard to the date of Christ's birth, he was unable to reconcile differing dates for the death of Charles Martel, and the chronology of the first book is unreliable.

Regino's independent account, beginning in his second book with the entry for 813, not only is one of the most important sources for the history of the ninth and early tenth centuries but also displays some very significant developments in the writing of history. Regino supplemented his narrative sources (probably the *Annales Prumienses* and *Annales Stablo*) with letters and official documents, especially when recounting the marriage scandal of *Lothar II. More important, Regino departed from the triumphalism of earlier chronicles, replacing the idea that the Carolingian Empire was the fulfillment of world history with the thesis that fortune, in conjunction with human virtue, influenced the course of events. This view had been the norm for history written in classical times and was probably known to Regino through the third-century A.D. *Epitome* of Justin. By adopting it, Regino was able both to relate Frankish history to that of earlier periods and to judge historical actions in context rather than against the strictures of Christian morality. Regino's analysis is not always reflected in the precise wording of his chronicle, since he also adopted the practice of quoting his sources accurately rather than paraphrasing them to fit his own conceptions. While Regino himself stopped his *Chronicle* in 908, a continuation ascribed to Adalbert of Magdeburg carried the narrative down to 967.

Regino's written work reflects the variety of concerns that faced an active churchman during the later ninth and early tenth century. His career as an abbot in Prüm and Trier demonstrates the difficulties and opportunities provided by a career as a high Church official, and his work as a historian demonstrates the continuing intellectual vitality of post-Carolingian Europe.

Bibliography: Sister M. P. LaRoux, trans., *The* De Harmonica Institutione *and* Tonarius *of Regino of Prüm*, 1967, reprint 1979; *Quellen zur Karolingischen Reichsgeschichte*, 3 vols., trans. and ed., R. Rau, 1955–1960.

Edward J. Schoenfeld

RICHARD I (THE LIONHEART) OF ENGLAND (1157–1199, R. 1189–1199).

Known mostly for his bravery and skill on the battlefield, for which he earned his nickname "the Lionheart," Richard spent most of his reign as the king of England fighting in France and in the Holy Land during the Third Crusade.

Born in Oxford the second son of *Henry II and *Eleanor of Aquitaine, Richard spent most of his youth in Aquitaine with his mother, whom he favored over his father all his life. He became the duke of Aquitaine at fourteen and learned the art of war, fighting to maintain control over those lands. At various times, Richard found himself either allied with or fighting against his father, Henry II; his brothers Henry, Geoffrey, and *John; and the kings of France, *Louis VII and *Philip II. Richard twice rebelled against his father, in 1173–1174 and 1188–1189. However, when his older brother Henry died in 1183, Richard became heir to the English throne.

In the autumn of 1187, when news reached Europe that *Saladin had taken the kingdom of Jerusalem, Richard took up the cross. Both Henry and Philip were initially shocked by Richard's decision, but the archbishop of Tyre eventually convinced the two of them to take crusader vows as well. While Richard wanted to go on crusade immediately, he was delayed in early 1188 by a rebellion in Aquitaine. His chances of leaving were pushed back further when Richard's enemy Raymond VI of Toulouse, who was one of Philip's men, came to the aid of the rebels. Richard quelled the rebellion, forced Raymond back, and began to take Toulouse, which prompted Philip to protect his vassal. Though Henry had not come to his son's aid earlier, at Philip's request, Henry now feared for his own lands and assisted Richard. During their peace negotiations, Richard realized Henry was willing to sacrifice some of his lands, so he struck his own deal with Philip and rebelled against his father. Henry died on 6 July 1189, with Richard still allied with Philip against him. Upon his father's death, Richard acted quickly to solidify his position as king so that he might go on crusade. After addressing immediate problems in France, Richard left for England, landing in Portsmouth on 13 August 1189. A month later, he was crowned king in Westminster. In early December, Richard returned to France; on 30 December, Richard and Philip swore to support each other, and their barons swore to remain faithful and keep the peace while the two kings were on crusade.

Richard began his crusade on 4 July 1190, first stopping in Sicily to meet up with Philip. While there, the two clashed as Richard sought to end his betrothal to Philip's half sister, to whom Richard had been betrothed as a child. Richard wished to marry Berengaria of Navarre, daughter of King Sancho VI. After Richard paid a hefty sum and made concessions of land in France, Philip freed him from the betrothal. Richard left Sicily on 10 April 1191, taking with him over 200 ships laden with men, horse, and siege weapons. On the way to the Holy Land, three of Richard's ships, which had separated from the fleet during a storm, landed in Cyprus, were plundered, and their crews taken hostage. Richard arrived at Cyprus on 6 May and immediately led a daring amphibious assault on a fortified beach. Richard pushed the defenders back, and five days later, Isaac Comnenus, the "tyrant of Cyprus," sued for peace. Richard married Berengaria a day later.

On 8 June 1191, Richard arrived at Acre, which fell on 12 July. From the start, he and Philip squabbled. Knowing Philip wanted to return to Europe, Richard suggested they take a vow to remain for three years or until Jerusalem was recaptured. Philip, however, feigned illness and left for France in early August. Richard remained in the Holy Land until 9 October 1192. During his crusade, Richard proved himself a brilliant general and fearless warrior, often entering battle at its thickest. While many of the crusaders wanted to quickly take Jerusalem and return to Europe, Richard's plan was to reestablish European strength to ensure that Jerusalem, once retaken, would be safe. Though Richard was militarily successful in the battles he undertook, he was unable to unify the various crusading factions. Many of the European crusaders only wanted to fulfill the letter of their crusader vows, and the French crusaders often refused to assist Richard. Unable to ensure victory as he wanted it, Richard settled for a negotiated peace. On 2 September 1192, Richard and Saladin signed the Treaty of Jaffa, which established peace for three years and eight months and, more important, allowed Christians to enter Jerusalem. Richard left for home on 9 October 1192.

The news from home had not been good. Philip's supporters who had returned to Europe earlier had started a smear campaign to defame Richard. In England, Richard's brother John had sought Philip's support in an attempt to take England for himself, a plot stopped by their mother, Eleanor of Aquitaine. And in France, Philip had tried to take Normandy while Richard was away but was unable to find enough support to help him attack the lands of a man gone on crusade. Hearing of the troubles at home, Richard intended to travel through Germany in order to avoid France. Shipwrecked, he was imprisoned by Leopold, duke of Austria, who eventually turned Richard over to the Holy Roman Emperor, *Henry VI, a friend of Philip's. As Henry held Richard prisoner, Philip and John continued to scheme against Richard. John first tried to stir up rebellion and then declared Richard dead. As with his earlier attempts, Eleanor of Aquitaine kept her youngest son in check. Richard eventually negotiated his freedom, paying Henry 150,000 marks of silver as ransom. He was set free on 4

February 1194 and arrived in England on 13 March. Upon learning of Richard's release, Philip is said to have warned John with the message, "Look to yourself, the devil is loosed." John fled to Normandy and eventually threw himself upon Richard's mercy, which he received.

While on crusade, Richard had left England and its well-established government machinery in the capable hands of such men as William Longchamp, Hubert Walter, and Geoffrey Fitz Peter. Once in England, Richard quickly quelled the little resistance there was and went about setting England in order. He revised the system of shrieval appointments and administration, established the royal customs system, punished John's collaborators, and invested much money in developing Portsmouth, making it one of the most important towns in England. He appointed Hubert Walter archbishop of Canterbury, left England in his charge, and returned to France in order to take revenge upon Philip. Richard's war with Philip lasted five years, with the fighting decidedly favoring Richard. It came to an end with Richard's death by infection on 6 April 1199, eleven days after he was hit by a crossbow bolt. Ironically, Richard was fighting a rebellious viscount in Limoges rather than Philip when he died.

While historians have debated Richard's character and his kingship, regarding him as a brutal man and a negligent king, current studies have called for a revision of both views. Richard's crusade and wars in France not only proved that he was skilled at war but demonstrated his ability at diplomacy and administration as well. Though Richard was absent from England for all but a few months of his reign, what he did do in England is telling. Upon his father's death, he had freed those unfairly imprisoned by his father and restored land to those who had lost it unfairly. He staffed churches his father had left empty in order to take their revenue. And in response to an attack upon Jews coming to his coronation, he demanded that all Jews be left in peace, putting them under his special protection. Additionally, Richard initiated the reforms mentioned above.

Though Richard's accomplishments as king of England can be easily overlooked, his role as crusader chivalric warrior cannot. Leading the Third Crusade, Richard influenced world events in a way no other king of premodern England would. Though he was unable to take Jerusalem, Richard assured the continued existence of the Latin kingdom of Jerusalem. His bravery, valor, and skill on the battlefield assured his place not only in history but in myth as well.

Bibliography: A. Bridge, *Richard the Lionheart*, 1989; J. Gillingham, *Richard I*, 1999; J. L. Nelson, ed., *Richard Coeur de Lion in History and Myth*, 1992.

John Paul Walter

RICHARD OF MIDDLETON. *See* RICHARDUS DE MEDIAVILLA.

RICHARD OF ST. VICTOR (D. 1173). One of the most important figures in the twelfth-century Parisian School of St. Victor, Richard is possibly the most mystical of the Victorines, though his mysticism still relies more on the workaday rituals of the authority of the Church than on deep numinous mystery.

Richard was the foremost disciple of *Hugh (or Hugo) of St. Victor in propounding the Abelardian (see Peter *Abelard) ideals of balancing emotional spirituality with reason, freedom with order. Together with Hugh, Richard was highly influential not only in perpetuating contemplative spirituality but also in the early development of the medieval university.

Richard's writings focus on mystical contemplation and devotion, dividing the steps to ecstasy into six parts, the first three preparatory for the more numinous or ecstatic final three: (1) Awareness of created things. This corresponds to Hugh's first stage, "reading." Awareness should lead to awe, or a primary feeling of unity with creation, which is introductory to the second stage. (2) Aesthetic sensibility. In this stage, beyond merely noticing the created world, the mystic or seeker comes to a deeper appreciation of form, substance, and design in God's work. (3) The sacramental stage. At this point the contemplative thought focuses on the "inner" reality of the creature being contemplated. God's revealing Himself through nature leads from level to level, each level glorifying God in a particular way; this level is about "knowing" the purpose and unique spiritual "is-ness" of the creature. (4, 5, 6) The inner knowing of stage three leads to a premystical stage of awareness (4) in which rational human thought plays a diminishing role. The soul is beginning its eventual total surrender to God. Stages five and six are mystical states reminiscent of the "dark night of the soul" or the "negative way" discussed by *Pseudo-Dionysius, but Richard emphasizes the need for repentance even in these elevated stages.

In his treatise "Benjamin Minor," Richard writes, "In order to reach this contemplation, compunction of heart is more needed than deep investigations of the mind, yearning of the soul more than reasoning, groanings more than proofs. We know, indeed, that nothing renders the heart more pure, nothing brings greater purity of soul, nothing more effectively drives away the clouds of error, nothing gives greater calm, than true repentance and compunction." Richard's mysticism thus maintains a tension between starkly individual spiritual encounter with Divinity and the humility necessary for true community. His emphasis on confession and penance for sin keeps the individual in line with the authority of Church, while simultaneously facilitating the soaring mystical flight his instruction suggests is possible.

Bibliography: S. Chase, *Angelic Wisdom: The Cherubim and the Grace of Contemplation in Richard of St. Victor*, 1995.

Zina Petersen

RICHARDUS DE MEDIAVILLA (RICHARD OF MIDDLETON, RICHARD OF MENNEVILLE) (C. 1249–C. 1307).

Franciscan philosopher and theologian, the place and time of his birth are uncertain. According to a late tradition, he was British and received his early education in Oxford—hence the

alternative English form for his name, Richard of Middleton. A couple of manuscripts cite his name as Richard of Menneville, which is a family name reported
in Northumberland but also in France; in this case, "Mediavilla" would be the
Latin form of a vernacular word.

In the year 1283—the first certain date about his life—he was in Paris, listed
as a member of the theological commission entrusted with the examination of
*Peter John Olivi's writings. The commission issued a censure that banned
Olivi's works from all Franciscan schools. At that time Richard was still a
bachelor, while in 1285 he had already acquired the title of master, according
to the address of a letter sent by Olivi to the commission. He should then have
been about thirty-five years old, the minimum age for becoming a master of
theology. He taught theology at the Franciscan studium in Paris until 1287,
producing three sets of quodlibetal questions and preparing his commentary on
*Peter Lombard's *Sentences*, which was eventually completed and released in
1295. In 1295, Richard was elected Provincial minister of the Franciscans for
France. Together with other Franciscan theologians, in 1296, he went to Naples
to teach at the court of the son of Charles II of Sicily, Saint Louis of Toulouse.
The time and place of his death are uncertain; however, according to the Franciscan tradition, he died around 1307–1308.

Richard became regent master in the aftermath of the 1277 condemnations
by Bishop Stephen *Tempier and Robert *Kilwardby, which gave the Bonaventurean tradition new prominence in Paris and Oxford; he was therefore a
privileged witness to the contemporary doctrinal and ecclesiastical controversies.
Aristotelianism and Augustinism, Thomism and *Bonaventure's teaching, the
relationship between Franciscans and Dominicans, and between regulars and
seculars, were all matter of debate and contention, whose outcome was to shape
the intellectual profile of the university and the identity of the religious orders
in the following century. Richard maintained in this turmoil a balanced position,
gaining respect, recognition, and the revealing honorary nickname of "Solid
Doctor." His main inspiration was the Franciscan teaching of Bonaventure, but
he never indulged in polemical excess against *Aquinas and Aristotelianism: in
fact, he had extensive knowledge of Aristotle and sometimes embraced Thomistic doctrines opposing Bonaventurean or Augustinian views.

He had particular interest in natural philosophy and emphasized the role of
experience in human knowledge. His intellectual openness contributed to the
development of the Franciscan philosophy and theology. According to many
modern scholars, Richard's psychology greatly refines the traditional Franciscan
teaching of the plurality of substantial forms in man. For him, the soul cannot
be properly defined, as Aristotle had done, as the first perfection of a body
capable of life, but insofar as absolutely considered, it is rather independent of
the body, while it is dependent on it if considered from the point of view of its
faculties. To define the rational soul as the substantial form of man does not
exclude the existence of other substantial forms.

In the treatise *De gradu formarum*, Richard makes use of several philosophical arguments to prove his point: Embryos do grow and move, which are faculties of the vegetative and sensitive forms, before they acquire the intellective form, or rational soul; if the rational soul were the only substantial form in man, a dead body would not retain the accidents inhering in the living body; all the individual characteristics that a man takes from his parents would not be explained by the existence of only one substantial form; and finally, a single substantial form would not account for the natural corruptibility of man. Richard held many other views—such as the doctrine of universal hylomorphism, the opinion that essence and existence are not really distinct, and the primacy of the will, either human or divine, over the intellect—which represent a refutation of Aquinas' opposing positions. Furthermore, in holding Bonaventure's thesis of the impossibility of eternal creation (creation *ab aeterno*), Richard developed his own original criticism of Aquinas' notions of creation *ex nihilo* (out of nothing) and eternity.

Bibliography: D. E. Sharp, *Franciscan Philosophy at Oxford in the Thirteenth Century*, 1964.

Roberto Plevano

ROBERT D'ARBRISSEL (C. 1047–1117). A celebrated preacher, Robert was the founder of the order of Fontevrault.

Born in Brittany around 1047, Robert came from a line of local parish priests. He may have been educated primarily by traveling as a wandering scholar, but little is known of his early life. By around 1079, he was in Paris, studying the trivium and finding his vocation in religion. Sylvester de la Guerche, the bishop of Rennes, summoned Robert there in 1089 to help in the clerical reform in Brittany. Robert preached against simony, lay investiture, clerical concubinage, and irregular marriages. He was also instrumental in the resolution of feuds. This phase of his career was short-lived, lasting only four years. In 1093, Bishop Sylvester died, and the reform came under attack in Brittany. Robert was forced to leave and went to Angers to study at the cathedral school under the poet *Marbod. After finishing his schooling, Robert, who had become more and more ascetic during his time at Angers, became a hermit, living in the forest of Craon, practicing mortification of the flesh in conjunction with prayer and meditation. Others who fled to the wilderness at that time and were known to Robert included Bernard of Tiron and Vitalis of Savigny.

Word of his asceticism soon brought Robert followers, and he organized this group into a community after receiving a donation of land from Renaud de Craon for the foundation of a house of canons regular of the Augustinian rule at La Roë. The bishop of Angers confirmed the grant in 1096, and Pope *Urban II recognized Robert as the head of the community at the same time. Urban also authorized Robert as an official itinerant preacher, although there is no evidence that Robert actually preached the First Crusade as he traveled throughout France.

Within two years, Robert had given up the direction of the community at La

Roë in order to spend his time as an itinerant public preacher, traveling through the northwestern part of France. He appealed to all classes as he excoriated the regular clergy for their corrupt practices while advocating poverty and the abandonment of the world. However, his critics attacked him for the large number of female followers he had attracted, especially since he was known to sleep with them to force himself to resist temptations of the flesh. In order to counteract this criticism, in 1101 Robert established a permanent order where men and women would be separated at Fontevrault in Poitiers. As with La Roë, the order became very popular and soon needed a prescribed administration. Two women were chosen to head the new order—Hersende de Champagne as prioress and Pétronelle de Chemillé as associate. These appointments also enabled Robert to resume traveling throughout western France, engaging in itinerant teaching and founding daughter houses for the main foundation at Fontevrault. Pope *Paschal II issued a bull in 1106, confirming the foundation and giving papal protection. Robert was able to use this papal imprimateur as he continued his travels, preaching and obtaining donations of land from the aristocracy for the order.

Over time, however, changes needed to be made to the organization of the order. After the death of Hersende de Champagne, Pétronelle de Chemillé was appointed prioress. The community was made into a double order with the men's order subordinate to the women's order. Pétronelle, as abbess, ruled the order. The women were placed under a modified version of the Benedictine Rule while the men continued to be governed by the Augustinian Rule.

In the last year of Robert's life, he traveled from one house to another of the order frequently with Pétronelle, overseeing administrative issues, while he also continued preaching throughout his travels. He died in February 1117 and was buried at Fontevrault.

Bibliography: J. Dalarun, *L'impossible sainteté: La vie retrouvée de Robert d'Arbrissel (v. 1045–1116) fondateur de Fontevraud*, 1985; J. Dalarun, *Robert d'Arbrissel fondateur de Fontevraud*, 1986; B. M. Kerr, *Religious Life for Women, c. 1100–c. 1350: Fontevraud in England*, 1999.

Sharon Michalove

ROBERT GUISCARD (ROBERT DE HAUTEVILLE) (1015–1085).

Duke of Apulia, Sicily, and Calabria, Robert, called Guiscard, or "cunning," dominated the Norman conquests of Italy and Sicily in the last half of the eleventh century. Robert was thrice excommunicated during a career in which he moved in and out of papal favor and attempted to seize the imperial throne of Constantinople.

Son of Tancred de Hauteville, Robert left Normandy in 1047, stealing horses from travelers in the hills outside Calabria. A formidable leader whose shout was said to horrify rival forces, Robert's power increased; he drew men to him with rewards and pillage. His brother, *Roger de Hauteville, joined him as he transformed from brigand to legitimate political power. Threatened by his growing strength, Pope *Leo IX attempted to expel Robert and his followers from Italy, but the papal army was defeated.

Receiving titular authority over Calabria, Sicily, and Apulia from Pope *Nicholas II, he subdued these regions and by 1078 was the reigning power in southern Italy. An unlikely candidate, Robert was cast in the role of papal vassal, variously against the Greeks and the German emperor. His bid for the throne of Constantinople, on behalf of an imperial imposter, obtained papal support, but he was called back to Rome by a desperate Pope *Gregory VII, cornered by the armies of Emperor *Henry IV. Breaking into the burning city, Robert freed Gregory, but Rome sustained grave damage. Robert died on a military venture the following year in 1085 and was immortalized in the fourteenth century as a champion of Christendom in Dante's *Paradiso.*

Bibliography: J. J. Norwich, *The Normans in the South, 1016–1130*, 1967.

Laura L. Gathagan

ROBERT KILWARDBY. *See* KILWARDBY, ROBERT.

ROBERT OF COURSON (C. 1155/1160–1219). An English theologian and cardinal in the Catholic Church, Robert served as a papal legate under Pope *Innocent III.

He was born in England between 1155 and 1160 but spent almost his entire life abroad. Like many other medieval Englishmen, he studied theology at the University of Paris. He was a student of Peter the Chanter in the 1190s and became part of a circle of theologians dedicated to bringing about moral and social reform in the Church. While there, he was a friend and fellow student of the future Innocent III in the early 1180s. He became a regent master of theology by 1200 and was still lecturing in 1210. He probably wrote his only extant work, a *Summa* important for the history of penance and usury, between 1204 and 1212.

While still teaching at Paris, Robert began a successful career in the Church. He became canon of Noyen in 1204–1209 and of Paris soon after. Innocent III made him a cardinal in 1212 and the following year announced the preparation of a major Church council to be held in Rome in 1215 (the Fourth Lateran Council). In anticipation, Innocent commissioned a number of papal legates to prepare the council and to preach a new crusade. He made Robert the legate to France, and from 1213 to 1215, Robert traveled around France convoking a number of local councils. These meetings gave him a chance to apply to ecclesiastical affairs outside the university some of the principles of reform worked out in Peter the Chanter's reforming circle. They were also a way to test out some of these reforms before they were proposed at the Fourth Lateran Council. Unfortunately, both Robert's personality and his policies raised some resentment among the French prelates; there were complaints about the fairness of his judgments and about his harsh actions against some of the clergy. Innocent III was forced to intervene three times either to moderate Robert's actions or to annul his decisions. One council had to be canceled because the French prelacy refused to attend.

As part of his duties as papal legate, Robert was responsible for revising the statutes of the nascent University of Paris in 1215. The statutes established, among other provisions, the age and qualifications of the masters, the curriculum, which included a prohibition against Aristotle's books on natural philosophy, and rules governing the conduct of students and masters. Here his reforming efforts were far more successful and less controversial. From 1215 to 1219, Robert was in Rome. He joined the Fifth Crusade and died during the siege of Damietta in 1219.

Bibliography: J. W. Baldwin, *Masters, Princes and Merchants: The Social Views of Peter the Chanter and His Circle*, 2 vols., 1970.

Kimberly Rivers

ROBERT OF SORBON (1201–1274). Robert was a French theologian and founder of the College of Sorbonne.

Robert was born in 1201 to humble parents in the small community of Sorbon, near Rethel, France. Best known for his scholarly activities, he studied at Rheims, possibly at Rethel (near Rheims), and then at Paris, where he became a regent master of theology by 1250. He must have taught there for many years because numerous witnesses attest to his presence there from 1250 to 1274. As a theologian, he wrote three works on penance and confession and a large number of sermons. He obtained several minor ecclesiastical posts, becoming archdeacon of Laon in 1266. He also had some connection to political affairs of the day through his position as chaplain to King *Louis IX of France.

Robert of Sorbon's greatest contribution to posterity was the foundation of the College of Sorbonne at the University of Paris. Probably erected by 1257, the college provided board and lodging for poor students studying theology at Paris. It held first sixteen, then thirty-six students. It seems to have been a popular foundation, as it received contributions from King Louis, Pope Alexander IV, and many of Robert's friends. The college became so entwined in the study of theology at Paris that by the sixteenth and seventeenth centuries the entire faculty of theology was known simply as the Sorbonne.

Bibliography: A. L. Gabriel, *The Paris Studium: Robert of Sorbonne and His Legacy*, 1992.

Kimberly Rivers

RODRIGO (RUY) DÍAZ DE VIVAR, THE CID CAMPEADOR (1043–1099). The Cid was Spain's epic hero whose military exploits against the Muslims are grounded in fact. Best known for conquering and defending Valencia, the Cid represented the paragon of the medieval warrior who balanced strength and wisdom (*fortitudo et sapientia*).

Born in Vivar, a village of Burgos (Castile), Rodrigo was of lesser nobility. Orphaned in 1058, he went to the court of *Ferdinand I of Castile and León, where he was educated alongside Prince Sancho. Rodrigo proved himself on the field in 1063 when the Castilians, with the aid of the Muslims, won a border dispute against the Aragonese. It was at this time the Christians gave him the sobriquet *Campeador* (roughly "one who stands out in battle"), and the Muslims gave him that of Cid ("lord"). In 1065, Sancho became king of Castile (Sancho II), naming Rodrigo his *alférez* (arms bearer). Rodrigo accompanied Sancho on his campaign to usurp his siblings' kingdoms (León and Galicia), but Sancho lost his life in the undertaking. *Alfonso VI of León took the crown of Castile.

As the Castilian *alférez*, Rodrigo swore in the new king and pledged his allegiance to him. However, Rodrigo's former alliance with Sancho put him in a precarious position, and members of the new king's retinue were hostile toward him, chiefly García Ordóñez. On a mission to collect tribute from Seville in 1080, García Ordóñez along with the Muslim king of Granada attacked the Cid, who captured them, freeing them three days later. In 1081, the Cid made a raid into the Muslim territory around Toledo and incurred the king's wrath. Alfonso banished him from Castile, and he went to serve the Muslim lord of Zaragoza, for whom he became adviser and military chief. Alfonso forgave Rodrigo in 1083, when the Cid rescued him from a Muslim betrayal. The Cid, however, feeling insecure at Alfonso's court, returned to Zaragoza, remaining there until 1087.

In 1084, when Alfonso attacked Zaragoza, the Cid, so as not to fight against his sworn lord, took no part in the fighting. He returned to Alfonso in 1087 to fight against the invading Almoravids and was granted as a legacy the lands he could conquer from the Muslims. However, the Cid incurred the king's wrath again in 1089 when he was unable to come to Alfonso's aid in a battle against the Almoravids. The king banished him once more, stripping him of the territories he had conquered. The Cid retaliated by conquering territory after territory along Spain's Mediterranean coast, and by 1090 he had set himself up essentially as a prince, establishing the rich seaport of Valencia as his abode. The Cid aided Alfonso in his campaign against Granada in 1092 but was still not forgiven. When Alfonso tried to conquer Valencia, Rodrigo retaliated by decimating the lands held by García Ordóñez; the king relented. The Cid successfully defended Valencia against an Almoravid attack in 1094, which proved the latter's first major upset in the peninsula. He maintained Valencia as a Christian enclave until his death.

The Cid's conquests, though sometimes more opportunistic than militarily sound, remained in the popular imagination and were woven into Spain's national epic, the *Cantar de mio Cid* (Song of My Cid), written presumably a century after Rodrigo' death. In addition to the fictional Cid's great prowess and wisdom, perhaps his most appealing feature is his crossing of social barriers: A warrior of the lowest rank of nobility conquers and maintains one of the richest cities of Spain and in essence becomes kinglike through his own actions.

Bibliography: B. F. Reilly, *The Contest of Christian and Muslim Spain: 1031–1157,* 1992.

Paul B. Nelson

ROGER DE HAUTEVILLE (ROGER I) (1031–1101). A younger son of the Norman baron Tancred de Hauteville, Roger joined his brother *Robert Guiscard in 1057 to assist him in what eventually became the conquest of southern Italy. Roger concentrated his efforts in Sicily, eventually taking control of the entire island and becoming count of Sicily and Calabria in 1072. His descendants ruled Sicily and southern Italy for almost two centuries.

Roger's conquest was remarkable because of its rapidity (the Muslim emirs he defeated had taken the island from the Byzantines in campaigns lasting from 827 to 902) and the small numbers of troops that were available to him (often fewer than 300 men). Roger was able to call on his brother Robert for reinforcements at crucial junctures, such as the capture of Messina in 1061 that opened the campaign, as well as the siege of Palermo in 1071–1072 that completed it. Accordingly, Roger became count of Sicily under the overlordship of his brother but was able to escape that obligation after Robert's death in 1085.

Since Roger's forces during the conquest had been small, it was not necessary to provide many large estates to reward his followers; thus, Roger was able to maintain most of the island under his direct control and build the foundation of the later kingdom of Sicily as a unitary state. Similarly, the small numbers of his forces encouraged Roger to reach understandings with factions already in place on the island; Muslims and Byzantine Greeks continued not only to live in Sicily but also to take leading roles in the military, public administration, and religion. Roger's appointment as papal legate in 1098 allowed him to continue his policies of coexistence by allowing his subjects to follow their Catholic, Orthodox, Muslim, and Jewish faiths without interference.

Roger created his policies in response to the circumstances and opportunities he found in Sicily; it would be a mistake to consider him more "enlightened" or "progressive" than other eleventh-century European rulers. Even so, the policies he established continued under his successors and laid the foundations for the kingdom of Sicily as a unitary state with an effective military force, a professional bureaucracy, and a tolerant religious policy.

Bibliography: J. J. Norwich, *The Normans in the South, 1016–1130,* 1967.

Edward J. Schoenfeld

ROGER II OF SICILY (1095–1154). Count of Sicily from 1105 and king from 1130, Roger was the son of *Roger de Hauteville, the first count of Sicily. Raised in a cosmopolitan world that included Muslim and Greek influences, he continued his father's policies in Sicily, expanded into southern Italy and North Africa, and made his court at Palermo the intellectual center of Europe.

Roger succeeded his brother Simon in 1105. The government at first was under the direction of his mother, Adelaide of Savona; Roger began his personal rule in 1122. He immediately began to trade his military support to his relatives, the successors of *Robert Guiscard as dukes of Apulia, in return for territory and privileges in southern Italy. Roger gained all of Calabria in 1122 before becoming duke of Apulia in his own right in 1127. Not content with control of the Norman territories in Italy, Roger also used his fleet to conquer most of what is now Tunisia, gaining command of the central Mediterranean and the increasingly profitable trade that passed through it. Roger continued the Norman antagonism to Byzantium by conquering the island of Corfu, raiding Thebes to carry off some of that city's silk workers, and even attacking Constantinople. Sicily thus became the leading economic and maritime power in the western Mediterranean, even though Tunisia was lost to the Almohads soon after Roger's death.

Roger's political ambitions included a title commensurate with his actual power, and he secured his coronation as king of Sicily by supporting the anti-pope Anacletus II in 1130. It was, however, only after Roger stymied the Italian expedition of Emperor Lothar II in 1136–1137 and then defeated a papal army in 1139 that a legitimate pope, Innocent II, recognized the title. Roger followed the acquisition of a royal title by acquiring Salerno in 1137 and Naples in 1139, thus completing the unification of southern Italy under a single, powerful ruler. The extensive and wealthy kingdom was then placed under a single legal and administrative system, promulgated at the Assizes of Ariano in 1140. While the Assizes recognized the diverse legal customs of Roger's Norman, Lombard, Muslim, Jewish, Greek, and Sicilian subjects, Roger provided unity for the kingdom by establishing himself as an autocratic monarch in the Byzantine tradition.

Roger thus continued his father's policy of coexistence between the manifold cultures that inhabited his realm. This was not, however, a policy of amalgamation, as the various ethnic groups were given roles that kept the other ethnic groups in careful check. For example, while Normans and Muslims dominated the military, Greeks controlled the navy. Similarly, the financial administration was mainly carried out by Muslims, but they reported to a chief minister who was invariably Greek (and whose concurrent position as commander in chief of the kingdom's navy brought his Arabic title the "Emir of Emir's" into the European languages as the word "admiral"). Lastly, although Sicily was part of Latin Christendom and looked to the pope for its doctrine, the Church administration was in the hands of Greeks whose desire to maintain their own Orthodox beliefs ensured that religious variety would continue to be tolerated.

The result was to make Sicily in many ways a unique realm within Latin Christendom. Cosmopolitan, tolerant, and well administered, Sicily provided a venue in which the various cultures of the Mediterranean could interact and in which Roger was able to make his court at Palermo a center of intellectual and cultural exchange between Byzantium, Islam, and western Europe. While the opportunities that Sicily provided for an ambitious ruler were indeed unique, Roger himself was only one of many medieval monarchs who tried to establish effective states based on the authority of the king. Roger's efforts may have foreshadowed, but did not surpass, similar efforts by *Henry II of England, *Philip II Augustus of France, *Frederick I Barbarossa in Germany, and *Alfonso X the Wise in Castile.

Bibliography: J. J. Norwich, *The Kingdom in the Sun 1130–1194*, 1970; J. J. Norwich, *The Normans in the South, 1016–1130*, 1967.

Edward J. Schoenfeld

ROGER OF SALISBURY (C. 1065–1139).

ROGER OF SALISBURY (C. 1065–1139). Bishop of Salisbury and chancellor of England, he served *Henry I of England as an adviser and chief justiciar.

Roger of Salisbury was born in Normandy, perhaps about 1065, in modest circumstances. Little is known of his early life. William of Newburgh, at the end of the twelfth century, tells the famous story that Roger caught the eye of Henry I, the youngest son of *William I the Conqueror, when, as a priest in the town of Caen, he said Mass very rapidly. This was probably in 1091. When Henry, now king of England, named him bishop of Salisbury, England, however, the formal certification of his election calls him a priest of Avranches.

Roger remained bishop of Salisbury until his death, but his principal importance was in government. He was one of the ablest courtiers of Henry I and the one on whom Henry relied most. His first important office was as custodian of what remained of the money King William had bequeathed Henry; and he earned Henry's respect by bringing order to his financial affairs. A few months after Henry became king, he made Roger chancellor, the highest-ranking member of the royal household. His nomination to Salisbury was announced before the end of 1101, though he may not have been formally elected to the see until 1102. Soon thereafter, he resigned the chancellorship. He was not consecrated bishop until August 1107, after the reconciliation between Henry and Archbishop *Anselm of Canterbury.

Henry I was often abroad, first securing and then governing his French lands. While away, he appointed regents to rule for him in England. During her lifetime, he usually named his wife, Queen Edith (also called Matilda). Roger of Salisbury was her regular collaborator in government from 1109 on at the latest, perhaps even from Henry's first absence in 1104. Henry also showed his great trust in Roger by giving Roger custody of his elder brother, Robert Curthose, duke of Normandy, after he was captured in 1106. Curthose remained in Roger's great castle of Devizes until 1126. After 1120, when both Edith and William, Henry's only legitimate son, were dead, Henry appointed Roger to govern England in his absences. This position, perhaps best characterized as viceroy, has led to Roger's recognition as the first of the great chief justiciars of twelfth-century England. Whatever one should call him, he clearly stood in the king's place when the king was out of the country and exercised all the royal powers, subject only to the king's control. His principal activities were financial and judicial. He was probably largely responsible for the development of the great office of the Exchequer during Henry's reign. It is scarcely surprising that he was quite unpopular: William of Newburgh's story of how he came to Henry's attention is told to disparage him, for example, not to praise him.

Roger founded a dynasty of clerical servants of the kings of England. He had a long connection with a woman named Matilda of Rambury. They had at least one son, Roger le Poer ("the Pauper"), who became chancellor early in King *Stephen of England's reign. They may also have been the parents of Adelelm, who became Stephen's treasurer and a high clerical official. Roger's nephews, probably his brother's sons, also received both ecclesiastical and secular promotion.

When Stephen succeeded Henry I in 1135, he inherited an able administrative staff headed by Roger of Salisbury. In 1137, during Stephen's continental campaign against his rival, Henry I's daughter, the Empress *Matilda, Roger again served as viceroy. As civil war began to brew in England, however, Stephen became suspicious of Roger's loyalty. In June 1139, he suddenly arrested Roger, Roger le Poer, and Alexander, bishop of Lincoln. Roger was thrown into a cowpen to humiliate him. His nephew, Nigel, bishop of Ely, and Adelelm escaped the trap and fled to Devizes, where Stephen besieged them. Threats to starve the bishops and to execute Roger le Poer led Matilda of Ramsbury to surrender the castle. The king seized the offices and most of the possessions of the Salisbury clan, and Roger died, a broken man, on 11 December 1139.

Bibliography: E. J. Kealey, *Roger of Salisbury, Viceroy of England*, 1972; F. J. West, *The Justiciarship in England, 1066–1232*, 1966.

Emily Tabuteau

ROLLO (D. C. 933). A Viking leader, Rollo founded the dynasty of dukes of Normandy who after 1066 were also the Norman kings of England.

"Rollo" is the Latinized version of his name, which was probably Hrolf. Little is known about him. He was probably of Norwegian extraction, although his men were mostly Danes. His band raided England and France with mixed success. In 911, after they were defeated at Chartres, the king of France, *Charles III the Simple, made Rollo count of the area around the mouth of the Seine so that he could protect it from raids by other pirates. As part of this agreement, called the treaty of St-Clair-sur-Epte, Rollo was baptized, but his conversion was probably politically motivated rather than stemming from sincere conviction. Allegedly, King Charles gave Rollo one of his daughters in marriage; but Rollo's son and successor William Longsword was born of Popa, a different Frankish woman, whom Rollo married "in the Danish manner," rather than according to Christian rules.

As ruler of the area that would be called "Normandy" after the "northmen," the Vikings who settled there, he expanded his rule well beyond the boundaries set by King Charles. No documents and few reliable stories survive about his rule. He may have made attempts to restore Church institutions, but this effort produced marked results only under his son and grandson, the next two rulers. It was also only under William Longsword that Normandy began to become integrated into the political system of tenth-century France. Rollo's date of death is usually reported as 933 but may have been as early as about 925.

Bibliography: D. Bates, *Normandy before 1066*, 1982.

Emily Tabuteau

ROSCELIN (ROSCELLINUS) (C. 1050–C. 1125). Roscelin of Compiègne, an eleventh-century French philosopher and theologian, was one of the first nominalists.

Roscelin was probably born in Compiègne, France, around 1050, where he would most likely have attended the Cathedral school at Soissons or at Rheims. His studies included *logica vetus*, that is, classical logic as expounded in Aristotle, Porphyry, and *Boethius. He became a priest sometime before 1090, but the date and location of his ordination are unknown.

He began teaching sometime around 1087, specializing in the application of Aristotelian methods of logic to philosophical and theological questions, a discipline then known as dialectics. In the eleventh century, however, dialectics was in its infancy, and using it to address questions of theology was regarded with suspicion. Roscelin was also an early figure in the development of nominalism, also called antirealism, a philosophy that states that the only substances are individual things and that universals exist only as words. Although he founded no nominalist school and attracted no nominalist disciples, his views were influential on his student Peter *Abelard, whose rejection of his teacher's position shaped his own philosophy. Roscelin's turbulent career, moreover, served to stimulate discussion of nominalism.

Roscelin was accused of teaching Tritheism, the doctrine that the Trinity was actually made up of three separate gods; he was consequently called to appear before the Council of Soissons in 1092. Apparently he successfully clarified his position and was not condemned by the Council. It is difficult, however, to determine precisely what Roscelin taught because we have very little of his original writing. Only a letter to Peter Abelard survives. Moreover, it is difficult to reconstruct his exact beliefs from the arguments posed against him by writers like Abelard and *Anselm of Laon; Roscelin's letter claims that Abelard grossly misrepresented his position, while Anselm freely admits that he is relying on secondhand and thirdhand accounts of Roscelin's words.

Simply having been accused of heresy, however, was enough to taint his reputation and perhaps imperil his safety. After the trial, he spent some time in England, where he became involved in a dispute about whether the children of priests were suitable candidates for the priesthood themselves. His vigorously expressed opinion that the children of priests were not fit for the priesthood was highly unpopular, and he left England under pressure from angry priests around 1094.

He went to Chartres, where he was welcomed by Bishop *Ivo, and then to Rome, where Pope *Urban II received him warmly. Being in the pope's good graces, he was able, over the years, to obtain teaching posts at Tours and Loches as well as a staff position as canon at Besançon. The relative dates of these positions are unknown, but it was at Loches, probably c. 1094–1096, that he taught Peter Abelard. The date of Roscelin's death is unknown; he disappears from the historical record after 1120.

The debate between nominalism and universalism was one of the most important intellectual issues of the Middle Ages, and Roscelin was an important figure in its early development. His application of this controversial approach of nominalism to the difficult topic of theology sparked generations of philosophical and theological disputation.

Bibliography: F. Picavet, *Roscelin, Philosophe et theologien, d'apres la legende et d'apres l'histoire*, 1911.

Anne Collins Smith and Owen M. Smith

RUFINUS (FL. LATE TWELFTH CENTURY). A professor, bishop, and finally archbishop, Rufinus was one of the most important Bolognese scholars of canon law in the latter half of the twelfth century. He is best known for his commentary on the *Decretum Gratiani*, a code of ecclesiastical law compiled by *Gratian between 1140 and 1151.

Little is known about the life of Rufinus. He was born in central Italy, probably near Assisi. He may have been a student of Gratian himself. By 1150, he was a professor of canon law at Bologna. After several years, he became bishop of Assisi. He wrote his famous commentary, called the *Summa decretorum*, from 1157 to 1159; it is not known whether he was a professor or a bishop at the time.

In 1179, Rufinus gave the opening speech at the Third Lateran Council, which had been called to repair a schism in the Church and to restore ecclesiastical discipline. He signed the Council's documents as bishop of Assisi. Between 1180 and 1186, he was made archbishop of Sorrento; he died sometime before 1192.

Rufinus was the first to undertake a serious commentary on Gratian's work. His commentary marked a departure from the traditional style, offering not a collection of glosses but an analytical treatise addressing each section of the *Decretum* in detail. Rufinus' treatment, however, was not entirely systematic; he skimmed over some topics and used others as springboards for extended digressions. Indeed, the style of his commentary was even more influential than its content, as subsequent commentators adopted his methodology.

In addition to his commentary on the *Decretum*, Rufinus' opening speech to the Third Lateran Council survives, as does the second version of a treatise on peace that he wrote between 1180 and 1186. He composed a collection of sermons for specific feasts and occasions, twenty-four of which survive in whole or in part.

The scantiness of our knowledge of his life can be partly ameliorated by reference to his work, which offers us a glimpse of his background, gifts, and personality. His writings display an impressive education in canon law, Roman law, theology, liturgy, and other subjects. His style is eloquent and skillful, characterized by clarity, originality, and expressiveness. As revealed in his writing, his personality is proud and passionate, ruthless in argumentation and criticism. Both his speech to the Council and his *Summa* reflect his immense respect for the authority of the Church.

Canon law was still very much in flux in the twelfth century. Rufinus' emphasis on Church authority and his method of commentary shaped the approach of generations of canon law scholars in his native Italy and beyond.

Bibliography: H. Singer, ed., *Die Summa Decretorum des Magister Rufinus*, 1902.
Anne Collins Smith and Owen M. Smith

RUPERT OF DEUTZ (C. 1075–1129). An exegetical theologian, Rupert became an abbot of the Benedictine house at Deutz.

Rupert was probably a child oblate and entered the Benedictine house of St. Laurent in Liège c. 1082. Apart from three intervals, Rupert remained at this house for most of his life. From 1092 to 1095, Rupert and several of his brethren there went into exile along with their abbot Berengar during the Investiture Controversy. These years were probably spent at Evergnicourt, a priory in the archdiocese of Rheims. Rupert refused ordination until 1106, when his simoniacal bishop was reconciled with Rome. A series of visionary experiences in his youth gave Rupert a new understanding of Scripture and encouraged him to become an expositor of Scripture.

Rupert's first treatise was *De divinis officiis* (On the Divine Office, c. 1111). This work was an allegorical interpretation of the liturgical year designed as a devotional guide for monks. *William of St. Thierry mildly rebuked Rupert for specific doctrines within this work and suggested that his teaching on the Eucharist resembled impanation (the doctrine that the body of Christ is impanated in the Eucharist after consecration). Rupert next wrote homilies on John, as well as *De trinitate*, a history of salvation in forty-two books.

In 1116, one of Rupert's confrères returned from studying with *Anselm of Laon and held views on God's will, namely, that God willed evil should happen, which he ascribed to his former master. Outraged both by Anselm's teachings and by the intrusion of dialectic into theology, Rupert wrote a work against Anselm, *De voluntate Dei* (On the Will of God) and wanted to debate him publicly. Rupert then traveled to Laon but was unable to debate with Anselm due to the master's death. Instead, he disputed Anselm's students over this issue. Next, he went to Châlons-sur-Marne and debated this topic with the noted teacher and friend of Anselm, *William of Champeaux.

After these debates, Rupert temporarily retired to the monastery at Siegburg. He was summoned to Liège in 1117 after a panel of masters and students had examined his works. He received no condemnation and wrote the treatise *De omnipotentia Dei* (On the Omnipotence of God). Nevertheless, the deteriorating ecclesiastical environment in Liège forced Rupert to leave for Cologne in April 1119. In the following year, Archbishop Frederick of Cologne appointed Rupert abbot of Deutz, a Benedictine house in the Rhineland. He held that post until his death in 1129.

Rupert continued to write at Deutz, composing a commentary on the Twelve Prophets, an Apocalypse commentary, and a commentary on the Song of Songs. In this latter work, Rupert interpreted the bride as the Blessed Virgin Mary, thereby giving this view widespread theological currency. Rupert also vigorously defended the Benedictine manner of life against the newer orders, in particular the Cistercians and the canons regular. He wrote a commentary on the Benedictine Rule and through his defense of his order provoked a polemical contest that soon involved *Bernard of Clairvaux, *Norbert of Xanten, and *Peter the Venerable.

Although a significant theological writer, many of Rupert's works were neglected until the Protestant Reformation. In the sixteenth century, some of the Protestant Reformers sought to find support for their doctrines in Rupert, especially with respect to his teachings on the Eucharist.

Bibliography: J. van Engen, *Rupert of Deutz*, 1983.

Andrew G. Traver

RUSHD, IBN (ABŪ AL-WALĪD MUHAMMAD IBN AHMAD IBN RUSHD, AVERROËS) (1126–1198).

Known in English as Averroës and in Arabic as Ibn Rushd, he was a Hispano-Arab Muslim philosopher, jurist, scientist, and physician. Considered by many to be the most important Islamic philosopher, Averroës sought to integrate Aristotelian philosophy with Islamic thought. Among Christian scholastics, Averroës became the premiere interpreter of Aristotle, and a school of thought known as Latin Averroism arose around his commentaries.

Born in Cordova, Spain, Averroës hailed from a distinguished family of Hispano-Muslim jurists and theologians. Both his father and grandfather served as judge of the Muslim community of Cordova, and the young Averroës received a thorough juridical education in addition to mastering the traditional Islamic sciences. While in Cordova, he also applied himself to the study of mathematics, astronomy, physics, and medicine. Averroës lived in a time of confused political conditions. Born during the reign of the Almoravid dynasty (r. 1056–1147), he found himself in the midst of a tripartite struggle for power in Spain and North

Africa. The declining power of the Almoravids was usurped by the Almohad dynasty (r. 1130–1269), and the latter were engaged at various times in a struggle with Christian Spanish rulers for control of Spain. In the midst of this turmoil, Averroës traveled to the Almohad capital Marrakesh, Morocco, in 1153. By this time, Averroës had already written the first version of his great medical compendium known in Latin as the *Colliget* as well as a few short commentaries on Aristotle's *Organon*, *Metaphysics*, and *Physics*.

In Marrakesh, Averroës was introduced to the Almohad prince Abū Ya'qūb Yūsuf (r. 1163–1184) by the celebrated Muslim philosopher Ibn Tufayl. According to his biographers, this meeting marked a turning point in Averroës' philosophic career. The prince, himself an avid student of Aristotle, asked him: "Is the sky a substance that has existed for all eternity or did it have a beginning?" Averroës was reluctant to answer this dangerous question (the eternity of the world being a contentious issue in Islamic discourse), but upon Ibn Tufayl's lead, he ventured an answer. The prince was impressed with the breadth of his learning, and thenceforth he enjoyed royal favor. Averroës was appointed judge of Seville in 1169 and was invited by Abū Ya'qūb Yūsuf to prepare a series of commentaries on Aristotle's works. He accepted both offers and for the next two years judiciously divided his time between administrative and scholarly duties.

Averroës' tenure as judge of Seville was short-lived, and he was called to return to his native city in 1171. He served as judge of Cordova for over a decade, and during this time he continued to write commentaries on Aristotle. These commentaries took a variety of forms, and he would often write a short paraphrase and medium and long commentary on the same text. A great part of the genius of Averroës' commentaries on Aristotle reside in his attempt to present Aristotle's arguments free from the Neoplatonic tradition that had informed so much of Aristotelian commentary in the Islamic world during the preceding centuries. Averroës proved to be able to distinguish between Aristotle's original points and those that previous commentators had attributed to him. Moreover, while he ably and critically used the classical commentators Themistius and Alexander of Aphrodisias and those of his Muslim predecessors, he was careful to let Aristotle speak for himself.

From 1174 to 1180, he produced a number of original works such as the *Decisive Treatise on the Agreement between Religious Law and Philosophy*, the *Examination of the Methods of Proof Concerning the Doctrines of Religion*, and his rejoinder to al-*Ghazālī's *Incoherence of the Philosophers*, the *Incoherence of the Incoherence*. Averroës held that the aim of philosophy is to establish the true, inner meaning of religious beliefs, and in these religious-philosophical polemical treatises, he posits that only the philosopher is capable of interpreting the doctrines of Islam. He posited that the Qur'an not only sanctions but obligates the use of demonstrative argument and that syllogistic thinking and the truth of Scripture do not ultimately conflict. Furthermore, he argued that the philosophical interpretation of revelation is the special provenance of the philosophers, since they are the highest of the three classes of persons, the other two being the dialectical theologians and the masses. In an attempt to return natural theology to the physics of matter and motion, Averroës also criticized the doctrines of Muslim philosophers such as *Avicenna. On the creation of the world, for instance, Averroës rejects Avicenna's theory of cosmic emanation and proposes instead a solution that relies upon the idea of an eternal creation.

In 1182, Averroës was called back to Marrakesh, and he succeeded Ibn Tufayl as Abū Yaʿqūb Yūsuf's chief physician. For several years after Abū Yaʿqūb Yūsuf's death, Averroës continued to enjoy Almohad patronage under Abū Yaʿqūb Yūsuf's son and successor Yaʿqūb al-Mansūr. In 1195, however, he, along with other intellectuals attached to the royal court, was banished. Several theories exist as to why he was banished, the most probable being that al-Mansūr, embroiled in a costly war in Spain, wished to gain the support of the orthodox religious establishment who held considerable sway over the populace. Thus, a public denunciation of the perceived opponents of religious orthodoxy would help in gathering such support. Averroës ended up in the small villa of Lucena located outside of Cordova. Shortly thereafter, a tribunal in Cordova condemned his teachings as being dangerous to religion, and copies of his philosophical works were publicly burned. Averroës' exile did not last long, and he was able to return to Marrakesh, where al-Mansūr repealed the edicts against him. It was here that he died in 1198.

No Muslim thinker had a greater influence on the medieval West than Averroës did. Among Christian Scholastics, Averroës was known as "the Commentator," and translations of his works had a significant impact on the development of Christian and Jewish philosophical, theological, and scientific thought from the thirteenth through the seventeenth centuries. His commentaries on Aristotle, in particular, greatly influenced medieval Christian and Jewish philosophy, and almost all of his commentaries and epitomes were translated into Latin in the second quarter of the thirteenth century. The widespread introduction of Aristotle into Europe was not without its problems, and Averroës' commentaries elicited both praise and condemnation from various camps within the medieval Christian West.

Averroës' treatment of Aristotle precipitated the development of a movement that was later termed "Averroism." This form of radical Aristotelianism caused a significant stir in European university centers throughout the thirteenth and fourteenth centuries. The views of the Averroists such as the individual immortality of the human intellectual soul and its unity among all humans (monopsychism), the attainability of happiness in this life, the eternity of the world, and the so-called double-truth theory were not easily reconcilable with Christian doctrine. From the Universities of Padua and Bologna, Averroist influence spread throughout Europe and became enough of an issue to engender critiques by both *Albertus Magnus and Thomas *Aquinas. In 1210, a provincial council at Paris declared both Aristotle's and Averroës' commentaries anathema, and in 1231 a papal injunction interdicted the reading of these works until their complete expurgation. Despite such condemnation, Averroism exerted a lasting influence on Christian Scholasticism and by the fifteenth century came to dominate the intellectual climate in Italian universities before becoming overshadowed by the intellectual shifts of the Renaissance.

Bibliography: O. Leaman, *Averroes and His Philosophy*, 1988; D. Urvoy, *Ibn Rushd (Averroes)*, trans. O. Stewart, 1991.

Erik S. Ohlander

S

SALADIN (ṢALĀḤ AL-DĪN BIN AYYŪB) (1138–1193). Saladin became the most famous of Islamic leaders to assault the Latin colonies in Palestine and Syria. His ascendancy led to the Third Crusade and a reduction in the Crusader territories.

Saladin was born in 1138 at Taqrīt, in Iraq, the son of Kurdish parents. His birth name was Yūsuf. In 1139, Saladin's father, Ayyūb, was made governor of Baalbeck by Zangī, the Syrian leader who was making increasing inroads into the Latin states. Saladin was raised in Baalbeck, though he reputedly also spent much time in Damascus. During the 1160s, by his own account, he fought alongside his father and uncle, Zangī, who served Nūr al-Dīn, the son of Zangī, who had taken control of Aleppo on the death of his father. Zangī made him his deputy, and Nūr al-Dīn in 1165 appointed him *shiḥna* (police chief) of Damascus.

When Zangī was despatched to support Shāwar, vizier of the Fatimid sultanate of Egypt, Saladin went with him. Shāwar's machinations with Amalric of Jerusalem led to Zangī ultimately taking over as vizier himself. Saladin succeeded Zangī as vizier on his death in 1169. In the same year, he fought off a combined Frankish and Byzantine attack on Damietta and established his power base in Cairo. As vizier of Egypt, Saladin consolidated his power by conquering areas of Gaza, Arabia, and Yemen—extending his control over the major trade routes to the east. In this, he became effectively the sultan of Egypt in his own right, although when he abolished the Fatimid dynasty altogether in 1171, he ordered that the name of the ʿAbbāsid caliph be mentioned in official prayers.

The subsequent biographical traditions established by ʿImād al-Dīn al Iṣfahānī, Bahāʾ al-Dīn, and especially Abū Shāma would represent Saladin's rise to power in terms of a natural succession to leadership of the *jihad* commenced by Zangī and Nūr al-Dīn against the Latin colonies. This is in many ways a retrospective view, however, and much of Saladin's imperialism can be understood in terms of complex processes of carving out holdings in the political landscape of the Levant, following the Seljuk and Zangid ascendancies and during a period when the ʿAbbāsid caliphs were little concerned with Syrian or Palestinian affairs. In fact, Saladin's increasing power after 1171 brought him into conflict with Nūr al-Dīn, though the death of the latter in 1174 came soon enough to defuse these tensions. Saladin's military power was sufficient to see him then take over control of Syria to become the principal opponent of Christendom.

That Saladin was occasioned to lead the successful assault against the kingdom of Jerusalem most particularly reflects the crucial importance of Egypt in the history of the Latin states. The Latin states had been established at a time when Egypt was divided from Damascus and Syria on political and sectarian grounds. Saladin's ending of Fatimid rule had the effect of returning Shiite Egypt to Sunni hands. This had little religious impact in Egypt where Shiite practice had had little deep impact in society, and as one chronicler put it, its passing did not even cause "two goats to lock horns." The Latin kingdom, however, no longer confronted politically separate neighbors. Saladin had persistently promulgated a view of *jihad* as a premise for his consolidation of Egypt and Syria, and after the breaking of the peace by the Franks in 1187, Saladin pursued his "counter crusade," culminating in the defeat of the armies of the Latin kingdom of Jerusalem at Ḥaṭṭīn on 4–5 July 1187. He followed this with the capture of Acre on 9 July, Beirut on 6 August, Ascalon on 5 September, and Jerusalem on 2 October. This rapid conquest of the Crusader states inspired the Third Crusade (1189–1191).

Following the capture of Acre by the crusaders, on 12 July 1191, after a siege of many months, Saladin's resources in Palestine were heavily drained. Saladin was defeated by *Richard I of England at Arsūf on 7 September 1191, which led to the truce between these two most romantic of figures in 1192—though the two never met. Saladin died the year after the truce, in Damascus on 4 March 1193. He was buried in a magnificent tomb, which survives in Damascus.

Saladin remains a figure of enormous significance both in Arabic and Christian historiography as well as legend. He was also to become revered as the founding father of the Islamic "counter crusade." Renowned for his skill at polo and attributed with chivalric qualities, he became the subject of both Arabic and Latin folklore. He was a noted patron of the arts. Saladin's name became widely known in the Latin West through the Saladin Tithe (1188), which preceded the Third Crusade.

Bibliography: P. M. Holt, *The Age of the Crusades: The Near East from the Eleventh Century to 1517*, 1986; M. C. Lyons and D.E.P. Jackson, *Saladin: The Politics of Holy War*, 1982.

Jonathan M. Wooding

SALIMBENE (1221–C. 1290).

SALIMBENE (1221–C. 1290). Born Balian de Adam in Parma, Italy, Salimbene became a Franciscan friar and priest as well as a renowned writer.

Despite his family's noble and material aspirations, he renounced these ambitions and entered the Franciscan Order when he was sixteen years old. These actions motivated a fellow friar to nickname him "Salimbene," meaning "good move," and reject his former sobriquet of "Ognibene," meaning "all good." His relationship with his family was already weak, but was completely severed after his ordination as a Franciscan, and his father even tried to kidnap him and separate him from the order.

Salimbene was most attracted to the Franciscan Spirituals. After the death of its founder Saint *Francis of Assisi in 1124, the order split between the Franciscan Spirituals, the faction intending to cling to the desires of the founder to reject material concerns in favor of a life of poverty, and the Franciscan Conventuals, who believed life mandated a more practical grasp of material concerns and renounced the ideal of poverty. Salimbene was also heavily influenced by the millenarian work of *Joachim de Fiore. Fiore claimed that history had been divided into three great ages, the first age ending with the birth of Jesus Christ, the second with the propagation of the Holy Spirit, and the third 1,260 years after the birth of Christ. Thus, Fiore prophesied the last age to end in 1260 with a coming of a great era of perfect peace and freedom.

After 1260, a disillusioned Salimbene rejected the literal nature of these teachings and began to compose his *Cronica*, also known as *The Chronicle of Salimbene de Adam*, which examines medieval political history from 1167 to 1288. This work is extremely valuable to historians because of its record of known historical events, such as the huge earthquake that devastated Parma in 1222, with which to corroborate the records of many of Salimbene's contemporaries. Salimbene knew many people, including the Hohenstaufen *Frederick II and Pope *Innocent IV, so his work provides valuable insights into the machinations of Church and state in the thirteenth century.

In fact, Salimbene's chief work for the Franciscans was not as a priest or a preacher but as an historian. His writings include a history of the Roman Empire, chronicles of the Franciscan Order, and treatises on Joachist philosophy. Salimbene's own personal standard dictated his research: "I intend to believe only what I can see." However, one can often see how Joachist philosophy affected his interpretation of historical events. The Mongol invasions of the Middle East, for instance, could be viewed within a Joachist framework for the apocalypse, and Frederick II's treatment of revolutionaries could be comprehended if one viewed Frederick as the Antichrist. Salimbene often defends his comments with the conclusion "and this I saw with my own eyes," perhaps to protect himself from critics.

In composing his histories, Salimbene traveled throughout France and Italy to study documents and people, often staying at different Franciscan monasteries and including religious ritual and discussions of Franciscan ideals in his work. Fellow Franciscans often distrusted Salimbene's wanderlust (one even termed Salimbene a "gadabout") even though he believed research and writing history to be part of his mission from God.

Salimbene had two special qualities as a historian. First, he had an ability to read between the lines of any document or see beneath the surface of those people he interviewed. Second, his talent for shrewd observation and meticulous detail enabled him to paint vivid pictures of events and people. Salimbene's detractors term him emotional and biased, noting his affection for the Franciscans and his reactions to personal situations. Nevertheless, Salimbene's objectivity must be viewed within the proper context, and he often criticized Franciscan "politicians" and the abstract qualities of Joachist philosophy. Though Salimbene's works were not well known until the nineteenth century, now they are considered to be indispensable for an understanding of medieval civilization.

Bibliography: J. L. Baird, G. Baglivi, and J. R. Kane, *The Chronicle of Salimbene de Adam*, 1986.

Alana Cain Scott

SAXO GRAMMATICUS (FL. THIRTEENTH CENTURY).

Saxo Grammaticus wrote a history of the Danish kings entitled *Danorum regum heroumque historia* (The History of the Kings and Heroes of the Danes), usually known as the *Gesta Danorum*. It is a synthesis of history, myth, and legend and is one of the greatest sources of northern heroic tradition outside of Iceland.

Little is known concerning the life of Danish Saxo. His sobriquets of "Grammaticus" and "Longus," which were posthumously conferred upon him, indicate that he was educated and most likely tall. It seems likely that he was native to Zealand since in his writing he highly praises the people there above other Danes. Saxo, himself, tells us that his father and grandfather were warriors and fought for King Valdemar I, who ruled over Denmark from 1157 to 1182. At some point, this son of warriors entered the household of one of Valdemar's closest advisers, Absalon, the bishop of Roskilde and archbishop of Lund, where he most likely became a clerk. In the preface to the *Gesta Danorum*, Saxo tells the reader that Absalon was eager to celebrate the achievements and fame of his beloved Denmark as other nations had taken pride in vaunting their heroes in a national history in Latin. To this task of writing the history for his *patria* he assigned Saxo, who humbly professes his inadequacy for the job but somehow managed to write a full sixteen books.

That Saxo enjoyed a good eclectic education is evident from his writing. He was familiar with Church history and Latin antiquity. He had read Dudo and *Bede and mentions both in Book One. Saxo was very likely familiar with medieval historians such as *Gregory of Tours, *Paul the Deacon, *Geoffrey of Monmouth, and *Adam of Bremen, among others. Moreover, scholars have long noted the debt that Saxo owes Latin poets and thinkers such as Virgil, Ovid, and Cicero. Of course, Saxo's biggest debt is to the folk traditions and lore of his own people and wandering Scandinavians, particularly, Icelanders. Indeed, modern scholars have found his history to be an invaluable source for comparison to other northern literatures, as the figures and events that he relates can be found in the Old English *Beowulf* and *Widsith* and in the Old Icelandic eddas and sagas.

Of the sixteen books of the *Gesta Danorum*, the first four recount the Danish kings who lived before the time of Christ, beginning with the eponymous Dan, the first king. Books Five through Eight cover the Danish heathen period until the establishment of the Church in Denmark; while the remaining books tell of the kings from the conversion to Saxo's own time. Throughout these many volumes, Saxo relates numerous stories, many concerning the exploits of Odin, Balder, and Scyld. Often these narratives differ greatly from their northern analogs. In addition, readers of Shakespeare's *Hamlet* will find the oldest source for that tragedy, though the figure of Saxo's Amlethus has little in common with the melancholy Dane of Elsinore. Like other writers of the Middle Ages, Saxo was greatly interested in the qualities necessary for a good king. Generosity, courage, great deeds, noble lineage, and a passion for revenge are prominent kingly virtues. Despite the fact that Saxo was entrusted to write this history by a church cleric, he does little in the way of Christian apologetics. Even the books that deal with history after the conversion do not overly emphasize Christian piety and humility.

Saxo outlived Bishop Absalon and King Valdemar. The *Gesta Danorum* was most likely completed after 1216 and dedicated to their successors, Archbishop Anders and King Valdemar II. The earliest complete manuscript dates from 1514, though four fragments from the fourteenth century, or perhaps earlier, exist.

Bibliography: Saxo Grammaticus, *History of the Danes*, ed. H. E. Davidson, trans. P. Fisher, 1979; Saxo Grammaticus, *History of the Danes*, http://sunsite.berkeley.edu/OMACL/DanishHistory (accessed July 18, 2001); I. Skovgaard-Petersen, "Saxo, Historian of the Patria," *Mediaeval Scandinavia* 2 (1969): 54–77.

Joseph Carroll

SIGEBERT OF GEMBLOUX (C. 1030–1112). A Benedictine monk, he was also a hagiographer and chronicler. His *De viribus illustribus*, a collection of ecclesiastic biographies, and his *Chronica*, a flawed but valuable chronicle, are important medieval contributions to their genres. Sigebert also took an active role in the Investiture Controversy, which was at its peak during his lifetime. On the side of the throne against the papacy, Sigebert condemmned Popes *Gregory VII and *Paschal II. He died at Gembloux in 1112.

Sigebert was educated at the monastery of Gembloux and taught at St. Vincent at Metz from about 1050 to 1070. There he composed the *Lives* of the saints of Metz as well as a *Sermon* and long poem on Saint Lucia's martyrdom. He further celebrated the area through biographies of Bishop Theoderic of Metz and King Sigebert III. In 1070, Sigebert returned to Gembloux and wrote a biography of Wicbert, the abbey's founder. He also composed another long poem in hexameters on the *Passion of the Theban Martyr Legion*, since Gembloux possessed the relics of its leader. His history of the abbots of Gembloux (*Gesta abbatum Gemblacensium*) offers insight into the effects of the Investiture struggle and uses biography to trace the abbey's history to 1048.

Two of Sigebert's three contributions to the Investiture Controversy survive. In a letter of 1075, he upbraids Gregory VII and defends married priests. Sigebert also attacked Pope Paschal II's call to punish citizens of Liège for their loyalty to the emperor and threw his support behind royal investiture. His lost letter refuted Gregory on the right of popes to excommunicate kings, as detailed in a letter the pope had written to Bishop Hermann of Metz in 1081.

In the last ten years of his life, Sigebert took on two vast projects. Biography as a genre reawoke with his *De viribus illustribus*, and therein are preserved the memory of many writers who otherwise would be unknown to us. This far-reaching compendium of Church writers, beginning with Marcellus and ending with the author himself, was continued and renamed *De scriptoribus ecclesiasticis* by a contemporary of Sigebert. The second work, the *Chronica*, sketches historical events from 381 to 1111. In an attempt to properly assign dates to events, Sigebert made many mistakes, for which scholars have treated him harshly. However, despite its flawed chronology, the *Chronica*, which was widely circulated and relied upon in the Middle Ages, remains a valuable historical document.

Bibliography: R. Witte, ed., *Catalogus Sigeberti Gemblacensis monachi de viris illustribus*, 1974.

Karolyn Kinane

SIGER OF BRABANT (C. 1240–C. 1284). A radical Aristotelian philosopher, siger was the founder of the Averroistic school of philosophy.

Siger was born c. 1240 in the duchy of Brabant. He probably began his early studies in Liège and entered the Faculty of Arts at the University of Paris c. 1255–1257. By 1266, he completed his master's degree, and he taught arts at Paris until 1277. In 1266, he was mentioned by a papal legate as a ringleader of a rebellious faction within the faculty. He became associated with *Boethius of Dacia and the "Averroistic" or radical Aristotelian movement at Paris. In 1270, Bishop Stephen *Tempier condemned thirteen philosophical propositions, many arising from the usage of *Averroës in the interpretation of Aristotle. In this same year, Thomas *Aquinas wrote *De unitate intellectus contra Averroistas* (On the Unity of the Intellect against the Averroists) against him.

In 1271, Siger was cited in a dispute within the Faculty of Arts over the election of a rector. In November 1276, he was cited for heresy by the inquisitor of France and summoned to answer this charge. In March 1277, Bishop Tempier condemned 219 philosophical propositions, several of which reflected Siger's teachings. Siger fled Paris in late 1276 and appealed to the papal court at Orvieto. He was killed by an insane secretary there, c. 1284. By the sixteenth century, he was acknowledged as the founder of the Averroistic school of philosophy.

As a philosopher, Siger believed that it was his duty to elucidate Aristotle, often relying upon his Arabic commentators *Avicenna and Averroës. Like Averroës and Boethius of Dacia, Siger separated philosophy from theology and sought to use human reason to bring philosophical considerations to their natural conclusions. As a natural philosopher, relying upon the usage of human reason, many of Siger's necessary conclusions thus came into conflict with the Christian faith. Siger's main philosophical conclusions against which his opponents Tempier, Aquinas, and *Bonaventure railed were: the eternity of the world, the unicity of the intellect for the human race, the denial of personal immortality, and the rejection of rewards and punishments in the afterlife.

However, Siger was a Christian, and like Boethius of Dacia, he never claimed that a philosophical conclusion contrary to faith was true. Thus, while reason may seem to indicate that the world is eternal, the Christian faith, using supernatural revelation and miracles, teaches creation *ex nihilo* and must remain true. He therefore never taught the "double-truth," as he believed that in cases of conflict between reason and faith, truth was on the side of faith.

Siger's primary works are his commentaries on Aristotle's *Metaphysics, Physics,* and *De anima.* He also commented upon the *Liber de causis* and wrote several independent works including *On the Intellective Soul, On the Eternity of the World,* and several scholastic *quaestiones.* Many of his Aristotelian commentaries and original works are now lost. Siger was an influential philosopher of the thirteenth century and was later, in the *Divine Comedy,* placed by Dante alongside Aquinas and *Albertus Magnus in the fourth heaven of Paradiso.

Bibliography: A. Maurer, *Medieval Philosophy,* 2d ed., 1982.

Andrew G. Traver

SIMON DE MONTFORT, THE ELDER. *See* MONTFORT, SIMON DE, THE ELDER.

SIMON DE MONTFORT, THE YOUNGER. *See* MONTFORT, SIMON DE, THE YOUNGER.

SĪNĀ, IBN (ABŪ ʿALĪ AL-HUSAYN IBN ʿABD ALLĀH IBN SĪNĀ, AVICENNA) (980–1037). An Islamic scientist, philosopher, and court physician, he was a prolific writer known primarily for his works on medicine and philosophy. Known in the West as Avicenna, his *Canon of Medicine* (*Kānūn fi ʾl-tibb*) became the standard medical text in the East and West from the twelfth to the sixteenth century, while his philosophical writing had an enormous impact on the development of Western medieval philosophy.

Bountiful information about Ibn Sīnā is available in authoritative biographies, as well as in his own autobiography, wherein he gives great detail about his first thirty years. Ibn Sīnā was born in his mother's home in 980 in the Persian city of Afshana, near Bukhārā. His father was a bureaucrat in the Samanid dynasty and gave careful attention to the education of his son. Although his father was an Ismaili, Ibn Sīnā's intellectual development was not limited in scope to Ismaili beliefs. Rather, he rapidly mastered a wide variety of religious and secular sciences. He is said to have mastered the Qur'an and religious sciences and to have explained the principles of logic to his teacher al-Nātilī at a very young age. After his fourteenth year, he was largely self-taught, and by the age of sixteen, he had taken over the role as teacher of natural sciences and medicine to more experienced physicians. After curing the Samanid emir of Khurāsān, he was granted free access to the royal library where he is said to have mastered all the known sciences by the age of eighteen.

When Ibn Sīnā was twenty-one, his father died, and he was faced with the choice of entering the service of Mahmud of Ghazna, the oppressive ruler who had recently captured Bukhārā, or to flee. He chose to leave his native city of Bukhārā and was the only one among his companions to survive the harsh journey across the desert to the Caspian Sea. Thereafter, Ibn Sīnā continued with his work in various cities of Persia, and to earn his living he served as court physician and even vizier to different princes. He eventually settled in Hamadān in the court of Shams al-Dawla; however, like all political figures, he was subject to the whims of political intrigues and, at one point, even was imprisoned. After the death of Shams al-Dawla, Ibn Sīnā went to Isfahan, where he spent fourteen uninterrupted years as court physician and teacher at a local school. He often accompanied the princes on their campaigns, continuing to dictate his scholarly works under the most strenuous of conditions. He depended primarily upon his memory and independent thought as he often lacked access to the original sources upon which he commented. On one such campaign with the prince 'Alā 'al-Dawla, in 1037, he became ill and died and was buried in Hamadān, where a modern, reconstructed mausoleum stands today.

Ibn Sīnā's corpus of works is quite extensive, including upwards of 276 works, though perhaps up to 100 of these are difficult to authenticate. His greatest works are about medicine and philosophy, but he also wrote about religious matters, Quranic exegesis, natural history, astronomy, mathematics, and chemistry, as well as pedagogical poetry.

Ibn Sīnā's greatest contribution is perhaps his *Canon of Medicine* in which he synthesized the works of the ancient Greek treatises of Hippocrates, Galen, and Dioscorides with the Arabic, Indian, and Iranian traditions. Ibn Sīnā combined philosophy and logic with the practical observations he gleaned from treating and healing people. He compiled a comprehensive work divided into five books that covers the nature of the human body, health and sickness, pharmacological properties of herbs, pathologies of organs, diagnosis and symptoms of illness including tumors, wounds, and fractures, and finally the production of medicines. He made important discoveries that have been accepted by modern scientists, including findings like the contagion of tuberculosis, brain tumors, and ulcers, as well as emphasis on good hygiene to maintain health.

His impact on the development of Western medicine is well documented. Ibn Sīnā's work was first introduced to the West through the mediation of *Averroës, who had appropriated it, and then through the translation of Averroës' version into Latin by *Gerard of Cremona in the mid-twelfth century. Later, when his *Canon of Medicine* was translated in its entirety, it formed the basis of the medical curriculum from the fourteenth to the sixteenth century. His importance to the medical sciences was undisputed for many years until his work was assailed by the likes of Leonardo da Vinci, Paracelcus, and later by Harvey, who made major discoveries about circulation in the 1620s.

Ibn Sīnā's contribution to philosophical inquiry was also quite extensive, though not as categorical as for medicine or the natural sciences. He attempted to synthesize the Aristotelian and Neoplatonist philosophies with the tradition of Abrahamic monotheism as revealed in the Qur'an. He composed his first philosophical work at age twenty-one, though his most influential work on philosophy is the *Book of Healing* (*Kitāb al-Shifā'*), which deals with logic, natural philosophy and natural sciences, mathematics, and metaphysics. Ibn Sīnā explored the principles behind the individual sciences through his use of logic and understanding of metaphysics, which was the science of being in his understanding. He also was not intimidated by the more esoteric understanding of wisdom as inner illumination.

His training in Islamic logic was a direct result of the Islamic tradition that revolved around commenting on the *Organon* of Aristotle. However, Ibn Sīnā did not limit himself simply to absorbing the tradition but was among the first medieval philosophers who sought to refine the tool of logic and develop it as a discipline unto itself. He chose to do this through his exploration of language, semantics, and hypothetical syllogism, as well as classification and logical definition.

In the realm of metaphysics, Ibn Sīnā placed the study of being (ontology) at the heart of his philosophical understanding that drew from the work of Aristotle, al-*Fārābī, and Plotinus, as well as the Islamic understanding of the unity of God. Parts of Plotinus' *Enneads* that Ibn Sīnā used, however, had been misattributed to Aristotle and were understood by Ibn Sīnā to be part of Aristotle's work *Metaphysics*. This misattribution set Ibn Sīnā down a difficult path of synthesizing and interpreting the contradictions of their views. Thus, he was one of the first to discuss the distinction between essence and existence, between necessity and contingency, between God and all that is not God, landing upon the theory of creation and emanation. For Ibn Sīnā, proving the existence of God is only possible in metaphyiisics, and not in physics, wherein God previously had been thought of as the prime mover. Saint Thomas *Aquinas further developed the distinctions outlined by Ibn Sīnā, between the uncreated being and created beings to a much greater degree than he, though it is clear that Aquinas depended heavily on Ibn Sīnā's earlier formulations.

The numerous Latin translations and manuscripts of the *Shifā'* and the *Kānūn* are testimony to his great influence on Western science and philosophy. For a period of time, he was thought to be a simple commentator on Aristotle, was translated by *Michael Scot, was used extensively by *Albertus Magnus and Saint Thomas Aquinas, and heavily influenced Roger *Bacon and *John Duns Scotus. Later philosophers reconsidered his work and placed Ibn Sīnā in the camp of the Neoplatonist and Augustinian philosophers. The wavering of subsequent scholars as to which school he belongs does not take away from the fundamental contribution he made to the development of Western medieval philosophy and, in particular, Thomistic thought.

Bibliography: W. Gohlman, ed., *The Life of Ibn Sina: A Critical Edition and Annotated Translation*, 1974; L. E. Goodman, *Avicenna*. 1992; D. Gutas, *Avicenna and the Aristotelian Tradition: Introduction to Reading Avicenna's Philosophical Works*, 1988.

Tom Papademetriou

SNORRI STURLUSON (C. 1178–1241). Icelandic saga writer, poet, and chieftain, Snorri wrote the *Prose Edda* as an attempt to preserve the techniques of skaldic poetry and northern mythological narratives. He also wrote the *Heimskringla*, a lengthy compilation of sagas detailing the lives of the kings of Norway from their legendary beginnings to the late twelfth century. Besides his literary accomplishments, Snorri was a powerful chieftain and lawspeaker during the Sturlung Age, a tumultuous period in Iceland's history that preceded the end of independent rule and overlordship of the island by the Norwegian crown.

Thanks to *Sturla Þórðarson, nephew to Snorri, much of the great chieftain's life is recounted in the *Íslendinga saga*. The reputation of Sturla Snorrason, Snorri's father, enabled him to place his son at the age of three under the fosterage of Jón Loptsson, the most powerful chieftain in Iceland at that time. Under his care, Snorri had access to the greatest library and thinkers on the island. His love for poetry and history developed at a young age, and his later tutelage at Oddi, a center for ecclesiastical and secular learning, was no doubt the intellectual wellspring for the *Heimskringla* and the *Prose Edda*.

After some shrewd business and political deals and a marriage to the daughter of a wealthy Icelander, the young and ambitious Snorri became a *goði* (chieftain). Soon he also held the prestigious office of *lögsögumaðr* (lawspeaker) and presided at the island's governmental assembly known as the *Althing*. Wishing further to increase his power, Snorri curried the favor of Norwegian nobility by writing skaldic poems to honor them. Encouraged by a warm response, he traveled to Norway, where he was eventually made a retainer of King *Hákon Hákonarson and Jarl Skuli. The Icelandic chieftain's loyalties to his homeland and his royal friends were severely tested when Hákon made known his desires to send a harrying force to subjugate Iceland. After suggesting a more diplomatic route, Snorri was charged with the duty of bringing the Icelanders in line. On his return home, however, he did little in the way of the king's mission and soon became embroiled in local disputes. After a bitter feud with his nephew Sturla Sighvatsson, Snorri was despoiled of his possessions and forced into exile. He stayed in Norway once more, but after the death of Sturla, he defied King Hákon's order prohibiting Icelanders to leave Norway, and he returned to Iceland. Shortly after that, two of Snorri's former sons-in-law who held disputes against him acted on behalf of the king. With a small band of men, they broke into Snorri's dwelling at Reykjaholt and killed him.

When not caught up in the political intrigues of thirteenth-century life, Snorri managed to write some of the greatest works the northern medieval world has ever produced. Though his name is never affixed to the oldest extant manuscripts, tradition and scholars have agreed on his authorship. His largest work, the *Heimskringla*, "the circle of the world," is so named in later manuscripts because it encompasses the vast history of the northern world. Drawing upon historical texts, skaldic tradition, hagiographic legends, and folklore, Snorri in the *Heimskringla* recounted the lives of the Norwegian kings from their earliest legendary sources to roughly his own time. Some of his concerns in this work were to present the cause and effects for the great events in northern political history and to give insight into the virtues and vices of many Norwegian rulers. The centerpiece of this collection of sagas is *Óláfs saga helga*, or the Saga of Saint *Óláfr Haraldsson, a retelling of the life of Norway's holy king who was instrumental in the country's final conversion to Christianity.

While the *Heimskringla* is Snorri's greatest achievement, he is probably better known for his *Prose Edda*, which continues to be a sourcebook for Norse mythology. His original intention, however, was for the work to be a kind of skaldic *ars poetica* that would preserve skaldic techniques and the pagan and heroic tales relied on by poets to create their elaborate metaphors. Among the many stories he recounts are the exploits of Thor against the Frost Giants, of Odin's stealing the mead of poetry, of Baldr's death by the trickery of Loki, and of Ragnarǫk, the downfall of the Gods. All of these tales have delighted and inspired poets, authors, composers and casual readers for centuries.

Bibliography: M. Ciklamini, *Snorri Sturluson*, 1978; *Prose Edda of Snorri Sturluson: Tales from Norse Mythology*, trans. J. Young, 1973; Snorri Sturluson, *Heimskringla: History of the Kings of Norway*, trans. L. M. Hollander, 1964.

Joseph Carroll

SOLOMON BEN JUDAH IBN GABIROL (AVICENBRON) (C. 1021–C. 1058).

Known also as Ibn Gabirol or Avencebrol, he was a celebrated Jewish poet and Neoplatonic philosopher of the Jewish Golden Age in Islamic Spain. His *Fountain of Life*, preserved in toto only in Latin translation, had a marked impact on Christian scholasticism.

The details of Avicenbron's biography are scarce. He was born in the Spanish city of Malaga and spent the better part of his early years in Saragossa. He was orphaned at a young age and dedicated himself to a life of poetry and philosophy quite early on. As a young man in Saragossa, he received a thorough Jewish education and acquired a deep working knowledge of the Arabic philosophic tradition. His poetic talents manifested at an early age, and by the time he was twenty, he had composed a sizable amount of Hebrew verse. His contemporary Moses ibn Ezra mentions that he was among the greatest poets of his generation and that he surpassed all of them in the literary quality of his work. His liturgical poetry is of particular excellence and is preserved in numerous Sephardic and Ashkenazic prayer books. In addition to his poetic genius, Avicenbron was an accomplished Neoplatonic philosopher, and his *Fountain of Life*, originally written in Arabic and preserved only in a Latin translation, represents the climax of Jewish Neoplatonic speculation.

Avicenbron was dependent upon the support of wealthy patrons for his livelihood, and in addition to composing many panegyrics for his patrons, he was fully engaged in the upper-class social life of his day. Due to his outspoken and somewhat haughty nature, he is said to have raised the ire of a number of influential men, and he became infamous for his virulent attacks on various prominent personalities. Around 1045, he left Saragossa, possibly for Granada. He died in Valencia in 1057–1058, possibly from the severe health problems he had experienced since early childhood.

Written as a dialogue between master and student, the *Fountain of Life* tackles questions of cosmology, ontology, and epistemology. Overall, the book is primarily devoted to a discussion of matter and form. Avicenbron proposes that all substances, either spiritual or corporeal, are composed of two basic elements: matter and form. In good Neoplatonic fashion, Avicenbron asserts that the First Essence, which can be identified with God, emanated the divine will, which, in turn, emanated substances composed of matter and form. Matter, which is the substratum undergirding all forms, is of two types, corporeal and spiritual. It is the combination of matter and form that causes outward multiplicity and thus creates the differences between created beings. Thus, for instance, a man is made up of matter and a number of forms such as "corporeality," "humanity," "rationality," and so forth; however, an animal, while sharing the form of "corporeality," does not have "rationality" and thus is more general in form, placing it lower in the hierarchy of being, which is classified according to the relative generality or complexity of the number of forms that inhere in a particular being.

Avicenbron's philosophical works did not have much of an influence on later Jewish thinkers. This is accounted for, at least partially, by the rise in popularity of Aristotelianism and the subsequent displacement of Neoplatonism among Jewish thinkers after the time of Moses *Maimonides. The response from Christian thinkers, however, was quite different, and the thirteenth-century Christian Scholastics were quite enamored with Avicenbron's philosophical work. His *Fountain of Life* was translated into Latin as *Fons vitae* under the aegis of Raymond, archbishop of Toledo, in the middle of the twelfth century. The book influenced both *Albertus Magnus and Thomas *Aquinas, the latter rejecting its doctrine of intelligible matter on grounds that it was contradictory. In addition to the Dominicans, two prominent Franciscans, *Bonaventure and *John Duns Scotus, also displayed an interest in Avicenbron's work. Curiously enough, his identity as a Jew did not seem to be recognized by his commentators, and at various times he was characterized as being either a Muslim or a Christian. In fact, it was not until the nineteenth century that the identity of the author of the *Fountain of Life* was identified as being the same as the celebrated Hebrew poet.

Bibliography: R. Loewe, *Ibn Gabirol*, 1989; J. Schlanger, *La philosophie de Salomon ibn Gabirol*, 1968.

Erik S. Ohlander

SORBON, ROBERT DE. *See* ROBERT OF SORBON.

STEPHEN (ISTVÁN) I OF HUNGARY, SAINT (C. 972–1038). Stephen was the king of Hungary from 998 to 1038 and a saint. A direct descendant of Árpád, who led the nomadic Magyar tribes to the central Danubian basin near the end of the ninth century, Stephen traditionally is regarded as the founder of the Hungarian state. In fact, he continued and expanded policies that his father Géza I (fl. 972–997) had initiated. Canonized in 1083, his feast day is 2 September.

The future king originally was given a traditional Magyar name, Vajk, but was baptised as Stephen a few years later. Géza designated Stephen heir to the throne by giving him control of Nyitra, the most important large administrative region (*ducate*) in the country. In 996, Stephen married Gisela, the sister of the future German emperor Henry II. Géza's promotion of Stephen as a successor was contrary to Magyar custom, which required that the throne pass to the eldest competent male of the entire Árpád family. Thus, Stephen faced serious rebellions during the first decade of his reign; these were supported always by the traditional nomadic and pagan elements within Hungary and occasionally by Byzantium. Stephen eventually established internal control by building a system of castles (*vár*) and recruiting a force of heavy cavalry, some of whom originally came from Germany with his wife. Traditional nomadic tactics survived only in specialized "ethnic" units provided by Szekelers, Khazars, and Pechenegs living inside Hungary, some of whom continued to practice paganism or Islam.

Much has been made of Stephen's commendation of Hungary to the protection of Saint Peter (i.e., the pope) when preparing for his formal coronation on Christmas Day 1000. In fact, this did not greatly impress contemporaries— Emperor *Otto III actually gave Pope *Sylvester II permission to accept the Hungarian offer, and Stephen had to go to war from 1027 to 1031 to resist *Conrad II's attempt to establish suzerainty over Hungary. Not until the Investiture Controversy did popes seriously try to support Hungary's claim of independence from the German empire, and it was still later generations that invested the crown of Saint Stephen with meaning as a symbol of Hungarian independence.

In addition to the war against Conrad, Stephen fought defensive wars against the Poles between 1015 and 1017 and, at about the same time, Pechenegs from the lower Danube. Stephen's only aggressive war, against the Bulgarians in 1018, was a joint campaign with the Byzantine Emperor *Basil II. Stephen eventually strengthened that connection with the betrothal of his son Emeric (Imré) to a Byzantine princess. Stephen also secured Hungarian interests in the Adriatic by marrying his sister to the Venetian doge, Otto Orseolo.

The major achievements of Stephen's reign were domestic. While Géza first introduced Latin Christianity to Hungary in 972, Stephen expanded and secured the position of the Church by endowing additional bishoprics and monasteries and introducing a system of regular tithes. His support of the Church included establishing hostels for the care of pilgrims traveling through Hungary to reach Jerusalem as well as the patronage of arts and literature. Stephen himself dictated a volume of *Admonitions* for his son, one of the earliest monuments of Latin literature in Hungary. Stephen also reorganized Hungary's administration, introducing a system of counties (*comitates*), each headed by a royally appointed official (*ispán*) recruited from important local clans rather than the Magyar tribal nobility. *Ducates* continued to exist, but all eventually were placed under members of the royal family. Further, Stephen transformed the king's traditional retinue (*udvar*) into a full-fledged court, established a chancery by attracting German scribes, and promulgated a written code of law.

Despite Stephen's efforts, the succession remained problematic. After the death of his son Emeric, Stephen favored the claim of his nephew, Peter Orseolo. But even having his own cousin Vazul blinded did not prevent a civil war after the king's death, and the descendants of Vazul eventually inherited the throne.

As the national saint and founding king of Hungary, Stephen compares to contemporaries and near contemporaries such as Henry II of Germany, *Edward the Confessor of England, and Saint *Óláfr Haraldsson of Norway; like them, some of his actions today appear incongruous in a saint. The actual events of his reign reflect the position of Hungary as a Western country with a diverse tradition and strong ties to Byzantium and eastern Europe, a position Stephen skillfully exploited to establish and maintain his independence and authority.

Bibliography: G. Györffy, *King Saint Stephen of Hungary*, trans. P. Doherty, 1994.

Edward J. Schoenfeld

STEPHEN II (III), POPE (C. 710–757, PONTIFICATE 752–757). He is
sometimes considered the third Stephen since the original Stephen II died four days after his election. Under his influence, weakened relations between Rome and Constantinople further deteriorated, and Rome aligned itself with the burgeoning Frankish Empire, an act that was to have ramifications in the Western Church for the next five centuries.

Stephen is chiefly remembered today because of his alliance with *Pepin III, king of the Franks. The Lombards had long threatened the stability of Italy.

With the accession of Aistulf in 749, the Lombard monarchy renewed its efforts to bring sections of Italy under its control. Stephen II was elected in 752 upon the death of Zacharias, the last Greek pope, in part because of his ability to deal with this critical situation. He appealed to Constantinople for support in the conflict as Aistulf laid seige to Rome, asserting his sovereignty over the duchy and levying an annual tribute on the people. Receiving no support nor even a promise of support from the East, Stephen exercised his only other option—he petitioned Pepin for aid against the Lombards. After one last attempt to persuade Aistulf to peace, Stephen embarked on a journey on 15 November 753 that would take him to the Frankish court. Pepin, a devout Christian, marched into Italy and defeated the Lombard armies, returning cities and duchies to the patrimony of Saint Peter. When Constantinople objected, Pepin renounced their authority in Italy and in effect founded the independent papal states.

Bibliography: R. Davis, trans., *The Lives of the Eighth-Century Popes* (Liber Pontificalis), 1992.

Clinton Atchley

STEPHEN HARDING. *See* HARDING, STEPHEN, SAINT

STEPHEN LANGTON. *See* LANGTON, STEPHEN.

STEPHEN OF ENGLAND (C. 1096–1154, R. 1135–1154). Due to a combination of nonroyal blood, poor judgment of both people and situations, political weakness, and lack of resolve, Stephen's reign is marked by civil war and political unrest.

Born the third son of Stephen, count of Blois and Chartres, and Adela, the daughter of *William I the Conqueror, little is known about Stephen before 1113. Sometime between 1106 and 1113, Adela sent Stephen to the court of his uncle, King *Henry I, where Stephen became one of Henry's "new men"—men who were raised up by the king, usually at the expense of his enemies. Henry made Stephen count of Mortain, and during the years 1113–1125, Stephen became one of the wealthiest Anglo-Normans as Henry continued to give him extensive lands in England and Normandy and arranged for him a marriage to the heiress Matilda of Boulogne.

Henry's death in December 1135 left the Anglo-Norman barons with a crisis: Henry's designated heir, his daughter the Empress *Matilda, was unacceptable to many of them because of her marriage to Geoffrey of Anjou. To further complicate the issue, the other two likely candidates, Stephen and Robert, earl of Gloucester, Henry's illegitimate son, were bitter enemies who were unlikely to support the other as king. While the barons debated whom they should support as king, Stephen, upon learning of his uncle's death, set sail for England. The people of London accepted him as king, and Stephen, with the help of his brother, Henry of Blois, bishop of Winchester, secured the support of officials in

Wincester, who controlled the governmental machinery and the royal treasury. Stephen's claim to the throne, however, was not secure until Hugh Bigod arrived and claimed Henry, on his deathbed, had designated Stephen his heir. While never confirmed, Bigod's news freed Stephen from his oath to support Matilda's claim, and the archbishop crowned him king on 22 December 1135. By April 1136, the majority of the Anglo-Norman nobles had accepted Stephen as king.

Stephen's firm hold on the throne was short-lived. Many poorly thought out actions demonstrated his weaknesses as a leader and alienated many supporters, including his brother Henry of Blois. With the Empress Matilda still exerting her claim to the throne, many nobles switched alliance and offered her their support. While fighting rebels in 1141, Stephen was captured by Robert, earl of Gloucester, and his son Earl Rannulf, who presented him to the empress. With Stephen in her power, she demanded to be recognized as queen. Many of the barons, while accepting her as heir, stalled by arguing that Stephen needed to free them of their oaths. The empress quickly proved dictatorial, which turned many of the nobles against her. As her support declined, Stephen's wife, Queen Matilda, using Stephen's Flemish mercenaries under William Ypres, attacked the region around London. Fearing the worst, a mob of Londoners turned on the empress, forcing her to flee. Conflicts broke out as various nobles came to the queen's aid, and the earl of Gloucester was himself captured. After a prolonged negotiation between the queen and the empress, Stephen and Robert were exchanged. Stephen refused to be reinstated, claiming that he had never been dethroned.

The following years were marked by additional conflicts, rebellions, and poor decisions on Stephen's part, which further undermined his position, both with his nobles and with the Church. In 1153, Henry Plantagenet (*Henry II), the empress' son, made his third invasion into England. While Henry's two earlier attempts had not been successful, both had improved his reputation as a warrior. This time, Henry came with an army strong enough to force his uncle into negotiations. In November of that year, three months after the death of Stephen's eldest son Eustace, Stephen accepted Henry as his heir. Stephen died on 25 October 1154.

Especially when compared to his predecessor and successor, Henry I and Henry II, Stephen's weakness as a monarch is readily apparent. Unable to inspire loyalty through a position of strength and all too capable of alienating his supporters through poor decisions, Stephen needed to create seventeen earldoms to buy support and had to make use of foreign mercenaries to ensure his army's loyalty.

Bibliography: H. A. Cronne, *The Reign of Stephen, 1135–1154: Anarchy in England*, 1970; R.H.C. Davis, *King Stephen, 1135–1154*, 3rd ed., 1990.

John Paul Walter

STRABO, WALAHFRID (C. 808–849).

Poet, abbot, and teacher at the Benedictine monastery at Reichenau in southeastern Germany, Walahfrid Strabo

(Walahfrid "the Squinter," in reference to an actual visual difficulty) represented one of a generation of scholars and writers associated with famous monasteries such as St. Gall, Fulda, Corbie, and Reichenau during the reign of *Louis the Pious following an age of court sponsorship under Louis' father *Charlemagne. Walahfrid edited in the early 840s a version of *Einhard's *Vita Karoli Magni* (Life of Charlemagne) in the preface to which he lamented that under Louis "the light of learning is less cared for and fading in many men." Though the decline alluded to is exaggerated (the political instability of the time notwithstanding), Walahfrid was nonetheless among the great poets of the Carolingian age and one of the foremost scholars of the ninth century.

Born to a humble Swabian family, Walahfrid entered the monastery at Reichenau by age fourteen in 822 and studied there under Wetti (whose vision would form the subject of Walahfrid's first poem), Tatto, and Grimald; in 826–827 he went to the abbey at Fulda to pursue studies under *Hrabanus Maurus (in turn a pupil of *Alcuin). From 829 to 838 at Aachen, he tutored *Charles (II the Bald), son of Emperor Louis and Empress Judith, at the end of which duty he was appointed abbot at Reichenau. He lost this position in 840 for supporting Lothar I; with Grimald's help he was reappointed in 842. Sent as an emissary by *Louis the German to Charles the Bald, Walahfrid died along the way, drowning in the Loire.

Walahfrid is primarily known for his verse, as he is the major Carolingian poet (and sole significant court poet) from the reign of Louis the Pious. He wrote two verse saints' lives or panegyrics: one of Saint Mamas (*Vita Mammae monachi*) and another of Saint Blaithmaic (Blathmacc mac Flaind, prior of Iona killed in a Viking raid of 825). Among his better-known poems are the *Visio Wettini* and *Hortulus*. The *Visio Wettini* (The Vision of Wetti) recounts his former teacher's vision of the otherworld experienced shortly before he died. It is Walahfrid's first known poem, composed when he was eighteen, and includes a famous portrait of Charlemagne (not named but spelled out in an acrostic—*Carolus imperator*—in the particular passage) suffering torments in hell for his sins of lust (he had kept concubines, and Louis the Pious' reign was one of reforms; Walahfrid elsewhere speaks more highly of Charlemagne). The *Hortulus* (The Little Garden, or *De cultura hortorum*, On the Cultivation of Gardens) was dedicated to Abbot Grimald and allegorically treats twenty-three plants or herbs, their characteristics, growth, and medicinal properties, and portrays with great wit a medieval monastic garden; Walahfrid composed it after leaving the difficulties of politics and serving as abbot at Reichenau. Among his other celebrated verse are the epigrams on friendship (*Cum splendor lunae fulgescat ab aethere purae* [When the Splendor of the Clear Moon Glistens from the Heavens], employing moonlight as a *pignus amoris*, pledge of love, between separated friends) and on the tibia of a doe slain by a hunting Louis the Pious (*Arboris est altix quondam vagina medullae* [What Once Sheathed Bone Marrow Now Is Foster-mother to a Tree]), and an elegy for the monastery at Reichenau (*Musa nostrum plange soror dolorem* [Sister Muse, Lament Our Pain]).

Walahfrid's prose works include a series of revisions or redactions (Einhard's *Life of Charlemagne*, Thegan's *Life of Louis the Pious*, the *Life* of Saint Gall, and Gozbert's *Life of St. Othmar*), the theological tract *De exordiis et incrementis quarundam in observationibus ecclesiasticis rerum* (on liturgical rites and observations), and a series of commentarial and glossarial works. Though Walahfrid is not responsible for the *Glossa ordinaria* as earlier legend held, he did compile an important edition of his teacher Hrabanus Maurus' commentary to the Pentateuch (St. Gall, Stiftsbibliothek MS 283; this nineth-century codex contains glosses in Old High German and Old English), a commentary to the Catholic Epistles, and glosses to *Isidore of Seville's *De homine et partibus eius* (On Man and His Parts). The latter activity, especially its connection to existing glossary traditions (such as that of the school of *Theodore and Hadrian at Canterbury), has also reserved for Walahfrid a role in the development of the German language.

Bibliography: P. Godman, *Poetry of the Carolingian Renaissance*, 1985; W. Strabo, *Opera omnia*, Patrologiae cursus completus, Series Latina, vols. 113–114, 1879.

Joseph McGowan

STURLA ÞÓRÐARSON (1214–1284). Icelandic historian, chieftain, and courtier, Sturla was the nephew of the similarly gifted and even more celebrated poet and historian *Snorri Sturluson.

Both were among the most prominent members of the Sturlung clan (descendants of the western Icelandic chieftain Hvamm-Sturla), whose name was later applied to the decline of the Icelandic republic ("the Sturlung Age") throughout those decades of civil war and clan feuding immediately preceding the island's capitulation to Norway in 1262. Imbalances of power among Iceland's thirty-six, and later forty-eight, local chieftains (*goðar*) who had legislative power at the Althing (national parliamentary assembly) formed the impetus behind these conflicts. Sturla was not only an active participant in the tumultuous events of the time, on the side of Icelandic independence from Norway as well as of postwar reconciliation, but also their chronicler.

Sturla was the illegitimate son of the chieftain Þórðr Sturluson and was fostered at an early age by his paternal grandmother, Guðny Bödvarsdottir. In his teens, Sturla served as his father's delegate to the Althing and as an aide to Bishop *Guðmundr when the bishop visited Sturla's home districts. Sturla showed leadership abilities early, organizing his brothers to deal with territorial disputes led by their own cousin, Snorri Sturluson's son Órækja. When Sturla was twenty-one, he went to live with his uncle Snorri. Later he named his first son after him and joined with his former rival Órækja in an attempt to avenge Snorri's death when he was slain in 1241 at the orders of the Icelandic chieftain Gizurr Þorvaldsson, acting for *Hákon Hákonarson, king of Norway. Twelve years later Sturla offered his daughter in marriage to Gizurr's son in an attempt at peacemaking; the wedding festivities ended in disaster, with the burning of Gizurr's homestead at Flugumyrr by elements dissatisfied with the reconciliation. On two occasions of political defeat in Iceland (1263 and 1277), Sturla suffered exile to Norway, where the pragmatic king *Magnús Hákonarson did not scruple to employ the rebellious but literate Icelander as historian and law-code reviser.

Sturla's *Íslendinga saga* (Saga of the Icelanders) covers events in Iceland from the death of Sturla's paternal grandfather and namesake Hvamm-Sturla in 1183 to the final annexation of Iceland in 1262–1264 by the Norwegian king Hákon Hákonarson. It forms the central narrative of the compilation called *Sturlunga saga*, amid a dozen shorter additional narratives by unknown authors chronicling related events. The recording of contemporary history was a new idea in Iceland in Sturla's time; it is a common assumption that these new chronicles reflect reality reasonably closely, since many of the people in the story would have been still alive when Sturla was writing and could have contradicted him publicly if they had disagreed with his account. All the same, Sturla did not pull any punches in *Íslendinga saga*: He portrayed its characters, including many of his real-life relatives, acting foolishly and heroically by turns, as the Icelandic republic's 400-year-old social structure fell to pieces around them. The saga recounts all the major events of the time, such as the battle of Örlygsstaðir (1238; the largest battle ever fought in Iceland), the ill-fated wedding at Flugumyrr (1253), and the death of Sturla's associate, the chieftain Þorgils Þkarði (1258). Among the most striking thematic elements of *Íslendinga saga* to the modern reader are the portentous dreams, which run like an ominous thread through the story. Characters see visions or dream dreams, often emerging from the experience reciting poetry. These warnings are not always taken seriously, though narrative logic strongly suggests that they should be: "Dreams are not worth noticing [Ekki er mark at draumum]," Sturla records his namesake and kinsman Sturla Sighvatsson as saying, after waking from a bad one just before the battle of Örlygsstaðir (1238), in which he was destined to die.

During his periods of exile at the Norwegian court Sturla was commissioned by King Magnús Hákonarson to write life histories of two kings of Norway: Magnús' father Hákon Hákonarson and Magnús himself. Since Sturla had firmly opposed the actions of Hákon toward Iceland and its independent chieftains—like Sturla's uncle Snorri, whom Hákon had ordered killed—these narratives, particularly the first one, are marked with ironic equivocation. Another Norwegian project Sturla was commissioned to complete was the revision of the existing law codes, a copy of which (called *Járnsíða*, Ironside) he brought back with him to Iceland; it became the basis of law in Iceland for the next ten years. Sturla also compiled a version of *Landnámabók*, the Icelandic Book of Settlements, known as *Sturlubók* (Sturla's Book).

Bibliography: E. Ó. Sveinsson, *The Age of the Sturlungs: Icelandic Civilization in the Thirteenth Century*, trans. J. S. Hannesson, 1953.

Sandra Ballif Straubhaar

SUGER OF ST. DENIS (C. 1081–1151). Abbot of the royal monastery of St. Denis from 1122, Suger has been credited as both the architect of the Capetian monarchy and the first to employ the Gothic style of architecture. Although scholars have begun to question the extent of these contributions, he was unquestionably an ardent and able administrator and builder. He was author of several works that remain testimonies to his life and times, including a valuable Latin *vita* of *Louis VI.

Suger was born of a very minor knightly family and entered the monastery of St. Denis as an oblate at the age or nine or ten, where he met fellow student the future King Louis VI. In his early twenties, after perhaps additional schooling at the monastery of Benoît-sur-Loire, he embarked on a promising ecclesiastic career: He became secretary to Abbot Adam of St. Denis in 1106, and between 1107 and 1109 he served as provost at monasteries in Normandy and Beauce. King Louis IV sent him to the court of Gelasius II at Maguelonne in the south of France in 1118, and he was later a royal envoy to Pope *Calixtus II in Rome. It was during his stay in Rome that he was named abbot of St. Denis, and the following year he attended the First Lateran Council before returning to take up his abbatial post.

St. Denis was the royal monastery of France; as such, it was a symbol of royal power, but Suger perceived that it had lost stature. In a memoir of his own abbatial administration, *Liber de rebus in administratione sua gestis* (On the Things Done in His Administration), he described how the monastery's lands and revenues had been mismanaged, and he related his struggle not only to recoup its losses but also to more fully exploit its property to increase revenues. He cleared forests and developed agricultural plots, established burgs and churches, and renegotiated rents. He also enforced the monastery's rights against the encroachments of the local nobility.

Suger also determined that St. Denis' church was too dilapidated and small to serve the needs of the monks and the increasing number of pilgrims who visited each year. Between 1135 and 1140, he rebuilt the west façade of the church, and in 1140 he began work on the east end, beginning construction of a new choir. He also started remodeling the nave, but the project was abandoned when he died in 1151. He wrote two short works describing his construction projects, particularly his redecoration of the abbey church: *Ordinatio* (c. 1140–1142) and *Libellus de consecratione ecclesiae sancti Dionysii* (c. 1144–1145). Part of his *De administratione* (1145–1148) also concerns his building projects. Many of the architectural elements he incorporated reflect the evolution from late Romanesque to Gothic style; as a result, St. Denis holds a central place in the history of the development of Gothic architecture. Suger's new church, resplendent as it was with stained glass, splendid hangings, and objects adorned with jewels, reflected his vision of the church as a heavenly symbol on earth, a fitting monument to God and to the saints, particularly Saint Denis.

Suger's role as a statesman was not at odds with his devotion to his monastery. Traditionally, St. Denis and the French monarchy had close ties; from its foundation by the Frankish king *Dagobert in the seventh century, the monastery had been the recipient of royal beneficence, receiving privileges, money, lands, and precious objects. Suger fostered the ties Louis VI had developed at St. Denis as a young pupil, becoming Louis' closest adviser for some twenty years. He effectively aided the king in extending royal dominion and systematizing royal administration, turning the administrative skill he had employed in reforming his monastery to the fortunes of the monarchy. The support of St. Denis, both the monastery and its patron saint, greatly increased the prestige of the Capetian house. And the king's support, in turn, enhanced the wealth and prestige of the royal abbey. Louis VI returned the crown of his father, Philip I, to St. Denis and in 1124 took up the monastery's standard when he left for battle. He also extended additional privileges to St. Denis, and it was Louis who decreed that the kings of France should be buried there. Suger's eulogistic biography of Louis, *Vita Ludovici Grossi regis*, in which Louis is depicted as an ideal Christian monarch, was the first of a long series written by monks of St. Denis to immortalize the Capetian kings.

Suger provided valuable continuity between the reigns of Louis VI and his son *Louis VII. Although he was engrossed with his building projects during Louis VII's turbulent early years as king, he once again took up his role of royal counselor in 1143. When Louis departed for the Second Crusade (1147–1149) against Suger's advice, he appointed Suger regent in his absence. Suger is believed to have written a history of Louis VII, *Historia Ludovici VII*, which exists only in a modified form in the work of a monk of St.-Germain-des-Prés.

As a statesman, Suger worked to strengthen royal power, to improve agriculture, commerce, and trade, and to reform the administration of justice. As abbot, he reformed the liturgy, improved the living conditions and life in general for his monks, and reestablished the prestige of his monastery. He forged new and stronger links between the monastery and the monarchy, enhancing the prestige and power of both. He rebuilt the abbey church into an extraordinary tribute not only to God and to his patron saint but also to his time. It reflects not only his passionate faith but also his creativity and drive. Inscribed in copper-gilt letters on the new doors, he left his own memorial: "For the glory of the church which nurtured and raised him, Suger strove for the glory of the church."

Bibliography: *Abbot Suger on the Abbey Church of Saint-Denis and Its Art Treasures*, ed. and trans. E. Panofsky, 2d ed., 1979; L. Grant, *Abbot Suger of St-Denis: Church and State in Early Twelfth-Century France*, 1998.

Marguerite Ragnow

SVEN I OF DENMARK (FORKBEARD) (D. 1014, R. 987–1014).

King of Denmark and briefly king of England, Sven's ambitious raids and campaigns and involvement in England, Norway, and Sweden mark him as a pivotal figure in medieval Scandinavian and English history.

Early in his life, he revolted against his father, *Harald I Bluetooth Gormsson and claimed the throne of Denmark. With *Óláfr Tryggvason, the future king of Norway, he embarked on raids in England in the 990s and collected the Danegeld. Years later, he engineered an alliance among Eiríkr Hákonarson, a Norwegian leader, King Óláfr Eriksson of Sweden, and himself that successfully defeated Óláfr Tryggvason at the battle of Svold. Thus, he gained overlordship of Norway. After the St. Brice Day massacre of the Danes in England, in 1002, in which Sven's sister and her husband were killed, Sven went on a raid to claim revenge and to win some monetary reparation. In 1013 he returned to England yet again. This time he turned a raid into a conquest as *Æthelred the Unready, who was generally an unpopular monarch, offered little resistance and soon fled the kingdom. Sven's reign as king of England was short-lived; he died on 3 February 1014. In England he was succeeded by his son *Cnut I and in Denmark by Harald II.

Contemporary sources for Sven were not too kind. *Adam of Bremen holds him up as a godless, ruthless ruler who was punished by God for his sins. Modern historians have been a little more favorable as they depict Sven as a nominal Christian king who was tolerant of heathenism, politically astute, and highly ambitious.

Bibliography: G. Jones, *A History of the Vikings*, 1984.

Joseph Carroll

SVEN ESTRIDSEN (C. 1020–1074). The nephew of *Cnut the Great, Sven ruled Denmark from 1047 to 1074, reorganized the Danish bishoprics, and founded the Estrid dynasty.

Sven was the son of Jarl Ulfr and Estrid, the sister of Cnut the Great. He spent a portion of his youth at Cnut's court in England, where he served as a hostage to ensure his father's good faith as Cnut's regent in Denmark. When Cnut murdered Sven's father at Roskilde in 1027, he ordered Sven to Sweden.

Upon Cnut's death in 1035, the Danish kingdom was given to Harthacnut and Norway to Magnús the Good. When Harthacnut died in 1042, Sven had support to become king in both England and Denmark, but he was passed over in favor of *Edward the Confessor in England, and Magnús asserted a claim to the Danish throne. Sven promised allegiance to Magnús, who was better equipped and experienced, but the Danish nobles acclaimed him king in 1043. Magnús promptly invaded the country, and Sven, ill equipped to defend his claim, was forced to flee to Sweden.

Sven fought with both Magnús and his successor, *Harald Hardråde, for the throne of Denmark for twenty years, a conflict that became the subject of several Old Norse sagas. During this time, Sven made several unsuccessful appeals to England for aid and even made himself a vassal of the Holy Roman Emperor *Henry III. Harald was successful in battle but failed to conquer Denmark, and the two rivals finally agreed to recognize each other's sovereignty in 1064. After Harald was killed at Stamford Bridge in 1066, Sven made several tentative attempts at his own invasion of England. In 1069–1070, a force led by his brother Osbeorn sacked York but then lost it again to the Normans. Sailing south, the Danes allied themselves with some Anglo-Saxon noblemen, including Hereward the Wake and Earl Waltheof, who were resisting the Norman occupation at Ely. Together they sacked Peterborough Abbey, but then the Danes took the treasure and a payment from *William I the Conqueror and returned home.

Sven made no further attempts to press his claims to England but contented himself with internal affairs. In 1060, he reorganized the Church government into new bishoprics, and he labored to free Denmark from the ecclesiastical control of the archbishoprics in Bremen and Canterbury, a goal accomplished only after his death with the foundation of the archbishopric at Lund. Sven was clearly a thoughtful strategist and a clever politician. He was respected for his knowledge of history and geography and advised *Adam of Bremen on these subjects in the composition of his *History of the Archbishops of Hamburg-Bremen.*

Bibliography: Adam of Bremen, *History of the Archbishops of Hamburg-Bremen*, trans. F. J. Tschan, 1959; P. Lauring, *A History of Denmark*, trans. D. Hohnen, 3d ed., 1995; M. Swanton, trans., *Anglo-Saxon Chronicle*, 1996.

Timothy Jones

SYLVESTER II, POPE (GERBERT OF AURILLAC) (C. 945–1003, PONTIFICATE 999–1003). Monk, arithmetician, statesman, and first French pope, Gerbert of Aurillac introduced Arabic mathematics to the West, and his collected letters uniquely document ecclesiastical politics about A.D. 1000.

Gerbert was born to free peasants living near Aurillac in south-central France about 945. At an early age, he entered the monastery of St. Géraud in Aurillac, where he studied Latin grammar and became a favorite of its abbot. In 967, Borel, duke of the Spanish March (Catalonia), arrived at Aurillac, and when he left, Gerbert accompanied him to further his education. In Spain, Gerbert studied with Hatto, bishop of Vich, who carefully trained him in mathematics. Because Gerbert later used Gobar numerals in his teaching, it is assumed that he also studied at a Muslim school—either Saragossa or Cordova, although the monastery of Santa Maria de Ripoll also incorporated Muslim mathematics in its curriculum. About 970, Borel went to Rome, and his delegation included Gerbert, who so impressed John XIII with his knowledge of arithmetic that the pope asked Borel to send Gerbert to Emperor *Otto I's court. In 972, Gerbert met Garamnus, archdeacon of the cathedral school at Rheims, who quickly recognized his talent and asked him to become *scholasticus* for his cathedral school. Gerbert accepted and moved to Rheims.

As *scholasticus* of Rheims, Gerbert sought to revise and expand the curriculum according to *Cassiodorus' outlines for study. In dialectics, he taught the *logica vetus*; in rhetoric, he used pagan writers, especially Cicero, as examples of accomplished oration. But Gerbert's real innovations occurred in his teaching of the quadrivium. Arithmetic had long been taught as an abstract study, one concerned with the properties of numbers, for example, that 6 is the perfect number. Under Gerbert, this theoretical study gave way to practical calculations like multiplication. He introduced Hindu-Arabic numerals, and reintroduced the abacus to Western mathematics. When teaching the proper use of the abacus, Gerbert emphasized the importance of decimal position in multiplication, a practice not then widespread. Gerbert also incorporated practical data in his geometry classes, using actual land surveys for his problems and models. For his astrology classes, he crafted mobiles and spheres to show the relative positions of the planets and stars. In music, he began the practice of establishing proper pitch with a monochord. Gerbert's enthusiasm, his innovative teaching, and his commitment to practical applications for learning resulted in Rheims attracting large numbers of students.

In 983, Emperor *Otto II, formerly Gerbert's student, placed Gerbert as abbot of St. Columban of Bobbio, a strategic site along the Po Valley. As abbot, Gerbert sought to implement Cluniac reforms, causing resentment among the community. His strict interpretation of land laws was resented as well by powerful landowners who had acquired *libelli* leases for much of the abbey's property. When Otto II died in 984, Gerbert was left without a champion in Italy, and he discretely returned to Rheims. From his experiences at Bobbio, however, Gerbert realized the importance of politics, and at Rheims he began to take an active interest in public affairs. With Archbishop Adalbero, Gerbert helped establish *Hugh Capet on the throne of the West Franks, effectively ending the Carolingian dynasty; they also worked to secure *Otto III's succession against a rival claim by Henry the Wrangler of Bavaria. After Adalbero's death in 989, political intrigue enveloped Rheims. Arnulf, the new archbishop, opened the city's gates to Carolingian loyalists; this treason led to Arnulf's deposition, and Gerbert was named his successor. Papal opposition to Arnulf's deposition, however, led to the excommunication of all who took part, including Gerbert. As Gerbert journeyed to Rome in 996 to protest his excommunication, John XV died suddenly. Otto's cousin was elevated to the Holy See (Gregory V), and he chose not to continue the quarrel with Gerbert. As Gerbert returned to Rheims, Hugh Capet died; Robert, Hugh's successor, showed Gerbert no favor, and political life at Rheims became untenable. In 998, the archbishopric of Ravenna fell vacant, and Otto appointed Gerbert. After the death of Pope Gregory a year later, Otto orchestrated Gerbert's election as Pope Sylvester II.

Sylvester's ties to Otto resulted in close cooperation between empire and Holy See. They devised a plan that would return the seat of empire to Rome, reform the papal hierarchy, and reestablish the power of seven palatine judges to consecrate the emperor and help elect the pope. Otto's death in 1002 prevented this program from being implemented, but Rome nonetheless extended its influence during Sylvester's papacy: The first archbishoprics in Poland were established;

episcopal sees in Hungary were created; and King *Óláfr Tryggvason was ordered to substitute the Roman alphabet for the runic if Norway were to be considered a Christian nation.

After Gerbert's death in 1003, legends connected his name to necromancy because he studied in Muslim Spain and invented curious machines as teaching devices. Other legends of Gerbert's diabolism are reported by *William of Malmesbury, who believed that Gerbert used magic to enchant his superiors. Far from proving that Gerbert was an enchanter, his election as pope shows that a dedicated man of acclaimed talents could reach the highest ecclesiastical office, even if he were from peasant stock. Gerbert's letters show a sophisticated grasp of theory and practice—in politics and schoolroom alike. From the example of his position as *scholasticus* of Rheims, we see how an outstanding teacher could attract large numbers of students and increase a school's prestige, even as official patronage for learning was diminished. Gerbert's teaching inspired students to devote themselves to learning; among his students were future abbots, founders of schools, and Pope Gregory VI.

Bibliography: R. L. Allen, "Gerbert, Pope Sylvester II," *English Historical Review*, n.s., 7 (1892): 625–668; H. P. Lattin, ed. and trans., *The Letters of Gerbert with His Papal Privileges as Sylvester II*, 1961.

James Countryman

T

TEMPIER, STEPHEN (D. 1279). Bishop of Paris, he is best known for his Condemnation of 1277, a list in which he pronounced 219 propositions in philosophy and theology to be heretical.

Very little is known of the life of Stephen (or Étienne) Tempier. He was born at Orléans; the date of his birth is unknown. He was a master of theology at the University of Paris for some time, serving as a chancellor of the university in 1263. He became bishop of Paris in 1268. He died on 3 September 1279.

Tempier is best known for his efforts to eradicate false teaching from the University of Paris. In 1270, he issued a statement condemning thirteen philosophical errors associated with Averroism. This proclamation, however, was overshadowed by his Condemnation of 1277, in which he condemned 219 propositions drawn from the writings of the University of Paris faculty. Those who taught or affirmed such propositions were to be excommunicated.

The Condemnation followed a request from Pope John XXI to inquire into possible heresy at the university; since the pope's letter was written in January and the list was issued in March, Tempier was probably already working on the project when the pope made his request. Tempier did not compile the list alone but engaged several masters of theology, including *Henry of Ghent, to assist him by examining selected works and drawing up lists of errors. His compilation of the propositions appears haphazard; he did not edit out propositions selected by more than one master, nor did he group similar propositions under category headings. Thus, the list is repetitive and disorganized. Nevertheless, it is also comprehensive and, for the most part, consistent. All the condemned propositions reflect the application of Greek philosophical concepts, mostly Aristotelian, to questions of theology in such a way as to conflict with orthodox Christian doctrine. Among the propositions condemned were assertions regarding human beings such as the view that all human beings share a common intellect so that individuals are incapable of understanding or free will, as well as assertions about God, such as the view that God knows only himself, cannot know individuals, and acts by necessity.

Tempier did not name specific masters in his condemnation, and scholars debate whether he intended to target specific propounders of Aristotelian philosophy. Certainly *Siger of Brabant and Thomas *Aquinas had included a number of the objectionable propositions in their teachings. Indeed, in 1325, shortly after Thomas Aquinas became a saint of the Roman Catholic Church, those articles of Tempier's condemnation that appeared to apply to Aquinas' teaching were retracted by Stephen of Bourret, bishop of Paris.

The Condemnation of 1277 is a watershed event in the history of the relationship between medieval theology and philosophy. An explicit differentiation between theology and philosophy became more pronounced. The focus of theology changed, as Henry of Ghent, *John Duns Scotus, and others sought to emphasize God's sovereignty and freedom and to redefine the relationship between God and human beings. The focus of philosophy changed as well, with philosophical inquiry turning away from the dangerous topic of theology and delving more deeply into questions concerning the natural world. In addition, the rejection of pure Aristotelianism led to experimentation with other techniques and approaches to studying the natural world. Hence, the Condemnation of 1277 is also a crucial point in the origin of modern science.

Tempier's condemnations marked a turning point in medieval intellectual history, affecting the direction of philosophy, theology, and science well into the modern period.

Bibliography: J.M.M.H. Thijssen, *Censure and Heresy at the University of Paris 1200–1400*, 1998.

Anne Collins Smith and Owen M. Smith

THEODORA I (C. 497–548). The wife of the Roman Emperor *Justinian, Theodora Augusta served as an adviser to her husband and may have influenced some legislation favorable to women.

She is a major figure in the work of the historian *Procopius, who was her contemporary. In addition to his *History*, he wrote a *Secret History*, which was published only in the sixteenth century. This latter work contains much about Theodora of a scurrilous nature; but it is well known that Procopius hated her, and so the problem for the modern reader is always how much to believe. Today's historians must wrestle with this problem, and their choice of what to repeat about Theodora may tell us more about them than about her.

She was apparently of lowly origins, the adopted daughter of an employee in the Hippodrome, a sort of sports arena used for chariot racing. She is said to have been an actress, which at that time probably meant that she was also a prostitute. She is described as striking and beautiful. A number of ancient statues are said to represent her. She is certainly depicted in a famous mosaic in the church of San Vitale in Ravenna, Italy, which faces an equally famous mosaic of Justinian. She became the mistress of an administrator and accompanied him to Africa (modern Libya), where they soon parted company; she made her way back to Constantinople, after a stop in Alexandria, Egypt, where she became a Monophysite, a variety of Christianity whose adherents were somewhat persecuted in the capital but quite powerful in Egypt and Palestine. On her return to Constantinople, she met Justinian, and they were married in the mid-520s. Soon after their marriage, he succeeded his adopted uncle Justin as emperor. He gave her his palace Hormisdas as a personal residence and also settled on her large sums of money.

Their reign is sometimes described as a partnership, and not only by Procopius, for Justinian seems to have consulted her frequently. On the famous occasion of the Nika riots in Constantinople in 532, when he seemed to think that all was lost and considered flight, she supposedly stiffened his resolve by pointing out that rather than flee he should fight to the death, for, as she said, "Purple is the best winding-sheet." She may well have been responsible for the improved fortune of the Monophysites, who captured several bishoprics during her reign.

Often described as the first feminist, with all the shifting meanings of that term, she seems to have taken an interest in the plight of women in the Roman Empire and to have donated time and money to improving their lot. She may have been the driving force behind some legislation favorable to women, especially in the 530s. She also helped found charitable institutions for women. She was a good friend to some of her husband's officers and their wives, but she could also be an implacable enemy and was reportedly responsible for the fall of the chief financial officer of the empire, John of Cappadocia. There are many scurrilous tales about her, more or less repeated by the various modern biographers; but her husband never abandoned her and seems to have depended on her in certain delicate situations: He would send an official letter, but she would send an oral instruction that revealed what the emperor really wanted done. On the other hand, she sometimes acted independently and may, for example, have been involved in the murder of Queen *Amalswintha in Gothic Italy and the deposition of Pope Silverius. She arranged the marriage of her niece Sophia to a nephew of Justinian, Justin; and this couple eventually became emperor and empress in their turn.

She was buried in the Church of the Holy Apostles in Constantinople. It is reported that Justinian was not as decisive, and not as successful after her death, and this may argue that he missed her advice. No historian ever reported that he was unfaithful to her, either before or after her death.

Bibliography: A. Bridge, *Theodora: Portrait in a Byzantine Landscape,* 1978; R. Browning, *Justinian and Theodora,* 1971; C. Diehl, *Theodora, Empress of Byzantium,* trans. S. R. Rosenbaum, 1972; L. Garland, *Byzantine Empresses: Women and Power in Byzantium,* AD 527–1204, 1999.

F.R.P. Akehurst

THEODORE OF CANTERBURY (THEODORE OF TARSUS) (602–690).

A monk trained in the East and living in Rome, Theodore was consecrated archbishop of Canterbury in 668, and upon his arrival in England a year later, he rigorously reorganized the Anglo-Saxon Church and established an important school in Canterbury with fellow scholar and churchman Hadrian.

Theodore was a native of Tarsus in Cicilia (in Asia Minor), and as a monk, he was well educated in Latin and Greek literatures, both secular and religious, and trained as an exegetical scholar. He was living in Rome when the English priest Wigheard from Canterbury arrived to seek consecration as its new archbishop. At the time, a severe plague had stricken many of England's leading churchmen, and when Wigheard died of the plague in 667, Pope Vitalian decided to make the appointment himself. He first chose Hadrian the African, but Hadrian doubted his ability and suggested Theodore, who was consecrated in 668. The two set off to England with the famed Northumbrian monk Benedict Biscop, and Theodore arrived in Canterbury in 669 and immediately set to work.

While still strong in the lower orders, the English Church lacked leadership and was in a state of chaos. Theodore made many appointments, and at the Synod of Hertford in 673, he reorganized the Church into smaller dioceses and made them dependent on the central authority of Canterbury. With the help of Hadrian, Theodore also established a school at Canterbury, which trained many great scholars of the age (like *Aldhelm) and laid the foundations for England's cultural achievements in the early Middle Ages. The great scholar and historian *Bede wrote sixty years later of the glorious learning and achievements of Theodore's prelacy, which ended when Theodore died at age eighty-eight in 690.

Bibliography: M. Lapidge, ed., *Archbishop Theodore: Commemorative Studies on His Life and Influence*, 1995.

Matthew Hussey

THEODORE OF TARSUS. *See* THEODORE OF CANTERBURY.

THEODORIC THE OSTROGOTH, THE GREAT (C. 454–526).

King of the Ostrogoths, Theodoric came to rule Italy in 493. The rule of law, religious toleration, and peace-weaving alliances with Burgundians, Franks, Visigoths, and other Germanic peoples marked his thirty-three-year reign.

Theodoric became king on the death of his father, Theodemir. The Ostrogoths, once rulers of territory from the Baltic to the Black Sea, having been defeated by the Huns, attempted to regain their land and power through uneasy ties to the Byzantine Empire. As a pledge of alliance, Theodoric was held hostage in Constantinople until the age of seventeen and later had a precarious relationship with the emperor Zeno. To put an end to Ostrogothic demands for money and land, Zeno encouraged Theodoric to invade Italy and oust Odawacer, who was ruler at the time. After he defeated Odawacer in battle, the two declared a truce and agreed to a joint rule. It was in 493, during this truce, that Theodoric murdered Odawacer, had his family and followers massacred, and made himself king of Italy, with Ravenna as his capital. He was ostensibly governing Italy in the name of Zeno, who limited his powers to some extent.

Nonetheless, he established a code of laws, which were administered by the Italians, although military service was restricted to Ostrogoths. Theodoric had developed a great admiration for Roman civilization during his youth in Constantinople. Like other Ostrogoths, an Arian Christian, he insisted on freedom of religion for the Catholic Italians. He aimed for peace and order, racial harmony, and the outlawing of oppression and violence that, for him, were *civilitas*. In part to establish this kind of order, he arranged marriages of one daughter to Alaric II the Visigoth and of another to Sigismund the Burgundian, while he himself married a sister of *Clovis. In addition, he improved the lives of the people through extensive public works and support of the arts.

In spite of his just and productive reign, there remained Italian resentment of what was perceived as alien rule. The emperor *Justinian in the East was eager to claim the Western Empire and found support among some highly placed officials in the service of Theodoric. The senator *Boethius, who was to have such profound influence on the intellectual life of the later Middle Ages and beyond, was one of those accused, along with his father-in-law Symmachus, of treason. During the imprisonment that resulted from what Boethius maintained was a false accusation, he wrote *The Consolation of Philosophy*. Both Boethius and Symmachus were among others executed as traitors, an act for which Theodoric later expressed regret.

On the death of Theodoric from dysentery in 526, his daughter *Amalswintha took the throne as regent for her ten-year-old son Athalaric. A splendid mausoleum was erected for Theodoric in Ravenna. Shortly after his death, however, Byzantium invaded and laid waste to Italy. In 540, the tomb was desecrated and the bones scattered; it later became the Church of Santa Maria della Rotonda. Soon after, the Ostrogoths ceased to exist as a people.

Germanic and Icelandic legends know Theodoric as Dietrich von Bern. He may also be the character named in the Old English poems *Deor* and *Widsith*, but this is uncertain. Some details of his reign are found in the writing of *Cassiodorus, who was his secretary, and in the letters of Sidonius Apollinaris.

Bibliography: J. Moorhead, *Theodoric in Italy*, 1992.

Patricia Silber

THEODULF OF ORLÉANS (C. 750/760–821). A bishop and writer of early-ninth-century France and a member of *Charlemagne's court, Theodulf's writings include poetry on sacred and secular topics, theological works, and exhortations to reform.

There is little historical information about the life of Theodulf of Orléans. He was probably born in Spain between 750 and 760, apparently of Gothic descent.

By 794, he had become a member of the court of Charlemagne, joining a group of intellectuals that included the renowned scholar *Alcuin.

Charlemagne appointed Theodulf abbot of Fleury and bishop of Orléans sometime between 794 and 798. As bishop, he encouraged reform among the clergy and the laity and promoted the establishment of parochial schools. He was also appointed a royal ambassador to southern France. After being implicated in a conspiracy involving Bernard, king of Italy, in 818, he was deposed by *Louis the Pious and exiled to Angers, where he died in 821. It is possible, but not certain, that he was murdered.

At the request of Charlemagne, Theodulf composed *De spiritu sancto* (On the Holy Spirit), defending the doctrine of double procession (the procession of the Holy Spirit from both the Father and the Son, rather than from the Father alone). This doctrine, which is central to the *filioque* controversy, had been debated at the Synod of Gentilly, held near Paris in 767; this Synod was the first occurrence of contention about the issue in the Western Church.

As a writer, however, Theodulf is best remembered for his poems, especially the still-popular hymn "All Glory, Laud and Honor to Thee Redeemer King." He also wrote poetry on secular topics, including letters in the form of poems that provide vivid portraits of court life. As a result of his observations in southern France, he wrote *Versus contra iudices* (Verses against the Judges), a work in poetic form encouraging reform both in the workings of the law courts and in the personal morality of the judges. Theodulf also wrote prose works on Church and theological matters such as baptism, the Creed, and the Mass. He attempted an emendation of the Vulgate text of the Bible by comparing it with Hebrew texts and the Septuagint.

Theodulf is among the finest poets of the Carolingian era; his sacred poems are still sung as hymns, while his secular poems provide valuable detail about life in the Frankish court. He exhorted clergy, laity, and secular judges to lead more moral and spiritual lives. The doctrine of double procession that he defended became official Church doctrine but ultimately led to the schism between the Roman Catholic and Orthodox churches in the eleventh century.

Bibliography: G. E. McCracken and A. Cabaniss, *Early Medieval Theology*, 1957.

Anne Collins Smith and Owen M. Smith

THEOPHANO (C. 960–991). Theophano was the daughter of Constantine Skleros and Sophia Phokas, niece of Nikephoros II Phokas. Not the purple-born princess the Ottonians had originally sought, Theophano married *Otto II and was crowned empress in Rome, Easter Sunday, 14 April 972. The birth of her first child, Adelheid, in 975, was followed by four others (including *Otto III's twin sister, dead in infancy). Her original dowry of the Byzantine lands in Italy theoretically made her husband master of the peninsula, but Otto never ruled even Capua-Benevento in any real sense. Nevertheless, the marriage signaled Byzantine acceptance of the Saxons as emperors of the West, and Theophano proved devoted to her husband's interests, traveling with him during his unceasing campaigns and using her ecclesiastical patronage to block Byzantine expansion in Poland.

When Otto II died, Henry the Wrangler seized his three-year-old son and claimed guardianship over him and then the crown. In June 984, he returned the boy to his mother; in 985 he exchanged his claim to the crown for Bavaria. Theophano, until her own death at Nijmegen, her son's birthplace, shared the guardianship with her mother-in-law *Adelaide but effectively sidelined her. In his wedding diploma, Otto had spoken of "the bond of legitimate marriage and the joint control of the empire." Theophano took him at his word. Byzantine influence on Ottonian art was once attributed almost entirely to the result of Theophano's marriage; it is now understood as the result of continuous Ottonian interest in things Greek.

Bibliography: A. Davids, *The Empress Theophano: Byzantium and the West at the Turn of the Last Millenium*, 1995.

Helen Conrad-O'Briain

THEUTBERGA (838/843–875). Daughter of Count Boso the Elder and Engeltrude, his wife, she was the much-maligned, childless wife of *Lothar II of Lotharingia. Lothar married her for political reasons in 855; by 858, he had begun attempts at divorce in order to marry his concubine *Waldrada, by whom he had a son. When Theutberga refused his demand for divorce, he accused her of premarital incest with her brother Hubert, lay abbot of St. Maurice-in-Valais, the charge of which she successfully cleared herself at a trial by ordeal. Lothar then imprisoned her until she agreed to enter a convent. However, nothing but divorce or annulment would allow him to remarry; therefore on 15 February 860 at a gathering of Frankish bishops and lay nobles she was forced to confess to incest and abortion. She then fled to the kingdom of *Charles II the Bald, who gave her a convent, but she did not take the veil. Within five years, Lothar was forced to take her back, and she was crowned queen in Lotharingia.

In her struggles with Lothar and his bishops, Theutberga had the backing of her powerful noble family. Her brother Hubert was virtual ruler of lands adjacent to Lothar's; a second brother was a count in Italy. For political reasons, she also received support from her husband's uncles. Popes *Nicholas I and Hadrian II fought her divorce on grounds of both marital indissolubility and the superiority of papal courts, while *Hincmar, archbishop of Rheims, wrote much on this particular case and marriage in general, as the Church began to move to gain control of marital cases.

Theutberga died in 875 at the convent of Avenay in Hincmar's diocese of Rheims. Both Lothar and Waldrada had predeceased her by many years.

Bibliography: S. F. Wemple, *Women in Frankish Society: Marriage and the Cloister, 500 to 900*, 1981.

Janice R. Norris

TREVET, NICHOLAS (C. 1258–AFTER 1334). An English Dominican and scholar, Trevet was a commentator on classical and theological works and a chronicler.

Trevet was born in England around 1258, the son of Sir Thomas Trevet, who served as an itinerant justice for *Henry III and *Edward I. Trevet joined the Dominican Order and was at the order's priory in Oxford by November 1297. From 1303 to 1307, he likely taught theology as a regent master in Oxford. From 1307 to 1314, he traveled to Italy and spent some time at the Dominican convent in Paris. In 1314–1315, he had a second stint as regent master in Oxford, and a papal letter confirms that he was lector of theology at the Dominicans' London convent in 1324. Trevet must have lived at least to 1334, because in his *Chronicles* he says that Pope John XXII (1316–1334) was pope for nineteen years.

Trevet's reputation rests on his commentaries on theological and classical works and on his historical writings. His earliest commentary was on *Boethius' *Consolation of Philosophy*, which had the widest circulation of all of his works. He also commented on several books of the Old Testament, including Genesis, Exodus, Leviticus, and the Psalms. In fact, he achieved such a solid reputation for these commentaries that several high-ranking Church officials asked him to write commentaries on selected works for them. Pope John XXII commissioned a commentary on Livy's *Roman History*, the first commentary on Livy to survive; Cardinal Nicholas Prato asked Trevet for a commentary on Seneca's *Tragedies*. The Livy commentary was especially popular in Italy in the early fourteenth century (it was read by Petrarch), as was another commentary on Augustine's *City of God*. Trevet was able to comment on such a wide selection of authors mainly because he used the same method for all genres; for each work, he discussed the authorship, place and date of composition, the subject, and the author's intention in a prologue, then moved through the text, explaining grammatical constructions and classical allusions. He did not feel obliged to discuss a work's historical or literary value. The popularity of his commentaries attests to the growing interest in classical studies in the fourteenth century.

From 1320, Trevet turned his obvious historical interests to writing chronicles of his own. He composed three important historical works: the *Annals of Six Kings of England* (c. 1320–1323), written in Latin and covering the reigns of *Stephen of England to Edward I; the *Historia*, a universal history in Latin from the Creation of the world up to the birth of Christ; and the *Chronicles*, a second universal history of the world from Creation until 1332. Composed in Anglo-Norman, it was dedicated to Princess Mary of Woodstock, daughter of Edward I. The *Annals* is a particularly useful source for the reign of Edward I, for which Trevet was an eyewitness.

Bibliography: R. J. Dean, "Nicholas Trevet, Historian," in *Medieval Language and Literature: Essays Presented to Richard William Hunt*, ed. J.J.G. Alexander and M. T. Gibson, 1976.

Kimberly Rivers

TROTULA (FL. LATE ELEVENTH CENTURY). A semilegendary woman who taught medicine at Salerno in the late eleventh or early twelfth century, she is credited with a gynecological text, *Passionibus mulierium curandorum* or *Trotula Major*, and with a guide to physical appearance, *De ornatu mulierum* or *Trotula Minor*; both texts were widely translated and used throughout Europe during the Middle Ages.

According to some, Trotula was married to Johannes Platearius, a physician, and was the mother of medical writers Mathias and Johannes, as well as holding a chair of medicine at the university at Salerno. The books attributed to her described and prescribed for diseases of women as well as dealing with more general subjects ranging from deafness to hemorrhoids. The work that came to be known as *Trotula Major* contains information on menstruation, conception, childbirth, and such contributors to healthful living as diet and exercise. It cites among other authorities Galen, Hippocrates, and Dioscorides. The *Trotula Minor*'s focus, however, is on cosmetic issues rather than on medical treatment. Among other pieces of advice in *De ornatu* are recipes for restoring the appearance of virginity to a woman who has had sexual intercourse. A number of manuscripts of both Trotula texts survive in many languages, including four in Middle English.

Although a strong tradition placed women among the healers at Salerno, an early and influential center for the study of medicine, many question whether the *Trotula* titles refer to an actual person. Three positions on whether Trotula really existed have emerged over the centuries. The first sees her as a well-attested member of the Ruggiero family, who died in 1097 and was honored with a funeral procession that stretched for two miles. The Ruggiero connection was posited in the seventeenth century, and the funeral added in the twentieth. No genuine evidence exists for any of this. Another theory that emerged in the twentieth century is based on a lost manuscript of medical texts; it claims that the famed physician was actually a man named Trottus. Since the theory stems from abbreviations found in a lost manuscript, there is little reason to accept it. The third and most recent position denies the existence of such a person altogether, maintaining that *trot* is a frequently found term referring—often derogatorily—to an old woman. Examples of unflattering references are found in Gower's *Mirour de l'Omme*, in Juan Ruiz's *Libro de Buen Amor*, and in the *Roman de la Rose*. The appearance of the name *Trotula* in the contents of Jankyn's book in the Wife of Bath's Prologue (*Canterbury Tales* III.677), however, confers some authority on Trotula by virtue of the other names cited: Tertullian, Crisippus, and *Héloïse. The most compelling case for Trotula's having been an actual person is found in an early-thirteenth-century manuscript containing a collection of Salernitan medical texts. Located in Madrid, this manuscript contains a work identified as *Practica secundum Trotum*. It begins with a prescription for bringing on menstruation and continues with both gynecological remedies and more general ones for many other health problems.

The sense of authority associated with Trotula almost certainly comes from the widespread knowledge of the *Trotula Major* and *Minor* as sources of medical advice. Nearly 100 manuscripts from the thirteenth to the fifteenth centuries indicate that at least some of the exemplars were meant for household use. The introduction to the *Passionibus*, for example, states that its prescriptions are meant for women to use and to share with other women who cannot read, because it is too difficult for women to discuss their ailments with a male physician. Later commentators claim that the contents of the texts are obviously the work of a woman, since a man could not have such knowledge of the female body. On the other hand are those who assert that no woman would be so immodest as to write explicitly about sexual matters.

Although variations exist among so many manuscripts, the treatments prescribed share an almost modern emphasis on the importance of hygiene, diet and exercise, and avoidance of stress as essential to good health. Especially unusual for the time is the absence of astrological calculation as a diagnostic tool. Among other assertions in Trotula is that failure to conceive may be as much the fault of the man as of the woman.

There is no doubt that women were involved in medical practice, particularly in Salerno, and in more capacities than that of midwife. There was also at the time a growing tendency to demand university credentials for the practice of medicine and to restrict these credentials to men. The result was a campaign of disparagement of women as physicians and, ultimately, charges of witchcraft against women who practiced medicine.

Bibliography: A. Barratt, ed., *Women's Writing in Middle English*, 1992; J. F. Benton, "Trotula, Women's Problems, and the Professionalization of Medicine in the Middle Ages," *Bulletin of the History of Medicine* 59.1 (1985): 30–53.

Patricia Silber

ÞORLÁKR ÞORHALLSSON (1133–1193). Declared as Iceland's first saint by the Althing in 1198, Þorlákr served as bishop of Skálaholt from 1178 until his death in 1193. Þorlákr, who had been abbot of two monasteries before being consecrated bishop, was known for his ascetic lifestyle, his generosity to the poor, his insistence on the celibacy of the clergy, and the sanctity of marriage. While Þorlákr's clash with Jón Loptsson over control of Iceland's proprietary churches was unsuccessful, it is credited with beginning the separation of power between Iceland's clergy and laity.

When Þorlákr was a child, his parents sent him to study at Oddi with the priest Eyjólfr, son of Sæmundr the Wise. After being ordained a priest, Þorlákr left to study abroad for six years, in Paris and at Lincoln. Upon his return, he lived with his family, who wanted him to marry. He broke his engagement off when, according to his *vita* (*Þorlákrs saga*), he was visited in a dream by an angel and joined the monastery at Kirkby (Kirkjaboe). He remained there until he left to found and become abbot of Iceland's first Augustinian monastery, at Þickby (Þykkvaboer). At thirty-five, Þorlákr left Þickby to become the abbot of

Wer (Ver). In 1174, he moved to Skálaholt when he was chosen to become the successor to the aging bishop Kloengr. When Kloengr died in 1176, Þorlákr traveled to the archdiocese of Nidaros in Norway to be consecrated. Although King Magnús initially opposed his consecration, Þorlákr was eventually consecrated bishop of Skálaholt on 2 July 1178 by Archbishop Eysteinn.

As bishop of Skálaholt, Þorlákr sought to institute Archbishop Eysteinn's ecclesiastical policies, which included an insistence upon the celibacy of the clergy, an end to the keeping of concubines by the laity, and an end to the proprietary church system, which was a system whereby wealthy landowners would build and oversee their own churches. Under this system, not only would the landowners keep half of their church's income, but they would appoint their own priests. Under Eysteinn's policies, while the landowners would still administer and make money from their churches, these churches would be under the authority of the Church. Þorlákr's institution of these policies, while first successful, brought him into conflict with Jón Loptsson, Iceland's most powerful chieftain. Their clash was not only over control of proprietary churches but also over Ragnheiðr Þorhallsdottir, who was both Jón's concubine and Þorlákr's sister. While Þorlákr lost the battle over the authority of the proprietary churches, Jón Loptsson eventually conceded on Ragnheiðr and arranged a marriage for her. Þorlákr died on 23 December 1193.

In the years following his death, many miracles were attributed to Þorlákr, who is attributed to have healed the sick, helped find lost items, protected sailors from storms, and cured livestock. These miracles were gathered into a book and read at the Althing in 1198 by Bishop Páll Jónsson, Þorlákr's successor and nephew, where he was declared Iceland's first saint.

Bibliography: G. F. Guðmundsson, *Þorlákur helgi: Life, Work, and Influence of St. Thorlák (1133–1193), Patron Saint of the Icelandic People*, 1993; "Thorláks saga helga," in *Origines Islandicae*, vol. I, trans. G. Vigfússon and F. Y. Powell, 1905.

John Paul Walter

U

ULRICH VON TÜRHEIM (C. 1210–C. 1260). Known for his continuations of *Gottfried von Strassburg's *Tristan* and *Wolfram von Eschenbach's *Willehalm* (*Rennewart*), Ulrich possibly composed the *Cligès* fragment mentioned by Rudolf von Ems (*Wilhelm von Orlens*). Records of the bishop and Cathedral of Augsburg document Ulrich's name between 1236 and 1244, though it is uncertain that this individual is the poet. Ulrich worked in the Swabian court of Henry VII and Conrad IV, sons of Holy Roman Emperor *Frederick II. Conrad IV patronized the *Willehalm* continuation. Other facts surrounding the poet are obscure.

Ulrich's continuation begins precisely where Gottfried's formulation ends. In his love for the Blond Isolde, Tristan has failed to consummate his marriage with Kaedin's sister Isolde, leaving the Arundel family up in arms. Tristan and his brother-in-law return to Tintajel to substantiate that Isolde the Blond is really the more beautiful woman. She wrongly attributes unfaithfulness to Tristan, who appears as a leper, and has him beaten. When he returns to Arundel, Tristan eventually consummates his marriage to Isolde of the Whitehands. He is mortally wounded while assisting Kaedin in the latter's own love affair, underscoring the disastrous results of immoral love.

Seeking her curative powers, Tristan sends for the Blond Isolde; a white sail signals her presence, black that she has not come. Isolde does arrive, but Isolde of the Whitehands purposely deceives Tristan, and he dies disconsolate. Upon discovering this, the Blond Isolde expires upon his grave. Symbolic of the couple's love, King Marke buries them in separate marble sarcophagi, planting a rose tree over Tristan's grave and a grapevine over Isolde's, which intertwine inseparably in perpetuity.

After 1243, Ulrich continued Wolfram von Eschenbach's *Willehalm* in *Rennewart*. Extant in forty manuscripts, this work consists of 36,500 lines. Fourteen additional renderings bring it together in a *Willehalm*-cycle following Ulrich von dem Türlin's *Arabel*, an introduction to *Willehalm*, and the *Willehalm* proper. *Rennewart* tells of this character's return to Orense, following the battle of Aliscans, and relates the important events of his life. When he suffers the loss of his wife Alise in his son's birth, Rennewart withdraws in sorrow to a cloister. Malefer is kidnapped and taken to his father's Saracen enemies, Terramer and his son Tibalt. Ultimately, Rennewart returns to fight for the Christians, facing Malefer in a duel. When the combatants recognize each other, Malefer becomes a Christian, the Saracens flee, the son succeeds his father, and Rennewart reenters his cloister. When again the Saracens return, Rennewart unsuccessfully attempts a reconciliation between Willehalm's wife Kyburg (Gyburg) and her ex-father-in-law, Terramer. Once again in his cloister, Rennewart dies in holiness.

Ulrich is probably best known for his *Tristan* completion, though the bulk of the scanty critical research pertains to *Rennewart*. He unsuccessfully attempted to imitate Gottfried's artistry and echoed numerous motifs from the *Tristrant* of Eilhart von Oberg. In the fifteenth century, the cycle was reworked in prose.

Bibliography: E. K. Busse, *Ulrich von Türheim*, 1913.

Kristine K. Sneeringer

'UMAR KHAYYĀM (OMAR) (1048–1131).

Esteemed Muslim mathematician, astronomer, philosopher, physician, and poet, Ghiyāth al-Dīn Abu'l-Fath 'Umar ibn Ibrāhīm al-Khayyāmī is famous for his scientific achievements, most notably his reform of the Persian calendar in 1079, an important book on algebra, and his poetry.

Born in the great medieval Persian city of Nīshāpūr, 'Umar Khayyam received a complete education in both the humanistic and exact sciences. He spent most of his life in the city of his birth, and his tomb is to be found there today. Although we know little about his early life, it is related that as a young student he excelled in the study of geometry, mathematics, and astronomy. It was in the latter two fields where he would produce the most lasting influence. The story of the "three-friends" made popular by Fitzgerald is to be rejected as pure legend. By the late 1060s, the young 'Umar found himself in Samarqand, where he composed his famous *Algebra* under the patronage of the chief judge (*qadi*) of the city, and also enjoyed the praise of the Qarakhanid ruler Shams al-Mulk (r. 1068–1080).

In 1073–1074, 'Umar Khayyām entered the service of the Seljuq Sultan Malik Shāh (r. 1073–1092) under the aegis of the powerful Seljuq vizier Nizām al-Mulk. He was appointed to head a council of eminent scientists in the reformation of the Persian calendar and the construction of an observatory at Isfahan. The new calendar, the "Jalālī," was completed in 1079 and turned out to be more accurate than the Gregorian calendar; it is still in use in Iran today. Khayyām actively participated in the learned circles surrounding the Seljuq court, although he was not a man without controversy. In fact, it is related that a number of his intellectual peers, including the great al-*Ghazālī, disliked him, and he was denounced on more than one occasion as a libertine and freethinker, although among the scientific elite he enjoyed a great deal of prestige and was in constant demand as a teacher and lecturer.

Although ʿUmar Khayyām maintained friendly relations with his royal patron Malik Shāh, he seems to have fallen into disfavor under the sultan's successor Sanjar (r. 1118–1157). Shortly after Sanjar's accession, Khayyām performed the pilgrimage and thereafter returned to his native Nīshāpūr, remaining there but for brief sojourns to Balkh and Marv. As with his early life, biographical information about his later activities is scarce. One of the few events recorded during this time relates to a weather prediction that he was commissioned to make for the Seljuq sultan in the winter of 1114–1115.

Khayyām was a prolific writer, but only a fraction of what he wrote is extant today. Overshadowing all else is Khayyām's *Algebra*, which contains solutions to and a detailed classification of geometric and algebraic equations of the third degree and discussions of cubic and quadratic equations. The most important theoretical innovation in this work surrounds Khayyām's contribution to the subject of algebraic geometry, as he elaborated a geometrical theory of polynomial equations, which had important consequences for the advancement of Arab algebraic theory. In addition to his *Algebra*, ʿUmar Khayyām wrote a number of other important mathematical treatises, including a study of the difficulties of Euclid's *Elements* in which he advanced a number of innovative geometrical proofs, and a treatise on cubic equations in which he further developed his new mathematical theories. The scope of his extant corpus includes, in addition to his famous *Algebra*, a number of philosophical treatises on free will and determinism, the universals of existence, theodicy, generation and corruption, and general metaphysics. Philosophically, ʿUmar Khayyām was a follower of *Avicenna; this is quite apparent in the subjects and their manner of treatment in his philosophical essays.

ʿUmar Khayyām's fame rested squarely on his reputation as a brilliant scientist. His Persian quatrains, made famous in Victorian England through the paraphrases of Edward Fitzgerald (d. 1883), are not mentioned at all in the earliest sources; his academic achievements in the fields of mathematics, astronomy, and philosophy overshadow all later mention of him in the medieval sources. Neither did Khayyām's work have any direct influence on the scientific or philosophical development of Europe, his *Algebra* was first translated into French in 1851.

Bibliography: J. A. Boyle, "Omar Khayyam: Astronomer, Mathematician and Poet," *Bulletin of the John Rylands Library* 52 (1969): 30–45; R. Rashid and B. Vahabzadeh, *Al-Khayyam mathématicien*, 1999.

Erik S. Ohlander

URBAN II, POPE (C. 1042–1099, PONTIFICATE 1088–1099). Noted for his involvement in the continuing Investiture Controversy with the Holy

Roman Emperor *Henry IV, he is best known for calling the First Crusade to free the Holy Land in 1095.

Before becoming pope, Urban was known as Odo of Lagery. Odo was born at Châtillon-sur-Marne into a northern French noble family. He studied at the cathedral school of Rheims (under Saint *Bruno, who later founded the even stricter monastic order of the Carthusians) and eventually became a canon and then archdeacon there. In the late 1060s, Odo entered the reformed Benedictine monastery at Cluny, in Burgundy. At Cluny, Odo rose to become a grand prior, that is, second in command to the abbot, in which position he served until he was sent to be an assistant to Pope *Gregory VII. The reforming spirit of his monastery heavily influenced him, and he became highly involved in the Gregorian reform of the Western Church. In 1078, Gregory appointed him to be cardinal bishop of Ostia, which made him the chief adviser of the pope.

Pope Gregory VII, who was in the midst of a struggle with the German emperor over control of Church appointments, made him legate to France and Germany in 1082–1085. In executing his duties as legate, he deposed bishops whom Gregory had condemned, filled vacant sees with bishops favorable to Gregory's cause, and at one point was even briefly captured by Emperor Henry IV. Following the death of Pope Victor III, Gregory VII's successor Odo of Lagery was elected as Pope Urban II on 12 March 1088 at Terracina. He immediately made clear his stand against clerical incontinence, simony, and lay investiture—the basic principles of the Gregorian reform.

Urban was unable to enter the city of Rome until November 1088 because the antipope Clement III (also known as Guibert of Ravenna), a rival claimant to the papal office who was supported by the emperor, controlled most of Rome. Urban then excommunicated both the antipope and the emperor, and troops loyal to the pope drove those of the antipope out of the city. By the next year, however, Clement was back in Rome, and the emperor's position was looking strong again, until Conrad, Henry IV's son, deserted his father and came over to Urban's side. Conrad helped Urban to return to Rome in 1094.

During his pontificate, Urban traveled a lot, holding councils throughout Italy and France. While in France in 1095, he became involved in the marriage case of King Philip I and his bigamous, incestuous wife Bertrade. In October, he dedicated the altar of the church at Cluny, and in November he called the famous Council of Clermont. At this council, Urban confirmed the excommunication of King Philip I for incest and continued the Gregorian reform against simony and clerical marriage. He also preached a crusade against the Muslims. The call for a crusade should be understood in the context of Urban's continuation of Gregory VII's ideas and policies. These included a concern over the schism between the Eastern and Western Churches and the enforcement of the Peace of God movement, an effort to limit the amount of violence and warfare among the laity of Christendom. Although the city of Jerusalem fell to the crusading army on 15 July 1099, Urban did not live to hear of this joyous event, for he died two weeks later, on 29 July 1099.

Urban's pontificate helped pave the way toward final victory for the Gregorian reform. He acted with a spirit of accommodation that helped advance the reform movement and bring the two sides closer together. At the same time, Urban sometimes went beyond Gregory's original measures. For example, he forbade bishops and clerics from becoming the feudal vassals of laymen, and he loosened the control some bishops had over monasteries in their diocese. In many ways, therefore, Urban had a profound influence on the outcome of the Investiture Controversy. Pope *Paschal II inherited from him a papal position that was much more secure than the position Urban had inherited from Victor III, and this helped him to finally bring the Investiture Controversy to an end.

Bibliography: J. Riley-Smith, *The First Crusade and the Idea of Crusading*, 1986; I. S. Robinson, *The Papacy 1073–1198: Continuity and Innovation*, 1990.

Ryan P. Crisp

V

VILLEHARDOUIN, GEOFFREY OF (C. 1150–1213). Marshal of Champagne and the author of *La conquête de Constantinople* (the Conquest of Constantinople), Geoffrey is important for the role he played as an adviser to the leaders of the Fourth Crusade and for the account he wrote of that adventure—which saw the crusaders start off to conquer Jerusalem and end up conquering Constantinople.

Born a younger son of Vilain of Villehardouin, a nobleman of Champagne, Geoffrey of Villehardouin, through personal connections, marriage, and his own talents, rose to become the marshal of Champagne in 1185. This position made him the chief logistical officer and the first deputy in administrative affairs to the count of Champagne. He was respected for his good sense and organizational skills and appears as a conscientious, pious, and chivalrous noble of his day in his own chronicle. Although his rank did not place him among the nominal leaders of the Fourth Crusade, he still attended most of their councils, offered advice to them, and served as a diplomat or emissary on several missions where he represented the leaders of the crusade. It was on his suggestion that the leadership of the crusade was offered to Boniface of Montferrat. He served as one of the emissaries sent to negotiate with the Venetians for ships to carry the crusaders. He was also sent as one of the diplomats who went before the Byzantine emperor, demanding his compliance with the Treaty of Zara. When the emperor refused to comply, Villehardouin's delegation declared war upon him.

La conquête de Constantinople, Villehardouin's history of the Fourth Crusade, is the most comprehensive and arguably the most important narrative of that expedition. It was also the first history of a crusade that has come down to us to be composed in French prose (earlier histories were all written in Latin, and earlier French writings on crusading topics were poems). At least some modern scholars have praised Villehardouin as a chronicler. They cite his skill at using and portraying numbers accurately and his good memory, which may have been supplemented by the use of actual documents and treaties while composing his work.

There has been much debate over the accuracy and veracity of Villehardouin's history. Some scholars accept his own assertion that he tried to tell the truth. Others believe that he suppressed part of the truth in order to avoid casting the leaders of the crusade, of whom he was one, in a bad light. Those scholars who view the events of the Fourth Crusade as a great conspiracy to conquer Constantinople are usually among the most unlikely to accept Villehardouin's explanation that it was all an accident and an unfortunate necessity. Whatever his "spin" on the Fourth Crusade, his chronicle remains one of the best surviving historical documents from medieval Europe.

Bibliography: D. E. Queller and T. F. Madden, *The Fourth Crusade: The Conquest of Constantinople*, 2nd ed., 1997.

Ryan P. Crisp

VINCENT OF BEAUVAIS (C. 1190–C. 1264). Vincent was the Dominican priest and scholar responsible for the writing of the massive encyclopedic *Speculum maius*, the most extensive gathering of knowledge yet compiled in the medieval period.

Very little is known of Vincent's life. However, conjecture places his birth at Beauvais, France, in the last decade of the twelfth century. He probably joined the Order of Preachers shortly after its establishment, and he likely enrolled in the Dominican studium generale of St. Jacques in Paris sometime in the early 1220s. He presumably returned to Beauvais upon the founding of its priory in 1225. The first solid evidence of his life dates from 1246, when he was named lector (a reader of and commentator on texts) at the Cistercian abbey of Royaumont, an appointment requested by King *Louis IX, who both befriended him and encouraged his scholarly pursuits. Two years previously the first edition of the *Speculum maius* appeared, in all likelihood compiled at Royaumont. Vincent remained at Royaumont, writing and preaching until 1259 or 1260. His whereabouts after then are not known, though he possibly returned to St. Jacques in Paris, where he probably died in 1264.

Vincent's work reflects the intellectual changes of the thirteenth century, the characteristic intellectual products of which are the encyclopedias and summas. Between the twelfth and thirteenth centuries, the intellectual outlook shifted from passive contemplative mental activity to active practical activity. Two of the religious orders that pioneered the shift were the Cistercians and the Dominicans; Vincent was involved with both: schooled by the Dominicans and working with the Cistercians at Royaumont. Moreover, compositional form from this period shows a marked change from that of the twelfth century. Whereas twelfth-century writers analyzed and harmonized their sources, thirteenth-century writers cited and credited their original sources. Moreover, accessing information became more of a preoccupation: Contents were being arranged alphabetically or chronologically, and tables of contents and marginal notes were now being provided.

It was in this age of change that Vincent began the *Speculum maius*. He conceived of it fundamentally as a practical aid for preachers—a manual, as it were, for students and preachers to combat heresies. Vincent's idea for the *Speculum* was not original. His most direct influence was likely the Cistercian monk Helinand of Froidmont's *Chronicon*. Yet Vincent's massive gathering of "all" knowledge and his interlinking of the three parts of the *Speculum* went unequaled until the eighteenth century. Moreover, Vincent was open to incorporating knowledge from the Greek, Arabic, and Hebrew sources that were then being translated.

Undergoing many revisions and expansions during Vincent's lifetime, the version of the *Speculum* that has come down to us is a tripartite one: The *Speculum naturale* (thirty-one books) deals with natural sciences (theology, cosmography, mineralogy, and agriculture, to name a few of the topics treated) and includes an account of the Creation and the Fall. The *Speculum doctrinale* (seventeen books) deals with those sciences aiding humankind with life on earth after the Fall, sciences such as logic, rhetoric, astronomy, medicine, and law. The *Speculum historiale* (seventeen books), by far the most popular part of the *Speculum maius*, covers world history up to the reign of Louis IX and has served as one of the best sources of history of that king's reign. A fourth *Speculum*, the *Speculum morale*, was added to the collection after Vincent's death, and though it appears that Vincent had planned on compiling it and that he and his helpers had begun gathering information for it, it cannot be attributed to him.

Vincent, however, was not just a compiler. He wrote theological treatises as well. He also began a four-part work dealing with the moral duties and virtues of the prince and the court and with the governance of the kingdom. Of the four parts, he completed only two: the *De morali principis institutione* and the *De eruditione filiorum nobilium*. He also wrote the *Liber consolatorius* for the king in 1260 upon the death of the crown prince.

Bibliography: W. J. Aerts et al., *Vincent of Beauvais and Alexander the Great: Studies on the* Speculum Maius *and Its Translations into Medieval Vernculars*, 1986; Vincent of Beauvais, *De morali principis institutione*, ed. R. J. Schneider, 1995.

Paul B. Nelson

VOGELWEIDE, WALTHER VON DER. *See* WALTHER VON DER VOGELWEIDE.

W

WACE (C. 1100–1175). A Norman verse chronicler and author of vernacular works, Wace served under Kings *Henry I, *II, and *III of England and was appointed canon of Bayeaux by Henry II between 1155 and 1160. His most famous work, the *Roman de Brut*, is a nearly 15,000-line verse history of the English kings.

Wace, born around 1100 on the Isle of Jersey, was the grandson of the chamberlain of Duke Robert the Magnificent. He grew up in Caen, was schooled in Paris, and then returned to Caen. He described his position in Caen both as a *clerc lisant* and *maistre*. Though his official position in Caen is not clear, he probably ran either a psalter school or a grammar school. While in Caen, he wrote numerous works in Norman French, such as political poems, pious works, chronicles, and translations of saints' lives.

The *Roman de Brut*, finished in 1155 and dedicated to *Eleanor of Aquitaine, is a history of the English kings based upon *Geoffrey of Monmouth's *Historia regum Britanniae*. While the *Roman de Brut* is modeled on Geoffrey's work in content and structure, Wace makes the material his own. In particular, Wace is famous for adding the Round Table to the story. Though still a chronicle, the style of the *Roman de Brut* is much closer to that of later romances and inspired later Arthurian writers such as *Chrétien de Troyes and Layamon. Due to the success of the *Roman de Brut*, Henry II asked Wace to create a work that would justify Norman rule over England. This work, the *Roman de Rou*, was unfinished when Wace died in 1175.

Bibliography: U. T. Holmes, Jr., "Norman Literature and Wace," in *Medieval Secular Literature*, ed. W. Matthews, 1967.

John Paul Walter

WALAHFRID STRABO. *See* STRABO, WALAHFRID.

WALDO, PETER (WALDES, VALDES) (D. 1217). The man now referred to as Peter Waldo ("Peter" was first given as part of his name in the fourteenth century, so it is probably a later addition) was the central figure in the twelfth-century heresy of Waldenses or Waldensianism in the region of southern France and northern Italy. Until disproved in the nineteenth century, Waldensian legend maintained that the religion as taught by Waldo was an ancient, pure Christianity established in the Alps by Christ's apostles soon after his ascension and that Waldo merely perpetuated the tradition. But twelfth-century Lombardy was the setting for many religious reform movements, most of which eventually became designated as heresies. Though Waldo was the only leader of one of these groups never to join an order or the priesthood, he was not the only creative theologian during his time. Also flourishing were the Cathars, the Humiliati, the Albigensians, and the Speronists; since Waldensianism shares features with each of these, it is difficult to identify definitively all the strands of heterodox ideas and their origins.

Waldo was, like his contemporary Saint *Francis, an advocate of poverty as an imitation of Christ, and he preached an ecstatic, extreme version of the apostolic life. Before his conversion to poverty, Waldo commissioned some monks to translate the Gospels for his own study. Through reading his own translated copies of the Gospels and other scriptural passages, as well as some of the writings of the Fathers, he became enthralled with the idea of perfection. His subsequent search for purity of life led to his conversion to poverty in 1173. He heard an itinerant singer (*jongleur*) perform a song of the legend of Saint Alexius, who gave up a wealthy inheritance and a beautiful bride in order to live in Christ-like poverty. Deeply moved by Alexius' example, Waldo immediately followed the injunction to sell all he had and follow Christ, giving up all of his possessions, which were considerable, since he had been a successful merchant. He also forswore his marriage, his home, and his two young daughters, whom he placed in a convent.

Waldo's beliefs attracted followers, and after a few years, the movement had grown into a formidable community of believers. Still accepted by the Church, they were given permission to beg and to travel but not to preach. Waldo and his followers decried this injunction and stepped up their preaching missionary efforts. Eventually they were excommunicated from the Roman Church, but they continued to grow into a heretical sect that proclaimed, among other things, the right of all worthy members (including women) to preach from the Scriptures without Church-sanctioned authority. Waldo also preached against the Catholic concepts of Purgatory, prayers for the dead, and indulgences. By the late 1180s, the Waldensians were actively persecuted as heretics. They became increasingly vociferous against the Roman Catholic Church, which they accused of apostasy. The Waldensian understanding of the Bible proscribed both the use of weapons and of oaths, which led them to refuse to participate in any Church rituals. Though very different from their founder's sect, there are still groups calling themselves Waldensians surviving today in Europe and North America, mostly affiliated with Calvinist Protestantism.

Bibliography: P. Stephens, *The Waldensian Story: A Study in Faith, Intolerance, and Survival*, 1998.

Zina Petersen

WALDRADA (D. 868/869). A concubine of the future *Lothar II of Lotharingia before his marriage in 855 to *Theutberga, she was briefly recognized as his queen in 862.

By 858, Waldrada had apparently produced a son and perhaps several daughters, and Lothar began his lifelong attempt to divorce the childless Theutberga in order to marry his concubine. In 862, having convinced local bishops to grant his divorce from Theutberga, Lothar formally married Waldrada and she was crowned queen.

However, Lothar's uncles *Charles II the Bald and *Louis the German had an interest in depriving Lothar of potential heirs to his kingdom. Ecclesiastics outside of Lotharingia, most particularly Popes *Nicholas I and Hadrian II, with *Hincmar, archbishop of Rheims, were struggling to control Christian marriage as both institution and sacrament, and Lothar's case became a focus of those struggles. Waldrada was accused of witchcraft, bewitching Lothar, and making her rival sterile. A papal synod and pressure from his uncles forced Lothar to return to Theutberga and have her crowned as his queen (865).

Waldrada then asked for and was granted absolution for her sins by the pope on condition that she separate from Lothar. In 866, she retired honorably to the monastery of Remiremont where she died in 868–889, while Lothar continued to press their marital case.

In 867, he gave their son Hugh the duchy of Alsace. After Lothar's death in 869, Hugh, with some local support, attempted to hold Lotharingia but was blinded in 885 and imprisoned in the monastery of Prüm. Waldrada's daughters, Gisla, Bertha, and Ermengard, retained the status of Carolingian princesses.

Bibliography: J. Bishop, "Bishops as Marital Advisors in the Ninth Century," in *Women of the Medieval World: Essays in Honor of John H. Mundy*, ed. J. Kirshner and S. F. Wemple, 1985.

Janice R. Norris

WALTER OF CHÂTILLON (GAUTIER DE LILLE, GAULERUS DE INSULIS) (C. 1135–1202/1203). The great twelfth-century Latin poet Walter of Châtillon was born in Lille and studied in Paris and Rheims. He taught at the cathedral school of Laon, and later at Châtillon-sur-Marne, but eventually went on to study canon law at Bologna. After his education, he served in the chancery of William of the White Hands, the archbishop of Rheims. Walter composed and dedicated his epic *Alexandreis* to William, perhaps to regain

William's favor after a falling out over a male lover. Walter died, probably of leprosy, in the first years of the thirteenth century.

Walter composed a number of Latin lyric poems in a twelfth-century "Goliardic" style, mostly on satirical and erotic topics. He also wrote a treatise against the Jews in dialogue form, the *Tractatus contra Iudaeos*. However, it is Walter's ten-book Latin epic on the life of Alexander that established his fame as a poet: The *Alexandreis* was composed in a five-year span somewhere between 1171 and 1181. Quintus Curtius' biography of Alexander was the main source for the epic, and Walter also appropriated a number of stylistic touches from classical authors such as Virgil and Ovid and infused the whole with a certain degree of twelfth-century Neoplatonism.

In the first book of the *Alexandreis*, Alexander is crowned as king of Macedonia upon the death of his father Philip. Walter also introduces us to the young Macedonian's mentor Aristotle, who warns him against the excesses of corruption and pleasure even as he instructs him in the arts of war and leadership. Walter paints Alexander as a questing, unbounded spirit, a figure of destiny already feeling in his youth the seductive pull of Pride. Burning with desire, Alexander ruthlessly destroys Thebes, walks triumphant through the landscape of Troy, and is unleashed upon Asia; however, he spares Jerusalem from destruction, as advised in a dream. The Persian king Darius rallies his kingdom but cannot intimidate the Macedonian, who cuts the enigmatic Gordian knot in the temple of Jove. As both leaders prepare their hosts for the great clash, Walter develops the contrast between the aging, corrupt—but still powerful and noble— Persian ruler and the young, burning, overly proud Macedonian king. Walter provides an extended description of the shield of Darius (modeled on similar descriptions in the *Aeneid* and the *Iliad*). This is one of three formal ecphrases in the poem: The others are the tomb of Darius' wife in Book IV and the tomb of Darius himself in Book VII.

In Book III, the Greeks and Persians clash in epic battle, Darius' forces receiving the worst. Walter models his poetry on the bloody single combats of classical epic. Darius flees the field, and Alexander captures his wife and family. In quick succession, Alexander marches through Damascus, Tyre, Gaza, and Egypt and finally crosses the Tigris into the unbounded reaches of the East. Darius' wife expires in captivity, and Alexander buries her in splendor, raising a magnificent tomb to her, engraved with an ecphrasis depicting the story of Creation and biblical history down to Ezra. Eventually Darius dies with courtly nobility in Book VII, and Alexander raises a glorious tomb in his honor, adorned with an ecphrasis representing the entire world, modeled on medieval *mappae mundi*. He presses on, even in the face of protests from his army, and encounters Talestris, queen of the Amazons. She comments on the incongruity between the Macedonian's puny appearance and his deeds of glory. The queen wishes to bear Alexander's child, and he obliges. Alexander is warned by the Scythian messengers not to continue his march into the East; they entreat him, unsuccessfully, to remember the limits of human endeavor. Alexander defeats Porus, king of India, but continues to press forward to find his glorious destiny, rather than turn back as his men wish. Finally, in Book X, Alexander's exploits rouse Nature herself to action. She travels to the underworld, enlisting the aid of Satan and Treachery to defeat Alexander. They move the hand of Antipater, who poisons Alexander in Babylon.

The *Alexandreis* had great influence in the Middle Ages; it survives in a large number of manuscripts, many of which are heavily glossed for use as school texts. The poem quickly became an important part of twelfth-and thirteenth-century literary culture and was translated into a number of vernacular languages.

Bibliography: M. Colker, ed., *Galteri de Castellione Alexandreis*, 1978; D. Townsend, *The* Alexandreis *of Walter of Châtillon: A Twelfth-Century Epic*, 1996.

Andrew Scheil

WALTHER VON DER VOGELWEIDE (C. 1170–1230). Known for his exemplary love poems and also as the composer of political and religious verse, Walther is the foremost lyric poet of the Middle High German "Blütezeit" (flowering.) Some ninety songs, 140 to 150 political proverbs, and one religious song survive him. His contemporary *Gottfried von Strassburg praises him as the leading "nightingale" of the day, and later political poets name him as their inspiration.

We know little about Walther. He may have come from lower Austria, but this is no more likely than any of several places throughout German-speaking Europe designated with the term "Vogelweide." Since the fourteenth century, tradition holds that he is buried in Würzburg, but there is no hard evidence for this. No one has discovered a family name "Vogelweide" in the thirteenth century, though the name is associated with a family of lesser nobility in a later century and Walther was sometimes called "Lord," a noble's title. Walther was acquainted with the lyric of France and Provençe, though his *opus* demonstrates a greater affinity with the works of vagrant Latin poets. He seems to have been educated in the Latin tradition, later admirers calling him "Master." Although his professional career ripened in Vienna, he spent most of his life as a wandering minstrel, relying on the generosity of his patrons for a living. For reasons that are unclear, he suddenly departed from Austria, meandering until King Philip of Swabia hired him. The courts of other rulers, Hermann I of Thuringia and Dietrich of Meissen, for example, also provided him with employment. He became known as a poet of political proverbs and subsequently plied his trade for Holy Roman Emperors *Otto IV and *Frederick II. In his old age he received a generous fief from the latter, over which he rejoiced openly. It is possible that Walther was a messenger/ambassador associated with Otto's court. The only fairly certain historical reference to Walther is noted in an account ledger of Bishop Wolfger von Erla. This records that the art-friendly churchman gave Walther five *solidi* with which to purchase a fur coat.

Walther's creative production can be grouped generally into three categories. His so-called *Leich*, a religious song, is dedicated to the praise of the Virgin Mary, though it also praises the Trinity. He is most famous for his love-lyric and his gnomic (political) poetry (Spruchdichtung). In opposition to his teacher Reinmar, who sang of the distant and unattainable woman and the longing pain associated with a man's unrequited desire for her, Walther illustrates an ideal love relationship as a happily and completely fulfilled condition, mutually attained by man and woman. This view reveals the influence of Heinrich von Morungen. In these poems, Walther rejoices in the beauty of nature, including the beauty of the female body and the shared joys of lovemaking.

Walther's political proverbs initiated a political poetics in the German language, which probably developed out of earlier oral tradition. Walther polemicizes on two planes; that is, which ruler is the legitimate one, referring to the double elections of Philip of Swabia and Otto IV and the double claims of Otto and Frederick II to the crown of empire; and between worldly and sacred authority, the emperor and the pope. Since Walther served in several courts, his worldview often vascillated accordingly.

Walther's influence lies in the expanded possibilities of lyric poetry, both in form and theme. This resulted in the creation of new genres in the German sphere such as the pastourelle, the exchange, the scold, and so forth. As the Middle Ages waned, Walther was never totally forgotten as many medieval poets were. Karl Lachmann published the fundamental critical edition of his poems in 1827, which has been updated by Carl von Kraus, Hugo Kuhn, and others, and most recently by Christoph Cormeau. Walther has been viewed as a servant of the prince in the Metternich era; he was exploited under Bismarck's reign for cultural purposes; under the Weimar regime, he was celebrated as a German nationalist; and the Nazis applied his art to the concept of the "folk." His poetry is memorialized in frescoes that adorn the walls of the castle Neuschwannstein of the mad King Ludwig the Bavarian, and Ulrich Müller traces his influence to contemporary music. We can still identify with Walther's feelings and visions as with few other medieval writers.

Bibliography: H. Brunner and S. Neureiter-Lackner, *Walther von der Vogelweide: Epoche, Werk, Wirkung*, 1996; G. F. Jones, *Walther von der Vogelweide*, 1968.

Kristine K. Sneeringer

WIDUKIND OF CORVEY (C. 925–AFTER 973). Widukind was a tenth-century chronicler of the Saxons and monk of the important Benedictine abbey at Corvey. His *Rerum gestarum Saxonicarum libri tres* (Deeds of the Saxons in Three Books) is an important source for the reigns of *Henry I and *Otto I of Germany as well as of a contemporary "non-Roman imperial ideal" (as a "Germanic" alternative to papal nomination or confirmation of emperors).

Widukind came from a noble Saxon family and entered the monastery at Corvey sometime in the early 940s. He began composition of his chronicle around 957, completing it in 968, then expanding it in 973 to cover the end of the reign of Otto I. Widukind seems to have spent his life at Corvey, though he is believed to have seen Otto in person, and the abbey at Corvey was often visited by major political figures of the day.

The *Res gestae Saxonicae* is the sole work of Widukind's to survive; his hagiographical works—lives of Saint Paul the Hermit (*Vita Pauli primi eremitae*) and Saint Thecla (*Passio Theclae virginis*)—have been lost. Employing historical models classical and biblical (Sallust, the Maccabees), Widukind's history is nonetheless largely secular and Germanic. The chronicle is dedicated to Princess Matilda, daughter of Otto I and later first abbess of Quedlinburg. Book I considers the origins of the Saxons and traces the history of the tribe up to the rise and reign of Henry I. The name "Saxon," he reports (I, 7) as deriving, according to custom, from the *cultelli* (short knives or swords) the Saxons carried that they called in their own tongue (or for Widukind *nostra lingua*) *sahs* (hence *Sahsones, Saxones*). He reports also of Saxon mercenaries in Roman Britain (I, 8) and the conversion to Christianity under *Charlemagne (I, 15). Typical of the work is his heroic portrait (I, 11) of the veteran soldier Hathagat in battle. Chapters 16 to 41 concern Henry I, in particular his wars with the Avars (Hungarians).

Books II and III concern the reign of Otto I; just like his treatment of Henry I, Widukind's account of Otto is filled with vivid battle scenes (in particular, the battle of Lechfeld against the Hungarians in 955; III, 44) and imbued with pride in Saxon lineage, and can be said to construct about the emperor an aura of charisma. The work as a whole is an important specimen of early medieval Latin narrative prose and repository of early Germanic history. Although his chronicle is more secular in its concerns (and a more modest accomplishment), Widukind's *Res gestae Saxonicae* places him in company with *Bede as a chronicler of a Germanic people.

Bibliography: A. Bauer and R. Rau, eds., *Quellen zur Geschichte der Sächsischen Kaiserzeit: Widukinds Sachsengeschichte, Adalberts Fortsetzung der Chronik Reginos, Liutprands Werke*, 1971; H. Beumann, *Widukind von Korvei: Untersuchungen zur Geschichtsschreibung und Ideengeschichte des 10. Jahrhunderts*, 1950; J. A. Brundage, "Widukind of Corvey and the 'Non-Roman' Imperial Idea," *Mediaeval Studies* 22 (1960): 15–26.

Joseph McGowan

WILLIAM IX OF AQUITAINE (1071–1126).

Known as the first troubadour, William was a controversial figure in his own time and an important influence on the poetry of Occitania (the south of France). Equally confident of himself as a warrior and a lover, he combined the arrogance of the nobility with the accomplishments of the courtly composer.

His late-thirteenth-century biographer characterized him with some accuracy as one of the greatest courtiers in the world and an accomplished poet and musician. Of the eleven songs attributed to him, one has been classified as dubious, but there is little scholarly doubt about the others. William has been called a "Janus-faced" poet because his corpus is divided between the ribald and the conventionally elegant. Three of his songs are "courtly," that is, polished and reverential celebrations of love and the woman he loves; one is a lament or *memento mori*; and of the remaining six, five (the "uncourtly") deal with sexual adventures of some kind and one is a parody of love songs. William's influence was substantial; his songs are daring, tender, sophisticated, boastful, always conscious of his high rank and visibility, possessive of both territory and love conquests. His poetry had a profound effect upon the lyric of love in his native Occitania (Provence), notably in the songs of later poets such as Marcabru, Jaufre Rudel, Raimbaut of Orange, and Peire Vidal, and extended into northern France as well.

William's life was as varied as his literary output. He was the first son of Count Guy-Geoffrey William VI and Audearde of Burgundy. At the age of ten he issued a document in his own name; five years later, after the death of his father, he became the seventh count of Poitiers, ninth duke of Aquitaine, ruling over one of the greatest territories in Carolingian France. His marriage to Ermengarde of Anjou in 1089 ended with his divorcing her two years later; his second marriage to Philippa-Mathilde of Toulouse produced two sons, William and Raymond, and a daughter, Agnes. Philippa-Mathilde retired to the abbey of Fontevrault shortly after the birth of their second son, about 1117. That he was manifestly unfaithful is attested not only in his songs but in the fulminations of chroniclers such as *William of Malmesbury and *Orderic Vitalis; he had a lengthy affair with a woman known as Dangerosa-Maubergeonne, the viscountess of Châtellerault. He arranged a marriage between his son William (X) and her daughter Ainor; their daughter *Eleanor became queen of France and England.

Political rivalries, skirmishes, and incursions, many of them unsuccessful or inconclusive, dominated William's career. In his wife's name, he invaded Toulouse; its count, *Raymond IV, had left on crusade (1097). He joined William Rufus of England against Philip of France in Normandy (1098); he set out for Constantinople to join the First Crusade, but after the massacre of his army in Turkey (1101), he made a brief pilgrimage to Jerusalem and returned to Poitou the following year. He fought with his neighbor the count of Anjou and took two bishops hostage to enforce the homage due him from their domains. He was excommunicated in 1114 for his failure to renounce his relationship with the viscountess of Châtellerault; his response was to imprison the bishop who pronounced the excommunication. He seems to have undergone a crisis of health in 1119, the putative date of a song renouncing worldly concerns. After recovering, however, he joined a crusade against the Moors in Spain (1120) and fought to contain a revolt in the County of Toulouse, which he lost in 1123. In 1126, he died and was buried in the chapter house of an abbey he had founded, Montierneuf.

William's songs evince an attitude that is both sensual and playful, and he expresses pride in his ability to produce both lyrics and music to good effect, just as he is successful in his courting (Songs 1, 6, 7). Two of his *companho* ("fellow-knight") songs speak of the urbane audience necessary to understand a well-made lyric (Song 1) and William's pride in his ability to produce a verse of high quality (Song 6). The same song, a boast of sexual prowess, introduces the boast or *gap* into the poetry of the south of France, as his song of farewell to chivalry introduces the *planh* or lament. He seems to have been the first to use the springtime/new life topos in vernacular poetry (Songs 7, 10), and his celebration of joy in Song 9 also incorporates courtly topoi such as the transformation of the lover through his submission and the discretion of his courtship.

Bibliography: G. A. Bond, ed. and trans., *The Poetry of William VII, Count of Poitiers, IX Duke of Aquitaine*, 1982; C. Jewers, "The Poetics of (S)Cat-Ology in Guilhem VII, Count of Poitiers, IX Duke of Aquitaine's Canso V," *Tenso* 11. 1 (1995): 38–63; S. G. Nichols, "The Early Troubadours: Guilhem IX to Bernart de Ventadorn," in *The Troubadours: An Introduction*, ed. S. Gaunt and S. Kay, 1999.

Judith Davis

WILLIAM I OF ENGLAND (THE CONQUEROR, DUKE OF NORMANDY, AND KING OF ENGLAND) (C. 1027/1028–1087).

A Norman, William claimed the throne of England after the death of *Edward the Confessor; he invaded England in October 1066 and was crowned king on 25 December 1066. His rule brought significant change to England.

William, born in 1027 or 1028, was the illegitimate son of Duke Robert I and Herleve, daughter of a tanner (or perhaps an undertaker) of Falaise. Before he departed on a pilgrimage to Jerusalem in 1035, Robert named William his heir; and when Robert died during the pilgrimage, William succeeded him as duke. His boyhood was turbulent, as the great men of Normandy fought each other for land and power and even for physical possession of the young duke. In one of these episodes, his guardian, Osbern, was killed in his presence.

William asserted his control over Normandy in a series of campaigns, beginning with a victory at Val-ès-Dunes in 1047 and the imposition of the Peace of God on the duchy in its aftermath. At first, he was helped by King Henry I of France, but by 1054, William and Henry were at odds, and William defeated the king at the battle of Mortemer. Thereafter, William's control over the duchy was unchallenged for a generation, and he was able to greatly strengthen Normandy's civil and religious institutions. By about 1060, he was one of the strongest rulers of northern France. About 1050, William married *Matilda of Flanders. It was an arranged marriage, but the spouses came to be very close. They had at least four sons and four daughters. King Henry died in 1060, and William's father-in-law became the regent for Henry's underage son and heir. In the same year, another opponent, Count Geoffrey Martel of Anjou, died. Because these deaths left William without a serious challenger in France, he was free to undertake the conquest of England when the opportunity presented itself.

Edward the Confessor, king of England, was the son of William's great-aunt. Between 1016 and 1041, he had spent part of his exile from England in Normandy. When he died in January 1066, William claimed the throne on the grounds that Edward had bequeathed it to him over a decade earlier, that he had sent *Harold Godwinson to Normandy to confirm the gift, and that Harold had sworn to uphold William's right to the throne. When Harold took the throne in 1066, therefore, William accused him of perjury and mounted an expedition to take the kingdom for himself. Recruitment of a large army from Normandy and other areas of France and preparation of the ships necessary to carry them across the Channel took months, so it was not until late September that William's expedition sailed. He was able to land unopposed at Pevensey because Harold was in the north of England. On 14 October, the English and French armies met in the battle of Hastings. Harold was killed, and William emerged triumphant. He was crowned king of England on Christmas Day 1066.

The Norman Conquest had profound effects on England. The Anglo-Saxon nobility disappeared, replaced by the king's French followers, who brought with them French constitutional and legal ideas. William's government of England cleverly combined useful institutions of both English and Norman origin. The striking monument of his administration of England is the Domesday Book, the great survey of the wealth of the English countryside, in 1086. The Church kept most of its lands after the Conquest, but it was brought into closer conformity with the developing standards of continental Europe, especially after William made *Lanfranc archbishop of Canterbury in 1070. French merchants settled in English towns and involved England in trade with the Continent to a greater extent than earlier. The English language and English arts and literature all came to incorporate French elements.

English revolts subsided after William's terrible harrying of rebellious northern areas in the winter of 1069–1070. Thereafter, he faced some threat from various Scandinavian claimants to England. His greatest problems, however, were caused by his eldest son, Robert Curthose, who wanted his father to grant him power in Normandy. As a precaution during his preparations for the 1066 campaign, William had declared Robert duke of Normandy; and Robert wanted the reality of power as well as the name. While she was alive, Matilda managed to keep her husband and son intermittently reconciled, but she died in 1083, and thereafter the two were constantly at loggerheads. William died, on 9 September 1087, as the result of an injury he suffered while campaigning against Robert. He left Normandy to Robert but England to William Rufus, his second son.

Bibliography: D. Bates, *Normandy before 1066*, 1982; R.H.C. Davis and M. Chibnall, eds. and trans., *The Gesta Guillelmi of William of Poitiers*, 1998; D. C. Douglas, *William the Conqueror: The Norman Impact on England*, 1964.

Emily Tabuteau

WILLIAM DURAND. *See* GUILLELMUS DURANDUS.

WILLIAM MARSHALL (C. 1147–1219).

WILLIAM MARSHALL (C. 1147–1219). From a landless household knight, William Marshall rose through his skills as a warrior and courtier to an earldom and ultimately the regency of England. The unique verse biography that records his career is a major source for the chivalric culture of the late twelfth century.

William was the fourth son of John Marshall, a minor Wiltshire baron and holder of the hereditary office of marshal. As a younger son, William could hope for no inheritance, but his family arranged a first-rate education in knightly skills at the household of his relative William de Tancarville, chamberlain of Normandy. In 1167, Tancarville knighted the young man and provided him with his introduction to battle and tournament. The next year, William entered the service of his maternal uncle, Patrick, earl of Salisbury, who was aiding Queen *Eleanor in putting down a rebellion in Poitou. When William was wounded and captured in an ambush, Eleanor herself paid his ransom.

This link with royalty set the pattern of William's career; for most of the next two decades, he would make his way as a retainer of one or another member of the royal family. In 1170, he joined the entourage of *Henry II's eldest son, also Henry, as tutor in martial skills and chivalry. He soon became an intimate of the younger Henry and followed him in his rebellion against the king in 1173–1174. After the rising failed, the younger Henry devoted himself to tournaments; William acted as captain of his household knights in these affairs. A prodigiously skilled combatant, William (in partnership with another knight) captured 103 opponents in one ten-month period of tourneying. Although estranged from his master briefly in 1182 because of rumors that he had bedded Henry's wife, William rejoined Henry's retinue during the latter's last rebellion. When Henry died in 1183, William undertook to fulfill his master's crusading vow and spent two years in the East. On his return, he joined the household of Henry II, who bore his son's loyal knight no ill will. William served the king capably in the wars against his rebellious sons and *Philip II of France that marked the last years of Henry's reign. In return, the king gave William his first landholding and the promise of marriage to Isabel de Clare, a wealthy heiress.

Although William had shortly before been his opponent on the battlefield, when *Richard I (the Lionheart) succeeded to the throne in 1189, he honored Henry's pledge. Through his marriage, William joined the ranks of the magnates, gaining lands in Normandy and Wales, the lordship of Leinster in Ireland, and claims to the earldom of Pembroke. Unsurprisingly, William became one of Richard's greatest supporters, serving as one of the four colleagues of the justiciar, William Longchamp, when Richard left on crusade in 1190. Longchamp proved unsuitable, and Marshall joined in the cabal that unseated him in 1191. When Richard's captivity led to Prince *John's bid for the throne of England in 1193–1194, William Marshall stood by Richard. In the last five years of Richard's reign, William aided the king in his recurrent wars and held various offices.

On Richard's death, William supported John's claim to the throne and was rewarded with the earldom of Pembroke. William's services as a captain in Normandy could not prevent John's loss of the duchy to Philip II in the campaigns of 1201–1203. William secured his Norman fiefs in 1205 by pledging Philip liege homage in France (though not elsewhere); this led to a rift later in the year when William accordingly refused to serve in John's projected expedition to Poitou. William fell from royal favor. He spent much of the years from 1207 to 1212 in unofficial exile on his estates in Ireland, where he clashed with John's justiciar. By 1212, difficulties with his barons, the pope, and Philip II convinced John that he needed William's support. William served him faithfully for the rest of the reign, commanding troops when invasion threatened in 1213 and playing a significant role in the negotiations that led to the Magna Carta in 1215. When that agreement failed and fighting broke out, William was one of the main leaders of the royalist party.

Thus, when John died in 1216, it was natural that William became guardian of his young heir, *Henry III of England. Under William's capable leadership, the rebels were defeated. Despite his advanced age, William himself fought lustily at the key royalist victory at Lincoln in May 1217. Once the rebellion was over, he restored order, reissued the Magna Carta, and ruled England as regent until failing health led him to resign in April 1219. With his end approaching, he fulfilled an old vow to join the Templars and died on 14 May 1219.

Bibliography: D. Crouch, *William Marshal: Court, Career and Chivalry in the Angevin Empire, 1147–1219*, 1990; G. Duby, *William Marshal: The Flower of Chivalry*, 1985.

Donald Fleming

WILLIAM OF AUVERGNE (C. 1190–1249).

The first great Parisian theologian to use Aristotelian and Arabic natural philosophy extensively, William of Auvergne was a prolific author.

He was born before 1190 in Aurillac (province of Auvergne). While a canon of Notre Dame in Paris, he became master of theology in 1223 and began to teach in 1225. In 1227, he went to Rome with a request for a collegiate election of the new bishop of Paris by the Cathedral canons. Such was his eloquence in the circumstance that Pope *Gregory IX at once ordained him a priest and appointed him bishop. William held the ecclesiastical office until his death in 1249.

A man of considerable political influence, he was close to France's royal family and continued to take an interest in university affairs. In 1229, he apparently failed to provide support for the university students and teachers, who were subject to ecclesiastical jurisdiction, in their confrontation with the Parisian civil authorities. The university went on strike for two years, and William came close to being dismissed, but by the end of the strike, he had regained the trust of the pope. During the strike, William appointed the Dominican Roland of Cremona professor of theology; it was the first time a mendicant order had a chair in the university. (The Franciscans as well later gained a chair in 1236 with *Alexander of Hales.)

William's copious literary production extends over the years of his university tenure and beyond. In his time, Aristotle's books of natural philosophy and metaphysics, together with Arabic commentaries and treatises, were gradually introduced into the curriculum of the Faculty of Arts, encountering intellectual opposition by theologians and ecclesiastical prohibitions by prelates. William sought to accommodate the newly read Aristotelian and Arabic philosophy into a general Augustinian interpretation of man and the universe. He manifested independent judgment and philosophical acumen in the evaluation of the new doctrines, rejecting or accepting them according to their compatibility with the Christian view of the world. However, the language and rational spirit of the Aristotelian science affected him deeply; moreover, his frequent use of Arabic sources like *Avicenna and *Avicenbron was an influence for the later theology.

In spite of his innovative studies, William did not know Aristotle's natural philosophy completely, due to its early stage of introduction to the West, and he failed sometimes to distinguish between Aristotle's genuine thought and the Arabic interpretations and additions. His theological view was that knowledge of God must be acquired through philosophical methodology and investigations. His main work the *Magisterium divinale ac sapientiale* (Teaching on God and Wisdom) is composed of different works, covering philosophical as well as practical and pastoral subjects: its purpose is the refutation of theological errors through rational arguments, and its form is indebted to Avicenna's treatises—with their continuous discussions—rather than the traditional scholastic arrangement of a series of questions. The most important parts of the *Magisterium* are the *De trinitate, De universo*, and *De anima*.

William's ontological views are close to *Boethius' and Avicenna's. He distinguishes, on the one hand, absolute and simple being, which is being by essence, uncaused, and necessary, and upon which all things depend for their creation and conservation, and on the other, secondary and composite being, which is caused, possible, and has being by participation. Creatures do possess the power to act, but their power is eventually dependent upon the overflowing power and will of the primary being. Against Aristotle and the Arab commentators, William holds that the universe was created in time. His Trinitarian theology takes its inspiration from Augustine: He interprets the psychological analogies to the Trinity in the light of the Aristotelian theory of knowledge. The "overflowing" divine essence, whose attribute is power, produces two emanations: by way of generation, the Son, or Wisdom, and by way of procession, the Spirit, or Love. The image of the Trinity can be found in every human soul through the attributes of life, knowledge, and love.

Bibliography: S. Marrone, *William of Auvergne and Robert Grosseteste. New Ideas of Truth in the Early Thirteenth Century*, 1983.

Roberto Plevano

WILLIAM OF AUXERRE (C. 1150–1231). William was proctor of Paris and considered one of the first scholastics to devise systematic treatises on the virtues, free will, and natural law.

Little is known of William's early life. By 1189, however, he was renowned in Paris as a master of theology. Because he used the other arts in his examinations of theological questions, some historians have speculated that he had been a disciple of *Richard of St. Victor. By 1220, William became archdeacon of Beauvais and proctor of the University of Paris at the Roman Curia. Sent as a royal envoy to Pope *Gregory IX in 1230, William was retained in Rome as adviser about the serious conflicts that were occurring between the citizens of Paris and their university. To battle perceived heresies taught at Paris, Gregory appointed a commission of three and charged them with correcting Aristotle's physical and metaphysical works. In addition to William, the other commission members were Stephen of Provins and Simon of Authie. Although Gregory encouraged formal education and established the University of Paris as an independent corporation, he nevertheless was concerned with establishing an orthodox curriculum for the university. To that end, Gregory requested that William be restored to his teaching position, and the pope expected him to continue his commission work as he and Godfrey of Poitiers reorganized the Paris curriculum to ensure that heresy was eliminated. William died before he could return to Paris and begin his assignment.

Although William wrote treatises on the Divine Office and on liturgical vestments, his academic fame rests largely on the *Summa aurea*, written between 1215 and 1225. Inspired by *Peter Lombard's *Sentences*, the *Summa* is divided into four books: (1) The One and Triune God; (2) Creation, angels and man; (3) Christ and the virtues; (4) Sacraments and the four last things. If now seldom read, the *Summa aurea* nevertheless was greatly influential to contemporary theologians like *Alexander of Hales and was very important as well to later scholastics like *Albertus Magnus, Thomas *Aquinas, and *Bonaventure. In his *Summa*, William posited theology as a science, one that was teachable in the same ways as other arts and sciences and one that established objective truths. Theology, William argues, proceeds from principles, which are also articles of faith, and it should use dialectic and the other arts to pursue its own end— making theology a living force in the world. With William's work, scholastic theology began to assume the shape of a rational exposition and interpretation of salvation history.

Bibliography: É. Gilson, *History of Christian Philosophy in the Middle Ages*, 1955; C. Ottaviano, *Guglielmo d'Auxerre, la vita, le opere, il pensiero*, 1929.

James Countryman

WILLIAM OF CHAMPEAUX (C. 1070–C. 1122).

Best remembered as Peter *Abelard's opponent in a pivotal debate about the nature of universals, William lived an eventful life as *scholasticus*, founder of the school at St. Victor, and bishop.

Early in his career, William studied under *Roscelin, *Anselm of Laon, and Manegold of Lautenbach. Some time before 1100, he became archdeacon of

Paris and head of the cathedral school of Notre Dame. Abelard reports that William was considered supreme master of dialectic in France, and William's reputation helped Paris to acquire great renown. Abelard went to Paris to study with William, and, while his student, the two publicly debated the thorny issue of the nature of universals. Contrary to his teacher Roscelin, who had espoused a nominalist position—that universals are not actually present in the world— William taught an extreme form of realism, asserting that an identical essential nature is wholly present in each individual of a species. Thus, individuals within a species differ only accidentally, not substantially. Abelard attacked this notion; he adopted a conceptualist position arguing that universals exist only in the mind as concepts and that these concepts have extramental existence only when represented in language. Following his disputes with Abelard, William changed his opinion of universals to a theory of indifference; that is, individuals are the same "indifferently" rather than essentially, and this lack of difference results in individuals being recognized as members of a species or genus.

After his disputes with Abelard, William withdrew from Paris and entered the abbey of St. Victor, which he reorganized following the canons regular of St. Augustine. About 1108, William founded a school of theology at the abbey. The school at St. Victor sought to bridge the gap between secular and clerical scholars, pointing to their common interests and pursuits. Its religious orientation was twofold: reformation of diocesan clergy by imposing on them the same obligations as religious orders, and the imitation of real monastic life within its walls. William himself taught free of charge to all comers, not only in dialectics but in grammar and rhetoric as well; his continuing reputation resulted in the school of St. Victor attracting large numbers of students. After 1113, William became bishop of Châlons-sur-Marne. Among the priests that he ordained was *Bernard of Clairvaux, who would later engage Abelard in his own series of disputes.

Only a few of his theological writings survive, and none of William's logical texts are extant; however, the influence of his teaching and the opposition it sparked from Abelard resulted in the first systematic attempts to define universals and to determine their relationships to language. William's contribution as founder of the school at St. Victor, which would become a distinguished center of learning and would greatly influence philosophy and theology over the next two centuries, is considerable.

Bibliography: J. T. Muckle, trans., *The Story of Abelard's Adversities. A Translation with Notes of the* Historia Calamitatum, 1954, reprint 1992; B. Radice, trans., *Letters of Abelard and Heloise*, 1974.

James Countryman

WILLIAM OF CONCHES (C. 1080–1154/1160). William was a product of the "Chartres school," the master of *John of Salisbury, and one of the most prolific commentators on Plato in the twelfth century.

William was born in Conches, in Normandy, studied under Bernard of Chartres, and became a master c. 1125. Little is known of his personal life, and historians even disagree about when and where he died. Like many of the thinkers associated with the school of Chartres, such as *Gilbert of Poitiers, Thierry of Chartres, and *Bernard Silvester, William was greatly concerned with classical learning, Christian humanism, and Platonic cosmology. However, William also found himself drawn to Arabian literature and philosophy through his interest in natural science and psychology. He also had an interest in cartography and produced several maps.

William seems to have taught primarily at Chartres, although he resided at Paris for a brief period. He found an opponent in *William of St. Thierry (Peter *Abelard's old foe), who, in his treatise *De erroribus Guillelmi a Conchis*, accused him of denying the permanence of the three Persons in the Trinity (modalism) and of relying on reason at the expense of faith. Soon thereafter, William accepted a position in the Norman court, and in this capacity he educated the sons of Geoffrey Plantagenet, including Henry Plantagenet, the future Angevin King *Henry II.

Originally scholars attributed several works to him, but in the last few centuries the authorship of many of them has been refuted. William did compile glosses on the grammarian *Priscian's *Institutiones grammaticae*. He also wrote glosses on Macrobius' *Dream of Scipio*, Martianus Capella's *Marriage of Philology and Mercury*, and *Boethius' *Consolation of Philosophy*. His glosses on the *Consolation* are interesting in that they pioneered a new format for such comments—separate sections of full text attached to the *Consolation* rather than interlinear or marginal remarks. In terms of content, however, they lack much originality. William also wrote two versions of glosses on Plato's *Timaeus*. In them, he attempted to harmonize the account of Creation of Genesis with Plato's cosmology.

William wrote a magnum opus of his own, *Philosophia mundi* (The Philosophy of the World), an encyclopedic text that discusses (1) nature and the divisions of philosophy; (2) God, angels, souls; (3) elements; (4) meteorology; (5) geography; and (6) creation. This work was later revised into his *Dragmaticon*, written in the form of a dialogue with Duke Geoffrey. A compilation of classical and biblical citations on ethics entitled *Moralium dogma philosophorum* may also be his work. William's legacy was both that as an interpreter of Plato and a composer of encyclopedic literature.

Bibliography: William of Conches, *A Dialogue on Natural Philosophy (Dragmaticon philosophia)*, trans. I. Ronca and M. Curr, 1997.

Alana Cain Scott

WILLIAM OF JUMIÈGES (D. C. 1070). A monk at the abbey of Jumièges in Normandy, he is the first reliable historian to have attempted to write the history of the dukes and the duchy of Normandy.

Little is known of his life. He tells us that he was a monk of Jumièges, one of the great ducal-sponsored abbeys near Rouen, but he cannot be identified in the documents of the monastery. He remarks that he had himself witnessed some of the events of the reign of Duke Richard III in the mid-1020s, which suggests that he was born about 1000. *Orderic Vitalis refers to him by his nickname "Calculus," but its meaning is not known. The first version of the history, which William may have begun in the 1050s, was completed about 1060; but he later added a few additional details and an account of the Norman Conquest of England that may have been requested by *William I of England. Because it describes the fall of York in late 1069, William cannot have died before 1070, but the date of his death is not known.

In form, William's work, which he entitled *Gesta Normannorum ducum* (The Deeds of the Dukes of the Normans), is an adaptation and continuation of the story of the dukes as it had been written by Dudo of St. Quentin in the first decades of the eleventh century, but it is more reliable. While he depends primarily on Dudo's account of early Norman history, he was skeptical about much of what Dudo said and reconsidered it in light of his own understanding. He also supplemented the information in Dudo's work from other sources. From the reign of Duke Richard II (996–1026) on, William's account is original. Much of his information must have come from his own observation or from oral accounts. He clearly used one charter of Jumièges and may have used others that are now lost, as well as other documentary sources.

The popularity of William's account of Norman history is shown by the large number of manuscripts of it that survive, forty-seven. How highly esteemed it was by Norman writers of the late eleventh and twelfth centuries is shown by the fact that it was continued by other Norman historians. While some of them were anonymous, the two most notable continuators were Orderic Vitalis and Robert of Torigni.

Bibliography: L. Shopkow, *History and Community: Norman Historical Writing in the Eleventh and Twelfth Century*, 1997; E. C. van Houts, ed. and trans., *The Gesta Normannorum Ducum of William of Jumièges, Orderic Vitalis and Robert of Torigni*, 2 vols., 1992–1995.

Emily Tabuteau

WILLIAM OF MALMESBURY (C. 1095–1143).

Respected in his own time for his learning, William is best remembered today for his achievements in historiography as the self-appointed successor to *Bede. He is also known for his elegant style of writing, which combines narration, description, and biography.

Born of a Norman father and an English mother, William became an oblate at Malmesbury Abbey at an early age, falling under the tutelage of his first abbot, Godfrey of Jumièges, in the abbey library. After Godfrey's death, William held the office of precentor at the abbey, and in that capacity, he supervised the library and extended its holdings. In 1140 he was offered the abbacy but refused. As a writer, William was the foremost historian of his day and the heir apparent to Bede. In 1125, he completed his *Gesta regum Anglorum* (Deeds of the Kings of the English), a secular history upon which much of his reputation today rests, which was intended to bridge the historical gap between Bede's time and his own. This text is also notable today as one of the earliest references to King Arthur; in it, he acknowledges King Arthur's historicity but laments the hyperbole and fantastic accounts associated with his name. His other important historical writings are the *Gesta pontificum Anglorum*, an ecclesiastical history of the English Church through 1125, and the *Historia novella*, a firsthand account of the history of England from 1128 to 1142. Although best known as a historian, William had a wide-ranging field of interests. He wrote or copied manuscripts dealing with a variety of subjects such as canon and civil law, scriptural exegesis, theology, hagiography, and the classics.

William deserves his reputation as a scholar for two reasons. First, he saw himself working in the traditon of Bede, and as such he contributed to the development of the historical method. Like Bede, he produced a corpus of historical works, two of which—the *Gesta regum Anglorum* and the *Gesta pontificum Anglorum*—exist in three recensions. His revisions of these texts allows us insight into his development as a historian as they reflect a more mature mind at work. His historiographical style, an admixture of Anglo-Saxon and Anglo-Norman traditions in which he consciously tries to entertain as well as edify, shows a particular influence by Suetonius and Bede. William was a man who traveled extensively and had a keen eye for observation. He was the first historian to make use of topography and visual evidence as historical sources. The second reason for William's importance for historians today is that although he often references other works that are now lost, his work is the only surviving witness of certain contemporary events and as such his work takes on increased significance. He wrote a first-rate account of the early years of the reign of King *Stephen of England that is invaluable to scholars today. Without William's achievement, our knowledge of this period of English history would be much diminished.

Bibliography: R. Thomson, *William of Malmesbury*, 1987.

Clinton Atchley

WILLIAM OF MOERBEKE (GUILLELMUS DE MOERBEKA) (C. 1215–C. 1286).
William was a translator of Aristotle and an archbishop of Corinth.

A native of Brabant or Flanders, William entered the Dominican Order and lived at the priory in Ghent. He studied at Cologne, perhaps under *Albertus Magnus. By 1260, he was sent to a priory at Thebes in Greece and later went to Nicaea. He was a chaplain and penitentiary for numerous popes including Clement IV (1265–1268), Gregory X (1271–1276), Innocent V (1276), Hadrian

V (1276), John XXI (1276–1277), and Nicholas III (1277–1280). He knew Thomas *Aquinas well, and both of them were at Clement IV's court together in Viterbo during 1267–1268. A zealous advocate of reunion between the Greek and Latin churches, William, as a personal adviser to Pope Gregory X, participated at the Council of Lyons (1274), held for the express purpose of ecclesiastical unification. Pope Nicholas III appointed him archbishop of Corinth in 1278, and he held that position until his death.

William was one of the most prominent translators of the second half of the thirteenth century. With respect to Aristotle, William either revised older Latin translations or, in the case of the *Politics* and *Poetics*, translated the text into Latin for the first time. By means of William's translations, the bulk of the Aristotelian corpus was made available to the Latin world. In addition to his well-known translations of Aristotle, William also translated other Greek philosophical and medicinal works, including those by Proclus, Simplicius, Themistius, Ammonius, Alexander of Aphrodisias, Ptolemy, Galen, and Hippocrates. His translation of Proclus' *Elementatio theologica* allowed Aquinas to see the true nature of the *Liber de causis*, a presumed Aristotelian text but actually an abridgement of the *Elementatio*. This work would provide inspiration for the Neoplatonic movement in the later Middle Ages.

William always favored a literal style of translation. Some scholars, such as Roger *Bacon, opposed these literal translations, while others, such as Aquinas, preferred them because they allowed him to see Aristotle's exact meaning. Many of William's Latin translations remained standard until the sixteenth century.

There was a long tradition that William translated many Aristotelian texts at the request of Aquinas. William, however, seems to have begun translating Greek texts before he met Aquinas and continued long after. Nevertheless, Aquinas requested to see several of William's translations and was, in many instances, the first person to use them.

Bibliography: M. Grabmann, *Guglielmo di Moerbeke, O.P. Il traduttore delle opere di Aristotele*, 1970; J. A. Weisheipl, *Friar Thomas d'Aquino: His Life, Thought, and Work*, rev. ed., 1983.

Andrew G. Traver

WILLIAM OF RUBRUCK (WILHEMUS RUBRUQUIS, WILLEM VAN RUYSBROECK) (C. 1215–C. 1295).

William was a Franciscan friar who went on a diplomatic mission for King *Louis IX of France to the court of the Mongol Khan from 1253 to 1255. When he returned safely to Europe, he wrote an accurate and perceptive account of central Asia and the Mongols.

The eruption of the conquering Mongol armies into Russia, eastern Europe, and the Middle East during the early thirteenth century created anxiety and confusion among the rulers of Europe. Some viewed the Mongols as the return of Gog and Magog, the harbingers of the Apocalypse. Others thought the Mongols were either lost Christians or potential converts to Christianity who would make wondrous allies against the forces of Islam.

At this time, King Louis IX, an avid crusader, became particularly anxious to make an alliance with the Mongols against the forces of Islam. After making several other abortive attempts, he assigned the Franciscan friar William of Rubruck to travel to the Mongol capital of Karakorum ostensibly as a missionary, but he was also to report to Louis IX. Departing from Constantinople on 7 May 1253, William reached the camp of Khan Batu and was sent on to the Great Khan Möngke at Karakorum. Utilizing the *Yam* system of post horses, the trip still took three and a half months and was a bitter experience during the winter. Arriving on 3 January 1254, William met with the Great Khan and succeeded in arousing some Mongol interest in an alliance in spite of having to work through a drunken and incompetent interpreter. Meanwhile, in 1253, Hulegu, Möngke's brother, had begun the savage conquest of the Islamic lands in Persia, Mesopotamia, and Syria. These Mongol attacks destroyed Baghdad and the ʿAbbāsid caliphate in 1258 and even threatened the existence of Islam, a Christian crusader's dream.

William of Rubruck began his return journey during July 1254. Eventually he reached the crusader outpost of Tripoli on 15 August 1255. William made an account of his journey, the *Itinerarium*, which noted geographical and ethnographic details with precision. His account revealed the existence of large numbers of Nestorian Christians in the Mongol lands and correctly identified the Caspian Sea as landlocked. He also looked for monstrous races and Prester John but upon failing to find them expressed skepticism about their existence. But in spite of the high quality of his account, medieval scholars generally did not utilize William's account in their own writings in the same degree as they used his contemporary *John of Plano Carpini's writings. Only Roger *Bacon made extensive use of it in his survey of human knowledge *Opus Maius*. Instead, William's narrative largely lay forgotten in a few manuscript copies until its rediscovery and publication by Richard Hakluyt during the latter part of the sixteenth century. Scholars of the history of travel and geography have admired its quality ever since.

Bibliography: Willem van Ruysbroeck, *The Mission of Friar William of Rubruck: His Journey to the Court of the Great Khan Möngke, 1253–1255*, ed. and trans. P. Jackson, 1990.

Ronald H. Fritze

WILLIAM OF ST. AMOUR (C. 1200–1272).

A canon lawyer and theologian, William was the most strident opponent of the mendicant orders.

William was born in St. Amour (Jura) c. 1200. He studied arts at the University of Paris and became a master of arts by 1228. He entered the Faculty of Canon Law and became a doctor in that discipline by 1238. He then commenced the study of theology, completing his doctorate c. 1250. He then became a regent master in theology and held that position until 1256.

William came to prominence during the general university strike of 1253.

According to university statutes, all members of the academic consortium at Paris were supposed to suspend classes when the university approved a strike measure; however, the three mendicant masters of theology, along with their students, remained at Paris and continued to lecture. When its members returned to Paris, the secular theologians, and especially William, proposed a series of restrictive decrees on the friars that sought to limit their number of teaching positions and bring them into fuller compliance with academic regulations. When the friars refused to obey these measures, the university expelled them.

In fall 1255, William continued to attack the friars through a series of disputed questions, which questioned the legitimacy of the mendicant interpretation of the religious life, especially with respect to individual poverty and mendicancy. At this juncture, *Bonaventure emerged as the chief mendicant apologist. William continued his attack throughout spring 1256 in a series of sermons directed against the friars and in the publication of his magnum opus, *De periculis novissimorum temporum* (On the Dangers of the Last Times). In this work, William attempted to prove, through recourse to Scripture, that the friars were actually the heralds of the Antichrist sent to usher in the Last Days. He also used it to argue that the radically Joachite (cf. *Joachim of Fiore) text of the condemned Franciscan Gerard of Borgo San Donnino was a blueprint for the mendicant orders, both Franciscan and Dominican. Gerard had prophesied in this work that the current Church structure would end in 1260 and be replaced with a ministry of friars. William's chief mendicant rival throughout 1256 was Thomas *Aquinas.

For a brief period of time, William had the sympathy of King *Louis IX of France and Pope *Innocent IV. However, the subsequent pope, Alexander IV, was inclined to support the friars and made William and his cohorts repent. William refused to do so and was instead tried at the papal curia in Anagni in fall 1256. Although William wrote a lengthy defense, exonerating himself of all wrongdoing, Pope Alexander evicted him from the university and asked Louis IX to expel him from France. William then returned to St. Amour, where he remained for the rest of his life.

William nevertheless continued to write and urged his colleagues within the theological faculty at Paris to beware of the friars. In his *Liber de antichristo* of the early 1260s, William lauded the fact that the year 1260 had come and passed without any major disturbance but still cautioned that the friars were false prophets. In 1266, William published his *Collectiones catholicae*, his response to the mendicant critics of *De periculis*, and sent a courtesy copy to Pope Clement IV. Clement responded by noting that he thought too much learning had made its author mad.

William kept in contact with his colleagues Gerald of Abbeville and Nicholas of Lisieux during the papal interregnum of 1268–1271, urging them to use this vacancy as an opportunity to publicize the dangers the friars posed. While both authors attacked the mendicant life, they found eminent critics in the persons of Bonaventure, Aquinas, and John *Peckham.

Many of William's arguments were translated into the vernacular within his own lifetime and can be seen in the works of Rutebeuf and *Jean de Meun. In the fourteenth century, William's polemic gained currency through John Wyclif and his followers and was once again used to question the validity of the mendicant life. In fact, William's depictions of the friars reappeared in the poetry of the Edwardian era, including the authors Chaucer and Langland. In the seventeenth century, many of his works were printed, and William was transformed into a "proto-Gallican" who fought for the defense and the independence of the French Church against papal intrusion.

Through his writings, William helped to shape the antifraternal tradition in the Middle Ages.

Bibliography: M.-M. Dufeil, *Guillaume de Saint-Amour et la polémique universitaire parisienne*, 1972.

Andrew G. Traver

WILLIAM OF ST. THIERRY (C. 1070–1148). William was an abbot, theologian, and mystic.

Born in Liège, William was educated in cathedral schools, probably at Rheims, in northern France, where he picked up the new scholastic learning and a broad knowledge of patristic sources from both the Eastern and Western Churches. In 1113, he entered the Benedictine monastery of St. Nicasius near Rheims. In 1119, William was elected abbot of St. Thierry, also near Rheims, where he wrote *De natura et dignitate amoris* (On the Nature and Dignity of Love) and *De contemplendo Deo* (On the Contemplation of God), which is modeled on Augustine's *Confessions*. About this time he met *Bernard of Clairvaux. Their friendship was sealed when the two spent a winter together in the infirmary at Clairvaux, recovering from illness and discussing the Song of Songs. The friendship was fruitful for both men. Bernard pushed William to clarify his mystical theology, while William urged Bernard both to defend the Cistercian Order (leading to the *Apologia*) and to enter the debate against Peter *Abelard (resulting in *On Grace and Free Will*, which Bernard dedicated to William). William was eager to join the more austere Cistercian Order, but Bernard refused to admit him to Clairvaux, arguing that he could do more good working for reform among his own monks. William continued his administrative duties and in 1130 attended the first general chapter of Benedictines in the Rheims province.

In 1135, William resigned his abbacy and secretly entered the Cistercian monastery of Signy as a simple monk. Here he wrote his best-known works and completed his *Meditations*, begun around 1120. In these, we see the working out in personal prayer of the ideas presented more formally in the treatises. William's *Exposition on the Song of Songs* shows both his indebtedness to and independence from Bernard's influence. He wrote disputations against Abelard and *William of Conches, both of whom he felt erred in questions of the Trinity and redemption. In *De natura corporis et animae* (The Nature of the Body and Soul) he uses medical texts and the work of Gregory of Nyssa to set out an anthropology that sees the human body as a microcosm of the universe and the soul as the image of God. Perhaps in response to Abelard's work, the related treatises *Speculum fidei* (Mirror of Faith) and *Aenigma fidei* (Enigma of Faith) instruct monks in the proper uses of faith and reason and contrast two ways of knowing God, by love and by understanding. In 1144, after an extended visit with the Carthusians at Mont Dieu, William wrote his most popular and influential work, *Epistola ad fratres de Monte-Dei* (Letter to the Brothers of Mont Dieu), the so-called *Golden Letter*. This guide to monastic spirituality circulated widely in Europe, often under Bernard's name. Following Origen, the book sets out three levels of spiritual development, with attention to the ascetical foundations of the contemplative life. A life of Saint Bernard was left unfinished at William's death on 8 September 1248.

William's theology is experiential and Neoplatonic. It synthesizes ideas from Latin Fathers like Pope *Gregory I the Great and Augustine of Hippo with those of Greek Fathers including Origin and Basil and Gregory of Nyssa, who were less well known in Europe. In brief, the soul learns to love when it experiences love and becomes more and more like God as it experiences God's presence. More fully, the human soul is stamped from birth with the image of the Trinity. The image is seen in the soul's three faculties: Memory represents the Father, reason the Son, and love the Holy Spirit. Sin, however, defaces the image, and its restoration requires a long process of grace and faith. In the beginning, or animal, state the soul is moved by authority and obedience. An ascetic life prepares it for more advanced stages of contemplation. In the rational stage, the soul, moved by hope, begins to understand God by will and intellect. In the spiritual stage, it is united to God by love. On earth, the soul moves back and forth between these two stages, which for William are not very different. According to his famous formula, "Love itself is understanding." After death the soul can achieve the unitive stage, a true likeness to God in which it loves and wills only what God also loves and wills.

Bibliography: J.-M. Déchanet, *William of St. Thierry: The Man and His Work*, trans. R. Strachan, 1972; B. McGinn, "William of Saint-Thierry: Spirit-Centered Mysticism," in *The Growth of Mysticism*, 1994.

Jill Averil Keen

WILLIAM OF TYRE (GUILLELMUS TYRI) (C. 1130–C. 1185). Archbishop of Tyre and the first comprehensive historian of the crusades, William's history of Jerusalem, the *Historia rerum in partibus transmarinis gestarum*, has served as the authoritative text of the crusading events for centuries.

Born in Jerusalem, probably to a merchant family from Italy or France, William presumably attended classes with the children of aristocratic families. He must also have come in close contact with speakers of many other languages, for he not only knew Latin, French (the language of the court), and Italian but also had a knowledge of Greek, Arabic, and even Hebrew and Persian. He spent twenty years in western Europe, studying the liberal arts and theology in Paris and Orléans, and law (both canon and civil) in Bologna.

William's high level of education, his language and interpersonal skills, and his church training led to a life of many accomplishments. He was elected canon of Tyre in 1161; he became archdeacon of Tyre in 1167. A year later, King Amaury of Jerusalem sent him as a diplomat to the Byzantine Emperor Manuel Comnenus to recruit support for Amaury's campaign against Egypt. In 1170, Amaury appointed William tutor to his son, Baldwin IV. William appeared to be on a track leading to the patriarchate of Jerusalem. After Amaury died (1174), William was appointed chancellor, a position he held for the rest of his life, as did he that of the archbishopric of Tyre from 1175. When Amaury's son Baldwin (d. 1185) assumed the crown in 1176, at the age of fifteen, William became his chief adviser.

However, William's fortune was soon to change. Due to Patriarch Amalrich's advanced age and failing health, William attended the Third Lateran Council in his stead (1178–1180). During his absence, two factions emerged in Jerusalem: one siding with Amaury's first wife, Agnes of Courtenay (Baldwin's mother), who had strong European ties; and another siding with his second wife, the Byzantine princess Maria Comnena, who had strong Eastern ties. William, probably for being allied with the latter faction, found himself out of favor upon his return to the East and was not granted the patriarchate of Jerusalem in 1180. From that time on, his expertise in political matters was not requested. He dedicated the rest of his life to performing church duties and revising his comprehensive history, which had originated as a requisitioned chronicle of King Amaury's reign.

Although best known for his monumental history of Jerusalem, William wrote two other works, neither of which is extant: an account of the Third Lateran Council and a history of the Muslim world, referred to as *Gesta orientalium principum*. For his history of Jerusalem, William employed a methodology resembling that of modern historians. He used both oral and written accounts of the events, as well as being eyewitness to many of them. He evaluated the material, judging and qualifying it before committing it to writing. The overall plan of the work is that of the conquest and rise, and the impending fall, of Jerusalem to the Muslims (to *Saladin). It best covers the years 1095 to 1184, though William added a prologue tracing the city's history back to 614, the year the Christians first lost control of the city. William's history circulated early throughout western Europe and was immediately recognized as the authoritative history of the Holy Lands.

Bibliography: P. W. Edbury and J. G. Rowe, *William of Tyre: Historian of the Latin East*, 1988.

Paul B. Nelson

WILLIBROD (WILLIBRORD), SAINT (658–739). The first archbishop of
Utrecht, apostle to the Frisians, and patron saint of Holland, Willibrod was one
of the leaders of the Anglo-Saxon missionary movement to northern Germany
during the eighth century and an innovative church administrator. His feast day
is 7 November.

The son of a hermit (Saint Wilgis), Willibrod was born in Northumbria and
educated by Saint Wilfrid of York at Ripon monastery. After Wilfrid's deposition and exile, Willibrod spent twelve years in Ireland, including studies under
Saint Egbert to train for missionary work. Ordained a priest in 688, two years
later Willibrod and eleven companions set out to carry on Wilfrid's work among
the Frisians and Old Saxons. Willibrod asked for and received the approval of
Pope Sergius I, an innovative step that began the close cooperation between
Anglo-Saxon monks, popes, and Frankish rulers that eventually characterized
the Frankish Church under the Carolingians. Willibrod also introduced the use
of suffragan (subordinate) bishops to the Latin Church and the practice of dating
from the birth of Christ to Frankish dominions.

The mission's progress initially was slow because of the opposition of the
Frisian leaders, who correctly saw that Christianization went hand in hand with
subordination to the neighboring Frankish kingdom. In fact, after Pope Sergius
consecrated Willibrod as archbishop (under the Latin name Clement) in 695,
Pepin of Heristal, the Frankish mayor of the palace, donated resources to Willibrod's archepiscopal seat in Utrecht. In 698, Pepin also established a monastery
at Echternach to further support Willibrod's activities. Willibrod's effort to
broaden the mission to include Denmark netted only thirty baptisms, and attempts to convert the Old Saxons resulted in violent retaliation and martyrdoms.
Frisian rebellions after the death of Pepin in 714 forced a hiatus until *Charles
Martel gained control of the Frankish state, but even Charles' military conquest
of Frisia did not substantially reduce the difficulty of making converts there.
The country was Christianized only superficially when Willibrod died at Echternach, and Willibrod's mission had to be carried forward, both by his successors
in Utrecht and by his former student and later rival, Saint *Boniface.

Willibrod was not the first missionary to attempt converting the Frisians and
Saxons, but because of the breadth of his activities and his innovative methods,
he ranks as one of the most important missionaries and saints produced by the
early medieval Church or by the English Church in any era.

Bibliography: J. H. Lynch, *The Medieval Church: A Brief History*, 1992.

Edward J. Schoenfeld

WOLFRAM VON ESCHENBACH (C. 1170–1220). German medieval poet
most famous for *Parzival*, Wolfran is also known for his *Willehalm, Titurel*, and
several songs. Wolfram was probably a ministerial vassal, as he calls himself a
knight by birth and by education. The extent of his formal education is not clear,
but he claims to be unlettered. This is obviously a subterfuge, however, because

his works illustrate knowledge of many subjects including theology, astrology, antiquity, French, and at least some Latin.

Wolfram is unnamed in any historical document, though the lords of Eschenbach, to whom he may have been connected, are witnessed historically as early as 1268. He includes himself in a reference to Bavarians but apparently lived in Middle Franken. Count Hermann of Thuringia was one of his patrons, and Wolfram names the counts of Wertheim as his lords; the lords of Dürne owned the castle Wildenberg, which Wolfram names in *Parzival*. His grave is reputed to have been at Frauensmünster, near Ansbach.

The most famous problems in Wolfram research deal with *Parzival*, completed between 1200 and 1210. Although we know with certainty that Wolfram's model was *Chrétien de Troyes' *Le conte du Graal*, Wolfram disclaims this. He fabulously alleges that Kyot, an unknown poet, supplied him with the story. A second problem deals with the grail. Wolfram's "thing" is a stone that fell from heaven, though this is somewhat unclear because of Wolfram's incorrect Latin usage. One scholar has shown that the grail-stone is a symbol for Christ, the cornerstone of the Church who also descended from heaven.

The religious is paramount in *Parzival*, noticeable in the poet's notion of love. Neither fighting battles nor the love of women wins success in the grail realm. Nevertheless, women and the grail are related because thoughts of love lead Parzival close to the grail. As he observes the pattern of three drops of blood in the snow, desiring thoughts of his wife mingle with thoughts of the grail, though love is the more prevalent. Parzival's development is as yet incomplete, because Parzival's priorities are wrong, wife first and grail second. The connection between love and grail reveals the close analogy that Wolfram draws between the feminine and God. Continuing the Parzival story, the story of Lohengrin (Loherangrin, Parizival's son) was added to the tale between 1283 and 1290 by another poet.

Wolfram's *Willehalm* (1210–1220) is another important work of the German Middle Ages, though it is incomplete. The source for this work was *La bataille d'Aliscans*, part of the Old French cycle surrounding the ninth-century hero Guillaume d'Orange (William of Orange). The heathen Terramer comes to Provence seeking his daughter Arabel, who has become a Christian, renamed herself Gyburg, and has been abducted and married by Willehalm. Wolfram questions the value of war against the Saracens for the sake of a woman or for faith, admonishing tolerance. He views the heathen as a sort of qualitative precursor to the Christian, the only significant difference being the Christian's baptism. Ulrich von dem Türlin's *Arabel-Willehalm* (1261–1269) introduces *Willehalm*, and *Ulrich von Türheim's *Rennewart* (c. 1250) continues it in many manuscripts.

Wolfram composed his two misleadingly named *Titurel* fragments c. 1220, at least partially contemporaneously to *Willehalm*. Having lost her mother, Sigune is raised by Parzival's mother Herzeloyde. Sigune and Schionatulander, the page of Parzival's father Gahmuret, are in love. One fragment consists of a dialogue between the lovers, then dialogues between Sigune and Herzeloyde, and Schionatulander and Gahmuret. The second fragment involves an episode concerning an allegorical dog and its leash. It is difficult to know what Wolfram's intention was because of the fragmentary nature of the transmission. His version constituted the basis for the more complete *Jüngerer Titurel* of Albrecht.

Of Wolfram's songs only a few survive. Although he composed a few, true *minnelieder*, his dawn songs were unique to his own personal style and imitated by his followers. Each includes a watchman, perhaps more allegorical than real, who guards the lovers and awakens them, warning them to part before the break of day and reminding them of the dangers of discovery.

Wolfram is remembered in the poetic "Wartburgkrieg" in the thirteenth century as a person of legendary proportions. He is recalled in modern times in Richard Wagner's *Parsifal* and in mythological frescoes in the Parzival chapel of the castle Neuschwannstein in southern Germany.

Bibliography: J. Bumke, *Wolfram von Eschenbach*, 1997; W. Hasty, ed., Introduction to *A Companion to Wolfram's Parzival*, 1999.

Kristine K. Sneeringer

WULFSTAN (WULSTAN) OF WORCESTER, SAINT (1008–1095).

Wulfstan was Benedictine bishop of Worcester at the time of the Norman Conquest of England, an able administrator and royal adviser, and fosterer of education.

What we know of his life is drawn from contemporary accounts by the monk Coleman and *William of Malmesbury. Wulfstan was born in 1008 in Long Itchington near Warwick and educated in the Benedictine abbeys of Evesham and Peterborough and in the household of Brihtheath bishop of Worcester, who later ordained him. Early in his career, he held the church of Hawkesbury in Gloucester. Wulfstan later became a monk of the cathedral monastery of Worcester, where he served for most of his career, first as a schoolmaster, then as precentor and sacristan. He became prior in c. 1050 and reluctantly accepted the bishopric in 1062 at the behest of King Saint *Edward the Confessor and his council. On his death on 18 January 1095, he was buried at Worcester.

At Worcester, Wulfstan earned a reputation as an energetic administrator. He regained alienated property, paid systematic visits to the holdings of his diocese, reformed finances, and raised the level of monastic observance. Under his care, the monastic community grew from twelve to fifty. He was also instrumental in caring for the Church fabric, initiating and carrying through a rebuilding program in c. 1086. Wulfstan also contributed to the development of a substantial scholarly tradition at Worcester. Under his leadership, the monk Hemming prepared a cartulary, the chronicle of Worcester was compiled, and many other manuscripts written and copied. Worcester fostered the careers of a flourishing school of chroniclers including John and Florence of Worcester. Worcester priory served as an important center of Old English culture and maintained its standing under the Norman regime.

Wulfstan lived in politically interesting times. Although he had initially supported *Harold Godwinson against the Normans, he was one of the first clerics to submit to *William I the Conqueror at Berkhamstead in 1066. Wulfstan retained his see and became William the Conqueror's adviser, administrator, one of few Anglo-Saxon bishops retained by the new regime. He helped with compiling the Domesday Book. After the Conqueror's death, Wulfstan supported the kingship of William I's heir William Rufus.

Wulfstan followed a simple way of life, dedicating many hours to solitude and prayer. He was personally austere and publicly humble. He was also known for his direct manner and plain speech. He supported the ambitious moral goals of the Gregorian reformers, including the celibacy of the clergy. In addition, he had a formidable reputation as a preacher. His sermons demonstrate pastoral responsibility, humanity, and a respect of Christian human life. Perhaps his most enduring pastoral achievement was his successful program to stop the merchants of Bristol from their customary capture and sale of slaves. Upon his death, miracles were reported at his tomb. After 1200, detailed accounts were kept of his miracles and cures to aid the process of canonization, granted by Pope *Innocent III in 1203. King William Rufus encased his tomb in gold and silver.

Bibliography: G. Márkus, ed., *The Radical Tradition: Revolutionary Saints in the Battle for Justice and Human Rights*, 1993; E. Mason, *Saint Wulfstan of Worcester, c. 1008–1095*, 1990.

Patricia Price

WULFSTAN OF YORK (WULFSTAN THE HOMILIST) (966–1023).

Bishop of London from 996 to 1002, bishop of Worcester from 1002 to 1016, and archbishop of York from 1002 to 1023, Wulfstan was, together with *Ælfric, one of the two greatest Old English prose stylists.

Wulfstan, like his contemporary Ælfric, was a product of the Benedictine reforms of the Anglo-Saxon Church begun by *Dunstan in the mid-tenth century and then continued by Æthelwold. Unlike Ælfric, though, who worked mostly as a homilist, hagiographer, and educator, Wulfstan is noteworthy as a sermon writer. In his best-known sermon, *Sermo Lupi ad Anglos* (Sermon of the Wolf to the English), he attacks the political and social disunity of the English in response to the renewed Scandinavian invasions of the late tenth and early eleventh centuries, taking as his inspiration *Gildas' earlier castigation of the British. In his sermons, Wulfstan uses a hortatory, zealous style quite distinct from Ælfric's usual quiet self-possession.

His other known works include the *Canons of Edgar*, attacking slothfulness and immorality in the secular clergy, and the *Institutes of Polity*, in which he sets out the theoretical organization of Christian society. He was also important as a legal writer, either drafting or supervising the drafting of "The Laws of

Edward," "The Laws of *Guthrum," many of the later edicts of *Æthelred the Unready, and a formal code for King *Cnut.

Bibliography: S. B. Greenfield and D. G. Calder, *A New Critical History of Old English Literature*, 1986.

David Day

Bibliography

GENERAL TITLES

Baldwin, John W. *The Scholastic Culture of the Middle Ages: 1000–1300*. 2nd ed. Prospect Heights, IL: Waveland Press, 1997.

Collins, Roger. *Early Medieval Europe, 300–1000*. Basingstoke: Macmillan Education, 1991.

Dictionary of the Middle Ages. Ed. Joseph R. Strayer. New York: Scribner, 1982.

Hollister, C. Warren. *Medieval Europe: A Short History*. Boston: McGraw-Hill, 1998.

Holmes, George, ed. *The Oxford History of Medieval Europe*. Oxford: Oxford University Press, 1992.

Lawrence, Clifford H. *Medieval Monasticism: Forms of Religious Life in Western Europe in the Middle Ages*. 2nd ed. London: Longman, 1989.

Le Goff, Jacques, ed. *Medieval Callings*. Trans. Lydia Cochrane. Chicago: University of Chicago Press, 1990.

Southern, Richard W. *The Making of the Middle Ages*. New Haven, CT: Yale University Press, 1992.

SPECIALIZED TITLES

Abbo de Fleury. *Questions grammaticales*. Ed. Anita Guerreau-Jalabert. Paris: Belles Lettres, 1982.

Abbot Suger on the Abbey Church of Saint-Denis and Its Art Treasures. Ed. and trans. Erwin Panofsky. 2d ed. Princeton, NJ: Princeton University Press, 1979.

Abels, Richard. *Alfred the Great: War, Kingship and Culture in Anglo-Saxon England*. London: Longman, 1998.

Abulafia, David. *Frederick II: A Medieval Emperor*. London: Penguin, 1988.

Adam of Bremen. *History of the Archbishops of Hamburg-Bremen*. Trans. Francis J. Tschan. New York: Columbia University Press, 1959.

Adamnan of Iona. *Life of St. Columba*. Ed. Richard Sharpe. Harmondsworth: Penguin, 1995.

Adelard of Bath. *Conversations with His Nephew*. Ed. and trans. Charles Burnett. Cambridge: Cambridge University Press, 1998.

Adler, Marcus N. *The Itinerary of Benjamin of Tudela*. 1907. Reprint, New York: P. Feldheim, 1964.

Aerts, W. J., Edmé R. Smits, and J. B. Voorbij. *Vincent of Beauvais and Alexander the Great: Studies on the* Speculum Maius *and Its Translations into Medieval Vernculars*. Groningen, The Netherlands: E. Forsten, 1986.

Alan of Lille. *Anticlaudianus, or the Good and Perfect Man*. Trans. James J. Sheridan. Toronto: Pontifical Institute of Mediaeval Studies, 1973.

———. *The Art of Preaching*. Trans. Gillian R. Evans. Kalamazoo, MI: Cistercian Publications, 1981.

———. *Plaint of Nature*. Trans. James J. Sheridan. Toronto: Pontifical Institute of Mediaeval Studies, 1980.

Alcock, Leslie. *Arthur's Britain*. London: Penguin, 1971.

Alcuin. *The Bishops, Kings, and Saints of York*. Ed. Peter Godman. Oxford: Oxford University Press, 1982.

Allen, Roland L. "Gerbert, Pope Sylvester II." *English Historical Review*, n.s., 7 (1892): 625–668.

Anderson, Earl R. *Cynewulf: Structure, Style, and Theme in His Poetry*. Madison, NJ: Fairleigh Dickinson University Press, 1983.

Anderson, Marjorie O. *Adomnán's Life of Columba*. Rev. ed. Oxford: Oxford University Press, 1991.

Angela of Foligno. *The Complete Works*. Trans. Paul Lachance. New York: Paulist Press, 1993.

Angold, Michael. *The Byzantine Empire, 1025–1204*. 2d ed. London: Longman, 1997.

Appel, Carl. *Bernart von Ventadorn, Seine Lieder mit Einleitung und Glossar*. Halle, Germany: Niemeyer, 1915.

Arden, Heather M. *The Romance of the Rose*. Boston: Twayne Publishers, 1987.

Ari Þorgilsson. *The Book of the Icelanders*. Ed. and trans. Halldór Hermannsson. Islandica 20. Ithaca, NY: Cornell University Press, 1930.

Armstrong, Regis J., and Ignatius C. Brady, trans. and eds. *Francis and Clare: The Complete Works*. New York: Paulist Press, 1982.

Arnold, Benjamin. *Medieval Germany, 500–1300. A Political Interpretation*. Toronto: University of Toronto Press, 1997.

Babinsky, Ellen L., trans. *The Mirror of Simple Souls*. New York: Paulist Press, 1993.

Bagge, Sverre. *From Gang Leader to the Lord's Anointed: Kingship in* Sverris saga *and* Hákonar saga Hákonarsonar. Odense, Denmark: Odense University Press, 1996.

———. "Ideas and Narrative in Otto of Freising's *Gesta Frederici*." *Journal of Medieval History* 22 (1996): 345–377.

Baird, Joseph L., Giuseppe Baglivi, and John R. Kane. *The Chronicle of Salimbene de Adam*. Binghamton, NY: Medieval and Renaissance Texts and Studies, 1986.

Baldwin, John W. *The Government of Philip Augustus: Foundations of French Power in the Middle Ages*. Berkeley: University of California Press, 1986.

———. *Masters, Princes and Merchants: The Social Views of Peter the Chanter and His Circle*. 2 vols. Princeton, NJ: Princeton University Press, 1970.

Barlow, Frank. *Edward the Confessor*. New ed. New Haven, CT: Yale University Press, 1997.

———. *Thomas Becket*. Berkeley: University of California Press, 1986.

Barraclough, Geoffrey. *The Origins of Modern Germany*. New York: Capricorn Books, 1963.

Barratt, Alexandra, ed. *Women's Writing in Middle English*. London: Longman, 1992.

Barrow, G.W.S. *Kingship and Unity: Scotland 1000–1306*. Toronto: University of Toronto Press, 1981.

Bartlett, Robert. *Gerald of Wales, 1146–1223*. Oxford: Clarendon Press, 1982.

Barton, John L. "The Mystery of Bracton." *Journal of Legal History* 14 (1993): 1–142.

Bates, David. *Normandy before 1066*. London: Longman, 1982.

Batselier, Pieter, ed. *Saint Benedict, Father of Western Civilization*. New York: Alpine Fine Arts Collection, 1981.

Bauer, Albert, and Reinhold Rau, eds. *Quellen zur Geschichte der Sächsischen Kaiserzeit: Widukinds Sachsengeschichte, Adalberts Fortsetzung der Chronik Reginos, Liutprands Werke*. Darmstadt, Germany: Wissenschaftliche Buchgesellschaft, 1971.

Beaumanoir, Philippe de. *The* Coutumes de Beauvaisis *of Philippe de Beaumanoir*. Trans. F.R.P. Akehurst. Philadelphia: University of Pennsylvania Press, 1992.

Beha, H. M. "Matthew of Aquasparta's Theory of Cognition." *Franciscan Studies*. 2d ser., 20 (1960): 161–204; 21 (1961): 1–79, 383–465.

Behrends, Frederick, ed. *The Letters and Poems of Fulbert of Chartres*. Oxford: Clarendon Press, 1976.

Benton, John F. "Collaborative Approaches to Fantasy and Reality in the Literature of Champagne." In *Culture, Power and Personality in Medieval France*, ed. Thomas Bisson. London: Hambledon Press, 1991.

———. "Trotula, Women's Problems, and the Professionalization of Medicine in the Middle Ages." *Bulletin of the History of Medicine* 59.1 (1985): 30–53.

———, trans. *Self and Society in Medieval France: The Memoirs of Abbot Guibert of Nogent*. New York: Harper & Row, 1970.

Beumann, Helmut. *Widukind von Korvei: Untersuchungen zur Geschichtsschreibung und Ideengeschichte des 10. Jahrhunderts*. Weimar, Germany: Hermann Böhlaus, 1950.

Billson, Marcus K., III. "Joinville's *Histoire de Saint-Louis*: Hagiography, History, and Memoir." *American Benedictine Review* 31 (1980): 418–442.

Birch, Debra J. "Jacques de Vitry and the Ideology of Pilgrimage." In *Pilgrimage Explored*, ed. Jennie Stopford. Suffolk, England: York Medieval Press, 1999.

Bishko, Charles Julian. *Studies in Medieval Spanish Frontier History*. London: Variorum Reprints, 1980.

Bishop, Jane. "Bishops as Marital Advisors in the Ninth Century." In *Women of the Medieval World: Essays in Honor of John H. Mundy*, ed. Julius Kirshner and Suzanne F. Wemple. Oxford: Basil Blackwell, 1985.

Bisson, Thomas N. *The Medieval Crown of Aragon*. Oxford: Clarendon Press, 1986.

Bjork, Robert E., ed. *Cynewulf: Basic Readings*. New York: Garland, 1996.

Bloch, Herbert. *Monte Cassino in the Middle Ages*. Vol. I. Cambridge: Harvard University Press, 1986.

Blum, Owen J. *St. Peter Damian: His Teaching on the Spiritual Life*. Washington, DC: Catholic University of America Press, 1947.

Blumenthal, Uta-Renate. *The Early Councils of Pope Paschal II, 1100–1110*. Toronto: Pontifical Institute of Mediaeval Studies, 1978.

Boase, Thomas S. R. *Boniface VIII*. London: Constable & Co., Ltd., 1933.

Boethius, A.M.S. *The Consolation of Philosophy*. Trans. Patrick G. Walsh. Oxford: Clarendon Press, 1999.

Boethius of Dacia. *On the Supreme Good, On the Eternity of the World, On Dreams*. Trans. John Wippel. Toronto: Pontifical Institute of Mediaeval Studies, 1987.

Bogin, Meg. *The Women Troubadours*. New York: Paddington Press, 1976.

Boncompagni, Baldassare. *Della vita e delle opere di Gherardo Cremonese*. Rome: Tipographia delle belle arti, 1851.

Bond, Gerald A., ed. and trans. *The Poetry of William VII, Count of Poitiers, IX Duke of Aquitaine*. New York: Garland, 1982.

Bonnet-Laborderie, Philippe, ed. *Actes du Colloque International Philippe de Beaumanoir et les Coutumes de Beauvaisis (1283–1983): Aspects de la vie au XIIIe siècle-Histoire-Droit-Littérature*. Beauvais, France: GEMOB, 1983.

Bostock, J. Knight. *A Handbook on Old High German Literature*. 2d ed. rev. Oxford: Clarendon Press, 1976.

Bougerol, Jacques G. *Introduction to the Works of Bonaventure*. Trans. José de Vinck. Paterson, NJ: St. Anthony Guild Press, 1963.

Bouvier-Ajam, Maurice. *Dagobert*. Paris: Éditions Tallandier, 1980.

Boyle, John A. "Omar Khayyam: Astronomer, Mathematician and Poet." *Bulletin of the John Rylands Library* 52 (1969): 30–45.

Bracton, Henrici de. *De legibus et consuetudinibus Angliae*. 4 vols. Ed. George E. Woodbine. Rev. and trans. Samuel E. Thorne. New Haven, CT: Yale University Press, 1915–1942.

Bradbury, Jim. *Philip Augustus, King of France 1180–1223*. London: Longman, 1998.

Bradley, Ritamary. "Beatrice of Nazareth (c. 1200–1268): A Search for Her True Spirituality." In *Vox Mystica: Essays on Medieval Mysticism in Honor of Professor Valerie M. Lagorio*, ed. Anne Clark Bartlett. Cambridge: D. S. Brewer, 1995.

Brady, Ignatius. "Petrus Manducator and the Oral Teachings of Peter Lombard." *Antonianum* 40 (1966): 454–490.

Braegelmann, Sr. Athanasius. *The Life and Writings of Saint Ildefonsus of Toledo*. Washington, DC: Catholic University of America Press, 1942.

Brand, Paul. "The Age of Bracton." In *The History of English Law: Centenary Essays on "Pollock and Maitland,"* ed. John Hudson. Oxford: Oxford University Press, 1996.

Bredero, Adriaan. *Bernard of Clairvaux: Between Cult and History*. Grand Rapids, MI: W. B. Eerdmans, 1996.

Brem, Ernst. *Papst Gregor IX bis zum Beginnen seines Pontifikats*. Heidelberg, Germany: C. Winter, 1911.

Bridge, Antony. *Richard the Lionheart*. London: Grafton, 1989.

———. *Theodora: Portrait in a Byzantine Landscape*. London: Cassell, 1978.

Brooks, Nicholas. *The Early History of the Church of Canterbury: Christ Church from 597 to 1066*. Leicester, England: Leicester University Press, 1984.

Brown, Sydney, and Jeremiah O'Sullivan, eds. *The Register of Eudes of Rouen*. New York: Columbia University Press, 1964.

Browning, Robert. *Justinian and Theodora*. New York: Praeger, 1971.

Bruckner, Matilda T. "Fictions of the Female Voice: The Women Troubadours." *Speculum* 67 (October 1992): 865–891.

Brundage, James A. "Adhémar of Puy. The Bishop and His Critics." *Speculum* 34 (1959): 201–212.

———. "Widukind of Corvey and the 'Non-Roman' Imperial Idea." *Mediaeval Studies* 22 (1960): 15–26.

Brunner, Horst, and Sigrid Neureiter-Lackner. *Walther von der Vogelweide: Epoche, Werk, Wirkung*. Munich: Beck, 1996.

Buc, Philippe. "Italian Hussies and German Matrons: Liutprand of Cremona on Dynastic Legitimacy." *Frühmittelalterliche Studien* 29 (1995): 207–225.

Bumke, Joachim. *Wolfram von Eschenbach*. Stuttgart: J. B. Metzler, 1997.

Burgess, Glyn S. *Marie de France: An Analytical Bibliography*. Supplement no. 2. London: Grant and Cutler, 1997.

Burnett, Charles, and Danielle Jacquart, eds. *Constantine the African and ʿAli ibn al-ʿAbbas al-Magusi: The* Pantegni *and Related Texts*. Studies in Ancient Medicine, 10. Leiden, The Netherlands: E. J. Brill, 1994.

Burns, Robert I. *Emperor of Culture: Alfonso X the Learned of Castile and His Thirteenth-Century Renaissance*. Philadelphia: University of Pennsylvania Press, 1990.

Burns, Thomas. *A History of the Ostrogoths*. Bloomington: Indiana University Press, 1991.

Burr, David. *Olivi and Franciscan Poverty. The Origins of the Usus Pauper Controversy*. Philadelphia: University of Pennsylvania Press, 1989.

Bury, John B. *A History of the Later Roman Empire from the Death of Theodosius to the Death of Justinian*. 2 vols. London: Macmillan, 1923.

Busse, Eberhard K. *Ulrich von Türheim*. Berlin: Mayer & Muller, 1913.

Butler, Alban. *The Lives of the Fathers, Martyrs, and Other Principal Saints*. 6 vols. New York: D. & J. Sadlier, 1846.

Butler, John. *The Quest for Becket's Bones: The Mystery of the Relics of St. Thomas Becket of Canterbury*. New Haven, CT: Yale University Press, 1995.

Bynum, Carolyn Walker. *Jesus as Mother: Studies in the Spirituality of the High Middle Ages*. Berkeley: University of California Press, 1982.

Cabaniss, Allen, trans. *The Emperor's Monk: A Contemporary Life of Benedict of Aniane*. Ilfracombe, England: A. H. Stockwell, 1979.

———. *Son of Charlemagne: A Contemporary Life of Louis the Pious*. Syracuse, NY: Syracuse University Press, 1961.

Cambridge History of German Literature. Ed. H. Watanabe-O'Kelly. Cambridge: Cambridge University Press, 1997.

Cameron, Averil. *Procopius and the Sixth Century*. Berkeley: University of California Press, 1985.

Campbell, Mary B. *The Witness and the Other World: Exotic European Travel Writing, 400–1600*. Ithaca, NY: Cornell University Press, 1988.

Capellanus, Andreas. *The Art of Courtly Love*. Trans. John Jay Parry. New York: Columbia University Press, 1960.

Carpenter, David A. *The Reign of Henry III*. London: Hambledon Press, 1996.

Cassiodorus. *An Introduction to Divine and Human Readings*. Trans. Leslie Webber Jones. New York: Octagon Books, 1966.

———. *Variae*. Trans. S.J.B. Barnish. Liverpool: Liverpool University Press, 1992.

Chadwick, Henry. *Boethius: The Consolations of Music, Logic, Theology, and Philosophy*. Oxford: Clarendon Press, 1981.

Chase, Stephen. *Angelic Wisdom: The Cherubim and the Grace of Contemplation in Richard of St. Victor.* Notre Dame, IN: University of Notre Dame Press, 1995.

Chibnall, Marjorie. *The Empress Matilda: Queen Consort, Queen Mother and Lady of the English.* Oxford: Blackwell, 1991.

————, ed. and trans. *The Ecclesiastical History of Orderic Vitalis.* 6 vols. Oxford: Clarendon Press, 1969–1980.

Chinca, Mark. *Gottfried von Strassburg: Tristan.* Cambridge: Cambridge University Press, 1997.

Chodorow, Stanley. *Christian Political Theory and Church Policy of the Mid-Twelfth Century: The Ecclesiology of Gratian's* Decretum. Berkeley: University of California Press, 1972.

Ciklamini, Marlene. *Snorri Sturluson.* Boston: Twayne Publishers, 1978.

Clarence-Smith, John. *Medieval Law Teachers and Writers: Civilian and Canonist.* Ottawa, Ontario, Canada: University of Ottawa Press, 1975.

Clot, Andre. *Harun al-Rashid and the World of the Thousand and One Nights.* Trans. John Howe. New York: New Amsterdam, 1989.

Cochrane, Louise. *Adelard of Bath: The First English Scientist.* London: British Museum Press, 1994.

Colish, Marcia L. *Peter Lombard.* 2 vols. Leiden, The Netherlands: E. J. Brill, 1994.

Colker, Marvin, ed. *Galteri de Castellione Alexandreis.* Padua, Italy: In aedibus Antenoreis, 1978.

Comins, Vicente Forcada. *San Ramón de Peñafort: Biografía.* Valencia, Spain: Provincia Dominicana de Aragón, 1994.

Cooperson, Michael. *Classical Arabic Biography. The Heirs of the Prophets in the Age of al-Ma'mūn.* Cambridge: Cambridge University Press, 2000.

Cormeau, Christoph, and Wilhelm Störmer. *Hartmann von Aue: Epoche, Werk, Wirkung.* Munich: C. H. Beck, 1993.

The Cosmographia of Bernardus Silvestris. Trans. Winthrop Wetherbee. New York: Columbia University Press, 1972.

Cronne, Henry A. *The Reign of Stephen, 1135–1154: Anarchy in England.* London: Weidenfeld & Nicholson, 1970.

Crouch, David. *William Marshal: Court, Career, and Chivalry in the Angevin Empire, 1147–1219.* London: Longman, 1990.

Curley, Michael J. *Geoffrey of Monmouth.* New York: Twayne Publishers, 1994.

Curtius, Ernst R. *European Literature and the Latin Middle Ages.* Trans. Willard R. Trask. Princeton, NJ: Princeton University Press, 1973.

Dalarun, Jacques. *L'impossible sainteté: La vie retrouvée de Robert d'Arbrissel (v. 1045–1116) fondateur de Fontevraud.* Paris: Cerf, 1985.

————. *Robert d'Arbrissel fondateur de Fontevraud.* Paris: A. Michel, 1986.

Dalven, Rae. *Anna Comnena.* New York: Twayne Publishers, 1972.

Damme, Jean-Baptiste Van. *The Three Founders of Cîteaux: Robert of Molesme, Alberic, Stephen Harding.* Kalamazoo, MI: Cistercian Publications, 1998.

Davids, Adalbert. *The Empress Theophano: Byzantium and the West at the Turn of the Last Millenium.* Cambridge: Cambridge University Press, 1995.

Davidson, Hilda R. Ellis. *The Viking Road to Byzantium.* London: Allen & Unwin, 1976.

Davis, Ralph H. C. *King Stephen, 1135–1154.* 3rd ed. New York: Longman, 1990.

Davis, Ralph H. C., and Marjorie Chibnall, eds. and trans. *The Gesta Guillelmi of William of Poitiers.* New York: Clarendon Press, 1998.

Davis, Raymond, trans. *The Lives of the Eighth-Century Popes* (Liber Pontificalis): *The Ancient Biographies of Nine Popes from* AD *715 to* AD *817*. Liverpool: Liverpool University Press, 1992.

Dean, Ruth J. "Nicholas Trevet, Historian." In *Medieval Language and Literature: Essays Presented to Richard William Hunt*, ed. J.J.G. Alexander and M. T. Gibson. Oxford: Clarendon Press, 1976.

Déchanet, Jean-Marie. *William of St. Thierry: The Man and His Work*. Trans. Richard Strachan. Spencer, MA: Cistercian Publications, 1972.

de Jong, Mayke. "The Empire as *ecclesia*: Hrabanus Maurus and Biblical *historia* for Rulers." In *The Uses of the Past in the Early Middle Ages*, ed. Yitzhak Hen and Matthew Innes. Cambridge: Cambridge University Press, 2000.

Delperrié de Bayac, Jacques. *Louis VI: La naissance de la France*. Paris: J. C. Lattès, 1983.

Devisse, Jean. *Hincmar, Archévêque de Reims, 845–882*. 3 vols. Geneva: Droz, 1975–1976.

Díaz y Díaz, Manuel C. "Introducción general" to *Etimologías, Edición Bilingüe*, by San Isidoro de Sevilla. Ed. José Oroz Reta and Manuel-Antonio Marcos Casquero. Madrid: Editorial Católica, 1982.

Diehl, Charles. *Theodora, Empress of Byzantium*. Trans. Samuel R. Rosenbaum. New York: Ungar, 1972.

Douglas, David C. *William the Conqueror: The Norman Impact on England*. London: Eyre & Spottiswoode, 1964.

Douglas, David C., and George W. Greenaway, eds. *English Historical Documents, Volume II: 1042–1189*. London: Eyre Methuen, 1981.

Douie, Decima. *Archbishop Peckham*. Oxford: Clarendon Press, 1952.

Dronke, Peter. "The Lyrical Compositions of Philip the Chancellor." *Studi Medievali* 28 (1987): 563–592.

———. *Medieval Latin and the Rise of the European Love Lyric*. 2d ed. 2 vols. Oxford: Clarendon Press, 1968.

Duby, Georges. *France in the Middle Ages 987–1460: From Hugh Capet to Joan of Arc*. Trans. Juliet Vale. Oxford: Blackwell Publishers, 1993.

———. *William Marshal: The Flower of Chivalry*. London: Faber, 1985.

Duckett, Eleanor S. *Carolingian Portraits: A Study in the Ninth Century*. Ann Arbor: University of Michigan Press, 1962.

Dudden, Frederick H. *Gregory the Great: His Place in History and Thought*. London: Longmans, Green, 1905.

Dufeil, M.-M. *Guillaume de Saint-Amour et la polémique universitaire parisienne*. Paris: A. et J. Picard, 1972.

Duggan, Charles. *Canon Law in Medieval England: The Becket Dispute and Decretal Collections*. London: Variorum Reprints, 1982.

Dunbabin, Jean. *Charles I of Anjou: Power, Kingship, and State-Making in Thirteenth-Century Europe*. London: Longman, 1998.

Dvornik, Francis. *Byzantine Missions among the Slavs: SS. Constantine-Cyril and Methodius*. New Brunswick, NJ: Rutgers University Press, 1970.

Eadmer. *The Life of St. Anselm of Canterbury*. Ed. and trans. Richard W. Southern. London: T. Nelson, 1962.

Easton, Stewart C. *Roger Bacon and His Search for a Universal Science. A Reconsid-*

eration of the Life and Work of Roger Bacon in the Light of His Own Stated Purposes. Oxford: Blackwell, 1952.

Edbury, Peter W., and John G. Rowe. *William of Tyre: Historian of the Latin East.* Cambridge: Cambridge University Press, 1988.

Egils saga. Trans. Eric R. Eddison. Cambridge: Cambridge University Press, 1930.

Einhard. *Vita Karoli Magni/The Life of Charlemagne.* Ed. and trans. Evelyn S. Firchow and Edwin H. Zeydel. Dudweiler, Germany: A. Q.–Verlag, 1985.

Elder, E. Rozanne, ed. *Benedictus: Studies in Honor of St. Benedict of Nursia.* Kalamazoo, MI: Cistercian Publications, 1981.

El-Hibri, Tayeb. "The Reign of the ʿAbbasid Caliph al-Maʾmūn (811–833): The Quest for Power and the Crisis of Legitimacy." Ph.D. dissertation, Columbia University, 1994.

————. *Reinterpreting Islamic Historiography: Hārūn al-Rashīd and the Narrative of the ʿAbbāsid Caliphate.* Cambridge: Cambridge University Press, 1999.

Emerton, Ephraim. *The Correspondence of Pope Gregory VII.* New York: Columbia University Press, 1932.

Erkens, Franz Reiner. *Konrad II (um 990–1039): Herrschaft und Reich des ersten Salierkaisers.* Regensburg, Germany: Pustet, 1998.

Evans, Gillian R. *Alan of Lille: The Frontiers of Theology in the Later Twelfth Century.* Cambridge: Cambridge University Press, 1983.

Evans, Joan. *Monastic Life at Cluny, 910–1157.* Oxford: Oxford University Press, 1931.

Evergates, Theodore, ed. *Aristocratic Women in Medieval France.* Philadelphia: University of Pennsylvania Press, 1999.

Falls, James S. "Ranulf de Glanville's Formative Years, c. 1120–1179: The Family Background and His Ascent to the Justiciarship." *Mediaeval Studies* 40 (1978): 312–327.

Fell, Christine. *Women in Anglo-Saxon England.* Bloomington: Indiana University Press, 1984.

Finnegan, Mary J. *The Women of Helfta: Scholars and Mystics.* Athens: University of Georgia Press, 1991.

Flanagan, Sabina, ed. *Secrets of God: Writings of Hildegard of Bingen.* Boston: Shambhala, 1996.

Flood, David. "The Theology of Peter John Olivi. A Search for a Theology and Anthropology of the Synoptic Gospels." In *The History of Franciscan Theology,* ed. Kenan B. Osborne. St. Bonaventure, NY: Franciscan Institute, 1994.

Fontaine, Jacques. *Isidore de Seville et la culture classique dans l'Espagne wisigothique.* 2d ed. 3 vols. Paris: Études Augustiniennes, 1983.

Fortini, Arnaldo. *Francis of Assisi.* New York: Seabury Press, 1981.

France before Charlemagne: A Translation from the Grandes Chroniques. Trans. Robert Levine. Lewiston, NY: Edwin Mellen Press, 1990.

Frank, Richard. *Al-Ghazālī and the Ashʾarite School.* Durham, NC: Duke University Press, 1994.

Frappier, Jean. *Chrétien de Troyes: The Man and His Work.* Trans. Raymond Cormier. 1957. Reprint, Athens: Ohio University Press, 1982.

Friedberg, Emil, and Aemilius Richter, contributors. *Corpus iuris canonici.* 2d ed. 2 vols. 1879. Reprint, Graz, Austria: Akademische Druck–U. Verlagsamstalt, 1959.

Gabriel, Astrik L. *The Paris Studium: Robert of Sorbonne and His Legacy.* Notre Dame, IN: University of Notre Dame Press, 1992.

Galston, Miriam G. *Politics and Excellence: The Political Philosophy of Alfarabi.* Princeton, NJ: Princeton University Press, 1990.

Garland, Lynda. *Byzantine Empresses: Women and Power in Byzantium, AD 527–1204.* London: Routledge, 1999.

Gathagan, Laura L. "The Coronation of Matilda of Flanders." *Haskins Society Journal* X (forthcoming).

George, Judith, trans. *Venantius Fortunatus: Personal and Political Poems.* Liverpool: Liverpool University Press, 1995.

Gero, Stephen. *Byzantine Iconoclasm during the Reign of Leo III.* Louvain, Belgium: Secrétariat du Corpus SCO, 1973.

Gertrude the Great. *Spiritual Exercises.* Translation, Introduction, Notes, and Indexes by Gertrud Jaron Lewis and Jack Lewis. Kalamazoo, MI: Cistercian Publications, 1989.

Gibson, Margaret T. *Lanfranc of Bec.* Oxford: Clarendon Press, 1978.

———, ed. *Boethius: His Life, Thought and Influence.* Oxford: Blackwell, 1981.

Gillingham, John. *Richard I.* New Haven, CT: Yale University Press, 1999.

Gilson, Étienne. *Héloïse and Abelard.* London: Hollis & Carter, 1953.

———. *History of Christian Philosophy in the Middle Ages.* New York: Random House, 1955.

Gjerset, Knut. *History of the Norwegian People.* New York: Macmillan, 1915.

Glaber, Radulphus. *Five Books of the Histories.* Ed. and trans. John France. Oxford: Clarendon Press, 1989.

Godman, Peter. *Poetry of the Carolingian Renaissance.* Norman: University of Oklahoma Press, 1985.

Goffart, Walter. *Narrators of Barbarian History (A.D. 550–800): Jordanes, Gregory of Tours, Bede, and Paul the Deacon.* Princeton, NJ: Princeton University Press, 1988.

Gohlman, William, ed. *The Life of Ibn Sina: A Critical Edition and Annotated Translation.* Albany: SUNY Press, 1974.

The Golden Legend: *Readings on the Saints.* Trans. William Granger Ryan. 2d ed. Princeton, NJ: Princeton University Press, 1993.

Golding, Brian. *Gilbert of Sempringham and the Gilbertine Order, c. 1130–c. 1300.* Oxford: Clarendon Press, 1995.

Goodman, Lenn E. *Avicenna.* London: Routledge, 1992.

Goodsell, Daniel A. *Peter the Hermit: A Story of Enthusiasm.* Cincinnati, OH: Jennings and Graham, 1906.

Grabmann, Martin. *Guglielmo di Moerbeke, O.P. Il traduttore delle opere di Aristotele.* Rome: Pontificia Università Gregoriana, 1970.

Grane, Leif. *Peter Abelard: Philosophy and Christianity in the Middle Ages.* London: Allen & Unwin, 1970.

Grant, Lindy. *Abbot Suger of St-Denis: Church and State in Early Twelfth-Century France.* London: Longman, 1998.

Gravdal, Kathryn. *Ravishing Maidens: Writing Rape in Medieval French Literature and Law.* Philadelphia: University of Pennsylvania Press, 1991.

Green, Judith A. *The Government of England under Henry I.* Cambridge: Cambridge University Press, 1986.

Greenaway, George W. *Arnold of Brescia.* Cambridge: Cambridge University Press, 1931.

Greenfield, Stanley B., and Daniel G. Calder. *A New Critical History of Old English Literature*. New York: New York University Press, 1986.

Gregory of Tours. *The History of the Franks*. Trans. Lewis Thorpe. Harmondsworth: Penguin, 1974.

———. *Lives of the Fathers*. Ed. and trans. Edward James. Liverpool: Liverpool University Press, 1985.

Grillparzer, Franz. *King Ottocar, His Rise and Fall, a Tragedy in Five Acts*. Trans. Henry H. Stevens. Yarmouth Port, MA: The Register Press, 1938.

Gross-Diaz, Theresa. *The Psalms Commentary of Gilbert of Poitiers: From* Lectio divina *to the Lecture Room*. Leiden, The Netherlands: E. J. Brill, 1996.

Guillaume Durand. *Pontificale*. In *Le Pontifical roman au moyen-âge*. III. *Le pontifical de Guillaume Durand*. Ed. M. Andrieu. Vatican City, Italy: Biblioteca Apostolica, 1940.

———. *Rationale divinorum officiorum*. Ed. V. d'Avino. Naples, Italy: Dura, 1859.

———. *Speculum iudicale*. Basel, 1574. Reprint, Aalen, Germany: Scientia, 1975.

Gutas, Dimitri. *Avicenna and the Aristotelian Tradition: Introduction to Reading Avicenna's Philosophical Works*. Leiden, The Netherlands: E. J. Brill, 1988.

Guðmundsson, Gunnar F. *Þorlákur helgi: Life, Work, and Influence of St. Thorlák (1133–1193), Patron Saint of the Icelandic People*. Reykjavík: Piló, 1993.

Gy, Pierre-Marie, ed. *Guillaume Durand, évêque de Mende (v. 1230–1296)*. Paris: Actes de la Table ronde du CNRS, 1992.

Györffy, György. *King Saint Stephen of Hungary*. Trans. Peter Doherty. New York: Columbia University Press, 1994.

Hackett, Jeremiah, ed. *Roger Bacon and the Sciences: Commemorative Essays*. Leiden, The Netherlands: E. J. Brill, 1997.

Hallam, Elizabeth M. *Capetian France, 987–1328*. London: Longman, 1990.

Hallberg, Peter. *Old Icelandic Poetry: Eddic Lay and Skaldic Verse*. Trans. Paul Schach. Lincoln: University of Nebraska Press, 1975.

Hallencreutz, Carl F. *Adam Bremensis and Sueonia: A Fresh Look at* Gesta hammaburgensis ecclesiae pontificum. Uppsala, Sweden: Almqvist & Wiksell, 1984.

Hampe, Karl. *Germany under the Salian and Hohenstaufen Emperors*. Trans. Ralph Bennett. Totowa, NJ: Rowman & Littlefield, 1973.

Haskins, Charles H. *Renaissance of the Twelfth Century*. Cambridge: Harvard University Press, 1927.

———. *Studies in the History of Medieval Science*. 2d ed. Cambridge: Harvard University Press, 1927.

Hastrup, Kristen. *Culture and History in Medieval Iceland*. Oxford: Clarendon Press, 1985.

Hasty, Will. *Adventures in Interpretation: The Works of Hartmann von Aue and Their Critical Reception*. Columbia, SC: Camden House, 1996.

———, ed. Introduction to *A Companion to Wolfram's Parzival*. Columbia, SC: Camden House, 1999.

Helbling, Hanno, ed. *Ekkehard IV. Die Geschichten des Klosters St. Gallen*. Weimar, Germany: H. Böhlaus Nachfolger, 1958.

Herren, Michael, "Classical and Secular Learning among the Irish before the Carolingian Renaissance." *Florilegium* 3 (1981): 118–157.

Hill, Boyd H., Jr. *Medieval Monarchy in Action: The German Empire from Henry I to Henry IV*. London: Allen and Unwin, 1972.

Hill, John Hugh, and Laurita Lyttleton Hill. *Raymond IV Count of Toulouse*. Syracuse, NY: Syracuse University Press, 1962.

Hillgarth, Jocelyn N. "Isidorian Studies, 1976–1985." *Studi medievali* 31.2 (1990): 925–973.

———. *Ramon Lull and Lullism in Fourteenth-Century France*. Oxford: Clarendon Press, 1971.

Hinnebusch, William A. *The History of the Dominican Order*. 2 vols. Staten Island, NY: Alba House, 1966.

Hoensch, Jörg K. *Premysl Otakar II von Böhmen, der goldene König*. Graz, Austria: Styria, 1989.

Hoffmann, Hartmut, and Rudolf Pokorny. *Das Dekret des Bischofs Burchard von Worms: Textstufen, Frühe Verbreitung, Vorlagen*. Monumenta Germaniae historica. Hilfsmittel 12. Munich: Monumenta Germaniae Historica, 1991.

Hollis, Stephanie. *Anglo-Saxon Women and the Church: Sharing a Common Fate*. Suffolk, England: Boydell Press, 1992.

Holloway, Julia Bolton. *Twice-Told Tales: Brunetto Latino and Dante Alighieri*. New York: Peter Lang, 1993.

Holmes, Urban T., Jr. "Norman Literature and Wace." In *Medieval Secular Literature*, ed. William Matthews. Berkeley: University of California Press, 1967.

Holt, James C. *Magna Carta*. 2d ed. Cambridge: Cambridge University Press, 1992.

Holt, Peter M. *The Age of the Crusades: The Near East from the Eleventh Century to 1517*. London: Longman, 1986.

Hrotsvit of Gandersheim: A Florilegium of Her Works. Trans. Katharina M. Wilson. Cambridge: D. S. Brewer, 1998.

Huddy, Mary. *Matilda, Countess of Tuscany*. London: J. Long, 1910.

Hugh of Saint-Victor: Selected Spiritual Writings. With an introduction by Aelred Squire. New York: Harper & Row, 1962.

Hunt, Richard W. *The Schools and the Cloister: The Life and Writings of Alexander Nequam (1157–1217)*. Ed. Margaret Gibson. Oxford: Clarendon Press, 1984.

Hunter Blair, Peter. *An Introduction to Anglo-Saxon England*. Cambridge: Cambridge University Press, 1966.

———. *The World of Bede*. London: Secker and Warburg, 1970.

Iohannis Scotti Eriugenae. *Carmina*. Ed. Michael W. Herren. Dublin: School of Celtic Studies, 1993.

Jacques de Vitry. *Life of Marie d'Oignies*. Trans. Margot H. King. Toronto: Peregrina Publishing, 1993.

Jenkins, Thomas A., ed. *The Espurgatoire Saint Patriz of Marie de France with a Text of the Latin Original*. 1903. Reprint, Geneva: Slatkine Reprints, 1974.

Jensen, Søren. "On the National Origin of Boethius of Dacia." *Classica et Mediaevalia* 24 (1963): 232–241.

Jewers, Caroline. "The Poetics of (S)Cat-Ology in Guilhem VII, Count of Poitiers, IX Duke of Aquitaine's Canso V." *Tenso* 11.1 (1995): 38–63.

John of Joinville. *Life of Saint Louis*. In *Chronicles of the Crusades*, ed. Margaret R. B. Shaw. Harmondsworth: Penguin, 1963.

John of Salisbury. *Policratus*. Ed. and trans. Cary J. Nederman. Cambridge: Cambridge University Press, 1990.

Jones, George F. *Walther von der Vogelweide*. New York: Twayne Publishers, 1968.

Jones, Gwyn. *A History of the Vikings*. New York: Oxford University Press, 1984.

Jónsson, Finnur, ed. *Den norsk-islandske skjaldedigtning*. Copenhagen and Christiania: Gyldendal, 1912–1915.

Jordan, Karl. *Henry the Lion: A Biography*. Trans. P. S. Falla. Oxford: Clarendon Press, 1986.

Jordan, William C. *Louis IX and the Challenge of the Crusade: A Study in Rulership*. Princeton, NJ: Princeton University Press, 1996.

Jover Zamora, José-María, and Miguel A. Ladero Quesada. *Historia de España Menéndez Pidal: Tomo IX. La Reconquista y el proceso de diferenciación política (1035–1217)*. Madrid: Espasa Calpe, 1998.

Judy, Albert G., ed. *De ortu scientiarum*. London: British Academy, 1976.

Kaldellis, Anthony. *The Argument of Psellos'* Chronographia. Leiden, The Netherlands: E. J. Brill, 1999.

Kaylor, Noel H. *The Medieval Consolation of Philosophy*. New York: Garland, 1992.

Kealey, Edward J. *Roger of Salisbury, Viceroy of England*. Berkeley: University of California Press, 1972.

Keil, Heinrich. *Grammatici latini*. 8 vols. Leipzig, Germany: B. G. Teubneri, 1855–1880.

Keller, John. *Alfonso X el Sabio*. New York: Twayne Publishers, 1967.

Kelly, Amy. *Eleanor of Aquitaine and the Four Kings*. Cambridge: Harvard University Press, 1950.

Kerr, Berenice M. *Religious Life for Women, c. 1100–c. 1350: Fontevraud in England*. Oxford: Oxford University Press, 1999.

Keynes, Simon. *The Diplomas of King Æthelred "the Unready" 978–1016: A Study in Their Use as Evidence*. Cambridge: Cambridge University Press, 1980.

Keynes, Simon, and Michael Lapidge, trans. *Alfred the Great: Asser's* Life of King Alfred *and Other Contemporary Sources*. Harmondsworth: Penguin, 1983.

Kibler, William W., ed. *Eleanor of Aquitaine: Patron and Politician*. Austin: University of Texas Press, 1976.

King, James C., and Petrus W. Tax, eds. *Die Werke Notkers des Deutschen*. Series. Tübingen, Germany: Max Niemeyer, 1972–1996.

Kitchen, John. *Saints' Lives and the Rhetoric of Gender: Male and Female in Merovingian Hagiography*. New York: Oxford University Press, 1998.

Kleiber, Wolfgang, ed. *Otfrid von Weissenburg*. Darmstadt, Germany: Wissenschaftliche Buchgesellschaft, 1978.

Klein, Thomas. "Heinrich von Veldeke und die mitteldeutschen Literatursprachen. Untersuchungen zum Veldeke-Problem." In *Zwei Studien zu Veldeke und zum Strassburger Alexander*. Amsterdam: Rodopi, 1985.

Klingshirn, William E. *Caesarius of Arles: Life, Testament, Letters*. Liverpool: Liverpool University Press, 1994.

———. *Caesarius of Arles: The Making of a Christian Community in Late Antique Gaul*. Cambridge: Cambridge University Press, 1994.

Koenigsberger, Helmut G. *Medieval Europe, 400–1500*. New York: Longman, 1987.

Kratchkovsky, I. "Les géographes arabes des XI et XII siècles en Occident." Trans. Morius Canard. *Annales de l'Institut d' Études Orientales de l'Université d'Alger* XVIII–XIX (1960–1961): 1–72.

Kritzeck, James. *Peter the Venerable and Islam*. Princeton, NJ: Princeton University Press, 1964.

Kuthan, Jiri. *Premysl Otakar II: König, Bauherr und Mäzen, höfische Kunst im 13 Jahrhundert*. Vienna: Böhlau Verlag, 1996.

Kuttner, Stephan. *Gratian and the Schools of Law, 1140–1234*. 1943. Reprint, London: Variorum Reprints, 1983.

————. *Harmony from Dissonance: An Interpretation of Medieval Canon Law*. Latrobe, PA: Archabbey Press, 1960.

Labande, Edmond-René. "Les filles d'Aliénor d'Aquitaine: Étude comparative." *Cahiers de civilisation médiévale* 19 (1986): 101–112.

Labarge, Margaret W. *Simon de Montfort*. London: Eyre & Spottiswoode, 1962.

————. *A Small Sound of the Trumpet. Women in Medieval Life*. Boston: Beacon Press, 1986.

The lais of Marie de France. Trans. Robert W. Hanning and Joan Ferrante. New York: Dutton, 1978.

Landgraf, Artur. *Introduction à l'histoire de la littérature théologique de la scolastique naissante*. Ed. Louis Geiger. Trans. Albert Landry. Montreal: Institut d'études médiévales, 1973.

Lapidge, Michael, ed. *Archbishop Theodore: Commemorative Studies on His Life and Influence*. Cambridge: Cambridge University Press, 1995.

————. *Columbanus: Studies on the Latin Writings*. New York: Boydell Press, 1997.

LaRoux, Sister Mary Protase, trans. *The* De Harmonica Institutione *and* Tonarius *of Regino of Prüm*. 1967. Reprint, Washington, DC: Catholic University of America Press, 1979.

Latini, Brunetto. *Li Livre dou trésor*. Ed. Francis J. Carmody. Berkeley: University of California Press, 1948.

————. *Il Tesoretto*. Trans. Julia Bolton Holloway. New York: Garland, 1981.

Lattin, Harriet Pratt, ed. and trans. *The Letters of Gerbert with His Papal Privileges as Sylvester II*. New York: Columbia University Press, 1961.

Lauring, Pelle. *A History of Denmark*. Trans. David Hohnen. 3d ed. Copenhagen: Høst, 1995.

Law, Vivien. "Grammar." In *Medieval Latin: An Introduction and Bibliographical Guide*, ed. F.A.C. Mantello and A. G. Rigg. Washington, DC: Catholic University of America Press, 1996.

Lawler, Traugott, ed. *The* Parisiana poetria *of John of Garland*. New Haven, CT: Yale University Press, 1974.

Lawrence, C. H. "The Letters of Adam Marsh and the Franciscan School at Oxford." *Journal of Ecclesiastical History* 42.2 (April 1991): 218–238.

Lawson, Michael K. *Cnut: The Danes in England in the Early Eleventh Century*. London: Longman, 1993.

Lazar, Moshé, ed. *Bernard de Ventadour, Troubadour du XIIe siècle, Chansons d'amour*. Paris: C. Klinckseck, 1966.

Leaman, Oliver. *Averroes and His Philosophy*. Oxford: Clarendon Press, 1988.

————. *Moses Maimonides*. London: Routledge, 1990.

Leclercq, Jean. *The Love of Learning and the Desire for God: A Study of Monastic Culture*. Trans. Catharine Misrahi. New York: New American Library, 1962.

Lees, Jay T. *Anselm of Havelberg: Deeds into Words in the Twelfth Century*. Leiden, The Netherlands: E. J. Brill, 1998.

Leonardi, Corrado. "La Vita e L'Opera di Uguccione da Pisa Decretista." *Studia Gratiana* 4 (1956–1957): 37–120.

Lerner, Robert E. "Poverty, Preaching, and Eschatology in the Commentaries of Hugh of St. Cher." In *The Bible in the Medieval World: Essays in Memory of Beryl Smalley*, ed. Katherine Walsh and Diana Wood. Oxford: Blackwell, 1985.

Levine, Robert. *The Deeds of God through the Franks: A Translation of Guibert de Nogent's* Gesta Dei per Francos. Suffolk, England: Boydell Press, 1997.

Levison, Wilhelm. *England and the Continent in the Eighth Century.* 1946. Reprint, Oxford: Oxford University, Press, 1998.

Lewis, C. S. *The Allegory of Love: A Study in Medieval Tradition.* Oxford: Oxford University Press, 1936.

Liber, Maurice. *Rashi.* Trans. Adele Szold. Philadelphia: Jewish Published Society of America, 1948.

Lindsay, Thomas. *Saint Benedict, His Life and Work.* London: Burns, Oates, 1950.

Lings, Martin. *Muhammad: His Life Based on the Earliest Sources.* London: Allen & Unwin, 1983.

Little, Andrew G. "The Franciscan School at Oxford in the Thirteenth Century." *Archivum Franciscanum Historicum* 19 (1926): 803–874.

Loewe, Raphael. *Ibn Gabirol.* London: Halban, 1989.

Lottin, Odon. *Psychologie et morale aux XIIe et XIIIe siècles, tome V: Problèmes d'histoire littéraire. L'école d'Anselme de Laon et de Guillaume de Champeaux.* Gembloux, Belgium: Duculot, 1957.

Luscombe, David. E. *The School of Peter Abelard: The Influence of Abelard's Thought in the Early Scholastic Period.* London: Cambridge University Press, 1969.

Lynch, Joseph H. *The Medieval Church: A Brief History.* London: Longman, 1992.

Lyons, Malcolm C., and David E. P. Jackson. *Saladin: The Politics of Holy War.* Cambridge: Cambridge University Press, 1982.

MacDonald, Allan J. *Berengar and the Reform of Sacramental Doctrine.* New York: Longmans, Green, 1930.

———. *Hildebrand, a Life of Gregory VII.* London: Methuen & Co., Ltd., 1932.

MacKinney, Loren C. *Bishop Fulbert and Education at the School of Chartres.* Notre Dame, IN: Medieval Institute, University of Notre Dame, 1957.

Maddicott, J. R. *Simon de Montfort.* Cambridge: Cambridge University Press, 1994.

Madigan, Shawn, ed. *Mystics, Visionaries, and Prophets: An Historical Anthology of Women's Spiritual Writings.* Minneapolis: Fortress Press, 1998.

Maimonides, Moses. *The Guide of the Perplexed.* Trans. Shlomo Pines. Chicago: University of Chicago Press, 1963.

Makk, Ferenc. *The Árpáds and the Comneni: Political Relations between Hungary and Byzantium in the 12th Century.* Trans. György Nóvak. Budapest: Akadémiai Kiadó, 1989.

Mālik ibn Anas. *Al-Muwatta.* Trans. ʿAʾisha ʿAbdarahman and Yaʾqub Johnson. Norwich, England: Diwan Press, 1982.

Malone, Sylvester. *Pope Adrian IV and Ireland.* Dublin: N. H. Gill, 1899.

Mandel, Oscar, trans. *Five Comedies of Medieval France.* Washington, DC: University Press of America, 1982.

Map, Walter. De nugis curialium: *Courtiers' Trifles.* Ed. and trans. Montague R. James. Rev. Christopher N. L. Brooke and Roger A. B. Mynors. Oxford: Clarendon Press, 1983.

Marbodi. *Liber decem capitulorum.* Ed. Rosario Leotta. Rome: Herder, 1984.

Marie de France. *Les fables.* Ed. and trans. Charles Brucker. Louvain, Belgium: Peeters, 1991.

Márkus, Gilbert, ed. *The Radical Tradition: Revolutionary Saints in the Battle for Justice and Human Rights*. 1st ed. New York: Doubleday, 1993.

Marrone, Steven. *Truth and Scientific Knowledge in the Thought of Henry of Ghent*. Cambridge, MA: Medieval Academy of America, 1985.

———. *William of Auvergne and Robert Grosseteste. New Ideas of Truth in the Early Thirteenth Century*. Princeton, NJ: Princeton University Press, 1983.

Mason, Emma. *Saint Wulfstan of Worcester, c. 1008–1095*. Oxford: Blackwell, 1990.

Masson, Georgina. *Frederick II of Hohenstaufen, a Life*. London: Secker & Warburg, 1957.

Maurer, Armand. *Medieval Philosophy*. 2d ed. Toronto: Pontifical Institute of Mediaeval Studies, 1982.

Maxwell-Stuart, P. G. *Chronicle of the Popes: The Reign-by-Reign Record of the Papacy from St. Peter to the Present*. New York: Thames and Hudson, 1997.

Mayeski, Marie A. *Dhuoda: Ninth Century Mother and Theologian*. New York: Fordham University Press, 1995.

Mayr-Harting, Henry. *The Coming of Christianity to Anglo-Saxon England*. London: Secker & Warburg, 1972.

McBrien, Richard P. *Lives of the Popes: The Pontiffs from St. Peter to John Paul II*. San Francisco: Harper San Francisco, 1997.

McCash, June Hall Martin. "Marie de Champagne and Eleanor of Aquitaine: A Relationship Reexamined." *Speculum* 54 (1979): 698–711.

McCracken, George E., and Allen Cabaniss. *Early Medieval Theology*. Philadelphia: Westminster Press, 1957.

McEvoy, James. *The Philosophy of Robert Grosseteste*. Oxford: Clarendon Press, 1982.

McGinn, Bernard. "William of Saint-Thierry: Spirit-Centered Mysticism." In *The Growth of Mysticism*. New York: Crossroad, 1994.

McGuire, Brian Patrick. *Brother and Lover: Ælred of Rievaulx*. New York: Crossroad, 1994.

McKitterick, Rosamond. *The Frankish Church and the Carolingian Reforms, 789–895*. London: Royal Historical Society, 1977.

———. *The Frankish Kingdoms under the Carolingians, 751–987*. London: Longman, 1983.

———, ed. *Carolingian Culture: Emulation and Innovation*. Cambridge: Cambridge University Press, 1994.

McLeod, E. *Héloïse. A Biography*. 2d ed. London: Chatto & Windus, 1971.

McNamara, Jo Ann, John E. Halborg, and E. Gordon Whately. "Clotilda." In *Sainted Women of the Dark Ages*, ed. and trans. Jo Ann McNamara, John E. Halborg, and E. Gordon Whately. Durham, NC: Duke University Press, 1992.

———. "Radegund, Queen of the Franks and Abbess of Poitiers (ca. 525–587)." In *Sainted Women of the Dark Ages*, ed. and trans. Jo Ann McNamara, John E. Halborg, and E. Gordon Whately. Durham, NC: Duke University Press, 1992.

McVaugh, Michael. "A List of Translations from Arabic into Latin in the Twelfth Century. Gerald of Cremona." In *A Source Book in Medieval Science*, ed. Edward Grant. Cambridge: Harvard University Press, 1976.

Mews, Constant J. *The Lost Love Letters of Heloise and Abelard. Perceptions of Dialogue in Twelfth-Century France*. New York: St. Martin's Press, 1999.

Moorhead, John. *Theodoric in Italy*. Oxford: Clarendon Press, 1992.

Morris, Colin. *The Papal Monarchy: The Western Church from 1050 to 1250*. Oxford: Clarendon Press, 1989.

Mortimer, Richard. "The Family of Rannulf de Glanville." *Bulletin of the Institute of Historical Research* 54 (1981): 1–16.

Mourret, Fernand. *Histoire genérale de l'église*. Vol. 4, *La chrétienté*. Paris: Bloud et Gay, 1928.

Muckle, J. T., trans. *The Story of Abelard's Adversities. A Translation with Notes of the* Historia Calamitatum. 1954. Reprint, Toronto: Pontifical Institute of Mediaeval Studies, 1992.

Munz, Peter. *Frederick Barbarossa, a Study in Medieval Politics*. Ithaca, NY: Cornell University Press, 1969.

Neale, John, trans. *The Symbolism of Churches and Church Ornaments*. London: Gibbings & Company, Ltd., 1893.

Nelson, Janet L. *Charles the Bald*. London: Longman, 1992.

———. "Public *Histories* and Private History in the Work of Nithard." *Speculum* 60.2 (April 1985): 251–293.

———, ed. *Richard Coeur de Lion in History and Myth*. London: Kings College, 1992.

Netton, Ian R. *Al-Fārābī and His School*. London: Routledge, 1992.

Newman, Barbara, ed. *Voice of the Living Light: Hildegard of Bingen and Her World*. Berkeley: University of California Press, 1998.

Newman, Roger Chatterton. *Brian Boru, King of Ireland*. Dublin: Anvil Books, 1983.

Nichols, Stephen G. "The Early Troubadours: Guilhem IX to Bernart de Ventadorn." In *The Troubadours: An Introduction*, ed. Simon Gaunt and Sarah Kay. Cambridge: Cambridge University Press, 1999.

Nichols, Stephen G., John A. Galm, and A. Bartlett Giamatti, eds. *The Songs of Bernart de Ventadorn*. Chapel Hill: University of North Carolina Press, 1962.

Nielsen, Lauge O. *Theology and Philosophy in the Twelfth Century: A Study of Gilbert Porreta's Thinking and the Theological Expositions of the Doctrine of the Incarnation during the Period, 1130–1180*. Leiden, The Netherlands: E. J. Brill, 1982.

Nineham, D. E. "Gottschalk of Orbais: Reactionary or Precursor of the Reformation?" *Journal of Ecclesiastical History* 40 (1989): 1–18.

Nithard. *Histoire des Fils de Louis le Pieux*. Ed. and trans. Philippe Lauer. Paris: H. Champion, 1926.

Noble, Thomas F. X. "Louis the Pious and the Frontiers of the Frankish Realms." In *Charlemagne's Heir. New Perspectives on the Reign of Louis the Pious*, ed. Peter Godman and Roger Collins. Oxford: Clarendon Press, 1990.

Nöldeke, Theodor. *Sketches from Eastern History*. Trans. John Sutherland Black. London: Adam and Charles Black, 1892.

Norwich, John J. *The Kingdom in the Sun 1130–1194*. London: Longmans, 1970.

———. *The Normans in the South, 1016–1130*. London: Longmans, 1967.

Obbard, Elizabeth R. *Poverty, My Riches: A Study of St. Elizabeth of Hungary, 1207–1231*. Southampton, England: Saint Austin Press, 1997.

O'Donnell, James J. *Cassiodorus*. Berkeley: University of California Press, 1979.

O'Donoghue, Bernard. *The Courtly Love Tradition*. Manchester, England: Manchester University Press, 1982.

Oesch, Hans. *Berno und Hermann von Reichenau als Musiktheoretiker*. Bern, Switzerland: P. Haupt, 1961.

Oman, G. "Al-Idrīsī." In *The Encyclopaedia of Islam*, ed. B. Lewis, V. L. Ménage, Ch. Pellat, and J. Schacht. New ed. Vol. 3. Leiden, The Netherlands: E. J. Brill, 1971.

O'Meara, John J. *Eriugena*. Oxford: Clarendon Press, 1988.

Orchard, Andy. *The Poetic Art of Aldhelm*. Cambridge: Cambridge University Press, 1994.

Osborne, Kenan B. "Alexander of Hales." In *A History of Franciscan Theology*, ed. K. B. Osborne. St. Bonaventure, NY: Franciscan Institute, 1994.

Ostrogorsky, George. *History of the Byzantine State*. Rev. ed. Trans. Joan Hussey. New Brunswick, NJ: Rutgers University Press, 1969.

Ottaviano, Carmelo. *Guglielmo d'Auxerre, la vita, le opere, il pensiero*. Rome: L'Universala tipografia poliglotta, 1929.

Pacaut, Marcel. *Louis VII et son royaume*. Paris: S.E.V. P.E.N., 1964.

Paden, William D., ed. *The Voice of the Trobairitz: Perspectives on the Women Troubadours*. Philadelphia: University of Pennsylvania Press, 1989.

Parsons, John Carmi, and Bonnie Wheeler, eds. *Medieval Mothering*. New York: Garland, 1996.

Patrologia cursus completus. Series Latina. Ed. J.-P. Migne. Paris: Garnier, 1844–1864.

Pearl, Chaim. *Rashi*. New York: Grove Press, 1988.

Pernoud, Régine. *Aliénor d'Aquitaine*. Paris: A. Michel, 1965.

———. *Blanche of Castile*. Trans. Henry Noel. New York: Coward, McCann & Geoghegan, 1975.

———. *La Femme au temps des cathédrales*. Paris: Stock, 1980.

Peter of les Vaux-de-Cernay. *The History of the Albigensian Crusade*. Trans. W. A. Sibly and M. D. Sibly. Suffolk, England: Boydell Press, 1998.

Peters, Edward. *The First Crusade: The Chronicle of Fulcher of Chartres and Other Source Materials*. 2d ed. Philadelphia: University of Pennsylvania Press, 1998.

Petersen, Erling L. *ʿAlī and Muʿāwiya in Early Arabic Tradition*. Copenhagen: Munksgard, 1964.

Petroff, Elizabeth. A. *Body and Soul: Essays on Medieval Women and Mysticism*. New York: Oxford University Press, 1994.

———. *Medieval Women's Visionary Literature*. Oxford: Oxford University Press, 1986.

Phillips, J.R.S. *The Medieval Expansion of Europe*. 2d ed. Oxford: Clarendon Press, 1998.

Picard, Jean-Michel. "Adomnán, and the Writing of History." *Peritia* 3 (1984): 50–70.

Picavet, François. *Roscelin, Philosophe et theologien, d'apres la legende et d'apres l'histoire*. Paris: Alcan et Guillaumin, 1911.

Pollock, Frederick, and Frederic W. Maitland. *History of English Law before the Time of Edward I*. Vol. 1. 2d ed. Cambridge: Cambridge University Press, 1968.

Powicke, F. Maurice. *Stephen Langton*. Oxford: Clarendon Press, 1928.

Prestwich, Michael. *Edward I*. New ed. New Haven, CT: Yale University Press, 1997.

Principe, Walter H. *Hugh of St. Cher's Theology of the Hypostatic Union*. Toronto: Pontifical Institute of Mediaeval Studies, 1970.

———. *Philip the Chancellor's Theology of the Hypostatic Union*. Toronto: Pontifical Institute of Mediaeval Studies, 1975.

Procopius. *Works*. Trans. Henry B. Dewing and Glanville Downey. 7 vols. London: W. Heinemann, 1914–1940.

Prose Edda of Snorri Sturluson: Tales from Norse Mythology. Trans. Jean Young. Berkeley: University of California Press, 1973.

Quellen zur Karolingischen Reichsgeschichte. 3 vols. Trans. and ed. Reinhold Rau. Berlin: Rutten & Loenig, 1955–1960.

Queller, Donald E., and Thomas F. Madden. *The Fourth Crusade: The Conquest of Constantinople.* 2d ed. Philadelphia: University of Pennsylvania Press, 1997.

Quinn, John F. *The Historical Constitution of Saint Bonaventure's Philosophy.* Toronto: Pontifical Institute of Mediaeval Studies, 1973.

Radbertus, Paschasius. *Charlemagne's Cousins: Contemporary Lives of Adalard and Wala.* Trans. Allen Cabaniss. Syracuse, NY: Syracuse University Press, 1967.

Radice, Betty, trans. *Letters of Abelard and Heloise.* Harmondsworth: Penguin, 1974.

Ramsay, Nigel, Margaret Sparks, and Tim Tatton-Brown. *St. Dunstan: His Life, Times and Cult.* New York: Boydell Press, 1992.

Rashid, Rushdi, and B. Vahabzadeh. *Al-Khayyam mathématicien.* Paris: A. Blanchard, 1999.

Reames, Sherry. *The* Legenda aurea: *A Reexamination of Its Paradoxical History.* Madison: University of Wisconsin Press, 1985.

Reeves, Marjorie. *Joachim of Fiore and the Prophetic Future.* New York: Harper & Row, 1976.

Reilly, Bernard F. *The Contest of Christian and Muslim Spain: 1031–1157.* Cambridge, MA: Blackwell, 1992.

———. *The Kingdom of León-Castilla under King Alfonso VI: 1065–1109.* Princeton, NJ: Princeton University Press, 1988.

———. *The Kingdom of León-Castilla under King Alfonso VII, 1126–1157.* Philadelphia: University of Pennsylvania Press, 1998.

Reuter, Timothy. *Germany in the Early Middle Ages c. 800–1056.* London: Longman, 1991.

Richard, Jean. "La papauté et la direction de la première croisade." *Journal des Savants* (April–June 1960): 49–58.

———. *Saint Louis: Crusader King of France.* Ed. Simon Lloyd. Trans. Jean Birrell. Cambridge: Cambridge University Press, 1992.

Richards, Jeffrey. *Consul of God: The Life and Times of Gregory the Great.* London: Routledge, 1980.

Riché, Pierre. *The Carolingians: A Family Who Forged Europe.* Trans. Michael Idomir Allen. Philadelphia: University of Pennsylvania Press, 1993.

Riessner, Claus. *Die "Magnae Derivationes" des Uguccione da Pisa.* Rome: Edizioni di Storia e Letteratura, 1965.

Riley-Smith, Jonathan. *The First Crusade and the Idea of Crusading.* London: Athlone Press, 1986.

Rindal, Magnus, and Knut Berg. *King Magnus Hákonarson's Laws of Norway and Other Legal Texts. Corpus codicum Norvegicorum Medii Aevi.* Vol. 7. Oslo: Society for Publication of Old Norwegian Manuscripts, 1983.

Robb, Fiona. "The Fourth Lateran Council's Definition of Trinitarian Orthodoxy." *Journal of Ecclesiastical History* 48.1 (January 1997): 22–43.

Roberts, Phyllis Barzillay. *Studies in the Sermons of Stephen Langton.* Toronto: Pontifical Institute of Mediaeval Studies, 1968.

Robertson, Howard S. "Structure and Comedy in *Le Jeu de Saint Nicolas.*" *Studies in Philology* 64 (1967): 551–563.

Robinson, Charles H. *Anskar: The Apostle of the North.* London: Society for the Propagation of the Gospel in Foreign Parts, 1921.

Robinson, Ian S. *The Papacy 1073–1198: Continuity and Innovation*. Cambridge: Cambridge University Press, 1990.

Roesdahl, Else. *Viking Age Denmark*. Trans. Susan Margeson and Kirsten Williams. London: British Museum, 1982.

Rogers, Elizabeth F. *Peter Lombard and the Sacramental System*. 1917. Reprint, Merrick, NY: Richwood Publishing Co., 1976.

Rorem, Paul. *Pseudo-Dionysius: A Commentary on the Texts and an Introduction to Their Influence*. New York: Oxford University Press, 1993.

Routledge History of Philosophy. Medieval Philosophy. London: Routledge, 1998.

Rudolph of Fulda. "The Life of Saint Leoba." Trans. C. H. Talbot. In *Soldiers of Christ: Saints and Saints' Lives from Late Antiquity and the Early Middle Ages*, ed. Thomas F. X. Noble and Thomas Head. Pittsburgh: Pennsylvania State University Press, 1995.

Runciman, Steven. *A History of the Crusades. Vol. 1.: The First Crusade and the Foundation of the Kingdom of Jerusalem*. Cambridge: Cambridge University Press, 1968.

———. *The Sicilian Vespers: A History of the Mediterranean World in the Later Thirteenth Century*. Cambridge: Cambridge University Press, 1958.

Salmon, Am[édée], ed. *Philippe de Beaumanoir*: Coutumes de Beauvaisis. 2 vols. Paris: Picard, 1974.

Sancti Columbani Opera. Ed and trans. G.S.M. Walker. Dublin: Dublin Institute for Advanced Studies, 1957.

Saxo Grammaticus. *History of the Danes*. Ed. H. E. Davidson. Trans. Peter Fisher. Cambridge: D. S. Brewer, 1979.

———. *History of the Danes*. http://sunsite.berkeley.edu/OMACL/DanishHistory (accessed on July 18, 2001).

The Saxon Mirror. A Sachsenspiegel *of the Fourteenth Century*. Trans. Maria Dobozy. Philadelphia: University of Pennsylvania Press, 1999.

Sayers, Jane. *Innocent III, Leader of Europe, 1198–1216*. London: Longman, 1994.

———. *Papal Government and England during the Pontificate of Honorius III (1216–1227)*. Cambridge: Cambridge University Press, 1984.

Schlanger, Jacques. *La philosophie de Salomon ibn Gabirol*. Leiden, The Netherlands: E. J. Brill, 1968.

Schmale, Franz-Josef, and Irene Schmale-Ott. *Frutolfs und Ekkehards Chroniken und die Anonyme Kaiserchronik*. Darmstadt, Germany: Wissenschaftliche Buchgesellschaft, 1972.

Schnell, Rüdiger. *Suche nach Wahrheit: Gottfrieds "Tristan und Isold" als erkenntniskritischer Roman*. Tübingen, Germany: Niemeyer, 1992.

Schoz, Bernhard W., and Barbara Rogers, trans. *Carolingian Chronicles: Royal Frankish Annals and Nithard's Histories*. Ann Arbor: University of Michigan Press, 1970.

Schrimpf, Gangolf, ed. *Kloster Fulda in der Welt der Karolinger und Ottonen*. Frankfurt am Main: Josef Knecht, 1996.

Schwertner, Thomas M. *St. Raymond of Pennafort*. Ed. C. M. Antony. Milwaukee, WI: Bruce Publishing Company, 1935.

Seymour, Michael C. *Bartholomaeus Anglicus and His Encyclopaedia*. Aldershot, England: Variorum, 1992.

Sharp, Dorothea E. *Franciscan Philosophy at Oxford in the Thirteenth Century*. New York: Russell & Russell, 1964.

Shopkow, Leah. *History and Community: Norman Historical Writing in the Eleventh and Twelfth Century.* Washington, DC: Catholic University of America Press, 1997.

Singer, Heinrich, ed. *Die Summa Decretorum des Magister Rufinus.* Paderborn, Germany: Ferdinand Schöningh, 1902.

Sinnema, John. *Hendrik van Veldeke.* New York: Twayne Publishers, 1972.

Sitwell, Gerard, ed. and trans. *St. Odo of Cluny, Being the Life of St. Odo of Cluny by John of Salerno and the Life of St. Gerald of Aurillac by St. Odo.* New York: Sheed and Ward, 1958.

Skovgaard-Petersen, Inge. "Saxo, Historian of the Patria." *Mediaeval Scandinavia* 2 (1969): 54–77.

Smalley, Beryl. "The Gospels in the Paris Schools in the Late Twelfth and Early Thirteenth Centuries: Peter the Chanter, Hugh of St-Cher, Alexander of Hales, John of la Rochelle." *Franciscan Studies* 39 (1979): 230–254; 40 (1980): 298–369.

———. *The Gospels in the Schools c. 1100–1280.* London: Hambledon, 1985.

Smyth, Alfred P. *King Alfred the Great.* Oxford: Oxford University Press, 1995.

Snorri Sturluson. *Heimskringla: History of the Kings of Norway.* Trans. Lee M. Hollander. Austin: University of Texas Press, 1964.

———. *The Saga of Harald Fairhair.* In *Heimskringla: History of the Kings of Norway.* Trans. Lee M. Hollander. Austin: University of Texas Press, 1964.

———. *Saint Olaf's Saga.* In *Heimskringla: History of the Kings of Norway.* Trans. Lee M. Hollander. Austin: University of Texas Press, 1964.

Somerville, Robert. *Pope Alexander III and the Council of Tours: A Study of Ecclesiastical Politics and Institutions in the Twelfth Century.* Berkeley: University of California Press, 1977.

Southern, Richard W. *Robert Grosseteste: The Growth of an English Mind in Medieval Europe.* Oxford: Clarendon Press, 1986.

———. *Scholastic Humanism and the Unification of Europe. Volume 1: Foundation.* Oxford: Blackwell, 1995.

Stafford, Pauline. *Queen Emma and Queen Edith: Queenship and Women's Power in Eleventh-Century England.* Oxford: Blackwell, 1997.

———. *Unification and Conquest: A Political and Social History of England in the Tenth and Eleventh Centuries.* London: E. Arnold, 1989.

Stancliffe, Clare, and Eric Cambridge, eds. *Oswald: Northumbrian King to European Saint.* Stamford, United Kingdom: Paul Watkins, 1995.

Steinen, Wolfram von den. *Notker der Dichter und seine Geistige Welt.* 2 vols. 1948. Reprint, Bern, Switzerland: Francke, 1978.

Stenton, Frank. *Anglo-Saxon England.* 3d ed. Oxford: Clarendon Press, 1971.

Stephens, Peter. *The Waldensian Story: A Study in Faith, Intolerance, and Survival.* Sussex, England: Book Guild, Ltd., 1998.

Stevenson, Francis. *Robert Grosseteste: Bishop of Lincoln.* London: Macmillan, 1899.

Stock, Brian. *Myth and Science in the Twelfth Century: A Study of Bernard Silvester.* Princeton, NJ: Princeton University Press, 1972.

Strabo, Walahfrid. *Opera omnia.* Patrologiae cursus completus. Series Latina. Vols. 113–114. Paris: Garnier, 1879.

Straw, Carole. *Gregory the Great.* In *Authors of the Middle Ages*, ed. P. J. Geary. Vol. IV, No. 12. Aldershot, England: Variorum, 1996.

Strayer, Joseph R. *The Albigensian Crusades*. Ann Arbor: University of Michigan Press, 1992.

Suger, Abbot of St. Denis. *The Deeds of Louis the Fat*. Trans. Richard Cusimano and John Moorhead. Washington, DC: Catholic University of America Press, 1992.

Sunnen, Donald. "Life and Letters at the Court of Hákon IV Hákonarson." *Medieval Perspectives* 8 (1993): 87–103.

Sveinsson, Einar Ólafur. *The Age of the Sturlungs: Icelandic Civilization in the Thirteenth Century*. Trans. Jóhann S. Hannesson. Islandica 36. Ithaca, NY: Cornell University Press, 1953.

Swanton, Michael, trans. *Anglo-Saxon Chronicle*. London: Dent, 1996.

Talbot, Charles H. *The Anglo-Saxon Missionaries in Germany*. London: Sheed and Ward, 1954.

———, ed. and trans. *The Life of Christina of Markyate: A Twelfth Century Recluse*. Toronto: University of Toronto Press, 1997.

Tarleton, Alfred. *Nicholas Breakspear (Adrian IV), Englishman and Pope*. London: A. L. Humphreys, 1896.

Tellenbach, Gerd. *Church, State and Christian Society at the Time of the Investiture Contest*. Trans. Ralph Bennett. Toronto: University of Toronto Press, 1991.

Thatcher, Oliver J. *Studies Concerning Adrian IV*. Chicago: University of Chicago Press, 1903.

Thiébaux, Marcelle. "Handmaid of God. Elisabeth of Schönau." In *The Writings of Medieval Women: An Anthology*. Trans. Marcelle Thiébaux. 2d ed. New York: Garland, 1994.

Thijssen, J.M.M.H. *Censure and Heresy at the University of Paris 1200–1400*. Philadelphia: University of Pennsylvania Press, 1998.

Thomson, Rodney. *William of Malmesbury*. Suffolk, England: Boydell Press, 1987.

"Thorláks saga helga." In *Origines Islandicae*. Vol. I. Trans. Guðbrandur Vigfússon and F. York Powell. Oxford: Clarendon Press, 1905.

Thorndike, Lynn. *Michael Scot*. London: Thomas Nelson and Sons, Ltd., 1965.

Tillman, Helene. *Pope Innocent III*. Trans. Walter Sax. Amsterdam: North Holland Publishing, 1980.

Topsfield, Leslie. *Chrétien de Troyes: A Study of the Arthurian Romances*. Cambridge: Cambridge University Press, 1981.

Torrell, Jean-Pierre. *Pierre le Venerable et sa vision du monde, sa vie, son ouevre, l'homme, et le démon*. Louvain, Belgium: Spicilegium Sacrum Lovaniense, 1986.

———. *Saint Thomas Aquinas: The Person and His Work*. Vol. 1. Trans. R. Royal. Washington, DC: Catholic University of America Press, 1996.

Townsend, David. *The Alexandreis of Walter of Châtillon: A Twelfth-Century Epic*. Philadelphia: University of Pennsylvania Press, 1996.

Turner, Ralph. *King John*. London: Longman, 1994.

Uguccione da Pisa. *De dubio accentu, agiographia, expositio de symbolo apostolorum*. Ed. Giuseppe Cremascoli. Spoleto, Italy: Centro Italiano di Studi sull'alto Medioevo, 1978.

Ullmann, Walter. *A Short History of the Papacy in the Middle Ages*. London: Methuen, 1972.

Urvoy, Domonique. *Ibn Rushd (Averroes)*. Trans. Olivia Stewart. Cairo: American University in Cairo Press, 1991.

Van Engen, John. *Rupert of Deutz*. Berkeley: University of California Press, 1983.

Van Houts, Elisabeth C., ed. and trans. *The Gesta Normannorum Ducum of William of Jumièges, Orderic Vitalis and Robert of Torigni*. 2 vols. Oxford: Clarendon Press, 1992–1995.

Vaughn, Richard, ed. and trans. *The Chronicles of Matthew Paris: Monastic Life in the Thirteenth Century*. New York: St. Martin's Press, 1984.

Vaughn, Sally N. *Anselm of Bec and Robert of Meulan: The Innocence of the Dove and the Wisdom of the Serpent*. Berkeley: University of California Press, 1987.

Veal, Johannes F. *The Sacramental Theology of Stephen Langton and the Influence upon Him of Peter the Chanter*. Rome: Officium Libri Catholici, 1955.

Verseuil, Jean. *Clovis ou la naissance des rois*. Paris: Criterion, 1992.

Vésteinsson, Orri. *The Christianization of Iceland: Priests, Power, and Social Change 1000–1300*. Oxford: Oxford University Press, 2000.

Vicaire, Marie-Humbert. *Saint Dominic and His Times*. Trans. Kathleen Pond. New York: McGraw-Hill, 1964.

Vincent of Beauvais. *De morali principis institutione*. Ed. Robert J. Schneider. Turnhout, Belgium: Brepols, 1995.

Vivell, Cölestin. *Frutolfi Breviarium de musica et tonarius*. Vienna: Buchhändler der Akademie der Wissenschaften, 1919.

Voaden, Rosalynn. "All Girls Together: Community, Gender and Vision at Helfta." In *Medieval Women in Their Communities*, ed. Diane Watt. Toronto: University of Toronto Press, 1997.

Wahlgren, Lena. *The Letter Collections of Peter of Blois: Studies in the Manuscript Tradition*. Göteborg, Sweden: Acta Universitatis Gothoburgensis, 1993.

Wainwright, Frederick T. "Æthelflæd, Lady of the Mercians." In *Scandinavian England: Collected Papers*, ed. H.P.R. Finberg. Chichester, West Sussex, England: Phillimore, 1975.

Walker, Ian W. *Harold: The Last Anglo-Saxon King*. Stroud, Gloucestershire, England: Sutton, 1997.

Wallace-Hadrill, John M. *Early Germanic Kingship in England and on the Continent*. Oxford: Clarendon Press, 1971.

———. *The Frankish Church*. Oxford: Clarendon Press, 1983.

———. *The Long-Haired Kings*. New York: Barnes & Noble, 1962.

Wallach, Luitpold. *Alcuin and Charlemagne: Studies in Carolingian History and Culture*. Ithaca, NY: Cornell University Press, 1959.

Warren, Wilfred L. *Henry II*. London: Eyre Methuen, 1977.

———. *King John*. 2d ed. London: Eyre Methuen, 1978.

Watt, William M. *Muhammad at Mecca*. Oxford: Clarendon Press, 1953.

———. *Muhammad at Medina*. Oxford: Clarendon Press, 1956.

———. *Muslim Intellectual: A Study of al-Ghazali*. Edinburgh: University Press, 1963.

Webb, Clement C. *John of Salisbury*. London: Methuen, 1932.

Webb, Geoffrey. "The Person and the Place—V: Herrad and Her Garden of Delights." *Life of the Spirit* 16 (1961–1962): 475–481.

Weisheipl, James A. "Albert the Great and Medieval Culture." *The Thomist* 44 (1980): 481–501.

———. *Friar Thomas d'Aquino: His Life, Thought, and Work*. Rev. ed. Washington, DC: Catholic University of America Press, 1983.

————, ed. *Albertus Magnus and the Sciences. Commemorative Essays*. Toronto: Pontifical Institute of Mediaeval Studies, 1980.

Wemple, Suzanne Fonay. *Women in Frankish Society: Marriage and the Cloister, 500 to 900*. Philadelphia: University of Pennsylvania Press, 1981.

West, Francis J. *The Justiciarship in England, 1066–1232*. Cambridge: Cambridge University Press, 1966.

Wetherbee, Winthrop. *Platonism and Poetry in the Twelfth Century: The Literary Influence of the School of Chartres*. Princeton, NJ: Princeton University Press, 1972.

Whittow, Mark. *The Making of Byzantium, 600–1025*. Berkeley: University of California Press, 1996.

Wicki, Nikolaus, ed. *Philippi Cancellarii Parisiensis Summa de bono*. 2 vols. Bern, Switzerland: Francke, 1985.

Wilks, Michael, ed. *The World of John of Salisbury*. Oxford: Basil Blackwell, 1984.

Willem van Ruysbroeck. *The Mission of Friar William of Rubruck: His Journey to the Court of the Great Khan Möngke, 1253–1255*. Ed. and trans. Peter Jackson. London: Hakluyt Society, 1990.

William of Conches. *A Dialogue on Natural Philosophy* (*Dragmaticon philosophia*). Trans. Italo Ronca and Matthew Curr. Notre Dame, IN: University of Notre Dame Press, 1997.

Wippel, John F. *The Metaphysical Thought of Godfrey of Fontaines: A Study in Late Thirteenth-Century Philosophy*. Washington, DC: Catholic University of America Press, 1981.

Witt, Ronald G. "Boncompagno and the Defense of Rhetoric." *Journal of Medieval and Renaissance Studies* 16.1 (1986): 1–31.

Witte, Robert, ed. *Catalogus Sigeberti Gemblacensis monachi de viris illustribus*. Frankfurt: Peter Lang, 1974.

Wolter, Allan B. "Reflections on the Life and Works of Scotus." *American Catholic Philosophical Quarterly* 67 (1993): 1–36.

Wood, Frances. *Did Marco Polo Go to China*. London: Secker & Warburg, 1995.

Wood, Ian. *The Merovingian Kingdoms 450–751*. London: Longman, 1994.

Wooding, Jonathan M., ed. *The Otherworld Voyage in Irish Literature and History*. Rev. ed. Dublin: Four Courts Press, 2000.

Wright, Craig. "Leoninus, Poet and Musician." *Journal of the American Musicological Society* 39 (1986): 1–35.

Yewdale, Ralph B. *Bohemond I, Prince of Antioch*. Princeton, NJ: Princeton University Press, 1924.

Yorke, Barbara. *Kings and Kingdoms of Early Anglo-Saxon England*. London: Seaby, 1990.

Yule, Henry, and Henri Cordier, eds. *The Travels of Marco Polo: The Complete Yule-Cordier Edition*. 2 vols. 1903. Reprint, New York: Dover Publications, 1993.

Ziolkowski, Jan. *Alan of Lille's Grammar of Sex: The Meaning of Grammar to a Twelfth-Century Intellectual*. Cambridge, MA: Medieval Academy of America, 1985.

Name Index

Main entries are in **boldface** type.

General Index

Contributors

F.R.P. AKEHURST, Department of French and Italian, University of Minnesota.

CLINTON ATCHLEY, Department of English, Henderson State University.

JOSEPH CARROLL, English Department, Rhode Island College.

HELEN CONRAD-O'BRIAIN, School of English, Trinity College, Dublin.

JAMES COUNTRYMAN, Department of English, University of Minnesota, Morris.

RYAN P. CRISP, Department of History, Ohio State University.

ELAINE CULLEN, Department of English, University of Minnesota.

JUDITH DAVIS, Department of Foreign Languages, Goshen College.

DAVID DAY, School of Human Sciences, University of Houston, Clear Lake.

HEIDE ESTES, Department of English, Monmouth University.

CONNIE EVANS, History Department, Baldwin-Wallace College.

DEANNA EVANS, Department of English, Bemidji State University.

DONALD FLEMING, Department of History, Hiram College.

JOEL FREDELL, Department of English, Southeastern Louisiana University.

RONALD H. FRITZE, Department of History, University of Central Arkansas.

LAURA L. GATHAGAN, Department of History, CUNY Graduate Center.

ANDREW GILLETT, School of History, Philosophy, and Politics, Macquairie University, Sydney NSW.

JAMES R. GINTHER, Department of Theology and Religious Studies, University of Leeds.

MATTHEW HUSSEY, Department of English, University of Wisconsin, Madison.

TIMOTHY JONES, Department of English, Augustana College.

GREGORY B. KAPLAN, Department of Modern Foreign Languages and Literatures, University of Tennessee, Knoxville.

JILL AVERIL KEEN, Postdoctoral Fellow, Center for Medieval Studies, University of Minnesota.

KAROLYN KINANE, Department of English, University of Minnesota.

DANIEL KLINE, Department of English, University of Alaska, Anchorage.

LEAH LARSON, Department of English, Drama, and the Communication Arts, Our Lady of the Lake University, San Antonio.

JAY T. LEES, Department of History, University of Northern Iowa.

JOSEPH McGOWAN, Department of English, University of San Diego.

OLIVIA H. McINTYRE, Letters Collegium, Eckerd College.

LINDA A. McMILLIN, Department of History, Susquehanna University.

SHARON MICHALOVE, Department of History, University of Illinois, Champagne–Urbana.

PAUL MILLER, Department of History, Louisiana State University.

PAUL B. NELSON, Department of Comparative Literature/Department of Spanish and Portuguese, Indiana University.

JANICE R. NORRIS, Department of History, Binghamton University.

ERIK S. OHLANDER, Department of Near Eastern Studies, University of Michigan.

TOM PAPADEMETRIOU, Department of Near Eastern Studies, Princeton University.

ZINA PETERSEN, Department of English, Brigham Young University.

ROBERTO PLEVANO, School of Philosophy, The Catholic University of America.

JANET POPE, Department of History, Hiram College.

PATRICIA PRICE, Postdoctoral Fellow, Center for Medieval Studies, University of Minnesota.

MARGUERITE RAGNOW, Department of History, University of Minnesota.

KIMBERLY RIVERS, Department of History, University of Wisconsin, Oshkosh.

WILLIAM B. ROBISON, Department of History, Southeastern Louisiana University.

ANDREW SCHEIL, History and Literature Program, Harvard University.

WILLIAM SCHIPPER, Department of English, Memorial University.

EDWARD J. SCHOENFELD, Department of History, University of Minnesota.

JANA K. SCHULMAN, Department of English, Southeastern Louisiana University.

ANDREA SCHUTZ, English Department, St. Thomas University, New Brunswick.

ALANA CAIN SCOTT, Department of Geography, Government, and History, Morehead State University.

PATRICIA SILBER, Department of English, Marymount College.

ANNE COLLINS SMITH, Department of Philosophy, Religion, and Classical Studies, Susquehanna University.

OWEN M. SMITH, Department of Philosophy, Religion, and Classical Studies, Susquehanna University.

KRISTINE K. SNEERINGER, Foreign Language Department, Lindbergh High School, St. Louis, Missouri.

ALEXANDRA STERLING-HELLENBRAND, Department of Foreign Languages, Goshen College.

SANDRA BALLIF STRAUBHAAR, Department of Germanic Studies, University of Texas, Austin.

EMILY TABUTEAU, Department of History, Michigan State University.

ALFONS TEIPEN, Department of Religion, Furman University.

ANDREW G. TRAVER, Department of History, Southeastern Louisiana University.

JOHN PAUL WALTER, Department of English, Saint Louis University.

KATHARINA M. WILSON, Department of Comparative Literature, University of Georgia.

JONATHAN M. WOODING, Department of Theology and Religious Studies, University of Wales, Lampeter.